IMPELLING SPIRIT

Revisiting a Founding Experience:

1539

Ignatius of Loyola and His Companions

Praise for *Impelling Spirit*

"Timely and masterful . . . This book is essential reading not only for those who want a deeper appreciation of Jesuit origins, but also for those who want a more profound and nuanced understanding of the role of *apostolic* religious life within the institutional Church."

—Theodore E. Kestler, S.J.,
Superior, Society of Jesus,
Region of Alaska

"Pedro Arrupe would have loved this book."

—Vincent T. O'Keefe, S.J.,
Former Assistant to Fr. Arrupe

". . . a fascinating study of the origins of the Society."

—Bernard McVeigh, O.C.S.O.,
Our Lady of Guadalupe Abbey

". . . a remarkable book for secular as well as religious readers."

—Professor Robert Waterman,
Gonzaga University

" . . . [Impelling Spirit] can be seen as a model in discerning the founding charism of any religious order or as a guide to personal discernment."

—Sister Mary Ellen King, S.S.A.,
Provincial Superior

IMPELLING SPIRIT

Revisiting a Founding Experience:

1539

Ignatius of Loyola and His Companions

An Exploration into the Spirit and Aims of the Society of Jesus

as Revealed in

the Founders' Proposed Papal Letter Approving the Society

Joseph F. Conwell, S.J.

© 1997 Joseph F. Conwell
All rights reserved
Printed in the United States of America

an imprint of
LOYOLA PRESS
3441 North Ashland Avenue
Chicago, Illinois 60657

Library of Congress Cataloging-in-Publication Data
Conwell, Joseph F. (1919–)
   Impelling spirit: revisiting a founding experience, 1539, Ignatius of Loyola and his companions: an exploration into the spirit and aims of the Society of Jesus as revealed in the founders' proposed papal letter approving the Society / Joseph F. Conwell, S.J.
    p. cm.
   Includes bibliographical references and index.
   ISBN 0-8294-0864-9
   1. Jesuits—History—16th century. 2. Jesuits—Spiritual life. 3. Ignatius, of Loyola, Saint, 1491–1556. 4. Cum ex plurium.
   I. Title.
BX3706.2.C66 1997
271'.53'009031—dc20   96-41076
                                                                                                    CIP

1 2 3 4 5 / 0 9 8 7 6

To

Ignatius
and his nine first companions,
but especially
to
all those Jesuits
of whom Ignatius often spoke,
who,
coming after the original ten companions,
would be better Jesuits than they.

cf. Nadal, *Apologia contra censuram [132]*

A Word Concerning Authorship

Most of the words in this book belong to me, much of the research that went into it, and all of the mistakes. Without the careful and painstaking critique, however, of my coworker and research associate, Sister Cecilia W. Wilms, Hermit, many of the words would have been inept, misleading, and ultimately boring. In her role of literary and scholarly midwife, her difficult task was to challenge, to support, to bolster, to supply wisdom, love, and prayer. She also provided much of the research, both locally and in her native Belgium, especially in monastic and other non–Jesuit religious sources. To her we owe the difficult tracing of references, the dogged sleuthing required for finding obscure passages in obscure books and articles. To her we owe order, exactness, precision, as in the bibliography. Without her this would have been a different book, if it would have been a book at all.

Joseph F. Conwell, S.J.

Contents

Foreword by Vincent T. O'Keefe, S.J.	xv
Preface	xix
Chronology of Principal Events	xxix

The Text of *Cum Ex Plurium*	1
Introduction	11
1. The Deliberation of the First Fathers	12
2. The Other Documents of 1539	16
3. Authorship of *Cum ex plurium*	21
4. Structure and Content of *Cum ex plurium*	26

SALUTATION	31
Chapter One: Pope Paul III and His Beloved Sons	33
1. Paul III	35
2. Paul's Beloved Sons	38
3. Masters of Paris	42

PART ONE	47
SECTION ONE: The Priesthood of Ignatius and Companions	
Introduction	49
Chapter Two: Their Choice to Be Poor	51
1. *Pauperes Christi* [*Poor* of Christ]	56
2. *Poor* Priests of Christ	58

Chapter Three: Their Choice to Be Priests	65
1. Ignatius, the Cleric, in the Context of History	65
2. Ignatius's Option for Priesthood	69
3. The Option of His Companions	71
4. Why *sacerdotes* Rather than *presbyteros*?	73
5. Peculiar Circumstances of the Ordination	75
6. The Spirit of Their Priesthood	79
Chapter Four: Their Choice to Join into One Body	81
Chapter Five: The Impelling Action of the Holy Spirit	89
Chapter Six: Free to Serve	97
1. The Dedication of Ignatius	103
2. The Dedication of All the Companions	106
Concluding Reflection	127

SECTION TWO: The Vineyard of the Lord

Introduction	129
Chapter Seven: Workers in the Vineyard	133
Chapter Eight: Planting and Tending the Vineyard	139
1. Publicly Preaching the Word	139
2. Exhorting in Private	150
3. Hearing Confessions	155
4. Directing the Spiritual Exercises	158
Chapter Nine: Tending the Weakest Vines	163
1. Caring for the Sick	163
2. Missionary Journeys	165
3. Teaching Christian Doctrine to Little Ones	176
4. Works of Charity	180
Chapter Ten: Stewardship of the Vineyard	183
1. Without Any Sign of Heresy	184
2. Without Any Sign of Avarice	199
3. Without Any Sign of Immoral Conduct	200
4. With Great Praise	202
Concluding Reflection	205

SECTION THREE: The Joy and Desire of Paul III

Introduction   209

Chapter Eleven: The Ancient Christian Way of Living   211
     1. *Conversatio* in Christian Tradition   213
     2. The Use of *conversatio* by the Companions   216

Chapter Twelve: *Ecclesia semper reformanda*
[A Church Always in Need of Renewal]   219
     1. The Need for Examples   219
     2. The Need for Renewal   223
     3. New Examples of the Ancient Christian Way
        of Living   227

Concluding Reflection   231

PART TWO   233

SECTION ONE: Companions of Jesus

Introduction   235

Chapter Thirteen: Prophetic Commitment   239
     1. *Pietas*   240
     2. *Religio*   242

Chapter Fourteen: *Vite institutum:* A Way that
Leads to God   247
     1. *Vite institutum*   248
     2. The First Followers   251

Chapter Fifteen: Companionship in Christ   255
     1. The Companions' Use of the Term *societas*   258
     2. Union in Christ: Society of Jesus   270
     3. Means to Preserve Union   276

Concluding Reflection   285

SECTION TWO: The Companions' Requests

Introduction   287

Chapter Sixteen: The Meaning of *vivendi formula*   291

Chapter Seventeen: The Evangelical Counsels	299
1. The Evangelical Counsels up to 1539	300
2. The Companions and the Evangelical Counsels	310
Chapter Eighteen: The Normative Teachings of the Fathers	319
1. The Meaning of *canonicis patrum sanctionibus*	319
2. Canon 13 of Lateran IV (1215)	322
3. The Unique Character of the Companions' *vivendi formula*	327
4. Blessing and Approving the *vivendi formula*	328
Concluding Reflection	331

PART THREE   333

SECTION ONE: The Companions' *propositum*

Introduction	335
Chapter Nineteen: The Meaning of *propositum* in Christian Tradition	339
1. The Transformation of Ancient Terminology	343
2. The Gradual Extension of *propositum* to Wider Areas	347
Chapter Twenty: The *propositum* of Ignatius	353
1. *Propositum* in the Earliest Writings of Ignatius	353
2. *Propositum* in the Autobiography of Ignatius	355
3. Ignatius's *propositum* and Christian Tradition	365
Chapter Twenty-One: Companions with the Same *propositum*	367
1. Genesis of a Religious Institute	367
2. From *propósito* to *el mismo propósito*	374
3. From *propositum* to *institutum*	376
Chapter Twenty-Two: The Summary of the Rule: The Formula of the Institute	381
1. Decree One: Chastity and Mission	384
2. Decree Two: Obedience to the Pope	387
3. Decree Three: Obedience within the Society	389

4. Decree Four: Poverty	390
5. Decree Five: Religious Observances	392
Concluding Reflection	395

SECTION TWO: Papal Approval and Commissioning

Introduction	397
Chapter Twenty-Three: Papal Approval and Commissioning	401
1. Approval of the Companions' Way of Living	401
2. The Papal Mandate	405

EPILOGUE: Impelling Spirit   411

Abbreviations	423
Endnotes	427
Bibliography	533
Index	561

Foreword

In its great impetus to religious life in the Church, the Second Vatican Council underlined clearly both the need for renewal and the two simultaneous processes it involves: (1) a constant return to the sources of Christian life (basically the following of Christ as proposed to us in the Gospel) and to the original inspiration of the institutes, and (2) an adaptation to the changed conditions of the times.

Joseph Conwell's book looks particularly to the constant return to the original inspiration of the Society of Jesus, to the spirit and aims of Ignatius of Loyola and his first companions. The methodology used is both fascinating and demanding. You know this book was not dashed off on weekends. It is clearly the result of long experience, persistent study, honest discussion and reflection, and, best of all, true Ignatian discernment.

A papal bull, *Regimini militantis Ecclesiae,* of Pope Paul III on September 27, 1540, gave official approval to the Society of Jesus, and this was confirmed and amplified by another papal bull, *Exposcit debitum,* of Pope Julius III on July 21, 1550. Certain paragraphs of this latter document (3–6) are known as the Formula of the Institute of the Society of Jesus, its foundational document expressing the way of life for all Jesuits. This is all very matter-of-fact business, and down through the centuries reference has been made simply and regularly—and, most of the time, uninspiringly—to the Formula. Jesuits study it at the beginning and end of their formative periods, but thereafter it has been looked on generally as something for the specialists. Only the Holy See can change anything in the Formula.

This book is about a draft for the papal bull of Pope Paul III mentioned above. Papal documents have a history all their own. Before they appear in a final, chiseled form, a process has been undergone involving drafts, debates, revisions, and, of course, various authors and contributors. Vaticanists have always taken particular delight in ferreting out these authors and contributors.

There is no secret about the authors of the draft we are considering since we know it was composed in 1539 by Ignatius of Loyola and his first companions. It is intriguing to note that they were drafting a letter granting official approval to their own Society.

Conwell prefers to call this draft *Cum ex plurium* (identifying it by its first three words, as was the custom for papal documents) instead of *The First Sketch of the Institute of the Society of Jesus,* as it is more generally known. The draft contains the five chapters which, in a revised form, became the Formula of the Institute, preceded by an introduction explaining the request for papal approval and followed by a conclusion approving and confirming the Society and urging the members to follow the Spirit wherever it leads. The obvious advantage of possessing *Cum ex plurium* is that it helps us immeasurably to understand the Formula and what the original spirit and aims of the first Jesuits were. We can see what the original discernment of these men was on how they conceived the way of life they were opting for and asking the pope to approve.

What Conwell does is to "unpack" *Cum ex plurium* so thoroughly that the Formula, the foundational document of the Society of Jesus, takes on a new life and vitality and can be described as "profoundly stirring and provocative, like the Declaration of Independence or the Gettysburg Address. . . . quite possibly the most exciting writing from the pen of Ignatius after the Call of the King and the Two Standards."

Conwell "unpacks" *Cum ex plurium* by enabling the reader to share in depth in a twofold discernment process: that of Ignatius and his companions with regard to the way of life they wish to follow and which they ask the pope to approve, and that of Pope Paul III as he discerns their discernment to see whether their call is from the Spirit.

The treatment of this discernment process helps to situate *Cum ex plurium* in its proper historical, cultural, spiritual, and theological context. It is no longer simply an austere–looking document. It has taken on flesh and blood, and we know its parents and the struggle involved in discovering and articulating a new way of commitment to God and his people.

We look into the lives of the main characters in this drama, their actions, and their writings. They are placed in the world and the Church of their times with particular emphasis on the idea and state of religious life in the Church. Particular emphasis is given to the Carthusians, to whom Ignatius was attracted, the renewal movement of the Cistercians within the monastic tradition, and the renewal movements of St. Francis and St. Dominic, who inspired Ignatius. Essential concepts and realities, like poverty, priesthood, the evangelical counsels, companionship, forms of ministry, serving the weakest and most marginal, a way of life leading to God, the rule, etc., are carefully analyzed and made understandable for today's world.

After following the author through the long and arduous discernment process which is the founding experience of Ignatius and his companions, the approval of Pope Paul III is stirring and inspiring. After a lengthy deliberation they put in writing their spirit and their aims, their proposal for a way of life leading to God, and asked the pope to judge them according to the norm of the Gospel and the living tradition of the church. According to this norm, their proposed way of life was judged to be the work of the Spirit, and they were exhorted to follow this same Spirit wherever it might lead them. This confirmed the conviction of Ignatius and his companions that the Holy Spirit inspires and impels each companion and that the Society as a whole is to follow this same "impelling Spirit."

This is a scholarly and inspirational book, thoroughly researched and written in a very readable and engaging style. The bibliography is an immensely valuable asset. As the author hopes, Jesuits old and young will find some of the hidden riches of the Ignatian heritage, throwing light on their origins and original inspiration.

Members of other religious families will find much light and help as they look into their own charisms and traditions. Lay readers seeking a fuller understanding of the Ignatian tradition or of the larger Christian tradition will also enjoy this book.

In my view, this book belongs with the best publications on the foundation of the Society of Jesus and its proposed way of life as a following of Jesus Christ in the service of the Church and the human family. After reading the manuscript, I felt I had read the Formula of the Institute of the Society of Jesus for the first time. It certainly would never be the same for me.

Vincent O'Keefe, S.J.
America House
New York, NY

Preface

A paradigm shift is coming about in our understanding of Ignatian and Jesuit spirituality, a shift from Ignatius as soldier–saint, a man of steely will, an orderly administrator, coldly rational, to Ignatius the mystic, man of passion and profound affectivity, responding to experience both rational and felt, a whole and holy man deeply in love.

This book reflects that paradigm shift, not only regarding our understanding of Ignatius himself but especially regarding contemporary Jesuits, a shift from the purely intellectual and rational to the mystical and passionate, a shift from pure reasoning to discernment, both personal and communal. Discernment, of course, is not pure affect: it is reasonable to *listen* to rather than simply to reason on the movements within, movements of *reason* and movements of affectivity.

We did not set out to write a book on this paradigm shift. After finishing the book, however, we recognized the need to abandon a paradigm that has betrayed Ignatius and his first companions and has long pervaded both the practical application of the Spiritual Exercises and the practical living out of the Constitutions of the Society of Jesus.

The title of the book, *Impelling Spirit,* itself reflects the new paradigm. If it is taken as referring to Ignatius and his companions, if it is his spirit or their spirit that is impelling, we are caught in the old paradigm. Rather, the impelling spirit is the Holy Spirit, passionate, creative, innovative, wildly beyond the rational, propelling, driving, pushing, blowing like an untamed hurricane with no predictable path.

Impelling Spirit is about the first draft of a covering letter, proposed as a letter from the pope, that failed to see the light of day. Ignatius of Loyola and his companions wrote it in the summer of 1539 after asking Pope Paul III to approve their way of life in the Society of Jesus. Although only proposed, it is not without lasting value; although unofficial, it is not without great authority; although non–binding, it is not without immense force. Buried in the archives, it was long forgotten; after its discovery and publication, it has been virtually ignored.

Into the covering letter, so as to become one with it, the companions inserted the Formula of the Institute of the Society of Jesus, the written expression of their way of life, which resulted from the discernment process they made in the spring of 1539. The covering letter itself consists of a salutation plus a single complex sentence introducing the Formula, and two concluding sentences after the Formula. As the first enthusiastic outpouring of what the founding members of the Society think the pope ought to say to them in reply to their request for approval, those three sentences deserve close attention.

I stumbled upon them one day, even though they were there for all to see. Missioned to write on the Society's Constitutions after ten years directing Jesuits in the last phase of their training, *tertianship,* I was convinced that the best place to begin was with the Formula, since it precedes the Constitutions. As I was flipping the pages of a book that compares in thought lines the three Latin versions of the Formula from 1539, 1540, and 1550,[1] the Latin word for *all* leaped out at me. *All!* Like *nothing* in John of the Cross! We have no way of knowing whether Ignatius first wrote the Formula in Spanish, but Antonio M. de Aldama's Spanish translation of the Formula of 1550 leads off with *Todo* [all].[2] I became excited and read the document in Spanish: *todo* or *todos* was in every chapter or decree of the Formula. Those few moments provoked an experience, not an exegesis. "*Nada,*" says John of the Cross, "hold back *nothing.*" "*Todo*" or "*todos*" says Ignatius, "*All* should give *everything.*" The Formula of the Institute, which I had often facetiously called "the world's most boring document," suddenly became alive. Enthusiastic now, I turned to the Latin text of the first draft. For the first time in my life I encountered the three sentences of the covering letter and discovered in them a gold mine of spirituality, a rich source of wisdom, a seedbed of motivation for impassioned ardor in the service of Christ. Here was a treasure worth exploring; forget the Constitutions for the moment.

Those three sentences provide the immediate background and context of the Formula of the Institute. An understanding of them helps to understand the Formula, and an appreciation of them is a stimulant to living more fully the ideals of the Formula and to meeting more completely the demands of the Formula. The Formula itself is a ringing document filled with all the overtones and undertones of the Call and the Two Standards meditations of the Spiritual Exercises, written ostensibly to outline for the Holy See and any others who asked about this manner of life the essential elements of the companions' way of living, "their way of proceeding." It is not written in dry, juridical language; far more is it like a recruitment brochure aimed to attract and challenge magnanimous and high–spirited men who want to live this way. Its five brief decrees demand that the whole Society and all those who belong to it, each and every one, give themselves wholly and entirely, all that they are and all that they have, to the service of God, *todo*, holding back nothing whatsoever, *nada*. That is a summary of the spirit of the Formula of the Institute. Only a Spanish hidalgo would have the inner arrogance and humility, the boldness and simplicity, the daring and the discretion to write a document addressed to future followers and to present it to the pope for approval as a way of life.

This book, however, is not on the Formula itself (except briefly) but on the salutation and the three sentences of the covering letter into which the companions inserted the Formula. Whereas the first draft of the Formula has received attention and has been the object of articles and other studies, the original draft of the covering letter has remained in almost total obscurity. Ignatius and his companions wrote the Formula, of course, but they also wrote these three sentences, so that the whole thing, the three sentences and the Formula, form their proposed draft of an apostolic letter approving their way of living. Better than any other document of the early Society, it expresses who the companions think they are and what they want to do, situates them where they think they belong in the Church, and outlines their hopes for the future.

The actual bull of approval a year later, *Regimini militantis ecclesiae*, changes or omits some of the words and expressions but retains the substance of both the Formula and the covering letter. The language, however, of the covering letter in the first draft is more informal, more human, more dynamic, less stylized than that of *Regimini*. In the opening sentence, for example, the companions are not "inspired by the Spirit," as they are in *Regimini*, but they portray the Spirit as actively impelling them, just as in the Formula they portray the Spirit as actively impelling those who wish to join the Company. In the concluding sentence they have the pope say boldly to them to go wherever the Spirit leads them. That is the way they envision the Society, then, now, and always: blowing with the Wind, the Holy Spirit of God.

Because the proposed papal letter of 1539 contains the proposed Formula, the editors of the *Monumenta Historica Societatis Jesu* [MHSI] have chosen to call this document *Prima Societatis Iesu instituti summa* [The First Sketch of the Institute of the Society of Jesus]. Because it also contains the introduction to the Formula and the conclusion, I have chosen instead to call it *Cum ex plurium* [*CEP*], according to the first three words of the document, as is customary with papal letters.[3]

The introductory and concluding sentences of *Cum ex plurium* represent the pope's reflection on the companions and their way of life, his discernment regarding their discernment. This book, therefore, is also about discernment, personal and communal, about listening to a call and judging the genuinity of that call, about distinguishing the whisper of the Spirit from sound and fury. As a case study in discernment the book does not so much present theory as document reality. Discernment, needless to say, is for everyone, not simply for Jesuits. The words about the Holy Spirit, drawn from this distinctively Jesuit document, are applicable to anyone.

Both the proposed Formula and the covering letter mention the Holy Spirit twice. These passages adumbrate the contents of this book. The first decree of the proposed Formula concerns the mission of the Society. It counsels that anyone who wishes to be a member should keep that mission in mind and strive to fulfill it with his whole heart and soul "according to the grace given him by the Holy Spirit and according to the special character of his own call" [*CEP* 2]. In this decree the companions manifest delicate sensitivity to the unique call of each member of the Company. Although all are called to the same mission, each is called by the Holy Spirit in his own way and according to his own particular grace. This general principle, applicable to every Christian, has profound significance for governance in the Society, demanding sensitivity in each member to the way the Holy Spirit operates within him, and sensitivity in the superior to the peculiar workings of the Holy Spirit in each companion. The second decree of the proposed Formula concerns the vow of each companion to go wherever the pope sends him, and cautions that those who wish to be members should reflect beforehand on whether they have the spiritual wealth to finish this tower once they begin to build it, "that is, whether the Holy Spirit, who impels them, has promised them enough grace, that they hope to carry the burden of this calling with his help" [*CEP* 3]. The decree recognizes that the Holy Spirit not only gives grace to each companion according to his calling, but impels each of the companions to do what he is called to do. It demands that each companion recognize this fact in his own case, be sensitive to the way the Spirit deals with him, and not outrun the Spirit, and it demands that the superior recognize the same fact and take it into account in his dealings with each companion. This is a principle of discernment for anyone and everyone.

    The two passages of the proposed covering letter that mention the Holy Spirit reflect these two passages of the proposed Formula. A passage in the introductory sentence refers to the first companions in their coming together, "with the Holy Spirit, as we believe, impelling you" [*CEP* 1]. Here the impelling action of the Holy Spirit moves from the companions as individuals to the whole Company. The Holy Spirit impels them as a body. The passage in the conclusion, on the other hand, speaks not only to the first companions, but calls upon all the companions to the end of time to follow their vocation "wherever the Holy Spirit leads" [*CEP* 8]. The impelling action of the Spirit moves from the original Company to the Company in each succeeding period of time. The exhortation, moreover, fits everyone.

The proposed papal letter in its entirety expresses the conviction of the companions that the Holy Spirit impels each companion, and that the Holy Spirit impels the Company as a whole. This conviction, moreover, is a Christian conviction, applicable to all persons and groups in every time and place. This conviction underlies every page of this book; it is the unifying force, the skeletal structure on which the flesh is built, the theme that ties together all the disparate elements in the book. Every page, once we cut through the historical background and context of each reflection, speaks of decision–making in the Spirit, personal decisions according to the grace imparted to each companion, communal decisions according to the grace imparted to the Company. To write in this manner of the Society of Jesus is not to claim that the activity of the Spirit belongs to the Society alone. It is rather to indicate the usual manner in which the Spirit operates in the Church; indeed we are doing nothing more than outlining the way of God with individual human beings as well as with human society in general and individual human societies in particular.

Because the Holy Spirit impels the Company as a whole, this book is also about companionship, companionship in mission. The paradigm of the first companions is an archetype not only for Jesuits who share companionship in mission with other Jesuits, or for Jesuits and their coworkers who share companionship in the same mission, but for all who share companionship in mission, all who labor valiantly in Christ's vineyard.

This book is, moreover, about a founding experience. Although ostensibly presenting the thoughts and feelings of Pope Paul III, the three sentences of the covering letter reflect much more deeply the vibrant founding experience of the first companions themselves. Even though the Society of Jesus is modeled on the life of Ignatius, ten companions conceive the Society and put it together. This fact has implications for the rest of the Society: the responsibility for the Society is on all of its members. Today's companions need not look back at the founders as the giants of the Society nor at the first years as the Society's golden age.[4] Each age has to interpret the Formula in new and creative ways: the founding experience is not completed but is an ongoing process. In the spirit of Vatican II today's companions need to search out "the spirit and aims" of the founders of the Society of Jesus, so that passionately following their spirit in our own day, we may live in companionship and walk in discernment. Other religious families might well find some truth here regarding their own founding experiences.

As a result, this book is also about religious roots. Unless we know where we come from we cannot discern where we are going. The founding experience reveals those roots and also reveals that the roots are planted within a Christian tradition. By seeing how the Spirit works in history we come to a better understanding of what the Spirit is doing in the world today. In this book, in order to see how the companions are unique even as they fit into the Christian tradition, we pay particular attention to the Carthusians to whom Ignatius was attracted, the renewal movement of the Cistercians within the ancient Benedictine tradition, and the renewal movements of Francis and Dominic who inspired Ignatius in a special way.

Because the companions expressed their experience in the vocabulary of their day, this book pays attention to the meanings of words, the growth and change and development, and sometimes the frozen sameness, of those meanings across the centuries. We need to avoid the pitfall of projecting on the past our own experience and ways of expressing ourselves. It is all too easy to misinterpret documents from an earlier era by reading them from our own point of view. Not every word that looks familiar has the same meaning now that it had 450 years ago. In Shakespeare, for example, who is born eight years after the death of Ignatius and so is more or less a contemporary, the mention in *Richard III* of Hastings's "conversation with Shore's wife" refers to his adulterous relationship with her, not to a talk they had together. Similarly, when the companions write that the pope hopes to find in them "examples of the ancient conversation," they mean *the ancient Christian way of living*. Furthermore, nowhere in the proposed letter do the companions call themselves a "religio," in the sense of a religious order, but carefully avoid that term lest they be forced, according to the canon law of the time, to adopt and accept one of the already established rules. They are not monks or canons regular, and these rules are not appropriate. Nor are they friars like the Franciscans and Dominicans. They are not like anything seen before, and so they call themselves "societas," a *company* or *companionship,* a word not used of religious orders at that time, but of pious associations. Those who belong to the Society need to understand better the meaning of that word at the time the Society was founded in order to enflesh that meaning today and live the full reality.

In order to discover the meanings of the words the companions use in drafting this letter to them from the pope, we explore their own writings, the historical context in which they find themselves, and the tradition in which the Church lives and moves. Since many readers will find the sources inaccessible because of the languages in which they are written, we hope through this study to make some of the hidden riches of the Ignatian heritage more available to Jesuits old and young, to other religious men and women as they explore their own charisms and traditions, and to the lay reader seeking illumination and understanding of the Ignatian tradition or the larger Christian tradition. Unless otherwise noted, all translations are my own.

This book does not supply a blueprint for the future any more than the Gospel provides a series of steps in the imitation of Christ. The Christian is called to imitate Christ, not in repeating his actions but in his obedience to the Father. The companions of today and tomorrow are not called to make the same decisions as the companions of 1539, but they are called to make all their decisions in the Spirit. That is a full–time task.

Acknowledgements

We wish to thank the Society of Jesus for granting us the time and financial support to do this work. We particularly thank the United States Jesuit Conference for financial aid and support. Special thanks go to our Jesuit brothers, mostly of the Oregon Province, for their support, assistance, and encouragement: to Tom Royce, provincial at the time, and his formation assistant, Pat Lee, for missioning me and my coworker, Sr. Cecilia Wilms, to this work in the first place, and to Frank Case and Steve Sundborg, succeeding provincials, for support in maintaining the work; to Pat Howell most of all, who generously read the manuscript in both its earlier and later forms and made major suggestions for its improvement; to Carlos Sevilla (California Province), who met with enthusiasm an early attempt that later became the foundation for a key part of the book; to Steve Dillard, who helped me acquire a computer and introduced me to its mysteries; to Nick King (British Province), who was the first to read part of the manuscript, critique it, and encourage us to proceed; to Mike McHugh, a true companion, who read what we sent and asked for more; to Fred Schlatter, who was particularly helpful when Renaissance Latin challenged all credibility; to John Padberg (Missouri Province) of the Institute of Jesuit Sources, who read most of the manuscript and urged its completion; to Ted Kestler, who thrust the manuscript on other members of the Society; to Jan Vanneste (Northern Belgium Province), who read and critiqued part of the manuscript; to David G. Kramp, M.D., his wife Ann, and Sister Mary Ann McGee, who read and critiqued and bore the pain of a long-awaited birth; to Sharon Prendergast of Gonzaga University's Crosby Library (now the Foley Center), without whom we would have been minus many books she secured through interlibrary loan; to Phil Fischer (Wisconsin Province) of the Institute of Jesuit Sources and to Brother Phillip Wertmans, of Our Lady of Guadalupe Trappist Abbey, who provided photocopies of articles difficult for us to obtain; to Herman Morlion (Northern Belgium Province), librarian of the Jesuit theologate in Heverlee, and to the librarians and staff at the Catholic University of Leuven, who helped in finding sources not easily available in this country; to Charlie O'Neill (New Orleans Province) and his colleagues from many provinces at the House of Writers in Rome for their hospitality and assistance during my stay with them in 1990; to Peter Byrne, rector of St. Michael's Institute, who refrained from imposing other obligations; to Kevin McGinley, dean of St. Michael's, who made life easier by providing the means needed to work; to Ed Schmidt (Chicago Province), who not only volunteered to copyedit *Impelling Spirit* but by his Jesuit insights and literary skills graciously simplified the manuscript, making it more reader-friendly; to

Jeremy Langford and Jill Mark Salyards of Loyola Press, for their openness, adaptability, and professional concern for the look and feel of the book; to all our friends, priests, religious, and lay persons, who cheered us on and supported us by their prayers; to many Jesuit companions who will remain unnamed, whose interest was both comforting and stimulating even when they wondered if many years of labor would produce a word in print.

Editorial Note

This book draws on much deep historical research and technical vocabulary of the Christian spiritual tradition generally and of the Ignatian spiritual tradition in particular. For clarity and precision, the author must use technical terms and make frequent reference to particular source material. In the case of sources, frequent reference is made to Spiritual Exercises of St. Ignatius, Constitutions, Formula of the Institute, Deliberation of the First Fathers, and a few other documents; even under careful scrutiny it is not always clear if the reference is strictly to a one-time event (the Deliberation of the First Fathers) or a repeatable experience (Spiritual Exercises) or to a written document (Constitutions) or to a specific edition or printing of that document. The typographical principle followed is that the term is capitalized when the text refers specifically to the Spiritual Exercises of St. Ignatius, to the Jesuit Constitutions, to the Deliberation of the First Fathers, to the Formula of the Institute; these terms are italicized only when a specific printed book by that name is being referred to; the same principle applies to various rules such as the Rule of St. Benedict, of St. Augustine, of the Theatines, etc., and to Giberti's Constitutions as well as the Dominican Constitutions and Capuchin Constitutions. Note too that Latin orthography up to and including the sixteenth century was not consistent, even within the same document, so that a *v* or a *u* might appear in certain settings interchangeably, as might *e* or *ae*.

Chronology of Principal Events

1491   Birth of Ignatius at Loyola

1506–17   Ignatius at Arévalo, as page of Juan Velásquez de Cuéllar

1512–17   [Fifth Lateran Council]

1517–21   Ignatius in service of duke of Nájera, viceroy of Navarre

1521   Ignatius wounded at Pamplona; recovers at Loyola; conversion experience

1522   Ignatius leaves Loyola; arrives at Montserrat, March 24
Ignatius at Manresa; begins to write the Spiritual Exercises

1523   Ignatius pilgrimages to Jerusalem (via Barcelona, Gaeta, Rome, Venice)

1524   Ignatius studies grammar in Barcelona
[Theatines founded]

1525   Pierre Favre and Francisco Xavier arrive in Paris

1526   Ignatius studies humanities in Alcalá; is investigated and jailed

1527   July: Ignatius studies in Salamanca; is investigated and imprisoned
Simão Rodrigues arrives in Paris

1528   February: Ignatius arrives in Paris, studies Latin at Collège de Montaigu
[Capuchins and Somaschi founded]

1529	First investigation of Ignatius in Paris; Ignatius starts studying philosophy
1530	[Barnabites founded]
1532	January: Ignatius receives a bachelor of arts degree Diego Laynez and Alfonso Salmerón arrive in Paris
1533	March: Ignatius receives his licentiate in arts degree; begins his study of theology Nicolás de Bobadilla arrives in Paris
1534	August 15: Ignatius and the six first companions take vows at Montmartre Autumn: Claude Jay, Paschase Broët, Jean Codure arrive in Paris [Alessandro Farnese elected pope, Paul III]
1535	March: Ignatius receives his master of arts degree; second judicial inquiry in Paris April: Ignatius leaves for Azpeitia to restore his health, then for Venice December: Ignatius arrives in Venice, studies theology, gives the Spiritual Exercises [Gasparo Contarini named cardinal]
1536	Several companions receive the master of arts In Venice, rumors about Ignatius's orthodoxy November 15: The companions leave Paris for Venice
1537	January 8: The companions arrive in Venice; work in hospitals [March: Commission of cardinals proposes reform: *Consilium de emendanda ecclesia*] Mid March: All but Ignatius leave for Loreto, then Rome April 3, Easter Tuesday: The group is introduced to Pope Paul III April 27: Permission for (1) pilgrimage to Jerusalem, (2) ordination of non-priests Early May: They return to Venice June 10: Minor orders; June 15: subdiaconate; June 17: diaconate June 24: Ordination to priesthood of Ignatius and five companions Companions disperse to various cities within republic of Venice

	October: All gather in Vicenza; disperse to other cities of Italy
	End of judicial process in Venice
	November: Ignatius has a vision at La Storta; with Favre and Laynez he enters Rome
1538	January: Favre and Laynez teach at the Sapienza
	Ignatius gives the Spiritual Exercises to Contarini, Ortiz, etc.
	Lent: Laynez and Favre alarmed at sermons of Fra Agostino
	April: The other companions arrive in Rome
	May 3: They receive extraordinary faculties to preach and hear confessions
	Spring: A persecution breaks out against the companions
	June: Testimonials from Ferrara, Bologna, and Siena
	July 7: Request for investigation into accusations
	Late July or August: Ignatius talks to Paul III in Frascati
	September–October: Judicial process in Rome
	November 18: Decree declaring the companions innocent of charges
	November: "Oblation to the pope"
	December 25: Ignatius celebrates his first mass
1539	Late March: Deliberation of the First Fathers begins
	April 15: Document "On Making a Vow of Obedience"
	Late April: Broët and Rodrigues leave for Siena
	May–June: "Decisions about the Company"
	June 20: Favre and Laynez leave Rome for Parma
	June 24: The Deliberation ends
	Drafting of the Formula of the Institute, during or after the Deliberation
	July–August: Tommaso Badia, O.P., evaluates the Formula of the Institute
	Ignatius and his companions draft covering letter, create *Cum ex plurium*
	September 3: Paul III orally approves the Society
1540	March 16: Xavier leaves for India
	September 27: Paul III officially approves the Society of Jesus with the bull *Regimini*
1541	March: Ignatius and Codure begin drafting the Constitutions

	April 8: Ignatius is elected general of the new Society
	April 22: The companions profess their vows
	August 29: Jean Codure dies in Rome
1542	Favre writes his *Memoriale*
1544–45	Ignatius drafts the *Constituciones circa missiones*
1546	August 1: Pierre Favre dies in Rome
1547	Juan de Polanco is chosen secretary of the Society
	Laynez responds to Polanco's request about the Society's beginnings
1548	Paul III approves the Spiritual Exercises
1550	July 21: New confirmation of the Society by Julius III, bull *Exposcit*
1552	August 6: Jay dies in Vienna
	December 2: Xavier dies on the island of Sancian off the coast of China
1553	Jerónimo Nadal entrusted with promulgating the Constitutions
1553–55	Ignatius dictates his Autobiography
1556	July 31: Ignatius dies in Rome
1562	September 14: Paschase Broët dies in Paris
1565	January 19: Diego Laynez dies in Rome
1577	Rodrigues writes his account of the origins and progress of the Society
1579	July 15: Simão Rodrigues dies in Lisbon
1585	February 13: Alfonso Salmerón dies in Naples
1589	Bobadilla writes his Autobiography
1590	September 23: Bobadilla dies in Loreto

THE TEXT OF *CUM EX PLURIUM*

One might try to translate *Cum ex plurium* by breaking it into shorter, sharper statements. To do so, however, invites the danger of losing the original sense of unity, of correct emphasis and proper subordination. Our deliberate choice has been to try to reflect the complexity of the original but also to break the sentences into sense lines for greater reading clarity. Main verbs and clauses containing main verbs are set off a few spaces to the left.

Paulus

Dilectis filiis
Ignatio de Loyola, Petro Fabro, Iacobo Laines,
Claudio Iayo, Paschasio Broet, Francisco Xauier,
Alfonso Salmeroni, Simoni Roderico, Ioanni Coduri,
Nicolao de Bobadilla,
magistris parisiensibus,
pampilonensis,
gebenensis,
seguntinae
toletanae,
bissentinae,
ebredunensis,
et palentinae
respectiue diocesum.

Cum ex plurium sermone saepe intellexissemus
vos sponte
pauperes Christi sacerdotes
e diuersis mundi regionibus
in vnum conuenisse
et Spiritu Sancto, ut credimus, impellente,
in hanc vnam voluntatem conspirasse,
ut, relictis seculi huius illecebris,
vitam vestram
perpetuo Domini nostri Jesu Christi
atque eius in terris vicarii seruitio dedicaretis;

cumque probate fidei viri
nobis saepius testati essent,
vos per plures iam annos
laudabiliter in vinea Domini exerceri,
predicando publice verbum Dei,
exhortando priuatim,
confessiones audiendo,
exercendo homines in meditationibus piis,
inseruiendo hospitalibus,
peregrinando,
pueros et personas rudes docendo

Paul

To his beloved sons,
Ignatius de Loyola, Pierre Favre, Diego Laynez,
Claude Jay, Paschase Broët, Francisco Xavier,
Alfonso Salmerón, Simão Rodrigues, Jean Codure,
Nicolás de Bobadilla,
Masters of Paris,
from the dioceses respectively of
Pamplona,
Geneva,
Sigüenza,
Toledo,
Vizeu,
Embrun,
and Palencia.

Since from the words of many we have often gathered
that you, of your own free choice
poor priests of Christ
from various parts of the world
have joined together into one body
and with the Holy Spirit, as we believe, impelling you,
have conspired together in this one desire,
that, having abandoned the snares of this world,
you would dedicate your lives
to the perpetual service of our Lord Jesus Christ
and of his vicar on earth;

since also men of proven faith
have frequently testified to us,
that for many years now
you have worked commendably in the Lord's vineyard,
by publicly preaching the word of God,
by privately exhorting,
by hearing confessions,
by directing people in holy meditations,
by serving in hospitals,
by pilgrimaging,
by teaching children and the uninitiated

ea quae ad christiani hominis institutionem sunt necessaria,
et omnia demum charitatis officia,
vbicumque terrarum fuistis,
non modo sine vlla haeresis
aut auaritiae
aut turpitudinis alicuius nota,
sed multa etiam cum laude obeundo:

cum hec, inquam, de vobis audiremus,
gaudebamus, vt par est,
ac magnopere optabamus,
multos, imo omnes, si fieri possit,
et praesertim clericos
veteris conuersationis exempla
(quod uos facitis) renouare;

dumque animo voluebamus
aliquod signum edere,
quo vestram hanc pietatem ac religionem
gratam esse nobis declararemus,
dilectus filius noster cardinalis Contarinus
narrauit nobis
hoc vestrum vite institutum
et a multis laudari
et a quibusdam ita probari,
ut illud etiam sequi velint,
vosque omnes valde cupere
ad conseruandam ac perficiendam
vestre Societatis in Christo vnionem,
illa omnia, que vsu comperistis
ad propositum vobis finem conducentia,
scripto iam et obedientie vinculo stabilire;

ideoque supplicare,
ut in his nostris pene assiduis
grauissimisque occupationibus
per aliquem a nobis delegatum consideretur
an vestra viuendi formula
euangelicis consiliis
et canonicis patrum sanctionibus sit conformis,
et comperta eius
cum christiane religionis puritate congruentia,

what is necessary for the instruction of a Christian,
and finally by performing every work of charity,
wherever you have been,
not only without any sign of heresy
or avarice
or immoral conduct of any sort,
but even with great praise:

since, I say, we kept hearing these reports about you,
we began to rejoice, as is only right,
and fervently to desire,
that many people, even all, if possible,
and especially the clergy,
would renew the models of the ancient Christian way of living
(as you are doing);

and while we were considering
giving some sign,
by which we would make clear
that your loving and zealous way of living was pleasing to us,
our beloved son, Cardinal Contarini
informed us
that your manner of life
was praised by many
and so welcomed by some,
that they would also like to follow it,
and that all of you profoundly desire
for preserving and bringing to perfection
the union of your Society in Christ,
that all that you have found by experience
conducive to the end proposed to you,
you now solidify in writing and by the bond of obedience;

and therefore you were requesting,
that in the midst of our almost incessant
and burdensome occupations
it be considered through someone delegated by us
whether your form of living
is conformed to the evangelical counsels
and the normative teachings of the fathers,
and after it has been found
to be congruent with the purity of the Christian religion,

de more a nobis benedicatur
atque approbetur;

que vestra petitio
cum animum nostrum
bene de vobis iam dudum sentientem reperisset,
illico negotium hoc
dilecto filio Thome Badie,
sacri nostri palatii magistro,
delegauimus;

qui, re mature perspecta,
nobis retulit
vniversum propositum Societatis vestre
pium sibi sanctumque videri,
summamque regule,
quam servare cupitis,
infrascriptis quinque capitulis contineri. [CEP 1]

... Quinque capitula formulae instituti ... [CEP 2–7]

Hanc vestram vite formam,
suprascriptis quinque capitulis contentam,
cum perlegerimus et
ad spiritualem profectum Societatis ipsius vestre
et reliqui christiani gregis
cuius cura nobis incumbit,
iudicauerimus fore opportunam,
vigore presentium
illam laude dignam esse declaramus
atque apostolica auctoritate
approbamus,
benedicimus,
roboramus,
et sub tutela huius sanctae sedis recipimus
atque confirmamus,
facultatem vobis concedentes
condendi particulares inter uos Constitutiones,
quas ad Societatis vestrae finem
et Jesu Christi Domini nostri gloriam
et proximi vtilitatem
conformes esse iudicaueritis.

according to custom it be blessed by us
and approved;

since this petition of yours
had found our heart feeling well-disposed
toward you for a long time already,
we immediately delegated this matter
to our beloved son, Tommaso Badia,
the Master of the Sacred Palace;

who, after carefully considering the matter,
reported to us
that the whole intent of your Society
seemed to him to be good and holy,
and that the summary of the rule,
that you desire to follow,
is contained in the five decrees written below. [*CEP* 1]

... *Five decrees of the Formula of the Institute* ... [*CEP* 2–7]

Since we have read this way of life of yours,
contained in the above five decrees,
and have judged that it would be suitable
for the spiritual growth of your Society
and of the rest of the Christian flock,
whose care falls upon us,
by the power of these presents
we declare it to be worthy of praise,
and by our apostolic authority
we approve it,
we bless it,
we validate it,
and we receive it under the protection of this Holy See
and confirm it,
granting you the faculties
to establish particular constitutions for yourselves,
that you judge to be in accordance
with the end of your Society
and the glory of our Lord Jesus Christ
and the help of the neighbor.

Agite igitur, dilecti in Christo filii,
vestram vocationem sequimini,
   quo vos ducit Spiritus Sanctus,
   et in vinea Domini posthac,
   sub protectione huius sanctae sedis,
tanquam boni agricolae viriliter laborate,
   Domino nostro Jesu Christo vobis fauente,
   qui viuit et regnat cum Spiritu Sancto
   Deus in seculorum secula. Amen. [*CEP* 8]

Ego G. Cardinalis Contarenus fidem facio
   quod Tibure legi quinque suprascripta capitula
   sanctissimo patri nostro,
   pretermisis prohaemio et epilogo ultimo,
   quae intellecta sanctitas sua approbauit
   ac concessit ut fieret bulla uel breue,
   prout melius videretur,
   iuxta relationem R.[di] Magistri sacri pallatii,
   cui per me sua beatitudo iniunxerat,
      ut, re bene considerata, referret quid sentiret.
   Idem manu propria scripsi et subscripsi. [*CEP* 9]

Press on, therefore, beloved sons in Christ,
follow your call,
    whithersoever the Holy Spirit leads you,
    and in the vineyard of the Lord from now on,
    under the protection of this Holy See,
work with all your heart like good vinedressers,
    with our Lord Jesus Christ on your side,
    who lives and reigns with the Holy Spirit
    God forever and ever. Amen. [*CEP* 8]

I, G. Cardinal Contarini, attest that at Tivoli
I read the above five decrees to our Holy Father,
leaving out the introduction and final conclusion.
His Holiness understood them and approved them,
and authorized that a bull or brief should be drawn up,
whichever seemed better,
in accordance with the report of the Master of the Sacred
    Palace,
whom His Holiness had instructed through me
to report what he thought
after due reflection on the matter.
I have written this with my own hand and signed it. [*CEP* 9]

Introduction

The founding of the Society of Jesus begins with a discernment process. Ignatius and his nine companions, unable to fulfill the vow they had made at Montmartre in 1534 to go to Jerusalem, offer themselves to the pope so that he might send them anywhere in the world. When he begins to send them two by two to various places at the beginning of 1539, they come together to discern whether the pope's action means an end to the companionship they have enjoyed since the first three were roommates in Paris in 1529. No eyewitness account tells the complete story of that deliberation and its subsequent events. We piece together the essentials from five documents of 1539 found in the first volume of the *Constitutions* [*C*] of the Society in the *Monumenta Historica Societatis Iesu C* 1–22:[1]

(1) The Deliberation of the First Fathers [*Deliberatio primorum patrum*] [*D* 1–9], *C* 1–7.
(2) On Making a Vow of Obedience [*De obedientiae voto faciendo*], *C* 8.
(3) Decisions about the Company [*Determinationes Societatis*] [*DS* 1–17], *C* 9–14.
(4) *Cum ex plurium* [*CEP* 1–8], *C* 14–21.
(5) A Letter of Cardinal Contarini to Ignatius, *C* 21–22.

Because of the intimate connection between the questions asked during the process of discernment and the content of the proposed covering letter from the pope approving the

Formula of the Institute, we shall consider more extensively the minutes of that discernment process before indicating the contents of the other documents.

1. The Deliberation of the First Fathers

The Deliberation of the First Fathers [*D* 1–9] contains the minutes of the discernment process that leads Ignatius of Loyola and his companions to found the Society of Jesus. It provides the immediate context of the proposed letter that is the object of our study. The Deliberation lasted from the middle of Lent 1539 until the feast of John the Baptist, June 24 [*D* 9].[2] The minutes concern only the first two questions raised.

(a) The Occasion. In the autumn of 1538 Ignatius of Loyola and his companions offer themselves to Pope Paul III to go wherever he might send them. In the spring of 1539 the pope sends two of their number to Siena. What about the rest? Are they to be scattered everywhere? What are the implications? What are the consequences both of their own offering and of the pope's decision? Near the middle of Lent in 1539 the companions come together to discuss the situation. The minutes reveal their concern, their faith, their perseverance in prayer, the questions they ask, the methods they use to find the answers, the answers they find, the decisions they make. They reveal themes that appear again when the companions propose their draft of the apostolic letter approving their way of life.

More important than the minutes is the Deliberation itself, the psychological and spiritual experience of the companions that the minutes reveal. The minutes begin with a sense of excitement and expectation evoking the thoughts and feelings of Jesus in Luke's Gospel, "When the days drew near for him to be taken up, he set his face to go to Jerusalem" (9:51),[3] or in John's Gospel, "Now before the festival of the Passover, Jesus knew that his hour had come to depart from this world and go to the Father. Having loved his own who were in the world, he loved them to the end" (13:1). In the opening sentence the chronicler or secretary for the group introduces key words we shall explore in detail later in this work:

> Toward the end of Lent, when the time was drawing near that we must be divided and separated from one another—an event we awaited with the deepest longing—in order that we might attain more quickly the goal we had already set in our hearts and pondered over and passionately desired, we decided to come together [*conuenire*] for some days before dispersing, to discuss together our vocation and manner of living [*viuendi formula*]. [*D* 1]

They are excited that some are leaving, yet sad to see them go. They long to be on the road themselves: it is time to fulfill their vow to go wherever the pope sends them.

The subject they discuss is broad. All are men of eloquence, all enthusiastic, some more exuberant than others. They have staunch opinions, firm convictions, strong emotions, and differing perspectives, for "some were French, others Spanish, others Savoyards, others Cantabrians" [*D* 1]. At the same time a glimmer of light and of hope breaks through the darkness. In the midst of all the enthusiasm and eloquence and conflicting positions, one experience stands out: "Common to us all was one mind and will, namely to seek the gracious and perfect will of God according to the scope of our vocation" [*D* 1]. They differ on what means would be better and more fruitful both for themselves and for others. Their failure does not surprise them. After all, they are "weak and fragile" [*D* 1], and better men than they have disagreed with one another and held different and contrary opinions.

(b) Seeking God's Will. They experience the need to focus more. "Since we differed in our judgments," the chronicler writes, "we became solicitous and watchful to find a truly open way by which we might all offer ourselves as a holocaust to our God, in whose praise, honor and glory we might surrender all we had" [*D* 1]. They agree to pray more and reflect more each day, "to cast all [their] concerns on the Lord, hoping in him" [*D* 1]. They propose some tough questions to think about and pray about during the day, and at night each one shares what he thinks about the question at hand [*D* 2].

(c) The First Question: Companionship. The first night they go right to the heart of the matter:

> The question was raised whether it would it be better, now that we had offered and dedicated ourselves and our lives to Christ our Lord and to his true and legitimate vicar on earth, so that he might dispose of us and send us wherever he judged we could produce more fruit, whether to [the Turks],[4] or the Indies, or heretics, or whatever believers or unbelievers; to repeat, would it be better for us to be bound and joined together in one body in such a way that no physical separation however great might separate us, or would it perhaps not be better. [*D* 3]

An example clarifies the question: two of them are about to set out for Siena at the behest of the pope. Should the rest have more concern for them, and vice versa, than for others "outside the Company," that is, those who do not share their companionship and are not part of their group [*D* 3]? The answer is resoundingly affirmative:

> Since the most merciful and gracious Lord had deigned to unite us to one another [*vnire*] and to gather us together [*congregare*], weak as we are and from different places and cultures, we should not sever the bonding [*unionem*] and gathering [*congregationem*] that comes from God, but should daily strengthen it and ground it, forming ourselves into one body, each having knowledge of and concern for the others to the greater profit of souls, since power that is itself united [*vnita*] has greater strength and fortitude to carry out difficult undertakings than power that is diffused into many parts. [*D* 3]

God has bestowed on them the gift of friendship with one another. Through God's grace that friendship has flowered into a group with a mission. Their Company has two complementary aspects: it is a companionship [*unio*] and it is a group with a purpose [*congregatio*]. The result: companionship in mission, a group of friends in the Lord. Thus a question about *companionship* leads to a decision about the Company, that is, about both companionship and mission. They cannot reject God's gift. They choose not to dissolve the Company but to strengthen and ground it more solidly. Nevertheless, they want nothing to come from their own heart or their own head but only what God might inspire and what the Apostolic See might confirm and approve [D 3].

(d) The Second Question: a Vow of Obedience. The second question is just as important, just as central, but even more difficult:

> Since we had all made a vow of perpetual chastity and a vow of poverty in the presence of the most reverend legate of His Holiness when we were in Venice, would it be better to make a third vow, namely, of obeying one of us, so that we might more sincerely and with greater praise and merit fulfill the will of the Lord our God in all things, and at the same time carry out the free will and command of His Holiness, to whom we had freely offered all we had, our will, our intellect, our ability, etc. [D 4]

Day after day of discussion brings no response. The question needs more focus, and they need more focus. They focus themselves by agreeing on three attitudes of mind and heart: (1) they will prepare and pray in such a way as to be confident that they will find joy and peace in the Holy Spirit regarding a vow of obedience, trying as best they can to be more inclined to obey than to command; (2) none of them will discuss the matter with any of the others outside the time they come together to share the results of their prayer, lest they be swayed by one another's opinions, but will seek the answer in prayer alone; (3) each will consider the matter as though he is not a member of the group, so as to be more objective concerning what might be more to the service of God and the preservation of their companionship [D 6].

Secondly, they focus the question by taking a negative stance and then an affirmative stance. One day they give reasons *against* making a vow of obedience, such as: obedience is not highly regarded today because it is badly practiced; and, we might be forced to accept an already existing rule which would frustrate our desires to work with people [D 7]. Another day they give reasons *for* making the vow, for example: without obedience the Company would not last long; obedience keeps a mission–oriented group together better than anything else; although they have committed themselves in obedience to the pope, he cannot and should not spend time taking care of all the numerous little details of their lives [D 7]. Many days they spend going back and forth examining the more serious arguments and spending time in prayer and meditation. Finally, with the help of God, they come to the unanimous conclusion:

> It is better and more necessary for us to give obedience to one of our Company, so that we might better and more exactly achieve our primary desire of fulfilling the divine will in all things, so that the Company would be preserved more surely, and finally proper provision could be made for whatever matters might arise, both spiritual and temporal. [D 8]

A question about mission leads to a decision about the Company, that is, about both companionship and mission. They choose to strengthen and ground more solidly by a vow of obedience their mission to do God's will, and in the process to preserve more surely the Company in both its companionship and its mission.

(e) Summary. As a document, the Deliberation tells the story of the companions' unanimous choice to maintain their companionship intact even as Pope Paul III begins to send them to different parts of the world, of their choice to follow a particular method of discernment in determining other more difficult questions, and of their choice to take a vow of obedience to one of their own. From other documents we learn further details of what happened and what they discussed once they had determined the two major questions of unity and obedience.

2. The Other Documents of 1539

On Making a Vow of Obedience [C 8], dated April 15, contains the statement, signed by each of the companions, that they have decided that "for the praise of God and the perpetuation of the Society there should be a vow of obedience in it," and they commit themselves "to enter the same Society if, with the Lord's favor, it should be confirmed by the pope." The unique character of this action reveals the importance of obedience to the companions; at no other time during the Deliberation do they commit themselves in this fashion to a particular decision they have made. To the final survivor amongst the companions,

Nicolás de Bobadilla, we owe a debt of gratitude for providing the context for this document in his Autobiography (1589):

> They reflected and decided that, after making a general confession, each companion would go to his own room and pray to God for fifteen days that he might reveal to them his holy will; at the end of the fifteen days they would receive communion at the end of a Mass celebrated by Master Favre, who was a sort of father of them all from hearing their confessions, so that he might ask each and every one of the companions if they wanted to be united and to form a religious order of all of them, if it pleased God and the Supreme Pontiff, and whether each one wanted to be a member of that religious order and society. They all found themselves to be of the same mind, and each responded affirmatively, and then was given the Eucharist of the body and blood of Christ. After this was done, they wrote their names and nicknames,[5] and these were given to the Supreme Pontiff Paul III [*B* 12].[6]

Decisions about the Company [*DS* 1–17] outlines the other questions they discuss in the Deliberation between May 4 and June 24.[7] The decisions regard what should be included in the Formula, their written way of living.

Cum ex plurium [*CEP* 1–8], the proposed papal letter approving the companions' way of living, contains the final immediate result of the Deliberation: the five decrees or chapters [*capitula*] of the Formula of the Institute which form the heart of the proposed letter [*CEP* 2–7].[8] The Formula was written either toward the end of the Deliberation as part of the communal effort, or shortly thereafter. The original manuscript is no longer extant. We know from the introductory sentence of *Cum ex plurium* that Pope Paul III asked a theologian his opinion on the Formula. *Cum ex plurium* is the response to the theologian's judgment that the way of life embodied in the Formula is good and holy.

Cum ex plurium opens with a salutation naming each of the companions, and an introduction sketching some of the circumstances surrounding the request of the companions for papal approval of their way of life. The introduction preceding the five decrees or chapters [*capitula*] of the Formula of the Institute is one long compound-complex sentence that accomplishes much in little space. That one sentence indicates Paul III's attitude toward this spontaneous and motley group of companions from various parts of the world who, under the impelling power of the Holy Spirit, form a company of priests living in the poverty of Christ, sloughing off the snares of the world and dedicating themselves in perpetuity to the service of Christ and his vicar on earth. By a wide variety of apostolic endeavors they gain such a good reputation that others desire to join them, and the pope sees in them the hope of genuine reform in the Church, especially amongst the clergy. The same sentence reveals that Cardinal Gasparo Contarini reported to the pope the companions' desire to perpetuate both the union they celebrate and the work they have begun by taking a vow of obedience, and their request that a judgment be made concerning their way of life, that the pope responded by delegating Tommaso Badia, the Master of the Sacred Palace, to evaluate their written way of living, and that Badia returned his judgment that their intent was good and holy and that an apostolic letter of approval should be drafted [*CEP* 1].[9] Following the five decrees [*CEP* 2–7] are two concluding sentences, the first containing the papal approbation and blessing, and the second a brief exhortation urging the companions to press on and to follow their vocation wherever the Spirit leads them [*CEP* 8].

Cum ex plurium, then, is the immediate response of the companions to Badia's judgment that an apostolic letter of approval should be drafted. They draft their own proposal for an apostolic letter addressed to themselves approving their way of life, including in the letter the Formula to be approved, and they write it in such a manner that it can become either a bull or a brief. They include the Formula within the letter, perhaps, as Aldama suggests,[10] because the Rule of Francis had been included in the bull of Honorius III, *Solet annuere*, in 1223.[11] Including the five decrees in a papal document would give them full papal authority.

At the end of the proposed papal letter, but not intended as part of it, is a memo in Contarini's hand, unaddressed but obviously intended for the companions [*CEP* 9]. It indicates that he read the five decrees of the Formula to the pope, but not the introduction and conclusion of *Cum ex plurium,* and that the pope approved them as read and ordered a brief or bull of approval to be drawn up, whichever would be more suitable, as the Master of the Sacred Palace had recommended.

A Letter of Cardinal Contarini to Ignatius [*C* 21], dated September 3 and written from Tivoli, indicates that Contarini had received from Ignatius through Antonio de Araoz the expanded form of the five decrees, that is, the Formula with the introduction and conclusion, along with a note from the Master of the Sacred Palace. He says that he made an oral presentation, then read the decrees to the pope, who graciously approved them. He adds that on their return to Rome they will have Cardinal Ghinucci draw up a brief or bull, whichever is more appropriate.[12] Contarini's note comes after *Cum ex plurium* in time, but it sheds some light on its creation.

Seeking further details from the companions themselves, we glean very little beyond Bobadilla's remarks regarding the vow of obedience. Two of the companions, Pierre Favre and Diego Laynez, leave Rome on a papal mission to Parma before the deliberations of 1539 are completed. Favre makes no mention of them in his *Memoriale*. In 1547, eight years after the event, Laynez writes a letter to the secretary of the Society, Juan de Polanco, on the origins of the Society; he mentions the deliberations, adding nothing to what is found in the official documents, but is silent about *Cum ex plurium* [*L* 49].[13] The Autobiography of Ignatius stops, for all practical purposes, with the end of the persecutions of 1538 [*A* 98].[14] In his memoirs written late in life, Simão Rodrigues, adds nothing significant [*R* 91–92].[15]

From Jerónimo Nadal, a second-generation companion, comes the tradition that when Contarini read the Formula to Paul III the pope responded, "The Spirit of God is here." We shall return to this remark in chapter five. Juan de Polanco, another second-generation companion who had made the Exercises under Laynez and entered the Society in 1541, provides information regarding the original intent of the companions and the role of Cardinal Contarini. Chosen by Ignatius in 1547 as secretary of the Society, he immediately set to work writing a history of the origins and first years of the Society, gathering his data from first-generation companions.[16] From him we learn that "in the absence of some of the companions, Father Master Ignatius and the others who were with him in Rome, to whose judgment the rest deferred, after putting in order their "form of life," desired to present it to the pope without any intermediary. Since the pope, however, wanted to leave Rome, they used Cardinal Contarini to propose it so as not to have to wait for the pope's return" [*PSH* 89].[17]

When Contarini returns to Rome, he delivers the document to the office in charge of papal briefs, following the plan he indicated in his letter to Ignatius. After a careful reading, the prefect refers it to the Chancery to be transformed into a papal bull.[18] During the course of a year the document undergoes some modifications. The framers of the new bull make a few changes in the Formula itself and adapt the rest of the letter to accord better with the style of a papal bull. Nonetheless, many of the words and ideas proposed by the companions in 1539 for an apostolic letter make their way into the papal bull approving the Society of Jesus in 1540, *Regimini militantis Ecclesiae* [*C* 24–32]. Many of their words and ideas also remain in *Exposcit debitum* [*C* 373–83], the bull of confirmation of 1550 that governs the Society today. The modifications that the framers of *Regimini* and *Exposcit* made in the first draft of the Formula have attracted the attention of writers on the Society. The original draft of the proposed covering letter of approval from the pope, however, namely the introduction and conclusion, has remained in almost total obscurity, the fate, no doubt, of most original drafts. This first draft, however, deserves a better fate, for it is written by the persons to whom it is addressed and reveals what those persons (Ignatius and his companions) suggest that the pope say to them in reply to their request that he approve their way of life.

To sum up, then, apart from the five documents of 1539 considered above, we learn little about *Cum ex plurium* or the events leading to its creation from the other writings of the companions themselves. Their almost total silence on *Cum ex plurium* reveals that the companions did not cling to it; they clung to the will of God expressed to them through the Holy Father. For Ignatius, what the pope approved was more important than what he, Ignatius, had written. For all of them, it was more important to live the spirit of *Cum ex plurium* than to quote it and to dream about it. At the same time, as we shall see, in one form or another *Cum ex plurium* lies deep at the heart of the Society and the Church and expresses the deepest longings and desires of the Christian spirit.

3. Authorship of *Cum ex plurium*

Jerónimo Nadal, a native of Majorca whom Ignatius had tried to recruit in Paris, entered the Society in 1545. He was close to Ignatius, who in 1553 gave him the task of promulgating the Constitutions. On at least two occasions Nadal indicates that the other companions assigned Ignatius the task of writing the Formula of the Institute.[19] Nadal is not always precise in his details, but with no evidence from other sources of that day, no one disputes his assertion even though it comes more than twenty years after the event. Who could better summarize the companions' way of life than Ignatius, who had fathered the others in that way of life?

Nevertheless, Heinrich Böhmer (1914) suggests that Cardinal Gasparo Contarini, who read the Formula of the Institute to Paul III in Tivoli, is the author of the introduction and conclusion of *Cum ex plurium*. Böhmer makes no argument for his contention. He appears to have assumed that Contarini was the author on the grounds that the text was found amongst his papers.[20] The editors of the *Monumenta* (1934), on the other hand, call Ignatius the principal author of the complete text arguing from similarities between expressions in *Cum ex plurium* and the Formula and expressions Ignatius uses in the Constitutions on Missions and the Declarations on Missions [*C* 159–64].[21] Other arguments will follow below. Aldama (1977), too, accepts Ignatius as author of the Formula; when he refers to the writing of the rest of the apostolic letter, that is, of the introduction and conclusion, he says either "St. Ignatius and his companions" or "the fathers."[22]

On the contrary, Georg Schurhammer (1961) asserts that Contarini wrote the introduction and conclusion, without, however, giving an argument for his conclusion beyond asserting that the wording of *Cum ex plurium* is too laudatory of the Society for Ignatius to be the author.[23] Jesús Iturrioz (1989), who rightly is impressed by Schurhammer's scholarly work in writing the life of Xavier, creates a scenario in which Contarini collaborates in preparing the introduction and conclusion. In this scenario Contarini "on his own initiative" includes the laudatory phrases.[24]

In reply to Schurhammer and Iturrioz, *Cum ex plurium,* as a matter of fact, is only echoing the laudatory words of both the governor of Rome and of the pope himself. After a long public investigation of their doctrine and conduct the previous year, the governor declared in a public decree that by reason of the charges and whispers against them Ignatius and his companions had not only not incurred any mark of dishonour either in law or in fact but their lives and doctrine had taken on a greater luster [*FD* 557].[25] Ignatius himself had asked for the formal investigation and wanted a formal decree from the governor. *Cum ex plurium* echoes the governor's remark in stating that the companions have labored unceasingly not only without any ignominious mark of heresy or avarice or immoral conduct of any sort but even with great praise. As for Paul III, even while the investigation was in progress, he had many times spoken favorably of them in public, even in their presence [*IR* 6].[26] Since Ignatius was determined that their apostolic work would suffer no harm from the false charges brought against them, he might well wish to introduce into a proposed papal letter a laudatory remark that the pope had made about them.

Ignatius as Principal Author

My own position is that all of the companions, by participating in the Deliberation, provide the basic material for *Cum ex plurium.* Someone must give it form. Others might contribute to discussions on the final text, but evidence points to Ignatius as the principal author, not only of the Formula, but of the introduction and conclusion as well. For internal evidence we compare *Cum ex plurium* (a) with the Deliberation of the First Fathers and also (b) with a letter Ignatius wrote to Isabel Roser on December 19, 1538. For external evidence we consider (c) Ignatius's diplomatic experience.

(a) The Deliberation and *Cum ex plurium*. The opening sentence of *Cum ex plurium* that introduces the Formula of the Institute reverberates throughout with echoes of the minutes of the discernment process, the Deliberation of the First Fathers, indicating they come from the same source. Each document begins with the same sense of excitement and anticipation. Each celebrates the same graces, almost always in the same words, their choice to come together, their common vulnerability, their diversity, their deep experience of unity. Each expresses a sense of their commitment to Christ and his vicar. Each moves from unity to obedience, and each contains a desire for obedience and the preservation of the Society. Throughout each runs a sense that the companions have submitted their lives to the movements of the Holy Spirit. The two documents are so similar in spirit and content and vocabulary that there can be no doubt that they come from the same source: the companions. For example:

	Deliberatio	*Cum ex plurium*
[coming together]	*inter nos conuenire* [1]	*in vnum conuenisse*
[diversity]	*ex diuersis regionibus et moribus* [3]	*e diuersis regionibus et moribus*
[unity]	*una communis mens et voluntas* [1]	*in hanc vnam voluntatem*
[commitment to Christ]	*dedicaueramus Christo* [3]	*dedicaretis . . . Christi*
[and to his vicar]	*et eius . . . vicario in terris* [3]	*atque eius in terris vicarii*
[submission to Christ]	*quod Dominus inspirauerit* [3]	*Domino praestante auxilium*
[and to the Holy Spirit]	*pacem in Spiritu Sancto* [6]	*Sancto Spiritu impellente*

(b) Letter to Isabel Roser and *Cum ex plurium*. Some months before *Cum ex plurium*, Ignatius wrote to a friend in Barcelona, Isabel Roser, outlining the works the companions were doing in Rome: preaching on every feast, lecturing twice a day, hearing confessions, directing the spiritual exercises. Then he says that they hope to increase the sermons and to teach children [*IR* 7]. *Cum ex plurium* also names the works the companions have been doing. Its list follows the same order as that of the letter to Isabel Roser. It omits lecturing, and it adds more works, inserting them into the order Ignatius had already established in the letter to Isabel Roser. The similarity of content and order suggests that the author of one is the author of the other:

	Ignatius to Roser	*Cum ex plurium*
[preaching]	*sermones*	*predicando*
[lecturing]	*lecciones*	
[exhorting]		*exhortando*
[hearing confessions]	*confessiones*	*confessiones audiendo*
[directing spiritual exercises]	*exercicios espirituales*	*exercendo*
[serving in hospitals]		*inseruiendo hospitalibus*
[pilgrimaging]		*peregrinando*
[teaching children]	*mostrar muchachos*	*pueros docendo*
[works of charity]		*charitatis officia*

(c) Ignatius's Training in Diplomacy. Ignatius was also better equipped than any of the other companions to prepare a document for papal signature, a task demanding tact and diplomacy. He had been educated as a courtier in the home of Juan Velázquez de Cuéllar, whose wife was a relative of Ignatius's mother. Velázquez was the chief treasurer of Ferdinand and Isabella and continued in that position after Isabella died. He wrote to Beltrán de Loyola, Ignatius's father, offering to take one of Beltrán's sons into his home, raise him like one of his own sons, and find him a position in the royal court,[27] possibly, as Iturrioz suggests, in the royal secretariat.[28] Beltrán sent Ignatius to the Velázquez home in Arévalo where he lived in a richly appointed palace adorned by objects acquired in the public auction of Queen Isabella's effects. Although Velázquez failed to place Ignatius in the royal court, the young Basque not only developed what he himself admits was a good hand [*A* 11] but also studied Latin and music and poetry and had access to a library filled with religious and secular literature. Furthermore, as one of the family of the royal treasurer, he also associated with members of the royal court [*A* 53]. If he picked up some of the vices of the court, he also acquired the gracious manner of a courtier[29] and felt at home with those of high station.[30] Upon leaving the household of Juan Velázquez, Ignatius became a gentleman of the house of the duke of Nájera, the viceroy of Navarre.[31] Ignatius was skilled in arbitration, and the viceroy sent him as a member of a delegation to settle a dispute amongst the towns of Guipúzcoa. He was not the chief negotiator, but he acquitted himself with distinction in bringing divergent minds together [*PV* 3].[32] As his letters indicate, Ignatius was not struck dumb by cardinals and kings. He had the knowledge and the skill to write a letter in the name of the pope.

The Latin Stylist. But did Ignatius have the skill to write the Formula and its covering letter in Latin? Others of the Company, certainly, had more skill than he. Various possibilities for a Latin stylist offer themselves. The *Monumenta* editors suggest that Jean Codure was at hand, who later assisted Ignatius in the writing of the Constitutions. So was Alfonso Salmerón, a bright young scholar more proficient in Latin than Ignatius. Favre was present, and so was Laynez, at least until June 20.[33] The editors apparently assume that the Formula was finished during the Deliberation, and that the covering letter was written at the same time. Iturrioz, on the other hand, seems to assume that the Formula was written after the Deliberation had concluded.[34] That would rule out Favre and Laynez, who left Rome on June 20, if not earlier. It would also rule out Codure, who arrived in Velletri on June 24 on a preaching mission [*EB* 417],[35] the day the Deliberation ended. Broët and Rodrigues had left for Siena in the latter part of April.[36] Left with Ignatius in Rome were Jay, Bobadilla, Salmerón, and Xavier. Consequently Iturrioz picks Xavier as the Latin stylist. Xavier is, in fact, a likely candidate. At first, after members of the Company began to leave Rome, those who remained took weekly turns in writing to them. Sometime after Favre left Rome, Xavier took over the task of writing for everyone, effectively becoming the first secretary of the Company [*EM* 40].[37] A nobleman like Ignatius, he was more familiar with curial protocol than the other companions. As a former teacher at the University of Paris, he not only knew Latin, the language of the classsroom, but knew how to organize and present arguments in a clear and forceful manner.

The Scribe. The manuscript containing *Cum ex plurium*, however, is not in Xavier's hand, nor in that of Ignatius. José Calveras has identified the writer, that is, the scribe, of the two manuscripts containing *Cum ex plurium* as Bartolomeo Ferrão, a Portuguese who was living with the companions.[38] One manuscript contains a memo by Contarini in his own hand, a note saying that he had read the five decrees of the Formula to the pope. That manuscript is preserved in the Vatican archives, bound in a volume containing Contarini's letters and other works.[39] In 1881 Dr. Franz Dittrich, who was doing research on the cardinal, published a number of documents and letters relating to Contarini which he had found in various archives. Included among the documents published was part of this manuscript from the Vatican. Dittrich erroneously dated it 1540, mistakenly thinking the five decrees of the Formula were identical with those found in *Regimini militantis Ecclesiae* and therefore omitting them. He published instead, edited with a number of glaring mistakes, the covering letter introducing and concluding the five decrees of the Formula.[40] Tacchi Venturi later published the entire document, well edited, and in parallel columns with *Regimini* for purposes of comparison.[41] The entire document has been edited anew and published in the *Monumenta*, *C* 14–21. The other manuscript has the same memo, but written in the hand of Antonio de Strada, who worked in the Society's secretariat from the beginning of 1539 until 1542. That manuscript is in the Society's archives in Rome.

4. Structure and Content of *Cum ex plurium*

The proposed covering letter from the pope begins with the name of the pope, added in Contarini's hand, and then the names of those to whom the letter is addressed. The introduction itself consists of one very long compound-complex sentence. Throughout the sentence the companions play a subordinate role syntactically, even though they are the subject of more subordinate verbs than is anyone else. The sentence contains four main verbs. Three of these have the pope as their subject, for he plays the primary role. The cardinal is the subject of the remaining verb: his role is entirely secondary. The first two verbs show the pope's reaction to what he has heard about who the companions are and what they have done: he *began to rejoice,* and he *began to desire.* The third verb indicates Cardinal Contarini's role: he *informed* the pope of the latest developments in the lives of the companions and of their request to the pope. The fourth verb gives the pope's prompt acquiesence to their request: he *delegated* someone to investigate and form a judgment. The conclusion consists of two short sentences, a blessing and an exhortation. Throughout the book a brief comment on the Latin structure will introduce each section of new material.

Cum ex plurium is not unlike a **three-act play.** The first lines are like a **prologue** introducing the characters in the drama. The long sentence whose function is to introduce the five chapters or decrees of the Formula of the Institute opens with three clauses beginning with *cum* [since]: since this, and since that, and since both (by way of repetition). Together they form a single unit, **three scenes in the first act of a drama.** The first *cum* clause is like a scene in which many different people report to the pope about who the companions are, their personal lives, their way of life; it covers matters that will eventually find their way into Part VI of the Constitutions. The second *cum* clause is like another scene in which more people report to the pope on the work the companions have been doing and the way they have been doing it; it deals with ministry, to be covered later in Part VII of the Constitutions. The third *cum* clause recalls the preceding two clauses (as though the pope is walking back and forth on the stage pondering over and soliloquizing about what he has heard) and presents two main verbs providing the pope's reaction to what he has learned: joy and a great longing that others would do what the companions are doing.

The second unit, **the second act,** opens with the pope reflecting on how he might give some public sign of his approval of the companions' way of life. His reflections are interrupted by a major event worthy of a main verb: Cardinal Contarini enters. He reports more immediate information regarding the companions: the desires of others to follow them and their own deep desires for unity, obedience, and the preservation of the group, matters later contained in Parts VIII, IX, and X of the Constitutions.[42] He also reports their specific request to the pope: that someone delegated by the pope would examine their way of life found in the five decrees of the Formula of the Institute as a prelude to giving his blessing and approval; they themselves suggest the norms for judging the written way of living [*viuendi formula*]. The desires of all the main actors have converged on the same goal.

The third unit, **the third act,** is brief and direct in its action, lengthy in its words. It provides through a main verb the papal response to the request of the companions: he immediately delegates someone to do what they have requested and the report comes back that their whole intent is good and holy. At this point come the five chapters or decrees of the Formula of the Institute (as though Cardinal Contarini had come on stage and was reading them to the pope), the outline of the companions' way of life. After he finishes reading, the **denouement** follows swiftly: in one sentence the pope gives his blessing and approval; in a second sentence he urges the companions to follow the lead of the Holy Spirit and invokes the favor of Christ.

To leave the analogy of a play and return to the theme of discernment, the companions chose to narrate a sequence of particular historical events in writing the proposed covering letter from the pope. Purposely or unpurposely, therefore, the narrative models, or models itself on, the experience of one who watches and monitors the discernment process of another, and that model has determined the outline of this book. An ordinary discernment process consists of three parts: (1) gathering data and reflecting on the data before the decision, (2) making the decision, (3) seeking confirmation of the decision. One who confirms the decision follows a somewhat similar process: (1) gathering data and reflecting on the data, (2) reflecting on the decision itself and/or the circumstances surrounding the decision, (3) confirming or rejecting the decision. (The confirmation of this new decision to confirm or reject comes from higher authority or from history.)

Viewed from this perspective, the letter divides naturally into the three parts or moments of the discernment process. After the salutation comes the main body of the letter. In Part One Pope Paul III is portrayed as reflecting on reports he has received on the lives and ministry of the companions, and as reflecting also on his own interior response to those reports. In Part Two the pope reflects first on his desire to manifest his esteem for the companions, and then he reflects on learning about their decision to seek approval for their way of living, and on the norms they suggest for judging that way of living. In Part Three the pope reflects on the advice he has been given, presents the companions' summary of their way of living, confirms their decision by granting his approval, and urges them to follow their call wherever the Holy Spirit leads them.

The approval of the pope marks a beginning rather than an end. In one sense, this new beginning brings discernment to an end. Approval, however, is a charge to carry out the decisions made in a spirit of ongoing discernment. Discernment once begun only leads to further discernment. The risks and the decision-making continue. As Robert E. Lee Prewitt muses in *From Here to Eternity*, "You decided one thing right, with much effort, and then you thought you'd coast a while. But tomorrow you had to decide another thing. And as long as you decided the way you knew was right you had to go right on deciding."[43] If the companions have surrendered to the impelling Spirit, they must continue to do so now and until the end of time. Discernment goes on; the Spirit continues to impel; listening cannot cease; generosity cannot end. The Company of Jesus is just beginning.

SALUTATION

1

Pope Paul III and His Beloved Sons

The proposed apostolic letter *Cum ex plurium* begins as follows:

> Paul
> [Paulus]
> **To his beloved sons,**
> [Dilectis filiis]
> **Ignatius de Loyola, Pierre Favre, Diego Laynez,**
> [Ignatio de Loyola, Petro Fabro, Iacobo Laines]
> **Claude Jay, Paschase Broët, Francisco Xavier,**
> [Claudio Iayo, Paschasio Broet, Francisco Xauier]
> **Alfonso Salmerón, Simão Rodrigues, Jean Codure,**
> [Alfonso Salmeroni, Simoni Roderico, Ioanni Coduri]
> **Nicolás de Bobadilla,**
> [Nicolao de Bobadilla]
> **Masters of Paris,**
> [magistris parisiensibus]
> **from the dioceses respectively of**
> **Pamplona** [Spain: Ignatius and Xavier],
> [pampilonensis]
> **Geneva** [Savoy: Favre, Jay, Broët],[1]
> [gebenensis]
> **Sigüenza** [Spain: Laynez],
> [seguntinae]
> **Toledo** [Spain: Salmerón],
> [toletanae]

Vizeu [Portugal: Rodrigues],
[bissentinae]
Embrun [France: Codure],
[ebredunensis]
and Palencia [Spain: Bobadilla].
[et palentinae]
[respectiue diocesum].

An apostolic letter is a legal document issuing from the Holy See. Like any legal document, it has its own format to follow, its own established words and phrases and clauses. The creativity of the writer consists in applying the established terminology and format to a particular situation. The first word is the pope's name. From the beginning, he holds center stage.

Various kinds of apostolic letters fit different occasions and purposes. Two of the most important kinds are bulls and briefs. A papal bull gets its name from the fact that at one time a major papal document was sealed with melted lead [*bulla*]. A papal brief, as the name indicates, is generally short, and its object is generally of less importance than that of a bull.[2] Both bulls and briefs begin with the pope's name, but a bull adds solemn and formal titles to the name. Since the companions are simply proposing a text, they omit the name entirely. In his own hand, Contarini adds the pope's name, totally unadorned. The letter can become either a bull or a brief.

Sometimes bulls and briefs mention other persons immediately after the pope's name and title. If he is addressing specific persons, he names them individually and calls them beloved sons [*dilectis filiis*] or beloved daughters [*dilectis filiabus*], or venerable brothers [*venerabilibus fratribus*], depending on their status. The letter often adds a title and/or a place to distinguish a person more precisely. Like *Dear Mom,* and *Dear Mr. Jones*, the phrases are stereotyped, although not devoid of meaning. The pope uses them whether he knows the persons or not: all bishops and archbishops are venerable, all others are beloved sons or daughters. The depth of meaning depends on the depth of the relationship between the pope and the persons themselves.

The proposed apostolic letter *Cum ex plurium* calls the companions "beloved sons" [*dilectis filiis*], names each of them (they are all founders), gives them the title of "Masters of Paris," and indicates the dioceses from which they come.

Paul III attracts our attention first. Who is he? What is his story? What does he know about the companions and how does he relate to them? What is the significance of the title "Masters of Paris," and why would the companions wish him to call them by that title? Reflections of this nature should lead to an appreciation of the real meaning contained for these persons in the stereotyped formula "beloved sons." Is Paul a loving father to them? Are they really his beloved sons?

1. Paul III

Paul III is born Alessandro Farnese in 1468, either at Canino or Rome. Since he lives in the heyday of the Italian Renaissance, he is extremely well educated. Innocent VIII names him apostolic secretary and notary at the age of twenty-three. Two years later in 1493, he is made a cardinal by Alexander VI, who has had an amour with Alessandro's sister Giulia. In 1499 Alexander VI gives him the bishopric of Corneto and Montefiascone. He is not yet ordained a priest, but the benefice supports his needs and desires.[3] By 1509, when Farnese, unordained and unmarried, is given the diocese of Parma, he has fathered three sons and one daughter.

The young Farnese is a good example of what disturbs Ignatius and his companions about the Church of their day. They profoundly oppose the greed for riches and the desire for honor that envelops much of the Church. The system of benefices based on money-producing titles and positions feeds both of these diseases. In theory the benefice system simply recognizes the right of the laborer in the vineyard of the Lord to receive just compensation for one's labor. In theory the income from a benefice is paid to the cleric who lives and works in the place. The reality, however, is far different. Many incomes go to absentees for work they do not do. Moreover, much of Farnese's personal life is an excellent example of what Ignatius and his companions object to in the life of the Church (and the earlier years of the pope's life may well remind Ignatius of his own younger years). His life, however, is not without Christian struggle. Although he does not break with his mistress until 1513, the first sign of moral change comes in 1509, when he appoints Bartholomeo Guidiccioni as vicar-general of Parma, a man learned in canon law and interested in reform, who will hold the post for nineteen years.

In 1516 Farnese holds a visitation of his diocese, a rare example of ecclesiastical energy. By 1519 his life has taken a new turn. He is ordained a priest on June 26, consecrated bishop a few days later, and celebrates his first mass at Christmas. In November he institutes a diocesan synod that introduces new constitutions for the reform of the clergy and makes older ones more stringent. It also puts into effect the reform decrees of the Fifth Lateran Council (1512–17).[4] Farnese, therefore, has become part of the reform movement even before Ignatius. Henceforth his moral conduct is without reproach, although he still lives after the manner of the churchmen of the Renaissance.

In 1534 Alessandro Farnese is elected pope. At the time of his election he is the dean of the College of Cardinals and has been a member of the college for forty years. At 67 he is the oldest of all the cardinals. Even though his health is poor, he is intellectually the most important of the cardinals and his election is no surprise. Right from the beginning Paul III talks about a general council to reform the Church. He is in favor of reform, but curbing the outlook and habits of a lifetime is not easy for him. His love of Church has not transformed his love of family. He appoints to the cardinalate his grandsons Alessandro Farnese and Guido Sforza, both in their early teens.[5] Caution and hesitation precede the pope's decisions, not for lack of courage but from shrewd calculation.

This is the man who will make the decision about the existence of the Society of Jesus. This is a man to whom, with all his faults, that Society relates with enthusiasm and love.

Paul III and the Members of the Company

Paul III meets the companions in an unexpected way. For reasons of health Ignatius had left the University of Paris in April 1535, gradually making his way to Venice where he continued his study of theology. His companions left Paris on November

15, 1536, on a pilgrimage to Loreto [*R* 36, 56], stopping to visit Ignatius in Venice at the beginning of 1537. After working for a couple of months in two Venetian hospitals, the companions decide to finish their pilgrimage and then to go to Rome to ask permission from the pope to make a pilgrimage to the Holy Land. They also want his permission to be ordained. Ignatius stays behind lest his presence stir the anger of a member of the papal curia, Dr. Pedro Ortiz, formerly a faculty member in Paris, who had been displeased with his activities there.[6] Nor does he wish to arouse the anger of a new acquaintance from Venice with whom he disagreed on religious matters, Gianpietro Carafa, cofounder of the Theatines and recently created cardinal.[7] Years later Laynez would comment that Carafa was, indeed, somewhat hostile, but not Ortiz [*L* 39].[8] Ortiz came to Rome in 1531; among other offices, he holds that of consultor in the hospice of St. James where the Spaniards find lodging.[9] Some of the companions seek him out and talk to him. Glad to see them, he recognizes their sincerity, welcomes them warmly, recommends the Parisian masters to Paul III, and arranges for an audience and a theological disputation which the pope enjoys having during his meals [*R* 58, *PV* 85].

Later Bobadilla, in his eighties, recalls that the audience takes place at the noonday meal [*B* 9]. They find themselves surrounded by theologians and learned doctors and bishops and cardinals [*EI* 119], all of whom put theological questions to them, now to one and now to another, and dispute with them [*R* 58]. The pope is pleased with all of them, but especially with Xavier.[10] To his statement that he will grant them whatever they ask, they reply that all they want is his blessing and permission to go to the Holy Land and to be ordained by any bishop whatsoever [*B* 9]. In his later years Simão Rodrigues writes that the pope opens his arms as though to embrace them all and says: "I experience great happiness and joy to see erudition like this joined with great modesty. . . . I believe, however, that you are not likely to get to Jerusalem." Simão adds in a biblical tone: "This he said either because he knew that the Venetians were going to arm themselves against the Turks, which happened a little later, or because he was the high priest that year" [*R* 58]. The pope grants them permission to go to Jerusalem, blesses them and urges them to persevere in what they have set out to do, gives them generous alms (as do the cardinals and others), gives the priests faculties to hear confessions, and grants permission to the rest to be ordained [*EI* 120].[11]

That is not the last time he sees them. Some months after their ordination in Venice in 1537, Ignatius, Laynez, and Favre go to Rome, and all the other companions return shortly after Easter in 1538. Paul III is absent at that time, but about a month after his return in July he and Ignatius have a long conversation regarding the persecutions the companions have been enduring in Rome during his absence [*IR* 5-6, *A* 98]. The pope counters the persecutions by inviting four of the companions to carry on theological disputations in his presence. He receives them enthusiastically: "The oftener you come, the better we like it" [*B* 11]. Ignatius himself indicates that they come for a disputation every two weeks [*IR* 6]. Later that winter Paul puts the companions in charge of teaching Christian doctrine to children in the schools [*IR* 10]. When Paul III makes his decision in September 1539 to approve the Society, he knows the companions personally, not through mere hearsay. He knows who they are, and he likes what he sees.

2. Paul's Beloved Sons

Paul III must have taken a close look at each of the companions. Paul was getting to know the little Basque with the beaked nose and balding head who seemed to be the "father" of this little band. Ordained on June 24, 1537, **Ignatius de Loyola** had not offered his first mass until after he knew they could not go to the Holy Land. Then he offered it at Christmas 1538 at the shrine of the manger in the church of Santa Maria Maggiore. Certainly he had not delayed for lack of devotion. Paul III felt the depth of that devotion when he and Ignatius talked for an hour in private toward the end of the summer of 1538. Ignatius, already in his late forties, begged him to urge the governor of Rome to expedite the investigation into the charges brought against the companions. He told the pope of all their hopes and desires and also of all the investigations that had been made into his own orthodoxy [*IR* 5]. Paul knew he was dealing with a man of decision and fiery love.

Paul had already come to know Favre and Laynez. Some months after the companions returned to Venice for ordination, the pope had summoned Favre and Laynez, probably at the urging of Ortiz, to teach theology at Rome's university, known as the Sapienza. (Ignatius had come along, probably again at the urging of Ortiz.[12]) **Pierre Favre,** eager and gentle, a quiet Savoyard of thirty-two, the first priest in the original group, father confessor to them all and destined to become father confessor to many more,[13] began expounding on the more obscure points of Sacred Scripture in January 1538. **Diego Laynez,** only twenty-six years old, dark, short, Spanish, began expounding on the work of the Tübingen theologian, Gabriel Biel, on the canon of the Mass [*MS* 2:735, 3].[14] According to Laynez's report, his first lecture had been disappointing both to himself and to his class so that even Ignatius was somewhat ashamed of him, but he kept getting better, to the satisfaction of all. His preaching had followed a similar pattern [*ML* 550].[15] Very likely Paul came to know Favre and Laynez well by inviting them to carry on theological disputations during his meal every couple of weeks [*IR* 6]. Even before the companions had completed their Deliberation, Paul had already sent Favre and Laynez to renew the city of Parma [*F* 19].[16] He held them in such high esteem that he later appointed them papal theologians at the Council of Trent [*EI* 362], although Favre died before he could get there [*PCh* 118].[17]

The first of the companions, however, at the Council of Trent was **Claude Jay** [*EI* 375]. About thirty-five, a schoolboy friend of Favre [*MF* 843–47], shy and modest, Jay would not blush to preach before kings [*PCh* 91]. In Ferrara he and Rodrigues made a deep impression on Vittoria Colonna [*R* 74 n. 27], and even Duke Ercole II made his confession to Jay and received communion from his hand [*L* 44, *PV* 92].[18] Paul's first assignment for Jay was Bagnorea not far from Rome, a town torn by strife and division. He was so successful there that he was sent to Brescia and Faenza and on to Germany [*PSH* 116–22]. The bishop of Augsburg, Cardinal Otto Truchsess, in whose service Paul III placed him, sent him to Trent as his personal substitute [*EB* 300].

The fact that Paul had already missioned **Paschase Broët** to Siena [*EB* 201–3], yielding to many petitions from Siena that he return to the place where he and Salmerón had done much good work the year before, occasioned the Deliberation of the First Fathers. About thirty-eight years old and from Amiens in Picardy, Broët had been a priest longer than any of the other companions, a veteran of ten years of ministry before joining them.

Paul III had already noted **Francisco Xavier** in the disputation in his presence on Easter Tuesday 1537.[19] Xavier was from Navarre in Spain, a Basque like Ignatius, thirty-three years old, wrenched from an ecclesiastical career which promised all kinds of dignities, and thrust on the road to sanctity. While the companions were working in the hospitals in Venice, a man who was completely covered with sores had yelled at him: "Hey, I'll love you; come and scratch my back." Francisco had done so but was suddenly struck with terror of contracting the disease. To overcome his fear he put his fingers into his mouth and sucked them. The next day he told the others jokingly that he had dreamed that he had caught the man's leprosy in his throat and that he had kept coughing and spitting in an attempt to get it out [*R* 44].[20] Later, in Bologna, he had worked so hard street preaching and hearing confessions all day long that his health had been impaired [*L* 45]. For the present Xavier was to stay in Rome, but before long Paul made him apostolic nuncio to the Indies and beyond, and to Ethiopia as well [*MX* 2:119–33].[21]

Alfonso Salmerón, twenty-three, had had to receive special permission from the pope to be ordained before the canonical age of twenty-four [*FD* 531]. After his ordination he had gone with Broët to Siena where the pair had made quite an impression preaching and hearing confessions and teaching catechism to little children [*L* 45]. This "boy" priest, the pope knew, had a reputation for brilliance. Salmerón's first assignment after the Deliberation was to teach at the Sapienza.[22] But soon Paul III missioned him to try to bring some relief to the land oppressed by Thomas Cromwell. In the early part of 1540 Paul appointed him apostolic nuncio to Ireland [*EB* 421–32].[23] Later he made him one of the papal theologians at the Council of Trent [*EI* 362].

The other companions had also gradually become familiar figures to the pope. **Simão Rodrigues,** twenty-eight years old and the only Portuguese in the group, was set to accompany Broët to Siena [*PCh* 9]. Perhaps the pope had already heard the story that while preparing for their first masses, he and Jay had gone to Bassano, where they lived with a hermit [*R* 62]. Simão had become ill and lay dying with a fever. Ignatius heard about it, and although he also was sick, he had gotten up and hiked with Favre the twenty-two miles to see the sick man, which rejuvenated him completely [*R* 62, *PSH* 72]. For some months before coming to Rome, Simão had labored effectively with Jay in Ferrara and with Jean Codure in Padua. When a new companion Ignatius had found in Venice, Diego de Hozes [*A* 92], overcome by work, got sick in Padua and breathed his last, Rodrigues had hurried there to be with Codure and console him at the death of his friend [*R* 68–69 n. 23]. Paul III so esteemed Rodrigues that he named him apostolic nuncio along with Xavier to go to faraway lands [*MX* 2:119–33]. Divine Providence, however, kept him in Portugal [*PCh* 31].

Perhaps when Paul looked at **Jean Codure** he mused a bit over the quality of those sometimes put in charge of the local churches. Codure was a Frenchman from Provence of uncertain age. He had worked hard in Padua with their new companion, Diego de Hozes, a dark, ugly man from Malaga [*R* 68] who seemed to have the face of an angel when he died [*L* 58]. But the day they had arrived in Padua the suffragan bishop had put them in chains and thrown them in jail (much to their delight, and especially that of Hozes who laughed all night long).[24] Next day the suffragan, his suspicions allayed, set them free and gave them every opportunity to help people by their preaching and hearing of confessions [*PV* 90]. Codure quickly became a favorite of Paul III. The pope named him confessor of Margaret of Austria, who was the daughter of Charles V and the wife of Ottavio Farnese, the pope's grandson.[25] Paul eventually directed the great zeal of Jean Codure toward the healing of the Irish people as his apostolic nuncio to that island, along with Alfonso Salmerón [*EB* 421–32]. While he was waiting to go there, the companions in Rome chose him to help Ignatius in writing the

Constitutions,[26] but he died on August 29, 1541, "called to a better society of Jesus."[27] Thereafter, Paul sent Broët on the Irish mission instead [*EB* 204–16].

The pope could not help but notice a particularly lively Spaniard in the group, **Nicolás de Bobadilla,** a regular participant in the disputations, who remembered them vividly when he was past eighty years old [*B* 11]. Now twenty-nine, he had worked with Xavier in Bologna, where the vicar-general had testified that both Bobadilla and Xavier had preached well and were particularly hard on Lutheranism [*MX* 2:133]. Bobadilla had left Bologna to help Jay in Ferrara. There he became a close friend of the duke, who was impressed by their preaching. The duke even offered as alms whatever they needed for the pilgrimage to Jerusalem [*L* 44]. Paul III eventually used this fiery eccentric in missions all over Europe. Before the year was over, he sent him on a secret mission to the island of Ischyia [*B* 14]. Later Paul was about to send him as nuncio with Rodrigues to India, but Bobadilla was sick at the time and the pope sent Xavier in his place [*B* 16].

This is Paul III and his beloved sons. In this instance "beloved sons" was no empty stereotyped phrase devoid of meaning. Paul had the highest regard for these men and employed them well in the Lord's vineyard. In return they loved him with all his faults and were deeply devoted to him. They looked to him for leadership, but they were not afraid to be critical of him, primarily by the example of their own lives.

3. Masters of Paris

The *inscriptio* of a papal bull or brief generally adds a title to the names of those to whom a pope addresses his apostolic letter. The one the companions chose for the pope to give them was unusual: *Masters of Paris.* In view of the fact that they had deliberately set aside academic careers for a more pastoral ministry, it might have been more usual for them to choose "clerics," as they were called in their ordination document [*FD* 530], or "priests," as in the document granting them faculties [*FD* 538], and more usual in this kind of letter.[28] Nor did they choose to be called "masters of arts and of philosophy" [*FD* 526] or "professors of sacred theology" [*FD* 544], as in earlier documents, vague titles coming from anywhere. They were Masters of Paris. They had come to Rome as poor pilgrims, but Dr. Pedro Ortiz had introduced them to Rome as masters from his university. As Masters of Paris, aware of all the latest theological views in a world filled with theological controversy, they were a source of excitement in Rome [*EI* 119–20]. As Masters of Paris they had disputed before the pope.

"Masters of Paris" was no mean title. That was not why they used it. When the governor of Rome cleared them of the charge of heresy, he had called them "Masters of Paris." It may have been a glamorous title for others; but, for themselves, "Masters of Paris" meant that they were orthodox. The University of Paris had the best educational system in all of Christendom. It may have concentrated on the head and missed the heart,[29] but the University of Paris was orthodox. As early as 1521 the theological faculty had condemned the teachings of Luther.[30] If the companions were to accomplish what they had set out to do, their reputations had to be unsullied. "Masters of Paris" meant that they were priests without theological blemish and with the best education possible.

No other university could match the logical progression of courses, the method of teaching, the personal concern for and direction of students, the skills in writing and speaking demanded of the students in Paris.[31] The course began with humanistic studies as a foundation to the study of arts. That is where Ignatius began when he arrived in Paris in February 1528, spending a year and a half laying a foundation in Latin, grammar, rhetoric, and poetry which would allow him to study for a degree. In October 1529 he began his work toward the master of arts. The first step was the bachelor of arts, mostly a study of logic, which Ignatius received in January 1532 [*FD* 386]. He devoted another year to the works of Aristotle: ethics and mathematics, physics and metaphysics, psychology, geometry, and astronomy. After the study of Aristotle the successful student received the licentiate, or license to teach. Ignatius achieved this in March 1533 [*FD* 389–91]. To teach at the University of Paris itself required the master of arts, which demanded more money than study. For financial reasons

Ignatius delayed until March 1535 [*FD* 395–97]. Meanwhile he had begun to study theology, not, however, with the purpose of attaining a higher degree. A master of arts who wished a doctorate could opt for medicine (seven more years of study), canon law (seven years), or theology (fourteen years). As a matter of fact, the study of theology could be reduced to twelve years, or even to five. The companions were not interested in spending that much time. Nor were they enthusiastic about the content of the advanced courses. Although most of its students were on the way to the priesthood, the University of Paris was not concerned with priestly formation. It was an academy, like that of Plato, not a seminary. Its concern was academics and titles and honors and the securing of benefices. Theology had become bogged down in obscure questions, dry speculations, sterile dialectics, pure academics divorced from practical living.

The countercultural attitude of Ignatius and his companions becomes evident at this point. They were not interested in honors and benefices but in being priests. On Sundays they skipped the required disputations[32] and spent the morning at the Carthusian monastery going to confession and participating in the Eucharistic liturgy.[33] They studied the kind of theology that would help them in the apostolate, and they became superb theologians in the process. But they had no patience for that which was not pastorally useful. Even so, Ignatius spent two years at the University of Paris studying theology; later, in Venice, he studied on his own. Except for Xavier, who received his master of arts in 1530, and Laynez, who received his in Alcalá in 1532, the others began their theological studies before receiving the master of arts in Paris in 1536.[34]

The degree of master of arts was by no means meaningless to the companions. In fact, they had the practice of calling one another "Master," e.g., Master Ignatius, Master Favre, Master Laynez. That practice may stem from the degree, a gentle reminder of competence and of the responsibility flowing from competence, but more than anything else the title reveals their understanding of who they are. Titles meant much to Ignatius, perhaps because he was a nobleman. Dominique Bertrand emphasizes the differences between *señor* [lord] and *maestro* [master, teacher] as Ignatius uses them. *Señor* contrasts with *siervo* [servant]. *Maestro* is contrasted to the learner, the disciple, the little child, and is oriented toward the elevation of the latter through the power of the word. Years later Ignatius wrote to Antonio Araoz, "for from little ones come the great ones" [*EI* 4:9].[35] Even today the French word for student is *élève,* one to be elevated. The student is not at the service of the master. The companions' use of the term *master* is an expression of their firm determination not to dominate.[36]

These "beloved sons" are a group of learned and well-trained men. All are capable of fencing theologically with the best minds of Europe. But they have come to serve, not to win glory for themselves. They are at the beck and call of Paul III. Today it would be like suddenly having at one's command ten PhD's out of the best universities in the world who have no ambitions other than to convert the whole world to Christ.

PART ONE

Part one is concerned with Paul III's gathering of data about the companions from his own experience and from that of other people. This gathering of data is not part of an investigation, but it indicates a growing awareness on the part of Paul III regarding the companions even before they ask him to confirm their way of living.

The three *cum* clauses of Part One bring us back to the theme of Paul and his beloved sons and the relationship that exists between him and them: what he has gathered about the companions from other people, and his reaction to what he has learned. The first *cum* clause answers the question: who are these men who call themselves the Company of Jesus? The second *cum* clause answers the question: what do they do, or what have they been doing? The third *cum* clause provides his own response to their presence in his life and the life of the Church.

SECTION ONE

The Priesthood of Ignatius and His Companions

The first *cum* clause answers the question: who are these men who call themselves the Company of Jesus? The clause touches upon matters Ignatius will develop more fully in Part VI of the Constitutions: "The personal life of those already admitted or incorporated into the Society."

Ignatius and his nine companions have degrees from the best university in the whole of Christendom; they can look forward to careers that would bring them honor and fame and fortune. Yet each of them, of his own accord, has chosen to live in a manner contrary to the prevailing culture. Each has freely and deliberately chosen to live in poverty in a world gone mad over wealth and power and dignity. Of his own accord—and not because of economic pressure or for the sake of social position and prestige or out of desire for a brilliant career—each has chosen to become a priest of Jesus Christ. They hail from different parts of Spain and France as well as Portugal; they speak Basque and Spanish and French and Portuguese, but share no common tongue facile to each; yet each has of his own accord chosen to associate himself with the others, and they have joined together into a single body.

The Holy Spirit is the impelling force behind this group of men who have freely chosen to throw in their lot together. Through that Spirit they have but one desire: to abandon all the enticements of this world, the traps, the snares, the illusions of this life, and to dedicate their lives forever to the service of Jesus, their Lord, and to the service of his vicar on earth.

THE FIRST *CUM* CLAUSE

Cum ex plurium sermone saepe intellexissemus
[Since from the words of many we have often gathered]

vos sponte
[that you, of your own free choice]

pauperes Christi sacerdotes
[poor priests of Christ]

e diuersis mundi regionibus
[from various parts of the world]

in vnum conuenisse
[have joined together into one body]

et Spiritu Sancto, ut credimus, impellente,
[and with the Holy Spirit, as we believe, impelling you]

in hanc vnam voluntatem conspirasse,
[have conspired together in this one desire,]

ut, relictis seculi huius illecebris,
[that, having abandoned the snares of this world]

vitam vestram [dedicaretis]
[you would dedicate your lives]

perpetuo [seruitio] **Domini nostri Jesu Christi**
[to the perpetual service of our Lord Jesus Christ]

atque eius in terris vicarii seruitio dedicaretis;
[and of his vicar on earth];

Structure: The principal verb of the first *cum* clause is *intellexissemus* [we have gathered]. Immediately dependent on *intellexissemus* are two infinitives, *conuenisse* [assemble, join together] and *conspirasse* [conspire or agree together]. Also immediately dependent on *intellexissemus* is another verb in the subjunctive, *dedicaretis* [you would dedicate]. Dependent upon *dedicaretis* is an ablative absolute, *relictis . . . illecebris* [having abandoned the snares], with the force of another subjunctive: you have conspired together to abandon and to dedicate.

2

Their Choice To Be Poor

The testimony here is about the choice the companions have made to form themselves into a company of poor priests in the first place, and then to offer themselves to the service of Jesus Christ and of the pope. From whom has Paul gathered his information, and what information has he gathered? *Cum ex plurium* provides part of the answer to the second question. Our immediate concern is who might have testified on their behalf.

Since from the words of many we have often gathered
[Cum ex plurium sermone saepe intellexissemus]

that you, of your own free choice

The pope knows the companions personally in a limited context. Others who have his ear or who have fairly easy access to him know them in other contexts. No records exist of oral testimony the pope has received, but from the facts we possess we can infer that the pope has heard fairly frequently about the companions.

Cum ex plurium names the most influential champion the companions have in Rome, Cardinal Gasparo Contarini, one of Paul III's most trusted advisers.[1] Fifteen years younger than the pope, he was born in 1483 of one of the oldest families of the Venetian nobility. He is a handsome man, extremely well-educated, having studied both philosophy and theology at the University of Padua. He was made a member of the Great Council of Venice, was sent to the Diet of Worms in 1521 (he did not meet Luther there), and was made Venetian ambassador to the Roman Curia in 1527. When he returned to Venice his house became the gathering place for politicians, philosophers, humanists, theologians, scholars of all kinds. Although a layman when named a cardinal in 1535, he is well versed in both the Fathers and the scholastics and wrote a masterly treatise on the episcopacy for a friend who was named a bishop. As the president of the pope's commission on reform he has become the heart of the reform movement. He made the Spiritual Exercises under Ignatius in late 1537 or early 1538 [PSH 78] and considers Ignatius a master of the affective life [PV 96]. Contarini's opinion means much to Ignatius and also to Paul III.

We know that in the spring and summer of 1538 the companions were under attack in Rome; we also know from a letter Ignatius wrote on December 2, 1538 [EI 134], to Pietro Contarini, whom Ignatius had directed through the Spiritual Exercises while in Venice [A 92], that Pietro had written to his relative, Gasparo, on their behalf.[2] We know from that same letter that Gasparo had gone to the governor of Rome to get some action as Ignatius had requested. We know, too, that "a friend" (to use Ignatius's word) spoke to the pope about the matter [IR 5].[3] We can infer that Gasparo was that friend and communicated the thought and feelings of his relative to the pope.[4]

We know, moreover, some of the friends they have in Rome besides Cardinal Contarini. To begin with, there are others close to the pope who, like Contarini, have made the Spiritual Exercises with Ignatius: Dr. Pedro Ortiz, Lattanzio Tolomei, and Pietro Codacio. Dr. Pedro Ortiz, the theologian from Paris whose anger Ignatius had feared in Rome, is the agent of Charles V in the matter of Henry VIII's divorce from Catherine of Aragon [PV 85]. Instead of an adversary, he has turned out to be a friend of the companions and their intercessor with the pope [L 39]. Ortiz made the Exercises with Ignatius at Monte Cassino [A 98] in the early part of 1538, and became so avid a friend of the Society that he would gladly have become a member, except that he was considered too obese to be able to engage in vigorous apostolic activity [PV 96].[5]

Lattanzio Tolomei, scholar, patron of the arts, and a friend of Michelangelo, has easy access to the pope as the ambassador to the papal court from the Republic of Siena.[6] He, too, made the Spiritual Exercises under the direction of Ignatius [*PSH* 78]. Tolomei pressured Paul III to send Paschase Broët, who had worked in Siena before, to reform a convent of nuns in that city [*EB* 203]. Helping to bring pressure were some of the leading citizens of Siena along with the archbishop himself, Francesco Bandini, and the Sienese theologian, Fra Ambrogio Catarino, O.P., the brother of the abbess. The pope's decision to send Broët occasioned the Deliberation of the First Fathers [*D* 3].

Pietro Codacio, the first Italian to join the company of friends, is another advocate from within the papal curia. Ordained a priest in 1532, he was soon brought to Rome and made an intimate part of the papal curia, where he possibly held the office of *maestro di camera*. Shortly after making the Spiritual Exercises under Ignatius, he decided to enter the Society in 1539 even though it was not yet canonically established. His ability in money matters and his knowledge of the curia become a real blessing to the struggling community.[7] No doubt all these enthusiasts of the Exercises have spoken to the pope about the companions.

Others in Rome able to testify on their behalf are: Dr. Robert Wauchope, a friend and former teacher from Paris [*EI* 133–34], named by Paul III administrator of the archdiocese of Armagh in Ireland; Reginald Pole, another Parisian friend, named a cardinal in 1536, one of the most distinguished members of the Sacred College;[8] and Cardinal Vincenzo Carafa, papal legate for the city of Rome during the pope's absence from the city, who had given the companions extensive faculties to preach and hear confessions [*FD* 537–39], probably influenced by his cousin, Cardinal Gianpietro Carafa, the other man whose anger Ignatius had feared.[9] The latter wrote the letter to Broët on behalf of the pope commanding him under holy obedience to undertake the task of reforming the convent in Siena [*EB* 201–3].

These men are some of the friends whom Ignatius, the man who wished to be unknown and unnoticed at Montserrat and Manresa, has acquired for himself in Rome.[10] Some or all of these may be intended in the words beginning the introductory sentence of *Cum ex plurium*: "Since from the words of many we have often gathered . . ."

Since from the words of many we have often gathered

that you, of your own free choice
[vos sponte]
poor priests of Christ,
[pauperes Christi sacerdotes]

from various parts of the world
have joined together into one body

In the salutation the pope calls the companions *Masters of Paris,* the objective sign and seal of their competence. Competence, however, is not what marks them as special. Many worldly men, after all, are competent. Something deeper is at stake. One who approves the decision of others has to discern whether the Spirit of God is at work in their lives. The personal lives of the companions flow from interior qualities on which their competence is based, the humility and generosity of priests *freely* choosing under the Spirit to be poor men of Christ, an indication of the shape their priesthood has already assumed for them, marking them as a breed apart.

Sponte [of your own free choice] is key, but its function is difficult to interpret. Placed as it is, between *vos* [you] and *pauperes* [poor], it seems to bear immediately on *pauperes* and to stress the spontaneity and freedom of the companions' choice to be poor.[11] At the same time, considering the content of the clauses, *sponte* embraces and bears upon everything after *vos:* the companions have freely chosen to be poor and have freely chosen to be priests and have freely chosen to join together into a single body.

Sponte is a strong word: freely, spontaneously, of their own accord, without reluctance, with their whole heart and soul. The norm of seeking what is more, found in the Principle and Foundation of the Spiritual Exercises [23], and the ideal of being one of the distinguished in the consideration on the Call of the King [97] immediately come to mind. These men hold back nothing.[12] They freely "desire and choose poverty with Christ poor rather than wealth" [167]. They freely choose, moreover, to be priests of Christ, priests because they want to be priests. They are not priests out of economic necessity or because custom dictates that one son in the family should follow an ecclesiastical career. They have not chosen either security or a career; they have joyfully chosen the priesthood of Christ because they want to preach his Word and live as he did. They have not chosen to be priests simply to glory in that fact but as a means to accomplish what they want to do. Lastly, they freely choose to band together. Ordained as secular priests from different dioceses, of their own free will they form a companionship. They join together into one body of their own free will, just as they are poor of their own free will and are priests of Christ of their own free will.

To understand and appreciate the revolutionary character of their banding together requires reflection on the larger historical background as well as the immediate historical context of their free choices, under the movement of the Spirit, to be poor and to be priests. We shall reflect first on their choice of poverty, then on their choice of priesthood, and finally on their decision to unite together. In the process we shall learn something of what Paul III learned about them.

Pauperes Christi sacerdotes ["*poor* of Christ, priests" or "*poor* priests of Christ"]. The companions were used to many names in Rome, not all of them complimentary. A letter written by the city of Montepulciano a few days before Contarini read the Formula to Paul III calls them pilgrim priests [*preti peregrini*].[13] Many of the people called them reformed priests [*preti reformati*], the name often used for the members of other groups of priests formed at that time.[14] Cardinal Contarini, for example, wrote on the back of the manuscript of *Cum ex plurium* in the Vatican archives: "Brief of His Holiness, Paul III, for the reformed priests of Jesus."[15] The words we are now considering express their own view of themselves, *pauperes Christi sacerdotes*: they are priests who are freely and unabashedly poor.

The phrase is not without its ambiguities, for *Christi* can be coupled with either *pauperes* or *sacerdotes*. The ambiguity may be deliberate. Whatever the case, paying attention to both phrases is worth the effort: (a) *pauperes Christi* [poor of Christ], in which case *pauperes* is a noun: the poor, or poor men of Christ, leaving *sacerdotes* standing in apposition to *pauperes*, an explanation of what kind of *pauperes* they are, not monks, not lay people, not the blind, the sick or the lame, but priests; (b) *Christi sacerdotes* [priests of Christ], in which case *pauperes* is an adjective modifying *sacerdotes:* poor priests of Christ, or a noun in apposition: poor men, priests of Christ.

1. *Pauperes Christi* [*Poor* of Christ]

The term *pauperes Christi* had been in use for centuries.[16] From the beginning it meant the involuntary poor, the indigent who had no money or property, who depended upon others for their sustenance, who were on the rolls of a certain church and cared for by that church. In Carolingian times "the poor of Christ" embraced widows and orphans as well as indigents, all of whom made up a sort of special class of people to be protected by the law and supported by the Church. Thus, Jacques de Vitry in the thirteenth century referred to all the poor, the sick, the wretched, the starving, lepers, etc., as *pauperes Christi*.[17] In other words, *pauperes Christi* refers to the little people, those called *anawim* in the Old Testament, for that is exactly what *pauper* means: one who has produced [*peperit*] little [*paucum*],[18] one who is considered a person of little worth. (Is there a slight glimmer here of why Ignatius later called his company "this least Society," just as Francis had called his group the "little" brothers?)

From the beginning, however, "poor of Christ" possessed within it the seeds of ambiguity. It could extend to a spiritual reality that went beyond the vulnerability of economic poverty. "Poor of Christ" became a title for monks, the voluntary poor, whose communities might or might not be poor. In the eleventh century the term also included individual hermits, in the twelfth century canons regular (clerics who lived in community according to the Rule of St. Augustine and served the apostolic needs of the local Church), and in the early thirteenth century a community of Carthusians.[19]

The Cistercians who, like the Carthusians, had adopted a very strict form of poverty, also call themselves "the poor of Christ" in their early documents.[20] Saint Bernard adds the significant word *servus* [servant, slave], calling himself "the servant of Christ's poor at Clairvaux."[21] Guigo I, the fifth

Carthusian prior after Bruno, also links *servus* with *pauper* (although he does not join either word with *Christi*). He calls himself "the useless servant of the poor Carthusians," and he calls the community the pope's "poor servants and sons at La Chartreuse."[22] In the Carthusians and Cistercians the terms indicate both a countercultural attitude and a profound acceptance of the status of *anawim*. The fact that *servitio* [service] appears along with *pauperes Christi sacerdotes* in the first *cum* clause of *Cum ex plurium* intimates that *pauperes Christi* applies as a technical term to the companions. It contains the idea of service of Christ through renunciation, and is linked with the adage of St. Jerome, "naked, follow the naked Christ."[23] This is certainly what the companions had in mind to do. In this respect Ignatius and his companions are very much in the line of these two renewal movements, the Carthusians and the Cistercians.

The twelfth and thirteenth centuries saw a burst of renewal activity centering on poverty, most of it coming from lay people, some of it orthodox and some quite unorthodox, all of it an attempt to imitate the simplicity of life of the apostles and the early Church.[24] In France the Waldensians or Poor Men of Lyons called themselves "poor of Christ" but strayed from the path of orthodoxy. The Poor Catholics of Durand de Huesca in southern France and Spain, and the *Humiliati* in northern Italy (Lombardy), both groups drawn from the Waldensians in order to convert them, eventually foundered but helped prepare the way for the Friars Minor, the Poor Clares, and the Dominicans.[25] Even the Cathars, for different reasons, called themselves "poor of Christ."[26] All these people lived actual poverty.

Bonaventure calls Francis "the poor man of Christ" [*Christi pauper*], and Francis calls all his followers "poor men of Christ."[27] The term does not appear in the Dominican tradition, but the reality does, for Dominicans follow the apostolic life that Augustine chose, which is "to leave everything for the sake of Christ and to preach him while serving him in poverty."[28] Whereas the Franciscans were a part of the poverty movement and differed from other groups by reason of their orthodoxy and fidelity to the Church, the Dominicans stood over against those of heretical bent even though they adopted the practices of poverty found amongst their adversaries. They were not part of the poverty movement, but were at the vanguard of a preaching movement that saw poverty as a guarantee of fidelity to the Gospel.

2. *Poor* Priests of Christ

As with Francis and Dominic, actual poverty was the companions' deliberate choice. If they wanted to be considered *poor of Christ,* it was in poverty that was real, not through some honorary title given to a group.

That they are poor *priests,* however, is doubly important. First, they are poor men of Christ who are priests: priest-type poor, not married-type poor, nor monk-type poor. Priesthood is for them the way to live out their poverty. Priesthood is the form of their poverty, the form in which it expresses itself, the form in which it is lived. Second, they are priests who are poor men of Christ. They are poor priests, not rich priests; they are vulnerable rather than untouchable; they have cast their lot with those "who are not" in order to confound those "who are." Poverty shapes their priesthood no matter how they exercise it. Ordination does not affect their poor mode of living; just the opposite. Poverty makes their priesthood more genuine. It makes their priesthood credible; it founds their competence on solid rock. It enables people to hear them. Perhaps that is why the phrase *pauperes Christi sacerdotes* is ambiguous. Poverty seems to be as much the form of their priesthood as priesthood the form of their poverty.

Francis of Assisi clearly chose poverty as an integral part of his following of Christ,[29] but he did not want to be a priest.[30] Ignatius also chose poverty first, but once he chose priesthood he not only did not reject poverty but even embraced it as an instrument for priesthood. His companions also chose to be poor with Christ poor, and they chose to be priests, and they chose to live the kind of poverty that would validate their priesthood. Whatever, then, may be said about the title, *pauperes Christi,* the companions clearly wanted to be *pauperes sacerdotes* [poor priests].

In the summer of 1539, when they were asking for papal approval, poverty was already a given. In the days of reflection together immediately preceding the writing of the five decrees of the Formula of the Institute, they may have given a great deal of time to the discussion of poverty, but the preparatory document, *Determinationes Societatis,* gives very little space to it. Adverting to the admission of candidates into their group they specify, almost curtly, that "whoever is going to enter should in fact be poor before admission to probation" [*DS* 9]. So much for personal poverty. As for the community, they can accept a house or church to live in, but with no right to the property itself [*DS* 15]. The community is poor just as the members are poor.[31]

The deeper motivations behind their choice of a radical personal and community poverty are not hard to find: to be like Jesus and to imitate the apostles.

Example of Jesus

When Ignatius left Loyola in 1522 he embraced poverty, no doubt as a form of penance in imitation of the saints [*A* 8, 14]. On the way to Montserrat he "had resolved to lay aside his garments and to don the armor of Christ." After some days at Montserrat, Ignatius arranged with his confessor to have his sword and dagger hung at the altar of Our Lady [*A* 17]. Then, "on the eve of the feast of Our Lady in March, at night, in the year 1522, he went as secretly as he could[32] to a beggar and, stripping off all his garments he gave them to the beggar. He dressed himself in his chosen attire and went to kneel before the altar of Our Lady. At times in this way and at other times standing, with his pilgrim's staff in hand, he spent the whole night. He left at daybreak so as not to be recognized" [*A* 18].

Like Francis of Assisi, Ignatius divested himself of his rich clothing, a symbolic action with deep meaning in the history of the Church.[33] When Francis threw off his clothes, that gesture was a "Yes" to Lady Poverty. His new garment was utter nakedness. By his action Francis spurned the wealth of the mercantile class to which his father belonged. When Ignatius threw off his clothes, he stripped himself of the garb of a nobleman, one who fought on occasion for honor and glory. (He was not a soldier [*sueldo* = soldier's pay], a mercenary, who fought for money.) In stripping himself, Ignatius not only turned his back on wealth but spurned as well the honor and glory that enthralled the noble class, with its penchant for military glory.

Francis threw off his clothes in broad daylight where everyone could see him. Ignatius did so at night, in secret, and he left at dawn, wanting no one to recognize him. From the beginning Ignatius's poverty was marked by a deep desire for a lack of esteem in order to counter his former vanity [A 1]. Putting on the armor of Christ meant more to him than burlap and a pilgrim's staff. The date is significant, March 24, the eve of the Annunciation, the celebration of the Incarnation when the Second Person of the Blessed Trinity "emptied himself, taking the form of a slave" (Phil. 2:7). Opprobrium—insults, injuries, reproaches—was the real armor of Christ. To take up the armor of Christ was to become wholly Christ's man. Ignatius wanted himself to be recognized henceforth only as Christ's servant, an anticipation of La Storta where he would experience the Father explicitly make him the servant of Christ.[34] His Manresa experience, reflected in the Spiritual Exercises, deepened his desire to be treated the way Christ was treated.

His companions discovered a half dozen years later in Paris that poverty and opprobrium are constant companions. They, too, wanted to be like Jesus. In the very first exercise of the Spiritual Exercises they confronted Christ as their Creator and Lord hanging on the cross, and they heard themselves asking, "What ought I to do for Christ?" [53]. In the Call of the King they saw "the synagogues, villages, and castles through which Christ our Lord passed as he preached" [91]. Contemplating Jesus demanded following him, and they reflected on offering to imitate Christ "in bearing all injuries and affronts, and any poverty, actual as well as spiritual" [98]. They contemplated Jesus "born in greatest poverty" and ready to die on the cross after many sufferings, including "injuries and insults" [116]. In the meditation on the Two Standards they heard him encourage them to both spiritual and actual poverty, "to a desire of reproaches and contempt" [146]; and they protested in their colloquies that they desired to be so chosen and placed beneath his standard [147]. They prayed over the Third Way of Being Humble, the desire and choice of "poverty with Christ poor rather than wealth; contempt with Christ laden with it rather than honors. Even further . . . to be regarded as a useless fool for Christ, who before me was regarded as such, rather than as a wise or prudent person in this world" [167]. That became their one desire: to be poor with Jesus who was poor and accounted a fool. Claude Jay illustrates their attitude in a letter he wrote to one of the companions:[35]

> The world seeks and treasures gold and silver and glories in them, but what gives pleasure to the servant of Christ is poverty, and he glories in it. . . . The world rejoices in human praise, but the servant of God is glad to suffer insults for the name of Jesus. The cross of Christ seems to the world to be foolishness, and the world calls fools those who carry their cross after Christ. But Paul used to say: God forbid that I should glory save in the cross (Douay-Rheims: Gal. 6:14). Therefore, dearest brother in Christ Jesus, we wish to follow naked the naked Christ.[36] Wherefore, that person is rich enough who is poor with Christ [*Ideo, satis dives est, qui cum Christo pauper est*]. . . . Abiding in this deserted place, I write to you as a hermit. Farewell in Christ. From St. Vitus, September 5, 1537, from Bassano.[37]

Example of Apostles

In the same Spiritual Exercises the Call of the King is imperative: "Come with me . . . labor with me . . . following me in the pain . . . follow me also in the glory" [95]. The response of the apostles was total: they left everything they had [275]. In the meditation on the Two Standards the companions of Ignatius watched Jesus send apostles and disciples throughout the whole world [145], charging them to encourage everyone not only to embrace spiritual and actual poverty but to desire reproaches and contempt and to seek the most profound humility [146]. In the Sermon on the Mount they heard Jesus link poverty with persecution [278], and they knew that in the call of the apostles they had found a paradigm of their own call to follow Jesus. They watched Jesus empower the apostles to care for bodily infirmities, and instruct them to be prudent and patient in an untrusting and untrustworthy world, to be like sheep in the midst of wolves, to preach in poverty and vulnerability: "Do not seek to possess gold or silver; freely have you received, freely give" [281]. The missionary discourse of Jesus in Matthew 10 became their charter, their rule of life.[38] They watched the apostles walking with Jesus, missing his meaning, abandoning him, doubting his resurrection, listening to his command to preach to the whole world, waiting for the coming of the Holy Spirit. From all these contemplations they came to know their own hearts.

The Companions' Practice of Poverty

For the companions poverty was no fantasy, but acted out. They chose poverty not to imitate the saints, as Ignatius had, but as the form of their service of Christ and his poor. They "had vowed to dedicate themselves to the service of the Lord in poverty," and they had confirmed and renewed this vow at Montmartre [*L* 30]. Laynez describes their choice of poverty thus: "It was not our intention from Paris on to start an official community but to dedicate ourselves in poverty [*dedicarse en pobreza*] to the service of God our Lord and to the profit of our neighbor, preaching and serving in hospitals, etc." [*L* 36].

Rodrigues confirms the testimony of Laynez some forty years after the event itself. In order "to give greater solidity to their determination, they would all bind themselves by the vow of poverty, of chastity, of sailing to Jerusalem, and on their return, with God's help, of working with all their might for the salvation of their neighbor. . . . They vowed besides that they would never accept anything for celebrating Mass, at the same time openly admitting that accepting a stipend for Masses or other liturgical ceremonies was quite legitimate. For themselves, however, in order to embrace poverty and evangelical perfection more closely, they wanted to rid themselves voluntarily even of legitimate things, so that, as far as possible, they could avoid the malicious lies of heretics and give them no grounds for saying that they did something out of a pretext of piety in order to gain much profit and make themselves richer and wealthier" [*R* 13]. Upon leaving Paris they gave away all their possessions and set out with nothing but the clothes on their backs, the rosaries around their necks, and a few books and notes in a handbag [R 26]. France and Spain were at war [R 25], and a few rough encounters in the first miles revealed the hazards in moving the Spaniards in the group through hostile territory [R 29]. After prayer, they decided not to beg their way, but to use the little money they had left to help them get to Venice [R 30].[39] In spite of this choice, they pilgrimaged in dire poverty.[40]

Not in their opinion. They had a much more radical idea of poverty. After meeting Ignatius in Venice and spending two and a half months there serving the poor in the hospitals, they continued on toward Rome. "This was the first journey they made in poverty, living on alms begged from door to door, sleeping sometimes in hospitals, at other times in haylofts, at times in cattle sheds, weary, with clothes, shoes and leggings soaking wet. . . . They were so committed to poverty and careful about it that they would not depart a hair's breadth from it, collecting only enough food for the present moment and reserving nothing for the next meal" [R 48].[41] They continued to live this austere poverty after their journey to Rome, a poverty that gave shape and form to their priesthood. At the same time, the priesthood began to give a new shape and form to their poverty. As they prepared for their first masses after ordination, they continued to live by begging alms, but they also began "to preach in the public squares with little or no preparation, more for our own mortification than anything else" [L 42]. They were in fact poor with Christ poor in every way, preaching in poverty and weakness after the manner of the apostles, *pauperes Christi sacerdotes,* poor of Christ, and priests of Christ.[42]

3

Their Choice To Be Priests

The preceding chapter considered the choice of Ignatius and his companions to belong to that class of people called the *poor of Christ* and also their choice to be *poor* priests of Christ. This chapter considers their Spirit-impelled choice to be *priests,* poor priests, to be sure, but priests nonetheless. In a world of too many priests and too little ministry, the choice to be poor priests of Christ [*pauperes Christi sacerdotes*] was not a light one.[1]

1. Ignatius, the Cleric, in the Context of History

The priesthood of the late middle ages was at one and the same time secularized, highly esteemed, and profoundly demeaned. The clerical class had become the catch-all for the holy, the talented, the zealous, the ambitious, the desperate, those who sought wealth, those who sought privilege, those who sought distinction.

Ignatius, Cleric. Ignatius knew the system from personal experience. He had received the tonsure[2] at an early age and had thus entered into the clerical state with all its privileges, but he had done so in the spirit of his times.[3] As a young man Ignatius appealed to clerical immunity when he and his clerical brother, Pero López de Oñaz, had gotten into some scrape and had been accused of "enormous crimes,"[4] a good example of an attempt to abuse a privilege. As a matter of fact, the privilege held good only under certain conditions that Alexander VI set down in 1493, and Ignatius did not meet the conditions on that occasion.[5] The conditions included wearing a proper tonsure and the sober garb befitting a cleric for four months preceding the crime. The evidence against Ignatius was that for years he had worn his hair down to his shoulders and had gone about in two-toned clothes and a colored hat, carrying a sword and dagger and other weapons, "an armed man" ready for a fight, "clothed in the insignia of secular warfare" [*FD* 242]. So much for Ignatius's claim, but it was one thing to belong to the clerical class and another to be able to enjoy its immunities and privileges.

The clerical state had not always existed, nor had its privileges.[6] In the earliest centuries of the Church distinctions within the Christian people were by functions rather than class. There were those who served at the altar, and those who served the Church in other ways.[7] Opportunites for education and culture were open to all. All took part in the development of Church structures and laws. Clerics were not distinguished from others by dress or manner of life. Although bishops held the preaching office, laymen were allowed to preach and administer church properties.[8] With the acceptance of the Church by the Roman Empire, however, distinctions that had been characteristic of the empire gradually became a part of church life. Clerics became a class apart and were exempt from taxes and immune from civil courts.[9] Over the centuries those exemptions continued.[10] In time men began to seek the clerical state for the privileges it entailed.[11]

Ignatius, Monk? When Ignatius was recuperating at Loyola he thought about becoming a Carthusian, but he was dreaming about penance, not privilege, a life of anonymity, not honor. He hesitated, however, because he thought he might be able to do greater penance outside the monastery "as he went about the world" [*A* 12]. What seemed to attract him to the Carthusians was the monastic element, not the priesthood. Monasticism, which took its rise in the third century, had indeed introduced a new state of life into the Church, but not one of privilege. Moreover, since in its origins monasticism was largely a lay movement the distinction that arose did not at that time drive a wedge between lay and cleric.[12] This mentality fitted well with the new outlook of Ignatius the convert.

Ignatius, Layman. Although as a younger man Ignatius had unsuccessfully claimed clerical exemption, on his way to Montserrat and Manresa he seems committed to avoid every form of privilege or distinction. One might say that at Montserrat Ignatius not only hung up his sword and disavowed his military career, but by embracing poverty he hung up his tonsure as well and disavowed an ecclesiastical career. From that moment until after Paris the only time he acknowledged the tonsure was when he had to indicate his state in life in seeking permission to make his pilgrimage to Jerusalem *[FD 290]*. The rest of the time he lived and acted as though he were a layman. As a layman Ignatius was in the tradition of all those stouthearted *pauperes Christi* of the twelfth and thirteenth centuries, laymen most of them, who saw danger in the wealth of the Church and the clergy, and who needed to see the Gospel lived as well as preached. He was in the tradition of Peter Waldo (Valdes), the poor man of Lyons, the merchant usurer who sold all he had and gave it to the poor and wanted to preach the Gospel to a twelfth century that would not listen to him because he was a layman and not properly educated.[13] He was in the tradition of Francis, the poor man of Assisi, the son of a cloth merchant, who stripped himself and pledged himself to poverty in order to imitate Christ and preach the Gospel to a thirteenth century that insisted that before anyone could listen Francis must at least appear to be a cleric.[14]

The Loyolas and Benefices. The tonsure or clerical state also meant the possibility of certain ecclesiastical sources of income not available to laymen, and ordination opened up even greater opportunities. In return for performing certain duties a suitable income was provided. The benefice came into being, income attached to a certain church or chapel or to a particular function like teaching or chanting the office.[15] A benefice was generally attached to *cura animarum* [the care of souls], or responsibility for the salvation of the people of a particular area, in other words, jurisdictional authority over the Body of Christ, belonging to the bishop in his diocese and to the pastor in his parish.[16]

The sustenance of its clergy was a legitimate concern of the Church, but the benefice system eventually fell prey to greed.

For centuries worldly men sought the clerical state and ordination for the income, not for ministry, and not even in order to perform the duties connected to the income. Those duties could be hired out at minimum salaries to clerics of lesser talent, uneducated, and, if ordained, barely able to read the Latin of the mass or breviary.[17] A disastrous change of mentality affected a large part of the Christian world. People came to think of priesthood in terms of *officium,* a duty to perform, "something to be done," and sharply distinguished it from *diakonia,* ministry, "something done to meet a need of the people."[18] Scores of men became priests who had no vocation to the ministry but who saw an opportunity for making a living if only by saying all the masses that needed to be said for the souls in purgatory.[19] Yet there were so many priests that many of them were destitute. An environment had developed in which one man could hold many benefices and do nothing[20] and other men would be in charge of ministries for which they had neither talent nor training. Unable to exist on their paltry incomes or greedy for further gain, the clergy would charge people for every religious act:[21]

> Money for baptism, money for confirmation, money for marriage, money for holy orders, money to go to confession, money to receive communion. They will not give extreme unction without money, nor ring the bells without money; no entering the church without money, no hearing of Mass in time of interdict without money, so that it appears that paradise is closed for those without money.[22]

No better breeding ground existed for ignorance and superstition and contempt for religion amongst the people,[23] and open concubinage amongst the clergy.[24]

Ignatius was no stranger to the benefice system. Martín García de Oñaz, his older brother, was the sole patron of the church of San Sebastián in Azpeitia, the village near the house of Loyola.[25] In 1512 he presented the name of Andrés de Loyola to the bishop of Pamplona as a recipient of a benefice in connection with the same church, and Andrés was established as an active cleric there [*FD* 223–24]. Some years later, after 1518, Iñigo's clerical brother, Pero López de Oñaz, who had been his companion in trouble in 1515, was named rector of San Sebastián, with attached benefice. Unlike many absentee prelates, both Andrés de Loyola and Pero López lived and worked at Azpeitia [*FD* 264]. The Loyolas were not profligate as the Borgias were. Nevertheless, Pero had fathered at least two children, perhaps four [*FD* 786–87]. He was not an isolated example of a slipshod view of chastity. Many a bastard son of both prince and prelate claimed a high rung on the ecclesiastical career ladder.[26] A new era was dawning, however, one that would see a Loyola (Ignatius) as general of the Society of Jesus use every pressure he legitimately could against a pope, and succeed, so that a Borgia (Francis) might remain fully in the Jesuit ranks and not be made a cardinal. Ambition and greed and unchastity could be bridled.

2. Ignatius's Option for Priesthood

At Manresa Ignatius wrote the rules for making a good election: one must first consider the service of God as the end to be attained, and then the choice of a way of life in which one can best serve God, not the other way around [169].[27] Ignatius's own election was clear: he chose to serve God, and the way he would serve God was in helping others, and the manner of his life would be that of a poor man. The driving force in Ignatius's life was not the priesthood, but the desire to "help his neighbor," to "save souls," "to help others." Even at Loyola he made his conversation such that the members of the household profited from it [*A* 11]. At Manresa a deeper eagerness to help others modified his desire to do penance [*A* 29],[28] and when he went to Jerusalem his desire was not only to visit the holy places but also to help souls [*A* 45].[29]

We do not know when Ignatius conceived the idea of becoming a priest.[30] We do know his desire to help people on the road to salvation was frustrated in Jerusalem [*A* 46–47], so he decided to go to Barcelona and study in order to be able to help others [*A* 50]. Later in his autobiography Ignatius indicates that even in Barcelona he was pondering on whether he should enter a religious order or continue to go about the world [*A* 71]. He says nothing about the priesthood. Laynez, however, says that when Ignatius realized that he was called to help others, he quickly wanted to be a conventual rather than an observant,[31] that is, he wanted more contact with people he could serve.

After two years he went to Alcalá to further his study, and in the process found some companions for his work in helping souls [A 56–58]. Inquisitors challenged their work and investigated their lives, yet "no error had been found in their teaching nor in their life, and therefore, they could go on doing the same as they did without any hindrance" [A 58]. Four months later another fruitless investigation took place, and after another four months Ignatius found himself in jail, where he had to wait another forty-two days before a notary informed him that they "should not speak about matters of faith until they had studied for four more years, because they had no education" [A 62]. Ignatius was in a quandary, "for seemingly they were closing the door for him to help souls, without giving him any reason except that he had not studied" [A 63].

Leaving Alcalà he went to Salamanca, one of the great medieval universities, only to undergo more or less the same experience: "After twenty-two days of imprisonment, they were summoned to hear the sentence, which was that no error was found in their life or teaching. Therefore they could do what they had been doing, teaching doctrine and speaking about the things of God, so long as they never defined that this is a mortal sin or this is venial, until they had spent four years in further studies" [A 70]. Ignatius tells us that "he found great difficulty in remaining in Salamanca, for it seemed to him that the door had been closed to helping souls by this prohibition not to determine mortal and venial sin." Although the inquisitors found no fault in his teaching on the Trinity, the Blessed Sacrament, and other matters, they forbade him to teach on a practical matter touching on the confessional [A 68, 70]. He found that when it came to helping people in spiritual matters the door was closed to laymen. Even so, he did not lose heart; rather, "he still felt the same desire that he had to help souls, and for that reason to study first and to gather some others with the same idea, and to keep those he had." And so he decided to pursue his studies in Paris [A 71].

The options Ignatius faced were not very attractive: abandon the good of souls or become a priest. According to his own principles, the service of God was the goal and the priesthood a means to that goal. We can only speculate that Ignatius may have been surprised at the mysterious ways in which God dealt with him as he gradually became aware of what he faced. If he wanted to help souls, as God was calling him to do, then he needed the Church to mission him, and since the Church was obviously not missioning laymen to that task, he would have to become a priest. Discernment does not offer a vision of the future; it only enlightens the next step along the path to God.

Good bishops[32] and good priests[33] did exist in the Church, even though the prevailing structures were not designed to produce them. The University of Paris was not a seminary, although a large proportion of its students were clerics. The university produced men capable of qualifying for the better benefices. Ignatius liked the University of Paris not because of its goals but because it had the best system of education in the world, far better than that he had experienced at Alcalá and Salamanca. Somewhere he also saw the possibility of a whole new way of being priest which would enable him to give himself totally to the task of helping others.[34]

3. The Option of His Companions

Perhaps the light began to dawn as he worked with those who became his companions. During this time in Paris he improved the Spiritual Exercises. He worked out the Principle and Foundation [23], which establishes the norm of indifference or openness to whatever is to the service of God. He created the masterful fifth annotation [5] which urges total generosity to God, offering him one's desire, freedom and whole person. He wrote the sixteenth annotation [16] which talks about going contrary to inordinate affections.[35]

In Paris Ignatius probably refined the rough outlines of the rules for election.[36] In the preamble to the election, Ignatius sets down the principle of choosing the service of God first and the way of life as a means to attain that end. Some, he says, choose first to get married or to seek a benefice and then try to figure out how to serve God in marriage or with the benefice, subverting the end (the service of God) to the means (marriage or benefice) [169]. That principle was important for Pierre Favre, the man who first joined him. Although as a boy of twelve Pierre had made a vow of perpetual chastity [*F* 4], as a young man he lived in much darkness of spirit. Alternating doubts and fears and scruples and anxieties with bursts of consolation [*F* 11–12], he was torn between marriage and medicine, law and teaching, becoming a doctor of theology, a lowly cleric, a monk [*F* 14]. Perhaps for Pierre's sake Ignatius wrote into the rules for election the second point on immutable elections, like priesthood and marriage, and mutable elections, like accepting benefices and temporal goods [171]. (None of these seems to have been particularly relevant to Ignatius at Manresa in his own interior struggle.) At any rate, after four years of spiritual guidance by Ignatius culminating in the Spiritual Exercises, Pierre Favre proceeded to ordination [*F* 14]. After associating with Ignatius for two years, he had already chosen to live in poverty [*F* 13].

Francisco Xavier had come to Paris no stranger to the benefice system. He had come to Paris to become a priest, but long before his "conversion" Xavier had set in motion the legal process to establish that he was of noble blood so that he might be eligible for some of the higher and more lucrative benefices.[37] He sought out a position as cathedral canon in Pamplona[38] and received the nomination to that office just before the companions left Paris.[39] Perhaps for his sake (and for the sake of the others as well) we find mention in the rules for an election the examples of receiving an office or benefice [178–83]. And perhaps for his sake, Ignatius added annotation 16 in Paris, which concerns what to do when one finds oneself inclined to an office or benefice for one's personal convenience rather than for the service of God [16]. At any rate, when Xavier received an offer from Pamplona he turned it down with joy. He considered it worthless [*R* 24]. He had already, along with the others, taken a vow of poverty at Montmartre.

Perhaps as he watched God at work in his companions, Ignatius saw how God was working in his own heart. Priesthood was a means to an end, an end he profoundly desired to attain, and as he saw it as a means to that end, he began to see the priesthood in an entirely different light. Priesthood was for ministry, not to enjoy privileges or fulfill an office or receive an income, but to give to others the gifts of God made available to the community of the Church. Ignatius had seen, as had Francis before him, that simply to be a Christian meant to be called to ministry, but neither of them had been allowed to respond to that call in total simplicity.[40]

4. Why *sacerdotes* Rather than *presbyteros*?

Sacerdotes: why use *sacerdos* (in grammatical plural) rather than *presbyter*? *Sacerdos* indicates a functional office held by certain persons within the community; it implies engagement in religious activities. *Presbyter*, on the other hand, indicates a position within the community. Is the choice of the word significant, or are these two words meaning *priest* interchangeable for Ignatius and the companions?

Sacerdos comes from *sacer* [sacred] plus *dare* [to give, grant, offer]. The neuter of *sacer* is also a noun, *sacrum* [a holy thing, a sacrifice]. *Sacrum dare* is to offer sacrifice, to perform religious mysteries. *Presbyter*, on the other hand, is from the Greek word *presbus* [old man]; it is the comparative form and means an older person, an elder.

In the New Testament the word most often used for the leaders in the early Church is *presbuteroi;* the Greek equivalent of *sacerdotes,* namely, *hieroi,* does not appear until the letter to the Hebrews, which contrasts Jesus to the priests of the Old Testament.[41] In Hebrews Jesus is high priest through his humanity, not through cultic selection. He is priest similar to the way he is king, in a complete reversal of the secular model of power.

The choice in this document to describe the companions as priests by using the word *sacerdos* rather than *presbyter* would seem to be significant. One stimulus[42] toward drawing this conclusion comes from a phrase in the will of Faustina de Jancolini, a woman who left her house to Ignatius and his companions (which Ignatius refused to accept). The will refers to the companions as *poveri preti sacerdoti di Jesu Christo* [poor priests, priests of Jesus Christ].[43] Side by side stand two words meaning priest, *preti* and *sacerdoti*. *Poveri preti* indicates that they are priests living in poverty. *Sacerdoti di Jesu Christo* indicates their priestly function in relationship to Jesus, perhaps their dignity as priests, their share in Jesus' sacerdotal ministry. *Preti* seems to suggest the class to which they belong, *sacerdoti* that they *exercised* their priesthood.[44]

A second stimulus comes from the fact that in the Middle Ages *sacerdotium* [priesthood] stood over against *imperium* [rule, government, empire], priestly power vs. imperial power.[45] The Gospel warning of Jesus to his apostles not to lord it over others but to serve others (Mark 10:42–45) had weakened to a whisper in the face of conflict with secular authority. The *sacerdotium* was in charge of the spiritual sphere just as the *imperium* was in charge of the temporal sphere. What was common to each was power. *Cura animarum* or care of souls (better understood as "pastoral charge" rather than as "pastoral care" or "spiritual care," as we use the words today) implied jurisdictional authority and, therefore, might also be called a sort of spiritual sovereignty.[46] Those who had the care of souls, the responsibility for the salvation of the people under their charge, not only served those people, but they had power over them.[47] If they were ordained, theirs was the responsibility to baptize, to celebrate the parish mass (which the people had to attend on Sunday), to hear their Easter confession and give them Easter communion, to preach, to marry, to bury.[48]

In renouncing benefices Ignatius and his companions had renounced the care of souls attached to the benefices, i.e., jurisdictional authority over a particular flock. They had renounced greed and they had renounced power, but in doing so they had not renounced ministry. Just as they had renounced receiving money for their services, so also they had renounced the power to demand anything of anyone. They had not renounced the power to serve. Their power was wholly for the purpose of freeing people to serve God. In paradoxical language, they were poor priests, *pauperes sacerdotes,* little people who were powerful people, each one vulnerable, needy, with the power to bring life, who, like Jesus, "is able to deal gently with the ignorant and wayward, since he himself is subject to weakness" (Heb. 5:2).

A third stimulus comes from the fact that the companions studied St. Thomas in Paris, and Thomas places much emphasis upon sacerdotal power, power over the body of Christ, the

Eucharistic body, and what we call today the mystical body, the Church.[49] This unfortunate development was probably inevitable in a time when all the ministries of the Church (overseer, elder, prophet, apostle, teacher) were funneled into the one reality of priest. Thomas maintains that the first and foremost power of the priest is over the Eucharistic body of Christ, i.e, the power to consecrate the host. This is the power exercised by priests who do not have the care of souls.[50] The second power, which is dependent on the first, is over the mystical body, the Church. This is the power of jurisdiction.

Care of souls was closely related to the administration of the sacraments, but from a juridical point of view. One of the major changes effected by the conflicts in the twelfth century between the diocesan clergy and the monks[51] on the one hand, and the monks and the regular canons on the other,[52] and by the conflicts in the thirteenth and fourteenth centuries between the mendicants and the diocesan clergy[53] was breaking out of the juridical straitjacketing of who had the right and the responsibility to administer the sacraments and approaching the sacraments from a purely pastoral or ministerial point of view, the feeding of the flock of Christ that was hungry and in need. Power used *for* the flock illumined the true meaning of power *over* the flock.

Whatever their theory of priesthood, Ignatius and his companions were interested in feeding the flock of Christ. Their practice and experience of priesthood was more important than their theory.[54] Their terminology may have come from Thomas but their understanding of power came from the Gospel experienced through the Spiritual Exercises. They chose to serve God by helping their neighbor, by working for the salvation of souls, and they did this before they became priests.[55] They chose to be priests so that they could more freely, more fully, and more universally bring Christ into the lives of people. They had come, not to rule, but to serve.

5. Peculiar Circumstances of the Ordination

Sacerdotes: The circumstances surrounding the ordination of the seven companions who were not yet priests are very illuminating with regard to their poverty, the priesthood they envisioned, and the way others saw them.[56] They had received proper papers to be ordained by any bishop outside of Rome, even one who was not living in his own diocese. The rite could take place outside the ordinary times and without observing the proper intervals. On the back of the document, in Cardinal Pucci's hand is written, "Gratis, by reason of their learning and pilgrimage" [FD 526–27].[57] Competence and lowliness were their trademark.

Time, Date, and Place of Ordination. The ordinary times for ordination were Ember Saturdays, the Saturday before Passion Sunday, and Holy Saturday, and the proper intervals stretched the process of ordination over a period of months or years. As pilgrims, hoping for a ship, any ship, to take them to the Holy Land, they could not delay over a long period of time. Their ordination was cast into the same sort of framework of haste that marked the departure of the Israelites from Egypt. Thus, they received minor orders on Sunday, June 10, 1537, and the subdiaconate on June 15, the feast of Sts. Vitus and Modestus, a very solemn festival in Venice. The following Sunday, June 17, they received the diaconate. A week later they were ordained priests on June 24, 1537 [FD 530–32], the feast of John the Baptist. The day was fitting for those who lived both sparingly and prophetically.

The place was Venice, gateway to the Middle East, starting place for all pilgrimages to Jerusalem. The place was as symbolic as the date: they were to be pilgrims for the rest of their lives. The ordination provided much consolation to them and to the ordaining bishop, Vincenzo Negusanti, who did not "charge them a penny, not even a candle" and who said that "in his whole life he had not celebrated an ordination with this much satisfaction" [L 41].[58]

Vow of Poverty. Another event of major importance also marked that day. For the companions, priesthood went hand in hand with poverty. They wanted the priesthood, but not the priesthood as a lucrative career. Since only one bishop could ordain them, Ignatius diplomatically saw to it that the other bishop who wanted to, Girolamo Veralli, the apostolic legate to the Republic of Venice, was included. Thus, immediately before the ordination ceremony, they vowed perpetual poverty in a solemn manner in the presence of the legate of the pope himself [*FD* 532].[59] This vow of perpetual poverty was most unusual, for they were secular priests. How unusual it was needs further explanation.

Titles for Ordination. To be ordained at that time (and until most recent years) the newly ordained had to be assured of support, a "title" it was called, something entitling him to a reasonable living.[60] Although a man could be ordained *sub titulo patrimonii,* meaning that he would live off his patrimony or inheritance, most priests were ordained for (*sub titulo*) a particular church or chapel and supported by its income or benefice, or for a diocese and supported by the diocese, by a benefice attached to the diocese.[61] A man could be ordained *sub titulo sufficientis scientiae* (or *literaturae*),[62] meaning that he had sufficient learning to hold a teaching office to which a benefice was attached or to which a salary or other emolument was attached. When the mendicant orders came into existence, their religious were ordained *sub titulo paupertatis* [under the title of poverty],[63] which meant that they depended upon the generosity of the people with whom they lived or whom they served and were not the responsibility of the bishop.[64]

The companions were offered two titles under which they could be ordained. The first was *sufficientis scientiae* [sufficient knowledge], which meant that they could support themselves by teaching or similar office. The second was *voluntariae paupertatis* [voluntary poverty]. Since they were secular priests without a community to support them, to be ordained under this title would be tantamount to being ordained without any title to a livelihood, and they would need a special dispensation.[65] Either title would suffice, or they could choose both. They chose both, and the papal legate granted the dispensation [*FD* 532].

The bishop's document attesting to the ordination gives no reason for their choice, nor do the accounts written by Ignatius and Laynez. A first glance suggests that they chose the title of *sufficient knowledge* so that they could support themselves by teaching.[66] Not these men. They looked for no support. They had already agreed in Paris that they would take no stipends for what they did. Begging was sufficient for them.[67] The title of *sufficient knowledge* was not a backup system for the title of *voluntary poverty,* in case they could not survive by begging. Rather, the two titles stand in paradox, the title of *voluntary poverty* rendering that of *sufficient knowledge* inoperative in practice, taking away what the other grants; they were a paradox enfleshed in their lives.[68] They humbly accepted the acclamation of their competence and of their right to sustenance, and they proclaimed loudly who they were and how they intended to live and how they understood priesthood for themselves.

On his sickbed in Loyola Ignatius had said to himself: "St. Dominic did this; therefore I have to do it" [*A* 7]. With regard to poverty the companions set out to do exactly what Dominic had set out to do. In a bull of February 11, 1218, Honorius III had commended the services of the new Order of Preachers to bishops throughout the world, describing them as men "who proclaiming the word of God faithfully and without cost [*gratis*], seeking only the profit of souls and following the Lord alone, have carried aloft the title of poverty [*paupertatis titulum*]."[69]

Faculties Granted at Ordination. Like everything else on that occasion, the faculties granted were extraordinary. The document outlining the faculties is dated from Venice, July 5, 1537, and is signed by the papal legate. He granted them permission throughout the various dioceses of the Republic of Venice (except in convents of nuns) to celebrate Mass, to administer the sacraments, to preach the Gospel, to lecture on Scripture both publicly and privately, and to hear the confessions of all who came to them, absolving even in those cases reserved to patriarchs, archbishops, bishops, and other ordinaries, (requesting their permission, of course, but even if it were not granted) [*FD* 533–34].[70]

Like the mendicants, who received a more universal mission not limited to a single diocese,[71] these new priests were granted the authority to work anywhere in the Republic of Venice. But they were even more free than the mendicants, for as diocesan priests their apostolic efforts were in no way limited by some monastic practices still remaining in the mendicant life.[72] They were also freer than the new orders of clerks regular, like the Theatines, who retained a number of monastic practices.[73]

6. The Spirit of Their Priesthood

The opening sentence of *Cum ex plurium* that introduces the five decrees of the Formula of the Institute contains only two phrases that tell us who the companions are: Masters of Paris and poor priests of Christ; everything else tells us something about their activity and its quality.

Like the two titles for ordination, the two phrases are paradoxical. *Masters of Paris,* like the title of *sufficient knowledge,* provides their external credentials, men of education and standing who might have the whole world at their feet. *Poor priests of Christ,* like the title of *voluntary poverty,* identifies their interior spirit and charism. Fortune and power are open to them, but instead they set them aside. Secular priests without position or rank, without income of any kind, without a diocese or ecclesiastical entity of any sort to support them, they are in the full sense of the word mendicants, or simply put, beggars who depend on the charity of others for their sustenance. With Christ they take their place among the weak and vulnerable. They voluntarily and joyfully choose to be without in order to be with Christ poor and with Christ's poor.

They are not laymen to whom the world will not listen and whose ministry can be brushed aside under the claim that they are not properly trained. Nor are they laymen to whom the world will listen, like Gasparo Contarini, because of wealth and rank and power and education but who could do no ministry without ecclesiastical preferment.

They are not monks. Not all monks are priests and not all monks are preachers, nor is any monk primarily a priest or a preacher and then a monk, but a monk first and foremost. In this company all are priests.[74]

They are neither secular canons, attached to some cathedral for the chanting of the office, nor regular canons, clerics who live a "full common life" with no private property and who follow some version of the so-called Rule of St. Augustine, nor are they mendicant friars who, though committed to a broader and more universal ministry, retain a good number of monastic practices.

They are not even clerks regular, dedicated like the Theatines to be priestly models, concerned primarily about liturgical cult and office and leaving their churches only occasionally.

They are priests, secular priests as yet, not religious, yet without bonds of support to any parish or diocese or community, so that their priesthood is not cultic, like that of the diocesan clergy, caring for a particular flock. The secular priesthood of the companions is oriented less toward a diocese than toward the universal Church, less toward the needs of a particular flock than toward the needs of all people everywhere, less toward cult than toward the ministry of the Word: preaching that is ordered toward completion in the sacraments, catechizing, giving the Spiritual Exercises, and toward the ministry of the spiritual and corporal works of mercy. It is a priesthood primarily prophetic in character, both in word and in deed.

They do not belong to the higher clergy, bishops and members of the cathedral chapter, recruited from the nobility and holding positions of power in cathedrals and wealthy churches, nor do they belong to the lower clergy, buried in the poorer parishes or chaplaincies with little or no benefice or hope of advancement. They have simply stepped outside the system. They are not ignorant and poor like many of the lower clergy, nor are they well-educated-and-rich like many of the higher clergy. They are well-educated-and-poor, and they are priests. In all their humility they stand tall because they are free.

They are also not alone. They are a company. They stand together. In Paris they had vowed to be poor with Christ poor; in Rome they have determined not to be separated from one another, not even by vast distances and differing missions. They are in the tradition of the voluntary poor, but they have decided to live like the involuntary poor.

The companions are aware that they do not fit the mold of contemporary priests, whether belonging to a religious order or belonging to a diocese. Pope Paul III, reflecting on what he learns from other people and what he observes for himself, is also profoundly aware that the companions are different. As primary discerner in the Church, his task is to see whether that difference comes from the Spirit of God.

4

Their Choice to Join into One Body

One day Francis of Assisi and seven companions broke into pairs and went off in four different directions to preach the Gospel. After a short time Francis had a great desire to see all of them, and he asked the Lord who "gathers the outcasts of Israel" (Ps. 147:2) to bring them together shortly in his mercy. And so it was done according to his desire. As Thomas of Celano narrates:

> It came about that . . . without any human message, they came together [*convenirent*] giving thanks to God. Coming together [*convenientibus in unum* (1 Cor. 11:20)], they celebrate the vision of their holy shepherd and marvel that thus they have come together [*convenisse*] with one desire [*uno desiderio*].[1]

Cum ex plurium uses the same vocabulary regarding Ignatius and his companions:

> Since from the words of many we have often gathered
> that you, by your own free choice
> poor priests of Christ,
>
> **from various parts of the world**
> [e diuersis mundi regionibus]
> **have joined together into one body,**
> [in vnum conuenisse]

and with the Holy Spirit, as we believe, impelling you,
have conspired together in this one desire . . .

The main verbs of the introductory sentence of *Cum ex plurium*, expressing the pope's joy and desire, *gaudebamus* [we began to rejoice] and *optabamus* [we began to desire], do not appear until much later in the sentence, yet the subordinate verbs in this part of the sentence ultimately depend on them. Why did the pope begin to rejoice and to have hope? Because from many people he had learned that these companions had freely chosen to be poor and had freely chosen to be priests of Christ; these two choices were considered in the two preceding chapters.

What else had he learned? He had also learned about the companions' coming together and about what they did when they came together. The first piece of information provides the material for this chapter, the second for the next. These pieces of information are expressed grammatically in balanced Latin clauses. A further balance occurs in the contrast: the diversity of their origins versus their unity of purpose. The pope has gathered that although the companions are from various parts of the world, they have come together into a single body [*in unum conuenisse*] by their own free choice.

In biblical terms God is the great gatherer. He gathers the people, the dispersed, the survivors, the outcast, all the nations. The coming together of the people is a sacred event. In First Corinthians it is a Eucharistic event (chapter 11), or a talent or gift-sharing event (chapter 14). In *Cum ex plurium* to come together marks a moment of prayerful discernment for men of widely differing gifts.

The word *convenire* combines *cum* [with] and *venire* [come], meaning "come together"; like its English derivative "convene," it implies coming together for a purpose. The conjugated form in this document, *conuenisse*, of itself has nothing to do with travel but has to do with the gathering of the companions as a body or with their forming themselves into one body [*in vnum*].

In other writings the companions reserve *convenire* and *congregare* to indicate their coming together at more solemn moments when they are faced with a decision or a decisive action. To express the simple fact of coming to a place the companions use, for example, "they arrived [*llegaron*]" [*EI* 119], "we reached [*llegamos*] Venice" [*L* 35], "we had come [*venissemus*]" [*F* 16], but when they meet to decide something they write, "they came together [*convenerunt*]" [*R* 64], "they come together [*conveniunt*] [*R* 78]," "we gathered [*congregamos*]" [*L* 47]. The Deliberation of the First Fathers emphasizes their sense of group identity through words that are strictly unnecessary: "we decided to come together with one another [*inter nos conuenire*] . . . to discuss together [*tractare inuicem*] our vocation and manner of living" [*D* 1]. They are a unit, a group, a company.

In vnum conuenisse [come together], therefore, highlights their experience of a process in which they discover an ever-deepening sense of unity. *Cum ex plurium* does not single out one event or a particular moment when they came together, in Paris or Venice or Vicenza or Rome, but indicates a process through which they came closer and closer together until they experienced oneness. They experienced what the Christians of Corinth failed to experience when they came together for the Eucharist.

Underlying the words of *Cum ex plurium* is a sense of astonishment that these particular men would have come together at all. They were not all from the same neighborhood; they were not all the same age; they were not all from the same country; they did not all speak the same language, not even those who were from the same country. The Deliberation of the First Fathers reveals that the companions experienced profoundly the paradox of their unity in diversity. These disparate personalities from three different countries (Spain, Portugal, and France), with four distinct mother tongues (Basque, Spanish, Portuguese, and French), came together to discuss their common vocation.[2] Almost immediately they experienced a split because of their cultural differences, at the same time finding they were of one mind and heart in seeking the divine will. The thought of disbanding brought to full awareness God's gift of a deeper unity in spite of their weaknesses and geographical and cultural differences. Their feeling of wonderment shines forth in Polanco's account: "seeing themselves hailing from many different nations yet bound together in spirit and called to the same vocation" [*PSH* 87].

A series of independent yet overlapping decisions and actions had resulted in the coming together of the companions on at least five different levels, the *physical* or *geographical,* the *social,* the *spiritual,* the *societal* or *communal,* and the *Societal,* not all of them intended here. Now they were requesting formal recognition and approval for that fifth level, encompassing and transcending the other four levels.

(1) Physical or Geographical

The first level is a prelude to the others. "From various parts of the world [*e diuersis mundi regionibus*]" describes them, no more. They came to Paris from various countries and provinces, each of his own free choice and for his own reasons.[3] What *Cum ex plurium* emphasizes is that profoundly disparate individuals have freely united to form a company.

Turned away from staying in Jerusalem in 1523, Ignatius had continually asked himself what should he do, and he decided to go to Barcelona to study [*A* 50]. In 1524 when he arrived in Barcelona he was thirty-two or thirty-three years old. For further study he went to Alcalá in 1526 [*A* 57], then to Salamanca in 1527 [*A* 64], and finally arrived in Paris in February 1528 [*A* 73]. Meanwhile in the autumn of 1525 Pierre Favre left the mountains of Savoy [*F* 6] and Francisco Xavier left the mountains of Navarre and each went to Paris to study for the priesthood. They both enrolled in the Collège de Sainte-Barbe.[4] Simão Rodrigues came to Paris from Portugal in 1527;[5] he too enrolled in the Collège de Sainte-Barbe. Diego Laynez of Almazán and Alfonso Salmerón of Toledo studied together in Alcalá, but in 1532 they left for Paris to do further study. Nicolás Bobadilla, from the diocese of Palencia in Old Castille, had also studied at Alcalá, leaving there after four years to finish his theological studies in Valladolid; in 1533 he came to Paris to study languages [*B* 3–4]. The first part of the group was assembled, and the social and spiritual coming together was already beginning even before the rest of the group arrived.

Not far from Favre's home village lived a young Savoyard priest by the name of Claude Jay. He had been ordained in Geneva on March 28, 1528, a few weeks after Ignatius arrived in Paris looking for companions. On a visit home in 1533 Favre persuaded him to come to Paris, which he did a year later, enrolling in the Collège de Sainte-Barbe. Toward the end of 1534 a new student arrived from Picardy, Paschase Broët. He had been ordained a priest in Amiens on March 12, 1524. After working for ten years he came to Paris to complete his studies and enrolled at the Collège de Calvi, where Bobadilla was teaching. At the same time, Jean Codure left the mountains of Provence in southern France and came to Paris to study for the priesthood. In 1534 he enrolled in the Collège de Lisieux, which was near the Collège de Sainte-Barbe. The companions-to-be were all assembled, but not all of them knew each other as yet.

(2) Social

The second level marks a new phase. Once they arrived in Paris, they found themselves thrown together by circumstances or drawn together by mutual attraction. In 1526, after a year of study, both Favre and Xavier were assigned to live in the same apartment as their tutor, Juan de la Peña [*F* 7]. In 1529 Ignatius was assigned the same tutor and the same apartment [*A* 82]. Sometime later Rodrigues became fascinated with Ignatius and moved in with them.

Laynez and Salmerón had more on their minds than study when they came to Paris. They also wanted to find Ignatius. The two friends had known him at least by reputation in Alcalá and wanted to search him out. On their arrival in Paris they ran into him at the hostelry and he helped them get settled. Bobadilla also knew about Ignatius. Shipwrecked on his journey to Paris, penniless, he sought out Ignatius who had a reputation for helping people [*PSH* 52]. Ignatius found him a teaching position in the Collège de Calvi and persuaded him to continue studying theology [*B* 5]. The more recent members of the group, however, Jay, Broët, and Codure, found their link through Favre, who introduced them to the others.

(3) Spiritual

The group gathered around the little Basque who was old enough to be the father of some of them, but very soon Jesus became the center and remained the center for all of them. Through the Spiritual Exercises, through spending time together in prayer and recreation, they bonded together in spite of their differences in age, national origin, language, and culture. Daily living with Ignatius gradually affected Favre and Xavier. By 1531 Favre was determined to follow Ignatius, and Xavier was won over in 1532 or 1533. At the same time Rodrigues was converted to the ideals of Ignatius. Not long after their arrival Laynez and Salmerón joined the group who met to pray at the Carthusian church on Sundays,[6] and soon Bobadilla brought to six the number of Ignatius's companions.

Making the Spiritual Exercises under the direction of Ignatius crowned their spiritual coming together. The first was Favre at the beginning of 1534, then Laynez and Salmerón, Rodrigues and Bobadilla, and finally Xavier in September of the same year. Each independently decided to live like Ignatius, following Christ in poverty and intent on going to Jerusalem to work for the salvation of others. Then they learned that their friends had made the same decision. Years later Rodrigues would enthusiastically proclaim: "When they learned that, words could not express what joy, what happiness, what consolation they experienced, what strength to persevere in their resolve" [R 9]. The physical, social, and spiritual coming together was not yet complete. Some months after Jay's arrival later in 1534 Favre directed him through the Spiritual Exercises, and he joined the other companions. Favre also became acquainted with Broët and directed him through the Exercises. Codure as well came under Pierre's influence, came to him for spiritual direction, and under Favre's direction, he, too, made the Spiritual Exercises.

They have not only come to the same place from many places, but this international group of students has come together as an international group of friends in the Lord. The process of their coming together has reached a new point, a sense of being united by and in the Lord.

(4) Communal

The process, however, is not yet complete. It is leading toward a sense of being bound together into one body. Although other friends shared much of their outlook, none shared their commitment. The companions gave themselves up to a project that was daring, dangerous, and demanding. They sought others who would do the same. Bonded together in a single purpose, the first seven companions, "those of us who came together [*convenimus*] that first time [*F* 15]," expressed who they were and wanted to be at Montmartre on August 15, 1534, in the vow that would send them either to Jerusalem or to the Holy Father in Rome. Each year in Paris the companions renewed their vows [*L* 30], and when they renewed them again at Montmartre in August 1536, Jay, Broët, and Codure came together with them [*R* 15].[7] Meanwhile, Ignatius had left Paris at Easter of 1535.

In the Deliberation of the First Fathers they recognize and celebrate their experience of friendship before Montmartre and their commitment at Montmartre in these words:

> Since the most merciful and gracious Lord had deigned to unite us to one another [*inuicem vnire*] and to gather us together [*et congregare*], weak as we are and from different places and cultures, we should not sever the bonding [*unionem*] and gathering [*et congregationem*] that comes from God.[8] [*D* 3]

They did not want to destroy that union; they did not want to destroy that body. They could not have become friends if they had not known each other or associated with one another. They could not have become one body if they had not become friends. From Venice Ignatius wrote a letter in the winter of 1536 to the confessor of the French queen referring to Favre and his *compañía* and the dangerous journey they were making from Paris in the midst of France's war with Spain [*EI* 110]; and the next summer he wrote to a friend in Barcelona, "Nine of my friends in the Lord have arrived from Paris" [*EI* 119]. They were a company of friends long before they gave themselves a name. Becoming one body, expressing their unity externally, cements and brings to perfection their unity in the Lord.

(5) Societal

The companions had no intent of becoming a religious order [*L* 36], but they were committed to follow the footsteps of Jesus in the Holy Land or the command of his vicar to go wherever he might send them. They were free spirits unburdened by organizational details. In Vicenza they formally recognized the fact that they were a company. Before they set out to seek new recruits in the universities of Italy [*L* 42], they asked themselves the question, what shall we respond if anyone asks us to what group [*congregación*] we belong? They betook themselves to prayer, and since they had no head but Jesus and no superior except Jesus whom they desired to serve, they decided to take the name of their head and to reply: the Company of Jesus [*PSH* 86].[9] Only when they could not go to Jerusalem, did they see through prayer and discernment that organization would be not a burden but an instrument of freedom.

To sum up, in the Deliberation of the First Fathers the companions recognized that despite their cultural differences a strong bond of companionship united them, a gift from God himself. Prayer and discernment confirmed the decision they had reached at Vicenza. They would be the Company of Jesus, and the time had come to ask for papal approbation for that name and their way of living. They wish to share their gift of companionship with countless others, to perpetuate throughout time the dynamic spirit of love that they have experienced for God and one another.

5

The Impelling Action of the Holy Spirit

The final piece of information the pope has gathered from others about the companions concerns what they did when they came together. At this point *Cum ex plurium* indicates a fundamental change in their experience. In sharp contrast to *sponte* [of their own free choice], we find a participial clause, *impellente Spiritu Sancto* [with the Holy Spirit impelling]. Each is joined to an infinitive, *sponte . . . conuenisse* [came together], and *impellente . . . conspirasse* [conspired]. These two infinitive clauses may, indeed, indicate some temporal sequence, but most of all they mark a clear distinction between two moments in the psychological experience of the companions:

> Since from the words of many we have often gathered
> that you, of your own free choice . . .
> from various parts of the world
> have joined together into one body,
>
> **and with the Holy Spirit, as we believe, impelling you,**
> [et Spiritu Sancto, ut credimus, impellente]
> **have conspired together in this one desire,**
> [in hanc vnam voluntatem conspirasse]
>
> that . . . you would dedicate your lives
> to the . . . service of our Lord Jesus Christ

The action of coming together they experience as free but graced, a genuine gift from God; the action of conspiring together they experience as so powerfully grace-filled that God's action fills their consciousness even as it enhances their freedom. Each of the companions has freely chosen to enter into relationship with the others; once the group is formed, they experience that the Holy Spirit sweeps the group along. When does that moment take place? After they have achieved the five levels of coming together outlined in the preceding chapter? Or somewhere along the line? To all appearances, it takes place after they freely chose to join together in one body; and yet, the one desire they share with one another and with the Holy Spirit, to dedicate themselves in companionship to the service of Christ and his Church, expresses itself concretely in the very joining together in one body. Freedom and grace are working hand in glove more than in temporal sequence. The psychological experience may vary, but freedom and the Spirit prevail and endure.

That there is some temporal sequence is clear, but when the group became conscious of the Spirit's activity in them as a group is harder to determine. We might, for example, have expected the sentence to read:

> with the Holy Spirit, as we believe, impelling you,
> [you] have come together from various parts of the world,
> and have conspired in this one desire . . .

But it does not read that way. By its position in the sentence the Holy Spirit clause reveals the authorship of the proposed letter, for it expresses better the experience of the companions (the real authors) than it does the conviction of the pope (the proposed author) drawn from observation or gathered from other people. Anyone reflecting on the series of events might discover the amazing providence of God bringing the companions together from different lands. That providence, however, is not what the companions have in mind in writing this sentence. In leaving their homes they are unaware of the Spirit of God at work bringing them together. In finding one another and becoming friends, in the longing of each to go to Jerusalem, they are not conscious of the Spirit's action on them as a group. Only after they experience their oneness and accept it do they begin to experience the activity of the Holy Spirit driving them, guiding them, goading them. The Spiritual Exercises have attuned them to the presence and action of the Spirit within each of them. As they progress toward their goal, they gradually become conscious of the Spirit's action within them as a group, but that moment is difficult to define precisely.

The Deliberation of the First Fathers reveals that the companions expect the guidance of the Holy Spirit in the group. After experiencing their shared desire to serve God but their division with regard to the appropriate means, they make a unanimous decision. They will apply themselves to more prayer and penance, will make every effort they can, and then they will cast all their concerns on the Lord, hoping in him [*sperantes in eum*]. They are convinced that God, who is so good and bountiful that he does not deny his good spirit to anyone who seeks him in humility and simplicity of heart, "will in no way desert [them] but be present to [them] according to his goodness much more abundantly than [they] request or comprehend" [*D* 1].[1]

Deciding they should not violate the union God has given them, they make every effort to set aside their own desires and inclinations so that nothing they affirm is from their "own spirit or understanding, but only, whatever it may be, that which God has inspired [*inspirauerit*] and the Apostolic See has confirmed and approved" [*D* 3].

At first they can reach no agreement regarding obedience. The minutes state, "Hoping in the Lord [*in Domino sperantes*], we began to discuss some means of solving the problem in a better way." They consider going off to some quiet place for thirty or forty days and spending time in prayer, fasting, and penance, "to this purpose, that the Lord would hear our desires and would deign to imprint on our minds the solution to the question" [*D* 5]. They understand prayer as a dialogue. They will be present to God and God will be present to them. They decide against going away. They continue their work with people, but they also open themselves to God in prayer, affirming that "each one would prepare himself in such a manner, would so give himself to prayers, sacrifices, and meditations, as to rely on [*niteretur*] finding joy and peace in the Holy Spirit regarding obedience" [*D* 6]. Throughout the Deliberation the companions are convinced that if they set aside their own wants and desires, God will reveal himself to them.[2] After many days of prayer and discussion, "with the Lord's help [*Domino prestante auxilium*]" they come to a unanimous and undisputed decision [*D* 8]. It is not reflection after the fact that reveals the Lord's help; they experience his help as he gives it.

In *Cum ex plurium* also the companions are concerned with experience during the fact, not reflection after the fact. Evidence is their remarkable use of the present participle active, *impellente:* "with the Holy Spirit *impelling* you." In the Formula of the Institute they use the same word in the present tense and add a present participle, telling those who wish to join them to ask themselves, "whether the Holy Spirit who impels [*impellit*] them has promised them enough grace that they may hope, with his help [*illo adiuuante*], to carry the weight of this vocation" [*CEP* 3]. They seek in others an experience similar to their own, an experience of the Spirit at work assisting them in the very act of entering into their vocation.

Papal briefs and bulls do not usually contain such exuberant phrases as *Spiritu Sancto . . . impellente*. Recognizing that God moves a religious founder is a stock idea in papal letters. The standardized phrases, however, are past, passive, and impersonal, and they usually refer to inspiration. For example, *Exponi nobis,* a brief issued by Clement VII in 1524, describes the founders of the Theatines and their companions in this way: *divina, ut creditur, inspiratione ducti* [led, as it is believed, by divine inspiration] [*BRT* 6:73a].

The basic idea is similar to *Spiritu Sancto . . . impellente,* but the passive and impersonal language draws attention to the founders as having been led in the past by a divine force, the force of inspiration. *Spiritu Sancto . . . impellente,* on the other hand, focuses on the Spirit as supremely active, driving them forward, not only in the past but continuing into the present. The bull of Paul III, *Dudum felicis,* approving the Barnabites in 1535 [*BRT* 6:191a], repeats the phrase from the Theatine brief word for word along with other phrases. The language, plainly standardized or stereotyped, not only expresses the experience of the observer rather than of the participant, it expresses the observer's experience of human beings rather than the observer's experience of God.

More like the phrase in *Cum ex plurium* is "with that Holy Spirit inspiring them [*spirante illo Spiritu Sancto*]" in the brief of Leo X to the Third Order of St. Francis in 1521 [*BRT* 5:764b]. The Holy Spirit is the active subject, as in *Cum ex plurium,* but the context is different. Although the participle is in the present, it refers to an event in the past. The event, once again, is inspiration, and those inspired are not founders but anonymous followers. *Spiritu Sancto . . . impellente,* on the other hand, refers to the past and to the present: the Holy Spirit has been and is impelling the companions. The Spirit is doing more than inspiring, breathing upon them or into them; the Spirit is blowing hard and driving them forward so that they are running before the wind. The Holy Spirit is the dominant figure, and the companion founders are called by their names.

The text of *Cum ex plurium* ascribes the experience to the pope: "as we believe [*ut credimus*]." The position of *impellente* in the sentence, however, reveals that the companions who wrote the document are really describing their own experience. Like Jesus whom the Spirit drove [*expulit*] into the desert (Mark 1:12), they are the ones who experience the impelling force of the Spirit. They are the ones who, after their coming together, experience the Holy Spirit driving them, impelling them, propelling them forward, blowing them ahead like a strong wind, not giving them much choice while giving them every choice, not just leading or persuading but driving them on. They are the ones who, after their coming together, experience the Holy Spirit impelling them to abandon the world and to become one in mind and heart in dedicating themselves to the service of Jesus Christ and of his vicar on earth.

A Legend Is Born

Six years after *Cum ex plurium,* five years after *Regimini militantis ecclesiae,* Jerónimo Nadal entered the Society. He soon became right-hand man to Ignatius. In 1553, three years after *Exposcit debitum,* Ignatius gave him the task of promulgating the Constitutions. Nadal probably knew little about *Cum ex plurium* except that Contarini had read the Formula to Paul III and the latter had orally approved the Society. He was familiar with *Spiritu sancto afflati* [inspired by the Holy Spirit], a phrase used in *Regimini* and *Exposcit,* but probably was unaware that it had evolved from *Spiritu Sancto . . . impellente* [with the Holy Spirit impelling] of *Cum ex plurium* through the influence of the stock phrase in the Theatine and Barnabite documents, *divina . . . inspiratione ducti* [led by divine inspiration]. That is why Nadal in 1554, fifteen years after Contarini read the Formula to the pope, could say that on that occasion the pope said, "The Spirit of God is here [*Spiritus Dei est hic*]."[3]

The remark is to be treasured, yet no one reported it before Nadal, not Ignatius when he wrote to his nephew Beltrán about the Society's approval about three weeks after the event [*EI* 149], not Salmerón when he wrote to the father of Diego Laynez on September 25, 1539 [*EI* 154], nor did any of the companions report it in any of their accounts of the oral confirmation, nor did Polanco when he wrote in 1547/48 that on that occasion the pope spoke "with a prophetic spirit" [*PSH* 89], nor did the same Polanco in 1564, ten years after Nadal's remark, when arguing that the Company was the work of the Holy Spirit [*PI* 10]; if Paul had explicitly stated, "The Spirit of God is here," that was the time for Polanco to testify to that fact. The only one who picks up the phrase is Ribadeneira in 1572, like Nadal and Polanco, a second generation member of the Company.

Nadal repeated the phrase to many different groups, on one occasion stating: "To this both he [Paul III] and Julius III have testified in their bulls of confirmation."[4] In their bulls the two pontiffs do not testify that Paul made the remark but that the companions were inspired by the Holy Spirit [*Spiritu sancto afflati*]. Nadal simply put the phrase in the bulls into the mouth of Paul III on the occasion of the oral confirmation. Nadal was more interested in truth than in historical precision: the words "The Spirit of God is here" reveal what the pope truly thought of the Society. Thus a legend is born, but legend speaks the truth.[5]

The "Conspiracy" of the Companions

The companions have freely chosen to be poor, have freely chosen to be ordained priests, have freely chosen to come together in companionship. Even as far back as Paris, they begin to experience a new power at work within the group, a power that does not take away their freedom but enhances it, a driving power that takes them in unexpected directions, the divine wind-breath, the Holy Spirit of God. Freely they choose to make themselves available to that power.

To what does the Holy Spirit impel them? To an action as remarkable as the experience itself of being impelled by the Spirit: to conspire together. The English falls short of the Latin. To "conspire" has many negative connotations in English, although it also means working together in harmony, agreeing together in thought or feeling.[6] In Latin the negative overtones are secondary and the primary meanings stress harmony and agreement. *Conspirasse,* following upon *Spiritu Sancto,* suggests breathing together with a breath received from the Holy Spirit. The holy breathing of the Holy Spirit fills their hearts with a single desire [*vnam voluntatem*]. That desire, to dedicate themselves in companionship to the service of Christ and his Church, we leave for the next chapter. Meanwhile, the passage recalls their experience of unity in diversity at the beginning of the Deliberation of the First Fathers when they came together to discuss their vocation and way of life, "Common to us all was one mind and will [*una omnium nostrum et communis mens et voluntas*], namely to seek the gracious and perfect will of God" [*D* 1]. Three months later they complete all their work "peacefully and with harmonious unanimity" [*D* 9]. Their unity of purpose hints at something to be treated later in *Cum ex plurium,* the union of their Company in Christ [*vestre Societatis in Christo vnionem*]. That kind of unity in that kind of diversity is an experience for them of the presence and activity of the Spirit of God.

6

Free to Serve

The Spirit of God is a freeing Spirit, a gentle warmth hovering over the waters of creation, a hot wind drying up the waters of the Red Sea, a life-giving breath arousing the dry bones of Israel bleaching on the plains. Ignatius and his companions move in a world that is not only shackled by sin but caught in the snares of its own loveliness. The Spirit of God breathes in them, moves in them, creates in them to choose freely to be free. They pray, they listen, they hear, they choose. They choose to be free so that they might serve the one who makes them free. The text expresses it well:

> have conspired in this one desire,
>
> **that, having abandoned the snares of this world,**
> [ut, relictis seculi huius illecebris]
>
> you would dedicate your lives to the perpetual service
> of our Lord Jesus Christ and of his vicar on earth;

The companions do not abandon the world; they love the world. They abandon the snares of the world. Snares [*illecebris*] is a deliberate translation. It might have been allurements or enticements, or even seductions. The world attracts the human heart, stirs the human appetite, allures and entices, even seduces, or especially seduces. The world is not seen as evil but as attractive, good but hopelessly inadequate to satisfy the human heart, good and beautiful and wonderful, and therefore seductive precisely because it cannot satisfy. The limited becomes a snare when the human heart, enraptured by it, refuses to admit the limitations and thereby becomes entangled and entrapped.

The clause, *relictis . . . illecebris,* seems to be an allusion to Mark's Gospel: "And immediately they left [*relicti*] their nets [*retibus*] and followed him" (1:18).[1] A net ensnares. A fish has to be very small to escape, to get through the snare. Whether Mark is using the net as a metaphor for the snares of this world is for the biblical scholar to decide. In Ignatian spirituality the goods of this world, riches and honors, for example, are snares, and only the humble can avoid becoming entangled and entrapped by them. Calling the attractions and enticements of this world snares is not meant to demean them but simply to relativize them and place them in proper perspective. Sin is not a snare; it is a chasm. Only good things are snares. What Saul had considered gain Paul considered hindrance after he had come to know Christ; relative to Christ everything else was rubbish (Phil. 3:8).

Contempt of the world has a long history.[2] Consistent in that history is the attitude of transcending earthly realities, not despising them in themselves but seeing them from a higher perspective, looking down upon them from the heights of heaven rather than looking down upon them from the level of earth.[3] The world is the non-Christian world, or more specifically, the pagan world in the early days of Christianity, the world with which the Christian had to break in order to follow Christ.

The *Life of Antony* (chapter 3) speaks of him as "free from all the chains of the world." Chains bind one down and are a constant burden. The things of this world may be good in themselves but relative to Christ they are extremely restrictive. That is why the early monks chose to leave (abandon) the world.[4] In language amazingly similar to that of Ignatius St. Augustine describes the life of the first cenobitical monks, "who, having despised [*contemptis*] and abandoned [*desertis*] the snares [*illecebris*] of this world, gathered together in a common life of chastity and holiness."[5] As one glances at the stories of those who fled from the world even the casual reader has to be struck by how many times the flight from the world is expressed by a subordinate clause: abandoning the world may be important, but something else is even more important.⁶ What Augustine seems excited about is not that the early monks of the desert had abandoned the world, but that they had lived together serenely in community.

A passage in an early Cistercian document provides another example. The first part of the sentence might substitute for the sentence thus far in *Cum ex plurium,* but the second part of each sentence goes off in a different direction, one in accordance with the Cistercian charism and the other in accordance with the Jesuit charism:

> Thus having rejected the riches of the world [*hujus saeculi divitiis spretis*], the new soldiers of Christ, poor with the poor Christ, began to consult with one another as to the question of the way by which, and with what work or occupation, they should provide in this life for themselves as well as for guests who would come, rich and poor alike, whom according to the Rule they should receive as Christ.⁷

Rejecting the riches of the world is only a beginning. The Cistercian, poor with Christ poor, chooses a life of prayer and hospitality. The Jesuit, poor with Christ poor, will choose a different form of prayer and a different form of hospitality. The deliberate choice of Ignatius and his companions will more closely resemble that of Francis and his companions as described by Honorius III in the first papal writing concerning the Franciscan Order:

> When our beloved sons, Brother Francis and his companions . . . having abandoned the vanities of this world [*abiectis vanitatibus huius mundi*], chose a way of life rightly approved by the Roman Church, and went about through various parts of the world, sowing the seed of the word of God after the example of the apostles . . .⁸

Many followed Francis "after renouncing worldly concerns [*saecularibus curis abiectis*],"⁹ but renunciation was not their goal. The supreme desire of Francis was "to be free of all that is in the world."¹⁰ Freedom was the goal, freedom to serve, freedom to spread the good news of Jesus. The importance of Francis was not that he abandoned the emptiness of the world, although that is an important prelude, but that he began to live a life that fed the whole Church and brought the Gospel to all parts of the world.

We see, therefore, that the Spirit of God is a freeing Spirit. It is also an engaging Spirit, moving the free to engage the world. Just as the Spirit hovers creatively over a world in chaos, so the Spirit sends those who are free to bring order out of chaos, filling it with light and peace, with joy and love. Freedom may be open-ended, but its seeks purpose, direction, life. The text indicates how the companions have chosen to direct their freedom:

> have conspired together in this one desire
> that, having abandoned the snares of this world,
>
> **you would dedicate your lives to the perpetual service**
> [vitam vestram perpetuo . . . servitio dedicaretis]
> **of our Lord Jesus Christ and of his vicar on earth;**
> [Domini nostri Jesu Christi atque eius in terris vicarii]

Pope Paul III had already learned from the companions themselves that they were completely at his service. These lines of *Cum ex plurium* prepare the way for introducing into the five decrees of the Formula of the Institute the fourth vow of obedience to the pope that will mark the unique character of the Society of Jesus. Their immediate progenitor is some lines from the Deliberation of the First Fathers written some days or weeks earlier:

> **we had offered and dedicated ourselves and our lives**
> [*nos vitamque nostram . . . obtuleramus et dedicaueramus*]
> **to Christ our Lord and to His true and legitimate vicar**
> [*Christo Domino nostro et eius vero ac legitimo vicario*] [*D* 3].

The title "vicar of Christ," although not biblical, is an ancient one, appearing in ecclesiastical writings of the third century. It had not always belonged to the pope exclusively; it was shared with bishops and emperors as well. It came to be the exclusive title of the pope in the time of Innocent III (1198–1216) whose policies of centralization gave increasing power to the papacy and took the place of other older titles such as "vicar of St. Peter" and "vicar of God."[11]

To *dedicate* is to give fully, to devote something or someone to the service and worship of God, or to set apart for a particular use or service. A deep interior attitude often begets an urge toward some external ritual act.

Service is not quite the same as ministry. The attitude of the servant, of the slave, is one of servitude, of loving servitude for the servant of Christ, of belonging wholly to another, namely, Jesus; the attitude of the minister is joyful compassion. The two, of course, can be joined in the same person.

Two sets of experiences shine forth through the words of *Cum ex plurium*, (1) the personal experiences of Ignatius in his conversion and in the vision he had at La Storta on the way to Rome and (2) the common experiences of Ignatius and companions in their vows at Montmartre and in the oblation they made of themselves to Pope Paul III. First, however, we need to reflect briefly on the Christian tradition of service that was the context in which Ignatius and his companions lived and acted.

Service in the Christian Tradition

Christian tradition approaches the idea of service with biblical images. The suffering Servant of Yahweh is one such image (Isa. 53). Jesus who comes to serve and not to be served is another, and the one who would be great among his followers is to be the servant of all (Mark 10:44–45). A servant or slave is one who belongs body and soul to someone else, in this case to God, and through God to God's people. In the total freedom of belonging, the servant loves in response to God's gift of love. If one begins with the secular norms of governance that Jesus rejected and then attempts to preserve and to sanctify them by imposing on them this biblical imagery, one can only wreak havoc, especially in the Church, where the power to rule is at the service of love and of freedom. To treat as subservient to oneself those who profess to be submissive servants of God and of his people is to deny love and to render one's actions manipulative, destructive, and tyrannical. If one begins, however, with the biblical image, it may transform the secular reality. Paul was the servant or slave of Christ [*Christou doulos*] (Gal. 1:10), just as Mary was handmaid of the Lord [*doulē kuriou*] (Luke 1:38). The Greek word immediately suggests dulia or veneration, a form of worship, reminding us of the fact that the service of God is not only linked with the worship [*latreia*] of God, but is identical with it.

Irenaeus links service and worship in a fairly lengthy passage full of uses of slave [*doulos*] and servitude [*douleia*] and servile [*doulikos*], in which he says that God first attracted us to be his slaves and then gave us our freedom. God does not need our service [*douleia*], but is good and merciful and rewards those who persevere in his service [*douleia*]. And then he suddenly changes from *doulein* [to serve] to *latreuein* [to worship], for to serve God is to worship God: "Just as God is in need of nothing, so also the human person needs communion with God. For this is the glory of a human being, to persevere in worshiping [*latreuein*] God."[12]

Early monasticism saw the monk as a slave of God, *doulos tou theou* in the East and *servus Dei* or *servus Domini* in the West. The monastic life itself was called a condition of slavery or servitude, the slavery of God, or the slavery of Christ, a liberating slavery that ennobled the one who embraced it voluntarily.[13] In a society and culture that lived with slavery as a reality, the monks transformed the term to mean the free surrender of oneself to God. Service and worship blend in the Rule of St. Benedict, where service is the very life that the monk leads. What Benedict wanted to establish was a school for the Lord's service [*dominici schola servitii*] (*RB*, Prol. 45), not simply a place where one learned how to serve but a situation in which one was actively engaged in serving at all times.[14]

Service and worship walk hand in hand through the whole history of Christian spirituality. Ignatius, original though he was, was also part of this tradition. If, in the manner of other Christian writers, he occasionally draws on the language of feudalism, he always does so in the context of the Christian biblical tradition (which feudalism, by itself, often distorted). Within this tradition, therefore, we should understand the Ignatian phrases in the Spiritual Exercises: "praise, reverence, and serve" of the Principle and Foundation [23]; "What ought I to do for Christ?" of the very first colloquy [53]; the proviso in the Call of the King [98] that imitating Jesus in bearing injuries must be for his greater service and praise; the proviso again in the prayer for the most perfect spiritual poverty in the colloquy after the Two Standards [147] that the Divine Majesty be served; and the *Suscipe* prayer in the Contemplation to Obtain Love [234] at the end of the Exercises that summarizes everything that could be said about service and worship:

> Take, Lord, and receive all my liberty, my memory, my understanding, and all my will, all that I have and possess. You Lord, have given all that to me. I now give it back to you, O Lord. All of it is yours. Dispose of it according to your will. Give me your love and your grace, for that is enough for me. [234]

These words find a new form of expression in *Cum ex plurium:* "you would dedicate your lives to the perpetual service of our Lord Jesus Christ and of his vicar on earth." *Service* in this passage draws its real strength from Christian tradition. The biblical force is there, the Irenaean emphasis on perpetual service as worship, the Lordship of Christ of the Benedictine tradition. The service of others is epitomized in the service of the one who takes the place of Christ.[15]

1. The Dedication of Ignatius

At Loyola, Ignatius gave himself to God. In the room where his conversion took place, there is today a striking sign: *Aquí San Ignacio se entregó a Dios* ("Here St. Ignatius dedicated himself to God"). A fascinating expression: the verb *entregar,* "dedicate," occurs in the Spanish translations of the Gospel for the Greek *paradidonai* to say that Judas *betrayed* Jesus, the chief priests *delivered* him to Pilate, Pilate *handed* him *over* to be crucified, and Jesus *gave up* his spirit. In each instance Jesus renders himself totally at the disposal of another. But the first three uses are enormously different from the final one: in the first three Jesus plays a passive role. In handing over his spirit to his Father, Jesus is totally engaged. To give oneself actively body and soul into the service of another is at the heart of service in the Christian tradition.

When Ignatius left his ancestral home, the service of Christ meant to him doing penance for his sins in imitation of the saints: "He thought of going to Jerusalem barefoot, and of eating nothing but plain vegetables and of practicing all the other rigors that he saw in the saints" [*A* 8]. But his experiences at Manresa transformed his attitude: "His firm intention was to remain in Jerusalem, continually visiting those holy places; and in addition to this devotion, he also planned to help souls" [*A* 45]. Serving God in penance [*A* 14] had become serving God's people.

Ignatius would later have the experience of not being allowed to stay in Jerusalem, and this experience made him cautious. His simple piety and simple theology saw all authority come directly from God. If it was not God's will that he walk in the footsteps of Jesus, he would seek God's will in the vicar of Christ. That he himself might be able to read the needs of God's people better than a half-committed pope, could not occur to Ignatius, for the pope was Christ's vicar. At the same time, Ignatius's service would never be servile. He was not afraid to contradict popes and princes: they could use a little illumination from human sources; but the final authority came from God, and when it was invoked Ignatius accepted it without question. He could still urge the contrary, but he could not disobey.

While at Manresa, his interior disposition deepened as he immersed himself in the challenge of Jesus. "What ought I to do for Christ?" he asked himself [53]. The answer came in the Call of the King: "All those who have judgment and reason will offer themselves wholeheartedly for this labor" [96]. Reason cried out for a total offering of himself. Could anything more be demanded than that, anything more be possible? Yes, came the answer. Even all allows for more: deeper intensity, greater enthusiasm, and an ever expanding generosity.

Ignatius was carrying much baggage from the past, but something could be done about that. Love demanded a fuller response that took into consideration his particular failings, his weaknesses, his vulnerability. The Call of the King anticipates the feelings, and even some of the language of *Cum ex plurium*, as the text continues:

Those who desire to show greater devotion and to distinguish themselves in total service of their eternal King and universal Lord will not only offer their persons for the labor, but go further still. They will work against their human sensitivities and against their carnal and worldly love, and they will make offerings of greater worth and moment, and say:

"Eternal Lord of all things, I make my offering, with your favor and help. . . . I wish and desire, and it is my deliberate decision [*determinación*], provided only that it is for your greater service and praise, to imitate you in bearing all injuries, and affronts, and any poverty, actual as well as spiritual, if your Most Holy Majesty desires to elect and receive me into such a life and state" [97–98].

In the triple colloquy at the end of the Two Standards, this ideal offering becomes a real request "for grace to be received under the standard" of Jesus [147]. To make the oblation is one thing; to experience its acceptance is another. Ignatius's disposition to give himself to Christ deepened as he experienced that acceptance in journeying as a poor pilgrim to the Holy Land, in the humiliating years of study after his return, and especially in the reproaches, slanders, injuries, and imprisonment he suffered while he battled his way through the charges brought by Church inquisitors that denied the very core of who he was.

The ritual expression of Ignatius's dedication occurred first in the all-night vigil at Montserrat, where Ignatius hung up his sword and dagger and clothed himself in the garments of a poor man. The ritual expression came again twelve years later in the vows at Montmartre and three years later still in his ordination to the priesthood in Venice.

At La Storta Ignatius experienced God's response to his offering, which for Ignatius was God's response to the whole Company as well. And La Storta confirmed Ignatius in the path he had chosen. The event occurred a few miles outside of Rome as Ignatius, Favre, and Laynez were on their way from Vicenza to Rome at the end of 1537. Ignatius begins the story by stating that "he had decided to spend a year without saying Mass after he became a priest, preparing himself and praying Our Lady to deign to place him with her Son." His prayer sounds like that of the Two Standards, and it appears that Ignatius had persevered in that prayer for fifteen years without a full sense that it had been heard and his request granted. He then continues: "One day, a few miles before reaching Rome, he was at prayer in a church and experienced such a change in his soul and saw so clearly that God the Father placed him with Christ his Son that he would not dare doubt it—that God the Father had placed him with his Son" [A 96]. His prayer was answered. From then on he knew that they were all called to be companions of Jesus.

Some twenty years later Laynez fills in some of the details concerning La Storta. Ignatius had told Laynez that "he seemed to see Christ with the cross on his shoulder, and the Eternal Father nearby said to him, 'I want you to take this man for your servant [*servitore*].' And so Jesus accepted him and said, 'I want you to serve us [*ci serva*].'"[16] The "I want" of the Father and the Son made it clear that Ignatius's service was their choice, not simply his. All the companions dedicated themselves to this same service of Jesus.

2. The Dedication of the Companions

(a) Before Montmartre

Each of the early companions of Ignatius had been so moved by the contemplations on the life of Christ in the Spiritual Exercises and by close association with Ignatius as to wish to go to the Holy Land with him. They longed to follow in the footsteps of Jesus, to walk the land he walked, to preach his word, to proclaim the good news of salvation, and to give their lives if necessary in his service. The totality of their disposition, the wholeheartedness of their dedication, is striking in their accounts.[17]

In his journal Favre writes of the confusion he experienced before his friendship with Ignatius, how he was dragged now one way, now another, by various spirits. "Freeing me, the Lord so filled me with the consolations of his spirit that I decided absolutely to become a priest totally dedicated to his service [*totus suo servitio dedicatus*] in a vocation so difficult and demanding that I would never be able to serve [*servire*] him worthily in it" [*F* 14]. For Favre the elements of complete and total dedication to the service of Christ are already there.

Rodrigues describes each of the companions in words that manifest not only his deep love for them, but their profound commitment to Jesus. Of Ignatius he says that he is a man who "has given himself totally [*totum*] to the divine service [*obsequio*]" [*R* 3].[18] Of Favre, Rodrigues says, "He consecrated himself to God with his whole heart [*ex toto corde*]" [*R* 4]; of Xavier, "He gave up his old way of life, and adopting a new one, gave himself completely [*totum*] to the salvation of souls and to a pilgrimage to the holy places of Jerusalem" [*R* 5]. Rodrigues describes his own commitment by saying first of all that he is not worthy to be listed amongst the others, and then speaks of himself in the third person, "He was a man driven [*impulsum*] by God and wondrously spurred on [*incitatum*] by God to change his former way of life to one of divine service [*obsequium*]. I will add besides that . . . not knowing what the other three had in mind, he decided to go to Jerusalem and to devote the whole course of his life to the salvation of souls" [*R* 7]. Rodrigues describes Laynez and Salmerón together: "Directed very fruitfully along the path of God by Father Ignatius, they made so much progress with the divine help, that without knowing what the other was doing, each of them decided to divorce the seductions of the world [*seculi illecebris*], to sail for Jerusalem, and to choose that kind of life which the others had already taken up" [*R* 8]. "To divorce" [*Nuntium remittere*, "to dissolve a marriage or "to break an engagement"] is strong language. The one divorced in this case is the seductiveness of the world, and the rejection is total and final.

Their interior dispositions are profound. The ritual dedication is soon to follow.

(b) Montmartre

Because the communal self-dedication of the companions to the service of God at Montmartre was a foundational experience for them, it serves as a guide in interpreting what they intended when they drew up the first draft of the Formula of the Institute and the proposed apostolic letter into which they inserted it.

The companions told the story of Montmartre time and again. To understand better the text of *Cum ex plurium,* we examine in each of the major accounts[19] (1) the language of dedication and service, (2) the object dedicated to service, (3) the totality of the dedication to service, and (4) the content of the offering that they made.

Witness of Favre

Favre's *Memoriale* of 1542 is the earliest witness to the event of Montmartre on August 15, 1534:

> On the feast of Mary's Assumption in August, all of us ... went to St. Mary's that is called Montmartre, near Paris, so that each might make a vow of going to Jerusalem at the time agreed upon, and after returning from there of placing himself under the obedience of the Roman Pontiff, and of beginning on the appointed day to abandon relatives and nets [*relinquere parentes, et retia*], except what was needed for the journey.[20] [*F*15]

The site and the feast are significant. In the triple colloquy [147] of the Spiritual Exercises after the Two Standards meditation the exercitant approaches Mary to mediate with Jesus for the grace to be received under his standard. Both the site and the feast indicate that the companions are asking Mary to mediate for them on this occasion.[21] The standard of Jesus is the deepest spiritual poverty, opprobrium, and injuries. A place of martyrdom marks their own witness to Jesus. With Mary they stand at the foot of the cross.

The vocabulary of dedication is missing, but the idea itself is inescapable in the determination that expresses their inner attitude and in the totality of their offering. Favre's phrase, "to abandon relatives and nets [*relinquere parentes, et retia*]," echoes not only *Cum ex plurium*'s "having abandoned the snares [*relictis illecebris*]" but also the Vulgate's "they forthwith left their nets and father [*relictis retibus et patre*], and followed him" (Douay-Rheims; Matt. 4:22).[22] The snares used in fishing are an apt figure for the snares and allurements of the world.

For Favre the content of the offering is in three equal parts: (a) to go to Jerusalem, (b) upon return to present themselves to the pope, (c) to do so in chastity and poverty. Just as there are no conditions attached to going to Jerusalem, so there are none with regard to presenting themselves to be at the service of the pope, nor to the giving up of persons and things. The commitment is total. *Parentes* [kinsfolk] is far more inclusive than *patre* [father]; it also means more than leaving existing relatives, for on that occasion they took a vow of chastity. Leaving their relatives and all the nets of this world simply means leaving everything. Since the remark about abandoning relatives and nets comes after mention of the pope, it suggests that for Favre their whole commitment to Jesus is contained in their service of the pope.

Witness of Laynez

In 1547 Laynez wrote a long letter to Polanco about the origins of the Society. He refers to Montmartre in two different passages that use strikingly similar language. In the first Laynez describes the life of the companions in Paris in the middle 1530s:

> We strengthened ourselves there, partly through prayer and frequent confession and communion, partly through our studies which were on sacred things, partly through making a vow to dedicate ourselves to the service [*dedicarse al servicio*] of the Lord in poverty. [*L* 30]

Dedication, service of Christ, poverty. He says nothing of the form the service of Christ took or would take (serving their neighbor, going to Jerusalem, presenting themselves to the pope), nor does he mention chastity, although it seems to be assumed in the very act of dedicating themselves to Christ in poverty. He returns to the same ideas later in narrating the events of 1537 and spells out the meaning of service of Christ:

> And since our intention from Paris on was not to found a religious order but to dedicate ourselves in poverty [*dedicarse en pobreza*] to the service of God our Lord [*al servicio de Dios nuestro Señor*] and the profit of our neighbor by preaching and serving in hospitals, etc., we made a vow some years earlier that in order to fulfill our intention we were resolved to go, if

we could, to the feet of the pope, the vicar of Christ, and to ask him for permission to go to Jerusalem, and if we could to remain there to our own profit and that of others, both believers and unbelievers, if our Lord would be served [*servido*]; and if there was no opportunity to go to Jerusalem within a year, or to remain there after going there, we made it clear in the vow that it was not our intention to oblige ourselves any further to go there, but to turn to the pope and make our obedience to him, going wherever he might send us. [*L* 36]

Dedication: they were handing themselves over first of all to Christ [*Dios nuestro Señor*]. Their own will, because they thought it was Christ's, was to go to Jerusalem, but even that will they handed over to Christ. If it was not his will, then they would go to the pope as Christ's vicar and go wherever he sent them. They would follow Jesus in poverty, like the apostles on their missionary journey. They had stripped themselves of all things. They would go where God allowed them to go, and they would go where the pope sent them to do what the pope told them to do. They were ready, in other words, for whatever mission the pope might have in mind for them. There were no conditions. Whether they went to the faithful, to heretics, or to unbelievers made no difference. Where Christ or his vicar wanted them was their preference.

Witness of Ignatius

Letter to Francesco Palmio. In 1553 Ignatius commissioned a letter to be written from Rome to Father Francesco Palmio in Bologna, in which he says that the companions who gathered in Paris

> did not go to Italy in order to found a religious order but to go to Jerusalem, and to preach, and to die amongst unbelievers; but then, when they were not able to find passage . . . they had to stay in Italy; and when the pope used them in the divine service [*seruitio*] and that of the Apostolic See, the time came when they began to talk about forming a body. [*EI* 5:259–60]

Even though the letter does not explicitly mention Montmartre, it does describe the intent of Ignatius and his companions in

Italy. Their intent was (1) to go to Jerusalem, (2) to preach (work for souls), (3) to die for the faith. Although no words refer to dedicating themselves to God, their willingness to die for the faith reveals the totality of their interior dedication. In more down-to-earth language the letter repeats the ideas of *Cum ex plurium:* "You would dedicate your lives to the perpetual service of our Lord Jesus Christ and of his vicar on earth."

Autobiography. In 1555 Ignatius dictated that part of his own story that tells of Montmartre.[23] In it he is characteristically brief:

> Already by this time [the end of Ignatius's stay in Paris] they had all determined what they would do, namely, go to Venice and to Jerusalem, and spend their lives for the good of souls; and if they were not given permission to remain in Jerusalem, then return to Rome and present themselves [*presentarsi*] to the vicar of Christ, so that he could make use of them wherever he thought it would be more for the glory of God and the good of souls. They also planned to wait a year in Venice for passage; but if there was no passage for the East that year, they would be free of their vow about Jerusalem and approach the pope, and so forth. [*A* 85]

Although again Ignatius does not specifically mention dedication to God, to intend to spend their lives in helping souls is sufficient sign of that dedication. "To present themselves" obviously means more than to introduce themselves to the pope. To what avail would they present themselves? Their discernment of what God called them to, made in deep prayer, was open to further discernment. They attached no conditions regarding places or persons. Wherever the pope sent them, and whether amongst the faithful, heretics, or unbelievers, they were ready to go.

Witness of Rodrigues

Rodrigues, on the other hand, is characteristically prolix. The General of the Society, Everard Mercurian, had asked him to give an account of the origins of the Society, and he did not want to leave out anything of importance [*FN* 3:8–135]. In 1577 at age sixty-seven (*anciano* they call him in Spanish), only two years before he died, he filled in the background outlined briefly by Laynez in his letter to Polanco in 1547.

Dedication to the Service of God and Neighbor. Rodrigues tells how in Paris the companions "daily became more and more inflamed with a new desire [*desiderio*] and a new zeal regarding their resolve," and they longed to carry out their "hearts' desires [*animorum desideria*]." They had decided "to give themselves wholly [*se totos tradere*] to the salvation of their neighbor," and so they gave themselves to prayer in order to overcome the obstacles that lay ahead [*R* 12]. He tells of their determination to take "vows of poverty, of chastity, of going to Jerusalem"[24] and of their commitment after their return of working for persons of faith or no faith at all, "preaching the divine word to all, and finally of administering the sacraments of confession and the Eucharist without receiving any stipend" [*R* 13].[25] Rodrigues expresses their desires for service in terms of worship: "They were all determined with amazing eagerness quietly to pour out life itself if need be, for any cause whatsoever respecting the greater worship and veneration of God" [*R* 14].

Dedication to the Service of the Pope. For Simão Rodrigues it was clear that, whatever they did, they would do it as a group. In Jerusalem they would decide whether to stay or to return "without breaking up the group" [*R* 14].[26] As a group they would offer themselves to the pope. Simão gives a more complete report than any of the others on what they intended at Montmartre when they vowed to present themselves to the pope. They had decided that on their return from Jerusalem, or if they were not able to go there,

> they would throw themselves at the feet of the Supreme Pontiff, would make him privy to their thoughts, would declare their lives consecrated to the salvation of souls, and finally they would humbly ask him what advice the Pontiff could give them. If, inspired by the divine majesty, he approved what they had undertaken, then, for greater success, they would ask for unrestricted faculties to preach, hear confessions, and celebrate the Eucharist anywhere in the world. Moreover, they would make every effort to make the Sovereign Pontiff understand that they were ready, at his command, without any wavering on their part, to proclaim the Gospel of Christ throughout

the whole world, even in the lands subject to the Turks or other tyrants opposed to the religion of Christ. [R 14]

This one passage has all the elements we are seeking: (1) consecration, (2) of their very lives, (3) in as total a way as possible, in readiness for any work in any place with anybody, (4) under the direction of the vicar of Christ.

The action of the companions combines audacity with prudence, religious enthusiasm with rationality. Deliberately calculated risk marks their approach, the kind of offering Jesus demanded when he said to the enthusiast who would follow him wherever he might go, "Foxes have holes, and birds of the air have nests; but the Son of man has nowhere to lay his head" (Matt. 8:20)

The Holocaust of the Companions. After the manner of the story of Abraham and Isaac, Rodrigues carefully details the preparations for the sacrifice: the choice of Mary as their intercessor at Montmartre [R 14]; the choice of the chapel built in honor of Mary by St. Denis, the patron saint of France, where he and his companions were martyred, as the proper place, "about a mile from the city, solitary, removed from all disturbance, and far from crowds of people"; and their method of readying themselves for the event: "To make their holocaust to God more fervently, they prepared themselves by fasting, meditating on divine things, expiating their sins, and other means of mortification" [R 15]. No word expresses better the totality of their dedication than holocaust [*holo*=whole; *kaustos*=burnt], a sacrifice that is wholly consumed by fire. Favre will use the term to describe their offering of themselves to the pope (see below, page 120).

The details of that holocaust are vivid in Simão's memory even many years later. He is the only one who gives us the details of the ceremony:

> No outsider was present, just the Fathers. Father Favre celebrated Mass, and before he gave communion to his companions, he turned to them and held the sacred host in his hands. They were kneeling on the floor with their minds fixed on God, and each in his own turn pronounced the vows in a clear voice that was audible to all. Then they immediately received holy communion [R 16].

Here is the historical basis for the liturgical setting of taking vows in the Society of Jesus, the ritual celebration of the interior dedication that is at the heart of Jesuit service. Rodrigues goes on in words that show that even more than forty years later he is still profoundly moved at the mere recollection of that event:

> That holocaust was offered with such eagerness, with such abnegation of will, with such hope in the divine mercy, by those first Fathers of the Society who at that moment truly committed [*devovebant*] themselves to God with their whole heart [*toto animo*], that often, when I think about it afterwards, an intense ardor fills my heart, a new flood of devotion swells up, and I experience incredible awe. Unending thanks and eternal praise to God for his wonderful gifts to us, because he was mindful of us and showed us his mercy [cf. Tob. 8:18]. [*R* 17]

Even the afterglow remains with him, the peace and joy of the rest of that eventful day, as Rodrigues brings his story to a conclusion: "When the ceremony was over, the Fathers spent the rest of the day with great joy and happiness . . . talking together about that burning zeal for the divine service [*obsequium*] with which they were on fire. At last, when the sun was already setting, they made their way home praising and glorifying God" [*R* 18]. A beautiful conclusion for a movie, but that is only the beginning of this story, not the end.

Witness of Bobadilla

Although Rodrigues's account of Montmartre is the most detailed, Bobadilla's is perhaps the most touching. He was a crusty man who wore his heart on his sleeve.

Letter to Francis Borgia. Bobadilla's first reference to Montmartre antedates the long account of Rodrigues by eight years. In 1569 he writes a letter to Francis Borgia, general of the Society at the time. More than any other account, it brings out the intercessory role of Mary in the event:

> Not without meaning did your Reverence write the long letter you sent me from Frascati, written on the day of the Assumption of Our Lady, the Virgin Mary, to whom I am

dearly devoted, because on that day our Company made its beginning on the Mount of Martyrs near Paris where the ten[27] of us made our first vows to go to Jerusalem. This holy feast is the root and origin of the Company . . . because Christ and his holy Mother took us as their sons, and as progenitors of this great Company. Blessed be God and his holy Mother for ever and ever. Amen. [*MB* 498]

For Bobadilla the central act of Montmartre is the vow to go to Jerusalem. What he introduces here, however, is something entirely new, unique, indeed, in the narratives about Montmartre: a sense of acceptance of their offering. "Christ and his holy Mother took us as their sons." The words echo in some way the prayer of the Two Standards in which Mary is the first intercessor to whom they turn. They echo even more the experience of Ignatius at La Storta where he sensed that the prayer of the Two Standards had been heard and accepted, and he experienced himself placed by the Father at the side of the Son carrying his cross.

Letter to Claude Aquaviva. On August 11, 1589, the year he wrote his autobiography, Bobadilla wrote to Fr. General Claude Aquaviva, recalling that "the first Fathers of our Company made a vow on Montmartre near Paris to go to Jerusalem. This vow Divine Providence . . . commuted to other better and more fruitful vows of pilgrimaging in religion" [*FN* 3:320–21]. Again, the central fact of Montmartre is the vow to go to Jerusalem, but in this account the vow undergoes a transformation. God commutes the vow into a new kind of pilgrimage. This remark of Bobadilla's about pilgrimaging is of enormous importance and will be treated later.

Autobiography. Bobadilla's account in his Autobiography[28] (1589) of their dedication to the service of God is marked by its brevity. Speaking of himself in the third person he writes, "He had made the Spiritual Exercises with Master Ignatius of Loyola, and knew that he would go in poverty to the holy sepulcher in Jerusalem" [*B* 5]. Once again for Bobadilla the central element of the vow is the pilgrimage. Essential to pilgrimage, however, is that it be done in poverty. In the sentences that follow he suggests rather than describes the disposition of heart of the companions, and comments on the significance of Mary in the event only by indicating that it took place on her feast.

Bobadilla makes no mention of the pope in any of his references to Montmartre. The rest of his autobiography, however, reveals what pilgrimaging in a religious order means to him. Paragraph after paragraph narrates mission after mission. The pope sends him here; the pope sends him there. He walks all over Italy, he goes to Flanders, he lives in Germany, he travels to Vienna, to Dalmatia, to Sicily. He preaches, he lectures, he reforms monasteries, he is official visitor, he acts as inquisitor, he argues with heretics, he founds colleges. To a friend he writes about those who spend their lives wandering from one place of pilgrimage to another wasting their lives in specious devotions, and then he comments: "My pilgrimages have not been undertaken in this spirit; they are true missions from my superiors, held first in their hearts and their desires, communicated to me by a word, which I have obeyed and put into execution. My pilgrimaging is not mere running around, as some have thought" [*MB* 637–38]. For Bobadilla, to pilgrimage in religion means to go where the pope sends him. In that sense, to serve the pope is to serve Christ.

Conclusion

Both Montmartre and La Storta are experiences relating dedication to service; both are experiences also relating dedication to worship.

The recollections of the companions, especially of Rodrigues and Bobadilla, reveal the deep forces at work within them. Their attitude of worship, their dedication of all that they had and were to God, manifested itself not only in a ritual that betokened dedication to service but in a life poured out in the service of their Lord and of his Church, in their willingness to go wherever the vicar of Christ might send them.

The choice of the chapel of the martyrs as the place to dedicate themselves to God during the Eucharist reflected the intensity of their "holocaust" [*R* 15], the depth of their desire to follow Christ, "to give life itself, if necessary," either amongst unbelievers or "for any cause whatsoever respecting the greater worship and veneration of God" [*R* 14].

Placing themselves at the side of Christ carrying his cross, and facing the Body of Christ at the moment just before communion, they made their vows. They were responding to him, not as life-giving Word of God as they might have at the Gospel, but as life-giving Bread, as the one whose body was broken and whose blood was poured out for them and for the rest of humanity. They were facing not just the Body of Christ, but the eucharistic body which is a symbol of the Church, the sign of the Kingdom, to which (or to whom) they wished to respond with the gift of their lives. They were facing the Mystical Body of Christ in all its terrible need and suffering on this earth, and they were facing all the persons who belong to that body in all their beauty and misery, and they wanted to respond to their cries for help.[29]

Again and again they interiorly repeated the offering made at Montmartre as they worked their way through their studies and pilgrimaged to Loreto, as they bathed the sick in the hospitals and begged their food in the streets. They expressed it ritually again at ordination, in the oblation to Pope Paul III, and in the submission of the five decrees of the Formula to the pope. Most of all, they lived that offering day after day.

The enthusiasm and indomitable spirit of the first companions shines through the words of Bobadilla in the letter (see above, page 115) that he wrote at age eighty to Claude Aquaviva:

> As to my own life, it is more death than life. I do not sleep well; I am unable to eat, for I have no teeth; catarrh and aches and pains are not lacking throughout my whole body; after eighty, labor and sorrow in abundance (Ps. 90:10). The remedy is patience, commending myself to God and the angels and blessed saints in heaven, and begging our Company and others to pray for me, and all who know and observe me to have compassion on me and to help and assist me both spiritually and corporally so that what little remains of this pilgrimage of mine may supply for that of Christ our Lord, so that I can say with the glorious Madonna: in all these and from all these I sought rest, and I shall abide in the inheritance of the Lord (Ecclus. 24:11), through the help of Christ the Lord, who with God the Father and the holy Spirit lives and reigns for ever and ever. Amen. [*FN* 3:321]

c) The Oblation to the Pope

Less than a year after the experience of Ignatius at La Storta, the companions as a group were to have their own La Storta–like experience of being accepted in service, this time in the service of the pope, to go wherever he might send them.

Whether there was a precise moment when the companions offered themselves to the service of the pope and experienced his acceptance of their offering, or whether the pope was always aware of the condition attached to their vow, or whether the understanding that they were at his service is something that gradually dawned on both sides, is not entirely clear.[30] Two passages in Favre [*EI* 132, *F* 18] and one in Bobadilla [*MB* 16] suggest a precise moment. There are sections in the Deliberation of the First Fathers [*D* 3, 7] and another document coming from the pen of Ignatius [Constitutions on the Missions 1544–1545, *C* 159–64] that imply the fact but give no indication of a moment. The silence in all the other writings, in Polanco, Nadal, Laynez, and especially in Ignatius's long letter to Isabel Roser, written shortly after the offering is supposed to have taken place, in which he mentions many much less significant events of those days, leads Antonio de Aldama to challenge a precise moment. He is inclined to think that when Paul III in the spring of 1539 began to send them on individual missions the companions awoke to the fact that they had been accepted, indeed, and in a way they had scarcely imagined possible, and that this experience was what Favre called, "as it were, the foundation of the whole Society [*quasi totius Societatis fundamentum*]" [*F* 18], and Ignatius a little later, "our origin and main foundation [*nuestro principio y principal fundamento*]" (Declarations on the Missions – 1544–1545 [*C* 162; *C* 2:214: *Const. Text. a*, P. VII, c. 2].[31] An argument from silence is not always convincing. Ignatius was concerned mainly with telling Isabel about the persecutions they endured. Moreover, Favre's language makes it extremely difficult to rule out a precise moment when the companions offered themselves to the pope. That is not the issue that concerns us here, but see the analysis that follows of the texts from Favre and Bobadilla.

Witness of Favre

Letter to Gouveia. During much of 1538 the companions endured persecution in Rome (see chapter ten for more details). On November 23, 1538, five days after the governor of Rome cleared the companions of false charges brought against them, Pierre Favre wrote a letter to Dr. Diogo de Gouveia, a native Portuguese and agent for King John of Portugal. De Gouveia had been the rector of the Collège de Sainte-Barbe when the companions were in Paris and for some years thereafter. On one occasion he had threatened to have Ignatius flogged for his "negative" influence on one of the students [A 78] but dissolved in tears at Ignatius's feet and implored forgiveness when he saw the accused man's humility [PV 64]. In February 1538 de Gouveia wrote to King John urging that he request the services of the companions for missionary work in India.[32] Favre replied in the name of all:

> Would that we could satisfy you, and satisfy our own hearts as well in their zealous yearning for the same things as you; but for the present something prevents us from responding to the desires of many others as well as to your own. You will understand this from what I now put down. We who have been bound together [*ad inuicem . . . colligati*] in this Society have dedicated [*deuouimus*] ourselves to the Supreme Pontiff, since he is the lord of the universal harvest of Christ; in this oblation [*oblacione*][33] we have made it clear to him that we are ready for everything that he might decide for us in Christ; if, therefore, he should send us where you are calling us, we shall gladly go there.[34] [*EI* 132]

Here we have the same burning desires that the companions manifested at Montmartre, the same dedication, this time expressed in terms of the pope as the one in charge of the harvest that belongs to Christ. They have dedicated themselves; they are ready for anything, to go anywhere the pope may decide for them because, as Favre puts it, "he has a better knowledge of the kinds of things that are expedient for the whole of Christianity" [*EI* 132].

Memoriale. Favre indicates the meaning of the oblation for the companions in a second passage, one he wrote four years later:

> It was also a remarkable gift, and as it were, the foundation of our whole Society, that in that same year after the judgment clearing us, when we presented ourselves as a holocaust to the Supreme Pontiff Paul III, so that he might determine how we might serve Christ to the edification of all who are under the authority of the apostolic see, in perpetual poverty, and ready to go, out of obedience to him, even to the farthermost Indies; [it was a remarkable gift], I say, that the Lord willed that he [the pope] would accept us and rejoice in what we had determined to do. [*F* 18]

Favre speaks of "what we had determined to do." For these resolute and determined men, there are no ifs in their attitudes or desires. What they propose is what they are convinced they have been called to do. They experience a vocation, not a plan. In that vocation they are fully committed, dedicated to the service of Christ.[35]

Holocaust is also religious language, a burnt offering made to God, an act of worship. Here it is a holocaust of themselves, and being burnt is clearly spelled out: perpetual poverty; readiness to go anywhere, even to the ends of the earth; obedience to the pope and not simply to God, a foreshadowing of *Cum ex plurium*. The companions have not heard the voice of the Father, as Ignatius did at La Storta, but they have heard the voice of the vicar of Christ, and to Favre there is no clearer call possible:

> Wherefore, I shall always be obliged, and so shall each of the others, to give thanks to the Lord of the harvest of the whole Catholic Church, that is, Jesus Christ our Lord, that he has deigned to declare through the voice of his vicar on earth (which is the clearest call possible), that . . . it pleased him that we should serve him and that he wanted to use us for all time to come. [*F* 18]

Favre is overwhelmed that Jesus repeats through his vicar what he had said to Ignatius at La Storta, that he takes the companions as his servants and all who are to follow them in the Society.

The experience is one of worship. It is at once a remarkable gift, a source and spring of gratitude (Eucharist), and an experience of communal self-giving and submission (also Eucharist). Favre sees this worship experience as the foundation of the whole Society [*quasi totius Societatis fundamentum*]. *Quasi* does not weaken the imagery but simply introduces it. Favre is aware that the solemn approbation of Pope Paul III in the bull *Regimini* lays the juridical foundation of the whole Society. But this profound act of worship, of total giving and total receiving (Eucharist), is the foundation that made that approbation possible.

Witness of Bobadilla

On July 4, 1539, Bobadilla wrote from Rome to the Duke of Ferrara about the desire of various people in Ferrara that some of the companions return there to work:

> This was not nor is it now in our hands, since we made an offering [*oblación*] to His Holiness for whatever he commands us, and he accepted this offering [*offerta*] with great affection.[36] He replied that it was his will that for the time being we should remain in the city and produce fruit there for the glory of God. [*MB* 16]

The offering, once more, is total. They have given themselves into the hands of the pope to be at his disposal. Just as Ignatius experienced that the Father placed him at the side of the Son carrying his cross in his service, so now all of them experience the pope's gracious acceptance of their offering of service. That service may be to go or to stay; they will serve wherever and however the pope may choose for them.

Deliberation of 1539

In order to plumb the sources on the companions' understanding of dedication and service, we return briefly to the Deliberation of the First Fathers.[37] The scribe of that document indicates the variety in their outlooks and opinions yet is able to state: "We were anxious and watchful to find a truly open way in which we might all offer ourselves as a holocaust to our God, in whose praise, honor and glory we might surrender all we had" [*D* 1]. The key question, of course, is whether they should stay united, bound together in one body, in such a way that nothing could separate them even if scattered over the face of the earth. What is more expedient,

> now that we had offered and dedicated [*obtuleramus et dedicaueramus*] ourselves and our lives to Christ our Lord and to his true and legitimate vicar on earth, so that he might dispose of us and send us wherever he judged we could produce more fruit, whether to [the Turks],[38] or the Indies, or heretics, or whatever believers or unbelievers; to repeat, would it be better for us to be bound [*inter nos deuinctos*] and joined together [*et colligatos*] in one body [*in vno corpore*] in such a way that no physical separation however great might separate us, or would it perhaps not be better. [*D* 3]

Service is a given, even without using the word. This passage is the immediate forerunner of *Cum ex plurium*'s "You would dedicate your lives to the perpetual service of our Lord Jesus Christ and of his vicar on earth." No question hedges their self-offering. The only question is whether they can carry out that offering *better* by staying united, and they decide that staying united would be more effective than separating.

A second and more difficult question faces them, whether they should take a vow of obedience to one of their own number,

> so that we might more sincerely and with greater praise and merit fulfill the will of the Lord our God in all things, and at the same time carry out the free will and command of His Holiness, to whom we had freely offered [*obtuleramus*] all we had, our will, our intellect, our ability, etc. [*D* 4]

The companions manifest parallel concerns: to fulfill the will of God in everything and to fulfill the will of the pope in everything. The totality of the offering can hardly be made clearer, especially that to the pope, couched in terms drawn directly from the *Suscipe* in the Spiritual Exercises, even though in the original context the words are part of a prayer directed to God. The question, therefore, comes down to: is obedience to one of us the best way to be obedient to God and to the pope? Their final, unanimous decision is affirmative. The reasons they give for their decision clarify the question even as they answer it. The arguments pro and con do not sway the companions, but rather the movements of the Spirit within do. First of all, through a vow of obedience to one of their own number, they "might better and more exactly achieve [their] primary desire of fulfilling the divine will in all things." Second, through this vow "the Society might be preserved more surely." Third, the vow will help them "to provide properly for whatever contingencies might arise, whether spiritual or temporal" [*D* 8]. In these three reasons their dedication to God and to the pope are so linked that to mention one implies the other. They do not choose that which *fulfills* the will either of God or of the pope. They choose that which is more *helpful* and more *needed* if they are to strive to fulfill the will of either: a vow of obedience to one of their own.

Witness of Ignatius

In 1544–45 Ignatius prepared a draft called Constitutions on the Missions. He also drew up a companion document called Declarations on the Missions containing comments and clarifications. Although written five or six years after *Cum ex plurium,* they shed abundant light on that document. Constitutions on the Missions opens with a one-page chapter explaining the vow of obedience to the pope. The lengthy title of the chapter is itself important:

> On the promise and vow that the Company has made to God our Lord and to his universal vicar to go to and fro [*discurrir*] through various parts [*por vnas partes y por otras*] of the world. [*C* 159 1o]

Discurrir means more than travel; it means gad, ramble, roam, the opposite of settling down. *Por vnas partes y por otras* means literally "through some parts and others," again the opposite of settling down. The vow does not envision traveling *to* a place but being on the move, "to do more work and do it more effectively in the fields of the Lord for the greater profit of souls with his divine favor and help, going wherever His Holiness thinks and judges that it would be more useful or more necessary to send us for that purpose, whether to believers or unbelievers" [C 159].[39]

Obviously, the intent is not simply to roam. The pope is to send them to a particular place, but also for a particular reason. The companions are not to be at the disposition of a particular bishop or city or abbot or other person [C 159] but at the disposition of the pope. Nor are the companions to stay anywhere forever regardless of the needs of other persons and places, "but in accordance with our intentions and desires to be scattered through diverse and different regions" [C 159–60]. The emphasis in "scattered" is not on the dispersion of the companions but on the multiplicity of places touched by their presence.

Ignatius then explains that the companions were from various places and various kingdoms, and did not know where to go. So as not to err in the way of the Lord, they made this promise and vow so that His Holiness would determine where they should go in accordance with their "promise and intention to roam [*discurrir*] throughout the world" [C 160]. The sentence does not end there. The words that follow reveal what the companions mean by *discurrir*:

> and where [they] did not find the desired spiritual fruit in one city or another, to pass to another and still another, traveling [*discurriendo*] thus through towns and other particular places to the greater glory of God our Lord and the greater spiritual profit of souls. [C 160]

The vow envisions a company always on the move in the spirit of the Gospel's missionary discourse (Matt. 10). Their handing over of themselves to God is made visible in the handing over of themselves to the pope for any mission. What they envision but do not state as a condition is that their going will be in terms of *more*. Their purpose is the salvation of souls and the glory of God: service and praise together, service that is worship. "This promise," Ignatius writes in the first declaration, "[is] our origin [*principio*] and main foundation [*principal fundamento*]"[40] [C 162].

Conclusion

Whatever the historical reality of the companions' self-oblation to the pope, whether a simple understanding of the heart between him and them or a formal declaration on their part, the fact is that Ignatius and his companions were available and ready to go wherever the pope might send them. That availability is the heart of the oblation, and it was a gift of God to them.

Dedicating oneself to God is an act of divine worship, as is dedicating oneself to the service of God in the service of people. Dedicating oneself in service ranks as a gift from God even as it stands as a gift of oneself to God. The worship and service of God through the service of people was precisely why the companions dedicated themselves to the service of the pope in vowing to go wherever he might send them.

Ignatius and his companions were generous, wholehearted men who set no limits to their love. They gave all they had. Strikingly they experienced their giving of themselves in service as a gift from the Holy Spirit, who was impelling them, gifting them, to give themselves in service. The impelling of the Spirit made them dedicate themselves to the service of the vicar of Christ. Their own generosity would have impelled them to go to Jerusalem, a human dream that went unfulfilled. But the dream of the Holy Spirit, the impelling breath of God, drove them to a different arena for the outpouring of their generosity. In the service of the pope they found where they should work and what they should do; they found the *magis,* the *more,* the greater glory, the more expedient, the greater fruit. Going where the pope would send them was not a *second best* for them; it was a *better* because the impelling power of the Spirit of God had bestowed it upon them.

Whether their offering of themselves to the pope took place in an audience,[41] or by a simple statement of Ignatius to the pope, or by mutual understanding as the months went by, the pope happily found at his disposal a group of ten priests who were completely devoted to going wherever he might send them and doing whatever he might ask them to do. In his struggles up to this time Paul III had not found himself endowed with many instruments of reform as willing and as capable as these men were proving themselves to be.

Concluding Reflection

The vocabulary and the ideas of the first *cum* clause bear an uncommon similarity to the vocabulary and ideas of the first four chapters of the Acts of the Apostles. In Acts the disciples come together with Jesus; the crowd comes together at the sound of the mighty wind; even the enemies of Jesus come together. Jesus talks to the disciples about the power of the Holy Spirit who will come upon them; the crowd comes from many different places and talks many different languages; when Jesus' enemies have gathered they talk to one another and plot (conspire?) against him. Like the early converts of Acts, the companions possessed nothing of their own; like the early converts they were of one mind and one heart; like the apostles "they were all filled with the Holy Spirit and spoke the word of God with boldness" (4:31).

Whereas the salutation, "To his beloved sons, etc.," is a simple presentation of facts, names, places, degrees, the first *cum* clause is a faith statement and a religious evaluation of the facts presented in the salutation. The persons are not just names: they enter into the faith experience of many people. The places are not just bits of geography: they are threads in a divine plan. The academic degrees are not simply signs of competence: they are attached to persons who are Christian to the core with qualifications that are much more profound than the degrees themselves. The word is abroad that these men, from these places, with these degrees are priests who have freely embraced poverty for the love of Christ, priests who have chosen a countercultural way of life. They have abandoned the snares of the world, rejecting paths of glory, paths of riches and of fame, and have opted to join the poor of Christ who down the ages have been poor with Christ for the sake of the Gospel. They have not acted on their own: they are a group, not just individuals, but a group with all the strength and vigor and resourcefulness and determination of a group Spirit-driven toward a single purpose. That purpose is not to seek their own advantage but the glory of their Lord. They have dedicated themselves to Jesus, and have placed themselves at the disposition of his vicar on earth to do whatever he might wish, to go wherever he might send them, to work with whatever class of people he might ordain. They are ready and willing and eager to lay down their lives for the sake of the Gospel. This is the word that is abroad.

But the report about them is not limited to who they are. The Acts of the Apostles is full of what the apostles did under the influence of the Holy Spirit. Trustworthy men have also reported to the pope on what the companions are doing, what they have done and continue to do. The second *cum* clause we are about to consider touches on what these men—qualified, poor, Spirit-driven—can do in the vineyard of the Lord.

SECTION TWO

The Vineyard of the Lord

When the companions come to Rome in the spring of 1538 they become alarmed at the sermons of an Augustinian monk, Fra Agostino Mainardi de Piamonte [*PSH* 84]. Laynez and Favre attend the sermons and are disturbed at what they hear. Recounting the event a few years later, Laynez writes that Fra Agostino "was at that time secretly, and is now publicly a Lutheran." The two companions first try to correct the preacher privately but without success. Next they warn some persons they know in the curia who are attending the sermons. Some of them turn antagonistic and a great persecution breaks out against the companions [*L* 53].

The fruit of the persecution is that it generates much of the testimony the pope accumulates regarding the companions. Letters, messengers, witnesses from Italy, Spain, and France bombard the pope, informing him of the good work the companions have done wherever they have been. He learns of their ministry of preaching in public. He hears of the ways they evangelize in private, exhorting others in whatever way they happen to need, hearing confessions, or directing people in the Spiritual Exercises. Word comes of their compassionate care of the sick and the dying in hospitals, of their boundless energy in moving from place to place, ever eager to move on to richer or more difficult harvests, of their work with the marginalized of society, children, the poor, those abandoned by everyone else.

The reports come from people who can be trusted, people who have proven themselves reliable in matters of faith. The reports are unanimous: these men known as the Company of Jesus are orthodox in matters of doctrine; they are not greedy and out to fleece the unsuspecting; what is more, they live blameless lives of prayer and penance, of fasting and keeping vigil.

THE SECOND *CUM* CLAUSE

cumque probate fidei viri
[since also men of proven faith]

nobis saepius testati essent,
[have frequently testified to us]

vos per plures iam annos
[that for many years now]

laudabiliter in vinea Domini exerceri,
[you have worked commendably in the Lord's vineyard]

predicando publice verbum Dei,
[by publicly preaching the word of God]

exhortando priuatim,
[by privately exhorting]

confessiones audiendo,
[by hearing confessions]

exercendo homines in meditationibus piis,
[by directing people in holy meditations]

inseruiendo hospitalibus,
[by serving in hospitals]

peregrinando,
[by pilgrimaging]

pueros et personas rudes docendo
[by teaching children and the uninitiated]

ea quae ad christiani hominis institutionem sunt necessaria,
[what is necessary for the instruction of a Christian]

et omnia demum charitatis officia,
[and finally by performing every work of charity]

vbicumque terrarum fuistis,
[wherever you have been]

non modo sine vlla haeresis
[not only without any sign of heresy]

aut auaritiae
[or avarice]

aut turpitudinis alicuius nota,
[or immoral conduct of any sort]

sed multa etiam cum laude obeundo:
[but even with great praise]

Structure: The principal verb of this subordinate clause is *testati essent* [have testified], followed by an accusative, *vos* [you], with an infinitive, *exerceri* [have worked]. A series of gerunds follows *exerceri,* all in the ablative: you have worked by doing this, by doing that, and by doing something else. The quality of performance is expressed by two parallel phrases: *non modo sine* [not only without] anything negative, followed by *sed etiam cum* [but even with] something positive.

7

Workers in the Vineyard

since also men of proven faith
[cumque probate fidei viri]

The phrase "men of proven faith" is not entirely original with this document. The legislation of Pachomius (4th century Egypt) employs similar phrases. In one passage a special task is given to the brothers "of proven faith," which certainly indicates those whose lives have proved the genuinity of their faith.[1] Innocent III uses the phrase in the same sense in a document granting permission to the *Humiliati* to preach in 1201,[2] and it surfaces without change of meaning three hundred years later in Pope Leo X's exhortation to Christian princes at Session IX of the Fifth Lateran Council on May 5, 1514.[3] Similar phrases, which seem to have the same value and meaning, appear frequently in the report of the proceedings at Manresa years later when the Church was investigating Ignatius's sanctity. In the testimony, for example, of Francis Puig, a priest and theologian, we often find a phrase such as "good and trustworthy men."[4]

A scriptural basis for the phrase "men of proven faith" may be found in Second Corinthians: "Try your own selves if you be in the faith; prove ye yourselves;" as well as in Hebrews.[5] In each case the gift of faith has been put under pressure and proven itself to be genuine.

since also men of proven faith

have frequently testified to us,
[nobis saepius testati essent]

Nothing requires us to think that the "men of proven faith" of this second *cum* clause are any different from the "many persons" of the first *cum* clause. We are simply confronted with a rhetorical device designed not only to balance the structures of the two clauses but to emphasize that the pope has an abundance of testimony regarding the character of the first members of the Company of Jesus. Nevertheless, it seems proper to produce here new witnesses who testify precisely about the work and the orthodoxy of the companions.

The summer of 1538 brings a flurry of testimonials and letters to people in high places on behalf of the companions who have been under attack since the spring. Paul III is absent, having left Rome for Nice on March 23 to attempt to bring peace between Emperor Charles V and King Francis I of France. No doubt the contents of the testimonials and letters are communicated to the pope when he returns to Rome on July 24.[6]

Bobadilla ignites some of the activity by writing on June 15, 1538, to Duke Ercole of Ferrara telling him of the work the companions are doing in Rome: preaching, hearing confessions, talking to people about God and salvation. Bobadilla also indicates that their work is being impeded through a calumny that he and Jay are fugitives from Ferrara [*MB* 2–4]. No doubt through the urging of the duke, the suffragan bishop and vicar-general of Ferarra, Ottaviano de Castello, writes a letter on behalf of Bobadilla and Jay on June 28, 1538, noting that for many months Bobadilla and Jay had "stayed in the city of Ferrara celebrating the liturgy, preaching the word of God publicly to the people and giving good example in the city of Ferrara, and they left here with our good grace and permission, not suspended, not excommunicated, but moved by devotion, and went elsewhere" [*MB* 4–5]. The bishop addresses the document "to all those who read this letter," which means that Bobadilla and Jay can show it to all those who might be able to bring it to the attention of the pope.

The next day, June 29, 1538, Francesco Cosci, the vicar-general of the archdiocese of Siena, writes a testimonial asserting that Salmerón and Broët "obtained our permission to feed our sheep with their doctrine, and they did so, establishing the truth of the Gospel not only by sound and Catholic preaching but also by the probity and sanctity of their lives, not only without an accusation from anyone but even without the least suspicion" [*EB* 200–201]. Cosci's letter is not intended to make Salmerón and Broët feel better, but to be read by those who will bring the matter to the attention of the pope.

We can infer a good many other things. Various city-states where the companions have worked have ambassadors to the papal states. Since the companions are beset by requests from bishops for their services [*IR* 6], surely the ambassadors are part of the pressure brought upon the pope.

Paul hears both complaints and praise from those who have been in Rome throughout the days of the persecution. Friends like Dr. Ortiz and others who have heard the companions' sermons in the churches or their lectures at the Sapienza are part of the crowd that swarms around the curia. Not least of the advocates on behalf of the companions is Bishop Benedetto Conversini,[7] the governor of the city, who is well acquainted with both sides of the persecution controversy. We can assume that he gives a full account to the pope when the latter asks him to bring the matter to a conclusion.

As we move along through the various works in which the companions are engaged still more witnesses will appear on their behalf. No doubt all these are but a fraction of those who speak to the pope about them, but these suffice to indicate that there are, indeed, plenty of persons of proven faith who can testify on behalf of the companions and who apparently do so.

have very frequently testified to us,

that for many years now
[vos per plures iam annos]
you have worked commendably
[laudabiliter . . . exerceri]

Some of the companions, the reports indicate, are veterans in the ministry, others relative newcomers who have accomplished much in a short time. By 1539, Broët, for example, has been a priest for fifteen years, Jay for eleven, Favre for five. The others have been ordained for a little less than two years, but they began to minister to the sick and the poor long before ordination. Ignatius, of course, has been engaged in ministerial activities of one sort or another for eighteen years. For two and a half years the companions have been laboring in city after city of Italy. They are no longer newcomers to the apostolate. Some of the friends mentioned above can testify about those years from personal experience, others from what they have heard from reliable witnesses. Besides the positive testimony of many regarding the work of the companions, a powerful negative witness is the number of times they have been officially cleared of heresy: in Alcalá, in Salamanca, in Paris, in Venice, and finally in Rome.

The amount of their labor is matched only by its quality. The list of their apostolic activities is staggering, but no more so than the list of activities Ignatius has performed from the beginning of his days at Manresa and for seventeen years thereafter. Though we associate Manresa with the Spiritual Exercises, Ignatius also began there the apostolic works that became characteristic of the early Society.

In 1606, during the canonization investigation at Manresa, many witnesses came forward to say that he had visited the poor, helped in hospitals, consoled the sick, exhorted people, urged them to the practice of frequent confession and communion, conversed with others on spiritual topics, and publicly taught Christian doctrine throughout the city, correcting and reprimanding public vices.[8] Margarita Capdepós, a carpenter's widow who was an eyewitness to Ignatius's life, at the age of ninety-six testified to the fact that Ignatius

> went about dressed in a sack like a penitent, that he stayed in the hospital of Santa Lucia along with the other poor people, serving them and particularly the sick with great humility and care in all their needs . . . he went to confession and communion frequently, said all the hours [of the divine office] and lived a life that was very strict and penitential, fasting all week, chastising himself with many disciplines . . . he went through the city publicly teaching Christian doctrine, and she was one of the many people who followed him; he also went throughout the city asking for alms with great humility from door to door, and she heard him say to the people that with what they gave him he supported many poor people, and he visited the sick throughout the city; and she remembered well that he urged people to frequent confession and communion.[9]

She presents a far more complete picture than the popular one, drawn mainly from Ignatius's Autobiography, of Ignatius as a solitary living in a cave, praying all day long (seven hours sufficed!), and appearing only to go to church and beg alms and talk to a few people on occasion.[10]

Even at Manresa we see grounds for Nadal's position that the life and grace of Ignatius is the model for what God wants to do in the Society and each of its members. Nadal sees the grace of God first transforming the person, and once the grace has taken root inside, transforming all his actions through it: "God first impressed the grace of this vocation on Ignatius and expressed it in his actions; through the ministry of this man he diverted it to others, and brought it about that this religious order also would exist in his Church."[11] Of course, Nadal sees the whole life of Ignatius as model. Certainly, what Ignatius does at Manresa as a layman sets the tone and, to some extent, the parameters of the apostolic activity of the Society about to be established.

>you have worked commendably
>
>**in the Lord's vineyard,**
>[in vinea Domini]

This biblical expression does not appear in other briefs and bulls drawn up near the time the Society was founded. It holds a prominent place, however, at the beginning of the Capuchin Constitutions of 1536: "To the end that our Order, as the Vineyard of the Most High Son of God, may the better stand fast in the spiritual observance of the Evangelical and Seraphic Rule..."[12] Ignatius and his companions use the word differently. For the Capuchins, the vineyard is the order itself; for the companions, the vineyard is the whole world in need of salvation.

Indeed, the biblical use of the word suggests that the vineyard of the Lord is the people especially dear to God for whom he has labored much, but who have not always been as fruitful as God might rightfully expect. In Isaiah we read:

>Let me sing for my beloved
>my love-song concerning his vineyard:

> My beloved had a vineyard on a very fertile hill.
> He dug it and cleared it of stones,
> and planted it with choice vines;
> he built a watchtower in the midst of it,
> and hewed out a wine vat in it;
> he expected it to yield grapes,
> but it yielded wild grapes... (Isa. 5:1–2)

Wild grapes, bloodshed, injustice describe for the companions as well a world that has turned away from God, a world that needs conversion. They see God as one who dresses the vine with compassion and love. They try to do the same.

For the companions the vineyard means the entire field of their endeavor, and they guard it jealously from anything that might diminish their apostolic effectiveness. For example, during the persecution of 1538, when "some thought they should be thrown to the flames, others that they should be exiled to the ends of the earth, and still others that they should be condemned to the galleys," they make every effort to avoid scandal: "Lest someone think they had taken flight, during that whole time no one left [Rome] for the sake of preaching and laboring in the vineyard of the Lord in some other place" [*R* 84].[13]

Although Ignatius does not employ the image of the vineyard in the Spiritual Exercises, he does evoke its spirit and message in the Call of the King and the Two Standards. These two exercises clearly form the backdrop for Part VII of the Constitutions subtitled, "On what pertains to those already admitted into the body of the Society in their relations with their neighbors, on their distribution in the vineyard of Christ our Lord." The opening sentence of Part VII picks up the theme: "Just as Part Six treats of what the members of the Society ought to observe in their own regard, so this seventh part deals with what ought to be observed with regard to the neighbor, which is the end most proper to our institute, the distribution of the members of the Society in the vineyard of Christ, to labor in that part of it and in that work which has been put in their care" [*C* 2:561]. The vineyard of the Lord is what the Society of Jesus is all about.

8

Planting and Tending the Vineyard

In Scripture God is the Lord of the vineyard. God owns the land, clears the stones, digs the soil, selects the vines for planting. Others may work at the divine command, but God is in charge. Ignatius and his companions acknowledge this and are grateful for it. They do not sit back and watch; they become involved.

Persons of proven faith testify that the companions have been engaged in many different works. The Spirit of God impels the companions primarily to various ways of carrying out the ministry of the Word of God: clearing the stones, digging the soil, planting the vines, tending the vineyard. The Spirit also impels them to a variety of works of charity: sharing the harvest of happiness. The ministry of the Word and the works of charity together present a picture of priests fully engaged in the Word made Flesh: in the Word that leads to Eucharist and finds its fulfillment in the spiritual and corporal works of mercy, the feeding and nurturing of the Body of Christ.

1. Publicly Preaching the Word of God

you have worked commendably in the Lord's vineyard,

by publicly preaching the word of God,
[predicando publice verbum Dei]

During the summer of 1538 the persecution of the companions in Rome is at its height. Pope Paul III, who is out of the city, has appointed Cardinal Vincenzo Carafa as papal legate for the city during his absence. On June 29, 1538, Duke Ercole II d'Este writes to an auditor of the Rota (one who hears judicial cases appealed to Rome) asking him to speak to Cardinal Carafa in favor of the companions and praising the work Bobadilla and Jay did in Ferrara "by publicly preaching and exhorting people to live good and holy lives." Moreover, "They have been a good example to everyone and . . . have become recognized as very good Catholics" [*MB* 7]. The duke expects the papal legate to report the contents of that letter to Pope Paul III on his return to Rome. Duke Ercole's words are not a routine letter of recommendation. In the context of the early sixteenth century they are a loud and extraordinary proclamation of praise.

Preaching Situation in Early Sixteenth Century

For at least a century the Church had suffered everywhere through the appointment of unworthy bishops who were not themselves capable of preaching or who did not appoint those who were.[1] Another problem was the number of mendicants who wandered about who were "not preachers but rapacious tax gatherers," that is, who sold indulgences for their own profit.[2] In a brief summary of the state of preaching in the late fifteenth and early sixteenth century, Erwin Iserloh says in part: "The duty of preaching on the part of clerics occupied in the care of souls goes without saying, but the frequent insistence on this duty by synods proves that it was not seldom neglected, less in cities than in the country. 'The poor peasants ask for bread but rare are the pastors who break it for them,' complained Cornelius de Suckis around 1500."[3]

As for bishops and their ineptness in the ministry of the Word, Erasmus had manifested his concern in 1515, long before Ignatius's conversion. He excoriated those prelates who had traded their holy vestments for battle dress, for whom violence and greed constituted a way of life, whose deeds belied their words, who failed to teach as Jesus did, by precept and example:[4] "The bishop is well versed in methods of warfare with arms and bombards, but he is dumb when it comes to teaching, exhorting, consoling. He is well armed with javelins and missiles, but absolutely unarmed with Holy Scripture."[5] A year later the Fifth Lateran Council tried to remedy the situation. On December 19, 1516, it issued a lengthy decree that demanded that no one preach who was not properly prepared and qualified and approved, and it called for preaching that was verified by an exemplary life.[6] Unfortunately, the council had more wishful thinking and pious posturing than a sincere effort at reform.

Ignatius arrived in Paris during a provincial council known as the Council of Paris (or of Sens) (1527–28). Among the many concerns of the council two are most pertinent for our purposes: (1) the council found that not a few priests of the diocese were "naked beggars,"[7] a condition of extreme poverty that was not likely to attract candidates of high quality to the priesthood; and (2) the council was conscious of the existence of those who, without permission, took upon themselves the office of preaching, who disseminated heretical ideas amongst the faithful and incited them to both civil and ecclesiastical disobedience.[8]

The day was coming when the high-sounding phrases of Lateran V about preaching would be brought to life and embodied in the lives of Catholic reformers who preceded Ignatius and his companions. For example, at the same time that the Council of Paris was meeting, Gian Matteo Giberti, the bishop of Verona, was establishing norms for excluding the unauthorized and ill-prepared from preaching in his diocese.[9]

One bishop, however, does not constitute a reform of the entire Church. In 1532 Gianpietro Carafa, who resigned the see of Chieti (in Latin, Theate) to become cofounder of the new order of Theatines, wrote a strong "memo" to Pope Clement VII urging that those appointed to preach or hear confessions should be diligently examined, especially about "their way of life, reputation, and Catholic belief."[10] Many preachers lived wicked lives, Carafa continued, but he was convinced that if stringent measures were taken the people would be wonderfully comforted, the heretics would have nothing to complain about, and the friars would make an effort "to bring order into their lives and beliefs."[11] Some took preaching seriously, however, as is evident from the Capuchin Constitutions of 1536: "Nor shall the office of preacher be conferred upon anyone unless it is evident that he is of holy and exemplary life, of clear and mature judgment, of strong and ardent will, because knowledge and eloquence without charity tend in no way to edification but often to destruction."[12]

Nevertheless, the efforts of a few did not change the general situation in the Church. In 1537, the year Ignatius and most of his companions were ordained, a papal commission on reform filed as part of its report the following remarks:

> We believe that the appointment of preachers and confessors from among the friars must also be given attention and corrected, first that their superiors take great care that they are qualified and then that they are presented to the bishops, to whom above all others the care of the Church has been entrusted, by whom they may be examined either directly or through capable men. Nor should they be permitted to carry out these tasks without the consent of the bishops.[13]

The Preaching of the Companions outside of Rome

When the companions first arrived in Rome in 1537 they were simply poor pilgrims who had eschewed ecclesiastical careers and preferments (Xavier had turned down an offer to be a canon in Pamplona [*MX* 2:37–39; *R* 24], Favre to stay at the University of Paris [*R* 23]). They were seeking only permission to go to the Holy Land and to be ordained. They must have been startled to find themselves invited to engage in theological discussions in the presence of the pope even before most of them were priests. Asking them questions on that occasion were papal legates, cardinals, bishops, learned men [*EI* 119][14], and theologians [*R* 58]. The pope was very pleased with them, granted them alms, and gave faculties to the priests in the group to hear confessions [*MF* 7–8]. The document granting faculties made no mention of preaching.[15]

A few weeks later, however, at the ordination in Venice of those not yet priests, Girolamo Veralli, the papal legate to the Republic of Venice, gave all the companions extensive faculties to preach and hear confessions throughout the Republic [*FD* 533–34]. His action was an example of the exercise of papal prerogative: the one granting the faculties was not the patriarch of Venice, but the papal legate. Moreover, he granted faculties that extended beyond diocesan boundaries. These priests were not members of a religious order that had expanded beyond diocesan boundaries but diocesan priests from various dioceses outside the territory in question, who were planning a pilgrimage to the Holy Land.

The faculties granted were truly extraordinary. Here were men without a parish, without a benefice of any kind, without *cura animarum* of any sort, some with no experience in hearing confessions, and yet the faculties they were given were broad indeed. Clearly the papal legate held Ignatius and his companions in high regard. And the companions wore this mantle of high regard with ease and humility. Only Ignatius even mentions the faculties [*EI* 121].

They left the city of Venice but stayed within the confines of the republic while they prepared to offer their first masses [*L* 41]. Laynez writes, "Carrying on the practice of begging alms, we began to practice preaching . . . more for our own mortification than for anything else, although there was always some fruit." Laynez surmises that the reason for the fruit was the fact that they *lived* in poverty, "twice a day begging alms in order to get bread for their survival, without wine or meat but sometimes a bit of oil or butter, in a shack without a bed or a door or windows, sleeping on a bit of straw even when sick" [*L* 42].

Ignatius had long wanted to preach in poverty. Two years before, on February 12, 1536, he had written to Jaime Cazador, an archdeacon in Barcelona, that he owed much to the people there but that God might call him to more humiliating and painful labors elsewhere. Whatever the case, it would always mean "preaching in poverty [*predicar en pobreza*], and without the luxury I now have while studying" [*EI* 96]. *Preaching in poverty* is basically a summary in three words of Jesus' missionary discourse to his apostles in Matthew 10. The desire of Ignatius to preach in poverty may well have had its origin in his reading of the lives of the saints while on his sickbed at Loyola. He would later remember his thoughts on that occasion: "St. Dominic did this, therefore I have to do it;

St. Francis did this, therefore I have to do it" [A 7]. In his desire to preach in poverty, Ignatius has taken a page out of Dominic's book as well as that of Francis, and it behooves us to pause a moment to look at those pages.

Preaching in Poverty: Dominic and Francis

In the days of Dominic and Francis there had been a cry for Gospel preaching, preaching of the Gospel that was authenticated: by word and by example [*verbo et exemplo*], by living in poverty.[16] Even though we are inclined to think of Dominic more in terms of preaching and Francis in terms of poverty, they both emphasized preaching, and they both emphasized poverty.[17]

Francis. Francis had already heard the Lord say to him, "Francis, go and repair my house, which, as you see, is totally destroyed,"[18] and he had already abandoned all his wealth and stripped himself naked[19] when he heard a priest reading the Gospel: "As you go, proclaim the good news, 'The kingdom of heaven has come near.' Cure the sick, raise the dead, cleanse the lepers, cast out demons. You received without payment; give without payment. Take no gold, or silver, or copper in your belts, no bag for your journey, or two tunics, or sandals, or a staff; for laborers deserve their food" (Matt. 10:7–10).[20] Francis responded: "'This is what I want . . . this is what I am looking for; this is what I long to do with all my heart.' . . . He immediately takes his shoes off his feet, puts aside his staff, and content with one tunic, exchanged his leather belt for a rope."[21]

Francis was committed to preaching in poverty, but his approach was different in spirit from that of Dominic.[22] Even his manner of preaching embodied a sort of poverty. He was probably more interested in moving people than in enlightening them. Thomas of Spalato heard Francis preach in Bologna on August 15, 1222, and later wrote of him that "he did not have the manner of a preacher [*praedicantis*], but more of a speaker at a public meeting [*concionantis*],"[23] by which he likely meant that Francis spoke more directly and familiarly and that his enthusiasm was so channeled to the Gospel that he had a profound effect on all his listeners, learned and unlearned alike. As Esser concludes, "Francis preached very impressively, but not in the academic manner."²⁴ Jacques de Vitry, another contemporary witness, saw the early Franciscans as an order dedicated to preaching:

> This is a religious order of truly poor men of the crucified one, and an order of preachers [*ordo praedicatorum*] whom we call Friars Minor. . . . They have no monasteries or churches, no fields or vineyards or herds of cattle, no house or other possessions, not even a place to lay their head. They attract many . . . to contempt of the world not only by their preaching [*predicatione*] but by the example of a holy life [*exemplo vite sancte*] and spotless conduct . . . and these, abandoning all their possessions . . . have put on . . . the habit of the Friars Minor.²⁵

Dominic. In 1206, about the same time that God was beginning to transform the heart of Francis, Dominic found himself quietly but quite dramatically thrust into a program of preaching in poverty. He was traveling as a priest companion to Diego, bishop of Osma (Spain), a close friend who had been prior of the cathedral chapter where Dominic was subprior. They came upon some Cistercians whom Pope Innocent III had commissioned to preach the Gospel to those being infected by the Albigensian or Catharist heresy. The Cistercians were discouraged: preaching was not their usual activity, nor could they handle all the pomp and display in their travel as papal legates. The pope, however, had chosen the Cistercians precisely because of their austerity and holiness: he wanted preaching by *word and example*.²⁶ Diego seems to have intuited the papal wishes immediately. He told them to abandon pomp, to preach the Gospel and to live the Gospel, to go barefoot and beg their living from door to door.

Peter, a monk of Vaux-de-Cernai and a contemporary historian, wrote a history of the Albigensians, along with a covering letter to Innocent III. According to this history, Diego advised the Cistercians in their perplexity "that setting everything else aside they should labor more ardently at preaching, and so that they might be able to stop the mouths of the malignant, following the path of humility, they should act and teach according to the example of the loving Master, and should go on foot, without gold and silver, imitating in all things the way of life of the apostles."²⁷ Here we are face to face with Matthew

10 again. The Cistercians were shocked, for one of the characteristics of the heretics was their insistence on preaching in poverty. Nevertheless, following the advice of Diego they dismissed their entourage, and Diego and Dominic led them in their venture of preaching in poverty. In little more than a year, however, the chief legate had returned to his monastery, another had died, a third had been assassinated, and Bishop Diego also had died. All of this left Dominic very much alone, but his dream had been conceived.[28]

The times were ripe for the dream. Many bishops were unequal to the task of preaching. Lay people were claiming the right to preach. Heresy was rampant. The Church responded to the situation with an ecumenical council, Lateran IV, in 1215. One of the canons of the council urges the bishops, especially those who have little talent for preaching (which they really ought to have), to provide "suitable men, powerful in work and word, to exercise with fruitful result the office of preaching."[29] Although the council fathers had in mind a much broader renovation of the preaching apostolate,[30] it was this decree that made the Dominicans, the Order of Preachers, possible. They were priests who by their institute were commissioned to preach, and to preach in poverty.[31] Their main work at first was to do battle against the heretics by preaching true doctrine. They also changed people's lives.

Preaching in Poverty: Ignatius and His Companions

Like Francis, Ignatius chose to be poor with Christ poor. Like Dominic, he wanted to preach, not simply in imitation of Jesus and the apostles but in order to bring the saving life of Christ to the people. Like the lay movements in the time of Francis and Dominic, he chose as part of his apostolic endeavor a poverty that authenticated his preaching. Like all these predecessors, Ignatius and his companions did not come in worldly trappings but on foot and begging from door to door. Their refusal from the beginning to accept stipends for their work shows that they were moved by the Gospel's missionary discourse: "You received without payment; give without payment" (Matt. 10:8).[32] Again, like these predecessors, Ignatius and his companions chose a life at variance with the traditional cloistered religious life but each in accordance with his own special gift. The lay movements, for example, had no head, no established place, no income, while Dominic saw to it that his community had a head, lodging, and revenue.[33] Dominic explicitly ruled out manual labor in order to be more acceptable to the Cathars and Waldensians, who considered time and energy ill-spent on manual labor when it could be spent preaching the Gospel.[34] Francis originally intended that the friars would earn a living by the work of their hands and beg only if necessary.[35] For their part, Ignatius and his companions recognized no head but Jesus, lived in a house that did not belong to them, and insisted on begging from door to door.

Their poverty, however, did not consist merely in a lack of material comforts. Even deeper was a poverty of language. They were, after all, unskilled as yet in Italian. Ignatius says that when he and three companions, Favre, Laynez, and Codure, were in Vicenza, "the four went to different piazzas and began to preach on the same day and at the same hour, first shouting loudly and summoning the people with their caps" [*A* 95]. Nadal, in fact, tells us regarding Ignatius that "the first word of his first sermon, although he was especially intent on talking Italian, came out in French. 'Hojourdi [*aujourd'hui*],' he said, which in Italian would be, 'hoggi [*oggi*],' that is, 'today [*hodie*]—holy Mother Church [*sancta Mater Ecclesia*], etc."'[36] Preaching, nonetheless, improved their language skill. When they went to Rome after Lent in the following year, 1538, six of them were soon preaching in Italian in six different churches in Rome [*L* 47], while Ignatius preached in Spanish to many persons of high quality, including a certain Dr. Jerónimo Arze, who said that he had never heard anyone preach quite like him, that "he was like one having authority, etc." [*PSH* 79].[37] Ignatius may well have preached the way Francis had preached.

Faculties to Preach

The truly astonishing aspect of their preaching, however, is the faculties under which they preached. Soon after their arrival around Easter, they made an effort to obtain faculties to preach, exhort, and hear confessions [*IR* 3].[38] Cardinal Vincenzo Carafa, the papal legate for the city of Rome during the pope's absence, granted all of them faculties as long as they lived "to preach the Word of God anywhere in the world [*ubique locorum . . . verbum Dei . . . predicare*], including Rome and its environs," whenever they were asked to do so or hoped that it would be profitable for Christ's faithful, "without needing to obtain anyone's permission." Furthermore, they were "to enjoy whatever privileges, graces, faculties, indults, and concessions belong to preachers of the Word of God either by law or custom" [*FD* 537–39]. These faculties went far beyond those mentioned above, which were limited to the Republic of Venice.[39]

Even Ignatius was impressed, calling the faculties "very broad, even though at that time they were spreading false rumors about us to the legate's vicar, obstructing the granting of the faculties" [*IR* 3]. After all the struggles and disappointments of Alcalá, Salamanca, and Jerusalem, Ignatius had finally achieved his objective, to be free to do whatever he wanted to do for God wherever he wanted.

These incredible faculties remind one of the license to preach [*licentia predicandi*] granted by various popes in earlier times to such persons as the Flemish monk Wedericus around 1075, Robert d'Arbrissel in 1096, and Norbert of Xanten in 1118.[40] Like the companions, all of them were itinerant preachers. Like the companions, what characterized the itinerant preachers of that time was not so much that they had no fixed abode, as that they had (1) no juridical bond to any determined church, and (2) often no territorial limitation to their ministry like that imposed upon the diocesan clergy;[41] moreover (3) some, like the three named above, held their mission from the pope.[42] The companions thus echo earlier precedents.

At the heart of the Dominican dream had been (1) being missioned by the pope, (2) to preach everywhere (implying being on the move), (3) in poverty, and (4) as one holding the office of preacher. As for Francis, after Innocent III approved the rule, he granted the friars the license to preach repentance everywhere as long as each one received permission from Francis himself.[43]

In view of this background, Favre's choice of language is significant when he comments on the faculties the companions received from Cardinal Vincenzo Carafa. In a paragraph filled with gratitude and praise of God, Favre says very simply,

"We received the faculties to be able as apostolic preachers to preach everywhere, and to hear confessions" [*F* 18].

The emphasis on mission was not new with Dominic, but institutionalizing it was. A new theological outlook had emerged, especially in view of Innocent III's activities and attitudes, that connected preaching not so much with the clerical state as with mission. St. Paul's "How are they to proclaim him unless they are sent?" (Rom. 10:15) dominated the thinking of the time. Applying it eliminated as preachers those who were ill-prepared, whether ordained or not ordained. Although those sent were usually clerics, it was not *priesthood* that ultimately dictated whether someone could preach or not. What gave the final nod was being *sent* by the pope or the bishop.[44]

The Preaching of the Companions in Rome

Armed with these faculties, dated May 3, 1538, some of the companions began to preach on Sundays and feasts [*IR* 3].[45] Although Laynez continued to be inclined to write off all this preaching activity as "our own mortification," he grudgingly admitted that at least it gave them a chance to urge more frequent confession and communion, and that the people of Rome responded affirmatively to that [*L* 48].

Years later Rodrigues recalls their preaching in Rome, "sometimes in churches, sometimes in the public streets, urging the people to do penance for their sins, to embrace our most gracious God with the fullest love, and to frequent the sacraments of confession and the Eucharist. The Roman populace was so moved to do this that all the Fathers could hardly satisfy the crowds that came." In the same paragraph he says that "at that time it was so unheard of and so unusual for clerics to ascend the pulpit that many people, overcome with astonishment, would say: 'We always thought that monks were the only ones who could preach [*R* 79].'"[46]

Ignatius, for his part, explained the reasons why the preaching of the companions produced results that exceeded their expectations:

> For all of the sermons there was quite a gathering of people, far more than we had expected for three reasons: first of all,

because the time was unusual, for we began immediately after Easter, at the time when the others quit who had preached for Lent and the principal feasts, and around here the custom is to preach only during Lent and Advent; secondly, because after enduring the labors and sermons of Lent, many people, because of our sins, are commonly more inclined to the relaxations and pleasures of the world than to more devotions of the same kind or even new ones; thirdly, because we pretend to no beauty and elegance of style, but even so we are convinced through many experiences that our Lord, through his great and infinite goodness, does not forget us, but helps and favors many others through us who are lowly and of no account. [*IR* 3]

No wonder their preaching was different. Not only did they preach in poverty without seeking a stipend of any kind, but, as the above report indicates, they filled a vacuum left by the other preachers and did not leave the flock untended; inelegant though they might be, God was profoundly at work in them. This was precisely what Ignatius had hoped for. Like Francis, he had no great desire to win acclaim in academic circles.[47]

2. Exhorting in Private

Planting choice vines is not enough to make a vineyard. The farmer must dig the earth and clear it of stones, plant a hedge and hew out a winepress and build a watch tower (Isa. 5:2; Mark 12:1). Preaching the Word of God is not enough; the people must be prepared, and there must be follow-through activities to foster the growth of the Word of God in people's hearts. The companions are not itinerant preachers who scatter the seed and leave it to the wind and the weather.

> you have worked commendably in the Lord's vineyard,
> by publicly preaching the word of God,
>
> **by privately exhorting,**
> [exhortando priuatim]

The phrase is somewhat opaque. It looks simple enough, but early Society sources shed little light on its meaning. A little reflection, however, on the times preceding the companions and on their preaching style can illumine the phrase. The nature of public exhortation reveals the meaning of private exhortation.

About the time Francis and Dominic began their work, Innocent III introduced a new distinction into the preaching vocabulary, based apparently on a distinction suggested in Scripture between books that required special expertise (and should be read only by priests) and those that anyone could understand (even a layman!).[48] The distinction was between preaching repentance, sometimes called *verbum exhortationis* [word of exhortation] (which competent laymen could do), and preaching doctrine (which laymen, no matter how competent, could not do). How the terminology developed is fascinating.[49]

The Word of Exhortation and the Thirteenth-Century Poverty Movements

Like today, the thirteenth century was a period of great wealth and great poverty. Mercantilism was on the rise, and society began to look upon merchants as respectable people, whereas in the eleventh century their profession had been considered ignoble.[50] The new dignity accorded the merchant distressed many people. The Church condemned usury, and although most merchants were not usurers, usurers were considered merchants and gave a bad name even to the innocent.[51]

Not unlike today, lay people then began to raise their voices against the accumulation of wealth. At the same time they criticized those who preached the Gospel but lived in luxury or relative ease.[52] They demanded that preachers live what they preach. Monks should not call themselves *pauperes Christi* [poor of Christ] in a time when poverty had become a fiction for some monasteries.[53] Some lay people were so serious about linking Gospel preaching and poverty that they gave up their own property to one degree or another and began to preach.[54] Some, like the Cathars, preached heresy; others, like the *Humiliati,* simply preached without permission.[55] These poverty movements were not initially preaching movements but an attempt to return to the *vita apostolica,* the life of the apostles and the early Church, a life of simple living and common sharing.[56] Since many who preached after the manner of the apostles did not live after the manner of the apostles, those who embraced poverty decided to embrace preaching as well.

Innocent III, who became pope in 1198, was able to salvage some of the lay preaching by making bold and creative efforts to reconcile those who went astray. His predecessor, Alexander III, had tried to reconcile the Waldensians. He refused them permission to preach, however, unless invited by the parish priests.[57] Since no one invited them, the Waldensians broke with the Church. Innocent, however, managed to reconcile to Rome a group of Waldensians under the leadership of Durand of Huesca, granting them the *licentia exhortandi* [license to exhort], as well as a group of priests and laymen who followed Bernard Prim.[58] He helped in the creation of the three orders of the *Humiliati* and granted that lay members, "with permission of the bishop of the diocese, might propose a word of exhortation [*verbum exhortationis*] to those who assembled to hear the Word of God, warning them and urging them to upright conduct and to works of piety, provided that they did not speak on the articles of faith and the sacraments of the Church."[59] This lay movement fostered that part of the reform of Gregory VII (1073–85) which insisted that preaching should be done both by *word and example*.[60] However, this movement also had the tendency (seen especially in the Waldensians) to make holiness of life the source and criterion of preaching rather than either ordination or mission.

Within this tradition of lay preaching and living poverty, we can place Ignatius as a layman, with his own special attitudes toward the Church.

The Experience of Ignatius and His Companions

The Spiritual Exercises are basically a call to *metanoia*, a total change of heart and life. Those who investigated Ignatius and his first companions at Alcalá and Salamanca were concerned about doctrine. They feared the esoteric doctrines of illuminism; what they found in Ignatius was a simple presentation of Christian truth designed to move the heart and change lives. Nonetheless they forbade the teaching of doctrine until Ignatius and his companions had studied more.

The conversation between Ignatius and the Dominican subprior at Salamanca reads like a time-traveler's excursion back into the thirteenth century. The Dominican wants to know how much they have studied and receives a frank reply. He further presses Ignatius:

> "Tell, then, what do you preach?" "We do not preach," said the pilgrim, "but we do speak familiarly with some people about the things of God; for example, after dinner with some people who invite us." "But," said the friar, "what things of God do you speak about? That is just what we would like to know." "We speak," said the pilgrim, "sometimes of one virtue, sometimes of another; and do so, praising it; sometimes of one vice, sometimes of another, condemning it." [A 65]

The distinction between lay preaching and lay exhorting comes to mind, but even in the thirteenth century no one could stop a person from saying a good word to a neighbor. The Dominican pushes on: you can know something through learning or through the Holy Spirit. Which is it? His concern is whether Ignatius and his companions are Alumbrados, *illuminati* or "enlightened ones," who bypass the Church, just as the Waldensians had in the thirteenth century, and claim their knowledge directly from the Holy Spirit. At this point Ignatius refuses to speak further except to one in authority.

At Alcalá and Salamanca Ignatius, as a layman, discovered that the Church he longed to serve looked upon him with suspicion. Like Waldo before him, he was eager but was "not sent."[61] Unlike Waldo before him, he would meet the demands of the Church, for like Francis and his little brothers he was "in all things obedient to the Apostolic See."[62]

After his studies in Paris and two years before his ordination, Ignatius preached in his home town of Azpeitia on his way from Paris to Venice. He preached with great fervor and considerable success in the hospital of the Magdalen on Mondays, Tuesdays, and Wednesdays, and sometimes on Sunday he preached in the parish church of St. Sebastian, always to good effect. He might teach the people prayers or exhort them about the commandments. If the crowd was too big he went out into the open, where he could be heard easily at three hundred paces. All this he did in the utmost poverty, living in the hospital and begging alms from door to door every day for himself and others. Many lives were changed by his activity.[63] All the terminology suggests that he was preaching "repentance," the word of exhortation that Innocent III had allowed to at least some laymen.

After their ordination to the priesthood the companions preached repentance, a change in the way people lived. Rodrigues remembers that "they urged people to detest sin, to keep the commandments of God and of the Church, exhorting them to frequent reception of the sacraments of confession and the Eucharist" [*R* 66]. Such preaching as this was "publicly exhorting." What they did in public they also did in private.

They had been "privately exhorting" long before their ordination. For Ignatius, private exhortation had been part of his stock-in-trade at least since Manresa, where he often urged people to frequent confession and communion.[64] For the other companions, exhorting others quietly in private began in their student days in Paris. Rodrigues recalls that "by their exhortation [*admonitionibus*] and example [*exemplo*] a good number of students and many of the people of Paris were moved to frequent the same sacraments" [*R* 19].

Private exhortation, however, was not always a one-way street. Two or three days after the companions left Paris to meet Ignatius in Venice, they encountered Rodrigues's brother and a close friend who had pursued them on horseback when they discovered they had left the city. The two tried hard to persuade Rodrigues to give up the life he had embarked upon, and he, in turn, tried to persuade them to join him in this new way of life. Both exhortations fell on deaf ears [*R* 31].

Perhaps the most important element in "privately exhorting" is what is suggested by coupling it with "publicly preaching." Privately exhorting is follow-up on publicly preaching, but it is more than that. It is also pre-evangelization or evangelization, preparing the ground so that someone might come to a sermon or be able to hear the message. The companions were not preachers who were separated from the crowd. They did not prepare their sermons in private, deliver them in public, and disappear again into privacy. What is far more likely is a cycle of private exhorting that led to public preaching that spilled over into more private exhorting, and so on. Both exhorting and preaching, moreover, led to the sacrament of penance or reconciliation.

3. Hearing Confessions

you have worked commendably in the Lord's vineyard,
by publicly preaching,
by privately exhorting,

by hearing confessions,
[confessiones audiendo]

In his old age Simão Rodrigues recalled the early days after the companions were ordained: "Italy was so much a stranger to the frequentation of the sacraments of the Eucharist and the confession of sins, that if someone went to confession and communion once a week everybody talked about it and wrote to their friends in other places as though something new and unusual had happened" [R 47].

The practice of confession had decreased in the later Middle Ages, so that by the time of the Reformation it was quite common that people received the sacrament only once a year, during Lent. Abuses also abounded, like charging for absolution or requiring the penitent to purchase masses from the confessor as a penance.[65] The theology of the sacrament had also weakened.[66]

Gianpietro Carafa complained to the pope in 1532 about the sad state of preaching. At the same time he maintained that the situation regarding confession, though hidden, was even worse: "Every insignificant and vile person sets himself up [as a confessor]. I have been repeatedly told that in several monasteries of conventuals some friars who are not priests at times set themselves up to hear confessions, in order to rob a few pennies. I will be silent about the scandals of revealing confessions and granting dispensations to remain in mortal sin and in all sorts of papal excommunications."[67] To offset abuses, the Rule of the Theatines, of which Carafa was the cofounder, contains the statement: "The sacraments are administered without charge by those whom the Superior shall select and those whom he shall allow."[68] In writing to the pope, Carafa then went on to describe the attitude of the people toward confession: "In this state [Venice] the majority of important people do not go to confession and communion each year.[69] If they are sometimes admonished by conscientious and anxious friends, they openly excuse themselves by saying that their confessors give them permission to do certain things that they know they should not do as good Christians.... I conclude that evil living and corrupt morals thrive only because of wicked confessors."[70]

Carafa's remarks reveal the context of the times in which the Capuchins manifest a deep and genuine concern to prepare good confessors:

> To remove every danger from subjects and Superiors, no Friar shall hear the confessions of seculars without the permission of the Chapter, or of the Father Vicar General. Since this office demands not merely a good and sufficient understanding but a ripe experience, it shall not be exercised save by those who are qualified. The Friars appointed to hear confessions shall do so only in particular cases, when charity demands.[71]

The companions apparently accepted the weakened theology of the sacrament prevalent at that time, or at least worked within its confines, striving to emphasize its positive elements. They vigorously rejected stipends and were adamantly opposed to a neglect of the sacrament. They were also well armed to handle any situation that might arise. Along with their faculties for preaching everywhere they had received abundant faculties for hearing confessions:

> Moreover, [you and any of yours may freely and lawfully] hear the confessions of any of Christ's faithful of either sex who wish to confess to you or any other of your company, without in any way requiring the permission of any rector of diocesan places or parochial churches or of anyone else, and after hearing them carefully, may absolve them of any sins, crimes, and delicts from which ordinaries of places can absolve either by law or by custom or in any other way, and to enjoin a salutary penance for whatever was committed. [*FD* 538–39]

The breadth of these faculties meant that, as far as confession was concerned, the companions had whatever powers bishops ordinarily possessed. Over the centuries the popes had granted extensive powers of absolution to priests of the mendicant orders who had been approved by their superiors, setting up long-standing conflicts between regular and diocesan clergy.[72] But now the companions, simply as diocesan priests, received these truly extraordinary faculties.

A good confession opened to a sinner the possibility of participating fully in the life of the sacraments. The document containing the companions' faculties to preach and hear confessions allows a still wider ministry:

> Likewise, by reason of these presents, we grant and confer by special favor the faculty upon you that you and any of yours may freely and lawfully administer the Eucharist and the other sacraments of the Church to the same faithful of Christ, without any prejudice to the rights of rectors of parochial churches, however, and with their consent. And we strictly forbid the same ordinaries and rectors, as well as any other persons whatsoever of whatever dignity, state, grade, order, or condition, to dare under any pretext whatsoever to impede or disquiet or disturb you or any of your company . . . under pain of immediate excommunication . . . and without any need for sentence to be passed. [*FD* 539]

For strangers in a strange land, that sweeping document must have provided some comfort.

While preparing for their first masses the companions not only preached but heard countless confessions in the various towns around Venice. The memory of feeding people starved for the sacraments stayed with Rodrigues all his life: "By the restoration and renewal of these sacraments very many improved their lives, and renouncing their former evil practices, they gave great thanks to God" [*R* 66]. *Restoration* and *renewal* are key words, indicating a quiet revolution in which the companions were engaged. Their own practice of frequent confession and communion before they became priests[73] and this early experience of the hunger of the people for the sacraments moved the companions to advocate frequent confession and communion (at least every two weeks). This position became a sort of hallmark of their apostolic activity along with other *preti reformati* of the time. What set them apart from the other *preti reformati,* however, was their work in guiding people through the reforming and renewing experience of the Spiritual Exercises.

4. Dirccting the Spiritual Exercises

you have worked commendably in the Lord's vineyard . . .
by hearing confessions,

by directing people in holy meditations,
[exercendo homines in meditationibus piis]

Exercendo [by exercising] is a strong word suggesting work on the part of the companions, but especially on the part of those with whom they worked. The Latin verb implies to drive on, to keep at work. The "holy meditations" are obviously the Spiritual Exercises. Each holy meditation was an *exercise,* and each actively engaged the *exercitant,* the one who did the exercise. To what extent all of the companions engaged in this work is uncertain; the written record up to 1539 indicates only Ignatius and Favre in terms of the full Exercises. The use of the phrase suggests that as far as the companions were concerned, the work of one was the work of all. In their work with people, the other companions may well have drawn on their own experience of the Exercises. Some people could handle only exercises from the first week. Nor would the companions hesitate to propose *holy meditations* not found in the Spiritual Exercises properly so called. They would choose whatever was useful or helpful to a particular person.

From earliest times Christians had been proposing holy meditations to one another. But the word *exercising* does indicate a special aspect of the Ignatian approach. Even here, however, Ignatius was not unique. The *devotio moderna* [modern devotion], a movement stressing practical spirituality, had preceded him by a hundred years, and he had drawn upon it consciously in his use of *The Imitation of Christ* by à Kempis, and perhaps unconsciously in many other ways. The *devotio moderna* was familiar with exercises to train a person in spiritual matters. Some reflections in a recent book on the *devotio moderna* help to situate Ignatius in his historical context:

> The notion of exercises, originally a military term, was applied to spiritual matters by the Church Fathers and especially the early monks, but the notion was first fostered by Franciscan devotional authors, and only came into widespread usage during the fourteenth century. . . . In origin it embraced fasting, prayer, meditation, and all the focused devotional activities of religious persons. With the Franciscans and their heirs it took on the additional meaning of empathetic meditation upon the life and passion of Christ. The New Devout assumed and developed both, adding an emphasis of their own on steady progress in battling the vices and acquiring the virtues.[74]

Whether he was conscious of his dependence on the *devotio moderna* is irrelevant, but once more we find Ignatius standing in the mainstream of Christian spirituality.[75] He was not a maverick, but he was creative, and what he contributed in terms of *exercises* was a unique purpose (the election), a unique arrangement (the four weeks) with key meditations, considerations, and contemplations, and a unique methodology (the director and the whole process of discernment embodied in rules drawn from Ignatius's own experience—even though their roots were in Christian antiquity).[76]

Ignatius, of course, directed people in the Exercises wherever he went, even while at Manresa.[77] On his return from Jerusalem, he picked up three companions in Barcelona through the Exercises and a fourth in Alcalá [*PSH* 35].[78] Reality ruled Ignatius's life. In those early days at Manresa more women came to see him than did men, with the result that more women than men made the Exercises. A radical change took place in Paris, where university life itself dictated that Ignatius would be moving amongst professors and students.[79] Here he stirred up a hornets' nest because of the change wrought in two teachers and a student he directed in the Exercises [*A* 77]. One of them, Pedro de Peralta, eventually became a canon of Toledo and a celebrated preacher,[80] and another, Juan de Castro, was destined to become the prior of the Carthusian monastery in Valencia.[81] Besides those students who eventually became his companions, Ignatius touched a number of others in the university who decided "to abandon the world completely and follow the way of poverty and the cross," some joining "the Franciscans, others the Dominicans, others the Carthusians" [*L* 29]. Some were professors, like Dr. Marcial and Dr. Valle and notably Alvaro Moscoso [*PSH* 51], for some time rector of the university and one day to be bishop of Pamplona and a theologian at the Council of Trent.[82] As for Dr. Marcial, since he was a doctor and Ignatius had taught him much, he thought that Ignatius should have the same title and set machinery in motion to have him named a doctor [*PSH* 51], but apparently this came to nothing.

Beginning with his time of study in Venice Ignatius chose for the Exercises those who might become members of the Company or those who might have a special impact on the Church or secular society. From Ignatius we learn that in Venice he gave the Exercises to Pietro Contarini, a relative of the cardinal, who a few years later became a bishop; to Gasparo de' Dotti, the vicar of the papal legate, Girolamo Veralli; to a Spaniard by the name of Roças; and to another Spaniard by the name of Hozes, who became one of the companions [*A* 92]. He also directed the priest Don Diego de Eguía and his brother, Estevan, both of whom he had met in Alcalá [*A* 57] and who had just returned from Jerusalem [*L* 35].[83] They both died in the Society. Estevan became a lay brother, and Diego was for a time Ignatius's confessor [*PCh* 18].

We have already detailed Ignatius's work with the Exercises in Rome, directing men of influence through thirty days of quiet prayer and reflection. He has moved far from the days of occasional instructions to the devout women of Manresa on the commandments and various methods of prayer. Meanwhile, Favre had directed three future companions in Paris, Jay, Broët, and Codure. In Rome he took over the direction of Francisco Estrada when Ignatius became ill.[84] Of the other companions not much is said for this period beyond the general remark of Polanco that at this time, after they had come to Rome, those of the companions who were in Rome were very active in a variety of works, including the Spiritual Exercises [*PSH* 96].

Conclusion

The works of the early companions are impressive; defending the Society some years later, Nadal summarizes their experience as they overcame their limitations:

> They were steadfast in prayer, but at the beginning hardly listened to in their sermons. Their spirit was great, their doctrine praised, but they were wanting both in speech and action. They were unskilled in Italian; they showed inexperience at first in dealing with people; they seemed more like peddlers than churchmen, for they preached in the public squares. But as this activity continued, many began to be not a little amazed, and a good number were moved to virtue and a change of conduct. At first, therefore, they could hardly collect enough bread to sustain life, and were forced to betake themselves to sheds on the outskirts of the city, later on they were flooded with food and hospitality, and were offered more than they were willing to accept.[85]

9

Tending the Weakest Vines

The ministry of the Word is directed toward planting and tending the vineyard of the Lord. Even healthy vines require much care. But some vines wither, those touched by disease, those on the edges beyond the reach of water, those without deep roots. The worker in the vineyard needs to take extra time and care in seeking them out, in digging and fertilizing and pruning. Ignatius and his companions were ministers of the Word. They tended the vines that bore much fruit, but they gave special care to the vines inclined to wither.

Persons of solid faith who spoke or wrote to Paul III about the companions told stories of their work with the marginalized. We turn now to those special ministries to the weak that the Holy Spirit impels them to undertake: (a) both before and after ordination they tended the sick poor; (b) after ordination they marched through towns filled with people hungry for the Word of God; and (c) from Paris on, but especially in Rome, they fed basic Christian doctrine to the abandoned and the neglected and the uninformed.

1. Caring for the Sick

From its earliest days the Church was careful that no one in the community be neglected. The most likely candidates for neglect were the powerless: strangers, the sick, the poor, widows, orphans, abandoned children, and the aged. As time passed, the hospice or *xenodochium* [place to receive strangers] welcomed all these people and cared for them. Over time, care of the sick and abandoned became more important than the care of strangers, and the Latin word, *hospitale* [asylum], replaced the Greek *xenodochium*. In the monasteries, hospitality meant more than caring for travelers; the poor, the sick, the disabled were also welcome.[1]

When Ignatius left Montserrat and made his way to the hospital of St. Lucy in Manresa, he was welcomed as a stranger. But the sick were also there, and he took care of them; the poor were there, and he begged both for himself and for them. Among the marginal of St. Lucy's were those poorly instructed in the faith, and he taught them Christian doctrine. In doing these things he was not an innovator but another in the long line of those who have fed Christ by feeding his brothers and sisters. Years later, when his companions rendezvoused with him in Venice, he introduced them to similar enriching experiences.

> you have worked commendably in the Lord's vineyard . . .
> by directing people in holy meditations,
>
> **by serving in hospitals,**
> [inseruiendo hospitalibus]

Before his companions arrived in Venice in January 1537 Ignatius had already directed Pietro Contarini through the Spiritual Exercises [*A* 92]. Contarini was then the procurator of the hospital for incurables in that city.[2] Experiencing the need in the hospitals probably suggested to Ignatius a good way for his newly arrived friends to spend their time while he finished his study of theology. Laynez laconically reports that as soon as they came to Venice they divided into two groups; four of the new arrivals plus Hozes went to work in the hospital of Saints John and Paul, and five in the hospital of the incurables, i.e, those with syphilis. Favre and Hozes especially occupied themselves in hearing confessions [*L* 35]. Rodrigues, who served in the hospital of Saints John and Paul, in his later years remembered well that "they waited on the indigent, made the beds, swept the house, cleaned out whatever was soiled, washed the pots of the poor who were sick, carried away the bodies of the dead honorably prepared for burial, dug their graves and buried them in a religious manner. Day and night they were present to everyone with such care, fervor, joy and happiness that all those living in the hospitals were greatly astounded" [*R* 42].

After stating that they had traded higher studies for toil and sweat, Rodrigues goes on to point out that "while the Fathers were doing these things, each one tried, in as manly a way as he could, to overcome the movements of repugnance stirred within them from the stench of the place, the filth, and the horrible sight of the wounds" [*R* 44]. That remark referred especially to the companions who worked in the hospital for the incurables. There the sick were beyond hope, waiting only to die. Schurhammer gives a graphic description of what faced the companions in the hospital of the incurables: "The 'French disease' began with a fever. Then the whole body was covered with ugly and repulsive sores two fingers wide. . . . They were often full of pus and exuded an evil smell that lasted for several months. They were so repulsive that frequently even the physicians fled away in disgust. . . . A kind of cancerous rot then set in and began to eat away one member after the other—nose, lips, gums, eyes, and so forth."[3]

For two and a half months they labored in Venice and then continued their pilgrimage to Loreto and Rome [*R* 48–49]. For them Venice was only the beginning of hospital work. After the ordinations in Venice, Jay and Rodrigues assisted the poor in the hospital in Ferrara [*L* 44, *R* 74], as did Broët and Salmerón in Siena [*L* 45]. When they gave up the idea of going to Jerusalem and gathered together in Rome, one of the works they did was preach and serve in the hospitals "for the love of God" [*L* 48].

The companions were so committed to serving the abandoned sick that they were unanimous in deciding that serving the poor in hospitals for a month would be one of the experiences required of all new members of the Society [*DS* 9].

2. Missionary Journeys

you have worked commendably in the Lord's vineyard . . .
by serving in hospitals,

by pilgrimaging,
[peregrinando]

What is pilgrimaging doing in the midst of a series of apostolic activities that are works of mercy? It is a simple enough word, but how does it fit in the context?[4]

Although historically pilgrimaging has taken a number of concrete forms, the word has three basic meanings: (1) to visit a sacred shrine, (2) to go into exile, (3) to go about preaching. The first is the more common meaning today. The second is far more profound and original, far more rooted in history. The third has its source in the Gospels (Mark 6:6),[5] although it is not without precedent in Buddhism.[6] Common to each is the sense of journey, of voyage, of leaving one place and going to another; each differs by its attitude toward place. In visiting a shrine, one is bent on going to, arriving at a sacred place; going into exile implies abandoning a place; itinerant preaching means always arriving and always leaving, going in a circle, never having a place that is one's own.[7] The meanings probably derive from the same military origin;[8] the soldier was both on the march and away from home.

Walking, after all, is what soldiers do, even more than fighting. The origin of the Latin *miles* [soldier, especially foot soldier] is obscure and uncertain (perhaps Etruscan), but it may be related, at least through popular etymology, to the Latin *mille* [thousand], as in *milia passuum* [a thousand paces], from which we derive the English *mile*.[9] The Latin word *peregrinatio* comes from *per* [through] and *ager* [field]. Going over the fields and through the woods probably meant sojourning or traveling in a foreign land, what we still call in military language, a "tour of duty."

To go on pilgrimage to a sacred shrine is what Ignatius set out to do when he left Loyola: to the shrine of Our Lady at Aránzazu, then to the shrine of Our Lady at Montserrat, and finally to Jerusalem. Ignatius also intended to go into exile when he left Loyola, and this was much more radical than going off to visit a shrine. He cut himself off from family and familiars and avoided places where he might be recognized. Although he did not set out to preach, he ended up preaching.

Later, at Montmartre, the companions chose to make a pilgrimage in the first sense of the word, to visit the holy city of Jerusalem; but the only pilgrimage they succeeded in making was from Paris to the sacred shrine at Loreto. But the second sense of pilgrimaging, going into exile, must also have been part of their experience, for they never ceased to pilgrimage, that is, to live as strangers in a strange land, constantly on the move; this kind of pilgrimaging required of them a profound detachment from everything and everyone on earth. As for the third sense of pilgrimage, some, at least, of the companions intended to stay in the Holy Land and go about preaching and converting unbelievers. Moreover, even before they gave up all hope of making a pilgrimage to the most sacred of all shrines, they began to go about preaching in Italy. Thus their lives model all three kinds of pilgrimaging. But which meaning is intended in this passage of *Cum ex plurium?*

Pilgrimaging: Visiting Shrines

After St. Helena's visit to Jerusalem, the holy places connected with Christ's life, death, and resurrection/ascension became the object of religious pilgrimage for many Christians. When the barbarian invasions of the fifth century made the shrines of the Holy Land inaccessible, other holy shrines took their place.[10] Sometimes the pilgrimage ended at the holy place, and the pilgrim returned home; sometimes, too, the pilgrimage to a holy place was part of voluntarily going into exile, and the pilgrim became a monk or hermit near the sacred shrine; sometimes also a pilgrim preached along the way, especially a pilgrim monk.

These journeys to holy places had a devotional and ascetic purpose that involved renunciation and risk. Often their purpose was directly penitential. An underlying assumption was that a pilgrim did not travel in luxury but in simplicity and poverty.[11] Pilgrimage also implied celibacy, at least as long as the pilgrimage lasted. Many pilgrims were monks; many others were married or single. Many a pilgrim journeyed alone, and certainly without a spouse; the spouse stayed home to take care of the house and the land and the family. In the meantime, married or single or monk, the pilgrim centered on Jesus alone. Unfortunately, however, not all pilgrims were chaste. In the thirteenth century Jacques de Vitry complained that when the civil courts began to impose pilgrimages for public crimes they filled the roads to holy places with an unholy gang of "wicked, impious, sacrilegious, thieves, robbers, murderers, parricides, perjurers, adulterers, traitors, corsairs, pirates, whoremongers, drunkards, minstrels, jugglers, and actors."[12] Penalties did not automatically transform hearts. For those, however, with hearts full of love or repentance, the pilgrimage meant an interior attitude of commitment and trust.

The Middle Ages provided the order of pilgrims [*ordo peregrinorum*], not a religious order but a special category of Christians, those on pilgrimage to a holy place. They wore a special garb, carried a staff and a soft leather pouch for money and food, were supposed to be received with hospitality (although they were frequently exploited and robbed), and sometimes given official letters of identification. They also traveled in large groups, sometimes as many as seven hundred at a time, in order to protect themselves from bandits.[13] A law regarding pilgrims regulated the protection to be given them.[14] The pilgrimage was still difficult, but even in a strange land one was not totally a stranger.

Those, however, who voluntarily chose to go into exile and to live permanently as expatriates wished to be treated as strangers in a strange land, with all the risks that involved, no language, no friends, no support but God alone.

Pilgrimaging: Going into Exile

In biblical terms the basic form of pilgrimaging is going into exile, and the paradigm for exile is Abraham, who was told by God to leave his country and his kindred and his father's house and to go to a land that the Lord would show him (Gen. 12:1). When Abraham sought a burial place for Sarah, he said to the Hittites who lived in the land, "I am a stranger and an alien residing among you" (Gen. 23:4).

The New Testament applies to Christians the language used of Abraham. The Letter to the Hebrews, for example, calls Abraham and his countless descendants "strangers and foreigners on the earth" (11:13).[15] Peter, writing to Gentile Christians, calls them "the exiles of the Dispersion" throughout Asia Minor (1 Pet. 1:1), and urges them "as aliens and exiles to abstain from the desires of the flesh that wage war against the soul"

(1 Pet. 2:11). The Greek words he uses for "aliens and exiles" are identical to those in the Greek Septuagint for "stranger and an alien" in the above passage concerning Abraham.[16] The Gospels transform this Abrahamic exile as the early Christians heard themselves being called to follow Jesus: "Everyone who has left houses or brothers or sisters or father or mother or children or fields, for my name's sake" (Matt. 19:29).

Exile is not simply inconvenient; it involves renunciation and a form of poverty. Voluntary exile or expatriation [*xeniteia*], freely becoming an alien, became an early Christian ideal.[17] The connection with early monasticism is obvious, a following of Christ by going off alone, in silence, in solitude, in humility, in poverty.[18] To be alone, *monos,* meant most of all, to be without a spouse.[19] The first act of pilgrimage, of exile, for the monk was chastity, a total commitment of oneself to Christ alone. It is the first act by which one alienates oneself from home and country and family and binds oneself to Christ, making oneself, like him, a stranger in a strange land. Whereas the monks of Syria tended to be constantly on the move, *gyrovagi* [wanderers in a circle],[20] the monks of fourth century Egypt lived as exiles in their own land. For those who had already left home and family and possessions there was no need for further geographical journeying. A further step, however, could still be taken. An exile from one's own country could become an exile from society itself, a hermit, for at the heart of exile is a profound experience of being alone: pilgrimage is an existential state of solitude. The Irish monks, in fact, of the sixth to the tenth centuries, went into voluntary exile, sailing far from their native land to find an ideal spot for a hermitage. In other words, to be an exile is a way of life, a permanent form of asceticism, a paradoxical achievement of "stability in pilgrimage."[21] Moreover, wherever they went, the monks preached, but they did not go mainly to preach, they went to find solitude. Some of them alternated periods of hermit life with their preaching. Being a hermit and preaching were simply two forms of being in exile. Moreover, one could always hope that living alone or preaching in a strange and barbaric land would lead to martyrdom,[22] the ultimate following of Christ.

Although the early Middle Ages saw many a pilgrim monk in the West, with the coming of the Crusades ideal and reality met head-on, and a new ideal was born.[23] The Crusades gave a new perspective to the mystical meaning of pilgrimage, that is, that the Church is always in exile and one must regain paradise through prayer and mortification. After the eleventh century that mystical ideal could be fulfilled in another way: in a journey that is interior, in the silence and quiet of the cloister, in what Jean Leclercq calls "pilgrimage in stability."[24] Geographical dislocation was not essential to being an exile. Nonetheless, the ideal pilgrim is always Abraham, whose name is constantly invoked.

Pilgrimaging: Going about Preaching and Healing

Besides going into exile and visiting shrines, pilgrimage has a third meaning, derived from the activity of Jesus and the apostles in the Gospel.[25]

When the people of Nazareth rejected Jesus, he said to them, "Prophets are not without honor, except in their hometown, and among their own kin, and in their own house" (Mark 6:4), words that echo the call of Abraham to leave his country and his kindred and his father's house. Immediately thereafter, Jesus, now an exile, "went about among the villages teaching" (Mark 6:6). He then sent the Twelve out two by two to preach and heal. Ched Myers points out that the orders Jesus gave them do not appear unique for this particular mission since he gave them "for the way" (*NRSV*: "for their journey"), that is, as normative for their lifestyle as his disciples:

> Their narrative significance lies not in some model of heroic asceticism . . . but in the emphasis upon the utter dependence of the disciples upon hospitality. [They] are allowed the means of travel (staff, sandals) but not sustenance (bread, money bag and money, extra clothes). In other words, they, like Jesus who has just been renounced in his own "home," are to take on the status of a sojourner in the land.[26]

In Matthew, the story of Jesus' sending the Twelve out to preach and to heal follows soon after the notice that although the Pharisees have categorically rejected him—"By the ruler of the demons he casts out the demons" (9:34)—still he "went about all the cities and villages" (9:35) teaching and healing.

Luke is no less poignant: those weeping and wailing for the daughter of Jairus jeer at Jesus (8:53), and he then empowers the Twelve, who "went through the villages, bringing the good news and curing diseases everywhere" (9:6). Moreover, when Jesus missions the seventy disciples (10:1–12), he does it in a context where the Samaritans refuse to receive him "because his face was set toward Jerusalem" (9:53). Thus one aspect of the pilgrimage of preaching and healing is a kind of exile.

As the Christian tradition developed, this *going about* preaching and teaching and healing became a new model for pilgrimage alongside that of Abraham's departure into the unknown. In the sixth century the primary desire of Columba and his companions may well have been to go into exile with Abraham, and preaching may have been entirely secondary to them, but the fact that *one* abbot set out with *twelve* monks suggests that they were not unaware that they were imitating Jesus and the apostles. They sought solitude, and they brought solitude, but they also brought the Gospel to the cities and towns and countryside. Hermits and other itinerant preachers of the late eleventh and twelfth centuries lived this kind of pilgrimaging. They had no goal, in the sense of reaching a sacred shrine, yet they had a goal: a continual going about while preaching the Gospel. This made the hermit at once an expatriate with Abraham and a companion of Jesus and the apostles. Popes understood them and gave the hermit-pilgrims the license to preach everywhere.[27] *Everywhere* at that time was much the equivalent of the *unknown*.

Dominic saw this kind of life as necessary, exciting, and willed by God. He, too, went about the villages and the towns preaching and teaching and bringing the healing power of the sacraments. And when he sent out his friars to do the same, he sent them, like the apostles, two by two. So did Francis. In the bull *Cum dilecti filii* of 1218, Honorius III describes the Franciscans as going "from one stopping place to another sowing the seed of the Word of God after the example of the Apostles."[28] The Franciscans went throughout the whole known world, like John the Baptist preaching repentance and proclaiming the Kingdom of God. Cloister had no meaning for them. "The monastery of the Friars Minor, if we may thus phrase it," writes Esser, "is the wide world."[29]

Pilgrimaging and the Companions

Many of the above comments about the meaning of pilgrimage apply to the early companions.[30] The companions' first impetus comes from a desire to make a journey to a holy place, but that desire has a deeper root, the attitude of the voluntary exile who wishes to follow Christ in total renunciation, in poverty, in chastity, in total trust in Divine Providence. Pilgrimaging in *Cum ex plurium* has little or nothing to do with visiting holy places, but everything to do with following Christ.[31]

Going into Exile and Visiting Shrines

From the early days of his conversion Ignatius conceived a desire to go to Jerusalem. Wanting to do it in a penitential manner, he dreamed of going "barefoot, and of eating nothing but plain vegetables and of practicing all the other rigors that he saw in the saints . . . with as much of disciplines and fasts as a generous spirit, fired with God, would want to perform" [A 8–9]. He wanted to visit the sacred shrines [A 45], and he also had a desire to give his life for the faith [PI 9].

Something deeper, however, stirring in his spirit made him call himself "pilgrim."[32] He intended his departure from Loyola as an act of expatriation. Even his brother had some inkling of this, recognizing that Ignatius was leaving home for good and giving up the life he had led up to that time [A 12]. Furthermore, Ignatius hoped not to be recognized [A 12, 18], but to be an unknown stranger. He gave away the money owed him, and as soon as he could he bought some sackcloth for a pilgrim's garment, and then gave his own garments to a poor man [A 16, 18]. He also took a vow of chastity [L 5]. At this stage Ignatius was very much a learner, but he had a way of doing spontaneously that which was in continuity with the whole Christian tradition. Laynez later wrote of him that "he determined to lead a very austere life; and therefore . . . he decided . . . to leave his house and totally renounce his land and his family and his own body, and to enter on the way of penance" [L 4]. The three elements in God's command to Abraham are present: "Go from your country and your kindred and your father's house" (Gen. 12:1).[33]

When the companions vowed at Montmartre to go to Jerusalem, they were certainly in the tradition of Abraham. Like Abraham, they were open to God's call, not knowing where they were going but sure that God would reveal to them the way.[34] When they left Paris on the first leg of their pilgrimage to Jerusalem, they had the pilgrim Ignatius as a model, but they were not slaves to that model. Ignatius had traveled through many cities and towns from Loyola to Jerusalem and back. On that pilgrimage Ignatius wore a rough pilgrim's tunic, had a staff and a gourd (a begging bowl, not a pouch for money and food), and carried some letters of recommendation, but he went alone and without money or food so that he might depend upon God alone [A 35, 42, 44]. Later, visiting Azpeitia on the way from Paris to Venice, he stayed in the hospital rather than his brother's home [A 87]; he was an exile without a land of his own.

Certainly the companions had abandoned all that was attractive in the world; they had left father and mother and home and country to follow Jesus, and they had done it in the utmost poverty. Men from various parts of Europe, they went to Italy where none of them knew the language. To get there they went far out of their way, through Germany, to avoid places where France and Spain were at war [R 25]. Even so, they often found themselves in danger among hostile people [R passim]. They were exiles, strangers in a strange land. We learn from Rodrigues that they were intent on a pilgrimage to the shrine of Our Lady at Loreto [R 36], just as Ignatius had first gone to Aránzazu and Montserrat; but they did not finish this pilgrimage until on their way from Venice to Rome [R 56]. They endured incredible hardships along the way, with their hope in God alone [R 49–55]. Polanco reports that "they came to Rome totally exhausted because of the poverty and the rain, walking barefoot, sometimes through water up to their chests, fasting daily" [PSI 9]. On their pilgrimage from Paris the companions wore no distinctive pilgrim costume to protect them other than their ordinary student garb. They carried enough money for the journey as far as Venice, but they had no letters of recommendation even though they were in hostile territory. They slept and ate where they could. They were a small group of foreigners, but they made no attempt to find a larger group to which they might attach themselves for protection. They had some sense of exile. After the visit to Loreto we hear of no more pilgrimages to sacred shrines before the writing of *Cum ex plurium.*

When we ask why Ignatius called himself "the pilgrim," we should not put much stock in his many travels. On all his journeys, after Manresa, his whole intent was to help his neighbor. He was constantly seeking the will of God. The outer journey was simply an external expression of what was happening in the depths of his being. When this much-traveled man returned to Rome his outer journey ceased. One suspects that it was the interior journey more than anything else that made him refer to himself as *pilgrim.* He had found stability in pilgrimage, but in Rome he found pilgrimage in stability.

Going into Exile and Going about Preaching and Healing

The evidence reveals that the "pilgrimaging" of *Cum ex plurium,* means more than visiting shrines and more than going into exile. Indeed, on August 26, 1539, a few days before Contarini read the five decrees of the Formula of the Institute to the pope, the leading citizens of Montepulciano wrote a letter inscribed, "To the very reverend brothers in Christ Jesus of the Company of pilgrim priests in Rome."[35] Not everyone knew the companions as the "Company of Jesus," but they did recognize that the companions were a company and that they were pilgrim priests. Since by then the companions had abandoned their pilgrimage to Jerusalem, those who called them pilgrim priests must have had a more profound reason for doing so.

"Pilgrim priests" was a pleasing name. Rodrigues liked it: when Francisco Xavier wrote a letter from Lisbon to Rome on October 22, 1540, Rodrigues signed it and inscribed it, "To our dear brothers in Christ, Master Codacio and Master Ignatius of Loyola, pilgrim priests" [*EX* 1:69].[36] Xavier and Rodrigues were waiting for a ship, ready to embark on a pilgrimage to India, but Codacio and Ignatius were settled in Rome and neither was going anywhere. Still, Rodrigues persistently addresses his friends in Rome as pilgrims. The following year he wrote two more letters from Lisbon after sickness had forced a change of plans and Xavier had already left for India, one on May 15, 1541, and the other on May 26, 1541, with identical inscriptions: "To our dear brothers in Christ, Master Ignatius and Master Pietro Codacio, of the Company of pilgrim priests in Rome at the Merangulo Tower" [*EB* 523, 526]. In these two letters Codacio and Ignatius are not singled out as "pilgrim priests," but the whole Company is. They are *all* pilgrim priests.

The title was won, it would seem, for two reasons: (1) they were clearly exiles, foreigners, men who had abandoned their homes and countries; (2) they were always on the move, willing to undertake any journey and any labor in order to help their neighbor as *they went about* the various cities and towns of Italy after the manner of Jesus and his apostles (Matt. 9–10). An incident in the earlier life of Ignatius illumines the second reason. The friars in the Dominican priory in Salamanca invited him to dinner along with his companion, Calixtus. After dinner the subprior took them to a chapel and told them that good reports were circulating about them, that they were going around preaching *a la apostolica* [*A* 64]. These words are significant in the mouth of a Dominican, one who came from a tradition in which apostolic preaching was understood as involving going from one town to another in poverty and other hardships.

That the companions considered themselves to be walking in the footsteps of Jesus and the apostles is supported by a letter that Bobadilla wrote many years later. On August 11, 1589, he wrote to Fr. General Aquaviva about the vow to go to Jerusalem that the companions had taken on August 15, 1534: "This vow Divine Providence . . . commuted to other better and more fruitful vows of pilgrimaging in religion" [*FN* 3:321]. Since all of the companions were to spend their days traveling all over the world, Bobadilla can mean only that fruitful travel that brought the companions to city after city and country after country after the manner of the apostles, preaching and teaching and healing through the sacraments, hearing confessions and attending to the poor and the sick and the dying. Their whole life was pilgrimage.

In their apostolic journeys through Italy the companions had been, in a sense, *gyrovagi* [wanderers], and they were now proposing to commit themselves to that kind of life. What they had done and proposed to do, however, was far different from what some ancient monks had done. They had not set out simply to wander as homeless exiles, like the Syrian monks of old, or to find a hermitage like some of the Irish monks of later centuries, and in the process do some preaching; rather they set out to preach, to bring the Gospel wherever they might go, and in doing so they had no other home than the pilgrimage itself, and they found solitude in prayer and in their own vulnerability and dependence on God.[37] Whereas the *gyrovagi* were in danger of falling into undisciplined wandering without a purpose, the companions had companionship in the Lord and a center in the vicar of Christ. Like Ignatius, they had all chosen to be pilgrims for the rest of their lives, finding stability in both the outer and the inner pilgrimage.[38]

Just as they agreed that serving in hospitals should be a part of the experience of each new member of the Society, so also they agreed that pilgrimaging should be part of that experience [*DS* 9]. To both experiences they gave the name of *ministry* [*DS* 9]. In both ministries they paid special attention to those neglected ones who had little or no familiarity with Christian doctrine.

3. Teaching Christian Doctrine to Little Ones

you have worked commendably in the Lord's vineyard . . .
by pilgrimaging,

by teaching children and the uninitiated
[pueros et personas rudes docendo]
what is necessary for the instruction of a Christian,
[ea quae ad christiani hominis institutionem sunt necessaria]

Although *pueros* frequently means "boys," in this context it refers to "children" of both sexes, as opposed to adults. The meaning of *rudes* is rough, unfinished, rude, crude. Like *pueros*, *rudes* includes both sexes. Also like *pueros*, *rudes* can refer to those in their younger years who are not yet fully grown, but the word is not limited to any particular age group. Men and women frequently came to hear Ignatius and the companions when they taught children. Commenting on the use of the term *rudes* in the Formula, Aldama suggests that it may have been inspired by St. Augustine's *De catechizandis rudibus* [On Catechizing the Uninitiated].[39] As in Augustine, so also here, the word does not suggest ill-breeding or stupidity but rather refers to those who are uneducated or unsophisticated or those who simply have not yet received instruction (who might well be refined and sophisticated and even educated), who have little or no knowledge of a particular field, who are inexperienced.[40] In this sense catechumens, no matter how brilliant, were among the *personas rudes* [uninitiated].

The plight of children in the closing years of the twentieth century is nothing new. Children, the least powerful of human beings, have always been amongst the most marginal in human society. Often abandoned, beaten, enslaved in one way or another, the hope of many has depended on the kindness of strangers.[41] The sixteenth century was no exception.

The children were not the only ones in need. In a period when bishops did not live in their dioceses and take care of their flocks, the people in general learned little about the faith in which they had been baptized. When ordinary priests were abysmally ignorant, the people shared that ignorance. When ignorance flourished, superstition abounded.[42] Even a worldly pontiff like Leo X was disturbed in 1516 by the nonsense that came from the mouth of preachers, false interpretations of Scripture, unfounded threats of evils to come, tales of fictitious miracles, false prophesies, all of which fed the gullible and misled the sensible.[43] Let one witness bear testimony for the whole age, Gian Pietro Giussano, the esteemed historian of the Ambrosian Church in Milan. In 1610 he wrote in a biography of Cardinal Borromeo (who was eighteen when Ignatius died), "The people had hardly any awareness of the fundamentals and principles of the Catholic faith, not knowing how to recite the Lord's prayer or the angelic salutation, scarcely even to make the sign of the cross, and much less did they have any knowledge of the articles of the faith and the commandments of God."[44] But the children were the most in need. If the Church was to change at all in a time crying out for reform, the faith of the children had to be protected and fostered.

The immediate response to the raw need of the people, both children and adults, was an ineffective decree on the part of Lateran V that Christian doctrine should be taught in the schools.[45] Among those leading the way twenty years after the council were Ignatius and his companions.[46] To the desperate need of children they responded eagerly with talent, zeal, and compassionate hearts. From their earliest days in Rome they worked with the most neglected, the most abandoned, the most marginal: street children, orphans (both boys and girls), fallen women and young women in danger of falling, Jewish converts rejected by their own people and not always welcomed by their Christian neighbors.[47]

The work in Rome was a continuation of the work Ignatius had begun in Manresa. At Manresa Ignatius shared the life of the powerless in the hospital of St. Lucy. As Polanco puts it, "He went to the hospital of the poor and joined the other shabby little people [*pauperculis*] there" [*PV* 14]. According to his own testimony Ignatius begged alms every day [*A* 19]. Eighty-four years later, at the age of ninety-six, Margarita Capdepós, a youthful eyewitness of Ignatius's activity, testified that he served the needs of the sick in the hospital, begged enough to support many of the poor, visited the sick all over town, and "went through the city publicly teaching Christian doctrine."[48] The people needed instruction as much as the poor needed food and the sick needed care.

The spiritually deprived became a major concern for Ignatius. In his mind no one could be more on the margin of society than an unbeliever, an infidel. He longed "to preach the faith and doctrine of Christ" to the Muslims of Jerusalem [*PV* 26]. But believers were also deprived, robbed of their Christian heritage for lack of instruction. On his return from Jerusalem, in the midst of his studies in Barcelona, "he did not altogether omit spiritual conversations [*colloquia spiritualia*] and the explanation of Christian doctrine" [*PV* 35]. He taught Christian doctrine again in Alcalá [*A* 57] and Salamanca [*A* 65] and got himself into trouble, as he did once more in Paris by reason of spiritual conversations and spiritual exercises [*et colloquiis et spiritualibus Exercitiis*] [*PV* 60]. When

Ignatius left Paris and returned to Spain, teaching Christian doctrine regained top priority, if it had ever lost that position in his heart. There in his homeland, he begged from door to door and proposed to teach Christian doctrine to the children, much to the consternation of his brother. Against his brother's protests that no one would come, Ignatius replied that if only one child appeared that would be enough. So many people, in fact, came to listen to him (including his brother) that the church overflowed and they had to take to the fields, some even climbing the trees in order to hear him better.[49] No explicit record exists that he taught Christian doctrine during his stay in Venice, but Ignatius may well include it in his remark that "he busied himself giving the Exercises and in other spiritual contacts" [A 92].[50]

The record regarding the other companions is less complete. Laynez reports teaching Christian doctrine to children only in Siena [L 45], but an explicit statement regarding one place does not rule out teaching in other places. In a passage that seems largely dependent upon Laynez's account, Polanco adds Bologna to the list [PV 93–94]. In fact, Polanco summarizes their work in such a way as to suggest that teaching children was something all the companions did:

> With some of them in Padua, and others in Ferrara, Bologna, Siena, and Rome, they began, to the edification of many, to share the Word of God as best they could with their neighbors in confession and through preaching, sometimes in the churches, sometimes in the piazzas, and to lecture and to teach Christian doctrine to children [*putti*] and simple folk [*persone simplici*], and to serve the poor, so that they were in good favor in those areas.[51] [PSI 11]

The terrible Roman winter of 1538–39 provides a good example of their work. When the companions gathered up the poor from around the city and brought them into their own home to feed them and warm them, they also taught them Christian doctrine [PSH 82].[52] Their purpose was not only to inform the minds of the poor but especially to touch their hearts.[53] Their concern for children and the uninstructed brought the Company as a whole its first commission from the pope even before the Society was founded. After the governor of Rome cleared their reputations in November 1538, Paul III had the governor order that the students in the city's schools come together so that the companions might teach them Christian doctrine [*IR* 10].[54]

The depth of their concern manifested itself in the Deliberations they made before writing *Cum ex plurium.* Anyone admitted to the Society should be led by the same spirit, and should at least be able to say to an unbeliever that Christ is savior, and be able to teach the faithful the Our Father and the commandments, etc.[55] Furthermore, they agreed that members of the Society should teach children and others the commandments and other rudiments of the faith for an hour each day over a period of forty days each year. When the others who were present wanted to bind themselves to this by a formal vow, Bobadilla demurred.[56] Nonetheless, the desire of all the companions to teach children reveals their insight into the close connection between mission and teaching Christian doctrine. Both are a response to Jesus' commandment to go and teach all nations. Both echo Jesus' concern for children and the "little ones" of society in whom lies the hope of the kingdom. Both aim at conversion. Whether one is sent to the faithful or to unbelievers, to children or to the sophisticated, it is all the same for Ignatius, who finds the presence and the mystery of God at work in the world in the simplest of scriptural prayers as well as in the most sophisticated doctrines. For him the purpose of mission anywhere is to introduce people to the life of God shared with us through the Son in the Spirit.[57]

Like serving in hospitals and pilgrimaging, teaching Christian doctrine eventually became a required experience before one could be admitted into the Society. Children were dear to the early companions, as were all those who were neglected and abandoned by the rest of society.[58]

4. Works of Charity

> by teaching children and the uninitiated
> what is necessary for the instruction of a Christian,

and finally by performing every work of charity
[et omnia demum charitatis officia ... (obeundo)]
wherever you happen to be ...
[vbicumque terrarum fuistis].

If the companions had kept journals, they would probably make exciting reading. We have no detailed firsthand account of all they did. If Nadal is correct in his summary written twenty years later, they were busy indeed. He indicates that in Vicenza they made the decision that during their wait to go to Jerusalem:

> With a passionate love for Christ, they would put all their effort into helping people, into sermons and lectures on Scripture, spiritual conversations, the Spiritual Exercises, the instruction of children and the uninitiated, hearing confessions, visiting the sick, rendering aid to slaves, reconciling opponents and enemies, taking care that abuses are eliminated and good works, both public and private, are established; bringing consolation to those in public jails and helping them when opportunity provides; and finally they would help their neighbor through all the works of charity, first and foremost through spiritual works but also corporal ones, striving most of all to bring about the frequent reception of the sacrament of penance and holy communion and the practice of prayer and good works, accepting no stipend or alms that could be connected with those works, doing nothing, however, without first receiving faculties from the ordinary of the place.[59]

The companions probably did not do all of these works in each place they visited, but the list gives some idea of all the activities they engaged in or were ready to undertake wherever they might be.[60]

Conclusion

Jesus first gave his apostles the power to heal, then he sent them to the lost sheep of the house of Israel, and finally he told them to preach the good news of the kingdom wherever they went (Matt. 10). These are the three works that capture the hearts of Ignatius and his companions: serving the sick, pilgrimaging in missionary fashion, teaching the basic truths of the kingdom of God. For Ignatius and his companions pilgrimaging means always being on that missionary journey of the apostles. Like the apostles, they do not stay in one place. Wherever they go they tend the sick and preach the kingdom; wherever they are, they exhort and hear confessions and give the Spiritual Exercises. Wherever they happen to be, they seek out the uninstructed and feed them whatever they can. What more can they do? Whatever needs to be done. Like the apostles, they have been given freely gifts to be given freely.

10

Stewardship of the Vineyard

With its widespread ignorance and superstition, ecclesiastical greed and clerical immorality, the early sixteenth century cried out for reform; but reform was not always provided. By the time Ignatius and his companions appeared on the scene in 1537, Lutheranism pervaded a good part of Germany and was the official religion of both Sweden and Denmark (which included Norway and Iceland). Calvin had just published his *Institutes of the Christian Religion* (1536). Monks were leaving their monasteries. Ordinary people were filled with confusion, easy prey to facile preachers and unscrupulous ecclesiastical con artists.

In this situation Ignatius and his friends discovered they were sheep in the midst of wolves, yet some people called them wolves. They were workers in the vineyard, not managers, but their stewardship of the vineyard was challenged: they were called heretics, they were fugitives by reason of heresy, they had been burned in effigy. They did not accept the charges in silence; rather they challenged the challengers.

Yielding to the driving power of the Holy Spirit can be dangerous. *Cum ex plurium* reports how the companions fared in those troubled times. If Pope Paul III received conflicting reports, he knew how to sift them, what to accept and what to reject:

> you have worked commendably in the Lord's vineyard . . .
> by performing every work of charity
> wherever you happen to be

> **not only without any sign of heresy**
> [non modo sine vlla haeresis . . . (nota)]
> **or avarice**
> [aut auaritiae]
> **or immoral conduct of any sort,**
> [aut turpitudinis alicuius nota]
> **but even with great praise:**
> [sed multa etiam cum laude obeundo]

The word we translate "sign" is the Latin *nota*, which means a mark, visible or invisible, by which something is recognized: a mark of distinction or of condemnation, a very evident mark or maybe a mere hint.¹ *Cum ex plurium* states that Ignatius and his companions have conducted themselves and their activities with: (1) no sign of heresy, (2) no sign of avarice, (3) no sign of immoral conduct, (4) great praise. Each deserves comment.

1. Without Any Sign of Heresy

A proper background for these remarks would amount to a full book on the religious ferment of the day, the effective as well as the ineffective attempts at reform within the Church of Rome along with the often fervent but misguided attempts that ended in heresy.² The temper of the times, its fear and concern about heretics are manifest in Gianpietro Carafa's *Memorial* to Clement VII in 1532 in which he instructs Bonaventura, a Franciscan friar, what he should bring to the attention of the pope: "Above all, report that the infection of Lutheran heresy as well as every other error against faith and good practices is being disseminated most effectively and made to increase by two kinds of people, namely apostates and conventual friars."³ A formal conviction on charges of heresy could mean imprisonment or death.

When Carafa wrote in 1532, the debate against Luther had long been raging and that against Calvin was about to begin. In Spain the Inquisition was at war with the Alumbrados [illuminists]. In England Henry VIII was rebelling. By the time they reached Rome, Ignatius and his companions had encountered at least the fringe of the heretical movements of the day. The companions were fresh and new and exciting. Had they kept themselves untainted by the heresy they had met? Were their fresh new voices orthodox?[4] Some did not think so. How welcome, then, in the midst of the persecutions of 1538, was a letter of recommendation on behalf of Bobadilla and Xavier written on June 26, 1538, by Agostino Zannetti, the vicar-general of Bologna. In it he testifies:

> Francisco Xavier and Nicolás Bobadilla, priests, with our permission preached in this city of Bologna with deep sincerity and in a Christian manner, without any hint of Lutheranism, in fact, attacking it with all their strength. In their sermons they have been very helpful to our city, and by their lives and conduct, which all approve, they have corroborated them. Wherefore, that they fled from this city as fugitives is false, but they left in order to take care of their own affairs and to sow elsewhere the good seed that they left with us. [MX 2:133]

This was not the first time the companions were cleared of the charge of heresy. And when we read in *Cum ex plurium* that the companions are free of heresy we can infer that a letter like Zannetti's did not go unnoticed in Rome. These words are not some empty formula found in every papal brief or bull; they press to the very heart of the companions' being, their identity, their surrender to Jesus and companionship with him.

Judicial Proceedings in Alcalá, Salamanca, and Paris

Ignatius had had clashes with Church authorities in his student days. To set rumors to rest Ignatius recounted some of these in a letter to King John III of Portugal on March 15, 1545, five years after the Society was confirmed:[5]

> In Alcalá de Enares, after my superiors investigated me three times, I was taken and put in jail for forty-two days. In Salamanca, after another investigation, I was not only put in jail but in chains, where I stayed for twenty-two days. In Paris, where I then went to study, it happened again. In all those five judicial processes and two imprisonments, through the grace

of God I never desired to take, nor did I take, any solicitor or procurator or lawyer except God in whom, through his favor and grace, I place all my present and future hope. [*IJ* 2].

Later Ignatius fleshed out these bare facts in the story he dictated to Luis Gonçalves da Câmara. In 1526 Ignatius and his pre-Paris companions were investigated in Alcalá. The investigators abandoned the project and left the process to the vicar Figueroa, who found no error in their lives or teaching, even after trying them twice four months apart in 1526 and 1527 [*A* 58–62].[6] They then faced a diocesan tribunal in Salamanca in 1527, but the tribunal found no error in their lifestyle or their teaching [*A* 67–70].[7] In his letter to King John Ignatius has a few comments to make:

> If Your Majesty wishes to be informed about why so much inquiry and investigation was made about me, be assured that it had nothing to do with schismatics or Lutherans or Alumbrados, for I did not associate with them or know them, but because I, unlettered, especially in Spain—they marvelled that I spoke and conversed so widely about spiritual matters.[8] [*IJ* 2]

In 1529 in Paris, Pedro Ortiz charged Ignatius with leading some students astray through the Spiritual Exercises [*FD* 548]. Ortiz was badly informed on the matter [*PSH* 68]. Ignatius went to the inquisitor of his own accord, but the inquisitor, Matthieu Ory, made light of the accusation and did not call him again [*A* 81].[9]

Second Judicial Inquiry in Paris

Ignatius continues in his letter to the king: "Seven years after the investigation in Paris another one was made in the same university; in Venice another; in Rome the final one against the whole Company" [*IJ* 2]. Again we learn more details from Ignatius's account to da Câmara. Before leaving Paris in April 1535 Ignatius heard that the Inquisition had started an action against him again, so once more of his own accord he confronted a new inquisitor, Valentín Liévin,[10] to have his name cleared. The inquisitor admitted a charge had been made but found it too unimportant to give it any attention. He asked to see the Exercises and praised them [A 86].

Escaping the hands of the Inquisition should have been a source of joy, but Ignatius was not satisfied. A new element had entered into the picture, the good name of his companions [IJ 2]. Ignatius did not mind calumny directed against himself, but falsity with regard to the group could be an obstacle to the work they wanted to do. The Paris inquisitor must have been taken aback by the vigorous way in which Ignatius pressed for a judgment in the investigation of his own orthodoxy. When the inquisitor made excuses, Ignatius brought his own witnesses and a public notary to the inquisitor's residence, and the whole thing was put in writing [A 86].

Judicial Process in Venice

The dates relating to this event need careful attention. Ignatius arrived in Venice at the very end of 1535; the companions left Paris on November 15, 1536, and arrived in Venice on January 8, 1537. During the year Ignatius was in Venice by himself he studied theology and, among other things, directed a variety of people through the Spiritual Exercises. Negative rumors about his orthodoxy began to float around the city and many said that his effigy had been burned in Spain and Paris and that he had fled from there [A 92–93]. Having learned a thing or two about tactics in Paris, Ignatius again took the initiative in order to be rid of the ugly rumors. Toward the end of 1536 he wrote to the inquisitor in Paris, Thomas Laurency, who replied on January 23, 1537, with a document that not only sheds more light on Paris but provided Ignatius with written testimony regarding his standing in that city. Laurency, a teacher of theology[11] and also secretary to the inquisitor at the time Ignatius had been investigated, testified that his predecessor, Valentín Liévin, had

> inquired into the life and moral conduct and teaching of Ignatius of Loyola, and we who were his secretary did not see that he ever found anything except what was Catholic and Christian. Furthermore, we know that the said Loyola and Pierre Favre and other friends we have seen always lived

> virtuously as good Catholics, nor did we ever see anything except what was fitting for the very best Christian men. Besides that, the Exercises that the said Loyola gives, as far as we can make out, seem to us to be Catholic. [*FD* 524]

Since all of the companions had already left Paris, Laurency called in two of their friends, Lorenzo García and Diego Cáceres, to testify concerning Ignatius and the others, and also to witness the document he sent to Ignatius in Venice.[12]

The judicial process in Venice was unusual for a number of reasons. The timing was unusual. The charges against Ignatius were made in 1536 and he began to gather data to refute the rumors in that same year. The companions were ordained in June 1537, but the investigation was not completed until October 1537. The investigator was Gasparo de' Dotti, an unusual man to be in charge. He was one of those Ignatius directed through the Exercises [*A* 92], either before or after the charges were made but certainly before the completion of the investigation, since the companions left Venice toward the end of July.[13] He was, moreover, the vicar-general for the papal legate to Venice, Girolamo Veralli. Veralli was eager to ordain Ignatius and his companions to the priesthood, but had to be content with receiving their vows of poverty and chastity on that occasion. As we have seen, he gave the companions extensive faculties to preach and hear confessions throughout the Republic of Venice. Clearly he was not particularly afraid that he might be harboring heretics.

De' Dotti's judgment emphasized that he wanted to put an end to rumors and charges once and for all. He says, in effect, that he has examined all the possible evidence, and "Father Ignatius of Loyola has been and should be absolved and freed from each and every one of the charges reported to us and to our office, as frivolous and empty and false . . . and silence should be imposed just as we now impose it" [*FD* 536–37].

Background of Judicial Investigation in Rome

De' Dotti's "final" judgment notwithstanding, in Rome in the spring and summer of 1538 all these old bones were to rise again, and in an extremely vicious manner.[14] When the companions came to Rome in the spring of 1538 they encountered the preaching of an Augustinian named Fra Agostino Mainardi de Piamonte, a secret Lutheran who later admitted to Lutheranism openly [*L* 53]. The companions contradicted him, and his friends began to attack them. One can feel the hurt in the words Ignatius wrote to his friend Isabel Roser a month after the ordeal was over:

> For eight whole months we have endured the most grievous opposition or persecution we have ever suffered in this life. I do not mean to say that they have molested our persons, or called us before a judge, or anything like that, but by spreading rumors among the people and calling us incredible names, they have made us suspect and hateful to the people, causing a great deal of scandal. The result was that we were forced to present ourselves to the legate and the governor of this city (for the pope had gone at that time to Nice) on account of the great scandal caused to many people. We began to name some who had turned against us and to summon them to state before our superiors the evils that they found in our life and teaching [*vida y doctrina*]. [*IR* 1]

At stake were the *word and example* of the companions. Almost in a rhythmic chant, the next pages present "word" as "teaching" [*doctrina, dogma*], and "example" as "life," "manner of acting," "conduct" [*vida, vita, costumbres, mores*]. After telling Isabel of the activities of the companions in Rome, Ignatius continues:

> So we presented ourselves, and two [of our opponents] were named and called, and one of them found himself before the judges in a position quite contrary to that which he had imagined.[15] The others whom we named to be summoned were so frightened that neither wishing nor daring to appear, they put a lot of obstacles for us about proceeding with the case before other judges. Since they were persons of substance . . . all of them members of the papal court and men of great influence, they associated with so many cardinals and other important personages in the curia, that they caused us to spend a great deal of time in this conflict.[16] At the end of all

this the principal persons were called and appeared before the legate and the governor and testified that they had heard our sermons and lectures, etc., and in all they said they spoke in entire justification of us both with regard to our teaching [*doctrina*] and our lives [*vida*]. At that, although the legate and the governor held us in high esteem, for the sake of these men and also for others, they wanted the affair to be shrouded in silence.[17] [*IR* 4]

The companions, however, pressed on. On July 7 they drafted a petition addressed to the pope, requesting a judicial process. They presented it to the cardinal legate since Pope Paul III had not yet returned from Nice. In proper form they give their names and places of origin, their competence as professors of theology, and state that in Rome they have tried every day to be helpful to the people by preaching, lecturing, and teaching [*FD* 543–44]. Nevertheless, they continue, for whatever reason some people have attempted to ruin their reputation, "claiming perhaps that the said petitioners are teaching erroneous doctrines and leading sinful lives." They state that their petition is not based on fear of their detractors, for their own good consciences rest secure. Their good works, however, "are being impeded," so that "it is to the public interest either that they should be punished properly, if they deserve it, or if they do not deserve punishment, that the evil of the rumors be made clear, lest they be spread amongst the people and cause scandal." Therefore, they ask that a complete inquiry be made regarding both themselves and their detractors, and that proper punishment should be imposed upon whatever guilty parties there may be [*FD* 544–45].

There follows, in the hand of Vincenzo Carafa, the cardinal legate, and signed by him: "By order of our Lord the pope, let the governor hear the case, let him cite witnesses and proceed as the petition requests, and let him administer justice." In yet another hand is written: "Presented to the governor on July 7, 1538" [*FD* 545].

But nothing happened.

Ignatius states in his letter to Isabel Roser: "We pleaded over and over again, according to what we thought was just, that what was good or bad in our teaching [*doctrina*] should be set down in writing, so that the scandal to the people might be removed, but we were never able to obtain this from them, neither as a matter of justice nor as a matter of law" [*IR* 4]. From that time on, however, because of the fear of justice, the talk against the companions ceased, at least in public [*IR* 5].

Pope Paul III returned from Nice on July 24.[18] Ignatius took a new approach. He indicates to Isabel Roser: "Since we were never able to bring it about that a judgment or declaration be made in our case, a friend of ours spoke to the pope after he returned from Nice, beseeching him that a declaration be made on the case."[19] A second step followed swiftly: "Granted that the pope agreed, when nothing happened two of our Company likewise talked to him" [*IR* 5].[20] Finally Ignatius himself pressed the point:

> After he [Paul III] left Rome for a villa in the country,[21] I went there and spoke earnestly to His Holiness alone in his room for an hour. Speaking to him at length of our resolves and intentions, I told him in detail of all the times a process had been instigated against me in Spain and in Paris, likewise of the times I had been jailed in Alcalá and Salamanca. I did this so that no one could give him more information than I had given him about myself, and that he would be more motivated to make an investigation concerning us so that finally a judgment or declaration would be made concerning our teaching. [*IR* 5]

Working under a shadow handicapped the companions. Ignatius was seeking a good name not for its own sake but as a means to an effective apostolate:

> Finally, since to preach and exhort it was very necessary for our men to be in good favor not only with God our Lord but also with the people, and not to be suspect regarding our teaching [*doctrina*] and manner of acting [*costumbres*], I begged His Holiness in the name of all that he enact a remedy, so that our teaching [*doctrina*] and actions [*costumbres*] would be investigated and examined by whatever ecclesiastical judge His Holiness decreed; for if they were to find evil, we would like to be corrected and punished; but if good, that His Holiness show us his favor. [*IR* 5]

Ignatius had another reason for wanting a definitive decision soon, but he could hardly spell it out to the pope at the moment. The time was at hand to admit that a year had passed in which they had not been able to secure passage for Jerusalem. Their vow now required that they offer themselves to the pope. They could hardly do so if they were under a cloud of suspicion, nor could they work well unless they were definitively cleared.[22]

The pope listened and took action. The governor also took action [*IR* 6], and even Divine Providence intervened [*IR* 7]. But more of that later. Let the investigation begin!

Judicial Inquiry in Rome

An inquiry is not a trial. *Process* is a better word, a judicial process to arrive at a decision to be put in writing. Ignatius and his companions are not accused; their accusers have already been called and the accusations retracted. No charges stand against them; rather, they are the petitioners, asking that the accusations against them that have been retracted be proven either true or false. The pope, moreover, who ordered the inquiry [*A* 98], often speaks publicly in their favor, even in their presence, for every two weeks some of the companions carry on theological discussions during the pope's dinner [*IR* 6]. The outcome of the process is clear before it begins. Even Divine Providence brings a few surprise witnesses. Ignatius continues his account to Isabel in these words:

> One rather amazing thing happened here in that regard, namely, that just as it had been reported and bruited abroad here about us that we were fugitives from many lands, especially from Paris, Spain, and Venice, at the very time that the verdict or judgment was to be passed in our regard, there appeared in Rome newly arrived the regent Figueroa, who had seized me once in Alcalá and twice brought proceedings against me, as well as the vicar-general of the papal legate of Venice [Gasparo de' Dotti], who also had instituted a process against me (after we began to preach in the Signoria of Venice), and also Dr. Ory who had himself undertaken proceedings against me in Paris, along with the bishop of

Vicenza where three or four of us preached for a short time, and all these gave testimony on our behalf.[23] [*IR* 7]

The process consists mainly in gathering depositions over a period of more than a month in the autumn of 1538. Witnesses are interrogated at home, in a church, in someone's office. Not all the depositions are kept in the same file and some appear to have been lost.[24] We have no direct testimony, for example, from Figueroa of Alcalá, or from de' Dotti of Venice, or from the bishop of Vicenza. The testimony of the judge from Paris, Matthieu Ory, is the last of the depositions we have.

Ambrogio Catarino. The first depositions are dated September 26, 1538. The first witness is a Dominican from Siena whose religious name is Ambrogio Catarino [Lancelloto de' Politi]. He is an expert theologian, well qualified to pass judgment on the orthodoxy of the companions. Asked about "the life, teaching [*doctrina*], learning, and moral conduct [*moribus*] of Ignatius, Pierre Favre, and other priest companions of theirs," he replies that he is best acquainted with Broët, Laynez, and Salmerón. What he has seen and heard suggests that he can only expect their companions to be like them even though he does not know them as well. His testimony is transcribed in the third person: "Regarding their teaching and their learning, he testifies that since he has often spoken with them about theological matters and about Sacred Scripture, he is fully aware of nothing except solid Catholic doctrine, and furthermore of great zeal for Catholic truth and against all heretics, both the ancient and the new" [*FD* 546]. He testifies that he has heard Laynez preach a number of sermons, "solid doctrine, both erudite and simple," edifying, and conducive "to reform of life and moral conduct" [*FD* 546–47]. As for Broët and Salmerón, they preached in Siena "without any problem or suspicion, and in many they produced fruit in the Lord." With regard to the other companions, he has talked to reputable men about them, and "heard nothing about them except good reports and a good reputation" [*FD* 547].

Pedro Ortiz. The next witness is our old friend Pedro Ortiz. As an old enemy who had reported Ignatius to the Paris inquisitor, he qualifies as an expert witness. He testifies that he has known

Ignatius since Paris, and the others since they first came to Rome as pilgrims, welcoming them and introducing them to the pope. Whatever damage he may have once done to Ignatius, he now quickly repairs. After referring to that incident, he remarks: "Nevertheless, from my frequent associations [*conversatione*] with him, I am aware of his great holiness and ardent zeal to make people turn back to God, his zeal for Catholic doctrine and against anything that smacks of Lutheranism or the other heresies that infect our times" [*FD* 548–49].

Ortiz qualifies as an expert witness on another ground as well. Shortly after Ignatius came to Rome he directed Ortiz through the Spiritual Exercises for forty days at Monte Cassino [*A* 98]. Ortiz enthusiastically refers to Ignatius's "great skill in directing souls which he does by spiritual exercises that are very adept at rooting out vices, bridling unruly passions, acquiring virtues, understanding and avoiding the wiles and temptations of the evil one, promoting divine grace and gifts." Lest anyone miss the point relative to the purpose of the judicial inquiry, Ortiz emphatically adds, "These exercises are Catholic and in accordance with Sacred Scripture and the teachings of the saints" [*FD* 549].

At this point Ortiz attacks head-on the charges brought against Ignatius of heresy and of being a fugitive from Spain. He testifies that Juan Rodríguez de Figueroa, the judge who had investigated Ignatius in Alcalá, happened to stop in Rome recently on his way from Spain to Naples. Ortiz says that he asked Figueroa about Ignatius, and Figueroa replied in the presence of three Spanish witnesses that "he had not found any heresy or error in him or in the companions he had at that time.... He said that if he had found any heresy or error in him, he would not have left it unpunished, but he held him for an upright man, and because at that time he did not know theology or scholastic teaching he forbade him to speak on matters of the faith and the Church, and that he should dress in the ordinary fashion of the day" [*FD* 549].

Ortiz now turns his attention away from Ignatius: "I have also known the rest of his companions, Masters of Paris, from the time mentioned earlier, and I find them upright and learned and well-trained to eliminate the heresies of our times; some of them I judge to excel in virtues both human and divine, and others to be very learned and especially well-trained in Catholic scholastic teaching, and to be in conformity with the traditions of the Church and of the holy doctors." Asked if he knew them culpable of any crime or heresy, he replies, "No, but I hold them to be Catholics, solid men and reputable, so help me God and my conscience" [*FD* 550].

Doimi Nascio. The last witness on the first day of interrogations is a priest from Amelia in Umbria, a doctor in canon and civil law by the name of Doimi Nascio, a man on the lookout for heresy. Like Ortiz, he had not been well-disposed to Ignatius at first. Also like Ortiz, he had later made the Spiritual Exercises under the direction of Ignatius.[25] Nascio testifies that, aware of the companions as new arrivals in Rome, he wonders about them. On his own, and also urged by Cardinal Gianpietro Carafa, he goes to listen to their lectures and their preaching, "precisely to watch and to see if they would stray from the right path and say something that would smack of heresy." Asked if he knows of any crime, especially heresy, of which any of them might be guilty, he replies "that they are rather opponents of the heresy of the Lutherans and others, and in their lectures and sermons they always oppose the sect of Luther, always holding with the Roman Catholic Church and adhering to it, as befits good and faithful followers of Christ" [*FD* 550–51].

Lattanzio Tolomei. The following week, on October 3, 1538, Lattanzio Tolomei, the legate to the pope for the Republic of Siena, makes his deposition. He, too, has made the Spiritual Exercises under the direction of Ignatius. Asked about his knowledge of Ignatius and the companions he says that he had known them in Rome and also in Siena, where they had preached the year before. The archbishop had commissioned him to examine them before they preached, and he had examined two of them. Moreover, "the archbishop himself, in the presence of many different learned men, wanted to hear them preach in his chapel, and from that it was concluded that they ought to preach because they were endowed with good, safe evangelical teaching [*doctrina*], and good lives and conduct [*moribus ac vita*]. . . . In Rome I have associated with them for some months, and I am thoroughly pleased with their teaching and their moral conduct and their way of life" [*FD* 552].

Matthieu Ory, O.P. The next day Ferdinando Díez, a Spanish doctor from the diocese of Palentia, makes his deposition, but adds nothing exciting to what other witnesses have already said [*FD* 553]. Last of all, on October 20, 1538, comes a providential witness, Matthieu Ory, O.P., who had examined Ignatius and his companions in Paris, and whom Paul III had recently named to a special office in Rome.[26] In their early days in Paris, six or seven of the companions had come to his lectures or those of his colleagues. In a fairly lengthy testimony he tells how Ignatius was brought before him in Paris for starting a new sect, and how he had examined him, and had also examined his companions. The testimony continues in the third person, "that in order to meditate they withdrew from people and practiced fasting, and although he told them that they could not start a new way of life without permission from the pope, after making sure of their morals, their lives, and their teaching, he found them free of every suspicion of heresy." After testifying that he found Ignatius not guilty, Ory ends on a supportive note, affirming that "he had not found anything bad in their lives and morals that would be contrary to the faith or to his office, and that he holds them to be good men of good conscience" [*FD* 554–56].

Formal Judgment of Governor of Rome

The witnesses have been heard, the depositions taken. All that remains is for Governor Conversini to draw up a formal judgment [*FD* 557]. Less than a month later it appears, November 18, 1538. In his decree Conversini explains that rumors have been bruited about and accusations made concerning the doctrine [*dogmatibus*] and manner of life [*conversatione vite*] of Ignatius and his companions, each of whom he names explicitly. Some have claimed that their teaching and exercises have been "erroneous, superstitious, and to some extent departing from Christian doctrine." He held an investigation, therefore, examining the accusers first of all. Then he received what were "partially public testimonies and partially judgments handed down in Spain, Paris, Venice, Vicenza, Bologna, Ferrara, and Siena," which were in favor of the companions and against the accusers. Finally, he had witnesses examined "who were without exception of the highest quality from a moral and doctrinal point of view and from their prominence in the community," and the conclusion was "that the murmuring and accusations and rumors spread against them have no foundation in truth." He therefore gives the following judgment or verdict:

> The aforesaid Don Ignatius and his companions have not only not incurred any stain [*notam*] of infamy either in law or in fact, but rather have achieved an even greater splendor in their lives and teaching [*vite ac etiam doctrine sane claritatem*], since we have certainly seen their adversaries make charges that were empty and far from the truth, and very solid men, on the contrary, bear excellent testimony on their behalf.

Finally, he gives the reason for handing down a verdict in the first place, "so that it may be a public testimony on their behalf against all adversaries of the truth, and may also serve as a source of tranquillity for all who might have conceived that unfavorable suspicion against them on the basis of these vilifiers and accusers." He also urges the faithful to accept Ignatius and his companions for what they are, Catholics: "and let every suspicion come to an end, in such a way that with God's help, which we hope for, they may persevere in the same manner of life and doctrine."

These final remarks are very important. Their aim is to bring peace to people of good will who may well have been disturbed at the continuing activity of the companions. For during this time they did not cease from their labors. In his letter to Isabel Ignatius testifies:

> We are very grateful to God our Lord that from the moment we began right up to the present point, we have never failed to have two or three sermons on every feast day; at the same time there were two lectures each day [Favre and Laynez at the Sapienza]; some of us were busy with confessions, others were occupied with giving the spiritual exercises. [*IR* 7]

Ignatius ends his account to Isabel in a remarkable way. There is no self-pity, no self-congratulation. An obstacle has been removed; there is work to be done. But their own efforts have not gone to waste, nor have God's. He is aware of the work that God has done through all that has happened:

> Now that the judgment has been given, we hope to expand our preaching and also our instructing of children; granted that the soil is barren and dry, and that the opposition against us has been great, we cannot say in truth that we have accomplished nothing, or that God our Lord has not been at work—more than our knowledge or understanding will ever be able to grasp. [*IR* 7]

A sigh of relief at last. All these accusations can now be put behind them.

Conclusion

The basis for the rumors against Ignatius was that he had, in truth, been investigated by ecclesiastical authorities in Spain, Paris, and Venice. None of them, however, had faulted his teaching. In fact, he had won the admiration of his judges, if he did not already have it. Even those persons who had reported him or been suspicious of him had become his friends and disciples. The advantage of the persecution of the companions and the official inquiry into the charges against them was that their names were cleared completely and they were free to go about their work without any cloud of suspicion hanging over them. As Ignatius wrote to King John III of Portugal almost seven years later, "In all those eight investigations, only through the grace and mercy of God, never was I reproved for a single proposition, not even a syllable, nor from then on, nor was I given a penance, nor was I sent into exile" [*IJ* 2]. One might conclude that Ignatius is about the most documented non-heretic in the history of the Church! This man whose ideal was the Third Way of Being Humble as expressed in the Spiritual Exercises [167] could not abide any attack on his reputation or that of the Society if it would interfere with the ability to do good for other people. Although he prized a good reputation for the sake of the work God called him to do, at the same time, he put the highest value on the humiliating experiences he had been forced to endure. To King John, a few years after the events, he comments: "The truth is, that the Lord who created me and has to judge me, is my witness forever, that for all the power and temporal riches there are under the heavens, I would not want that all that I have said would not have happened to me, with the desire that much more will happen in the future to the greater glory of his Divine Majesty" [*IJ* 2]. The letter to King John ends in a remarkable passage, one that reveals not only how Ignatius dared to address a royal sovereign, but how deeply he was convinced of the value of being despised for the sake of Christ:

> And so, my lord in our Lord,[27] if anything of the sort should happen there, be prepared, with the boundless mercy and grace that the Divine Majesty has given to Your Majesty in order to serve and praise him better, to recognize his graces. Know how to distinguish the good from the bad, taking profit from everything. The greater desire we can achieve on our part, without offense on the part of our neighbor, to clothe ourselves in the livery of Christ our Lord, (which is opprobrium, false testimonies, and every other kind of injury), the more we will make progress in the spirit and achieve spiritual riches. By them alone, if we live in the spirit, our soul desires to be distinguished. [*IJ* 3]

Ignatius and his companions were alive in the spirit. They did, indeed, experience the Holy Spirit driving them in all that happened to them: the good and the bad, the pleasant and the painful, all was joyful.

2. Without Any Sign of Avarice

The principal vices of the Renaissance were avarice, luxury, and ambition, especially amongst the clergy. This we conclude from sermons of the day, often based on the First Letter of John, the concupiscence of the eyes, the concupiscence of the flesh, and the pride of life (1 John 2:16). Perhaps the text itself made the preachers expect these vices; perhaps the reality drove them to the text.[28] Actually, the principal characteristic of the lower clergy was not their immorality but their poverty. Stripped of their proper benefices, parish priests were forced to demand stipends from their people for every sacred action performed on their behalf.²⁹ As the lower clergy scratched and scraped and clawed their way to survival, the higher clergy were concerned about piling wealth upon wealth. A thorough condemnation of the clerical avarice of the times is found in a sermon by John Colet, dean of St. Paul's Cathedral in London, delivered on February 6, 1512, at the opening of the Convocation of the clergy of Canterbury province. Referring to the "lust of the eye," he maintains that covetousness has so darkened the eyes of the minds of priests that they are blind to everything but gain and then concludes, "Every corruption, all the ruin of the Church, all the scandals of the world, come from the covetousness of priests."³⁰

The companions, on the other hand, took the opposite course: poverty. In Paris they vowed not to accept even legitimate stipends. The deeper they entered into evangelical poverty, the more they sought to abandon even legitimate sources of income, "so that, as far as possible, they might avoid the malicious lies of heretics and give them no grounds for saying that they did something under the appearance of piety in order to bring in bigger and richer and more abundant gains" [*R* 13]. A remark of Lattanzio Tolomei during the judicial process in Rome summarizes the experience of people regarding the companions. He says that after examining two of them in Siena regarding their competence to preach, "I later wanted closer contact with them, and I saw that they had an abhorrence of money and were leading holy lives" [*FD* 552]. No charge of avarice arose in any of the judicial inquiries concerning Ignatius, nor was avarice charged against his companions. From the beginning of his life of begging at Manresa, evidence indicated that Ignatius gave to others much of what he begged.³¹ When the companions discovered they could not make the pilgrimage to Jerusalem, they returned money given them for their passage [*A* 93, *R* 58]. Close observation revealed no shred of avarice in any of them.

3. Without Any Sign of Immoral Conduct

No one could justly charge the companions with avarice, the "lust of the eye." What about the "lust of the flesh?" Undeniably, the lives of the clergy were not always edifying. What is forbidden by ecclesiastical decree reveals what is being done: the carrying of arms, going about at all hours of the night (especially with musical instruments and singing lewd songs), participating in dances and other public spectacles, patronizing taverns and joining in drinking parties, tarrying with prostitutes.[32] In the same sermon quoted above Colet charges:

> As to . . . the lust for the flesh—has not this vice, I ask, inundated the Church as with the flood of its lust, so that nothing is more carefully sought after, in these most troublous times, by the most part of priests, than that which ministers to sensual pleasure? They give themselves to feasting and banqueting; spend themselves in vain babbling, take part in sports and plays, devote themselves to hunting and hawking; are drowned in the delights of this world; patronize those who cater for their pleasure.[33]

In a context where clergy and sexual improprieties were almost synonymous, reputations were in peril. Fingers could easily point at Xavier when a woman who came to him for confession and spiritual direction was found pregnant. Fortunately the guilty party was found. Jean Codure had a similar experience, but his spiritual daughter was discovered with another man [A 97]. Anyone who observed the lives of the companions knew they were not caught in the web of worldliness. As an old man Rodrigues tells the story of one who did observe them carefully, an old woman who spied during the night on Rodrigues and Jay and discovered that they arose in the middle of the night to pray. When asked about them she replied: "Obviously they are saints, and to be commended for their incorrupt morals, their spotless lives, and the purity of their teaching. They do not eat, nor do they drink, the whole night they pray and pour out their supplications. I have seen them, I myself have often seen them while I was spying on them very carefully" [R 74]. This simple soul was not alone in her opinion. Confirming every word is the testimony of Ambrogio Catarino, the distinguished Dominican professor of Scripture in Siena, in the judicial inquiry in Rome. Asked about the lives and teaching of the companions he knew, he replied that he "had not seen anything or heard anything about them except that which pointed to lives and conduct that were proper and religious, profoundly spiritual and exemplary," so he was "not able to think otherwise of their companions," with whom he "had spoken but did not know as well" [*FD* 546].[34]

4. With Great Praise

Schurhammer does not think that the companions are the authors of *Cum ex plurium* since they were not likely to report anything laudatory about themselves. *Cum ex plurium*, however, was written in 1539, very much in the context of the long persecution of 1538, during which the companions had sought out testimonies (words of praise) from every friend they could find. Ignatius was not displeased when he reported to Isabel Roser in late 1538 that the pope spoke highly of them in public [*IR* 6]. They needed a good reputation amongst people in order to be able to preach and exhort effectively.

Religious orders had fallen on bad times, and the companions did not need to find themselves typed along with the crowd. In the heat of passion Carafa probably overstates his case when he says that "all monastic orders are prostrate and afflicted,"[35] but even the very sober *Consilium de emendanda ecclesia* says in more measured tones, "Another abuse must be corrected with regard to the religious orders, for many have become so deformed that they are a great scandal to the laity and do grave harm by their example."[36] In that sort of situation, praise was important. The witnesses who wrote and spoke on behalf of the companions, especially the duke of Ferrara, were not interested simply in turning aside the charge of heresy; they were enthusiastic about the work the companions had done and wanted them to return to their cities to do more. One of the witnesses quoted above in the judicial inquiry in Rome, Doimi Nascio, who began by trying to smell out some heresy in their lecturing and preaching, testifies that he "associated with them frequently," and comments, "I swear by my faith that never have I been able to dig up a thing except what was worthy of all praise [*degna de ogni laude*] . . . and I assure you that I have been amazed at the good and holy lives they lead" [*FD* 551]. A few days later Lattanzio Tolomei adds his testimony in the same investigation, "In the places where they stayed in Siena they were greatly praised [*multum laudabantur*] because of their holy and good lives and because of their moral conduct and their excellent teaching . . . and that is the truth" [*FD* 552].

And that is the truth. As a consequence of the truth the companions find themselves in 1539 plagued [*infestados*] with requests from bishops and others to come to their various countries to work [*IR* 6]. There can be no better recommendation than the truth.

Concluding Reflection

The smoke and the fury, the fire and the confusion that manifest the presence of the evil one described in the images of the Spiritual Exercises [140], could not stand for long against the calm and simplicity of truth. Men of truth and goodness testified against the lies and slanders of envious men, and truth prevailed. The truth made Ignatius and his companions free, free to labor once more in the vineyard of the Lord, digging, planting, fertilizing, pruning, tending most carefully the weakest vines.

Cum ex Plurium outlines the works in which the companions had engaged before the persecution against them began. The list of their activities is remarkable, showing how deeply they were immersed in the priesthood. In fact, they did almost everything that bishops did.[1] They participated in the bishops' ministry of the Word by preaching, exhorting, hearing confessions, giving the Spiritual Exercises. They participated in the bishops' compassionate concern for the suffering members of the flock by serving in hospitals, by moving from one town to another to seek out those who were lost, by carefully instructing in the faith the little ones who were most despised and abandoned.

All of these concerns were to become "experiments" for novices, for followers who wished to join the companions: (1) making the Spiritual Exercises for a month, (2) working in a hospital, (3) making a pilgrimage, (4) doing the lowliest tasks around the house, (5) preaching and hearing confessions, and (6) teaching Christian doctrine to children and the uninitiated [*C* 2:52–57]. These experiments were not to discover whether the novices could do something difficult or even to see whether they could successfully perform the works of the Society, the ministry of the Word and the service of marginal people. Rather, these experiments were to probe their hearts, the depth of their constancy and commitment, to see whether, in the words of the Formula, "they have the spiritual resources to build this tower to completion, according to the Lord's counsel (Luke 14:30), that is, whether the Holy Spirit who impels them, has promised them so much grace that with his help they may hope to bear the weight of this vocation" [*CEP* 3].

One cannot do everything. No matter how skilled and eager the workers, they must make choices that put limits to their ministries. A number of new orders were founded in the sixteenth century with specific apostolic goals. The Theatines (1524) were concerned with reforming the clergy and with the sick and the poor. The Capuchins (1528) devoted themselves to the eremitical life but also engaged in the corporal works of mercy. The Somaschi (1528) took care of orphans and taught Christian doctrine. The Barnabites (1530) worked to reform the evil morals of their day and devoted themselves to a penitent life and to missions amongst the people. The Ursulines (1535) were founded for the education of girls. The Brothers Hospitalers (1571) cared for the sick poor. The Oratorians (1575) were concerned primarily with preaching and hearing confessions. The Camillians (ca. 1582) ministered to the sick. Ignatius and his companions did not specify a field of ministry but limited themselves to what was *more* for God's glory. Thus they had constant need for discernment so they would make their choices in terms of the Gospel.

Masters of Paris, they did not hesitate to challenge one of the more renowned preachers of their day on the grounds of heresy, and through their preaching thwarted him from plundering the vineyard of the Lord. *Priests of Christ,* they sowed the seed of the Word of Christ and administered his sacraments, exhorting, consoling, teaching, guiding in the ways of the Spirit, preparing the future. *Poor men of Christ,* they lived with the poor of Christ, taught the poor of Christ, cared for the poor of Christ. The last of all and the least of all, they gave succour to the last and the least. *Pilgrims,* strangers in a strange land, they sought out strangers and befriended them, welcomed the homeless, consoled those bereft of family and friends. Like Abraham, they practiced hospitality. *Companions of Jesus,* with Jesus they welcomed the little children, the ignorant, the neglected, the searching. They taught them the rudiments of the faith. They showed them the Father's love. Like Jesus, they "went about doing good and healing all who were oppressed by the devil" (Acts 10:38). Like Jesus, they were accused of being instruments of Beelzebul. Like Jesus, they were put on trial. Like Jesus, they were innocent. Like Jesus, they learned obedience through what they suffered. God did not abandon Jesus but raised him from the dead and gave him a name above all names. Nor did Divine Providence abandon Ignatius and his companions but rescued them and raised them up, and also gave them a name.

SECTION THREE

The Joy and Desire of Paul III

Few people are certified nonheretics. The persecution of the companions in 1538 results in a solemn declaration freeing them from any suspicion that hinders their work. The decree declares that they are genuine Catholics who teach solid doctrine and give good example by their lives. Adversity has its advantages. The decree says more. The companions not only enjoy a reputation as solid and untainted. They also, to repeat the words of the governor of Rome, "have achieved an even greater splendor in their lives and teaching [*vite ac etiam doctrine*]" [*FD* 557]. The persecution makes the lives of the companions shine with a new brilliance, and Paul III's praise alerts people to that brilliance long before the investigation ends. Far from wishing to condemn the companions, the pope is so aware of the Spirit at work within them that he sees in the companions hope for the reform of the Church. He is of this frame of mind some months before they ask him to give official approval to their way of living.

Paul III had been struggling with reform and renewal for four years before Ignatius and his companions appeared on the Roman scene. Like everyone else, Paul had limited vision, but he could recognize the creative possibilities in other people. He was pleased to have any help he could get and pleased to encounter help in both the manner of living and the lived example of these pilgrim priests or reformed priests. He would have been very happy to find many more like them. Paul III envisioned more than a change of laws; he sought the interior renewal of each member of the Church, especially the clergy. To see what this renewal meant specifically, we need to probe the workings of the sixteenth-century heart.

THE THIRD *CUM* CLAUSE

cum hec, inquam, de vobis audiremus,
[since, I say, we kept hearing these reports about you]

gaudebamus, vt par est,
[we began to rejoice, as is only right]

ac magnopere optabamus,
[and fervently to desire]

multos, imo omnes, si fieri possit,
[that many people, even all, if possible]

et praesertim clericos
[and especially the clergy]

veteris conuersationis exempla
[would recreate examples of the ancient Christian way of living]

(quod uos facitis) renouare;
(as you are doing)

Structure: The section consists of eight clauses containing a total of twenty-nine words, nine of which are verbs. The opening *cum* clause introduces the main verbs, *gaudebamus* [we began to rejoice] and *optabamus* [we began to desire]. *Gaudebamus* stands alone, but *optabamus* introduces three accusatives as subjects of the same infinitive: *multos* [many], *omnes* [all], and *clericos* [clergy] as subjects of *renouare* [renew]. The object of the infinitive *renouare* is *exempla* [examples], followed by a descriptive genitive, *veteris conuersationis* [of the ancient Christian way of living].

11

The Ancient Christian Way of Living

After a third *cum* clause that summarizes the preceding two, we finally come to two of the main verbs in this long and very complex sentence, *gaudebamus* [we began to rejoice] and *optabamus* [we began to desire]. They are revealing words. They suddenly plunge us into the pope's heart and lay bare his own feelings: (1) his delight in the companions, in who they are and what they are doing, and (2) his longing that others, too, might do what they are doing.

> **since, I say, we kept hearing these reports about you,**
> [cum hec, inquam, de vobis audiremus]
> **we began to rejoice, as is only right,**
> [gaudebamus, vt par est]
> **and fervently to desire,**
> [ac magnopere optabamus]

When Pope Paul III returned to Rome from Nice he began to hear reports about Ignatius and his companions. In July or August 1538 in a private conversation at Frascati Ignatius told the pope of the times he had been investigated in Spain and Paris and Venice. Not only did the pope not condemn the companions in any way, but, as Ignatius writes to Isabel Roser, he "received it all in good part, praising our talents and the way we applied them in good causes." Paul, indeed, did more than praise: "After encouraging us for a time (certainly with the words of a true and genuine pastor), he took great care in ordering the governor . . . to take immediate action on our behalf." Furthermore, "He spoke in public many times in our favor, also in the presence of the Company, (for every two weeks some would go to carry on a disputation while His Holiness was eating)" [*IR* 6].

What words of praise and encouragement did the pope use? The only record suggesting an answer is *Cum ex plurium*. The words attributed to the pope in *Cum ex plurium*, "We began to rejoice . . . and fervently to desire, that many people, even all, if possible, and especially the clergy, would recreate examples of the ancient Christian way of life (as you are doing)," provide a foundation for interpreting his conversation with Ignatius at Frascati and of his public comments concerning the companions: (1) when he praised their talents and the way they applied them, he told Ignatius how glad he was to hear what they were doing, and he praised their ability to apply the Gospel to the concrete circumstances of the day; as a true pastor, he urged them to continue to create for the Church fresh new models of how to live the Gospel; (2) when he spoke of the companions in public he commended their example to others and urged all his hearers, especially priests, to be examples themselves of Gospel living in their daily lives.

This passage provides part of the historical context in which the companions decide to ask for papal approval of their Company: papal enthusiasm that sees in their example hope for a profound renewal in the Church. It has the advantage, moreover, of locating the document in a context of living, feeling people. We learn more from *Cum ex plurium* about the circumstances surrounding the Society's approval than we do from either of the papal bulls solemnly approving it.

We need to examine one by one the words the companions attribute to the pope. In doing so, we shall follow the order in which they appear in Latin.

and fervently to desire,

that many people, even all, if possible,
[multos, imo omnes, si fieri possit]

and especially the clergy,
[et praesertim clericos]
would recreate examples of the ancient Christian way of living
[veteris conuersationis exempla . . . (renouare)]

Each word of the final line is packed with meaning. In this and the next chapter we shall repeat the line, highlighting the words we wish to discuss. We begin with "of the ancient Christian way of living" [*veteris conversationis*].

Today the English word *conversation* normally means some sort of dialogue. A twentieth-century reader of Shakespeare might easily miss the significance of a line in *Richard III* about Hastings and "his conversation with Shore's wife," in which Richard means the adulterous affair Hastings had with Shore's wife.[1] Shakespeare was born less than ten years after Ignatius died. For centuries before either of them, *conversatio* was not so much a word about talking as a word about doing. In the patristic period and the Middle Ages *conversatio* more frequently meant way of life, manner of living, conduct, or morals: the exterior manner of acting that is visible to other people.[2] In *Cum ex plurium*'s context, *veteris conversationis exempla* means models of the ancient way of living, and specifically of the *Christian* way of living.

1. *Conversatio* in Christian Tradition

From earliest times Christians have been called to be pilgrims. A pilgrim, an exile, alone in a strange land and often amongst people who are hostile, is called not to conform to the attitudes and actions of strangers, to the local *conversatio* [way of living], but to live according to the Gospel of Christ: "Beloved, I urge you as aliens and exiles to abstain from the desires of the flesh that wage war against the soul. Conduct [*conversationem*] yourselves honorably among the Gentiles, so that though they malign you as evildoers, they may see your honorable deeds and glorify God when he comes to judge" (1 Pet. 2:11–12). In other words, the Christian way of living [*conversatio*] is countercultural. Paul puts it thus: "We proclaim Christ crucified, a stumbling block to Jews and foolishness to Gentiles, but to those who are called, both Jews and Greeks, Christ the power of God and the wisdom of God" (1 Cor. 1:23–24).

The martyrs of the early Church (and of the Church throughout the ages even to the present day), beginning with the apostles themselves and the people they instructed and baptized in the faith of Jesus, are the best examples of that ancient Christian way of living. Good examples also are those members of the early Christian community who lived in communion with one another, sharing all they had (Acts 4:32). The virgins and the widows and the ascetics of the early Christian ages, by their choice to bear witness to Gospel values in a radical sort of way, became examples for others of the Christian way of living. The movement to the desert and the beginnings of monastic life, which "in a variety of ways expressed a rejection of the conventional worldly values,"[3] provided more radical examples of Christian living. In rejecting conventional values the monks were simply trying to take the Gospel seriously, to live out in a striking manner the Gospel call to everyone. The proper conduct for a monk is the conduct proper for a Christian.

Christian literature often used *conversatio* to translate the Greek *askēsis* meaning either the ascetic life that is proper to all Christians or, more specifically, the monastic life.[4] To identify the monastic life as the ascetic life is to state that monasticism is not an aberration, is not something outside the stream of Christianity, is not contrary to the Gospel: for a monk *conversatio*, the ascetic life or way of living as a Christian, takes the form of the monastic life. To identify *conversatio* with the monastic life exclusively would mean that the practice of asceticism is not essential to the life of ordinary Christians. Earlier we referred to the words of the Pachomian legislation concerning brothers who were considered of proven conduct and faith [*probatae conversationis et fidei*].[5] They had lived like good Christians in the monastery: they had followed the monastic observance, which was nothing more than the Christian observance or Christian manner of life, a radical departure from worldly values.

To lead a life counter to the dominant culture is not easy. It has to be learned and is always a gift. The monastic rule gets one started along the right path. *Conversatio* as the way of living in a monastery is obviously a dynamic process with a beginning, a middle, and an end. Benedict uses *conversatio* that way in his Rule,⁶ which he wrote so that "by observing it in monasteries, we can show that we have some degree of virtue and the beginnings of monastic life [*conversationis*]" [*RB* 73.1]. For one who has made progress there are other guides to help one arrive at the perfection of Christian living. The Rule of Benedict continues: "But for anyone hastening on to the perfection of monastic life [*conversationis*], there are the teachings of the holy Fathers, the observance of which will lead him to the very heights of perfection" [*RB* 73.2].⁷

Benedict's Rule makes a close connection between the monastic life [*conversatio*] and faith.⁸ *Conversatio* is the external manifestation of the faith that lies deep within.⁹ *Conversatio* that flows from faith is bound to differ from *conversatio* that does not flow from faith. Faith that has gone awry, moreover, will manifest itself in *conversatio* that is negative and destructive. Benedict views with dislike the gyrovagues, wandering monks "who spend their entire lives drifting from region to region." He says of them, "Always on the move, they never settle down, and are slaves to their own wills and gross appetites." For Benedict their manner of living is a "disgraceful way of life [*conversatione*]" [*RB* 1.10–12].

The follower of Benedict makes a commitment to a way of life governed by Christian faith by promising "stability, fidelity to monastic life [*conversatione morum*], and obedience" [*RB* 58.17]. Unfortunately, in the course of time *conversatio morum* gradually slipped into *conversio morum*, and it began to look as though Benedict was looking for a conversion in moral conduct when someone entered the monastery. What Benedict expected was not a single moment of conversion [*conversio*] but a lifelong way of living [*conversatio*]. The monastery provided an environment in which one could either begin to live the Christian life or continue to live the kind of life that was expected of all Christians.¹⁰

Some seven hundred years later Francis of Assisi used identical terminology in addressing his community: "The friars' way of living [*conversatio*] amongst people should be such that whoever hears or sees them would devoutly praise and glorify the

Father in heaven." The little brothers heard him so well that when they went out to preach, "seeing their humble and holy way of living [*conversationem*], and hearing their words . . . many came to them and fervently and humbly put on the holy religious habit."[11] Moreover, Francis told his friars, few though they were, that he had a vision of a great multitude who wished to join them in their "way of living [*in habitu sanctae conversationis*]" and in following their rule.[12] *Sancta conversatio*, the holy way of living proper to a Christian, had become a synonym for the religious life. Francis would be the last to say that he was adding anything to the Gospel intended for all Christians.[13]

As for Dominic, the minutes of his canonization process in 1233 preserve the testimonies concerning his "life, activities, and death [*vita, conversatione et transitu*]." One of the persons who testified was William of Monferrato, a close associate, who "lived [*conversabatur*] with him day and night." William believed that Dominic had always preserved his virginity. His conviction was based on observation that included more than listening to Dominic talk, "the good manner of living [*conversationem*] he saw that he had."[14] All of the testimonies, in fact, are based on the fact that the witness had lived [*conversatus*] with Dominic for a long time. Years later Stephen Salagnac (+1291) said of Dominic, "This holy man was a canon by the vow of his profession, a monk by the austerity of his life [*conversationis*], and an apostle by his office of preaching."[15] Once again, *conversatio* is a way of living, not a way of talking. *Conversatio* as living action is *exemplum*, a model for living.

2. The Use of *Conversatio* by the Companions

During the time of Ignatius (and Shakespeare) *conversatio* was undergoing a transformation. Sometimes it meant "conversation" in the modern sense of the word, but it frequently also meant a way of living or way of acting, a way of being with or way of dealing with people.

Ignatius uses *conversatio* and its cognates in the Spiritual Exercises. For example, in the second exercise of the first week of the Spiritual Exercises the exercitant is asked to recall the sins of a lifetime, including "the associations [*conuersación*] which I have had with others" [56]. Since in that context "conversation" does not satisfy the meaning of the text, translators variously render *conuersación* as "relations," "relationships," "intercourse," "dealings," and so on. In the examination of conscience with regard to words, Ignatius affirms that one may speak of the fault of another in the case of "a public error infecting the minds of those with whom we live [*conversa*]" [41]. On the other hand, when he refers to intimate prayer in the third annotation [3] or to the colloquy with Christ on the cross at the end of the first exercise [54], he does not use some form of *conversar* in the sense of dialogue, but rather some form of *hablar* [talk]. Also, Ignatius says of the risen Jesus, "He appeared to the disciples on many occasions, and discoursed [*conuersaua*] with them" [311]. Obviously, Jesus did far more than converse or discourse with the disciples on the road to Emmaus, with Thomas in the upper room, with Peter by the lakeside; he dealt with them in an intimate fashion that went far beyond the words he spoke to them.

Certainly *conversar* implies much more than merely carrying on a conversation. As Ignatius dictated to da Câmara: "At this time he associated with [*conversava*] Master Pierre Favre and Master Francis Xavier, whom he later won for God's service by means of the Exercises" [*A* 82]. Pierre Favre's *Memoriale* confirms this point in the way he uses *conversatio*. In recounting his experiences up to 1539, Favre expresses his gratitude to God for the grace of rooming with Ignatius: "For when it was thus ordained that I should tutor this holy man, I modeled myself on his exterior way of living [*exteriorem conversationem*], and then on his interior way [*interiorem*]" [*F* 8]. Pierre was not mimicking Ignatius's way of speaking, as is clear from the context:

> Since we were living in the same room, eating at the same table, sharing the same purse, and since he was my guide in spiritual matters, providing me with a way of ascending to a knowledge of the divine will and also of my own, we finally were made one in desires, in will, in the firm determination of choosing this life that we now have. [*F* 8]

Favre explains the way they lived, frequenting confession and communion, daily making an examination of conscience:

"About four years passed for us in this way of living [*in tali conversatione*], associating [*conversantes*] with others also who were of the same mind" [*F* 10]. Their conversation or dialogue did not last for four years, but their way of associating did.

To sum up, accustomed as Pope Paul III is to the conversation typical of the salons of noblemen and churchmen alike in his day, he is delighted to encounter in the companions that holy way of living [*conversatio*] typical of the Christian who lives the Gospel. False worldly values in sixteenth-century Rome of fame and fortune, sensual delights and domineering power had obscured that holy way of living to which the Spirit calls Christian people in every time and in every place. Passion had gone astray; hospitality was misdirected; power was abused; the wealth of the few had become destructive of the many. If reform was to come to the Church, as Paul greatly desired, he needed and welcomed contemporary models of how to live the Christian life. He needed not only good talkers, preachers who could move others by their word, but also those who by the example of their lives could stimulate change and bring new life to the Church.

12

Ecclesia semper reformanda
[A Church Always in Need of Renewal]

1. The Need for Examples

Because Pope Paul III sees the Spirit of God guiding the companions along ancient paths in fresh, new ways, he begins to see these poor priests of Christ as possible leaders in establishing new examples for his people. As the text states, the pope hopes that people "would recreate *examples* [*exempla*] of the ancient Christian way of living."

Characteristic of the Middle Ages and of the Renaissance was a desire for *exemplars,* models of behavior, heroes and heroines. The verb *eximere,* from which *exemplar* derives, means "to take out, take away, remove." That which has been taken out is a sample [*exemplum*], a specimen, hence an exemplar, an image, a portrait, a copy, a pattern, a model. The Middle Ages so pursued models of behavior as to create a whole literary genre, a rhetorical device called *exemplum,* defined by Jacques Le Goff as "a brief narrative, presented as true and intended for use in a speech, generally a sermon, in order to convince an audience by means of a salutary lesson. The story is brief, easy to remember, and convincing. It uses rhetoric and narrative effects, and it seizes the imagination."[1] The edition of the *Lives of the Saints* that Ignatius probably used at Loyola has a picture of Jesus crucified at the beginning of this book of heroes and heroines.[2] The serious acceptance of Jesus as role model is the first and final act of conversion.

Preachers knew a living example was far more powerful than a literary one and they appealed to good example as the solution to the problem of reform. In John O'Malley's study of the preaching during this period he talks about "the final quality the preachers propose as distinguishing the life of the true Christian, especially if he is a public man. He should be an example to others." O'Malley describes the "mirror-literature" of the time: "the mirror of the good pope, of the good cardinal, of the good bishop," etc., and then he continues: "In panegyrics of the saints . . . the preachers consistently commend the saints' *praecepta* and their *exempla*." He ends with a summary statement:

> The example of God's great deeds, the example of Christ's love and humility, and the example of the learning and virtue of the saints supplied the Christian people with an almost inexhaustible resource of incitements to good and holy living. But more was needed—the good example of contemporaries, especially of leaders in society like princes, bishops, cardinals, and popes. This is what the preachers so often found wanting, and this is what they deplored. This is what they wanted to see remedied by a reform of Church and society.[3]

At least one of the members of Lateran V (1512–17) recognized the root of the problem of reform. In a speech during the fourth session Archbishop Christopher Marcellus of Corfu addressed himself to Pope Julius II and said that the reform of the Church was up to the skill and example of the pope. Whether he was simply repeating the admonition to Timothy (1 Tim. 4:12) and Titus (2:7) is hard to say, but he told Julius that if he would live a virtuous life others would follow his example and the Church would be renewed in all her parts.[4]

In the eleventh session of Lateran V, in its decree on preaching of December 19, 1516, the council demanded that those who proclaimed the Word of God should be chosen because of the good example of their lives [*vitae exemplaritate*].[5] Although Luther soon called for a reform in doctrine, the real need was for a reform in living. The scandalous lives of the clergy, from the pope on down, caused more harm to the Church than any deviations from the truth.

Bad example was more destructive than bad thinking. Josse Clichtove (1472–1543) attempted interior renewal of the clergy, but in his vision he separated the priest from the people. His spirituality was patterned on monastic spirituality, even though monasticism was not basically sacerdotal. His theology of priesthood centered on ritual rather than on the Word, on cult rather than on mission. As a form of renewal it was not sufficiently concerned with ministry.[6]

Alessandro Farnese, elected Pope Paul III in 1534, was deeply committed to reform. When it came to "reform in head and members,"[7] however, his love for his own family blinded him to "reform in the head."[8] Nevertheless, he was convinced of a profound need for "reform in the members." In the first consistory of his pontificate, on March 3, 1535, Paul III urged the cardinals to be examples to others by the lives they led.[9] Soon he began to appoint cardinals who were known both for their learning and for the example of their lives. In 1535 he raised a layman, Gasparo Contarini, a man closely associated with reform, to the rank of cardinal; in his treatise, *De episcopis,* Contarini demands great sanctity of a bishop because "his life has been set before others as an example" [*exemplar*].[10] Paul followed this action in 1536 by naming as cardinals other men dedicated to reform, like Gianpietro Carafa, Reginald Pole of England, and Jacopo Sadoleto, bishop of Carpentras.[11] Around these men he established a reform commission under the leadership of Contarini,[12] placing on it those who passionately favored real change, men like Bishop Gian Matteo Giberti of Verona (sometimes called "the bishop *par excellence* of the Catholic reform"),[13] Bishop Federigo Fregoso of Gubbio, the Benedictine Gregorio Cortese, abbot of San Giorgio Maggiore in Venice, and the Dominican, Tommaso Badia, the Master of the Sacred Palace. Paul also appointed to the commission Girolamo Aleandro, archbishop of Brindisi and papal nuncio, who was interested in reform from an intellectual point of view but lacked the passion of the others.[14] Significantly, Paul did not appoint to the commission those curial canonists who took a more conservative approach and were satisfied with enforcing existing law. What Sadoleto said of Fregoso applied to many of the new appointments: "His life and his learning provide us a solid example of fidelity to the ancient discipline."[15] The thought is close to that contained in *veteris conversationis exempla . . . renouare*. Aleandro for his part praised Paul for calling back to life the ancient model [*vetus exemplum*] and for imitating the examples of the ancient pontiffs and gave assurance to the pope that people would return to the ancient religion.[16]

In its report, "A Plan for the Reform of the Church,"[17] the commission first addresses Paul III, challenging him by stating that the Holy Spirit has given him the role of rebuilding the Church[18] (the same role God gave St. Francis in a vision[19]). Then the authors bluntly point out abuses that must be eliminated. First "is the ordination of clerics and especially of priests, in which no care is taken, no diligence employed, so that indiscriminately the most unskilled, men of the vilest stock and of evil morals, adolescents, are admitted to Holy Orders and to the priesthood."[20] Twice the document speaks about bad example: (1) Cardinals whose work demands their presence in Rome are appointed to bishoprics but are unable to care for the flocks put in their charge. "This practice is especially injurious in the example it sets."[21] (2) Religious orders are in a sad condition, "for many have become so deformed that they are a great scandal to the laity and do grave harm by their example. We think all conventual orders ought to be done away with."[22]

Almost a century earlier, Thomas à Kempis had been aware of the bad example of many, even as he stated that the apostles, martyrs, confessors, virgins, and the Fathers of the Desert "are given as models [*in exemplum*] to us religious and their examples more powerfully spur us on to advance in holiness than the multitude of the lukewarm can entice us to become lax."[23] Ignatius had his own examples from a later time in Francis and Dominic. Dominic was "an example to the friars in all things [*exemplum in omnibus fratrum*]," and was "relentless in pursuing and refuting heretics both by word and by example [*tam verbo quam exemplo*]."[24] Francis was conscious that he was to be a good example to the rest of the friars.[25] He also wanted the friars to be good examples to others.[26]

It is no surprise, therefore, that Paul III is delighted to hear from reliable sources that Ignatius and his companions are outstanding examples of Christian living,[27] nor is it a surprise that he wishes everyone else also would be an example.

2. The Need for Renewal

Even before the companions ask Paul III to confirm their way of living he is well disposed toward them, for he discerns the presence of the Spirit in their lives, and he begins to hope great things from them: "and fervently to desire, that many people . . . *would recreate* examples of the ancient Christian way of living.

The longing for renewal is the heartbeat of the Church. John the Baptist preached a change of heart, a return to the way of the Lord, and Jesus did the same. Periodically the Church experiences a strong need and urge for reform. From time to time an increasing awareness arises of a vast discrepancy between the form of life of the contemporary Church and that of the apostles, martyrs, and early Church Fathers.[28] In earlier ages the desire for renewal centered primarily on personal and monastic reform; in the eleventh and thirteenth centuries the desire extended to the reform of the entire Church.[29] The cry of the Spirit of God in the sixteenth century also was for general reform. Because of their openness to the Spirit, Paul III finds in the companions an impetus to his own desire to renew the Church.

"Ancient" translates *vetus,* something old, of long standing, former, earlier. "Old" suggests wear and deterioration, but there might also be a suggestion of maturity: an old cloak is one thing and old wine something else. In the Corpus Christi hymns of Thomas Aquinas *vetus* means old and worn out and out of date and is in direct contrast with *novus* [new]: "At this table of the new [*novi*] King, the new [*novae*] law's new [*novum*] Pasch puts an end to the old [*vetus*] Pasch. The new [*novitas*] displaces the old [*vetustatem*]."[30] But *vetus* can equally signify that which has proven itself over the years. Renewal has to embrace both meanings, that which is dated and worn out, and that which deserves respect, admiration, and veneration. The New [*Novum*] Testament has surpassed the Old [*Vetus*], but we deeply venerate the Old. A profound discontinuity exists between them, yet also a profound continuity. Renewal breaks with the past, and yet it reaches back to draw the past somehow into the present.

To reform or renew [*renovare*] means to break out of accumulated practices and customs, to discard what is harmful, to add what is helpful, to give new life to what is wasting away, to adjust and accomodate according to the times and circumstances, to change by growing so that a reality becomes more fully itself. Renewal implies something old and something new, a new way of doing in the present that which, once new and exciting, has become dulled and corroded with time. John XXIII called it *aggiornamento*, bringing up to date that which has become tired and worn out.[31]

The Church, when genuinely concerned about Gospel living, does not seek to restore itself to its primitive splendor exactly as it existed in an earlier age. That is to fall into the trap of a literal primitivism or fundamentalism.[32] Nor is it enough to make adaptations here and there in order to make an ancient reality fit better into a modified modernity. The Church's consciousness of itself is in evolution, as is its consciousness of the mystery of Christ entrusted to it.[33] The challenge in each era is to express the Church's experience of itself as it slowly evolves; what is always at stake is a radically new vision of an ancient reality that is in continuity with the ancient vision of that same reality. The spirit and vision of the Church incarnates itself in the concrete circumstances of each evolving age, always a challenge.[34]

Renewal as idea (philosophy of history) and renewal as reality are not the same. The reformer may fall short of his words and ideas, as in Lateran V (1512–17). The reformer also may accomplish far more than his philosophy envisions: a genuine transformation that breaks with the past even as it continues it.[35] Reform is not always thought out; it is simply lived. Reform is often spontaneous and non-reflective; the reformer simply does what needs to be done. Every age needs someone who will not waste energy in fruitless endeavors or in trying to fit into patterns that are already established, but who will simply live the Gospel, creating whatever new structures are necessary to make Gospel values flourish in a society where the old structures are toppling.

Renewal in the Early Sixteenth Century

The end of the fifteenth century and the early sixteenth century witnessed a great desire for renewal in the Church. Not everyone agreed, however, on what it meant or how to bring it about. It was a time of extraordinary piety, it was a time of extreme superstition. It was a time of strong faith but also of enervating heresy.[36] There were holy prelates and power-hungry prelates who lived like princes and fought like pirates. There were prelates who lived in evangelical poverty and prelates whose avaricious grasp of benefices knew no bounds, prelates who valiantly tried to reform their dioceses and prelates who neither knew nor cared about the state of their dioceses, having never set foot in them. There were fervent priests and worldly priests. There were priests who led devout lives of prayer and penance and priests who led dissolute lives of debauchery and drunkenness, celibate priests and priests who lived in open concubinage.[37] There were religious orders, like the Carthusians and Camaldolese, that flourished, and new ones like the Theatines and Capuchins that offered hope for the future;[38] but most of the religious orders were much in need of reform themselves.[39]

Even the preachers who graced the papal pulpit had a low opinion of the prelates who graced the papal curia.[40] As for priests, the injunctions in Giberti's Constitutions, which he drew up for the diocese of Verona sometime after 1527, hint at widespread scandalous activities amongst the city clergy. The city, moreover, was a trap for rural priests: "Many country priests, when they come to the city . . . have gone into taverns from bad motives or in innocence, seduced by the allurements of the innkeepers, procurers and prostitutes tarrying there . . . and have let loose the reins of indulgence and have committed vain and execrable wrongs."[41] Finally, with regard to religious, Gianpietro Carafa manifested his concern for the state of monastic orders, "on which the salvation or destruction of the world depends: salvation if their condition were healthy, as when they were founded, and ruin because they are now broken down and deformed."[42]

The end of the fifteenth century and the beginning of the sixteenth was also a period of rebirth, marked by the rediscovery of ancient values. Many people yearned to return to the sources, to that which was real and solid and enduring. For some thinkers of the time, however, to renew meant to turn back the clock, to dust off the statue stored in the closet and put it back on the pedestal where it was before. As John O'Malley has shown, Giles of Viterbo could speak of the need for continual innovation, meaning the need to return to the past, to recapture a previous age, to find again a particular truth, or reestablish an ancient practice.[43] Moreover, in his prayer for the Fifth Lateran Council, Raphael Brandolini begged that God might reform the city of Rome, that he might call back her customs, institutions, rites, and disciplines "to their ancient integrity [*ad veterem integritatem*], to their original holiness [*ad pristinam sanctitatem*]."[44]

Most of those who spoke at Lateran Council V thought that reform meant to get back to basic norms, to restore the ancient customs, the laws that would put order into the Church and renew morals. As one bishop put it: "The norm of our whole life has been prescribed for us from the prescriptions of the evangelical law, and from the actions of Christ our legislator, so that in them, as in an archetype and exemplar, we can see what we ought to flee and what we ought to follow."[45] The heavy-handed legalism of this passage is obvious. The Gospel is not good news that sets people free, but law that tells them what to avoid and what to do. Christ is legislator rather than shepherd or savior. For most reformers of the very early sixteenth century, to renew the laws would be to renew the Church, and to renew the laws meant to return to the ancient statutes.

The call of Lateran V for observance of laws fell on deaf ears. Luther began to call for something more than a reform of laws, namely, the reform of dogma itself. Adrian VI (1522–23), however, who became pope a year after Luther's excommunication, was not interested in reforming dogma or laws but in reforming lives. As Robert McNally has noted, reform for Adrian was more religious and personal than legal and structural, "its aim was more renewal of the institution through renewal of persons than the renewal of persons through the renewal of the institution."[46] At least Adrian wanted to get at the heart of the matter.

3. New Examples of the Ancient Christian Way of Living

The way of living of Ignatius and his companions stirs something deep within the heart of Paul III. He longs for the Church to come alive, and he yearns to see others do what these reformed priests are already doing: bring new life to ancient patterns, creating new ways of living the ancient way. Again, according to the text the pope hopes for people who "would recreate examples of the ancient Christian way of living (*as you are doing*)."

A verse of the First Letter to Timothy provides a summary of this whole section:

"Let no one despise your youth, but set the believers an *example* [*exemplum*] in speech [*verbo*] and *conduct* [*conversatione*], in love [*caritate*], in faith [*fide*], in purity [*castitate*] [emphasis added]."[47] Timothy, in spite of his youth is to be a model [*exemplum*] for believers. The writer addresses Timothy's impact on the faithful, not on the rest of the world. That impact is to come: (1) in word and action (Timothy is to be a model not only by his preaching and by practicing what he preaches but by his whole way of living); (2) in love and faith (he should live out in love for others his faith that comes from the Word received from God); and (3) in purity (the way he lives will have greater impact than anything he says).

The import and impact of the above sentence is far richer and stronger than in the Douay-Rheims version: "Let no man despise thy youth: but be thou an example of the faithful in word, in *conversation,* in charity, in faith, in chastity [emphasis added]." Whenever *conversatio* is used in the Latin Vulgate, the Douay-Rheims version of the New Testament translates it simply as *conversation,* e.g., Phil. 3:20: "But our conversation is found in heaven." The Greek here is *politeuma,* which would be better translated as citizenship (*JB, NRSV*), or commonwealth (*RSV*), or homeland (*NAB*), or possibly heavenly behaviour, as de Bhaldraithe suggests.[48]

The passage from Timothy provides a format for viewing the apostolic activities of Ignatius and his companions described in the preceding chapters of this book: preaching, exhorting, hearing confessions, giving the Spiritual Exercises, serving in hospitals, pilgrimaging, teaching Christian doctrine to children and the uninitiated, and performing other works of charity, without any sign of heresy or avarice or bad conduct of any kind. Their ministry of the Word falls under *verbo,* but it is ratified by *conversatione,* that is, by the example of their lives. The Word leads them to act and calls others to action as well. They ratify by action, by the way they live, the Word they preach, and what they preach in turn ratifies the way they live, so that Word and action become one in a spiral that leads to God. *Conversatio* includes everything they do. Even their ministry of the Word becomes *conversatio* [Christian living], a model [*exemplum*] for others, because it is linked with action, doctrine lived to the full, so that they are *exempla* in both word and deed:

in speech [verbo]:	*in conduct [conversatione]:*
preaching publicly	serving in hospitals
exhorting privately	pilgrimaging
hearing confessions	teaching children
Spiritual Exercises	works of charity

in faith: without any sign of heresy
in love: without any sign of avarice
in purity: without any sign of immoral conduct

Like Timothy the companions were concerned with preaching and teaching the Word of God. That Word, which expressed their own faith, governed their way of living [*conversatio*] by love, so that theirs was truly Christian conduct [*conversatio*]. They were a model [*exemplum*] for others, not simply for believers, but also for heretical Christians or those entirely outside the faith.

The Companions as Examples of the Ancient Christian Way of Living

When the companions were ordained in Venice in 1537, the ordaining prelate spoke to the people about the need to inquire into the life and behavior [*conversatione*] of those about to be ordained. He admonished the companions themselves that they were to build the house of God by preaching and example. After imposing hands on their heads in silence, he begged the heavenly Father that those ordained might be models of Christian conduct by the example of their way of living [*exemplo suae conversationis*]. When they received their priestly vestments, he prayed that each of them might lead by example the flock entrusted to them.[49] Unlike many in their day, Ignatius and his companions took their ordination seriously. The reports that come to Paul III speak eloquently of that.

In judicial proceedings and private letters the words and deeds of Ignatius and his companions are constantly linked together. De' Dotti, for example, vicar-general of the papal legate to Venice, declares on October 13, 1537: "The said Father Ignatius has been and is a priest of a good and religious life and of sound doctrine, of the highest standing and reputation, who has exhibited learning and good example in this city of Venice up to this very day" [*FD* 537]. On June 28, 1538, the vicar-general of Ferrara writes of Bobadilla and Jay that they had stayed in his city, "celebrating the liturgy, preaching the Word of God publicly to the people, and giving good example" [*MB* 5]. The very next day the duke of Ferrara also writes to the same effect [*MB* 7]. In the Roman inquiry the Dominican, Ambrogio Catarino, testifies of Broët, Salmerón, and Laynez that they were "very zealous, and powerful in example" [*FD* 546]. In this respect the most stirring witness is Doimi Nascio, the priest who had tried to trap them in heresy. He does not use the term good example, but his words trumpet the idea: "I assert to you that I am amazed at the good and holy lives that they live. I have been dealing with religious orders a large part of my life, and never have I been so convinced, or even nearly so, regarding the good and holy and religious life of anyone as I have been of theirs" [*FD* 551].

In the decree proclaiming the innocence of the companions, the governor of Rome stresses that the public should have knowledge of those who contribute to the salvation of many "by the example of their life [*vite exemplo*] and teaching" [*FD* 556]. Those who sow weeds have attacked the companions concerning "the doctrine and manner of life [*conversatione vite*] and the Spiritual Exercises they give to others" [*FD*

556]. Their preaching, their *conversatio* [exemplary Christian behavior], their influence on others, are at stake. Their living in communion with one another and with others, especially the poor, distresses their critics, who charge them with starting a religious order without papal approval [*IR* 8]. Many men can preach; living what they preach makes the companions models for others. Their good example is not limited to an isolated incident or two; their whole lives are their good example. In them and in their whole way of living others can see an example of how to live as Christians.

Thus, the words, *veteris conversationis exempla . . . renouare*, are an intregral part of *Cum ex plurium*, the proposed papal letter approving the way of life of the companions. They say that Ignatius and his companions are living the Gospel to the full, like the martyrs of the early Church, like the early Christian ascetics, like the monks who took to the desert in search of God, like Benedict and Francis and Dominic and others who have founded and renewed religious orders down the ages. Their way of living, their *conversatio*, is like the *conversatio* of the Christians of old.

Concluding Reflection

The way the companions have of abiding in the world, their way of being present, their way of living, of acting, their preeminently Christian behavior, is the ancient *conversatio* renewed. We can see how their lives of constant apostolic activity profoundly renew the patterns of the ancient *conversatio* by comparing the companions' *conversatio* with the monastic life as it began to develop from the end of the third century onward.[1] A monk, according to the etymology of the word, is a person without a spouse, a person with an undivided heart. That is true of the companions, though they are far from being monks: they are totally bent on the service of Jesus Christ, their Lord. What they are renewing is the whole idea of *conversatio*.

The first step in monastic life is *apotagē*, or *apotaxis*, renunciation. The monk must renounce not only evil and Satan, but some good aspects of life as well, summarized in family and riches, what is called *cosmos,* the world. The world, though good, is a source of care and of division. Renunciation, therefore, invites to embracing both chastity and poverty. The purpose is to be *amerimnos,* without care in the world (1 Cor. 7:32-35), to be wholly available for the service of God. That is precisely why the companions renounce the world, but their availability to God takes a different form. For the monk renunciation involves far more than an interior attitude. It also means physical separation, so that the second step characteristic of monastic life is *anachorēsis,* withdrawal from the world. This suggests the desert and the constant battle to maintain both inner and outer solitude and silence, *hesychia*. The desert of the early Jesuit companions is their own heart, prayer, recollection, quiet, maintained not only in the long hours of journeying from one town to another, but even in the midst of their incessant activity once they have arrived. One aspect of the monk's search for solitude and silence is the desire to imitate the angelic life, *bios angelikos*, a life undivided, freed from cares, intent only on the service of God. That idea will find an echo later in the Jesuit Constitutions.[2] This withdrawal of the monk allows of different dimensions, but basically it is a withdrawal from the familiar into that which is strange and unfamiliar. It is *xeniteia*, the state of being a stranger, an exile in a land that is not one's own. Henceforth one is a pilgrim, a foreigner, one whose customs are out of tune with the customs of the land, the natural result of renunciation. That is what the companions choose: to pilgrimage in religion, to use the later phrase of Bobadilla;[3] and in doing so they renew and transform the whole idea of exile.

Indeed, by the way they live [*conversatione*], Ignatius and his companions are creating new [*renouare*] examples [*exempla*] of that ancient way of living [*veteris conversationis*] of which the letter to Timothy speaks. Insofar as they exemplify in their own lives that ancient way of living, they renew or recreate the examples of past ages, bringing them to life again in the context and circumstances and limiting conditions of their own sixteenth century. Ignatius and his companions do not live *like* the apostles or the ancient hermits or the monks of old, that is, they do not model their external conduct on that of those ancient folk. Rather, they live their faith in all the freshness of its meaning in their own day. The words attributed to the pope in *Cum ex plurium*, "*veteris conversationis exempla . . . renouare*," express the hope that they will not be alone in living the ancient way, that all Christians, and especially the clergy, will live out the Gospel in a way that will be vigorous and inviting to others. Ignatius and his companions, unhindered by outworn customs that choked the vitality of religious and priestly life, come as a breath of fresh air to the pope. From them could come new life into the Church. In its deepest being the Church knew what to do, but found itself frozen, fearful of any threats to the status quo. This band of companions who are unafraid of decision offer an example that others might follow.

PART TWO

Part one dealt with the first part of a discerner's task, the gathering of data and reflection on the data to see if the Spirit of God is at work. It described the life of the companions as reported by others to the pope, their interior attitudes and disposition, their work, their reputation. Many recognized them as models of the ancient Christian way of living.

Part two considers the circumstances surrounding the decision to be confirmed or rejected as well as the decision itself, again to see whether the Spirit of God is present. It consists of two clusters of clauses. The first cluster considers different responses to their way of life: (a) the desire of the pope to commend it, (b) the desire of some to follow it, (c) the desire of the companions to preserve it. The second cluster concerns a request the companions address to the pope to bless and approve their way of life and treats of the norms for discerning whether the Spirit of God is present and active.

In each chapter of the two sections of part two the central theme is the lives of the companions. From different perspectives each chapter reveals new richness in their way of perceiving and of living the Christian life.

SECTION ONE

Companions of Jesus

This section continues to lay bare the heart of the pope: he is enthusiastic about the companions and wishes to show some sign of his approval. It also lays bare the hearts of the companions. Through a main verb, *narravit,* we learn that Cardinal Contarini makes a special report to the pope. He reveals the response of others to the companions' way of life. He reveals as well the immediate longing of the companions themselves.

First we consider from a new perspective the way of life of the companions that the pope desires to approve visibly as a model for others, focusing on two qualities of their commitment: *religio* and *pietas.* Then we reflect, again from a new perspective, on the way of life of the companions. Lastly we examine the companionship these friends in the Lord enjoy and how they wish to maintain and develop their manner of living in companionship. They wish to reduce to writing what their experience has taught them is conducive to their purpose. They also wish to bind themselves by vow to live in the way experience has taught them is fruitful.

THE *DUMQUE* CLAUSE

dumque animo voluebamus
[and while we were considering]

aliquod signum edere,
[giving some sign]

quo [. . . declararemus],
[by which we would make clear]

vestram hanc pietatem ac religionem
[that your loving and zealous way of living]

gratam esse nobis declararemus,
[was pleasing to us,]

dilectus filius noster cardinalis Contarinus
[our beloved son, Cardinal Contarini]

narrauit nobis
[informed us]

hoc vestrum vite institutum
[that your manner of life]

et a multis laudari
[was praised by many]

et a quibusdam ita probari,
[and so welcomed by some]

ut illud etiam sequi velint,
[that they also wanted to follow it]

vosque omnes valde cupere
[and that all of you profoundly desire]

ad conseruandam ac perficiendam
[for preserving and bringing to perfection]

vestre Societatis in Christo vnionem,
[the union of your Society in Christ]

illa omnia,
[that all]

que vsu comperistis
[that you have found by experience]

ad propositum vobis finem conducentia,
[conducive to the end proposed to you]

[. . . iam . . . stabilire]
[you now solidify]

scripto iam et obedientie vinculo stabilire;
[in writing and by the bond of obedience]

Structure: The cluster of clauses contains one of the main verbs of this long compound-complex sentence, *narrauit* [he informed]. It begins, however with two subordinate clauses. The verb of the first subordinate clause is in the indicative, *voluebamus* [we were considering], and introduces an infinitive, *edere* [to give], with its object. The verb of the second subordinate clause is in the subjunctive, *declararemus* [we would make clear], and introduces an accusative with an infinitive, *esse* [to be]. The subject of the infinitive, *vestram hanc pietatem ac religionem,* not easy to translate, provides the material for the first chapter. The main verb, *narrauit* [he informed], introduces an accusative, *institutum* [manner of life], as subject of two infinitives, *laudari* [to be praised] and *probari* [to be welcomed], and a third accusative with an infinitive, *vos cupere* [you desire]. *Cupere* itself introduces another infinitive at the end of the cluster, *stabilire* [to solidify]. A prepositional phrase containing two gerundives, *conseruandum* [to be preserved] and *perficiendam* [to be brought to perfection], expresses the purpose of *stabilire*.

13

Prophetic Commitment

This chapter continues to answer the question: what words did Paul III use to praise the companions even before the end of the Roman inquiry into their orthodoxy and orthopraxis? Picking up the last lines already considered, the text continues:

> would recreate examples of the ancient Christian way of living (as you are doing);
>
> **and while we were considering**
> [dumque animo voluebamus]
> **giving some sign**
> [aliquod signum edere,]
> **by which we would make clear**
> [quo (. . . declararemus)]
> **that your loving and zealous way of living**
> [vestram hanc pietatem ac religionem]
> **was pleasing to us,**
> [gratam esse nobis declararemus]

Paul III, anxious for reform, is pleased with the companions. The companions can introduce this remark into the proposed letter only if the pope has revealed his mind and heart to them, or if someone else has reported a public or private comment the pope has made. The text pictures the pope as mulling over a sign he might give of his pleasure in the companions. In them his dream for the Church is taking concrete form. He has already given a sign of his esteem by appointing them teachers of Christian doctrine in the schools of Rome [*IR* 10]. Now he wishes to do more. He wants to show that he is pleased with their *pietas* and *religio*.

Pietas is not easy to translate, nor is *religio*. Piety simply will not do, nor will *religion*.[1] Together, however, they sum up the life of a prophet: that loving fidelity to God and to God's Word that is the proper response to God's own loving fidelity to his Word and promise. A prophet is one whom the Spirit of God impels to speak and to live the truth. By word and act the prophet defies false gods, challenges public morality, and confronts human sinfulness with justice and compassion. The weight of God's Word is not easy to bear. *Cum ex plurium* has already outlined the prophetic manner of living the companions have chosen in response to the impelling action of the Holy Spirit.

Context is important here. The demonstrative pronoun "this" [*hanc*] is the key to understanding the phrase which in its fullness reads "this loving and zealous way of living of yours [*vestram hanc pietatem ac religionem*]". "This" forces us to look back at the companions' prophetic way of living: their total commitment to the service of Christ and his vicar (1st *cum* clause) and the zealous way of life their works manifest (2d *cum* clause). Any temptation to equate *pietatem* with the first *cum* clause and *religionem* with the second must yield to the fact that each word refers to the reality described in each clause. In translating we have treated the two words as a hendiadys, the expression of an idea through two nouns, better translated in English by a noun and an adjective, for example, "God's merciful goodness," for "the mercy and goodness of God." Thus *vestram hanc pietatem ac religionem* means something like *this loving and zealous way of living of yours*.

We look now more closely at the words to see how they can have those meanings. We also examine how the companions use them, for use frequently determines meaning.

1. *Pietas*

Pietas has a noble history. The ancient Romans praised *pietas* as reverence and respect for the gods, but also for one's country and one's parents. *Pietas* does not appear in Latin translations of the Gospels, but it appears in the pastoral letters, where it is not limited to cult, as it often is with the Greeks, nor to the fulfillment of the law, as in Judaism. It is not one virtue among many others but comprises a whole manner of life, a way of living the Gospel to the full.[2] *NRSV* and Douay-Rheims translate it as *godliness,* the lived relationship of a human being to God as creator and redeemer. As the centuries pass *pietas* grows, sometimes containing but always surpassing its ancient roots. *Pietas* expresses proper reverence and respect for God but also an attitude of goodness and kindness and love toward all others.[3]

Pietas does not appear frequently in the companions' writings, though Ignatius uses it on occasion and Rodrigues more frequently. For example, Rodrigues says that the companions, by their rejection of stipends, wished to avoid giving any occasion for heretics to accuse them of seeking riches "under the appearance of piety [*pietatis*]" [*R* 13], under the pretense of seeking God. In simple words Rodrigues also paints a picture of the companions exhausted on their pilgrimage to Loreto. One of them, like Jesus, looking around, was "moved by compassion [*pietate*] for the others who were so weak and feeble and deprived of human help" [*R* 49]. The comment of Rodrigues that in Pavia Codure and Hozes "discharged the duties of piety [*pietatis officia*] very carefully" [*R* 68], reveals how far beyond the ancient conception *pietas* had grown. Today we might say that they "discharged their priestly duties with untiring zeal." In this context *pietas* includes their worship and reverence of God and deep compassion for people, both prayer and fasting and an abundance of good works. That sort of zeal attracted other men to the Society. Twice Rodrigues links *pietas* with *studium* [zeal, eagerness, desire], adding in each case a word suggesting fire. He speaks of those priests who want to join the companions, describing them as endowed with virtue and "on fire with a burning zeal [*pietatis studio incensi*]" [*R* 83].

In the evolution of the word, this expansion of *pietas* beyond one's own circle is less striking, however, than the extension of *pietas* to express God's attitude toward us. *Pietas* is no longer a simple human virtue but a divine attribute, the kindness and goodness and benevolence of God toward human beings.[4] Thus Rodrigues refers to the "remarkable providence and compassion [*pietas*] of God" [*R* 2]. Ignatius uses the Spanish cognate *piedad* in the Spiritual Exercises in this sense of God's faithful and enduring love. In the colloquy at the end of the meditation on hell he writes, "He has shown me, all through my life up to the present moment so much pity [*piedad*] and mercy" [71]. Ignatius uses piedad in this same sense when he writes to Gianpietro Carafa in 1536, "Beseech him [God] that through his usual mercy [*piedad*] and bountiful grace . . ." [*EI* 118]. Although in his early letters Ignatius's favorite word in relation to God is *bondad* [goodness] rather than *piedad,* in this instance, however, he had used *bondad* in the preceding line.

If *pietas* resides primarily in God, then our *pietas* toward others is but a reflection of God's.[5] In the Contemplation to Attain Love in the Spiritual Exercises Ignatius uses *piedad* to express that reflection in us of God's unconditional love when he lists all the good gifts that descend from above after the manner of divine power: "justice, goodness, piety [*piedad*], mercy, and so forth" [237]. The passage evokes the covenantal love between God and his people expressed in the Hebrew word *hesed,* variously translated pity, mercy, compassion, designating the mutual relations that exist between relatives, friends, and allies. *Hesed* often joins with *emet,* truth, fidelity, sense of loyalty. The fidelity of God calls forth the fidelity of the people, the *piety* of God (his fidelity to himself and all he has created) challenging his people to a similar *piety,* steadfastness in love and service.[6]

Thus for the companions *pietas* evokes images of fidelity and compassion and commitment and dedication and selfless self-giving. *Pietas* embraces not only all that the first *cum* clause contains about the extraordinary commitment of the companions to the service of Christ and his vicar on earth, but also all the zealous works the second *cum* clause enumerates.

2. *Religio*

In ancient Rome *religio* was sometimes a synonym for *pietas*.[7] The ancients disagreed on the etymology of the word, Cicero arguing for *relegere* [to go over again, to reread],⁸ Massurius Sabinus for *relinquere* [to leave behind],⁹ and Lactantius for *religare* [to bind].

Lactantius (c.240–c.320 A.D.) sounds almost contemporary with modern psychology in his emphasis on bonding. He writes, "The name of religion [*religionis*] is taken from the bond of fidelity [*pietatis*], because God has bound man to himself [*religauerit*] and secured him in fidelity" [*pietate*].¹⁰ The link Lactantius makes between *pietas* and *religio* offers a key to understanding and appreciating their presence together in *Cum ex plurium*. St. Augustine (with modern etymologists) opts for Lactantius when he writes: "That is the true religion [*religio*] by which the soul binds [*religat*] itself in reconciliation to God alone, from whom it has sundered itself by sin."¹¹

Whatever the derivation, the most basic meaning of *religio* relates a person in some way to the gods or God. It expresses reverential awe, an awe that could be exaggerated or perfectly balanced. For non-Christian Latin authors *religio* comes to imply interior exactness, possibly scrupulosity or excesssive anxiety, even superstition. In its better moments *religio* moves toward a respect for what is sacred, conveying the idea of religious feeling and awe. *Religio* also becomes objectified as the religious observances themselves.¹² For Christians, however, worship is such an all-absorbing occupation, going far beyond ritual and ceremony, that they begin to use *religio* for a way of life in the service of God. The Epistle of James speaks of religion that is worthless and religion that is pure and undefiled (James 1:26–27).¹³ Religious cult and ritual are empty unless they accompany concern and action for others. *Religio* is superficial unless it becomes a way of life. *Religio* is the Christian life, the life demanded by baptism.

As time passes and Christians develop a variety of ways of manifesting and expressing the Christian life, the monastic way of life gradually becomes a favored way of living out the ascetical or *religious* life. Benedict does not use the word *religio* in his Rule. Nevertheless, terms such as *religio* [religion, religious life] and *religiosus* [religious person] begin to be applied in a technical sense to monks or to those who choose to be engaged in more ecclesiastical, as opposed to secular, roles in society.¹⁴ Determining whether an author is speaking precisely of the monastic life or in general of the ascetical life is not always easy, for the monastery was simply a place where one might more easily lead the life of asceticism [*religio*] to which all Christians are called.[15]

Over the centuries four basic meanings develop for *religio:* (1) the Christian or ascetical way of life, (2) religious fervor, genuine devotion and commitment to God, (3) the kind of life lived in a monastery, and (4) a religious order or body of people living in a manner (following a rule) approved by the Church.

In the Carthusian *Consuetudines, religio* has all four meanings: (1) the Christian religion or way of life [80.12]; (2) religious observance or fervor [55.1]; (3) the religious life lived in a monastery [35.1]; (4) the religious order itself [22.2; 36.1; 41.3].[16] The first three meanings are clear also in early Cistercian documents. All three, in fact, can be found in one paragraph of the *Exordium parvum* that uses *religio* four times.[17] In the Franciscan sources perused for this work, on the other hand, *religio* refers mainly to the last three meanings found in the Carthusian documents. The same is true of papal documents concerning the Dominicans and the Dominican Constitutions themselves. Some of these meanings blend into each other. One author, for example, translates *religio* in Canon 13 of the Fourth Lateran Council (1215) as *religious order,* while another translates it *religious rules and foundations.*[18] The religious order, after all, consists of persons living a particular way of life, and religious observance implies the religious way of life and blurs into religious fervor.

Thus, within the Christian religion [*religio*] is the religious life [*religio*], as opposed to life in secular society, and within the religious life [*religio*] are many ways of life or religious orders [*religiones*], each with its own particular way of leading the religious life. We conclude that by the thirteenth century the use of the term *religio* has become standardized. The same meanings prevail in the papal and conciliar documents of the early sixteenth century,[19] and remain current to the present day.

The Companions and religio

Ignatius and his companions inherit the language of the Middle Ages. Although a first glance suggests that they use *religio* only for religious order, and the religious life followed by the religious order, Rodrigues shows that they are familiar with religious fervor and commitment, a zealous way of living completely dedicated to God and neighbor.

Ignatius. In Jerusalem the Franciscan provincial tries to discourage Ignatius from staying there, arguing that his order [*religión*, the Spanish cognate for the Latin *religio*] has to ransom captives imprisoned by the Turks [A 46]. In Alcalá, Figueroa tells Ignatius and his temporary companions to wear different clothing, for "since they were not religious [*religiosos*], it did not seem right for them to go about all in the same habit" [A 58]. In Barcelona Ignatius sometimes ponders over whether "he would enter a religious institute [*religión*] or go about the world. When thoughts of entering an institute [*religión*] came to him" [A 71], he considers entering a decadent one so he might suffer more. Writing to Isabel Roser about the persecutions they suffered in Rome in 1538, Ignatius divulges a false accusation that they "were forming a community or religious order [*congregación o religión*] without apostolic authority" [IR 8].[20] In this sense of "religious life" Ignatius uses the Spanish word *religión* when he writes in the Spiritual Exercises, "to enter religious life" [14], and "to choose religious life" [15], "strongly praise religious institutes [*religiones*]" [356], and "praise the vows of religion]" [357]. In all of these religious order and religious life are more or less interchangeable.

Rodrigues. Simão Rodrigues writes about a priest whom the Society refuses to admit. He becomes a Capuchin, "where he passed his whole life in great religious fervor [*in summa religione*]" [R 96]. Rodrigues twice refers to waiting for a whole year to find a ship to Jerusalem in order to fulfill their vow: "The Fathers therefore, since all hope of sailing that year had been taken away because of the outbreak of war, decided to wait a whole year in order to evince the binding force [*religionem*] of their vow and to discharge their promise" [R 61]. *Religio* here draws on Lactantius's definition of that which binds a person to God, but the whole passage evokes also a sense of commitment and fidelity on the part of the companions, of a desire on their part to fulfill the vow. It evokes, not scrupulosity, but that whole range of sentiments that bespeak consecration to the service of God. Rodrigues joins *pietas* with *religio* when he tells of his work with Codure in Pavia and how they labor "that the hearts of the citizens of Pavia would be formed in genuine *pietate and religione*" [*R* 70]. Both words evoke the covenant response to God's enduring love [*hesed*], zeal for God and zeal for their neighbor. What they live themselves they try to communicate to others. Consciously or unconsciously, they are models for others, and are moving others to create new models of the ancient Christian way of living.

From all the evidence we conclude that *religio*, like *pietas*, embraces not only the way of life that produced the good works of the second *cum* clause, but also the profound devotion to Christ and his vicar envisaged in the first *cum* clause. Put the two together and we have a way of life marked by extraordinary commitment and fidelity to both God and his people.

Conclusion

In the context of *Cum ex plurium*, *religio* cannot mean "religious order" or "religious life"; at this point Paul III knows the companions as secular priests. "Religious fervor" comes closer, provided it embraces this whole way of living in a worshipful manner, their whole way of living the Gospel. Linked with *pietas*, which refers to their loving fidelity in the service of Christ and his vicar on earth, *religio* refers to the fervent and zealous way they have lived out that *pietas* in practice. Their *religio* is not primarily cult, ceremonies, and observances. But their *religio*, pure and undefiled, includes a long list of activities straight out of the Gospel, like preaching, teaching, works of charity. Their *pietas* and their *religio*—their loving and committed way of life, their prophetic commitment to serve Christ and his vicar in serving people with love—this is what Pope Paul III finds pleasing.

14

Vite institutum:
A Way That Leads to God

After reflecting on how Pope Paul III regards the companions, we turn now to how other people respond to their manner of life. We consider first their manner of life and then the response they receive.

> and while we were considering giving some sign
> by which we would make clear
> that your loving and zealous way of living
> was pleasing to us,
>
> **our beloved son, Cardinal Contarini,**
> [dilectus filius noster cardinalis Contarinus]
> **informed us**
> [narrauit nobis]
> **that your manner of life**
> [hoc vestrum vite institutum]
>
> was praised by many . . .

Contarini's action forms the third independent clause in this long sentence at the beginning of *Cum ex plurium.* The first two stood side by side in part one, section three: "We began to rejoice . . . and kept desiring . . ." The sole source for our knowledge of Contarini's action in this instance is

Cum ex plurium itself. Other documents reveal that he had made the Spiritual Exercises under Ignatius and was a close friend of all ten companions before they asked for papal approval. None of the other sources narrating the events preceding the oral approbation of the Society, however, mention this visit to the pope.

In this and the following chapter we are dealing only with what *Cum ex plurium* indicates Contarini said [*narravit*] to the pope. His remarks cover two areas, what other people say about the companions' way of life and the desires of the companions themselves. The next chapter considers the companions' desires. The present chapter considers Contarini's remarks about other people: (a) many people hold in high esteem the manner of life [*vite¹ institutum*] of the companions; (b) some do so to such an extent as to want to join them.

In other words, many people see the Spirit of God at work in the companions, and the same Spirit who impels the companions impels some of these people to wish to join them in companionship. The manner of life of the companions is what people admire; their manner of life is what the companions write down in the five decrees that form the heart of *Cum ex plurium,* the five decrees now known as the Formula of the Institute [*formula instituti*].

1. *Vite institutum*

Latin and English are not far apart on the meaning and use of *institute*. To institute [*instituere*] means to establish, to determine, to organize, to initiate, to instruct. An institute [*institutum*], on the other hand, is that which has been established. It can be an organization or a rule, an institution; or in the plural: a set of precepts or a summary of laws, for example, the *Institutes* of Justinian, which summarized law in the Byzantine empire, or the *Institutes* of Cassian, which set down the principles of monastic life. In English an institute can be a meeting, like the pastors' institute or teachers' institute, especially one in which some instruction takes place. In Latin *institutum* can be a plan, a use once current in English but now obsolete.[2] The step from plan to plan of life is slight, with *vitae* [life] or without it.

Institutum *in Christian Tradition*

In his Latin translation or paraphrase of Athanasius's *Life of Antony*, Evagrius reaches for *institutum* to translate that ever-evasive word, *askēsis*, the ascetical life or the life of a monk.[3] Evagrius also uses *institutum* to translate other Greek words, for example, *politeia*, with the same sense of monastic life or ascetical life: "to find an example in the life [*ex instituto*] of the great Elijah."[4] These meanings come together in an important work in the monastic tradition, the *Institutes* of John Cassian. *Institutum* as Evagrius uses it is one of Cassian's most important words: an ascetical teaching, monastic doctrine, a principle that has been established on how to live the monastic life.[5] Cassian founded a monastery in Marseilles. The purpose of his book, *Instituta coenobiorum*, is to place his monks within the established monastic tradition. The *Institutes* are the ascetical teachings that the fathers of the desert in Egypt and the monks of Palestine and Mesopotamia established and observed and handed down. When instructions or teachings become normative, they make up a rule of life.[6]

The Middle Ages continue to use *instituta* in the sense of precepts or laws, as in *instituta canonica* [canonical precepts or decrees] and *canonum instituta* [decrees of the canons].[7] Far more than dry decrees, however, *instituta* are principles of living. As *religio* grew from cultic practices to a way of life and came to mean a religious order, so also *institutum* grew from a precept to a teaching to a whole way of living, and it also came to designate a religious order, or formally approved religious body.[8] More frequently, however, *institutum* refers to the rules and customs and practices of a religious order or approved religious group, the rule in all its ramifications, the whole manner of living proper to a particular order or religious body. For example, a Latin life of St. Bruno (+1101), the founder of the Carthusians, says that the Father, Son, and Holy Spirit dwelt in Bruno, "for the architect of this sublime and difficult way of life [*instituti*] for future ages himself also needed to excel in the special gift of heavenly grace."[9]

Context, of course, determines how to translate. A Cistercian document, for example, refers to the Rule of Benedict as *instituta* [precepts, teaching, instructions = rule].[10] As *institutum* in the singular can mean a whole way of life, so *instituta* in the plural can mean the established instructions on how to live that way of life. The Cistercians entitled one document: "The Institutes [*Instituta*] of the Cistercian Monks Who Departed from Molesme."[11] Subtle and not so subtle shifts in meaning are taking place here. Whereas the *instituta* of Benedict mean his Rule, the *instituta* of the Cistercians indicate the customs that have grown up in the manner of living out the Rule.

The Companions of Ignatius

The presence of *vite institutum* in *Cum ex plurium* indicates that even though Ignatius and his companions are setting out on a new venture, they have already established a way of living that other people recognize as a particular way of living the Christian life.

Even when the various companions-to-be come to know Ignatius in Paris, they discover he is already living in a way they can adopt as their own manner of living. Favre, for example, describes his confusion before he had set his heart "on the way of life [*instituto vitae*] that the Lord had given [him] through Ignatius" [*F* 14]. Rodrigues recalls the days of the companions in Paris when they were making the Spiritual Exercises: "After each of them freely and of his own accord had decided to dedicate himself wholly to the service of God and to the aforesaid way of life [*vitae instituto*], then it came to him that others also had consecrated themselves completely to a similar way of living [*vivendi rationi*]" [*R* 9]. Further on he indicates that during the period when they were falsely accused in Rome Paul III had investigated them thoroughly: "The Pontiff, who did everything wisely and prudently, had already seen to it secretly that the life [*vitam*] and manner of living [*institutum*] of the companions should be examined" [*R* 84]. In this passage *vitam* may refer to their moral conduct, and *institutum* to their way of living that distinguishes them from others. On the other hand, in this context both nouns likely mean a way of life. Prior to

1539, the way of life of the companions is not yet a "religious institute" nor have they written down their "institute" in the sense of rules and decrees and customs, but beyond all doubt they have established their manner of life [*institutum*].[12]

To sum up, through normal usage new meanings evolved for *institutum:* customs, precepts, instruction, way of life, religious order, religious observance. *Institutum* evolved from a day-to-day way of living to a rule, a way of life to be lived. What the Society of Jesus calls the Formula of the *Institute* is the written form of the way of life Ignatius and his companions lived. *Institute* is, indeed, a governing norm, but the word refers primarily to a manner of living, a way of life, a particular way of being Christian.

2. The First Followers

The companions describe their institute in the Formula as "a certain way to him (God) [*que via quedam est ad illum*]" [*CEP* 2]. How did other people respond to it?

> Cardinal Contarini informed us
> that your manner of life
>
> **was praised by many**
> [et a multis laudari]
> **and so welcomed by some**
> [et a quibusdam ita probari]
> **that they also would like to follow it,**
> [ut illud etiam sequi velint]

We have already seen how some people lavished praise on the companions. Their way of life impressed people. Their way of life challenged and rejected the base standards and ideals of the times; their way of life enflamed and satisfied the deepest longings and desires that people experience. Some were so impressed that they wanted to join the companions. In the letter he wrote to Isabel Roser in late 1538, Ignatius mentions "four or five who are determined to be in our Company, and they have persevered in this determination many days and many months" [*IR* 8]. We have met some of them already.[13]

Polanco lists Pietro Codacio among those Ignatius directed through the Exercises in his early months in Rome [*PSH* 83]. Da Câmara informs us that on that occasion Codacio went three days without food, although he loved to eat and enjoyed delicacies.[14] A priest from the town of Lodi in Lombardy, he knew the papal curia inside out. Although his income was abundant, he abandoned it all and used his considerable talents running the financial affairs of the young Society as its first procurator [*PCh* 11].[15]

Another early new companion was Bartolomeo Ferrão, who is of special interest since *Cum ex plurium* is written in his hand.[16] A Portuguese of noble birth from the town of Castellobranco in the diocese of Guarda, he made the Exercises and joined the companions in 1538. He was so indifferent (in the sense of the Spiritual Exercises) that Ignatius nicknamed him *El Intentable,* perhaps "the man who is ready for anything." Upon Ferrão's death Polanco succeeded him as secretary of the Society.[17]

A third new companion was Francisco Estrada, who was born in the town of Dueñas in the diocese of Palentina, Spain. With the help of Dr. Ortiz, he took a position in the household of Cardinal Gianpietro Carafa, though he was only in his teens;[18] he met Ignatius at the cardinal's. When the cardinal let him go he took off for Naples to engage himself in some military fashion. On his way he encountered Ignatius, who was returning from Monte Cassino after directing Dr. Ortiz through the Spiritual Exercises there. Ignatius turned Estrada's life around by bringing him back to Rome and introducing him to the Exercises. As a scholastic Estrada was expert in adapting them to different people. He also was an eloquent speaker.[19]

Ignatius was somewhat modest when he mentioned four or five who wanted to follow them. Dr. Ortiz himself wanted to join the Company, but his excessive corpulence made him unfit for its rigorous labors [*PV* 96]. We have already seen the desires and troubles of Miguel Landívar and Lorenzo García.[20] They had a hard time giving up. García wrote from Paris to Ignatius in February 1539, regretting his part in the persecutions of 1538, asking for news, and ending with the statement: "Since I am no good for anything else, I will ask you to take me as cook" [*EM* 16]. Diego de Cáceres delivered the letter, a young student who worked so closely with the companions that in 1539 he actually signed the document *Determinationes Societatis* [*C* 13], but he did not persevere [*PV* 68]. Others, too, wanted to join the Company, for example, the brothers Diego and Estevan Eguía, who had made the Exercises under Ignatius in Venice and wanted to follow his way of life [*PSH* 62]. Antonio Araoz, the nephew of Ignatius who brought *Cum ex plurium* to Tivoli for Contarini to read to the pope, also wanted to join. He made the Exercises before the confirmation of the Society [*PSH* 147], living with the companions for almost a year during that period.[21]

These names are enough to show that the new Company was attracting both priests and young students facing many years of study. Whether the companions accepted them or not, whether they persevered or not, is irrelevant; they wanted to join the Company. Their desire to join caused trouble for Ignatius. He comments to Isabel Roser, "We do not dare to admit them, for this is one point, among others, that they are making against us, that is, that we are accepting others, and that we are establishing a community [*congregación*] or religious order [*religión*] without apostolic authority" [*IR* 8]. They had, indeed, been looking for like-minded people. Laynez tells us that while waiting for passage to the Holy Land in 1537 they scattered throughout the various universities of Italy "to see whether our Lord would deign to call any student to our way of life [*instituto*]" [*L* 42].[22] Laynez had also, however, made something else clear: "Our intention from Paris on was not to start a community [*congregación*], but to dedicate ourselves in poverty to the service of God our Lord and the profit of our neighbor by preaching and serving in hospitals, etc." [*L* 36]. Finding new companions for their work was one thing; establishing an official ecclesiastical organization was something else. When they started thinking about a religious institute they had to be more cautious about receiving men into their house. Plenty, however, still thought so highly of the way they lived that they wanted to join them and share their life and labor.[23]

Conclusion

The institute [*institutum*], the way of life, marks the difference between one religious order [*religio*] or approved religious group and another. Although *religio* itself means a way of life, a radical manner of living the Gospel, each order or religious group differs from the others by its own common manner of living out the Gospel and the commitment shared by its members: its spirit, its emphasis, its life of prayer and penance, its approach to the apostolate, in short, by its institute. What is striking about the companions is that they had an institute by which they lived long before they dreamed of seeking approval from the apostolic see.

15

Companionship in Christ

The year 1538 is difficult for the companions. Their pilgrimage to Jerusalem has already been on hold for some months. They spend the summer defending themselves against the false charges of persecutors. The investigation establishing their innocence takes most of the autumn. The next year, 1539, is positively overwhelming. The pope, who treats them generously, is thinking how to commend them publicly. People speak highly of them. Priests and young laymen want to join them. What is going on in their own hearts? To what is the Spirit of God impelling them now?

After reviewing the papal attitude toward the companions and the enthusiastic reception people have given them, *Cum ex plurium* considers their own desires:

> Cardinal Contarini informed us
> that your manner of life
> was praised by many
> and so welcomed by some
> that they also would like to follow it,
>
> **and that all of you profoundly desire,**
> [vosque omnes valde cupere]
> **for preserving and bringing to perfection**
> [ad conseruandam ac perficiendam]
> **the union of your Society in Christ,**
> [vestre Societatis in Christo vnionem]

The youthful enthusiasm and idealism of the young Society is obvious. The companions have strong desires, based on experiences that no one can deny or ignore. One of their most profound experiences is of their companionship as gift. They call themselves *compañeros* [companions] when they write in Spanish, *socii* [companions] when they write in Latin. When they speak of themselves as a group or association or community they mean more than an organization. They call themselves in Spanish *compañía* [a fellowship] and in Latin *societas* [a companionship]. *Societas* means far more than a society. It implies a group of friends who share their lives and aspirations, their hopes and joys and sorrows, for they are one in mind and heart and spirit. Note that *societas* is not capitalized in the manuscript of *Cum ex plurium*; we owe each capital *S* to the twentieth-century editors of the *Monumenta* edition of *Cum ex plurium* we are using. The discerning reader must decide each instance whether *societas* refers to the group or to the companionship of the group. In any case, even when it refers to the group, *societas* implies and enfolds the companionship of the group. This should become evident as we proceed.

In his report to Pope Paul III, according to *Cum ex plurium*, Cardinal Contarini first indicates the purpose the companions have in mind: to preserve their union in Christ and to bring it to perfection, that is, enable it to have its full and proper effect. He then indicates how they wish to achieve that purpose: to put in writing whatever experience has taught them is conducive to their end, and to confirm the same by the bond of obedience.

Cardinal Contarini's remarks echo the prayer experience of the companions in the Deliberation they made after the pope started sending them to various parts of the world: (1) the sense of deep union they enjoyed, and their desire to preserve and increase that union; (2) the need of a vow of obedience to preserve that union and accomplish all they wanted to do in the service of God and the pope. Hence, in commenting on *Cum ex plurium*, we need at times to take a close look at the Deliberation of the First Fathers, for that document is the parent of *Cum ex plurium*.

The Deliberation of the First Fathers reveals the profound experience the companions have of their union in Christ. The Deliberation also begins with an expression of their yearning [*desideriis*] to achieve the goal they have long desired [*desideratum*] with their whole heart and soul. Their purpose in deliberating is to talk about their common vocation and way of life [*viuendi formula*]. After several days they find they have a wide variety of positions and opinions about their vocation. They are, after all, of many different native stocks. About one basic reality, however, they all agree: "Common to us all was one mind and will, namely to seek the gracious and perfect will of God according to the scope of our vocation" [*D* 1]. They disagree, however, on the means they should use. With united hearts and minds, then, but divided opinions, they place all their trust in God, in whose praise, honor, and glory they would surrender everything they have [*D* 1]. They find the way not in emphasizing their differences but in embracing the gift of union amongst themselves and in choosing to live in obedience to one of their own number.

Their intent is to perpetuate the union in Christ that God has created in them. Even as the companions are about to become a community in dispersion they desire to preserve the union they have experienced and to make it operative. As they say in the Deliberation of the First Fathers in the answer to their first question about union, "Power that is itself united has greater strength and fortitude to carry out difficult undertakings than power that is diffused in many parts" [*D* 3]. Language both reveals and conceals experience. By the way they use the word *societas,* the companions reveal that in the Company they experience power united [*virtus vnita*].

The experience of union and a desire for it are not unique to Ignatius and his companions. The Prologue to *The Ancient Constitutions of the Order of Friars Preachers* begins in this fashion: "Our Rule commands us to have one heart and one soul in the Lord, so it is right that we who live under a single Rule and by a single profession should be found uniform in the observance of our canonical religion, so that the unity we are to maintain inwardly in our hearts will be fostered and expressed by the uniformity we observe outwardly in our behaviour."[1] This passage emphasizes the union or communion a community should have.

Long before the Dominicans, the Cistercians had expressed the same longing but with a different emphasis in the *Carta*

Caritatis: "Anxious to avoid a future wreck of their mutual concord, in this decree the aforementioned brethren made clear, ordained and recorded for their successors by what bond, in what way, and, most importantly, by what charity their monks, scattered in body throughout abbeys in diverse parts of the world, should be indissolubly joined together in spirit."[2] The Cistercian passage emphasizes the need for union and communion even when the community sends some members to new foundations in other parts of the world.

1. The Companions' Use of the Term *societas*

We limit our inquiry primarily to the writings that come before September 3, 1539, the date of the oral confirmation of the Society. How do the companions speak of themselves before that time, and what do they experience? After that date they might well use the term *Society* when speaking of some earlier event, the way many refer to "Indians" who lived in the New World before Columbus. Rodrigues, for example, consistently calls each of the companions "Father" even before their ordination. When he says, however, "While the seven first Fathers persevered, (for the rest had not yet joined their company [*eorum societatem*])" [*R* 12], he is not reading back into an earlier time the term *societatem,* for he does not say that the others had not yet joined "*the* Society" but "*their* company" or "*their* companionship."

A. *Letters of Ignatius (1532–39)*

Since the early letters of Ignatius are the oldest documents we have concerning his activities and those of his companions, they are of particular importance here. They precede his Autobiography by some years, and terminology that developed later does not compromise them.

Ignatius wrote in Spanish; he used *compañía* [companionship, company, society, *societas* (Latin)] and *compañero* [companion, *socius* (Latin)] long before the juridical establishment of the Society.[3] Although bands of condottieri, mercenaries of the fourteenth to the sixteenth centuries who hired themselves out to the highest bidder, called themselves *compañía*, nothing in the writings of Ignatius indicates that he has this military use of the word in mind. *Compañía* and *compañeros* come from the Latin *cum* [with] + *panis* [bread]: those who share bread. The root of *societas* and *socius* is *sec*, which also occurs in the verb *sequor* [follow]: one who follows another, complies with or conforms to another, one closely associated with another. The two sets of words have to do with sharing: sharing bread, sharing in some common purpose, sharing in the same life and the same aspirations.[4]

In the first paragraph of the Autobiography Ignatius says that before the battle of Pamplona "he confessed to one of these companions in arms" [*A* 1]. These are men whose lives closely entwine with his, who struggle together, eat together, and live or die together. He trusts one enough to make his confession to him. Had Ignatius drawn on the military for *compañía*, he would have done so to indicate not a fighting unit but the close companionship fighting men share.

(1) Letter about Pierre Favre and Companions

In a letter Ignatius sent toward the end of 1536, addressed to the confessor of Eleanore of Austria, wife of King Francis I of France, he writes that "Master Pierre Favre with a company of his is facing a rather difficult journey. . . . He and his company may find themselves in grave or even extreme need" [*EI* 110]. Here *compañía* is the equivalent of *compañeros*, a group of which Favre is a member. The use of *compañía* suggests that in his difficult enterprise Favre is not without companionship: they are a band of men with their own identity and a sense of unity and purpose, not casual companions traveling together by chance.

Ignatius calls this same company "my friends in the Lord" in a letter he writes from Venice to Juan de Verdolay noting their safe arrival from Paris [*EI* 119]. *Compañía* both hides and reveals their friendship, the life they share. In that same letter to de Verdolay, however, Ignatius uses *compañía* in a vague and general sense: "Here certain parties [*compañías*] have sought to join us . . . and we have had to refuse them rather than increase our numbers, for fear of lapses" [*EI* 122]. This remark likely refers to people like Miguel Landívar, whose weaknesses they could catalogue. Here *compañía* implies no sense of shared aspirations and companionship even though referring to men who long to share the aspirations and companionship of Ignatius and his friends.

(2) Letter to Gianpietro Carafa

A deeper experience, however, than friendship lies at the base of *compañía*. A company is a gift from God, a gift to nourish, as the companions decided in the Deliberation of the First Fathers [*D* 3]. Another letter of Ignatius provides the background for his reflection on this subject. He probably wrote the letter in Venice in 1536 and addressed it to Gianpietro Carafa, cofounder of the Theatines, who was living in Venice when Ignatius arrived there but left for Rome before the end of 1536. Whether Ignatius sent the letter is not certain. These uncertainties about details do not detract from the importance of the ideas Ignatius expresses in the letter.[5]

Writing about a religious group of men who are striving valiantly to live in poverty on freewill offerings without begging, Ignatius does not employ a juridical title such as *religio* [religious order]. Instead, he twice uses the word *compañía*, the equivalent of the Italian word Carafa himself had used a few years before in writing to Gian Matteo Giberti about the Theatines, "This poor *compagnia* will survive forever, if it pleases God."[6] Carafa, too, recognized that the gift is God's to give. In his letter Ignatius critiques both the Theatine order and its founder. In doing so, he reveals his own idea of the meaning of *compañía*.

Ignatius has three points to make in this letter. In the first point he expresses the fear that the company will not expand and grow:

> The first is, I think I have enough arguments based on sound reasons and plausible conjectures to fear or to think (speaking in true peace, love, and charity) that the company [*compañía*] God has given you will in no way spread itself abroad [*no se esparziese*]; whereas, if there were more companions, it would be better for the greater service and praise of the Lord.[7] [*EI* 115]

The company is a gift from God. Its nature is to grow, to expand, to embrace more people, to have a wider impact on society. Ignatius fears that the company he is writing about will not expand and thus will fail to meet the greater needs of God's people.

When Ignatius writes that the company should spread itself abroad, he is describing what Francis did and what Dominic did. His own *compañía* would follow their example after arriving in Venice not long after he wrote this letter to Carafa. They immediately divided into two groups and went to work in hospitals. Later they scattered themselves two by two around cities near Venice, not only to work hard in the vineyard of the Lord but also in the hope that their work might attract others to join them [*L* 42].

Since Ignatius appeals to the example of Francis and Dominic in his second and third points, we can use them to illustrate the first point as well: that their vocation is a gift meant to multiply. In the *Legend of the Three Companions* Francis says to his six companions: "Let us consider, dear brothers, our vocation to which God has mercifully called us . . . that we should go throughout the world exhorting everyone, more through example than by word" [*LTS* 36]. That is precisely what they did, going two by two, preaching the Word of God and astonishing people by the lives they lived. In the *Golden Legend* we read that while Dominic was at prayer Peter and Paul appeared to him and told him to go and preach, "and in an instant he seemed to see his sons, setting out two by two and spreading throughout the world."[8]

In the second point of his letter Ignatius is gently critical of the superior's personal style of living. Faithful to his own principle in the Spiritual Exercises [22] always to give the best interpretation possible to a person's actions, Ignatius suggests that the superior's better clothing and other appointments reflect his background and are "more for the sake of visitors than for the others in the community [*compañía*]" *[EI* 116]. Little bond exists, however, with those who come and go. What of those who stay, who share the same life? The companions of the community [*compañía*] deserve a closer bond. Without using the words, Ignatius wonders what effect the superior's way of living might have on the members of the community, whether it builds up companionship within the order he has founded.

He first recalls "how St. Francis and St. Dominic and others in the distant past dealt with their men at the time they got started and gave a method and example to their *compañías*." Then he invokes a principle of discernment:

> Many things are lawful to a man that are not expedient, as St. Paul says of himself, so that others may not take occasion to grow lax but be stirred by example to make progress, especially those of one's own household who always pay more attention to words and deeds when they are the deeds and words of their superior and leader. [*EI* 116]

Ignatius suggests that the superior and his *compañía* are not sufficiently *compañeros*. They should share their poverty together the way Francis shared poverty with his *compañía* and Dominic with his.

Francis does not use the vocabulary of companionship in his Rule but of brothers [*fratres:* friars]. We find it, however, in the *Legend of the Three Companions*. The title indicates the three men are companions [*socii*] of Francis rather than of one another (although that is also true).[9] The story also tells of the companions [*socii*] with whom he associated [*sociaretur*] before his conversion in a companionship [*societate*] not always good for him. Later, joined [*sociatus*] by two brothers, he lived at Portiuncula where a third asked him to receive him into their company [*societatem*] (or companionship). He had already chosen the Gospel as the rule of all who wished to join their company [*societati*].[10] The Dominican *Constitutiones antiquae* generally uses *socius* in the sense of a friar who is with another friar. The word neither affirms nor denies the intimacy of friendship, but implies some degree of companionship. When a novice enters, he is to put off his secular clothing, don religious garb, and be received "into our company (companionship) [*societatem*] in chapter." An incorrigible member, on the other hand, is to be dismissed "from your company [*societate*]."[11] *Societas* is not a title for the community, but indicates a characteristic or quality of the community: a group living in companionship.

In commenting on this other community, Ignatius must recall his own reflections on companionship in his earlier days. In his Autobiography, a document written for the instruction of the Society, Ignatius has a remarkable passage that reveals his understanding of companionship:

> So at the beginning of the year '23, he set out for Barcelona to take ship. Although various people [*compañías*] offered to accompany him, he wanted to go quite alone, for his whole idea was to have God alone as refuge. One day some persons were strongly urging him to take a companion [*compañía*], since he did not know either the Italian or the Latin language. They told him how much this would help him and praised a certain person highly. He replied that even if the companion were the son or the brother of the Duke of Cardona, he would not go in his company [*compañía*]. For he wanted to practice three virtues—charity, faith, and hope; if he took a companion [*compañero*], he would expect help from him when he was hungry; if he fell down, the man would help him get up. He himself, too, would trust the companion and feel attachment to him on this account. But he wanted to place that trust, attachment, and expectation in God alone. [*A* 35]

Ignatius clearly understood the purpose of companionship, but at that time he wanted to place his trust in God alone. Reflection on his experience in Jerusalem changed Ignatius radically in at least two ways: he saw that some learning was necessary if he wanted to fulfill his dream and he began to look for companions to fulfill it with him. After his return from Jerusalem, he studied in Barcelona, and then "he set out alone for Alcalá, though he already had some companions [*compañeros*]" [*A* 56]. Later, these men joined him in Alcalá and went with him to Salamanca. When he left for Paris, he did not forget them. In Rouen, he helped a sick man board a ship to Spain, and "He also gave him letters directing him to the companions [*compagni*] who were in Salamanca" [*A* 79].

After Ignatius finds Favre and Xavier and the others in Paris, the vocabulary of companionship flows from him like a river. For the rest of the story he refers to the others only as companions:

the companions, for example, bought him a little horse for his journey to Spain [A 87]; while there he performed several errands for the companions [A 89], and visited their hometowns [A 90]; when the nine companions came to Venice, they split up to work in hospitals, then went to Rome together; at the end of their pilgrimage the companions returned from Rome with plenty of alms for the journey to Jerusalem, but even so, the companions returned to Venice begging on foot [A 93]. Sharing in everything, they were not unaware of their differences, nor of their weaknesses. They mixed nationalities together to leave no one in a vulnerable position. Thus Ignatius underlines the need for supportive companionship.

The third point Ignatius makes in the letter touches on poverty and ministry. The word for community throughout this paragraph is not *compañía* but "your holy profession [*profesión*]." Ignatius moves from what they should be, a company of companions, to their profession, what they should do. They professed to be priests; let them exercise their priesthood more freely and that will take care of poverty. If, indeed, Ignatius is writing to Carafa, the *compañía* in question is the Theatines, of which Carafa was a cofounder. The Theatines made no pretensions of being a new religious order, although the Apostolic See eventually recognized them as such. They tried, rather, to provide a model for the secular clergy as a way of bringing about clerical reform. They lived in community under the three vows, and practiced a life of prayer and apostolic activity. To live in poverty, they refused ecclesiastical benefices. Choosing not to beg, they depended entirely on the good will of the people for their livelihood.[12] The Theatine ideal was to combine somehow the life of an ordinary priest with the monastic life.

The letter of Ignatius gives the impression that the Theatines did little apostolic work. "First, they do not beg what they need, having no way to support themselves; second, they do not preach; third, they do not practice the corporal works of mercy, like burying the dead and saying masses for those who die, etc." [*EI* 117]. Since they do none of these ministries, they make little impression on the people on whom they depend for sustenance. Francis and Dominic depended on Divine Providence, but they also took the means to see that their houses could maintain themselves and grow for the greater service and praise of God.

We are beginning to understand better why Ignatius thinks the group will not spread. Perhaps he did not understand the Theatines. Perhaps in his judgment they were at home too much, too much engaged in quiet contemplation, not enough with the people. But perhaps he did understand them. As the historian of the Theatines, Pio Paschini, remarked, "The love of solitude dominated everything else for the clerks regular in the first decade of their foundation." He quotes Carafa as writing from Venice on October 9, 1532: "We willingly stay at home, filled with a marvelous love to flee from anything practical, for such is the need in these evil days."[13]

Ignatius's style of companionship is to be with his fellow workers and with the people as well. Rodrigues describes the experience of the companions: living in hovels and begging their food, preaching, taking care of the poor, administering the sacraments, surviving as best they can. The love, the concern, the willingness and openness and generosity, the companionship they experienced is transparent [R 66]. Sharing poverty means more than sharing a drafty room and little to eat; sharing poverty is sharing life. Ignatius tells of the time they had scattered through various towns of Italy before going to Rome:

> While he was still at Vicenza, he learned that one of the companions, who was at Bassano, was ill to the point of death. At the same time he too was ill with fever. Nevertheless, he set out and walked so vigorously that Favre, his companion, could not keep up with him. On that journey he had assurance from God, and he told Favre so, that the companion would not die of that illness. On their arriving at Bassano, the sick man was much comforted and soon recovered. [A 95]

Rodrigues matches this story with one about himself and Jean Codure when the latter's companion, Diego de Hozes, succumbed to sickness during their labors in Padua and eventually died. "This left Codure alone in Padua, profoundly moved by a desire for his companion [*socii*], and deeply distressed by the weight of many serious matters. Well then, what kind of love existed amongst the companions [*socios*], how on fire was their love? To console Codure and to help him carry his burden, one of the two companions [*sociis*] who were at Ferrara, a nearby town, immediately came to him. Wonderful it is how much the coming of this Father soothed the heart of Codure, what powerful encouragement it gave him" [*R* 69].

These incidents reveal the companionship [*compañia*] the Company enjoyed even before the juridical establishment of the Society [*Compagnia: A* 80, 100]. These experiences were not yet available to Ignatius when he wrote his letter to Carafa, but he had a clear idea of what companionship meant. Either he misunderstood the Theatines or feared their way of life was such that shared companionship would not happen.

(3) Letter to Isabel Roser (December 19, 1538)

Two years after the letter to Carafa, Ignatius's own company and the companionship that had begun in Paris were solidly established. In his letter to Isabel Roser recounting the story of the persecutions in Rome, Ignatius uses *Compañía* six times. The word refers to the group made up of himself and his companions. It is a special group, bound together in love, and their oneness is evident in each phrase:

> More than a year ago three of our Company arrived here in Rome. . . . Four months after our coming, we decided to gather all of our Company in this city. . . . After [Paul III] returned from Nice . . . two of our Company talked to him. . . . The pope . . . spoke in public many times in our favor and in the presence of the Company. . . . The duke of Ferrara . . . wrote to his ambassador and to our Company several times. . . . Four or five [young men] are determined to be part of our Company. [*IR* 2–8]

The Company, the Companionship, is already a fact, even without thought of making it a juridical reality. They have experienced their union; the Church has not yet blessed it.[14]

B. Letter of Favre (November 23, 1538)

A few months before the Deliberation of the First Fathers, Pierre Favre wrote in the name of the companions to their former principal in Paris, Diogo de Gouveia, in response to a request for help in India, "We who have been bound together to one another in this Society [companionship] have dedicated ourselves to the supreme pontiff" [*EI* 132]. Again, the Society [companionship] exists before they ask themselves whether they should establish it juridically. Significantly, the word "Society" is used in conjunction with "bound together to one another [*colligati ad inuicem*]," thus emphasizing the reality of the group, the body bound together, the *Company*, as well as the quality of the group, its *companionship*. They are bound to one another in this companionship in which they have devoted themselves completely to the work of Christ in the person of the pope.

C. The Deliberation of the First Fathers (Lent 1539)

(a) Bound Together. The vocabulary of Favre is particularly significant when we compare it to that of the first question in the Deliberation of the First Fathers:[15]

> To repeat, would it be better for us to be bound [*inter nos deuinctos*] and joined together [*colligatos*] in one body [*in vno corpore*] in such a way that no physical separation however great might separate us, or would it perhaps not be better.[16] [*D* 3]

The sense of the words in this passage is identical to the sense of the words in Favre's letter to Gouveia. Favre's "bound together to one another in this Society (companionship) [*ad inuicem in hac Societate colligati*]" becomes in the Deliberation "bound and joined together in one body [*inter nos deuinctos et colligatos in vno corpore*]." The words in the Deliberation emphasize their sense of unity. "To be bound and joined together" means "to be closely united amongst ourselves." The addition of the words "in one body" intensifies the sense of unity.

The image is of intertwining after the fashion of the Holy Trinity, the way the three divine persons relate so closely to one another as to live in one another. For the companions, however, union comes before joining. United in friendship, they have joined together in a single body, in a common enterprise. The question they address to themselves is: should they be joined in such a manner that the union of the body can in no way be destroyed no matter how physically separated the members of the body are?

(b) *Societas:* **Company or Companionship.** The same question is then concretized and put in another way:

> Should we be concerned about those who go there [Siena], or they about us, and keep in touch with one another, or perhaps should we have no more concern for them than for those who are outside our companionship [*Societatem*]? [*D* 3]

For the first time in the Deliberation we encounter a form of the word *Societas*. Since this second form of the question is simply a concretization of the original question, we have to understand the word *Societas* in the context of that question. In this context, those "outside the Society" are those who are outside the experience of being "bound and joined together in one body," that is, "outside the companionship."[17]

(c) *Societas:* **the Companionship of the Company.** *Societas* does not mean simply "the group" but embraces the companionship the group enjoys. This is clear from the response that God's gift of union was so great they could not lightly set it aside:

> Since the most merciful and gracious Lord had deigned to unite us to one another [*inuicem vnire*] and to gather us together [*congregare*], weak as we are and from different places and cultures, we should not sever the bonding [*unionem*] and gathering [*congregationem*] that comes from God, but should daily strengthen it and ground it, forming ourselves into one body, each having knowledge of and concern for the others to the greater profit of souls, since power that is itself united [*virtus ipsa vnita*] has greater strength and fortitude to carry out difficult undertakings than power that is diffused into many parts.[18] [*D* 3]

In the answer to the foundational question about joining together formally, the same peculiar configuration of ideas appears as in the question itself: to unite and to join [*vnire et congregare*], union and community [*unionem et congregationem*]. This is not simply the figure of speech known as hendiadys (two words for one idea) meaning *unite* and *union*. Uniting really comes first, and joining together comes second. In the Deliberation the companions recognize that God first united them in a peculiar kind of union, *union in Christ*: they became *friends in the Lord*, and then God brought them together in a company. They were first friends, and then at Montmartre they joined each other in a common enterprise. Not all friends band together for a particular purpose. These friends, however, united with one another, find themselves in a close-knit association that has a purpose other than pure friendship.

In 1542 Favre, the first companion of Ignatius, began a spiritual diary called his *Memoriale*. In recalling the years preceding the foundation of the Society, he uses *societas* in a significant manner. Referring to his tutor-roommate, Master Juan de la Peña, and their other roommate, Francisco Xavier,[19] Pierre expresses his gratitude to God for granting him "such a tutor and such companionship [*societatem*]" [*F* 7]. It is significant that in this first use of *societas* in the *Memoriale* the word indicates the quality of communion rather than merely designating a group. The next sentence is something of a surprise: "I refer especially to Master Francisco Xavier, who is of the Society [*Societate*] of Jesus Christ" [*F* 7]. This qualifying sentence makes clear that although Pierre appreciated the tutor, the companionship he cherished most was that of Xavier, a companionship that existed even before either one of them knew Ignatius. In a context that stresses companionship [*societatem*], Favre significantly names the group [*Societate*] he and his companion would join. He reveals that in the group the experience of companionship is not only maintained but deeply anchored.

In the light of Favre's experience we can understand the desire of the companions to "strengthen and confirm [*confirmare et stabilire*]" their union [*D* 3], a phrase that anticipates *Cum ex plurium*'s "preserving [*conseruandam*] and bringing to perfection [*perficiendam*] the union of your Society in Christ" [*CEP* 1].[20]

(d) *Societas*: a Body of Companions United in Companionship. We grasp the full force of the meaning of *societas* when we examine its position in the paragraph quoted above in which it first appears in the Deliberation of the First Fathers. The paragraph opens with the original question on unity, then rephrases the question, and then concludes with the answer to the question. *Societatem* finds itself in the rephrased question, between the question with its two verbs and the answer with its two verbs and two nouns.

In that position, *Societatem* summarizes the two verbs in the question, "bound and joined in one body [*inter nos deuinctos et colligatos in vno corpore*]." In the same way it looks forward in summary to the two verbs of the answer, "unite and join [*inuicem vnire et congregare*]." It also summarizes in anticipation the two nouns in the answer, "union and association [*unionem et congregationem*]." *Societas* is being united and joined together; *Societas* is the union and association; *Societas* is the one body of those united and joined together in love.[21]

2. Union in Christ: Society of Jesus

Out of the experience of the Deliberation of the First Fathers the companions choose to name themselves and their religious organization a society. *Societas* or *compañía,* although not in common use then for a religious order, was a common name for various associations of people committed to religious purposes.[22] The word captures and aptly expresses the companions' experience of their identity. Their experience, however, goes deeper: their closeness, their bondedness, their union is *in Christ,* and that is why they choose to call themselves the Society of Jesus. The Deliberation of the First Fathers does not use *Cum ex plurium*'s phrase "the union of your Society in Christ [*vestre Societatis in Christo vnionem*]" or "the union of your companionship in Christ," but it leaves no doubt that union in Christ is what they experience. The Deliberation acknowledges that they had offered and dedicated themselves to Christ, who is the basis of their union [*D* 3]. They are one in him, and without him they have nothing to share. None of the other documents written before the oral approbation of the Society on September 3, 1539, says anything about the union of the companions in Christ. Other documents, written after 1539 but about the events preceding that approbation, however, do shed light on it, and illumine as well their choice of a name for their company.

Once again, keep in mind that the manuscript of *Cum ex plurium* has no capital *S* when it uses any form of *societas*. *Societas* can mean "Society" or "companionship," and either meaning implies friendship, love, and interpersonal commitment.

Favre's Memoriale (1542)

A passage in Favre's *Memoriale* centers on the activity of Jesus in bringing the Society into being. Favre recognizes that regardless of the amount of work they had done, praying, reflecting, deliberating over whether the company should continue in being and what sort of company it should be, in the end it is Jesus' Company. Reflecting on their offering of themselves in holocaust to the pope that he might send them where he thought they could serve Christ, Favre exclaims, "It was also a remarkable gift, and as it were, the foundation of our whole Society . . . that the Lord willed that [the pope] would accept us and rejoice in what we had determined to do" [*F* 18]. Significantly, Favre sees that it is Christ's will that has brought the Society into being. Christ's action is the foundation of the whole Society: Christ has formed both the group and the companionship of the group. Without using the same words, the passage anticipates *Cum ex plurium*'s "union of your Society in Christ [*vestre Societatis in Christo vnionem*]."

Polanco (1547)

Although Polanco's concern in this passage is about the name of the Society rather than union, he picks up Favre's theme of the activity of Jesus amongst them:

> Its name is the Company [*Compañía*] of Jesus, and it took this name before they arrived in Rome. Discussing amongst themselves what name they should give to someone who might inquire what association [*congregación*] they belonged to, which consisted of 9 or 10 persons, they began to give themselves to prayer and to reflect on what name would be most appropriate. Since there was no head amongst them, and

since they had no leader except Jesus whom alone they desired to serve, it seemed to them that they should take the name of the one they had for a head, calling themselves the Company [*Compañía*] of Jesus. [*PSH* 86][23]

Jesus is the head, the one who unites all, who directs all, from whom comes all the vision, the commands, the decisions that affect the life of the companions. He creates the companionship, maintains it, fosters it, and makes it flourish. He is the guiding force, the unifying force, the impelling force that directs their lives. The name comes from that center of unity, the head, Jesus.

Ignatius enforces Polanco's view of how the companions experienced their relationship to Jesus in the Spiritual Diary he wrote in 1544–45. Praying about the poverty the newly founded Society should practice, Ignatius wrote, "the thought of Jesus came to me, and an urge to follow Him. Deeply in my soul I thought that since he is the head of the Society [*Compañía*], that very fact is a greater argument for proceeding in total poverty than all the other human reasons."[24] Union with Jesus is the driving force in Ignatius.

Laynez (1559)

Polanco explains the deeper question why they called themselves the Society of *Jesus,* but does not explain why they chose the name *Society.* Diego Laynez, the second father general, does that. In an exhortation to about two hundred Jesuits in Rome on July 2, 1559, he explains (1) when the companions decided to call the Society after Jesus; (2) why they named the Society after Jesus; and (3) the sense in which they used *Society.*

(1) Speaking in Italian, Laynez touches once more on the Deliberation of the First Fathers. He locates in the Deliberation the decision about the Society's name:

> The first question was whether there should be an association [*congregatione*]. This we agreed upon unanimously. . . . Then he [Ignatius] said that it seemed like a good idea to him that the association [*congregatione*] should be called the Company [*Compagnia*] of Jesus, if the rest of us were content. We said

that we were, and it was proposed to the Apostolic See and was approved. So the first foundation was this holy name. [*FN* 2:133 {6}]

In this passage Laynez uses association [*congregatione*] as Polanco used it in the passage quoted above. *Congregatio* implies some unifying element among the persons in a group. In his letter to Isabel Roser Ignatius refers to the charge that the companions were trying to establish an association [*congregación*] or religious order [*religión*] without proper authorization [*IR* 8]. Laynez denies that the companions planned even from Paris to start an association [*congregación*, a community of some sort, not necessarily synonymous with a religious order] [*L* 36].

Congregatio is an assembly. Applied to a religious order, it usually refers to the *community*, as *congregation* refers to a parish or to a liturgical assembly. In ecclesiastical usage *congregatio* was a synonym for a synod; it meant a religious community, especially a monastic community, and was a synonym for a monastery. It referred to a chapter of canons and even to a university meeting.[25] *Congregatio* was not, in the early part of the sixteenth century, used to distinguish a religious community of simple vows (there were none) from a religious *order* of solemn vows, as became customary later. (The 1983 code of Canon Law makes no distinction between solemn and simple vows or between an order and a congregation, referring to all religious communities as religious institutes.[26]) The companions used *congregatio* to signify their number gathered as a community, especially a community assembled to act. *Congregatio* was a good word to express the external reality of assembling. *Societas* was a better word to express the interior communion of a group.

Laynez and Polanco do not disagree about the time for choosing the name of the Company. Polanco puts the decision at Vicenza, but in Vicenza they had not even thought of becoming an approved religious organization. As soon as that question arises, they have to consider again the matter of a name for the group, the consideration that Laynez places in Rome. Although this passage reveals the union of the companions in their prayer and discussions, it only hints at their union in Jesus in the choice of his name to designate their company.

(2) Laynez, however, immediately touches upon their union in Jesus in indicating the reason for choosing that name:

> The primary reason for this name was our Father [Ignatius], as I shall now tell you. As we were on the way to Rome from Siena our Father received many spiritual consolations, especially from the most holy Eucharist that he received every day from Pierre Favre or me. We said Mass every day, but he did not. He told me that it seemed to him that God the Father had imprinted these words on his heart: "I shall be propitious to you [plural] in Rome." Since our Father did not know what these words might mean, he said: "I don't know what is going to happen to us; perhaps we shall be crucified in Rome." Then on another occasion he said that it seemed to him that he saw Christ with the cross on his shoulder, and next to him the Eternal Father, who said to him: "I want You to take this man for your servant." And so Jesus took him and said: "I want you [singular] to serve us." For this reason, because he had great devotion to this most holy name, he wanted the community [*congregatione*] to be called the Company [*Compagnia* (Italian)] of Jesus. [*FN* 2:133 {7}]

That the words of the Father are in the plural is significant: he will be propitious to all the companions. Their union is something even the Father cannot ignore. What is more, in this vision at La Storta Ignatius experiences the answer to his personal prayer of the Two Standards in the Spiritual Exercises [147] to be placed at the side of the Son bearing his cross. He hears Jesus choose *him*. Also, by choosing the name of Jesus, this sense of union with Jesus, this sense of being chosen personally by him, is communicated to the companions who had themselves made the same prayer.

(3) Laynez makes clear the way he understands the meaning of *Compagnia*. His emphasis is not on group or organization but on companionship, on union:

> If St. Paul calls all Christians the Company [*Compagnia*] of Jesus, we can still call ourselves that. In the First Letter to the Corinthians St. Paul says: "God is faithful; by him you were called into the fellowship [*Societatem*] of his Son, Jesus Christ

our Lord" (1 Cor. 1:9). And John in his First Letter says: "we declare to you what we have seen and heard so that you also may have fellowship [*societatem*] with us; and truly our fellowship [*societas*] is with the Father and with his Son Jesus Christ" (1 John 1:3). [*FN* 2:134 {8}]

The companionship is with one another, but also with Christ. The union, the communion, the companionship, is in Christ, and through him with the Father and the Holy Spirit.

The Greek word for *societas* in the above passages from Paul and John is *koinōnia*. *Koinos* means "common," and *koinōnia* "communion, association, partnership." It expresses mutuality of experience, as in joint ownership, sexual intercourse, or the giving and receiving of alms. It speaks of sharing. The *koinōnia* of which Paul writes, fellowship or participation in a shared life with the Son, is the experience of Eucharist, *koinōnia* in the cup, *koinōnia* in the bread (1 Cor. 10:16). Although here the Latin Vulgate does not use *societas* but *communicatio* and *participatio,* those additional words only bring out more fully the sense of inner communion contained in *societas*. What is important is that *koinōnia* indicates an interior union with Christ. As one may participate in his life, so also one may know "the sharing [*koinōnian/societatem*] of his sufferings" (Phil. 3:10). In John, *koinōnia* [*societas*] stresses the interior union all Christians enjoy, not only with the Son, but also with the Father and the Holy Spirit.

Conclusion

The union dear to the companions is not merely union, but "union in Christ," a union founded on Christ's love for them and their love for Christ, seen in the Scriptures and experienced in a deeply personal way by each during the Spiritual Exercises. More than that, the union and joining together, the union *and* community of the Deliberation of the First Fathers has in *Cum ex plurium* become the union *of* the community: "the union of your companionship in Christ." They not only experience and embrace union with Christ and one another, but they experience the union of the group in Christ that binds the group to Christ and to one another.

The name the companions choose for their religious community expresses their companionship with one another and with Jesus in a common enterprise. They are not just an organization but a union with and in Jesus, in whom they share life and love, talent and energy, joy and pain, laughter and tears. This union, this communion, this companionship names them not the Order of Jesus but the *Company* of Jesus, the *Society* of Jesus.

3. Means to Preserve Union

The companions recognize that the Spirit of God is now urging them to preserve the union which God has given them. But while they find their companionship in Christ highly desirable personally, a gift they should not set aside, the apostolate remains the Society's main purpose:

> and that all of you profoundly desire
> for preserving and bringing to perfection
> the union of your Society in Christ,
>
> **that all**
> [illa omnia]
> **that you have found by experience**
> [que vsu comperistis]
> **conducive to the end proposed to you,**
> [ad propositum vobis finem conducentia]

The End beyond the End

The companions have an end beyond the end of preserving the Society: the service of Christ and his Church. They wish to write down and commit themselves by a vow of obedience to everything that experience has taught them is conducive to that end. They wish to do this to preserve the Society and make it grow. They are convinced that united they can serve Christ and his Church more effectively than if they are not united. The Society will make them more effective instruments of service and help them use all the other instruments God has given them for his service. The attitude of the companions echoes the ending of the Principle and Foundation of the Exercises: "I ought to desire and elect only the thing which is more conducive to the end for which I am created" [23].

Their theological position points toward the answer to a technical question. When we translate the phrase, *ad propositum vobis finem conducentia*: "conducive to the end proposed *to* you," do we mean that someone else has proposed the end to them, or that they have proposed the end to themselves? Cicero has a complicated little phrase: *cum id mihi propositum initio non fuisset*. He does not mean, "since it was not proposed to me from the beginning" by someone else. He means that he had not intended it from the beginning, he had not proposed it to himself. Cicero speaks in a context where he proposes or does not propose a course of action.[27] So also the companions. They have decided upon a course of action and they intend to carry it through. Like Cicero, they had not intended it from the beginning; they had not proposed it to themselves. Unlike Cicero, however, they have had a course of action proposed to them by someone else, a purpose in life that is a gift to them, a goal to which they have been called, not something they conceived for themselves. Their experience is that of the apostles at the Last Supper: "You did not choose me but I chose you. And I appointed you to go and bear fruit, fruit that will last" (John 15:16). We read in Hebrews, "Let us run with perseverance the race that is set before us [*propositum nobis*]" (Heb. 12:1). We have, indeed, decided to run the race, but God has set the race before us; we could not have imagined the race for ourselves even in our wildest dreams.

The end the companions have determined upon is not one they have established for themselves but an end given to them. The pope did not propose it, nor did anyone else. The end they seek has been proposed to them and for them by God. No other interpretation is possible, for when they write down what experience has taught them, they state explicitly not only what the goal is but who established it. In the first decree of the Formula they spell out what the service of Christ and the Church means to them, saying that anyone who wants to be a part of the Society

> should keep in mind that he is a member of a community founded for this most of all, that it aim principally at the advancement of souls in Christian life and doctrine, and the propagation of the faith through the ministry of the Word, through the Spiritual Exercises, and by works of charity, and specifically through the instruction of children and the uninitiated in Christianity, and let him take care always to have before his eyes first God, and then the nature of this institute, which is a certain way to him, and to strive with all his strength to attain this end proposed to him by God.[28] [*CEP* 2]

They experience their union in Christ as God's own work. In both the introductory sentence of *Cum ex plurium* and in the Formula the companions express not only their experience of themselves but their experience of God at work in their lives and at work among all those their lives touch and will touch in time to come.

The First Means: Setting down Their Way of Life in Writing

>> that all
>> that you have found by experience
>> conducive to the end proposed to you,
>
> **you solidify now**
> [... iam ... stabilire ...]
> **in writing**
> [scripto]

The companions choose to preserve their union and bring it to perfection by writing down all that experience has taught them is conducive to the end that God has given them. The result is the first draft of the Formula of the Institute, five brief decrees [*capitula*] outlining the way of life for which they seek papal approval.[29] If a document can be exuberant with subdued enthusiasm, such is the first draft of the Formula. It is, in fact, a highly sophisticated piece of work, profoundly stirring and provocative, like the Declaration of Independence or the Gettysburg Address. "A true *magna charta* of the new order," Tacchi Venturi calls it.[30] Chapter 22 of this book will consider the Formula in more detail; the brief summary which follows here will simply introduce the content.

Decree one addresses itself to all who choose to join in serving "the Lord alone and his vicar on earth" under the banner of the cross and describes this venture in brief detail. In a surprising move it links the mission and works of the Society with a solemn vow of chastity. This decree is a ringing challenge to the spirit of the age that invited churchmen to commit themselves to career and wealth and power rather than to ministry, to the attractions and blandishments of sensuality rather than to the gift of oneself to God. Everything they describe, experience has taught them. At this point, they add something new, obedience to one chosen from their number, and they outline his powers and duties and the limits of his power.

Decree two explains their relation to the pope and the vow to go wherever he sends them, and it challenges stouthearted men to weigh well the demands and not to outrun the Spirit.

Decree three moves to obedience to the general, outlining the loving and gentle way in which he is to exercise his authority and the gentle and humble way in which the companions are to find Christ in him.

Decree four expands on what it means to keep God always before their eyes, to serve God alone: the all-demanding poverty that seeks first the kingdom of God and trusts completely in a loving providence.

Decree five describes what it means to keep the nature of this institute always before their eyes and indicates some ways it differs from other institutes, leaving no room for comfortable preconceptions of religious life. A concluding paragraph warns those who come after them to be mindful of elements they consider important, especially that no one should be admitted to this life without a long probation. The warning ends with a prayer that Jesus look with favor upon these "weak beginnings."

Though this brief summary cannot communicate the spirit of the document, this Formula is quite possibly the most exciting writing from the pen of Ignatius after the Call of the King and the Two Standards. According to Jerónimo Nadal, it was mainly through these two meditations, the Call of the King and the Two Standards, that Ignatius learned the aim and purpose of his life, a purpose now shared by the whole Society.[31] In his commentary on the Formula, Aldama cites Nadal and then elaborates on the two exercises in a very stirring manner, recalling in detail the mission of the apostles in Matthew's Gospel, the paradigm for the life and work of the Company.[32]

The Formula may well have been written first in Spanish and then translated into Latin, but we have only the Latin. In Aldama's Spanish translation of the Formula[33] the very first word is *Todo* [all]. *Todo* appears a surprising number of times throughout the document. *Todo* for Ignatius and his companions is like *nada* [nothing] in John of the Cross some years later. "Nothing," says John of the Cross. "Everything," "Everyone," says Ignatius. *Todo* and *todos* suggest that the whole Society and all those who belong to it, each and every one, are to give themselves entirely, all that they are and all that they have, all their being, to the service of God, *todo,* holding back nothing, *nada*. That is a summary of the spirit of the Formula of the Institute.

The Second Means: the Bond of Obedience

> you solidify now
> in writing
>
> **and by the bond of obedience;**
> [et obedientie[34] vinculo stabilire]

The second means the companions choose to preserve their union and bring it to perfection is to bind themselves by obedience to observe all that experience has taught them is conducive to the end that God has given them. The question about obedience is more difficult than the question about unity. They see obedience as a way of opening the future, of freeing them to act more fully, more powerfully:

> Since we had all made a vow of perpetual chastity and a vow of poverty in the presence of the most reverend legate of His Holiness when we were in Venice, would it be better to make

a third vow, namely, of obeying one of us [*obediendi alicui ex nobis*], so that we might more sincerely and with greater praise and merit fulfill the will of the Lord our God in all things, and at the same time carry out the free will and command of His Holiness, to whom we had freely offered all we had, our will, our intellect, our ability, etc. [*D* 4]

"Obeying one of us" is a remarkable phrase in that it suggests the companionship they already enjoy. They do not write "obeying a superior." "Obeying one of us" implies that the one they obey is the superior, but it states clearly that the superior is to be "one of us." "One of us" is by no means an outsider; neither is he some lofty figure of heroic stature barely accessible to the ordinary person. If they are to obey someone, he is to be one of the companions.

The reasons the companions indicate for obeying are also remarkable: to be able to fulfill in everything the will of God more sincerely and with greater praise and merit, and to be able to fulfill as well the will and command of the pope. The reasons they give are not ascetic but are purely apostolic: the better service of Christ and his vicar. This is something new.

If we consider the history of obedience, we find that the early centuries of Christianity highly recommended obedience as an ascetic practice. Obedience removed obstacles to growth in the Christian life. For the Desert Fathers and Mothers, the one who commanded did so in the Holy Spirit, and the sole claim on obedience was the spiritual perfection of the one who commanded. Those who obeyed saw in him or her one who engendered life in the Holy Spirit, not one who represented God. Cassian was more mystical: obedience was a means to union with God. At the same time, another and more practical side of obedience came to light: the good government of the monastery. These two united in Benedict, spiritual perfection and good government: the directions and commands of the abbot, who stood in the place of Christ, marked the path the monk should follow on the way of life.[35] For the companions, the path to follow is the path of mission; the question was whether obedience will be a help to mission. The discussions produce an answer broader than the question.

In their Deliberations Ignatius and his companions struggle with ascetical problems, juridical problems, ministerial problems, practical problems, even a problem of public relations. One said, "It seems that this name of religious order [*religionis*] or obedience [*obedientie*] does not . . . have the good reputation among Christian people that it ought to have."[36] Again, another said, "If we want to live under obedience we may be forced by the pope to accept an already established rule." Also, "If we give obedience to someone, not many will enter our community [*congregationem*] to work faithfully in the vineyard of the Lord, in which few real workers are found . . . [M]any seek their own profit and their own will rather than that of Jesus Christ and the complete denial of themselves" [*D* 7]. The final objection reveals the speaker's own outlook: he is concerned about the vineyard of the Lord rather than his own interests, and for him obedience is a way of seeking the will of Jesus.

After many days of deliberation their response is affirmative regarding obedience, "We concluded: it is better and more necessary for us to give obedience to one of our company," and the response is a masterful synthesis with respect to mission ("so that we might better and more exactly achieve our primary desire of fulfilling the divine will in all things"), companionship ("so that the Company would be preserved more surely"), and the practical ("and finally proper provision could be made for whatever matters might arise, both spiritual and temporal") [*D* 8]. We need to reflect further on the response the companions receive from the Holy Spirit during their prayer on the question of obedience.

(a) Mission. The primary concern is the accomplishment of ministry. The bond of obedience in *Cum ex plurium*, will stabilize them more solidly in what they desire to do. It is not a chain that weighs them down and shackles their freedom. Rather, it is a like a rope tying mountain climbers together so they can act more freely and accomplish more fully what they want to do. The way they pose the question in the first place suggests this interpretation. An argument one of the companions uses in favor of obedience is:

> If our community [*congregatio*] had some job to do, no one would have a particular responsibility without the sweet yoke

of obedience [*suaui obedientiae jugo*]; each would push it off on someone else, as we have often experienced. [*D* 7]

"A sweet yoke," a burden, a responsibility, but one that makes life easier, more fruitful, more free. When they went off in twos and threes after ordination, they had taken weekly turns at the office of superior [*R* 63]. They had already experienced, therefore, that "obeying one of us" has as its purpose, not to shrug off responsibility by placing it on the superior but to shoulder responsibility willingly by ridding one of reluctance, of laziness, of everything that shackles freedom and makes it difficult to act, especially in concert with others.

(b) Companionship. The second concern returns them to the issue of companionship and its preservation: obedience will more fully guarantee the preservation of the Company and the continuation of mission made possible through companionship. Someone had argued:

> If this community [*congregatio*] were without obedience [*obedientia*], it could not last or persevere for a long time, but that is contrary to our first intention of preserving [*conseruandi*] forever our companionship [*Societatem*]. Since, therefore, a community is preserved by nothing better than by obedience, it [obedience] seems necessary for us, especially for us who have vowed perpetual poverty and are engaged in difficult and continual labors, both spiritual and temporal, in which companionship is less easily preserved. [*D* 7]

Without obedience, difficult and continual labors exhaust the spirit, especially for those who have few creature comforts, and tend to develop a spirit of self-sufficiency, a "loner" mentality. With obedience, one's work becomes part of the common effort, contributes to the common enterprise, and those who are exhausted and otherwise without support draw away from isolation and find themselves instead to be companions.

(c) The Practical. The third concern embarks upon new territory, good government:

> Although we have given all obedience, both universal and particular, to the Supreme Pontiff and pastor, he would not

be free to attend to all our particular problems, which are innumerable, nor would it be proper for him to do so even if he could. [*D* 7]

They want themselves to be a gift to the pope, not a burden. Obedience would maintain good order and, although they do not explicitly state it, would make them free and available through the good management of their needs.

Conclusion

This triple response is something new, and yet it is very, very old, for it is the practical application in their particular circumstances and way of life of the synthesis established by Benedict: the commands of the superior point out the path to follow on the way of life.[37] What is new is the relation of obedience to mission, and the preservation of companionship in mission through obedience. Maintaining good order through obedience is not new, but doing it for the sake of mission is. On April 15, 1539, each of the companions signed a document stating that he is in favor of a vow of obedience. The statement reads in part: "I have freely come to the determination that in my judgment it would be more expedient for the praise of God and the perpetuation of the Society for there to be a vow of obedience in it" [*C* 8].

This statement echoes the response to the question on obedience in the Deliberation of the First Fathers. What is "more expedient for the praise of God" is the equivalent of "fulfilling the divine will in all things." As in the Deliberation, the language of this statement leaves no doubt of their conviction that obedience would contribute to the preservation of the Society. The bond of obedience is a bond of union.

Concluding Reflection

Now that they have put behind them the trials and false accusations of 1538, now that their darkness has given way to light, the companions find themselves in a period of deep consolation. Pope Paul III is pleased with them and eager to enlist their support. Other people are pleased with them, some to such an extent that they want to join them in their way of life. The companions are excited about the way God is dealing with them. They want to perpetuate what they have begun. They want to make their way of life available to others. They move now from union and intimacy toward generativity, from companionship in Jesus to a Pentecost of fruitfulness in the apostolate.

The next steps in their long discernment process are clear: it is time to organize themselves in an official manner, to write down their way of life so all can see and understand it, to choose one from among them to whom they owe obedience. What that might mean, time and circumstances will make clear. Cardinal Contarini has intervened with the pope on their behalf. As we shall see, the pope's theologian, Tommaso Badia, has approved their way of life. The next step is not theirs to decide. Now it is up to the pope.

SECTION TWO

The Companions' Requests

This section continues to center on the report that Cardinal Contarini has made to Pope Paul III. It reveals that Ignatius and his companions, undismayed by a papal investigation of the orthodoxy of their teaching and the morality of their lives, recognize that the Holy Spirit is moving them to ask for another papal investigation. They want a papally authorized examination of what they have written down as their form of living [*viuendi formula*]. Does that *form of living* conform to the evangelical counsels and the canonical sanctions of the fathers? If it does, they want the pope to approve and bless it. These sixteenth-century requests raise some questions for twentieth-century minds. What is a form of living? Is it the same as a rule? The twentieth-century mind has to be open to some surprises concerning the choices of the companions vis-à-vis other religious orders. Also, what *evangelical counsels* are they talking about? What is the spirit with which the companions approach the evangelical counsels? Are the evangelical counsels a help or a hindrance in view of what the companions are trying to accomplish? Lastly, what are the *canonical sanctions of the fathers?* Have we suddenly moved from the realm of religious fervor and idealism into the realm of canon law? And what does it mean to be approved and blessed? Although aware of juridical implications, the companions continue to move in the world of the Spirit.

The companions are now seeking the freedom a papal approval would bring them. They use terminology that shows they want to break with the past and strike out on a new path. They wish to avoid legalism and juridicism and live in a way that frees them to work at what they do best, helping their neighbor wherever the pope wishes to send them. Their minds are not narrow, their hearts are not mean-spirited, their ideals are not bound by anything but the person and the love of Jesus.

THE *IDEOQUE* CLAUSE

ideoque supplicare,
[and therefore you were requesting]

ut in his nostris pene assiduis
[that in the midst of our almost incessant]

grauissimisque occupationibus
[and burdensome occupations]

per aliquem a nobis delegatum consideretur
[it be considered through someone delegated by us]

an vestra viuendi formula
[whether your form of living]

. . . (sit conformis)
[is conformed]

euangelicis consiliis
[to the evangelical counsels]

et canonicis patrum sanctionibus sit conformis,
[and the normative teachings of the fathers]

et comperta eius . . . (congruentia)
[and after it has been found to be congruent]

cum christiane religionis puritate congruentia,
[with the purity of the Christian religion]

de more a nobis benedicatur
[according to custom it be blessed by us]

atque approbetur;
[and approved]

Structure: Supplicare [to request] continues the series of infinitives after *narrauit* [narrated]; it introduces *ut* [that], which in turn introduces two clauses containing the requests. The verb of the first request is impersonal, *consideretur* [it should be considered]; the subject is a long question introduced by *an* [whether]. The subject of the question is *viuendi formula* [way of living]. Linking the first request with the second is an ablative absolute, *comperta . . . congruentia* [its congruence having been determined]. The verbs of the second request are *benedicatur* [be blessed] and *approbetur* [be approved], with *viuendi formula* understood as the subject of both verbs.

16

The Meaning of *viuendi formula*

By the beginning of 1539, time and war have made it impossible for the companions to fulfill their vow to go to Jerusalem. Discernment, they know, is always open to further discernment: time and war have revealed the will of God to them. Ready to go wherever the pope might send them, they are convinced that God is calling them to maintain the unity of their companionship through a bond of obedience. Aware of obstacles in their path, they throw themselves vigorously into the task of removing the obstacles. They are eager for the pope to bless their union and send them on their way. In asking the pope to confirm their way of living as manifesting the presence of the Spirit they use the term *viuendi formula* [form of living], a term of the utmost importance in understanding the Society of Jesus. Prior to reflecting on the meaning of this term we will briefly consider the context of their request.

> **and therefore you were requesting**
> [ideoque supplicare]
> **that in the midst of our almost incessant**
> [ut in his nostris pene assiduis]
> **and burdensome occupations**
> [grauissimisque occupationibus]
>
> it be considered through someone delegated by us

The pope's busy schedule in 1539 is not likely to gain much sympathy from jaded hearts of the twentieth century. The statement's intent, however, is not to impress someone with all the pope has to do but rather to acknowledge the companions' gratitude for his attention to them and their needs. A study of the pope's schedule enables us to locate *Cum ex plurium* more securely in the context of the events of the times.[1] In the spring and summer of 1539, Paul III's engagement calendar includes half a dozen projects which he must have taken time to consider at Tivoli, a favorite papal retreat outside Rome.

(1) Preparing a General Council (Trent, 1545–63). In spite of his background as a Renaissance pope, Paul is eager to bring about reform in the Church. He has struggled and struggled with this council. He originally planned it for Mantua in 1537, shifted it to Vicenza in 1538, but had to postpone it to 1539. He has been busy from early January 1539 sending envoys and letters to Emperor Charles V, to Francis I, and to other Catholic princes, addressing their negative responses. He has also sent letters to all the bishops and is negotiating with the Lutherans. On April 21 he nominates three conciliar legates, but a month later his hopes for convening a council dim, and he postpones it indefinitely. He sends out more letters on June 10, and now he has to read their answers as they come in.

(2) Work of the Reform Commission. In the spring of 1539 Paul increases the commission from four to eight members, assigning two cardinals to each of the four departments to undergo reform: the Rota, the Penitentiaria, the Cancellaria, and the Dataria. The wide differences among the members make him put pressure on them in a consistory on March 5; in a private meeting he tells them to bring about reforms even at the cost of lessening revenues, a difficult concession. He has made every effort to get Giberti, the zealous bishop of Verona, to come to Rome, for his presence would be a boon to the reform movement. At least, after much negotiation, he persuades his old vicar-general from Parma, Bartolomeo Guidiccioni, to come to the curia.

(3) War with the Turks. The Turks remain a constant threat. Plans to renew the crusade in early 1539 collapse. The papal treasury is exhausted. Paul thought a salt tax would be the solution but, like other salt taxes, it has not been popular nor is it always collectable.

(4) Family Troubles. Late in 1538 Paul III lays claim to the duchy of Camerino. The emperor, Charles V, is deaf to Paul's complaints on January 1, 1539, that both Florence and Siena did not support the pope. A few days later, however, the duchy surrenders and Paul calls off his troops. The duchy is destined for Ottavio Farnese, his grandson, but not for now. Meanwhile, he has married the same Ottavio to Margaret of Austria, widow of Alessandro de' Medici and natural daughter of the emperor, and he has had some busy days trying to reconcile the reluctant sixteen-year-old widow-bride and her thirteen-year-old husband.

(5) Heresy and Schism. Germany is a worry, for Protestantism is making inroads into the Church there. England is also a worry; after excommunicating Henry VIII in December 1538, Paul is now trying to determine what to do about him, for hope is dwindling that a council can pressure him into seeking reconciliation with the Church.

(6) Miscellanea. The ordinary demands of Paul's schedule do not lessen because of crises. He needs to watch and encourage the new religious orders. The Capuchins have some problems, and he comes to their defense. And now this new company, whose members have longed to go to Jerusalem and find the Turks frustrating their attempts to do so, who dispute in his presence every couple of weeks, who teach the faithful and do not hesitate to challenge heretics, who want to convert the infidels and are ready to set the world on fire, want to become official.... People in Siena have asked him to send two of their company there, and he has been dealing with Cardinal Filonardi who wants him to send a couple of the company to Parma to renew the people, and Cardinal Cupis has been after him to send Codure to preach in Velletri, and now these men have been sent.... How good now to be at Tivoli for a few days before setting out on an exhausting journey to Loreto and Camerino and absence from Rome for over a month....

> that in the midst of our almost incessant
> and burdensome occupations

> **it be considered through someone delegated by us**
> [per aliquem a nobis delegatum consideretur]
>
> whether your form of living is conformed

The request of the companions leaves no room for half measures. They did not ask the pope to examine their form of living, for he had other work to do; nor did they request that he delegate someone to make the examination. Their request, rather, goes to the heart of the matter immediately: that their way of life *be examined,* and they specify that the examiner should be someone the pope delegates.

Popes often refer matters of importance to experts for their recommendation; papal documents rarely refer to the experts or identify them. Innocent III (1198–1216) normally delegated someone to examine newly emerged groups.[2] Leo X's 1517 bull, *Ite et vos,* dealing with the separation of the Conventuals from the Friars Minor, says "some cardinals were delegated" to look into the matter, and that they have given him their judgment "after a thorough and protracted examination of the issues" [*BRT* 5:694a].[3] *Cum ex plurium,* on the other hand, not only refers to a papal delegate but names him a few lines later.[4] Not so the formal bulls of approbation which will follow, *Regimini militantis ecclesiae* (1540) and *Exposcit debitum* (1550); neither of these has any reference to an expert who has reported to the pope on the *viuendi formula* of the companions.

> it be considered through someone delegated by us
>
> **whether your form of living**
> [an vestra viuendi formula]
>
> is conformed to the evangelical counsels

As noted above, the term *viuendi formula* (usually spelled *vivendi formula*) is a key term in understanding the Society of Jesus. It refers to the content of the five decrees of *Cum ex plurium* describing the way of life of the companions. The same *viuendi formula* will appear again under different modifications in the papal bulls *Regimini militantis ecclesiae* (1540) and *Exposcit debitum* (1550). The usual name for it is the *Formula of the Institute*. *Viuendi formula* has its own history preceding *Cum ex plurium*. The etymology of the term is revealing as is its use.

Etymological Reflections. Our purpose here is simply to get a feel for the terms *formula* and *forma* [form], from which it derives, to illumine more clearly the document we are considering. The *American Heritage Dictionary* relates *forma* to the Indo-European root *mer-bh*, connected with the Greek *morphē* [form, beauty, outward appearance]. *Harper's Latin Dictionary*, on the other hand, relates *forma* to the Sanskrit root *dhar* [support], related to the Greek *thrēnus* [footstool] and to *thronos* [throne], in either case something to rest upon in security and comfort. Both derivations are illuminating.

(For some in the monastic tradition, the image that spontaneously accompanies *forma* is that of the choir stall. Niermeyer, who gives the French meaning first and then the English, identifies as one of the meanings of *forma: banquette, stalle de choeur,* stool, choir stall, and for *formula: couche, lit, sorte de chaise longue,* couch, underframe of a bed, sort of restchair.[5] Stools and thrones and choir stalls and beds are excellent and much needed supports for human beings, in which they find not only support but rest and renewed strength.)

Whether the companions reflected on the etymology or not is irrelevant. The *formula viuendi* provided and continues to provide support and rest and vigor for the companions of Ignatius, as well as beauty and grace.

The Sanskrit root *dhar* has even more treasures to reveal, for it points to a heavily loaded Sanskrit word, *dharma*, that which is solid, enduring, unchanging, forever dependable: the teaching, the law, the truth, the whole religion or religious outlook on life. *Dharma* in India is comparable to *torah* for the Jewish faith. Jesus is the Society's equivalent of *dharma*. If he is the living example, the model, the pattern of living, he is also the living *dharma*, whereas the *formula viuendi* is the verbal expression of what being a companion of Jesus means; in that sense it is the rock on which the Society of Jesus is built; it is the teaching; it is the law; it contains the Society's truth; even more than the Spiritual Exercises, the written *viuendi formula* is the summary of the Society's religious outlook on life; and yet it is none of these, since Jesus alone is all of them.

Reflections on Usage. *Viuendi formula* is not a term unique to the Society of Jesus. Its relatives, *vivendi forma, vitae forma,* and *vita* (along with other terms found in *Cum ex plurium*), appear in a treatise as the late fourth century turns into the fifth.[6] It came into its own as a technical term in the thirteenth century when many documents concerning emerging religious groups used cognate phrases with apparently no change of meaning:

vita	*vivendi forma*	*vivendi modus et formula*
forma vite	*vivendi modus*	*forma seu dogma vivendi*
vite forma	*modus vivendi*	*regula seu vivendi formula*
vite formula		*dogma seu forma Vite*

Whatever variant is used, except *vita*, each expression has at least two components: (1) some word denoting life [*vita*] or living [*vivendi*] and (2) some word denoting form [*forma, formula*] or manner [*modus*] or norm [*dogma, regula*].

Each expression signifies the rules of governance for a particular group, as does *vita* standing alone.[7] Some documents, in fact, use one of the expressions in connection with *regula* [rule] either as a synonym for *regula*, as in *regula seu vivendi formula*, or interchangeably with it. This use of *regula*, however, gives the word a sense beyond its normal meaning. During the twelfth century *regula* generally meant one of the ancient rules that had stood the test of time, the rule of Benedict or of Basil or of Augustine. To profess a *vita* was different from professing a *regula*. *Vita* in its various forms indicated a canonical status inferior to a *regula* in the sense of one of the ancient rules. Nevertheless, groups extended the term *regula* by analogy to indicate their own norms of governance.[8]

For the moment we center our discussion on terms linking *vita* and *forma*. The earliest use of one of these terms seems to be in the *propositum* or plan of life of the *Humiliati* in 1201: "You, therefore, beloved sons in the Lord, should observe the form of living [*vivendi formam*] that we have taken care to examine diligently, to correct prudently, and to approve in a wholesome manner."[9] The date is significant. The term appears during the reign of Innocent III (1198–1216), who has a lasting influence on terminology relative to the religious life, and a few years before Lateran IV (1215), the dominant legislative force in religious life until the Council of Trent (1545–63). Thirteenth-century documents employing the above terminology mostly pertain to penitential groups, which by and large are lay groups, although clerics belong to some of them. Since they consist of people who share the same life [*vitam*], some are called fraternities. All the documents pertain to the early stages of development of new religious movements, some of which eventually become religious orders (for example, the Franciscans[10] and Carmelites[11]).

In 1405 Innocent VII approved a Dominican third order called the Brothers and Sisters of Penance. Throughout the bull of approbation, *Sedis Apostolicae providentia,* Innocent uses *forma, vivendi forma, vivendi formula,* and *vivendi modum* [*BRT* 637–42]. The terminology continues into the sixteenth century. In 1524, Clement VII used the variant form *vivendi modus* to express a communal way of living, in his brief *Exponi nobis* approving the Theatines as a legitimate way of life within the Church [*BRT* 6:73b]. In 1535 Paul III used the same expression in approving the Barnabites [*BRT* 6:191b]. What the popes recognize is that the Theatines and the Barnabites have chosen a Gospel way of living. Both groups shared with the lay movements of the thirteenth century a radical departure from the approved religious orders of the Church's first millenium. They were so new, in fact, that the Theatines had not even thought of themselves at first as a religious order.[12]

Viuendi formula and the Society of Jesus

Ignatius and his companions were the newest phenomenon on the religious scene. They were priests, not laymen, but their approach to religious life was so radically different from the ancient orders that at first they were not even called clerks regular, as were the Theatines, but were recognized still as secular clergy. Their terminology was not that of the ancient orders but of the newer movements.

The scribe of the Deliberation of the First Fathers reports that the companions "decided to come together . . . to discuss [their] vocation [*vocatione*] and *viuendi formula*" [*D* 1]. His words indicate that their vocation and their form or way of living are identical, that is, they experience within themselves a call [*vocatio*] from God to live in a particular way or according to a particular pattern [*vivendi formula*]. The call and the manner of living out the call are the same from two different points of view, and both are called "vocation." Eight years later, in 1547, Laynez comments, "After praying, we came together, and proceeding article by article in what pertains to our vocation [*nuestra vocación*], each one presented reasons for and against" [*L* 49]. When Polanco, on the other hand, wrote of the origins of the Society in 1547 he says that they engaged themselves in "organizing their way of living" [*la forma de vivir suya*] [*PSH* 89]. *Forma de vivir* is a good Spanish translation of *vivendi formula*. What Laynez calls "vocation" and Polanco "way of living" are identical.[13] Thirty years later Rodrigues puts the matter even more simply, "They decided to tell the Pontiff what kind of life [*vitam*] they desired to establish in God's honor and in the service of the Apostolic See" [*R* 91]. Their vocation, their life, their form of living are all the same.

By asking the pontiff to approve their *viuendi formula,* the companions are requesting that the five decrees containing it be transformed into papal law. This papal law would be deeply intrinsic to the Society, its very heart, and far more important than the Constitutions, yet to be written. The Formula is what the Society is all about; the Constitutions implement the Formula. A general congregation can approve or modify the Constitutions; only papal action can change the Formula. In other words, the companions wish to make a covenant among themselves, and between themselves and the pope as head of the Church, binding the whole Society to live in a certain manner within the Church.[14] The Society and its members make a commitment to a particular manner of living the Gospel, a commitment first to Jesus as the Society's head, and then to the whole Body of Christ, the Church. Each member of the Society, furthermore, makes a commitment to each of the other members, and to the deepest part of his own heart, to live according to that way of life the first fathers conceived and outlined in the Formula of the Institute.

17

The Evangelical Counsels

When Cardinal Contarini spoke to the pope on behalf of the companions, he also passed on to the pope a request: that the written version of their form of life [*viuendi formula*] be examined by someone delegated by the pope to see if that form of living conformed to the evangelical counsels and the normative teachings of the fathers.

> it be considered. . .
> whether your form of living
>
> **is conformed**
> [. . . (sit conformis)]
> **to the evangelical counsels**
> [euangelicis consiliis]
>
> and the normative teachings of the fathers,

In this last decade of the twentieth century no one is shedding blood in theological controversy over the evangelical counsels, a term that has slipped from our vocabulary, except for occasional reference to "the threefold evangelical counsels," a restrictive phrase indicating poverty, chastity, and obedience, "the three vows of religion." Before these terms surfaced, committed Christians put all their efforts into living the Gospel, and the Gospel contains more than three counsels.

The material on the evangelical counsels is like a massive tangle of string ensnarled almost beyond hope. To write an adequate treatment of the evangelical counsels might take several books. *A first book* might be about the origin of the name, and the distinction between counsels and precepts, a distinction that is not always obvious. When the term *evangelical counsels* first emerged is uncertain. Innocent III uses *con silia evangelica* in a document approving the Poor Catholics in 1208. Identical language appears in two bulls concerning the Poor Lombards in 1210 and 1212.[1] Jacques de Vitry uses it ten years later in reference to the Friars Minor in the thirty-second chapter of his *Historia occidentalis*. *A second book* might be about the gradual emergence over the course of the centuries of three counsels in particular from all the others found in the Gospel: (1) poverty: not owning anything as one's own, (2) chastity: not marrying, not having a genital relationship of any sort, (3) obedience: not doing one's own will. They are not specifically Christian but appear in the monastic traditions of other religions also. Someone needs to make a careful analysis of the patristic exegesis that seeks to uncover them in the Gospels, especially since contemporary exegesis sometimes differs markedly from the ancient interpretations. *A third book* might consider the problem of how the three evangelical counsels mentioned above gradually came to be expressed in the form of vows, how those vows became the three "vows of religion," and whether this development was an advance over the ancient monastic way of commitment or tended to confuse the unattainable with the achievable. *A fourth book* might reflect on the gradual evolution that took place in the Church that created various distinctions within the Body of Christ, the distinction, for example, between clergy and laity, between religious and non-religious, the consecrated life and that which is not consecrated, and whether these distinctions have been helpful or harmful or both.

1. The Evangelical Counsels up to 1539

To better understand what the evangelical counsels mean for Ignatius and his companions, we shall begin with Francis of

Assisi and then look briefly at the time before Francis and the time between Francis and Ignatius.

Following Jesus: Francis of Assisi

Although Francis says nothing about a way of living conformed to the evangelical counsels, he expresses the same idea in a simpler way: "to live according to the form of the holy Gospel [*vivere secundum formam sancti Evangelii*]," to have the Gospel as the pattern for one's life.[2] This meant that Francis and his friars are subject in all things to the Word of God.

Numbering neither the evangelical counsels nor the precepts, Jacques de Vitry (ca. 1170–1240) praises the Franciscans for their diligent efforts in renewing "the religion of the primitive church, its poverty and humility . . . by eagerly and thirstily drawing pure water from the evangelical spring, so that, deliberately imitating the life of the apostles, they work to fulfill in every way not only the evangelical precepts [*euangelica precepta*] but also the counsels [*consilia*]."[3] De Vitry sees the Franciscans simply as trying to live the Gospel. Francis's first biographer, Thomas of Celano, aptly expresses this Gospel attitude of heart:

> His highest purpose, his chief desire and supreme aim was to observe the holy Gospel in every way and by every means; and perfectly, with all watchfulness, all zeal, entire desire of mind, full fervour of heart, to follow the teaching and the footsteps of our Lord Jesus Christ.[4]

The *Earlier Rule* of 1221, in a lapidary sentence that surely reflects the original rule of life [*propositum vitae*], no longer extant, that Innocent III approved in 1209 or 1210, puts the matter succinctly in the prologue: "This is the life of the Gospel of Jesus Christ."[5] The original Rule placed Jesus at the center of Franciscan life and probably read like this: "The rule and life of these brothers is this: to follow the teaching and the footsteps of our Lord Jesus Christ."[6] The opening lines of the first chapter of the *Earlier Rule* contain a few more words that were probably inserted into the original text under the influence of Innocent III:[7]

> The rule and life of these brothers is this: to live in obedience [*vivere in obedientia*], in chastity [*in castitate*], and without anything of their own [*et sine proprio*], and to follow the teaching and the footsteps of our Lord Jesus Christ.[8]

Dino Dozzi shows that to live in obedience, in chastity, and without anything of one's own is not synonymous with following the teaching and the footsteps of our Lord Jesus Christ.[9] At this point the *Rule* presents a series of quotations from the Gospels. Dozzi sees in each of them three distinct moments constitutive of the life of the friars:

1) leaving,   leaving things [*sine proprio*],
                                    leaving family affection [*castitas*],
                                    leaving one's own will [*obedientia*],
2) following Jesus,
3) receiving reward
   of discipleship.

The three evangelical counsels are only introductory to the following of Jesus; they do not constitute the following of Jesus.

The *Later Rule* (1223) rearranges the words (whether inserted or not) into a smoother and stronger sequence to set off the primacy of the Gospel, making Jesus, and Jesus alone, the center and norm of the friars' life, with everything else subordinated to him:

> The rule and life of the Friars Minor is this: to observe the holy Gospel of our Lord Jesus Christ by living in obedience, without anything of their own, and in chastity.[10]

This last text is a hinge. It links two approaches to Christian living, one old and one new, the observance of the Gospel and the practice of the threefold evangelical counsels, and subordinates the new to the old. The old is more biblical and more spontaneous, the new the result of much reflection. The old prevailed from the earliest days of the Christian era down to the time of Francis. The new began about a century before Francis and has continued to the present day.[11]

Following Jesus: Early Christianity

The first centuries of Christianity were conscious of but one Christian vocation: to follow Christ, to be perfect as the Gospel requires. Today, as then, all Christians have that same vocation. The invitation is to listen to the Word of God and after hearing [*audiens*] it to be obedient [*ob-audiens*] to it. The Christian response to the Gospel depends not only on what God has spoken within the Christian community and on what the Christian community has heard, but also on what God has spoken to each member of the community and on what that member has heard interiorly. The *Life of Saint Antony* provides a classic example.[12] Over against the Word of God, in the perspective of early Christianity, stands the "world," understood in a negative sense.[13] One pole of this global reality, the Word of God, calls for submission, and the other pole, the world, calls for renunciation. The model is Jesus, who was obedient unto death, the model of submission, the model of renunciation.[14]

The Rule of Benedict is a good example of the Gospel approach to Christian living.[15] The prologue reads, "Clothed then with faith and the performance of good works, let us set out on this way, with the Gospel for our guide, that we may deserve to see him *who has called us to his kingdom* (1 Thess. 2:12)" [Prol. 21]. The Gospel way is central for Benedict. In a chapter replete with quotations from Scripture, Benedict provides a long list of tools for good works, making no distinction between command and invitation (chap. 4). Sixty-first on this list is an admonition to obey the abbot; sixty-fourth, "treasure chastity." He does not list poverty. Nevertheless, Benedict devotes the whole of the next chapter to obedience (chap. 5), and spends a whole chapter on whether monks should have anything of their own (chap. 33). Chastity does not have its own chapter; some matters are so obvious as to be taken for granted.[16] De Vogüé shows that for Benedict Christ-like obedience [*RB* 7.34], "the way we go to God" [*RB* 71.2], is simply a way of giving oneself to God, and so is disappropriation, having nothing as one's own.[17] Chastity, too, is a way of giving oneself to God.

Benedict, then, is a good example of the older approach to Christian living. The Rule mentions what we call the evangelical counsels only in the context of the whole Gospel, of all of Scripture: "What page, what passage of the inspired books of the Old and New Testaments is not the truest of guides for human life?" [*RB* 73.3]. The Word of God is primary; the counsels are subordinate to the Word.[18]

The Triad Takes Shape

As time passed, the evangelical counsels that we know as poverty, chastity, and obedience began to be considered as embodying in a special way all that the Gospel contains. Two key texts, often cited but rarely quoted beyond a line or two, illustrate the new approach.

(1) Letter of Odo, Abbot of St. Genevieve (1148)

The first text is a personal letter written in 1148, often cited as the first explicit reference to the evangelical counsels as we know them.[19] The author is Odo, the abbot of St. Genevieve in Paris, an abbey following the Augustinian rule. Although the terminology is still developing, Odo sheds light on the later classic terminology. Odo's triad, moreover, is all-embracing, providing a rich setting for the three vows that will come later. Odo does not use our contemporary term poverty [*paupertas*], but sharing [*communio*]: "In our profession," he says, "we promise three things, as you well know, chastity, sharing [*communionem*], obedience."[20] *Communio* immediately suggests poverty, the sharing of goods, but the first sentence of the Rule of Augustine intimates that *communio* means more than that:

> The reason you have been gathered together into one community [*in unum*] is that you may live in harmony [*unanimes*] in the house, and that you may have one soul and one heart [*anima una et cor unum*] in God.

The second sentence of the Rule suggests that unity includes the sharing of goods: "And do not call anything your own [*proprium*], but let all things be common [*communia*] among you."[21] Unity, sharing their lives together, includes, but is not exhausted by, the sharing of goods.

Abbot Odo warns against a narrow and legalistic interpretation of chastity, sharing, and obedience. Such an interpretation could lead to immature complacency. The abbot's view is that their profession is open-ended and all-embracing:

> Someone might say: "The profession that I made under God's inspiration, I have kept up to now with his help; for I maintain chastity of the body [*castitatem corporis*]; having nothing of my own [*proprium*], I live sharing with others [*communiter vivo*]; doing what is commanded me, I observe obedience [*obedientiam*]." Well, if it is as he says, well and good, but even so the one who says this should not be secure: for if we attend more carefully to the words of profession, and if we inquire a little more subtly what lies within, we shall clearly see that we have perhaps not even begun what we stupidly thought we had brought to perfection.[22]

(a) Chastity. Odo examines a twofold chastity, of the body and of the spirit, maintaining that any form of sinfulness is far worse than the loss of bodily integrity, "for as often as we consent even to the least sin, as often as we love something other than God, we corrupt the chastity of our mind, because, abandoning the Creator, the spouse of the soul, and joining ourselves to a creature in illicit love, we somehow commit spiritual fornication."[23] Having burst the bubble of complacency, Odo settles juridically for that integrity of the body that avoids carnal acts and that integrity of the mind that in no way consents to carnal desires. In the process, however, he deepens the meaning of chastity by giving it a larger context. He makes no comment on precepts and counsels, but he reflects on chastity in terms of the demands of the Gospel.

(b) Sharing [*communio*]. Odo also enlarges the technical meaning of *communio* by dwelling on its religious meaning. His remarks are a commentary on the first sentence of the Rule of Augustine (itself reminiscent of the early Christian community in Acts 4:32):

> Because one sees that he has nothing external as his own [*proprium*], he thinks he observes sharing [*communionem*] perfectly. Maybe he makes note that he has no bread of his own, no

> garment of his own, but does not pay attention to having his own will [*propriam voluntatem*]. He pays attention to sharing a house with others, but does not notice he has no common love [*communem dilectionem*] with others. . . . Let no one think that by living in one house or sharing one table, or even by participating in the one body and blood of the Lord one fulfills the profession of sharing with others [*communionis*], if one clings to his own will [*propriam . . . voluntatem*] or by evil conduct drives a wedge into fraternal unity [*fraternam . . . unitatem*].[24]

In this sense Odo sees little difference between a life of sharing and obedience, or between a life of sharing and chaste love, which expresses itself not only in marriage but also in fraternal love in community. Each demands a total giving of oneself to God. To be without anything of one's own while retaining one's own will or spurning the brotherhood, is not to respond to the call of the Gospel.[25]

(c) Obedience. Nor does Odo find much difference between chastity and obedience. Obedience for Odo is simply to set aside all earthly fear and all earthly love and follow commands out of love of God alone. To obey in what is difficult and contrary to nature demands a joyful and cheerful will; to obey in what is easy and brings pleasure demands not seeking the delight of doing one's own will, "for whoever for the love of God once abandons the allurements and the shackles of the world, sins without a doubt if he still goes back to them on occasion out of his own free choice."[26]

For Odo, then, chastity, sharing, and obedience are extremely broad in their Gospel context and suffer markedly if approached from a juridical and reductionist viewpoint.

(2) Letter of Innocent III (1202)

The second key text is a letter from Innocent III (1198–1216) to the abbot of the Benedictine monastery at Subiaco. Innocent immersed himself in every aspect of the life of the Church, including the spiritual health of monks. He made a series of canonical visits to monasteries living under the Rule of Benedict, received reports from legates, listened to complaints from bishops and from the monks themselves.[27] In 1202, a half century after Odo's letter and a few years before meeting Francis, he visited the monastery at Subiaco, and upon his return to Rome he wrote a letter to the abbot expressing concern about several deficiencies he had witnessed during his visit, setting down criteria for genuine monastic living.[28]

Writers often cite this letter in reference to the genesis of the classical triad of poverty, chastity, and obedience.[29] Closer examination reveals that Innocent does not use those precise terms, nor is an equivalent triad obvious at first sight. Innocent does not write about *poverty* or about *vows;* he mentions several elements in monastic life, some of them more important than others: not clinging to riches, having nothing of one's own, control of the tongue, mortification, detachment, good example, obedience, the renunciation of property, chastity. Three times he refers to acting according to either "monastic discipline," or "the ancient custom of a monastery," or "the rule [*regulam*]." He is talking about obedience, obedience to the rule as well as to the abbot, even though he does not state that explicitly in each instance. The letter is taken so seriously that it is included in the *Decretals* of Gregory IX. The critical passage authors most often quote is the conclusion of the final sentence:

> The renunciation of property [*abdicatio proprietatis*], as also the custody of chastity [*custodia castitatis*], is so connected to the monastic rule [*regulae monachali*], that not even the Supreme Pontiff can dispense in its regard.[30]

The reference to the monastic rule is an oblique reference to obedience; the terminology has not yet evolved into its classical form. The import of the passage is twofold: it becomes normative for Benedictine reform and it declares "poverty," chastity, and obedience essential to the religious life without prejudice to other possible essentials.

A serious question remains. Has he substituted the abdication of property for sharing [*communio*] as though one is equal to the other, or has he focused his attention on one particular aspect of sharing? As head of the Church, Innocent III is determined to safeguard Gospel living in the monasticism of his day and at the same time, aware that the Gospel is for everyone, he engages himself equally in the struggles of various lay movements that outspokenly champion evangelical poverty.[31] Nevertheless, in countering an abuse he draws attention away from the Gospel to the abuse and its cure and helps to bring about a radical shift within the ecclesial psyche from an emphasis on sharing life together to an emphasis on the nonpossession of property.

To sum up, Odo is dealing with a triad already in existence, apparently in the profession formula of his monastery, but does not want the terminology to place limits on the full reality of what his monks profess. Innocent, on the other hand, wants to insist that certain elements of monastic life are more important than others and even the pope cannot set them aside. Far from wanting to limit monastic profession, he is trying to emphasize the totality of the commitment. The words of Innocent, however, are more open to a legalistic interpretation than are those of Odo.

Precisely how and when poverty [*paupertas*] takes the place of sharing [*communio*], the renunciation of property [*abdicatio proprietatis*], and having nothing of one's own [*sine proprio*] is uncertain. In the thirteenth century Thomas Aquinas uses both *paupertas* and *absque proprio*. In his *Summa theologica* Thomas writes that the foundation of charity "is voluntary poverty [*voluntaria paupertas*] so that one may live without anything of one's own [*absque proprio*]."[32] *Communio* emphasizes the sharing of life, including the sharing of goods; *abdicatio proprietatis* emphasizes getting rid of property and not acquiring it; *sine proprio* underlines not having anything of one's own; *paupertas* implies having little. Except for *communio* none of the terms explicitly demands sharing; living in community, however, implies the sharing of goods not personally owned, and *paupertas* suggests that there is little to share.

Further Developments

In 1243, Pope Innocent IV (1243–54) wrote a letter to the abbess of the Poor Clare convent in Prague, which reads in part:

> The *Rule* [of St. Benedict] itself does not bind the Sisters of your order to anything other than obedience, the renuncia-

tion of property, and perpetual chastity, which come under the various elements of any religious order [*quae sub alia cujuslibet religionis existunt*].[33]

Some commentators read *substantialia* rather than *sub alia*, finding a more explicit witness to the bond between the three vows and the essentials of religious life than the text may, in fact, warrant[34]. Innocent's letter states no more than that obedience, the renunciation of property, and perpetual chastity are *among* those elements that are found in every religious order. The letter is really more a fatherly and informal commentary on Canon 13 of Lateran IV (1215) than a solemn declaration of Christian doctrine. Hearsay, furthermore, is intermingled with Innocent's own thoughts, for Innocent is quoting what his predecessor said to the cardinal protector of the order.[35] In a papal bull, however, even hearsay is in danger of being transmuted into a principle of canon law.

How the three vows come to be considered the substantials of the religious life requires further research into the religious developments underlying the terminology of this whole period. No one can doubt that in the twelfth and thirteenth centuries the three elements of poverty, chastity, and obedience gradually became more important as an expression of the religious life. Without anyone's intending it, the focus also gradually shifted from following Jesus to the means of following Jesus. That these three elements constitute the substantials of a religious order is either an entirely new view of religious life or a new expression of a view already widely accepted. The terminology, in any case, would endure, with the consequent danger that the shift of focus might also endure.

By the time of Ignatius and his companions, the formulas expressing religious commitment have evolved through various stages: simple commitment, promise, vows. Two characteristics mark the formulas of the new religious orders of the sixteenth century. They express commitment in terms of *vows*, and the vows are *poverty, chastity,* and *obedience*. Furthermore, a cursory survey of bulls and briefs approving new religious orders in the first half of the sixteenth century reveals two consistent practices on the part of the Church: (1) if the new order has already chosen a rule, the bull or brief mentions the rule according to which the members are going to live;[36] (2) if there is no mention of a rule, the bull or brief indicates that the members will live according to the three substantials of the religious life, the vows of poverty, chastity, and obedience.[37] What is the meaning of substantials: the elements that stand under [*substant*] or at the base of the religious life? or the elements that constitute the substance [*substantia*] of the religious life? Whatever the intent of the word, the full reality of any religious order is found in the Gospel, and the papal bulls and briefs do not deny that.

2. The Companions and the Evangelical Counsels

The companions present conformity to the evangelical counsels as a norm for discerning whether the Spirit of God is present in their way of living. But what do the companions mean by the evangelical counsels when they ask Paul III to have his delegate determine whether their way of living conformed to them? Ignatius has no treatise on the evangelical counsels, nor do the other companions. Remarks in the Spiritual Exercises, however, reveal some suppositions of Ignatius, and the Deliberation of the First Fathers along with the discussions immediately after reveal some of the ideas the companions share. The most revealing evidence of their approach to the evangelical counsels appears in the five decrees of the Formula of the Institute in which they outline their form of living.

The Spiritual Exercises

In the Spiritual Exercises Ignatius occasionally mentions the vows of poverty, chastity, and obedience, or the religious life, but he subordinates each statement to some other thought. The context reveals what the evangelical counsels mean to him more than the words he uses. He does not emphasize the vows themselves or the generosity vows require but the centrality of God and the need for discernment before embracing vows.

(1) The consideration of the Call of the King [91–98] is a parable in pictures, similar to Francis's simple image of follow-

ing in the footsteps of Jesus. In it Ignatius speaks of various ways of responding to the call of Jesus. He observes that in response to Christ's call, "all those who have judgment and reason will offer themselves wholeheartedly for this labor" [96], but he also presents a more radical response: actively removing, by a deliberate choice, the obstacles that stand in the way of offering one's whole person [97].[38] "The offerings of greater worth and moment" contain two conditions: "provided only that it is for your greater service and praise" and "if your Most Holy Majesty desires to elect and receive me into such a life and state" [98].

For Ignatius the person of Jesus is central. The response to his call is radical or more radical, not in relation to Jesus but with respect to all that is not God.[39] Moreover, the response a person freely gives depends primarily on God's choice and God's gift. God initiates the call, not the person who receives the call.

(2) Jesus is not only central. He is the primary example of how to live a human life. After the contemplations on the incarnation and Jesus' infancy that follow the Call of the King, Ignatius presents two attractive contemplations, one on "how the child Jesus was obedient to his parents at Nazareth" and "next how they found him in the temple" [134]. The Introduction to the Consideration on States of Life follows immediately:

> We have already considered the example which Christ our Lord gave us for the first state of life, which consists in the observance of the commandments. He gave this example when he lived in obedience to his parents.
>
> We have also considered the example he gave us for the second state, that of evangelical perfection, when he remained in the temple, separating himself from his adoptive father and human mother in order to devote himself solely to the service of his eternal Father. [135]

At Nazareth Jesus responds to God with his whole person in his obedience to Mary and Joseph, but in the temple episode his response is more radical, a deeper listening to and hearing [*ob-audiens*] and responding to his Father's voice. He does not allow even his love for his parents to be an obstacle in the service of his Father. In these sections Ignatius does not mention counsels or vows or religious life. The term Ignatius uses is *evangelical perfection*. The focus is always on Jesus and the Gospel.

(3) The fourteenth and fifteenth annotations, which Ignatius wrote after he had finished his theological studies, introduce the subject of vows, both in general and in particular.[40] Here Ignatius manifests himself not only as a wise and shrewd director of souls, but also as a prudent guide of other directors of souls. He cautions a director not to allow an exercitant in a burst of fervor to make any vow that might prove ill-considered and precipitous.[41] One can "advise another to enter religious life, which entails the taking of vows of obedience, poverty, and chastity." Even so, "one ought to bestow much thought on the circumstances and character of each person, and on the helps or hindrances one is likely to meet with in carrying out what one wishes to promise" [14]. If the exercitant should not outrun God, the director should not outguess God. God is central, not the vows, which are only means to God.[42] Proper discernment requires that the director, as well as the exercitant, have a listening attitude, coupled with a profound knowledge of the exercitant and of the immediate context of the exercitant's experience.

(4) The fifteenth annotation goes a step further, admonishing the director not to move the exercitant "toward poverty or any other promise more than toward their opposites, or to one state or way of life more than to another." As Ignatius explains, "It is more appropriate and far better that the Creator and Lord himself should communicate himself to the devout soul . . . disposing it for the way which will most enable the soul to serve him in the future" [15]. Primary for Ignatius is that the service of God, whether in one state of life or another, is God's free gift and call. A person should not choose a state of life because it is easier or more difficult or better, or because to do so would be more generous, but solely because God calls that person to one rather than the other.[43]

The Practice of the Companions

Vows are commonplace in the worldview of the companions. They are used to them, comfortable with them, and they do not question their appropriateness in certain situations.

Ignatius, for example, makes a vow of chastity shortly after his conversion, probably at the shrine of Aránzazu on the way to Montserrat.[44] Favre promises perpetual chastity to God at the age of twelve [F 4]. At Montmartre each of the companions makes a vow of poverty [L 30], not binding while studying in Paris, and allowing them to retain what they need [*viaticum*] for the pilgrimage to Jerusalem [R 13]. On leaving Paris, they distribute their surplus to the poor [R 29]. Experience soon teaches them not to beg from door to door (too dangerous for the Spaniards since France was at war with Spain) but to set apart enough of the viaticum to enable them to get to Venice [R 29–30]. After they leave Venice for Loreto and Rome, they begin to practice poverty [R 48]. Their ideal of poverty is not a life of simplicity, "not having much," but "not having anything at all [*sine proprio*]." Very likely they also have a vow of chastity [R 13] and a vow to go to the Holy Land [F 15, R 13]. Prayer and fasting, pilgrimaging and working with the poor are a part of their lives [L 36–37], an attempt to live out the Gospel, especially as experienced in and through the Spiritual Exercises. At their ordination in Venice they make solemn vows of poverty and chastity [*PSH* 70]. They continue to live according to the Gospel, living in obedience and taking turns in the role of superior [R 63].

Already having these two solemn vows, they decide to come together to discuss their "vocation and manner of living" [D 1], in that period called the Deliberation of the First Fathers. After prayer they conclude to confirm their practice of obedience by a vow of obedience [D 8]. They decide that those seeking to join them should make a vow of obedience to go wherever the pope might send them [DS 1] and should be actually poor before being admitted to probation [DS 9]. They decide that they can accept a house or church on loan without right of ownership, and must return it without dispute whenever the owner chooses to take it back [DS 15], meaning that the community as well as its members is to be without anything of its own [*sine proprio*], a provision far beyond the practice of the monastic communities, and even of the mendicants. They have no discussion on chastity, for chastity is a given. They have freely given themselves and with great affection bound themselves to Jesus.

The Five Decrees of the Formula of the Institute

The request the companions made to Paul III through Cardinal Contarini was not simply that someone he delegated should examine their way of living [*viuendi formula*] to see if it conformed to the evangelical counsels. They wanted that person to examine the written version of their way of living.

In the Formula of the Institute, the companions sketch their revolutionary vision of the religious life. They break new ground and lead the way by example. For a Church in dire need of reform in head and members, scourged by internal dissensions regarding faith in Jesus, and at war with those who did not believe in Christ, the Formula reads almost like an act of faith not only in Christ but in the Church. Like the Rule of Francis, the *viuendi formula* of the companions expresses a vision that refuses to be contained by the three vows. For Ignatius and his companions, too, the center is Jesus. In the Formula both *Deus* [God] and *Dominus* [Lord] refer to Jesus, for example, "to place all trust in God and his vicar" [*CEP* 3]. The pope is Jesus' vicar, not the vicar of God the Father. Jesus is the head of the Company, and he is the one who has called them together and given them work to do.

In the time of the companions, religious commitment expresses itself in terms of the evangelical counsels and by means of vows. Children of their times, they express their *viuendi formula* in the terminology of the times, using it as a way of following Jesus, their head, without reserve. In the Formula they introduce the vows not as a sacred or privileged triad but only in the context of Jesus and the Gospel and each in its proper place.[45] Their way of living is a way to God [*via quaelibet ad illum*] that puts no limits on the counsels or on the vows: they embrace the evangelical counsels not to limit the service of Jesus but to open themselves to the fullness of Gospel living, to the endless surprises and the countless risks the Gospel presents. At the side of Jesus carrying his cross, they are ready for anything.[46]

Chastity. The Formula begins with ministry and immediately presents chastity in the context of a ministry that is universal and all-extensive. Chastity is one aspect of a proposed way of living, a life of service to Christ and his vicar; like the other vows it is presented as wholly subordinate to that service, as a means to express that way of living in service. Just as the Gospel (Jesus) was primary for Francis, so Jesus and his service is primary for Ignatius and his companions. Just as Francis had a vision that was wider than the vows, so also does Ignatius. The Formula places Christ at the center of the companions' lives in the opening words:

> Whoever in our Society, which we desire to be designated by the name of Jesus, wishes to serve God under the standard of the cross and serve the Lord alone and his vicar on earth, after a solemn vow of perpetual chastity....[47] [*CEP* 2]

The centrality of Jesus in the outlook of Ignatius and his companions is palpable here. Jesus is the Lord whom alone they serve. The centuries-old search of monks for God alone takes a new shape in the service of Jesus alone. As aloneness was of the essence of a monk, one without spouse, so for the companions chastity embodies the centrality of Jesus in their lives, their total dedication to Jesus and to his work discovered through his vicar on earth. The vow of chastity is caught up in a larger vision of service of Jesus alone. Chastity is a means of service, expresses commitment, and embodies the love of him of whom it is said there is no other. Soon after, anyone who wishes to serve is told to "take care to have always before his eyes first of all God, and then the nature of this, his institute, which is a sort of way to him, and to pursue with all his energy this end proposed to him by God" [*CEP* 2]. Once again, Jesus is the center. The one who wishes to serve him is to serve with all his heart, with all his strength. That is the context of the vow of chastity.

Obedience. The theme of the service of Christ in a ministry as wide as the Church continues with an expansive view of obedience. The companions are to be aware that the whole Society and each one in it "are at the service of God [*Deo militare*] under faithful obedience to His Holiness Paul the Third and his successors" [*CEP* 3]. In obeying Christ's vicar they serve Christ himself [*Deo militare*]. Jesus is the central figure. Furthermore, they bind themselves by vow to go wherever the pope sends them, ruling out any possibility of refusal or of offering excuses. The demand is so lofty that those who wish to join them should ask themselves whether they have the spiritual resources to respond in this manner, "that is, whether the Holy Spirit who impels them is promising them so much grace that they can hope, with his help, to carry the burden of this calling" [*CEP* 3]. The Spirit who impels them to serve Jesus in chastity is the Spirit who impels them to serve the pope in obedience. Chastity and obedience are at the service of ministry and blend into the same reality.

Concerning obedience within the Company, the superior "should always be mindful of the kindness, gentleness and love of Christ, and the pattern of Peter and Paul." The subjects should be obedient to the superior "in everything pertaining to the observance of the rule and they should recognize and venerate Christ as present in him" [*CEP* 4]. Jesus is the model for the superior's style of governing. Jesus is the focus in the subject's relation to the superior. Jesus is at the center of the life of the companions. Their lives embrace far more than the vows: they envelop the Son of God whom they are to venerate in the superior.

Poverty. By 1539 *paupertas* [poverty] has replaced *communio* [sharing] and *sine proprio* [having nothing of one's own] in religious language, which is unfortunate, for loving union and having nothing of their own both as persons and as community is precisely what the companions have in mind:

> Since we have learned from experience that a life as far removed as possible from every taint of avarice and as similar as possible to evangelical poverty, is more joyful, more simple and more suitable for edifying the neighbor, and since we know that our Lord Jesus Christ will provide his servants who seek only the kingdom of God what is needed for food and clothing, let each and every one vow perpetual poverty. [*CEP* 5]

The companions do not spin theories; they write out of their experience. In Gospel poverty they do not cling to things but accept all from Jesus, who is at the center of their poverty. If they echo Francis here, it is because they have responded to the same Gospel.

When we reflect on the vows thus described, little distinguishes the full reality of one vow from the full reality of the other. Each means total transparency to God, revealed in Jesus in the Gospel: *obedience* the fullness of listening to God's word, *chastity* the fullness of self-donation to God and to his people, *poverty* the fullness of possessing God alone.

Gospel Context of Everyday Living. In a culture that delighted in elaborate display, the Formula approaches prayer and liturgy in a modest fashion. Anything elaborate could hinder the companions' ministry,[48] "since according to the nature of our vocation, besides other necessary duties, we frequently have to spend a great part of the day and even of the night in comforting the sick both in body and in spirit" [*CEP* 6]. They follow the Gospel pattern of Jesus, who withdrew for quiet but responded to need whenever it presented itself.

The Formula affirms that in the spirit of the Gospel the companions engage in fasts and mortification but impose nothing by rule; with the freedom of the children of God they can occupy themselves more fully in the ministry of the Gospel. The Formula closes with an admonition that the training of each new member should be long and careful, "and when he shall appear to be prudent in Christ and conspicuous in learning or in the sanctity of his life, then let him finally be admitted to the service [*miliciam*] of Jesus Christ" [*CEP* 7].

Conclusion

From the time of God's call of Abraham, the human response has been a stretching process, an effort to be faithful to oneself by surrendering entirely to the divine reality deep within the human heart. Since the human cannot respond wholly to the divine at any one moment, the response is a process rather than an act, a stretching to attain rather than an attainment.

Monasticism has always recognized this fact. For the first millenium of Christianity, the expression of Gospel commitment was to a process, the following of Jesus. By joining a monastic community the early monks committed themselves to living the life of the community. Even when the rule required an oral or written expression of commitment, that expression aimed at embracing a life rather than binding to precise obligations. When making a commitment to live a fully Christian life according to the Gospel under the direction of an elder in a community of unmarried persons who shared goods in common, the monk did not express commitment in terms of vows of poverty, chastity, and obedience. Followers of the Rule of Benedict, for example, promised stability, fidelity to the monastic life [*conversationem morum*], and obedience. Even when poverty, chastity, and obedience became common usage in profession formulas, the old monastic orders retained their ancient expression of commitment to the monastic life and process.

Rooted in the Gospel, the evangelical counsels presuppose that a person always has more to offer. An understanding of the counsels that views them as particular and attainable, denying the universality of religious commitment and the nature of religious commitment as process, is detrimental to the full life of the Gospel and weakens the richness of the ancient tradition.[49] The use of the term *religious* for certain Christians obscures the universal call to holiness. To promise or vow something particular can obscure the baptized person's commitment to the whole of the Gospel. Whether we read Matthew or Paul, Cassian or Benedict, Francis or Odo or Ignatius and his companions, the call is always to magnanimity. The struggle to stretch goes on. Religious commitment is an on-going process, a reaching toward freedom, the freedom of the children of God, a call to liberty in Christ and in the Spirit.

18

The Normative Teachings of the Fathers

A second norm for discerning the presence of the Spirit of God is whether the companions' written form of life conforms also to the normative teachings of the fathers.

> it be considered . . .
> whether your form of living is conformed
> to the evangelical counsels
>
> **and the normative teachings of the fathers,**
> [et canonicis patrum sanctionibus]

1. The Meaning of *Canonicis patrum sanctionibus*

Canon, a Latin noun from the Greek word *kanōn* [rod], means a measure, a rule, a model, a standard. It came to signify the body of truth necessary for salvation, as opposed to the imperial laws, which are subject to change. In Church parlance *canon* referred equally to doctrinal norms and disciplinary norms. Disciplinary norms are norms of action, as opposed to doctrinal norms, norms of belief. Between the Council of Nicea (325), however, and the end of the Second Lateran Council (1139), *canon* referred almost universally to a disciplinary decision, whether of a council or a pope. The Third

Lateran Council (1179) called its disciplinary decrees *capitula* [chapters], and other councils did the same up to but not including the Council of Trent.[1] This fact suggests that the five decrees [*capitula*] of the Formula of the Institute are not simply convenient divisions or chapters; the five "chapters" are disciplinary decrees in the sense that their primary purpose is to outline a program of action rather than a creed.

The adjective *canonicus* means regular, according to a rule, canonical, standard. It came to mean having the force of law in the Church. Both *canon* and *canonicus* intimate the solidity of truth more than something juridical.

Sanctio, another Latin noun, has the same root as *sanctus* [holy, sacred, inviolable], and means a decree or ordinance. Although it also can mean sanction, a coercive measure to bring about compliance with a law, its primary meaning is the decree or ordinance itself. In ancient times it even referred to doctrinal decisions of the popes.[2] *Sanctio* contains no suggestion of the tentative; rather, it is that which has been rendered sacred, fixed unalterably, made inviolate and irrevocable. Because modern usage employs *sanction* for both condemnation and permission, one might easily interpret the phrase *canonicae sanctiones* in papal and conciliar documents to mean canonical decrees imposing coercive measures or canonical decrees granting permissions. A closer reading, however, suggests that the phrase refers to established teaching rather than to any particular decrees.[3] In a papal bull of 1335, for instance, Benedict XII writes: "Although in the case of monks who act as proprietors, except for administrators, plenty has been provided through established teaching [*canonicas sanctiones*], since the giving up of property is integral to the monastic rule . . . we decree . . ."[4] In this passage the *canonical sanctions* are not concessions, penalties, or particular coercive measures of popes or councils, but long-established, time-honored monastic teachings on how to deal with monks who have acquired property for themselves.

The *fathers*, therefore, in the phrase, "normative teachings of the fathers," are our religious ancestors, those who have gone before us, the fathers of the Church in the widest possible sense. The term includes those we call the Fathers of the Church from the beginning of Christianity to the last of the Fathers, St. Bernard (1091–1153). It also includes the popes who have enacted decrees on the religious life, the conciliar fathers of provincial as well as ecumenical councils, those participating in synods and chapters of abbots, the monastic fathers and others whose teachings have become normative and have the force of law in the Church. The *fathers,* in this sense, form a good part of the living tradition in the Church.

The question, therefore, is: does the form of life of the companions fit into the living tradition of the Church or is it an aberration from that tradition?

The viuendi formula of the Companions

Papal directives concerning the Theatine Rule confirm the above interpretation of the meaning of *canonicae sanctiones* and provide part of the linguistic context in which the companions write *Cum ex plurium.*[5] Clement VII's brief approving the Theatines in 1524, authorized them to draw up "statutes, ordinances and constitutions" covering everything about their way of life, all that was "lawful and proper, reasonable and not contrary to Christian practice and the revered norms [*canonibus*]" [*BRT* 6:74a]. *Cum ex plurium* puts the same matter in a positive way and in question form: is the *viuendi formula* of the companions in accord with the evangelical counsels and the established teachings?

Regarding the evangelical counsels, we have seen above that the five decrees of the Formula embrace them in a fresh and new way: they view the counsels as relating to and enhancing ministry. Regarding the established teachings of the fathers, this book has taken considerable care to locate the spiritual position of Ignatius and his companions in the flowing stream of the living tradition of the Church, with Antony and the desert tradition of the East, with the western tradition of Benedict and the Carthusians and Cistercians, with the freshness of Francis, and with the originality of Dominic within the Augustinian tradition. Regarding specific legislation on the part of the Church, the *viuendi formula* not only meets the requirements of conciliar decrees but often goes far beyond them.[6]

A problem remains. The companions recognize that their very existence contradicts positions the Church has taken in the past, as we are about to see.

2. Canon 13 of Lateran IV (1215)

In their early deliberations, one of the objections to a vow of obedience is that the companions "may be forced by the Supreme Pontiff to live under another rule that has already been established and constituted" [*D* 7], a possibility they clearly do not relish. They have good grounds for their fear. Both Canon 13 of the Fourth Lateran Council (1215) and Canon 23 of the Second Council of Lyons (1274) forbade the creation of new religious orders.

The Fourth Lateran Council, commonly called in canon law "the Great Council," had the same force for the time of Ignatius as the Council of Trent had for the twentieth-century Church before Vatican II.[7] Attending the council were 412 bishops and about 800 abbots and priors.[8]

The politico-religious context of the council's Canon 13, which treats religious orders, is the subject of scholarly dispute. Some say the decree represents the initiative of bishops opposed to Innocent III's tendency to accept too many disparate groups under the umbrella of the Church and of abbots opposed to establishing new and competing religious orders.[9] Others maintain that the initiative for the canon came from Innocent III as part of his effort to bring order and harmony and a certain amount of healthy uniformity into the religious life of the Church.[10] Likely all parties had something to gain. Whatever the context, the decree did not have in mind religious orders as they are today, organizations having a multiplicity of religious houses.

In those days, except for the Cistercians, each religious house was autonomous; the houses were in no way federated with one another. The Cistercians, who followed the Rule of Benedict, had not only numerous houses presided over by individual abbots but also a system of governance tying these monasteries together; they were the only group that would fit the twentieth-century idea of a religious order.[11] In contrast, for the Benedictines, who followed the same rule, each house was independent from every other house, and similarly for the canons regular. Except for the Cistercians, then, to found a religious house was to found an autonomous religious community.[12]

Moreover, terminology was different in 1215 because reality was different. A good many terms that have fixed meanings today were fluid then. *Religio, ordo, propositum, regula, institutio, approbatio, confirmatio* were all in evolution largely because of the advent of the two world-wide mendicant orders, the Franciscans and the Dominicans. So also were *constitutiones, institutiones, instituta, statuta, ordines, traditiones, consuetudines, observantiae, usus,* and others.[13]

At the time of Lateran IV, *religio* was a very important term, indicating a way of life, a way of religious observance.[14] It embraced a range of meaning including (1) the Christian or ascetical way of life, (2) the religious fervor associated with that kind of life, (3) the way of life lived in a monastery, (4) a religious order or body of people living a way of life (following a rule) approved by the Church.

At the same time, *ordo* was synonymous with *religio*.[15] For some centuries *ordo monasticus* [monastic order] had referred to those who followed the monastic life and *ordo canonicus* [canonical order] to those who lived as canons regular.[16] For almost a hundred years before Lateran IV papal documents consistently referred to those in the *ordo monasticus* as following either the Rule of Benedict or, on occasion, the Rule of Basil, and to those in the *ordo canonicus* as following the Rule of Augustine.[17] Both monks and canons regular were considered *regulares:* those who follow a rule. A practice existed, therefore, of limiting the rules available to a religious community. Much of the authority of these rules derived from their antiquity: they had, as it were, become public law, as canonical as the canons of the conciliar fathers.[18]

During the same period military orders arising from the Crusades, groups dedicated to fight for the Holy Land and defend the faith, had proliferated. Most of these religious knights vowed chastity, obedience, and to have nothing of their own.[19] New groups were now asking for recognition: hospitalers, those seeking to redeem captives, and various poverty movements connected with preaching.[20] Too many rules had brought bewilderment into the Church and confused the pagan peoples who still needed to be converted.[21] Canon 13 simply established as law the existing practice of limiting the rules available to a religious community.

Lateran IV's Canon 13 and Its Meaning

The text of Canon 13 of Lateran IV reads:

> Lest too great a diversity of ways of religious observance [*religionum*] lead to grave confusion in the Church of God, we strictly forbid anyone in the future to found a new manner of observance [*religionem*], but whoever should wish to enter the religious way of life [*religionem*], should choose an observance already approved. Similarly, whoever would wish to found a new religious house [*religiosam domum*], must accept a rule and institution [*regulam et institutionem*] from one of the approved ways of religious observance [*de religionibus approbatis*].[22]

An examination of the language of Canon 13 reveals:

1. *Religio* is not a religious order as understood in the twentieth century but a way of religious observance followed by a person or religious group.
2. *Regula* is the rule, a primary element in determining the way of religious observance that is being followed. Usage shows that the approved rules are those of Benedict, Basil, and Augustine, understood not as establishing a juridical bond but as pointing in a general direction. Carthusians, for example, were considered under the Rule of Benedict.[23]
3. *Institutio* may mean constitutions, statutes, ordinances, institutions, etc. In Canon 13, however, usage after Lateran IV shows that *institutio* means the basic organization of a religious house: novitiate, profession, election, internal order, etc. Statutes, constitutions, etc., are often called *institutiones* in formulas of profession in use at this time. Such *institutiones* are not included in Canon 13.[24]

The result of Canon 13 is: (1) no new rules (in the above sense) are allowed; (2) anyone entering religious life should follow a rule already approved; (3) a new religious house should accept an approved rule and *institutio,* that is, basic organization of the house. The *institutio* always corresponds to the rule, that is, those in the *ordo monasticus* do not choose an *institutio* from the *ordo canonicus* or vice versa. Groups of canons with the same rule, however, or monasteries with the same rule need not have the same *institutio*.[25]

The decree contained a large amount of flexibility even as it established limitations. It did not restrict bishops from approving new religious houses, but, to avoid the proliferation of rules, it limited the choice of rule [*regula*] in a general way. As for *institutio*, a wide choice was available from within the broad scope of *ordo monasticus* or *ordo canonicus*. The shape of any new religious group would depend largely on the creative imagination of the founder.

A good example is the case of the Poor Clares, to whom their cardinal protector gave the Rule of St. Benedict in 1219.[26] In his letter *In divini timore*, mentioned above in chapter 17, Innocent IV, with fatherly compassion, addresses the concern of Agnes of Prague and her community that they are bound by two different rules, that of St. Benedict and the Form of Life Francis has given them. He explains that they had been given the Rule of Benedict "so that through it, as the principal approved rule, your own religious order would be authenticated."[27] That does not mean, he says, that you are bound to observe the Rule, and he supports his position by the remark of his predecessor in the presence and hearing of the Cardinal of Ostia. The content of that remark, analyzed above in chap. 17, is similar to that of Innocent III in his letter to the monastery of Subiaco, also discussed above in the same chapter. It is very much in line with what Hugolino had said to the Poor Clares in giving them a rule: "we give you the *Rule of Saint Benedict* to be observed in all things which are in no way contrary to that same *Form of Life* that was given to you by us and by which you have especially chosen to live."[28] The Rule of Benedict authenticated them, classified them as part of the monastic family; the Form of Life Francis gave them governed the way they lived.

The decree did not slow down the birth of new religious groups but strengthened the papal hand with regard to religious.[29] For the next fifty years or more popes were quite willing to approve new orders.[30] Many new communities sprang up, most of them mendicants, most of them following the Rule of St. Augustine. The bishops were not pleased; the abbots were not pleased; succeeding popes had either thoughtfully or carelessly accepted Innocent's policy of open arms and open heart to those who wanted to follow the Gospel. Some people said the pope should tighten the reins.

And so, sixty years later, in the constitution *Religionum Diversitatem,* the Second Council of Lyons (1274) suppresses all orders, mendicant or otherwise, founded since Lateran IV (1215) and not confirmed by the pope and again forbids establishing any new orders except under the conditions set down by Lateran IV. Mendicant orders founded since Lateran IV and approved by the pope are to receive no new members, and those remaining in them cannot preach, hear confessions, or conduct funerals.[31] The decree explicitly leaves untouched the Dominicans and Franciscans and postpones action regarding the Carmelites and the Hermits of St. Augustine.[32]

The meaning of a decree is one thing, its practical implementation another. In interpreting Canon 23 of Lyons II and the earlier canon of Lateran IV, the practice of the Church is critical. Many interpreted Lateran IV's Canon 13 as completely forbidding the establishment of new orders, and not a few founders suffered because of it. The popes, however, did not act as though bound by this prohibition; they interpreted the decree as reserving to the Roman Pontiff the right of approving new orders.[33]

Since Innocent III had orally approved the Rule of Francis before Canon 13 of Lateran IV, it was technically one of the approved rules along with those of Benedict, Basil, and Augustine. The rule of the Minims, who were founded by Francis of Paola in 1493, while quite original, shows considerable influence by the Franciscan rule.[34] When Clement VII approved the Theatines in 1524, he told them to write their own statutes [*BRT* 6:74a]. One of the cofounders, Gianpietro Carafa, drew up a rule, basing it on the Rule of Augustine.[35] The Capuchins, approved in 1528, accepted the Rule of St. Francis [*BRT* 6:113b], but they were already Friars Minor in search of a stricter observance of the rule. In 1533 Clement VII also told the Barnabites to write their own statutes [*BRT* 6:160b]; the rule that Paul III eventually approved in 1542 based itself on that of Augustine.[36] The Somaschi were founded in 1534, but not until 1568 did Pius V give them the Rule of Augustine [*BRT* 7:730b].[37]

3. The Unique Character of the Companions' *viuendi formula*

The implications of Lateran IV's Canon 13 and of Canon 23 of Lyons II provide the remote background prompting the concern of Ignatius and his companions: "We may be forced by the Supreme Pontiff to live under a rule that has already been established and constituted" [*D* 7]. The Deliberation of the First Fathers mentions the dilemma but gives no account of a discussion concerning it. The experience of the Company is something new, and under canon law current in the sixteenth century nothing new can come into existence. The companions live by begging, and the Church frowns on the multiplication of mendicant orders. Nonetheless the action they take is bold: at the end of the long Deliberation, the five decrees of the Formula of the Institute stand as their response to the problem of accepting one of the ancient rules:

1. The companions see too great a difference between themselves and existing orders to use the same terminology as the others and to choose one of the approved rules.[38]
2. They set aside the rules the Church approves and requires, and choose to walk their own path.
3. In place of rule [*regula*] they use another legislative tool, form of living [*viuendi formula*] and way of life [*vite formam*], originating earlier but still current in the sixteenth century.[39]
4. In their *viuendi formula*, moreover, they set aside the ordinary observances of common life, like choir, common habit, and common penances, common to the approved rules.[40]
5. Nowhere in *Cum ex plurium*, including the five decrees outlining their way of living [*viuendi formula*], do the companions call the Society a religious order [*religio*].
6. Nor do they refer to the members of the Society as clerks regular, after the fashion of the Theatines and Barnabites.[41]
7. The companions do not shrink from the prospect that others might judge the Company juridically inferior to the established orders.

8. The companions prefer to call themselves a companionship [*societas*], a company, a society.

Perhaps they reflect in this manner: if the Church does not recognize our Company as meeting the requirements of a religious order, well and good, as long as we can do what God calls us to do; if our Company does meet the requirements, our experience that the approved rules are inadequate for our purposes is not our problem but a problem and a challenge for the Church. Perhaps they have sufficient knowledge of the history and practice of canon law to know that its restrictions sometimes baffle the Church. Their experience of the Holy Spirit's impelling them tells them that the Holy Spirit can break down the strongest barriers. They are emboldened to trust that the creative power of Jesus' life-giving Spirit will work impellingly in the creative imagination of the vicar of Christ.

To sum up, the proposed Society of Jesus does not conform to any existing group: its members are not monks, nor are they like other religious or diocesan clergy. The best way to describe them is in paradox: a company of secular priests with religious vows and a rule, committed to go wherever the pope sends them to help their neighbor for the glory of God. Nonetheless, the Church has a great capacity for opening the boundaries of her own categories.

4. Blessing and Approving the *viuendi formula*

The clause continues the papal narrative of the request the companions made through Cardinal Contarini:

> whether your form of living is conformed to . . .
> the normative teachings of the fathers,
>
> **and after it has been found to be congruent**
> [et comperta eius . . . (congruentia)]
> **with the purity of the Christian religion,**
> [cum christiane religionis puritate]

according to custom it be blessed by us
[de more a nobis benedicatur]
and approved;
[atque approbetur]

To be conformed to the Gospel and the normative teachings of the fathers is to be congruent with the purity of the Christian religion. Although their company does not fit the usual categories, the companions are confident that their *viuendi formula* will pass the test. They, therefore, make a further request, that the pope bless their way of living and give it his full approval.

Before Lateran IV (1215) bishops had the right to approve new religious foundations.[42] The pope, of course, was also free to do so. Canon 13 of Lateran IV made no change in this regard, nor did Canon 23 of Lyons II. Only in the fourteenth century did Pope John XXII (1316–34) declare that the Holy See had the exclusive right to approve religious foundations.[43]

For the group to receive the blessing and approval of the pope would put an end, once and for all, to all the accusations that have dogged the companions' footsteps. They would fulfill their desire to work in freedom, and the whole world would lie open before them as the vineyard in which to cultivate the Kingdom of Christ. What happens to their requests is the subject of the next part of this book.

Concluding Reflection

The Spirit at work in the Church and the world of the sixteenth century is the same Spirit at work in the Church and the world of the twentieth century. We turn to Vatican II and its decree on the renewal of religious life to evaluate the activity of Ignatius and his companions and the wisdom they manifest in *Cum ex plurium*.

The conciliar fathers of Vatican II are clear and to the point when they state under number two of *Perfectae caritatis* that the up-to-date renewal of the religious life comprises both (1) a constant return to the sources of the whole of the Christian life and to the primitive inspiration of the institutes and (2) their adaptation to the changed conditions of our time. With regard to returning to the sources, they maintain that the following of Christ as presented in the Gospel is the final norm of the religious life and must be the supreme rule of all institutes. With regard to the primitive inspiration, they note that each founder's spirit [*spiritus*] and aims [*propriaque proposita*] should be faithfully accepted and retained, as also the sound traditions of each institute. With regard to adaptation, they say that each institute should absorb what is going on in the life of the Church and should see to it that its members understand human nature, the conditions of the times, and the needs of the Church in order to make apostolic decisions; they also say that adaptations without spiritual renewal are meaningless since religious life is ordered to the following of Christ.

Granted that Ignatius and his companions are beginning and not renewing a religious institute, the way they begin follows Vatican II's recommended pattern for renewal. Moreover, the way they begin is a way of renewing religious life and the Church in their day.

Section one of part two is a reflection on their spirit [*spiritus*] and their aims [*propriaque proposita*] their prophetic zeal and enthusiasm, their sense of companionship in Christ, their readiness to bind themselves in obedience in order to serve God and the Church more fully. (The same is true of the whole of part one: their commitment to the Church in poverty and priesthood, their vigorous labor for all in the Church but especially the most marginal, their example of genuine Christian living.)

Section two of part two considers their eagerness to submit their way of living to the judgment of the Church. In *Cum ex plurium* they even suggest the norms to use: the Gospel and the whole of Christian tradition. Return to the sources of Christian life, they say, and judge whether our way of living reflects the Gospel and all the wisdom the Church has gathered through all the ages.

As for adaptation, throughout the book we see the companions participating in and even initiating life-giving movements within the Church. Working closely with people, they come to know them personally. They experience the superstition of the common people, the lack of good preaching and teaching, the inadequacy of sacramental preparation and administration, the aspiration for a deeper knowledge of God in prayer. They come to know firsthand the needs of the Church. They know by experience that the Church is starving and can be fed only by the Spirit. Their way of living does not copy the past; it confronts both Church and world and adapts to the needs of the times. At the center they place the service of Christ and his Church: vows, prayer, obedience, common life, whatever, they make everything subservient to the service of God and his people.

Section one of part three will take up the aims of the companions more in detail and will reflect more fully on their capacity to be innovative in adapting to the times and its needs.

PART THREE

Part one considered the pope's perception of the spirit and aims of those destined to become the founders of the Society of Jesus. Both the Spirit within and the spirit created within them drive them to proclaim the Word of God in a variety of ways and to astonishing labors with every class of people, but especially with those abandoned by others. The pope recognizes in them a foundation for hope in the renewal of the Church.

Part two reflected on the movement towards incorporation of their spirit and aims in an association approved by the pope. The companions come to a profound experience of God's gift of union and they long to preserve that unity. They write down what they are all about, their spirit, and their aims. They ask, finally, to be approved.

Part three considers how the pope responds, first a more immediate response and then a more general one.

SECTION ONE

The Companions' *propositum*

Section one concerns the immediate response of Pope Paul III to the request that someone he delegated might examine the written *viuendi formula* the companions had chosen to follow, and the results of that response. The opening of section one considers his appointment of an examiner and the judgment the examiner makes regarding the form of living of the companions. The examiner expresses himself in terms of their aims or intent [*propositum*], for their spirit is obvious from their intent. *Propositum* is a word loaded with meaning, and so we investigate its meaning in Christian tradition. Next we examine the meaning of the term in the early writings of Ignatius and follow the growth of Ignatius's own *propositum* from Loyola to Paris where he meets his companions. After reviewing the role of the *propositum* in the genesis of any order, with special reference to the Carthusians, Cistercians, Franciscans, and Dominicans, we follow the genesis of the Society of Jesus, watching the companions of Ignatius as they grow into and clothe themselves with his *propositum* so that it also becomes their own, and finally we view the *propositum* as the companions express it in each of the five decrees of the Formula of the Institute.

THE *QUE* CLAUSE

(... cum) **que vestra petitio**
[since this petition of yours]

cum animum nostrum bene ... (sentientem reperisset)
[had found our heart feeling well-disposed]

de vobis iam dudum sentientem reperisset,
[toward you for a long time already]

illico negotium hoc ... (delegauimus)
[we immediately delegated this matter]

dilecto filio Thome Badie,
[to our beloved son, Tommaso Badia]

sacri nostri palatii magistro, delegauimus;
[the Master of the Sacred Palace]

Structure: The first word of this part of the sentence, *que* [which] (an alternative form of *quae*), conveys the sense of "and this" as in "and this petition of yours" [*que vestra petitio*]. *Petitio* is the subject of *reperisset* [had found], a verb in the subjunctive introduced by *cum* [since]. The construction is clumsy in English but not in Latin and is the equivalent of "and since this petition of yours had found ..." The clause in the subjunctive serves to introduce the fourth and final main verb of the sentence, *delegauimus* [we delegated].

THE *QUI* CLAUSE

qui, re mature perspecta,
[who, after carefully considering the matter]

nobis retulit
[reported to us]

vniversum propositum Societatis vestre
[that the whole intent of your Society]

pium sibi sanctumque videri,
[seemed to him to be good and holy]

summamque regule,
[and that the summary of the rule]

quam servare cupitis,
[that you desire to follow]

infrascriptis quinque capitulis contineri.
[is contained in the five decrees written below]

Structure: Another relative pronoun, *qui* [who], introduces the verb *retulit* [reported]. *Retulit* introduces an accusative with an infinitive, *propositum . . . videri* [the intent seems], and another accusative with an infinitive, *summam . . . contineri* [the summary is contained].

19

The Meaning of *propositum* in Christian Tradition

Prior to exploring the meaning of *propositum* we need to consider the appointment of the pope's delegate.

> **since this petition of yours**
> [que vestra petitio]
> **had found our heart feeling well-disposed**
> [cum animum nostrum bene . . . (sentientem reperisset)]
> **toward you for a long time already,**
> [de vobis iam dudum sentientem reperisset]
> **we immediately delegated this matter**
> [illico negotium hoc . . . (delegauimus)]
> **to our beloved son, Tommaso Badia,**
> [dilecto filio Thome Badie]
> **the Master of the Sacred Palace;**
> [sacri nostri palatii magistro, delegauimus]

That Pope Paul III is well disposed to the companions comes as no surprise. No pope is likely to invite theologians every two weeks to carry on theological disputations while he is eating dinner unless he finds what they say worth hearing. We do not know whether they discussed their petition with him ahead of time, nor do we know whether Cardinal Contarini had done so on their behalf. The request by the companions may have come to Paul as a surprise, not so much as a request to approve their way of living, for he had already given them permission to add to their numbers [R 83], but as a request to approve it in written form.

The man to whom Pope Paul III delegates the task of determining whether the written *viuendi formula* of the companions conforms with the evangelical counsels and the normative teachings of the fathers is a Dominican theologian, Tommaso Badia, Master of the Sacred Palace. His opinion will have a major impact on the future of the Company of Jesus.

Master of the Sacred Palace is the title of the pope's official theologian, who is always a Dominican.[1] Tommaso Badia, born in Modena in 1483, the same year as Contarini, was appointed to the office on February 17, 1529, by Clement VII, Paul III's immediate predecessor.[2] Badia was known for both his piety and his learning. When Paul III in July 1536 invited some cardinals together to plan for a general council, Contarini asked the pope to invite Badia also, and he did so. Badia's theological outlook is rigorous. He forbade publication of Cardinal Sadoleto's commentary on the Epistle to the Romans, even though Sadoleto worked with him on the reform commission that was drawing up a list of abuses for the proposed council to address.[3] Two cardinals on the reform commission, Contarini and Aleandro, esteemed Badia enough to choose him as their confessor.[4] The pope sent him to the conference at Worms in 1540, and he acted as Contarini's theologian at Ratisbon in 1541. When the pope wanted to make him a cardinal, he pleaded against it, and even on the day of the consistory itself he begged Cardinal Pole to intervene on his behalf so that he could remain a simple religious, a desire the pope denied him.[5]

Such a man could understand what Ignatius and his companions had in mind; he also could be trusted to give a negative judgment if he thought the matter deserved one.

> **who, after carefully considering the matter,**
> [qui, re mature perspecta]
> **reported to us**
> [nobis retulit]

that the whole intent of your Society
[vniuersum propositum Societatis vestre]
seemed to him to be good and holy,
[pium sibi sanctumque videri]

The Jesuit historian Daniel Bartoli, writing some hundred years later, says that Badia kept the Formula for two months.[6] Two months seems a long time for a capable theologian to study a short document. The material is complex, however, and deserving of reflection. If Bartoli is correct, the companions had little time to produce the Formula. The Deliberation of the First Fathers ended on June 24. On September 3 Cardinal Contarini presented the written *viuendi formula* to the pope. For Badia to have the Formula for two months, July–August, the companions had to complete it by the last days of June or the first days of July. Perhaps Bartoli was incorrect. The *viuendi formula* is a sophisticated document, and the companions may have needed more than a few days to complete it. Perhaps Badia did not receive it until mid July or even later.

Throughout August and into September Paul III was holding frequent consistories at St. Mark's, the church connected with the papal palace in Rome. According to the Jesuit historian Tacchi Venturi, he held consistories on August 4, 8, 18, and 27. Perhaps, in view of the pope's schedule, Badia felt little pressure to make his report; perhaps he had to be present at the consistories; perhaps he abandoned Rome during the August heat. We do not know when he delivered his judgment. We do know that sometime after August 27 Paul III took a few days at Tivoli and returned to Rome on September 5.[7] By that time Badia had returned the five decrees of the Formula and his response.

Tommaso Badia was satisfied. He summarized his judgment in terminology once used about his own Order of Preachers: the *propositum* of the Society is good and holy.[8]

We turn now to the meaning of *propositum*. This word, difficult to translate, is a rich word with a long history of consistent use from the earliest ages of Christianity. Capable of meaning a simple proposal or even a question or problem, it is used throughout the Christian tradition to signify the profound religious act by which a person makes a commitment to God, or to God and the community. Ignatius and his companions may be original and innovative but they are not out of tune with the Christian spiritual tradition that preceded them. In order to understand their use of the term *propositum* we need to see its use in the history of Christian thought before them.

Propositum is the past participle of *proponere,* a compound of *ponere* [to place] and *pro* [before]. A *propositum* is that which has been placed before someone. It means "something proposed or intended but not yet carried out."[9] The authors of the ancient Roman empire established the basic meaning of *propositum;* Christian writers transformed it.

Caesar (44 BC) wrote that in one of his battles "each side appeared to hold to their *propositum.*" They resolutely adhered to their battle plans. In this sense *propositum* can mean intent, determination, resolve, purpose. The mind slides easily between the inclination of will in the person and the object to which the person is inclined. Thus, Brutus (42 BC) wrote to Cicero of an old man who "in no way can be deterred from his resolve [*proposito*]." Each of these meanings has something to do with what the person set out to do. Building on this concept, non-Christian authors of the Christian era gave *propositum* a new meaning: a deliberately chosen way of acting (mode of conduct, practice) or way of living (way of life). "Way of acting" is intended in the remark of Phaedrus (+40), "You must change your conduct [*propositum*] and your way of life [*vitae genus*]." Way of living is what Velleius Paterculus (+30) has in mind in describing someone as a sort of secular saint, a man of brilliant mind and profound personal integrity, "a man of genius, most holy in his way of living [*proposito*]." Seneca (+65) intends the same sense, although his view was more negative when he wrote to Lucilius, "Let this not be the case, that you call yourself a philosopher or contemplative: give a different name to your way of life [*proposito*], ill health and impotency; worse, call it sloth."[10]

Propositum is such a common term throughout the Christian ages that an exhaustive discussion of its use would take volumes.[11] We select various authors or documents for two purposes: (1) to illustrate the way Christians used and often transformed the terminology of ancient Rome; (2) to illustrate the gradual extension of *propositum* to wider areas without changing its basic meaning.

1. The Transformation of Ancient Terminology

The present level of research places St. Cyprian (+258) as the first Christian author to use *propositum*. He, however, uses it as though it is a common term in everyday use, both in the sense of way of acting[12] and way of living. Even so, his way of using it intensifies the meaning of *propositum* and transports it beyond its pagan roots. The first time Cyprian uses *propositum*, he cautions a colleague against thinking that fervor is lacking in the Church because those who have lapsed into adultery have been treated gently and penitents have been offered the hope of experiencing peace. "Nonetheless," he maintains, "virginity is not therefore lacking in the Church, nor is the glorious commitment [*propositum*] to chastity [*continentiae*] languishing because of the sins of others."[13] As a resolve to live in chastity, *propositum continentiae* indicates a way of living. Reflection on this particular way of living will provide deeper insight into the Christian transformation of *propositum*.

(a) A Publicly Approved Way of Living in the Church

St. Ambrose (+397) called the resolve to live in chastity the commitment to virginity [*propositum virginitatis*].[14] It is an example of a response to a call from God within the Church. In the depths of human consciousness it is more than a proposal or a resolution; it is a commitment. At the same time, within the community, it is a way of life or manner of living in response to God's call.

The existence of virgins within the Church from the earliest times is undisputed. We do not know, however, when the Church first sanctioned a commitment to virginity by a public ceremony. The earliest references to public consecration of virgins are from the fourth century, from Ambrose himself.[15]

The Leonine Sacramentary, named after Leo I (+461), is the oldest witness to the Roman rite of consecration of virgins. One of the most ancient prayers, the collect of the mass for the consecration of virgins, uses the phrase "the resolve to live in holy virginity" [*virginitatis sanctae propositum*]. Following the collect is a long Eucharistic prayer in the form of a preface that uses equivalent phrases, "the commitment to celibacy" [*continentiae propositum*] and "the espousal of virgins" [*proposito virginum*]. This prayer has been used throughout the ages[16] and is part of the renewed rite of the Consecration of Virgins in use today. At one point the bishop prays: "Lord, look with favor on these your servants, who place in your hands their resolve [*propositum*] to live in chastity . . . lest the ancient enemy . . . snatch them from the commitment [*proposito*] of being virgins."[17]

The long practice of the Church regarding the *propositum virginitatis* illustrates a number of important points:

1. *Propositum* as a religious commitment is a strong word indicative of a self-offering.
2. *Propositum* is the most ancient form of commitment, older than consecration, profession, promise, and vow, and has the same sense of irrevocability about it.
3. *Propositum* precedes the public expression of the commitment.
4. The public expression of commitment is grounded in the initial *propositum*, sets it seal upon it, and is meaningless without it.
5. The public expression of commitment becomes a matter of public interest, takes on a juridical aspect, and is subsequently subject to public law.
6. In the Church, the public expression removes the commitment from the purely private realm of conscience and makes it a matter of ecclesial interest and ecclesial intent, i.e., it becomes in some way a *propositum* of the Church deserving of ecclesial support and at the same time takes on a juridical aspect and is subject to ecclesial law.

The ancient Romans had combined *propositum* with various genitives. Seneca (+65), for example, used "*propositum bene faciendi*" [the intent to do well], and Quintilian (+95) *"propositum bellandi"* [the intention of waging war].¹⁸ These were hardly vocations in the Christian sense of the word. Throughout the centuries *propositum* combines with nouns in the genitive or with adjectives to specify a particular way of living. *Propositum continentiae, propositum virginitatis, propositum castitatis,* and *propositum virginale* indicate the virginal way of living. *Propositum viduitatis* or *propositum vidualis castitatis* express the call to live in chastity as a widow. *Propositum monachi,* or the plural *propositum monachorum,* is the call to be a monk; *propositum canonicorum* is the call to be a canon.¹⁹ In the course of time *propositum* combines with *serving God,* with *poverty,* with *religion,* with *entering a monastery,* with *penance,* with *pilgrimage,* and with many other terms that indicate a way of living to which God calls someone.²⁰ The English word *vocation* contains the same double element as *propositum:* (1) a subjective, driving element, a *calling;* and (2) the objective *way of life* to which one is called.

(b) Reneging on a Publicly Approved Way of Living in the Church

The Christian viewpoint has so intensified the meaning of *propositum* that closely connected to the public celebration of a commitment to God is the condemnation of those who do not keep the commitment.

No one should back out on a commitment to God. Innocent I (+417) argues that if a contract between two human beings cannot be dissolved, how much less can a promise made to God be dissolved without penalty! If Paul condemns those "who have gone contrary to their commitment to widowhood [*proposito viduitatis*]," how much more should virgins be condemned who have broken their promise!²¹ St. Augustine (+430) maintains that "it is bad to renege on a commitment [*proposito*], but it is worse to fake a commitment [*propositum*]." He condemns widows and virgins who break their commitment to chastity and calls their action a "betrayal of their commitment [*propositi fraus*]."²²

Down the ages saints and popes and synods and councils condemn in the same fashion those who abandon their *propositum.*

Gratian (+ca. 1159) gathered many of these condemnations into his summary of canon law.[23] The document does not make pleasant reading. Nonetheless, the very vigor of the condemnations throughout the ages bears witness to the depth of the commitment the community expected from those who freely committed themselves to God in a way of living. On the other hand, no one can create a call from God or make a commitment for someone else. No doubt some young women, even many, did not embrace the life of virginity in total freedom; their families chose it for them to avoid the problems inherent in arranging marriages.[24] The rigorous condemnation of those who lapsed, therefore, may at times have been misplaced.

Conclusion

In Christian writers the meaning of *propositum* far transcends moral conduct or an attitude of mind and heart. The object of a Christian *propositum* might be something to be accomplished once and for all, like fasting on a particular day or making a pilgrimage to Jerusalem; or it might be something unattainable except in constantly pursuing it, like virginity or poverty, or living a life devoted to prayer and fasting or to the service of the poor. In either case, whether the call is to perform a particular action or live a way of life, the Christian *propositum* involves a sense of commitment that goes far beyond the meaning of the ancient writers of pagan Rome. That which transforms a *propositum* and makes it religious is a sense of its relationship to God. Intent, determination, resolve, and purpose are all very good, but the word is transformed by the fact that what the Christian has set out to do is to fulfill God's will or answer God's call. Often for Christians their vocation is at stake. A *propositum* is not tentative; it is not a suggestion or a mere wish. It represents a decision and the determination to execute the decision. A Christian *propositum* is a determination to follow Christ in some way in living out the values of the Gospel. When the *propositum* is a way of life, it means a determination to follow Christ not just today or tomorrow but by offering a holocaust of one's whole life. Manifesting that intention publicly tends to guard the person against going back on the resolution.[25]

2. The Gradual Extension of *propositum* to Wider Areas

A *propositum,* although deeply personal, can also be shared, both the subjective attitude of mind and heart and the objective reality, the purpose, the way of life.[26] A gradual evolution in the use of *propositum* marks the movement from personal commitment to the commitment of a community.

(1) Latin Translation of Scripture

In Scripture, *propositum* means personal commitment. Jerome made *propositum* a biblical expression by using it in his translation of Scripture known as the Latin Vulgate. He uses the word four times in the Old Testament, nine times in the New. Generally it means purpose or plan, either God's or that of some human person. In the Second Letter to Timothy, however, the term is linked with teaching [*doctrina*] and conduct [*institutio*], and means manner of life or aim of life: "Now you have observed my teaching, my conduct, my aim in life, my faith, my patience, my love, my steadfastness" [2 Tim. 3:10, *NRSV*]. The *propositum* is Paul's. He reminds Timothy of what he has witnessed: Paul's own word and example and whole way of living.

(2) Latin Translation of Eastern Monastic Writings

(a) Anthony the Hermit (+356) is a good example of personal commitment. St Athanasius (+373) wrote a life of Anthony in Greek that Evagrius of Antioch (+393) translated into Latin a few years later, *Vita Antonii.*[27] A common word in Athanasius is *askēsis* meaning the practice of virtue or the practice of mortification, constant exertion or labor, but also a way of life. When *askēsis* means way of life Evagrius sometimes uses *propositum,* sometimes either of two synonyms, *institutum* or *conversatio:* "He maintained his way of life [*propositum*] assiduously" (chap 7).[28] In each passage Anthony's personal *propositum* is the monastic life, a life that he lives alone. Others will share it only in the sense that they are committed to the same way of life.

Evagrius freely uses *propositum* to translate other Greek words, for example, in the preface, where it means Antony's intent, namely, the monastic way of life. Elsewhere it means what Antony has decided to do, as in "wanting to turn him from his good decision [*proposito*]" (chap. 5). To turn Antony from his decision (subjective) was the same as to turn him from what he had decided upon (objective), namely, the monastic life. Translating the sense of one passage rather than the words, Evagrius cautions not "to grow weary of the task [propositi] undertaken" (chap. 16).[29] The task in question is, of course, the monastic life.

(b) The sense of shared commitment begins to develop in the Latin translation of the Rule of St. Basil (+379), which Rufinus of Aquileia (+410) made from the Greek.[30] Those who have the same personal *propositum* do more than live side by side; they share their life together.

After *Interrogatio 3* Rufinus inserts, "*cum fratribus eiusdem propositi* [with brethren of the same way of life]." He freely translates *Responsio 3* in this manner: "I see that in many ways it is useful to lead a common life with those who are of the same disposition [*voluntatis*] and spiritual outlook [*propositi*]." In *Responsio 10* he translates: "When we all come together [*convenimus*] with the same outlook [*prospectu*] and purpose [*proposito*]."

(3) Rule of the Master (6th Century)

When a personal way of living becomes a communal way of living, it is still called *propositum*. The Rule of the Master[31] uses the term eight times, always referring to the way of living common to all the members of the community. The Master cautions against chanting the divine office in the presence of secular folk "making fun of our way of life [*propositum*]" [*RM* 58.5]. Throughout the rule the context makes clear that the way of life the Master has in mind is the monastic life, the vocation to be a monk. Context, therefore, determines whether *propositum* means a personal resolve or way of living, or whether it should sometimes be rendered by some word designating a particular way of living, e.g., monastic life or religious life, or even the life of the monastery.

(4) The Carthusian Consuetudines (12th Century)

Reading the Carthusian *Consuetudines,* or *Book of Customs,*[32] is instructive in this regard, for the work draws on the whole monastic tradition. The French translation renders *propositum* in various ways that sum up the totality of the Carthusian way of living: *observance* [observance], *règle* [rule], *vie* [life] [22.2, 41.4, 41.5]. Eight of eleven times, however, in which *propositum* appears in the *Consuetudines,* the French translation renders it *vocation* [vocation]. Sometimes it means the personal vocation of each one, for example, "to defend his vocation" [20.3], sometimes their common vocation, as in "the humility of our vocation" [Prol.3], sometimes the personal vocation they share in common, for example, "Mass is rarely sung here because our principle endeavor and calling [*propositum*] is to spend time in the silence and solitude of our cell" [14.5]. A shared commitment still demands a personal response and personal effort. When *propositum* indicates something more than a single attainable goal, it demands the whole of a person's being.

In the *Consuetudines* a distinction appears between the Carthusian vocation [*propositum*] to contemplation, which they share with others, and their manner of living it out [*institutio*] [80.7]. The monks are not, for example, to undertake religious exercises and penances that do not belong to the Carthusian *institutio* [35.1]. Lateran IV (1215) later makes a similar distinction between *regula* [rule] and *institutio.* Although *propositum* and *institutio* are distinct, sometimes the two seem identical. The resolve to be a Carthusian embraces both the *propositum* to the contemplative or monastic life and the particular *institutio* or way the Carthusians have of leading the contemplative life. Together they make up the institute [*institutum*].

In the *Consuetudines, propositum* ranges from personal commitment to a way of living to the way of life shared by many, embracing every aspect of that shared way of life. The same is true of *propositum* in other Carthusian sources and in the Cistercian, Franciscan, and Dominican sources perused for this book.[33]

(5) Lay Movements of the Early 13th Century

Although in a particular context the term *propositum* can mean the monastic life, the term remains the property of all Christians. In the context of the new lay religious movements of the early thirteenth century, *propositum* moves from indicating a particular way of living to include also the norms governing that way of living. Thus, we have the *propositum* of the *Humiliati* in 1201, the *propositum conversationis* of the Poor Catholics in 1208, the *propositum* of the Poor Lombards in 1210 and again in 1212, and so forth.[34] Each *propositum* is the rule of life for the members of the group. The pope is concerned about confirming each of the members and all of them together in their *pio proposito*, in doing what they have set out to do, and he speaks of their desire "to remain and persevere in their intent [*proposito*]."[35] The *propositum* of the *Humiliati* in 1201 is also called a *vivendi forma*.[36]

Propositum, therefore, like the various forms of *vivendi formula*,[37] is associated with the earlier moments of an endeavor. In fact, *vita* and *propositum* are synonyms in a passage written by Anselm of Havelberg (+1158) about the founding of the Knights Templar in the previous century: "Pope Urban first confirmed their rule [*vitam*] and way of life [*propositum*], on the advice of many bishops."[38] The way a group lives [*vita*] demands a rule [*regula*], norms for that way of living; so also a commitment that people have [*propositum*] eventually demands an established manner of group living [*institutum*].

At the same time that lay groups seek a more intense religious life in Europe, a similar phenomenon appears in Asia Minor. In answer to a request from lay hermits living on Mt. Carmel, Albert, the patriarch of Jerusalem, replies: "It is to me, however, that you have come for a rule of life [*vitae formulam*] in keeping with your avowed purpose [*propositum*], a rule you may hold fast to henceforward."[39] These lay hermits would eventually become the Carmelites.

Propositum, therefore, moves from a simple resolve of one person, through the public expression of that resolve and the way of living resolved upon, to a shared or communal way of living and the written expression (rule) of that communal way of living.

(6) Papal Documents of the Sixteenth Century

In the intervening centuries the use of *propositum* does not change. A few references show that the term is alive and well in the sixteenth century. The bull of Clement VII approving the Theatines (*BRT* 6:73b) in 1524, calls what they have set out to do, their *vitae propositum*, a way of living [*vivendi modum*] in common. The presence of *vitae* emphasizes that the commitment of the Theatines is not a transient endeavor but their whole way of living. In one breath Pius V in 1568 praises the Somaschi's "holy life [*vitam*] and splendid way of living [*vivendi modum*] and the aim of their way of life [*instituti propositum*]" (*BRT* 7:730b). These last two words form a fascinating combination: both *institutum* and *propositum* indicate a way of living. *Propositum* is more primitive: what is a deep-felt resolve in the beginning has become a way of life. *Institutum* is a stage along the way: the way of life has become established and provides a norm for others. *Propositum* is resolve that looks to the future; *institutum* looks to the present, the resolve already concretized in actual living.

Conclusion

A *propositum* concerning a lifelong quest demands a certain way of living, and so the way of living is also called *propositum*. When the endeavor or *propositum* takes on its own peculiar shape, when it has become institutionalized in its own particular way, then it becomes *institutum*. The way of living is not necessarily a *religio*, an order approved by the Church; but it can be an *institutum*, an established way of life whether recognized as a religious order or not.[40] *Propositum*, an eager youngster, has matured into an adult; a way of life to be lived has become a lived way of life. This growth takes place because from the beginning *propositum* has contained the seed of *institutum*. *Propositum* frequently indicates something that has not yet been completed; rarely does it indicate something not yet begun. An effort already undertaken easily becomes a way of life. *Propositum*, then, is a word rich in meaning and it has its roots deep in the Christian tradition. In its weakest sense it is a proposal to do something, a question of Shall I or Shall I not. But once the determination is made, and once it is clear that the resolution is in accordance with the will of God, a *propositum* is the driving force in a person's life, or in the life of a group.

20

The *propositum* of Ignatius

What do the companions mean by *propositum?* Does it mean the same for them as it does for the pope's delegate? In this chapter we consider (1) the way Ignatius uses *propósito* in the Spiritual Exercises and in his letters before the writing of *Cum ex plurium,* and (2) Ignatius's *propositum* as he describes it in his Autobiography.

1. *Propositum* in the Earliest Writings of Ignatius

The Spiritual Exercises

The earliest use that Ignatius makes of *propósito* and its cognate forms is in the Spiritual Exercises. He wrote the bulk of the Exercises at Manresa in 1522 but made some additions while in Paris (1528–35), in Italy (1537–39), and in Rome (1539–41).[1] The vocabulary of the Exercises provides an easy introduction to the meaning of *propositum.*

Propositum (*propósito* in Spanish) is a noun, but it received its start in life as a participle, *proposed.* In its first stage, before a decision is made, that which has been proposed is expectant, undecided, awaiting resolution, and this openness is expressed through various forms of the verb. After a decision is made to follow through on what has been proposed, the *proposed* becomes a noun and enters a second stage as a purpose, a plan, a project demanding effort and determination.

353

In the Spiritual Exercises the verbal forms of *propositum* or *propósito* can mean a proposal, something to be considered [178–82] (Manresa), but after a decision has been made, *propositum* and *propósito* become nouns and take on the force of deep commitment as in the fifth rule for the discernment of spirits more proper to the First Week [318] (Paris), and also in the sixth rule: "in time of desolation we ought not to change our former plans [*propósitos*]" [319] (Rome). When a decision has been made, even the verbal forms of *propositum* and *propósito* take on the aura of commitment, as in the passages about determining to avoid sin [24] (Manresa). Ignatius also warns that the evil spirit is at work if a train of thought ends up in something "less good than what the soul was originally proposing to do [*tenía propuesta*]" [333] (Rome), or, as de Nicolas translates it, "less good than the soul had already planned to do."[2]

A *propositum* in the Spiritual Exercises arises only in the atmosphere of prayer. In the Exercises *propositum* marks a human decision, but the decision reaches its fullness only when it flows from the grace of God.

Letters of Ignatius

Once, in a letter to his brother Martín García de Oñaz[3] in 1532, Ignatius uses *á propósito* [*EI* 80] much after the manner of Cicero's *ad propositum* [to come to the point].[4] Again, in a letter to Teresa Rejadell in 1536, he uses the phrase *que hazen al propósito* [which are much to the point] [*EI* 102]. In these passages he uses an accepted secular phrase. More to the point, in both of these letters, as well as in two others he wrote before 1539, he uses *propósitos* in a way consistent with its traditional use in the Church.

Ignatius writes from Paris about Martín's decision [*determinada uoluntad*] to send his son to Paris to study theology and prays, "May the supreme goodness be pleased with all our resolves [*propósitos*] ordered in his service and praise" [*EI* 77–78]. To Teresa he explains that the enemy of human nature brings charges of vainglory against one who mentions to others "anything that God our Lord has given [that person] by way of deeds or resolves [*propósitos*] and desire" [*EI* 102].[5]

In 1537 Ignatius wrote from Venice to Juan de Verdolay in Barcelona, twice using the word *propósitos*. He tells him that his companions "went to Rome for Holy Week with a few others who followed along with the same resolves [*en los mesmos propósitos*] as they had" [*EI* 119] and that the pope urged them "to persevere in their designs [*propósitos*]" [*EI* 120]. From the favors granted by the pope, we can conclude that their *propósitos* included: (1) a pilgrimage to Jerusalem, (2) poverty, (3) priesthood, and (4) doing priestly work.

Ignatius wrote to Isabel Roser on December 19, 1538, that during much of the year the companions had been under much pressure from persecution in Rome. He had talked to Paul III at Frascati after the pope had returned from Nice, "telling him at length about our resolutions and intentions [*propósitos e intenciones*]" [*IR* 5].[6] Ignatius poured out his soul to the pope. If he and his companions were to preach and exhort, they had to have spotless reputations. Ignatius outlined all the desires and hopes of the companions, the way they wanted to live, something of what they wanted to do and hoped to accomplish: their *propósitos*. *Propósitos* does not indicate some possibilities the companions have in mind, but what they have set out to do.

In summary, in none of the letters does *propósitos* suggest something under consideration, to be accepted or rejected, but rather something already decided. Each assumes commitment, process, action, perseverance. *Propósitos* in Ignatius entails far more than Caesar's plan of battle; what is at stake is fulfilling the will of God.

2. *Propositum* in the Autobiography of Ignatius

The foundational experience of the ten companions depends upon the earlier mystical experiences of Ignatius: his experience of Jesus, of the Father, and of their life-giving Spirit.[7]

Jerónimo Nadal expressed the conviction that God deals with founders and their followers according to a certain pattern. God moves a person like St. Francis along a particular path and in a particular manner, and then moves the person's followers along the same path and in the same manner. One of the ways we have of knowing the particular grace of an institute, therefore, is by studying the life of its founder or founders. God has moved and continues to move the followers of Ignatius after the pattern of Ignatius's own life.[8]

Both the spirit [*spiritus*] and the aims [*proposita*] of Ignatius and the first companions are vitally important to our investigation. The story of Ignatius reveals his spirit, and the story of Ignatius and his companions reveals the spirit of the group. At the same time the stories lay bare their intentions, the aims that have captured their hearts and minds, the *proposita* that drive them on. We can, therefore, come to a better understanding of how the early companions came to draft their *propositum*, the five decrees of the Formula of the Institute, for papal approval: (1) by seeing the inner growth in Ignatius as he moves from dream to determination to execution to frustration to new and clearer formulation of that which he has set out to do [*propositum*], and (2) by watching the development of the companions as they move from friendship to sharing a common *propositum* to disappointment to enthusiasm for a *propositum* creatively renewed. In following the stories we shall watch carefully the use of the varying forms of *propositum* and its synonyms.

Loyola

God is at work in human events. A French canonball shatters the leg of Ignatius at Pamplona. He can find no books at Loyola except the *Life of Christ* and the *Lives of the Saints*. At this turning point in life he unwittingly goes through a process of discernment:

Reading the Movements. The first interior movements Ignatius experiences at Loyola on his sickbed are provisionary. He keeps proposing grand projects to himself. Now he serves a certain lady far above his station; now he performs heroic deeds in the cause of Christ after the manner of St. Francis and St. Dominic [*A* 6–7]. "Thus he pondered over many things that he found good, always proposing [*proponiéndose*] to himself what was difficult and burdensome; and as he so proposed [*proponía*], it seemed easy for him to accomplish it" [*A* 7]. He lives in fantasy, in enthusiastic yet unresolved engagement. He dreams of great and difficult deeds, but he makes no decisions or commitments. Movements are at work, but no discernment. Two sets of voices whisper within him, coming from two sets of experiences: his experience of the world of chivalry and his experience of the ideals of the saints. Years later the Deliberation of the First Fathers will begin in the same fashion: different voices coming from good people with different backgrounds and experiences. He notices, finally, that he is left "dry and unsatisfied" after dreaming about the lady, "satisfied and joyful" after dreaming "of going to Jerusalem barefoot, and of eating nothing but plain vegetables and of practicing all the other rigors that he saw in the saints" [A 8].[9] Yet the vision remains vague and imprecise, lacking in focus, lacking in realism. The Deliberation of the First Fathers will begin in the same way: great ideas, but no resolution, a normal way for discernment to begin, else there is nothing to discern.

Making the Decision. Gradually his dreaming changes to serious thinking "about his past life and about the great need he had to do penance for it." Thinking becomes "the desire to imitate the saints," and desire leads to decision, "promising with God's grace to do what they had done. But the one thing he wanted to do was to go to Jerusalem as soon as he recovered . . . with as much of disciplines and fasts as a generous spirit, fired with God, would want to perform" [A 9]. He has two *proposita* to go to Jerusalem and to do penance (disciplines and fasts).

Finding Confirmation. Decisions need confirmation. "He began to forget the previous thoughts with these holy desires . . . and they were confirmed by a spiritual experience. . . . One night . . . he saw clearly an image of Our Lady with the holy Child Jesus. From this sight he received for a considerable time very great consolation, and he was left with such loathing for his whole past life and especially for the things of the flesh that it seemed to him that his spirit was rid of all the images that had been painted on it. Thus from that hour until August '53 when this was written, he never gave the slightest consent to the things of the flesh" [A 10]. His whole life is in a process of transformation, especially his sexuality. He does not mention yet a commitment to celibacy.

Readiness for Action. His decision and its confirmation leave nothing tentative about what he desires to do. "Not worried at all, he persevered in his reading and his good resolutions [*propósitos*]." In his excitement about the future, however, he pays little attention to his impact on others. The *proposita* to go to Jerusalem and to do penance he subsumes into a single *propositum,* "to serve [*servir*] Our Lord. He often thought about his intention [*propósito*] and wished he were now wholly well so he could get on his way" [A 11].

Movements for Further Discernment. During this period he reflects on what he should do "after he returned from Jerusalem, so he could always live as a penitent. [H]e thought he might enter the Carthusian house in Seville, without saying who he was, so that they would make little of him; and there never to eat anything but plain vegetables." Perhaps he should be a permanent pilgrim as well as a permanent penitent. He fears the Carthusians might restrict his penance. He does not shun institutional structures, but he sees the possibility of greater freedom for greater penance going about the world in a life of perpetual pilgrimage. For the moment, doing penance and going to Jerusalem summarize his service to Christ, but those decisions are open to further discernment, and so "he instructed one of the household servants who was going to Burgos to get information about the rule of the Carthusians, and the information he obtained about it seemed good" [A 12].

Taking Action. The account of Ignatius hints that he has not revealed all the implications contained in his *propositum.* After his vision of Our Lady and the Child, "his brother [Martín][10] as well as the rest of the household came to know from his exterior the change that had been wrought inwardly in his soul" [A 10]. His brother is dismayed. When it is time for Ignatius to go "his brother took him to one room and then another, and with much feeling begged him not to throw himself away; also to consider what hopes had been placed in him by the people, and how much he could achieve, and other such words, all with the purpose of dissuading him from his good intention [*buen deseo*]" [A 12]. His brother is aware that Ignatius is embarking upon a whole new way of life. Like Abraham, Ignatius leaves his country, his relatives, and his father's house, to go to a land which God will show him (Gen. 12:1).[11]

Aránzazu

Ignatius is ostensibly on a journey to Navarrete to visit the duke. On the way he stops at a shrine of Our Lady of Aránzazu. He spends the night in a vigil of prayer "that he might gain fresh strength for the journey" [A 13]. The vigil is a time of special grace. Twenty-two years later, in 1554, he wrote to Francis Borgia encouraging him in his work of restoring the monastery attached to the shrine: "As for myself, I can say that I have a special reason for desiring it; for when God our Lord showed me mercy that I might make a change in my life, I recall that I received some help to my soul while making a night vigil in that church" [*EI* 7:422]. This comment about a special grace at Aránzazu may refer to a vow of chastity.[12] If so, it situates more precisely the site of the vow of chastity that Laynez says Ignatius made on the way to Montserrat:

> In order to carry out this intention [*propósito*] of his [of renouncing his former way of life and doing penance], he decided to go to Catalonia to Our Lady of Montserrat. Because he had more fear of being conquered in the area of chastity than in other things, while on the way he made a vow of chastity to Our Lady to whom he had a special devotion, although at that time it was not well-conceived. But Our Lord, who gave him that pure intention [*intención*], and who used his most holy Mother as an instrument to help this poor creature, seemed to accept this sacrifice and took him under his protection.[13] [*L* 5]

The vow of chastity is a radical response to the radical change God wrought in Ignatius through the vision at Loyola of Our Lady and the Child. That vision confirmed his *proposita*, and after that moment "he never gave the slightest consent to the things of the flesh" [A 10]. He may see the vow as a third *propositum* added to pilgrimage and penance. Pilgrimage has a penitential aspect, and chastity is an integral part of pilgrimage. The aim is clear; the direction is set: a penitential pilgrimage to Jerusalem in chastity.

Montserrat

The *propositum* of Ignatius continues to unfold. "Coming to a large town before Montserrat, he decided to buy there the attire he had resolved to wear and use when going to Jerusalem . . . cloth from which sacks are usually made, loosely woven and very prickly. Then he ordered a long garment to be made from it, reaching to his feet. He bought a pilgrim's staff and a small gourd and put everything in front by the mule's saddle" [*A* 16]. The slow rhythm of the mule lulls him into daydreaming, "thinking as he always did of the exploits he would perform for the love of God," his head full of the romances of his day. "Thus he decided [*se determinó*] to keep a vigil of arms one whole night . . . before the altar of Our Lady of Montserrat, where he had resolved [*tenía determinado*] to lay aside his garments and to don the armor of Christ. So leaving this place, he set off, thinking as usual of his resolutions [*propósitos*]" [*A* 17].

Arriving at Montserrat, a shrine of Our Lady outside Barcelona, Ignatius reveals his decision [*determinación*] for the first time to his confessor [*A* 17]. After making his general confession he asks his confessor to hang his sword and dagger at the altar of Our Lady. He himself goes secretly at night, strips himself of his nobleman's clothing, gives it to a poor man and dons the rough burlap of a pilgrim. In stripping himself he renounces his nobility and the military way of life it involves and chooses to live in poverty, just as Francis, by doing the same, renounced a merchant's life of wealth. From now on he begs his daily bread. Poverty is not a new *propositum,* but, like chastity, a way of being a pilgrim.

At this point Ignatius has made some firm determinations of a religious nature; they are not mere "proposals" or "options" that he might easily change or set aside, but firm resolutions to perform certain actions of a religious character or to live in a particular manner in following Christ. Inexperienced though he is, he is not so rash as to continue without revealing to a confessor what he wants to do. His primary *propositum* is to serve God. The particular manner in which he is resolved to serve God is to be a pilgrim, living a life of penance in chastity and poverty. The movements of grace have been wonderfully harmonious: his energy is concentrated, his life unified and centered. He is still a novice, however, in serving God. Later, as he dictates his story, Ignatius muses for a moment on the state of his soul before Montserrat:

> On the way something happened to him which it would be well to record, so one may understand how Our Lord dealt with his soul, which was still blind, though greatly desirous of serving him [*con grandes deseos de servirle*] as far as his knowledge went. Thus, he decided [*determinaba*] to do great penances no longer with an eye to satisfying for his sins so much as to please and gratify God. So when it occurred to him to do some penance that the saints practiced, he determined [*proponía*] to do the same and even more. [A 14]

He has made some progress: pleasing God means more to him than satisfying for his sins. Doing penance, however, still holds him enthralled. In his reflections Ignatius makes this judgment upon himself at this stage of his journey: "From these thoughts he derived all his consolation, not looking to any interior thing, nor knowing what humility was or charity or patience, or the discretion that regulates and measure these virtues. His whole intention [*intención*] was to do such great external works because the saints had done so for the glory of God, without considering any more particular detail" [A 14].

Deseo, intención, determinación, propósito all mean the same; they all well up from a deeply religious interior and center on external works. The time for growth has come.

Manresa

When Antony was converted, he went off into the desert to pray. From Montserrat Ignatius goes off to a little town called Manresa, apart from the main thoroughfares where he might be known to travelers, but not totally apart from other people. In the desert Antony led a harsh and ascetic life; Ignatius does the same. He thinks he has turned aside to jot a few notes [A 18], but he soon discovers that God has turned him aside to turn him around. Ignatius does not choose Manresa; Manresa happens to him. There he fasts and prays and begs his food and works with the poor and the sick and those ignorant of Christian doctrine. There he experiences God at work within him, and begins to write the Spiritual Exercises. There he discovers "helping souls," a new *propositum,* serving the people of God. There he realizes that he should temper his penance to the needs of others. There he becomes a "man of the Church."[14]

Nevertheless, during his days at Manresa Ignatius struggles against the temptation to abandon his new way of life. One of his great heroes is St. Humphrey (Onuphrius), whose hair so covered his body that he looked like a beast. Having left his monastery to follow the example of Elijah and John the Baptist, Humphrey survived in the desert for seventy years eating nothing but herbs.[15] Ignatius tries to imitate him. He lives on a sparse diet, lets his hair grow long and his nails. In this milieu he hears the tempter whisper, "How can you endure this life for the seventy years you have yet to live?" Antony struggled with demons, Humphrey with nature's elements; Ignatius struggles with temptations and scruples and dark despair, until God's mercy saves him [*A* 19–25].

During this time, "besides his seven hours of prayer, he busied himself helping in spiritual matters certain souls, who came there looking for him" [*A* 26]. An interior change in him takes place through a rather odd experience:

> He continued to abstain from eating meat and was so determined about it that he would not think of changing it for any reason; but one day, when he got up in the morning, edible meat appeared before him as if he saw it with his ordinary eyes, though no desire for it had preceded. At the same time he also had a strong inclination of his will to eat it from then on. Although he remembered his previous intention [*propósito*], he had no doubt about this, but rather a conviction that he ought to eat meat. Later when telling this to his confessor, the confessor told him to consider whether perhaps this was a temptation; but examining it carefully, he could never doubt about it. [*A* 27]

What is noteworthy is not that Ignatius abandons a *propositum,* but that he ceases to imitate the saints blindly and begins to listen to how God wants *him* to live, giving him a firm will [*voluntad*] to serve him [A 27]. The real *propositum* is service of God.

Through his various experiences he begins to see the fruit in being at the service of God's people. He abandons extremes [A 29]. His desire for penance does not fade, but becomes subordinate to the new *propositum* of serving people. His aims, expanding and evolving, are clearer. More draws him than going to Jerusalem and doing penance. He is leading a life of prayer and penance and prayerful discernment; he lives in poverty and chastity; self is receding for the sake of others. He is ready to go to Jerusalem.

Jerusalem

Ignatius arrives in Jerusalem happy and resolute. His *proposita* continue to evolve, but without any loss of continuity. "His firm intention [*propósito*] was to remain in Jerusalem, continually visiting those holy places; and in addition [*también tenía propósito*] to this devotion, he also planned to help souls." He is in for a shock. The Franciscans in charge of the holy places and in charge of pilgrims to the holy places provide a severe challenge to his first *propositum*. Ignatius tells the Franciscan guardian "of his intention [*intención*] to remain there because of his devotion; but not the second part about wanting to help souls" [A 45]. Nevertheless, "on the eve of the departure of the pilgrims, he received a summons from the provincial . . . and the Guardian. The provincial spoke kindly to him, saying that he knew of his good intention [*intención*] to remain in those holy places . . . but . . . he judged it was not expedient."[16] Ignatius replies that he is "very firm in his purpose [*propósito*]" and that unless someone could oblige him under pain of sin "he would not abandon his intention [*propósito*] out of any fear" [A 46]. The provincial says he can produce papers indicating his power to excommunicate. Ignatius obediently leaves "since it was not Our Lord's will that he remain in those holy places" [A 47].

The *propositum* of pilgrimaging in Jerusalem for the rest of his life is badly shaken, but Ignatius gives no indication of panic, of self-recrimination, of plaguing questions. Neither does the provincial's authority destroy Ignatius's intent to be a pilgrim [*propositum peregrinationis*]. It does, however, reveal to Ignatius that his own *propositum* to be a pilgrim, precisely here in the footsteps of Jesus and God's will for him need to be reconciled.

Studies in Spain

After leaving Jerusalem Ignatius thinks about "what he ought to do" and decides to study. He does not call study a *propositum,* one of his aims, but he chooses to study "so he would be able to help souls" [A 50]. Serving God's people is by now a fundamental *propositum* in his life; study goes with the territory of serving God's people, just as chastity and poverty go with the territory of being a pilgrim. In Barcelona he continues his life of prayer, poverty, penance [A 55], and chastity. He also finds some companions, although he does not mention them until later [A 57]. His choice to study and his choice to share companionship suggest that in prayer Ignatius continues to break away from a literal imitation of the saints. He learns that trust in God supposes a readiness to accept what God provides. By studying he can become a better instrument in the hand of God for serving God's people; he can also become a better instrument by joining forces with others as his companions. Study is his immediate concern; but after study, what then? His prayer concerns whether "he would enter a religious institute or go about the world." He makes no mention of the Carthusians. He thinks of religious life in terms of self-renunciation and helping others [A 71].[17] Pilgrimage still attracts him, but now his prayer centers on "going about the world" rather than following Jesus in the Holy Land itself. His *propositum* remains the service of God, but he can serve God in a variety of ways.

On the advice of his teacher Ignatius goes to the university of Alcalá for further study [A 56]. The *propositum* to serve the people of God, unrevealed and unchallenged in Jerusalem, is now challenged in Alcalá. Gossip and rumors bring inquisitors who imprison him for forty-two days and then proclaim that he should not teach until he has studied four more years [A 62]. He is puzzled "for seemingly they were closing the door for him to help souls, without giving him any reason except that he had not studied" [A 63]. Ignatius leaves the jurisdiction of the authorities in Alcalá and moves on with his companions to Salamanca. In Salamanca they meet similar opposition, are investigated, imprisoned, and told what they can teach and not teach. As a result, "he found great difficulty in remaining in Salamanca, for it seemed to him that the door had been closed to helping souls by this prohibition not to determine mortal and venial sin" [A 70]. He responds vigorously to the closing of the door, packing powerful feelings in the laconic expression: "So he decided [*se determinó*] to go to Paris to study" [A 71].[18]

In Spain the experience of trying to serve God's people has been painful. No one, in truth, has tried to turn him permanently away from his *propositum* to be of service to others; they have only confirmed the necessity of study. He reflects on the events and chooses three precise means for his purpose, "to study first and to gather some others with the same idea [*del mismo propósito*] and to keep those he had" [A 71]. In his third objective he fails: one of those companions he already had went off to to the West Indies a couple of times and came back a very rich man, another became a bishop in Chiapas in Mexico,[19] and the third "began to live in such manner that he seemed to have forgotten his earlier resolution [*primo proposito*]" [A 80].[20] He succeeds in the other two objectives: he equips himself academically and he finds in Paris companions after his own heart, men with the same aims [*des mismo propósito*], like-minded persons willing to make the same commitment.

3. Ignatius's *propositum* and Christian Tradition

In his desire to imitate the saints Ignatius inserts himself into a long Christian tradition of surrendering to and serving God. Caught in the culture of his own day and limited by it, he is at the same time psychologically and spiritually a throwback to the earliest ages of Christianity, setting out to live in his own way the Gospel message, to follow in the footsteps of Jesus. Unsophisticated in his knowledge of the Christian tradition, he has the popular image of the saints as his model. Even so, his desire to do penance puts him with the earliest ascetics of the Christian era. His desire to go to Jerusalem as a penitential pilgrim places him at the side of hundreds and thousands who journeyed there by land and by sea to do penance for their sins. He is yet unformed in the life of the Spirit, but his instincts are correct.

Without reflection he spontaneously enters into the experience of the past. He picks up ancient trails in the Christian tradition but refuses to follow any of them exactly. Listening to his own experience and finding in it the presence of the Spirit, he follows the ancient paths in his own way. Ignatius leaves his ancestral home, takes a vow of chastity, gives his clothes to the poor, and retires into an out-of-the-way place where no one will recognize him. He is determined to do penance and go to Jerusalem. Whether he is aware of it or not, he is following the pattern of the ancient monks: renunciation [*apotaxis*], withdrawal [*anachōrēsis*], solitude and quiet [*hesychia*], expatriation [*xeniteia*], in order to place himself entirely at the service of God. If he is inventive and creative, it is not in finding a new way to God, for the way is always Jesus, nor even in the way to follow Jesus, which is always through the renunciation of self and the world, but in the concrete way in which he lives out his single-heartedness [*haplotēs*].[21]

Like the original monks, Ignatius is a layman,[22] unsophisticated in his knowledge of the Gospel and of the laws of growth in the Body of Christ. Like them, he plunges with his whole heart and soul into a life of prayer and penance. Despite his choosing this demanding way of living, he neither protects nor supports himself with the vast array of juridical forms available throughout the history of Christianity. Even his unsophisticated eye can recognize that these forms are sadly deficient as practiced in his own day. He is in the stream of Christian tradition but also determined not to be overcome by the treacherous forces tugging and pulling within the stream.

21

Companions with the Same *propositum*

The Spirit of God is inviting Ignatius along a path long before he realizes that the path is leading to a new religious institute. Is this path unique, is the impelling action of the Spirit in him unique, just as the resulting religious institute is unique?

The genesis of a religious institute follows a pattern: conversion or insight, commitment, seeking companions of the same mind-set, groping steps to carry out the commitment. Before reflecting on Ignatius and his activities in Paris we turn to the beginnings of those earlier religious orders we have studied that offer similitarities and parallels with the experience of Ignatius and his companions. Their beginnings provide a glimpse of how the Spirit works in successive ages in the Church and in the world. In each instance *propositum* at first means what someone has resolved or determined or set out to do [*intentio* or *determinatio*] but eventually becomes an established way or mode or manner of living [*institutum*]. Similar language and similar experiences make more intelligible the beginnings of the Company of Jesus.

1. Genesis of a Religious Institute

Carthusian Beginnings

Many similarities and dissimilarities exist between Ignatius and St. Bruno, the founder of the Carthusians, the order

Ignatius often thought of joining. Quite unlike Ignatius, Bruno was a distinguished schoolman, the master and chancellor of the schools at Rheims in France. Like Ignatius, however, he abandoned his career. But whereas Ignatius became a hermit, living in a cave by himself on the edge of a small town, Bruno joined a group of hermits in the forest of Colan far from other habitations, some of whom later were among those who established the Cistercian Order at Cîteaux. Bruno eventually separated himself from the group in the forest in 1084. After some experimentation he began with six companions, as did Ignatius centuries later. Bruno's companions were a school teacher named Landuin, two canons of St. Rufus, Stephen of Bourg and Stephen of Die, Hugh the Chaplain, and two laymen, Andrew and Guerin.[1] We read in the anonymous *Vita antiquior* of Bruno:

> He and the six other good men with him determined [*deliber-averunt*] to renounce the world and its pomps, and to seek the barren advantages of the desert in order to do constant penance, and there, having abandoned all the riches and delights and honors of this world [*relictis omnibus divitiis et deliciis et honoribus hujus mundi*], [they determined] to take up their crosses, and naked to follow the naked Christ along the narrow way that leads to life.... With the Holy Spirit inspiring them [*sancto spiritu inspirante*], they proposed [*proposuerunt*] to approach the ... bishop ... to give themselves over to the execution of their holy and wholesome intention [*propositum*].[2]

The actions, the spirit, the vocabulary, the penance, the deliberation, the renouncing of the world, the inspiring action of the Holy Spirit, approaching the proper authority figure to present a holy *propositum,* the eagerness to put their *propositum* into execution, we encounter again in Ignatius and his band of poor men of Christ. Small wonder that the companions used to meet at the Carthusian monastery in Paris to share in the liturgy, go to confession, and receive communion together.[3]

The story is slightly different in a second life [*Vita altera*] of Bruno written in the sixteenth century, but the vocabulary remains the same. The *Vita altera* joins *propositum* with *desiderium* [desire], a combination that will appear again in the story of Ignatius and his companions. Bruno and his companions requested the bishop to designate a place where "they could fulfill their desire [*desiderium*], to serve God alone worthily." The bishop replied: "I not only do not disapprove of your desired undertaking [*propositum et desiderium*], but I recommend it vigorously."⁴

Bruno and his companions came to the Grande Chartreuse around June 24, the feast of John the Baptist, the hermit of the Judean desert.⁵ Ignatius and his companions chose to be ordained priests on June 24, 1537, and on June 24, 1539, they ended the Deliberation in which they decided to seek approval as a religious institute. At the Grande Chartreuse Bruno "taught [*instituebat*] them [his companions] admirably by word and example," just as Ignatius would do centuries later in Paris, and thus became "the architect of this sublime and difficult institute [*instituti*] for future ages."⁶ As they settled in Bruno and his companions established a way of living that others could follow. The words might have been written of Ignatius and his companions:

> These seven, then . . . wishing to subjugate to themselves . . . the world that they had left and everything in it . . . established [*instituerunt*] a rather difficult way of living [*vivendi normam*], which they followed themselves and imposed upon those who were to come after them.⁷

A call from God [*vocatio*] gives birth to desire [*desiderium*]; desire becomes resolve [*propositum*], and resolve becomes a way of life [*institutum*] with its own rule [*norma vivendi*]: a calling, a vocation [*vocatio*] to be lived. The circle is complete.

What Ignatius would find in pilgrimage, Bruno found in solitude. Nonetheless, Bruno had his own kind of pilgrimage. After many labors in establishing his community, and spending some years in Rome where he had been called, he founded a monastery in Calabria in Southern Italy, and there, "humbly persevering in his aim [*proposito*] of leading a life of solitude until the end of his life . . . he clung to God at all times, and there he happily ended the course of his pilgrimage."⁸

Cistercian Beginnings

In 1098, at the time of Bruno and his six companions, another group of men were dreaming about a new way of life. Once more desire [*desiderium*] joined with intention or determination [*propositum*]. Some of the monks at Molesme, a monastery following the Rule of Benedict, "realized that, although life in that place was a godly and upright life, they observed the Rule they had vowed to keep in a way short of their desire [*desiderio*] and intention [*proposito*]."[9] As a result of their conversations, Robert, the Abbot of Molesme, and six of his monks, Alberic, Odo, John, Stephen, Letald, and Peter, visited the papal legate in France. To him they presented the manner of life to which they were convinced God was calling them. After deliberation his response was that they "persevere in this holy endeavor [*sanctum propositum*]."[10] Returning to Molesme, they informed the other monks, and,

> after common deliberation [*communi consilio*] . . . twenty-one monks went out to try to carry out jointly [*communi . . . assensu*] what they had conceived with one spirit [*uno spiritu*]. Eventually . . . they reached their goal [*desiderio*]. . . . Realizing that the asperity of the place accorded well with the strict design [*proposito*] they had already conceived [in their minds], the soldiers of Christ found the place almost as though divinely prepared, to be as alluring as their design [*propositum*] had been dear.[11]

Their desire not to be restricted in the service of God, their presenting to proper authority how they want to live, their common deliberation and their sense of unity, their deep desire to carry out their *propositum*, these are themes common to the early Cistercians and to Ignatius and his companions.

As with Bruno and his companions, the aspiration [*desiderium*] becomes a determination [*propositum*] that is eventually established [*institutum*] for others to follow. Chapter 15 of the *Exordium parvum* is entitled, "The Institutes [*Instituta*] of the Cistercian Monks Who Departed from Molesme."[12] The terminology is consistent, just as the call of God is consistent. To both the call and the lived response we give the name *vocation*. From this small Cistercian beginning would grow a vast complex of monasteries all over the world.

Franciscan Beginnings

Many parallels also exist between Ignatius and St. Francis in the early years after their conversions. The similarity in vocabulary is striking.

In 1208, Francis of Assisi underwent an interior change and set his life in a new direction. According to Thomas of Celano, his first biographer, he sold his horse and all his goods (successful merchant that he was), offered the money to a priest, and "told him in detail what he had decided to do [*propositum*]" [1C 8–9]. The change was no passing fancy; he was fully determined. His father imprisoned him, but "he was only made all the more ready and eager to carry out his holy intention [*propositum sanctum*] . . . nor could he be dissuaded from his resolve [*proposito*]" [1C 12–13]. Two years after his conversion Francis began to pick up companions of the same mind. One of them, a man by the name of Bernard, imitated what Francis had done, then went to Francis and "revealed to him his resolve [*propositum*]" [*LTS* 27]. Francis was grateful to God for giving him "a needed companion [*socium*] and faithful friend" [1C 24]. Peter, Giles, Philip, and Sylvester followed.[13] When his companions were six in number Francis began to talk to them about growing into a countless multitude from all parts of the world and spreading to the ends of the earth [1C 27]. When the group numbered eight in all, he divided them into four groups of two each and sent them off in four different directions, urging them to be "confident that the Lord will fulfill his purpose [*propositum*] and his promise" [1C 29]. He had come to realize that the *propositum* he had conceived he had really received: it was God's own *propositum*. Soon thereafter he asked God to call them back together [*congregare*], and in a short time they came together [*convenirent*]. "When they had assembled [*convenientibus vero in unum*] . . . he began to open his intention [*propositum*] to them and to indicate what God had revealed to him" [1C 30].[14]

What began as a simple change of heart matured and expanded as prayer and experience revealed God's word to him. Four more joined the group. Seeing that God blessed them daily, Francis "wrote out a way of life [*vitae formam*] and rule [*regulam*] for himself and his brothers, present and future, in a few simple words." He and his brothers took what he had written to Rome to be confirmed by Innocent III. In Rome he met his own bishop from Assisi, and "when he heard their story and understood their intent [*proposito*]" he promised to help them. Francis also approached another bishop, who heard him out and "greatly praised his desire [*voluntatem*] and intent [*propositum*]" [1C 32]. This bishop, however, tried to persuade him to become a monk or a hermit, for he was afraid Francis "might withdraw from his lofty purpose [*proposito*]," but when Francis refused to budge, he promised to help him. Innocent III received them and assented to their request, blessed them and said: "Go with the Lord, brothers, and to the extent that the Lord will deign to inspire you [*prout Dominus vobis inspirare dignabitur*], preach repentance to all" [1C 33]. Celano tells the story of the work they did, the effect they had on people, and comments:

> How enflamed the new disciples of Christ were with the fire of charity! How the love of holy companionship flourished amongst them! . . . quiet conversation, a modest smile, a happy look . . . a humble spirit, a pleasant tongue, a gentle response, the same resolve [*propositum*], prompt obedience, an untiring hand. [1C 38]

In this comment Celano creates an image of a community of friars who mirrored what he was to write about Francis: "His highest purpose [*summa intentio*], his chief desire [*praecipuum desiderium*], and supreme aim [*supremumque propositum*] was to observe the holy Gospel in every way and by every means" [1C 84].

Some of the themes common to Francis and Ignatius are conversion, abandoning home and espousing poverty, finding companions of the same mind, wanting to evangelize the whole world, enjoying a sense of unity with companions, and presenting a *propositum* to papal authority for approval. The life of Francis so moved Ignatius that he said, "What if I should do what St. Francis did?" [*A* 7].

Dominican Beginnings

Meanwhile, Dominic of Guzman was hard at work in southern France.[15] A canon of St. Augustine attached to the cathedral church of Osma in Spain, he had been recruited by Bishop Diego of Osma to preach against the Cathars. No great conversion stirred Dominic, but other aspects of his life would find parallels in the experience of Ignatius some three hundred years later.

The first companions to join Dominic in his preaching had all died or returned home, but the time was coming when he would no longer work alone. Some of those who were with him we know: William of Claret and Dominic of Spain [*Lib.* 31], Stephen of Metz, a man by the name of Noël, and a certain Friar Vitalis. In 1214 Dominic and his companions had not yet started a preaching order but it was a topic talked about [*tractatum*] in their meetings [*Lib.* 37], just as later on Ignatius and his companions came together to talk about [*tractare*] their vocation [*D* 1]. Like the Society of Jesus later on, an order of preachers was something new, for preaching was the prerogative of bishops. In 1215 the Order of Preachers was born. The first members to make profession in the hands of Dominic were Peter Seila and a man named Thomas, in April 1215 [*Lib.* 38]. About two months later Dominic and his six companions[16] established at Toulouse the first religious community in the new order. They had the approbation of Bishop Fulk:

> We establish as preachers in our diocese friar Dominic and his companions who have committed themselves [*proposuerunt*] to go about on foot in evangelical poverty after the manner of religious and to preach the word of evangelical truth.[17]

Events were moving rapidly. In September 1215 Dominic in the company of Bishop Fulk went to Rome and talked to Pope Innocent III, who "confirmed him in his holy resolve [*proposito*]"[18] and told Dominic to have the community choose one of the established rules [*Lib.* 40–41]. On his return in 1216 after the Lateran Council (1215), Dominic and his companions chose to follow the Rule of Augustine and "they determined [*proposuerunt*] and established [*instituerunt*] not to have any possessions" [*Lib.* 42].[19] Later in 1216 Dominic visited Rome again to seek from the pope all he wanted "according to their intent [*propositum*] and determination" [*Lib.* 45]. Honorius III granted his request in the bull *Religiosam Vitam* (1216).[20] Dominic's *propositum* did not end with papal approval. He, too, had a world-wide endeavor in mind. In 1217 Dominic gathered the friars together and after invoking the Holy Spirit he told them that "it was his heart's resolve [*propositum*] to send them all throughout the world, few though they were" [*Lib.* 47].[21]

Some themes in Dominic common to Ignatius are, of course: finding companions in ministry, discussing with them a revolutionary religious institute, the desire to preach in poverty, seeking approval from Rome, dreaming of world-wide horizons for an apostolate. This is the other man whose life so moved Ignatius that he said, "What if I should do what St. Dominic did?" [*A* 7]

2. From *propósito* to *el mismo propósito*

Seven years have now passed since the events at Loyola. Ignatius is the same, but he is different. Like Francis of Assisi he has discovered that both religious and secular events reveal the will of God to the person who listens in prayer. Because religious authorities interfere with his work for others, Ignatius leaves Spain for the University of Paris where he hopes to be able to study more freely and to seek out others with the same aims [*del mismo propósito*] [*A* 71], the same mind and heart, the same dreams. Seven more years and some months he will pass in Paris. While he studies he will find six companions, and they in turn will find three more.

Arriving in Paris early in 1528, Ignatius begins to carry out his objectives. After a year he changes colleges and begins to share a room with Pierre Favre and Francisco Xavier [*F* 7–8]. In a journal Pierre describes his own experience of "living in the same room, eating at the same table, sharing the same purse." Ignatius becomes his spiritual guide. Pierre comments: "We finally were made one in desires, in will, in the firm determination [*proposito*] of choosing this life [*vitam*] that we now have" [*F* 8].²² Favre describes the first four years with Ignatius and concludes:

> I now found myself strong in the Lord alone concerning the resolves [*propositis*] in which I had persevered for more than two years, namely, following Ignatius in a life of poverty, and . . . I was waiting for nothing more than the end of my studies and of his studies and those of Master Francisco and of the others who were of the same mind [*eiusdem animi*] and purpose [*propositi*]. [*F* 13]

Ignatius has succeeded in his second objective, to find others who are *del mismo propósito* [of the same intent]. He does not name them, but Favre writes of "all of us who then shared the same determination [*determinatione*] . . . Ignatius, Master Francisco, I, Favre, Master Bobadilla, Master Laynez, Master Salmerón, Master Simão; Jay had not yet come to Paris, Master Jean and Paschase had not yet been won over" [*F* 15]. Rodrigues comments only on Jay: "He came to the first seven as a companion of the same resolve [*eiusdem propositi*]" [*R* 10], but Ribadeneira writes of all the newcomers: "Then three others, Claude Jay, Jean Codure, and Paschase Broët, companions with the same resolve [*eiusdem propositi socii*], were added to the first seven."²³ All are studying for the priesthood.

The vows that the first seven of them take at Montmartre in Paris on August 15, 1534, reveal how Ignatius endeavors to reconcile his *propositum* with God's will: they are to be pilgrims, pilgrim priests, and pilgrim companions. The first *propositum* of Ignatius is still deep in his heart. Nevertheless, Ignatius's Jerusalem experience cautions them to nuance carefully at Montmartre the haunting idea of pilgrimage:

> They had all determined . . . [to] go to Venice and to Jerusalem, and spend their lives for the good of souls; and if they were not given permission to remain in Jerusalem, then return to Rome and present themselves to the Vicar of Christ, so that he could make use of them wherever he thought it would be more for the glory of God and the good of souls. [*A* 85]

The trip to Venice to find a ship bound for Jerusalem is a one-time project; the service of souls is a lifelong task. Moreover, an alternative to Jerusalem now exists: the pope might determine their pilgrimaging. A radical change of circumstance also exists: whether in Jerusalem or sent on the road by the pope, the pilgrims will be priests. Furthermore, a profound evolution has taken place in the context of pilgrimage: whereas on his first pilgrimage Ignatius had set out alone, it was now a group of companions who would pilgrimage together. Before, he was like his hero St. Humphrey, who had no one to give him food or drink[24] and had no help in his struggle against the evil one except "divine solace." By now Ignatius has learned that relying on God can mean relying on other human beings. Ignatius is now part of a group of companions who are tied together by love and deep mutual concern. They are now "friends in the Lord" [*EI* 119].

3. From *propositum* to *institutum*

The commitment of the companions to the service of Christ and the help of souls is a commitment to more than doing; it is a commitment to living. Their aim, their *propositum*, implies a manner of life, which they sometimes call *institutum* or *institutum vitae*, sometimes *ratio vivendi*. Favre, for example, describes how confused he was before he committed himself "to the way of life [*instituto vitae*] that the Lord gave [him] through Ignatius" [*F* 14]. Simão Rodrigues, in turn, mentions the next two companions together, Diego Laynez and Alfonso Salmerón, "because both of them came together from Spain to Paris for the purpose of study, both at almost the same time embraced the same decision [*sententiam*] and the same way of life [*vivendi rationem*]" [*R* 8]. Each chose what the other chose, the same way of life the other companions embraced.

By mid 1534 all six of the new companions have made the Spiritual Exercises under the direction of Ignatius, except for Xavier, who waits until September. Rodrigues comments:

> After each one of them freely and of his own accord had decided to dedicate himself wholly to the service of God and

to the aforementioned way of life [*vitae instituto*], then it was revealed to him that there were others who had consecrated themselves to a similar way of living [*vivendi rationi*]. When they learned that, words could not express what joy, what happiness, what consolation they experienced, what strength to persevere in their resolve [*proposito*]! [*R* 9]

In this passage all of the companions are of one mind and one heart and with the same goals [*del mismo propósito*]. The *propositum* they share is not a single project but a lifetime effort. They do not share a common project while living different sorts of lives; they also share a way of life [*vitae institutum* or *vivendi ratio*]. The commitment of each is personal and final but is stronger for being shared. Rodrigues remarks in words reminiscent of the Acts of the Apostles (2:42–47): "The first seven Fathers persevered . . . and day by day, more and more stirred up by their new desire and the new ardor of their calling [*propositi*], they began to talk about the time when they would leave Paris and begin to put into execution the desires of their hearts" [*R* 12]. Rodrigues reveals how deep the commitment of each one is to the common *propositum* and *ratio vivendi* when he narrates that Ignatius must leave Paris for Venice via Spain in order to try to improve his health. They will miss him, but his absence will not affect their determination. "For just as each one by himself, freely, before he had heard of the vocation or determination [*propositum*] of any other, began to aspire to this one norm of living [*vivendi normam*], so he [each of them] firmly decided within himself that, even if the others defected, he would put his hand to the plow and not look back" [*R* 21].

Elements of the Companions' vitae institutum

In their different accounts of Montmartre Rodrigues [*R* 13], Laynez [*L* 36], and Favre [*F* 15] all include poverty as part of the pilgrimage to Jerusalem. Rodrigues mentions chastity, and he and Laynez speak of preaching the Word of God, to which Rodrigues adds "administering the holy sacraments of confession and the Eucharist without any stipend" [*R* 13]. They are indicating elements of their way of life once they get on the road.

Rodrigues also suggests some of the elements integral to their way of living in Paris itself: "After the Fathers began to talk amongst themselves about entering upon this way of life [*vitae instituto*] they judged that the frequentation of the sacraments should always be linked with their scholarly studies" [*R* 19]. Laynez fills in more details in his description of how the companions live after Ignatius leaves Paris:

> We strengthened[25] ourselves there, partly through prayer and frequent confession and communion, partly through our studies which were on sacred things, partly through making a vow to dedicate ourselves to the service of the Lord in poverty ... and in renewing and confirming this vow each year on the feast of Our Lady in August at St. Mary of Montmartre. [*L* 30]

Laynez is describing more than a simple *propositum*. He speaks of something already established [*institutum*] as the environment in which they can carry out the *propositum*. His description contains at least four elements: (1) prayer, (2) frequentation of the sacraments, (3) studying theology, and (4) the vow of serving the Lord in poverty, all aimed at the service of God and the help of the neighbor.[26] At this point Laynez adds a fifth element, which he does not name, although he elaborates on it at length:

> We renewed our vow, staying afterwards to eat together in charity. We continued this throughout the year, from time to time having a potluck meal now at one house, now at another, which, with visiting and encouraging one another, helped us to survive. The Lord helped us especially in our studies in which we made steady progress, dedicating them always to the glory of the Lord and the help of the neighbor, maintaining a special love for one another and helping each other even in temporal matters when we could. [*L* 30]

The potluck meals jolt us into realizing that they share companionship rather than community under the same roof; they are a *societas*, not a *communitas*. *Societas* means companionship as well as society.

Departure from Paris

The companions now seek confirmation of their way of life. "Before their departure [for Venice] the Fathers approach two outstanding scholars, doctors both of them, in order to outline the nature of their endeavor [*propositi*]; they praise it, approve it, extol it; they also indicate that it is fraught with difficulties and dangers" [*R* 23]. The companions are aware that Paris is a time of training for the future, yet they do not think of themselves as religious, for Laynez states explicitly, "Our intention [*intención*] from Paris on was not to found a religious order [*congregación*]" [*L* 36]. They leave Paris in the middle of November 1536 and are ordained in Venice the following summer. After some months of tireless labor in Italy they gather in Vicenza. They recognize that in their companionship they are bound together in such a fashion as to be a company. If anyone asks them who they are, they are the Company of Jesus, for Jesus is their only head.

This Company of Jesus gathers together in Rome in 1539. The time has come to recognize that Jerusalem is only a dream. Rodrigues summarizes their experience of the event called the Deliberation of the First Fathers and indicates that all of the elements of their *institutum vitae* are beginning to fall into place:

> Having gained a time of quiet pregnant with opportunity, the companions decided to explain to the pontiff the kind of life [*vitam*] they wanted to lead [*instituere*] to the honor of God and in the service of the Apostolic See. . . . They committed all their energy, their whole life, to procuring the salvation of their neighbors, both believers and unbelievers. They add something new, that one is to be selected as superior general to be in charge of the others, as it is now; then solemn vows of obedience, poverty, chastity to be pronounced, and finally of special obedience to the Supreme Pontiff and his successors. Many other things besides were decided upon conducive to their endeavor [*propositum*] and their purpose [*finemque*], that I will not repeat at length since they can be read in the first document [*diplomate*] of the Society.[27] [*R* 91]

The document Rodrigues has in mind is the Formula of the Institute, orally approved by Pope Paul III on September 3, 1539, and solemnly approved in *Regimini militantis ecclesiae* on September 27, 1540. The Formula spells out their *propositum;* it has not changed substantially since Ignatius first set out for Jerusalem, but, like a child growing into an adult, it has evolved naturally into a mature way of living [*institutum*]. Serving God and helping souls is still there, but now as priests; the pilgrimage is still there, but going wherever the pope might send them; chastity is there, and poverty, the whole way of life [*institutum*] freshly united through a bond of obedience, a difficult way of life filled with renunciation and the way of the cross.

Ignatius is not the lone founder of the Society of Jesus. He has companions who embrace his *propositum* and make it their own, and together they form the Company whose Formula they ask the pope to approve. The time has finally come to turn to the Formula.

22

The Summary of the Rule: The Formula of the Institute

Using as his norms the Scriptures and the living tradition of the Church, the Dominican theologian Tommaso Badia recognized that the *propositum* of the companions was good and holy. Furthermore, he indicated that the five decrees that the companions had submitted contained a summary of the rule they wished to follow. He recognized that the five decrees did not contain the whole rule. He recognized, in other words, that it was a living rule to be lived by *living* people, and that not all that it contained could be written down:

> that the whole intent of your Society
> seemed to him to be good and holy,
>
> **and that the summary of the rule,**
> [summamque regule]
> **that you desire to follow,**
> [quam seruare cupitis]
> **is contained in the five decrees written below.**
> [infrascriptis quinque capitulis contineri]

In monastic terminology, the *propositum,* that which one's heart is set upon, is the monastic life; the guide that points out the way to lead that life is the rule [*regula*], whether it is the Rule of Benedict or the Rule of Basil. Ignatius and his companions, on the other hand, under the impelling power of the Spirit, have determined their *propositum* over a period of years. They have formulated how to live out that *propositum*. They have elaborated a rule [*regula*], and a summary of that rule [*summam regule*] is found in the five decrees of the Formula. The terminology is risky. As noted above, "rule" was, strictly speaking, limited to the approved rules of the time of Lateran IV (1215), the Rule of Benedict or the Rule of Basil for monks and the Rule of Augustine for canons.[1]

In 1209, Francis of Assisi had asked for approval of a new rule. Francis did not want to accept one of the ancient rules canonized by the use of centuries; the Gospel was sufficient. In presenting the Gospel as norm for his friars, he used *vita* [life], terminology that was also current in the twelfth and thirteenth centuries to indicate legislation governing the lives of penitents or of lay people who lived in a religious manner. These groups called their norms of governance a rule [*regula*] by way of analogy with the ancient rules.[2] Francis, however, clearly wanted his *regula* to be on a par with the ancient rules, for he had by-passed his bishop (who was favorable to him) and had come knocking at the pope's door asking for the approval of his rule.[3] Six years before Lateran IV (1215) Innocent III orally approved the rule Francis presented to him. Strictly speaking, therefore, it was an approved rule before the Lateran Council adopted Canon 13, even though papal confirmation of the rule did not come until 1223.[4] Although in one sense it could in no way claim the antiquity sanctifying the other rules, in another sense it could: no rule is older than the Gospel, and Francis and his friars saw themselves as restoring the original Gospel ideal. They acted as though equal to the "older" orders, and the Roman curia treated them as equal. Even so, at the beginning of the thirteenth century many experienced the Franciscan rule as fresh and new.[5]

Dominic, too, came knocking on the papal door just before Lateran IV was to meet, armed with the approval of his bishop for the new Order of Preachers and asking for papal confirmation. Unlike Francis, Dominic did not insist on a new rule, and Innocent III told him to go home and choose a rule and write appropriate constitutions; he said nothing about *institu-*

tio. Dominic chose the Rule of St. Augustine, which he had already been following as a canon regular, as the approved rule of the new Order of Preachers,[6] and wrote his own *institutiones* or *constitutiones,* drawn largely from the Premonstratensians.[7] Honorius III confirmed the Order of Preachers in 1216.[8] The Constitutions Dominic wrote soon took on all the force and authority and vitality of an original rule equal in power to one of the ancient rules.[9] The Dominicans, in fact, did not hesitate to call the Constitutions their rule [*regula*][10] and were somewhat distressed that the Franciscan *regula* was recognized as "approved" whereas theirs was not.[11] In the course of time the Dominicans developed to such an extent as to break the bonds of schematization and become a "new" religious order.[12]

In writing a *viuendi formula* [way of living] the companions declare emphatically that they are *not* of the same nature as the ancient orders. Moreover, in Decree Three of the Formula the companions call their *viuendi formula* a rule [*regula*]: "All shall vow obedience to the superior of the Society in all things which pertain to the observance of our rule" [*CEP* 4].[13] By calling their *viuendi formula* their *rule* the companions say that they have no desire to accept an already approved rule. Nevertheless, whether they are conscious of it or not, the companions draft their *viuendi formula* in the manner of an ancient rule, and as such the Formula will serve the same purpose as the great rules of the past.[14] Their choice to write a *viuendi formula* rather than to adopt an ancient *regula* explains why the first members of the Company of Jesus are not called *regulares,* followers of a rule, for they do not follow one of the ancient rules, or even a *religio,* for they stand outside the approved *religiones;* they are a breed apart. A summary of how they intend to live [*summa regule*] is contained in the Formula. They do not particularly care about terminology except that they be called the Company of Jesus. What else they are called makes little difference, as long as they are allowed to carry out the *propositum* God has given them.

The five decrees of the Formula summarize the *propositum* of the companions and are their rule of life, "which is a way that leads to God" [*CEP* 2]. They reflect the commitment the companions made at Montmartre, the experience of La Storta that the Father had accepted their offering, and the conclusions they made in the deliberations of the spring of 1539. Written shortly after those deliberations, the five chapters follow the same order and cover the same matters.

The summary of the rule is a norm, not a straitjacket. It is designed to assist the companions in leading their way of life. It assumes prayer and listening to God, prayer and listening on the part of the superior, prayer and listening on the part of each companion. After listening to God and to each companion, the superior has responsibility to decide in the light of what he has heard.

1. Decree One: Chastity and Mission

The first topic in the Deliberation of the First Fathers was whether the companions should split up since Paul III was beginning to send them to different parts of the world. Their response was a resounding "No," an affirmation to maintain the unity God had given them. Whatever they do, they will do in companionship. Decree One of the Formula, employing the imagery of La Storta, takes off from that conclusion and goes to the core of their *propositum* immediately:

> Whoever in our Society, which we desire to be designated by the name of Jesus, wishes to serve God [*Deo militare*] under the standard of the cross and serve the Lord alone and his vicar on earth . . .[15] [*CEP* 2]

Service in companionship. The text images Ignatius and his friends as companions at the side of Christ carrying his cross in the service of the Father for the salvation of the world. To be serving in companionship at the side of Christ, continuing in the present the work he came to do, this is their desire [*deseo*], their intention [*intención*], their determination [*determinación*], their resolve [*propósito*].

Their *propositum* is service, but they choose to serve in companionship: (1) companionship in Jesus, that takes its name from him, (2) companionship under the standard of the cross of Jesus, (3) companionship in serving Jesus [*Deo militare*], (4) companionship in the service of Jesus alone [*soli Domino*], and (5) companionship in the service of the vicar of Jesus. Everything else in the Formula concerns the means to carry out this aim [*propositum*].

It is precisely in this context of (1) companionship, (2) service of Jesus in the service of the Father, and (3) service of the vicar of Christ that the companions introduce the vow of chastity. Chastity, therefore, relates to these three elements. It is a vow taken within the companionship binding the companions together in a triple bond of love: (1) a deep commitment to one another who share the same *propositum;* (2) a radical interior commitment to Jesus and the Father after the manner of Jesus' own commitment to the Father; and (3) a commitment to the vicar of Christ, which means a commitment of enduring and selfless love to the Church and the world, to all people, believers and unbelievers alike:

> Whoever in our Society . . . wishes to serve God . . . after a solemn vow of perpetual chastity, should keep in mind that he is a member of a community founded for this most of all, that it aim principally at the advancement of souls in Christian life and doctrine, and the propagation of the faith through the ministry of the Word, through the Spiritual Exercises, and by works of charity, and specifically through the instruction of children and the uninitiated in Christianity . . . [*CEP* 2]

The purpose of the companionship, in other words, is to bring people to the Father and the Son in and through the Church. In an age where priesthood was most often a career opportunity, where it was not infrequent for an ecclesiastic to take a mistress and lunge at the ladder of success, to take a solemn vow of chastity and plunge into the ministry of love carried on by Jesus and the apostles was bold, daring, and a challenge to the sexual immorality of the times.

The full context of the vow of chastity includes not only the persons to whom the companions relate but also the works the companions do. Those works are all in the same line as the works Ignatius did at Manresa: the primary instruments of the new Company of Jesus are the ministry of the Word and works of charity; the limits, if any, are hard to discern.[16] In contrast, some founding documents of the sixteenth century indicate an institute has the "three substantial vows of religion, poverty, chastity, and obedience," and is founded to do certain limited works.[17] In the Formula each vow stands in its own proper context.

In its specific context the vow of chastity has a richer motive than that which moved Ignatius on the way to Montserrat, "because he had more fear of being conquered in the area of chastity than in other things" [L 5]. In the Formula it is not a vow of fear but a vow of love. Chastity marks the impelling presence of the Spirit linking the companions to one another who are sent, to the Father and the Son who send them, and to those to whom they are sent. Chastity has to do with service and mission. Gone is the awkward commitment to the external aspect of things characteristic of Ignatius immediately after his conversion; the Father has drawn him and all his companions into the interior life of Jesus carrying his cross for the life of the world. The words of the Formula are a call to enter into that experience. The final version of 1550 is more nuanced, "to serve the Lord alone and the Church, his spouse, under the Roman Pontiff, his vicar on earth." Jesus is carrying his cross in his mystical body.

In the Constitutions Ignatius treats of the vows (Part VI) before he treats of mission (Part VII): again the vows are ordered to mission. The opening words of the Formula, "Whoever in our Society . . . wishes to serve God, etc.," are reflected in the opening words of Part VI: "So that those already admitted . . . might apply themselves more fruitfully according to our institute in the divine service and the help of their neighbor, etc." Both passages concern what those in the Society are called to do in order to serve God. Once again Ignatius begins with chastity. The opening passage in the Formula about mission and chastity, I am convinced, is the basis for his intriguing statement in the Constitutions that chastity needs no explanation "since it is clear how perfectly it should be observed, striving to imitate in it angelic purity through cleanliness [*limpieça*] of both body and mind" [C 2:520].[18] One wonders if Ignatius's choice of *limpieça* [cleanliness] is an attack against the Spanish concern at that time for blood purity [*limpieça*], that is, the concern to be free of any stain or taint of Jewish blood,[19] replacing that concern with a desire for Gospel purity, to be without fault in every way. Jesus lauds cleanliness in the beatitude: "Blessed are the pure [in Spanish, *limpios*] in heart" (Matt. 5:8). The pure in heart are those with no mixture of moral fault, those who are centered wholly on God.

The angel's purity consists in the angel's total and loving transparency to God, singleness of purpose and direction, unhesitating and powerful decisiveness in God's service, and unhesitating readiness to be sent [*angelos* = messenger of God]. That is the cleanliness or limpidity of which Ignatius speaks: freedom in relation to other human persons and transparency to Jesus alone, a loving relationship to Jesus and to everyone else in Jesus, so that the mind is wholly bent on Jesus in the ministry of the Word, and the bodily labor of the works of charity center entirely in him. Nothing created comes between the person and Jesus: the whole person is in his service, unhesitating, decisive, clear, ready to be sent.

2. Decree Two: Obedience to the Pope

The context for the decisions of the companions to perpetuate the gift of unity God had given them and to take a vow of obedience to one of their number was the pope's own decision to send them to various places two by two. The next decision they made was that members of the Society should make a vow to go wherever the pope might send them [*DS* 1]. Decree Two takes up that vow of obedience to the pope. The vow shatters the prevailing image of the pope as a temporal ruler. It challenges not only the pope but the kings and princes who lead armies against him, for it assumes a vision of the pope in his Gospel role as spiritual leader of the Christian people. For the companions, this vow transforms the idea of pilgrimage dear to them from the beginning. Like Decree One, Decree Two begins with companionship:

> All the companions should be aware . . . that this whole Society and each one individually . . . are at the service of God under faithful obedience to His Holiness Paul the Third and his successors . . . [*CEP* 3]

What the Formula announces is something communal. The works of the Society are not for private entrepreneurs, lone rangers, or solitary commandos. The companions are companions, and they serve Christ under his vicar:

> Whatever His Holiness commands, for the good of souls and the propagation of the faith, we are bound to execute immediately as far as we can, without any evasion or excuse, whether he sends us to the Turks, or to the new world, or to the Lutherans, or to any other unbelievers or believers whatsoever. [*CEP* 3]

Without saying so, the companions are describing here an imitation of angelic purity, an imitation of the angel's enduring openness and readiness to go at God's slightest command, the singleminded, unencumbered, and unhesitating response of an angel's intellect and will to whatever God desires.

Paul III had said to the companions: "Why do you want so much to go to Jerusalem? Italy is a good and true Jerusalem if you want to produce fruit in the Church of God" [*B* 11]. Decree Two nuances the *propositum* conceived at Montmartre and accepted at La Storta. If Italy is a good Jerusalem, so is the whole world. Pilgrimaging to the city where Jesus carried his cross is no longer part of their dream; they dream now of pilgrimaging throughout the world for the helping of souls. Nicolás Bobadilla would be the last of the companions to die, at the age of ninety or ninety-one. His life is a marvelous example of a lifelong pilgrimage and a symbol of the change that took place in their idea of pilgrimage. He certainly knew what the vow of obedience to the pope was all about. Bobadilla was missioned to India but became sick, and Xavier went in his place. Instead he spent his life walking the roads of Europe. He was sent all over Italy and Sicily, to various parts of Germany, to Dalmatia, to Vienna, and to Prague. The year before his death he wrote to Father General Aquaviva, the fifth general of the Society, on August 11, 1589:

> Recalling (as I often do recall) this holy feast of the Assumption of the glorious Madonna, especially in my old age, I cannot omit writing to Your Paternity in view of the fact that on

this day the first Fathers of our Company made a vow on Montmartre near Paris to go to Jerusalem. This vow Divine Providence . . . commuted to other better and more fruitful vows of pilgrimaging in religion. [*FN* 3:321]

The reality was better than the dream. In the years between Loyola and Rome, going to Jerusalem, walking where Jesus had walked, was transformed into going wherever Jesus needs to walk, going to heretics, to believers, and to unbelievers, going to the ends of the earth. Helping souls was not a stay-at-home cottage industry. It called for a pilgrimage that never ends and it called for the vicar of Christ to be in charge.

Decree Two is on obedience to the pope, but it ends on obedience to the superior and the Society: to thwart ambition or any refusal on their part, each one promises not to negotiate with the pontiff regarding where he might go. Availability to the pope for pilgrimage is like the total and loving availability of the angel to be sent anywhere by God. Human beings, however, are not angels. In humans corruption is always possible. That is why Decree Two stresses obedience rather than chastity. To imitate the openness and availability, the flaming love and devotion, the readiness of an angel to discharge any duty in God's service, let everyone "leave the whole matter to God, his vicar, and the superior of the Society" [*CEP* 3].

3. Decree Three: Obedience within the Society

Decree Three returns to the solution to the second question addressed in the Deliberation of the First Fathers, a vow of obedience to one of their own number: the companionship can best be maintained and the *propositum* can best be carried out through obedience to one of themselves whose office it is to keep the *propositum* in mind at all times:

> All shall vow obedience to the superior of the Society in all things pertaining to the observance of our rule. He should, furthermore, command whatever he knows to be opportune for the attainment of the end proposed [*propossiti* (*sic*)] to him by God and the Society. . . . As for the subjects, both

> because of the great usefulness of order, and because of the vigorous exercise of humility, which cannot be praised enough, they should be ready to obey the superior at all times in everything pertaining to the Society's institute, and should recognize Christ as present in him and give him fitting veneration. [*CEP* 4]

In the Deliberation of the First Fathers they had agreed that God called them to preserve their companionship, and that they should take a vow of obedience to one of their number for three reasons: (1) to carry out better their desire to fulfill the divine will in all things, i.e., better carry out their *proposita*; (2) to preserve the Society better, i.e., preserve their companionship; and (3) to take care of details, i.e., to preserve good order. In the Formula the companions affirm that it is up to the superior to keep the *proposita* in mind at all times, an admonition against the prevailing attitude of rulers who neglect the common good for their own private gain. They also maintain that it is up to the rest to obey for the sake of good order and for the sake of humility: the service of Jesus cannot be chaotic nor power seeking. This second admonition contains a two-pronged countercultural thrust: (1) against self-seeking as manifested in clerical career hunting, and (2) toward seeking the will of God revealed in the Gospel.

To be accepted as companions at the side of Christ carrying his cross implies that the prayer of the Two Standards has been answered, to be poor with Christ, humiliated with Christ, and humble with Christ. As companions at the side of Christ they are to recognize in the superior Christ who is companion of all. Chastity and obedience blend into the same reality, the love and service of Jesus alone.

4. Decree Four: Poverty

Decree Four reaches out with open arms and embraces with enthusiasm the condition under which the companions have learned they can best carry out their *propositum*: poverty, which is the environment, the ambience, the breath of life to a pilgrim. Ignatius knew poverty from Montserrat and Manresa;

the others committed themselves at Montmartre, tasted poverty after reaching Venice when they began to beg from door to door, and came to relish it:

> Since we have learned from experience that a life as far removed as possible from every taint of avarice and as similar as possible to evangelical poverty is more joyful, more simple and more suitable for edifying the neighbor . . . let each and every one vow perpetual poverty . . . [*CEP* 5]

In their countercultural rejection of wealth they have experienced joy in poverty in a world where avarice dominates even life in the Church. Poverty is not only more joyful, as Francis had shown centuries before, it also provides a more uncluttered life, a life more fully centered on God. Poverty is not doing something difficult in imitation of the saints; it is not giving up or giving away. Poverty is union with Christ. Poverty is a tool for service, for helping people. It verifies in act what is said in word. They experience that poverty validates their preaching, their exhorting, their giving of the Spiritual Exercises, their work with the sick and the poor and the abandoned. The poverty they choose is total:

> They cannot, either individually or in common, for the maintenance or use of the Society, acquire any civil right to any real property or produce or income, but should be content to be happy with the use only of necessary things, at the good pleasure of those who own them, and to accept money and the value of things given to them in order to buy what they need. [*CEP* 5]

This is poverty indeed. Most religious orders owned a church they served or a house to live in, but these men choose to be totally without. They have no house or city designated as the residence of the superior or of anyone else.[20] They are totally at the mercy of benefactors. In poverty they once more come close to the purity of the angels, that utter detachment regarding the whole of creation that lets nothing get in the way of the service of God.

5. Decree Five: Religious Observances

The companions left no minutes of the final meeting of their 1539 Deliberation, which took place on June 24, but Decree Five and the concluding paragraph of the Formula fill in the gap.[21] They contain two of the most remarkable passages in the whole of the Formula. In a few brief strokes they sweep away a good part of the support systems traditionally connected with the priesthood or the religious life. These two passages were so creative, so daring, so radical that officials in the papal curia feared the companions might be called Lutherans. (The two passages quietly disappeared from the Formula in 1540, but remained a silent part of the *propositum* nonetheless.) Decree Five begins with a quiet look at priesthood:

> All the members who are in sacred orders, although they can acquire no right to benefices and incomes, are nevertheless obliged to recite the divine office according to the rite of the Church but not in choir, lest they be led away from the works of charity to which all have dedicated ourselves. For this reason they should not use organs or singing in Masses or other rites; for these, which laudably adorn the religious worship of clerics and other religious and have been found to arouse and inspire souls by reason of the hymns and ritual, we have found to be no little hindrance to us, since according to the nature of our vocation we frequently have to spend a great part of the day and even of the night in comforting the sick both in body and in spirit. [*CEP* 6]

The passage is strikingly countercultural. The companions affirm their commitment to priesthood, a way of being in the Church; they reject priesthood as a source of income. They affirm the value of the divine office; choir, with all its beauty, they set aside. They embrace liturgy but reject liturgical splendor, not because it is splendid but because it interferes with their apostolic work.

The second countercultural passage, located in the concluding paragraph of the Formula, considers certain elements that up to that time were a normal part of religious life:

> no fasts, disciplines, baring of feet or head, color of dress or kind of food, penances, hairshirts and other bodily mortification are to be imposed on the members under pain of mortal sin; we do not prohibit them because we condemn them, but only because we do not wish our men to be crushed by too many burdens undertaken at the same time, or to have some excuse for not carrying out the task we have set for ourselves [*quae nobis proposuimus*]. Each one, if the superior does not forbid it, can practice these things devoutly to the extent that he recognizes them necessary or useful for himself. [*CEP* 7]

These men, whose leader had set out to live a life of penance, dismiss out of hand common penances, a common habit, and ordinary practices supportive of community in monasteries. Like Ignatius, they subordinate everything to the *propositum* of helping souls. They find no need to seek out great and difficult deeds; the *propositum* itself is difficult enough.

A final remark about Decree Five and the concluding paragraph serves as a comment on the other decrees as well. Even within the established religious framework Ignatius and his companions are countercultural. They make no absolutes of anything found in the religious tradition. They impose no obligations. Rather everything they choose to take upon themselves is in the service of Jesus: the vows, prayer, mortification, their whole approach to the religious tradition. They choose nothing for itself; they simply rearrange all the elements of religious life so that they are in the service of their ministry to God's people.

Concluding Reflection

What Ignatius began with has been sifted and rearranged and given new emphases. Imitating the saints has disappeared or been subsumed into serving Jesus. Doing penance [*propositum penitentiae*] has become secondary; envisioned at first as a way of serving God, its role now is to serve the work they are doing, the help of souls. Serving God [*propositum serviendi Deo*] has itself been transformed into serving the neighbor. Living in chastity [*propositum continentiae*], at first perhaps linked with fear, is a spontaneous self-giving to Jesus guaranteeing freedom to pilgrimage in service to the end of one's days. Going to Jerusalem [*propositum peregrinationis*], which meant to be where Jesus had been, has been transformed into going wherever Jesus needs to be. Being poor, which had its own glamor for a man of noble blood, is experienced now as a happier way, a clearer and purer way, a way more apt to have an impact on people. From one turned in upon himself and his own sinfulness, Ignatius has become the leader of a Company, priests who labor in loving companionship for the good of others, reaching out in all directions to the uttermost ends of the earth.

The *propositum* of Ignatius has grown and evolved and been transformed. Purified through the divine action, it has become the *propositum* of the Society. Badia in the papal Curia does not pass judgment on the *propositum* of Ignatius but on the Society's *propositum*, and that, he says, is good and holy. The love and commitment of one man has been subsumed into the love and companionship of many. The seed has been transformed into the fruit, and the fruit is destined to drop more seeds to produce more fruit.

SECTION TWO

Papal Approval and Commissioning

After the five decrees of the Formula of the Institute the companions add a final paragraph, and the proposed apostolic letter is complete. The final paragraph consists of two sentences. The first approves the way of living [*viuendi formula*] of the companions. It sets the tiny Company in the context of the whole Christian world and sees it as a gift to the whole Church. The second sentence is like an explosion. Urging them to get moving, it recalls the impelling action of the Holy Spirit at the beginning of *Cum ex plurium,* and commands them to let the Spirit take them wherever the Spirit will.

THE *HANC VESTRAM* SENTENCE

Hanc vestram vite formam [. . . cum perlegerimus],
[Since we have read this form of life of yours]

suprascriptis quinque capitulis contentam,
[contained in the above five decrees]

**cum perlegerimus
et** [. . . iudicauerimus fore opportunam],
[and have judged that it would be suitable]

ad spiritualem profectum Societatis ipsius vestre
[for the spiritual growth of your Society]

et reliqui christiani gregis
[and of the rest of the Christian flock]

cuius cura nobis incumbit,
[whose care falls upon us]

**iudicauerimus fore opportunam,
vigore presentium**
[by the power of these presents]

illam laude dignam esse declaramus
[we declare it to be worthy of praise]

atque apostolica auctoritate
[and by our apostolic authority]

approbamus,
[we approve it]

benedicimus,
[we bless it]

roboramus,
[we validate it]

et sub tutela huius sanctae sedis recipimus
[and we receive it under the protection of this Holy See]

atque confirmamus,
[and confirm it]

facultatem vobis concedentes
[granting you the faculties]

condendi particulares inter uos Constitutiones,
[to establish particular Constitutions for yourselves]

quas [. . . conformes esse iudicaueritis]
[that you judge to be in accordance]

ad Societatis vestrae finem
[with the end of your Society]

et Jesu Christi Domini nostri gloriam
[and the glory of our Lord Jesus Christ]

et proximi vtilitatem
[and the help of the neighbor]

conformes esse iudicaueritis.

Structure: The sentence begins with an accusative, *Hanc vestram vite formam* [this form of life of yours], the object of the subordinate verb *perlegerimus* [we have read]; the same phrase serves as the accusative with an infinitive, *fore,* after another subordinate verb, *iudicauerimus* [we have judged]. The pronoun *illam* [it] refers to the same *hanc formam* phrase and stands as the object of a series of independent verbs: *declaramus* [we declare], *approbamus* [we approve], *benedicimus* [we bless], *roboramus* [we strengthen], *recipimus* [we receive], and *confirmamus* [we confirm].

THE *AGITE* SENTENCE

Agite igitur, dilecti in Christo filii,
[Press on, therefore, beloved sons in Christ]

vestram vocationem sequimini,
[follow your call]

quo vos ducit Spiritus Sanctus,
[whithersoever the Holy Spirit leads you]

et in vinea Domini posthac,
[and in the vineyard of the Lord from now on]

sub protectione huius sanctae sedis,
[under the protection of this Holy See]

tanquam boni agricolae viriliter laborate,
[work with all your heart like good vinedressers]

Domino nostro Jesu Christo vobis fauente,
[with our Lord Jesus Christ on your side]

qui viuit et regnat cum Spiritu Sancto
[who lives and reigns with the Holy Spirit]

Deus in seculorum secula. Amen.
[God forever and ever. Amen.]

Structure: The sentence has three independent verbs, all imperatives: *agite* [drive, march, move], *sequimini* [follow], and *laborate* [labor]. *Agite* stands alone. *Sequimini* has *vocationem* [calling] as its object and leads into a subordinate clause introduced by *quo* [whither]. The *laborate* clause contains an ablative absolute, *Domino . . . favente* [the Lord favoring].

23

Papal Approval and Commissioning

1. Approval of the Companions' Way of Living

Cum ex plurium is a *proposed* apostolic letter containing the companions' written *viuendi formula* in the five decrees of the Formula of the Institute. Its conclusion reveals what they hope the papal response will be.

> **Since we have read this form of life of yours,**
> [Hanc vestram vite formam . . . (cum perlegerimus)]
> **contained in the above five decrees,**
> [suprascriptis quinque capitulis contentam]
>
> [cum perlegerimus]
> **and have judged that it would be suitable**
> [et . . . (iudicauerimus fore opportunam)]
> **for the spiritual growth of your Society**
> [ad spiritualem profectum Societatis ipsius vestre]
> **and the rest of the Christian flock**
> [et reliqui christiani gregis]
> **whose care falls upon us,**
> [cuius cura nobis incumbit]
>
> [iudicauerimus fore opportunam]

The Company has an ecclesial dimension. The unity the companions enjoy is not for themselves alone. Their way of life has power for good beyond their own growth. The Holy Spirit has created the Company for the Church, and the Church needs to recognize that the Company belongs to all of God's people. As the pope continues to prepare for a general council, here is a ready instrument for reform and renewal. The ecclesial dimension of the Company includes the thrust of the Church toward those outside the Church, either to bring them in or by mere presence to touch and bless and transform their lives. Reference in *Cum ex plurium* to the pope's concern for Christians without acknowledged concern for non-Christians strikes an odd note in post–Vatican II ears. Yet the Formula itself stresses the readiness, even the eagerness, of the companions to work amongst those who do not believe in Christ as well as with those who do. The global responsibility of the Church is so obvious to them, and the possibility of working amongst non-Christians is so real to them, that the companions take both for granted.

> **by the power of these presents**
> [vigore presentium]
> **we declare it to be worthy of praise,**
> [illam laude dignam esse declaramus]
> **and by our apostolic authority**
> [atque apostolica auctoritate]
> **we approve it,**
> [approbamus]
> **we bless it,**
> [benedicimus]
> **we validate it,**
> [roboramus]
> **and receive it under the protection of this Holy See**
> [et sub tutela huius sanctae sedis recipimus]
> **and confirm it,**
> [atque confirmamus]

Like bells intoning the joyful tidings of victory, the verbs ring out. Each has its own special timbre, its own special pitch, its own special sound. *Declaramus:* we make clear [*claram*]. If the governor's decree about their innocence has left any doubt in any mind concerning them, we now make it clear that their form of life [*vite formam*] is worthy of praise. *Approbamus:* we manifest it as proven [*probam*]; we assent to it as good; we favor it; we establish it. *Benedicimus:* we speak [*dicimus*] well [*bene*] of it; we hold it as holy and make it holy; we bless it. *Roboramus:* we give it strength [*robur*]; we put our seal upon it; we validate it. *Recipimus:* we take [*capimus*] it under our wing; to be for it is to be for us; to be against it is to be against us; we receive it and all who follow it under the protection of the Holy See. *Confirmamus:* we firm it up [*firmamus*]; we go one step further, and insist on all that we have said; we confirm it.

>**granting you the faculties**
>[facultatem vobis concedentes]
>**to establish particular Constitutions for yourselves**
>[condendi particulares inter uos Constitutiones]

The companions ask for no rule [*regula*], no institution [*institutio*], from one of the approved ways of religious observance as demanded by Canon 13 of Lateran IV. They have written their own way of living [*viuendi formula*] and call it their rule [*regula*]. They wish now to write their own Constitutions touching on more specific points. The *viuendi formula* the pope approves is papal law, to be changed only by papal authority; the Constitutions are to be more familial, norms for governance within the family of the Society, and subject to change by the Society itself.

>**that you judge to be in accordance**
>[quas . . . (conformes esse iudicaueritis)]
>**with the end of your Society**
>[ad Societatis vestrae finem]
>**and the glory of our Lord Jesus Christ**
>[et Jesu Christi Domini nostri gloriam]
>**and the help of the neighbor.**
>[et proximi vtilitatem]
>
>[conformes esse iudicaueritis]

It is up to the companions to judge what to include in the Constitutions. They have already, according to *Cum ex plurium,* reflected on what experience has taught them is conducive to the end of the Society and have expressed the major points in the Formula of the Institute. The Constitutions in no way take the place of the Formula, but complement the Formula and enable the companions to carry out the Formula more expeditiously. The norms are both simple and profound:

1. The end of the Society, of the companionship that is God's gift to them. Whatever fits that purpose, whatever helps toward that goal, that satisfies the norm. Echoes of the Principle and Foundation [23] of the Spiritual Exercises resound: to use whatever might "help me toward my end, and rid myself" of whatever might hinder me. The Principle and Foundation, however, goes farther still: whatever is "more conducive to the end for which I am created," not simply what fits and what helps, but what helps more [*magis*]. Time-honored customs and attitudes stand or fall before that norm.
2. The glory of our Lord Jesus Christ. He is at the heart of the companionship; he is the head of the Company, the life of the companions. Whatever obscures or denies his glory is unacceptable; what merely proclaims his glory is not enough; whatever proclaims it better is the norm the companions seek.
3. The help of the neighbor. The Company is not self-centered; it is centered on Jesus, the risen Lord, and Jesus lives on in his brothers and sisters. Jesus engages the problems and the trials, the hopes and the joys of every age in and through men and women and children everywhere. Whatever is more conducive to the life and growth and happiness of the neighbor, the Company can embrace; the Company has no interest in anything else.

The norms are simple. In a few words they express an abundance, in fact, a superabundance. The end of the Society, after all, *is* the glory of Jesus and the help of the neighbor, and the glory of Jesus *is* that neighbors help one another. To recognize and respond to the neighbor is to recognize and respond to Jesus. In the words of Jesus himself: "By this everyone will know that you are my disciples, if you have love for one another" (John 13:35), and in the words of Irenaeus: "For the glory of God is the human person fully alive; the life, moreover, of a human being is the vision of God."[1]

On March 4, 1541, the six companions who were in Rome gave Ignatius and Codure the task of writing the Constitutions [C 34 {1}].[2] The two began working on March 10 and finished a preliminary draft two or three weeks later. All six signed the document. Although they had not yet elected anyone to the office of general, they empowered the general to give official explanations of the Constitutions [C 43 {33}]. A few days later, on April 8, they elected Ignatius general, an office he did not accept until April 19. On April 22 they made their solemn profession.[3] Codure died on August 29; Ignatius was left to work on the Constitutions alone for the rest of his life. He continued to modify them and clarify them to the very end, not writing them in stone, leaving them open-ended, adaptable to the ever-changing needs of changing times.

2. The Papal Mandate

Beyond the papal blessing and approval, do the companions hope for something else from Pope Paul III? The words of *Cum ex plurium* reveal not only their own interior but also the way they conceive of their relationship to the Holy See. The concluding lines of the letter are consistent with all that preceded, and all that preceded leads to the conclusion.

>**Press on, therefore, beloved sons in Christ,**
>[Agite igitur, dilecti in Christo filii]
>**follow your call**
>[vestram vocationem sequimini]
>**whithersoever the Holy Spirit leads you,**
>[quo vos ducit Spiritus Sanctus]
>**and in the vineyard of the Lord from now on,**
>[et in vinea Domini posthac]

> **under the protection of this Holy See,**
> [sub protectione huius sanctae sedis]
> **work with all your heart like good vinedressers,**
> [tanquam boni agricolae viriliter laborate]
> **with our Lord Jesus Christ on your side,**
> [Domino nostro Jesu Christo vobis fauente]
> **who lives and reigns with the Holy Spirit**
> [qui viuit et regnat cum Spiritu Sancto]
> **God forever and ever. Amen.**
> [Deus in seculorum secula. Amen]

The first sentence of the final paragraph returned to the theme of praise from the earlier part of *Cum ex plurium*. The second sentence begins with a trumpet flare, and then, in a great symphonic surge, returns to the themes of the Holy Spirit and working in the vineyard of the Lord. The cadence and the sound of *Agite, igitur* suggest a sharp command from Pope Paul III: Press on, therefore! Get moving! Go to it! Just do it! *Agere* means to set in motion, to drive, to impel: the word asserts vigorous action, and it implies invigorating living. "*Quid agendum*" [A 50], Ignatius had asked himself after he had to leave Jerusalem, "What should I do?" Fifteen years later the answer is clear: go where the pope sends you. *Agite, igitur!* The companions see the pope bursting with emotion: I release you at last to do all that you have longed to do for years: now on your way!

We can hear the companions respond in the words of St. Paul, longing for their goal as he had longed for the resurrection from the dead: "I press on to make it my own, because Christ Jesus has made me his own" (Phil. 3:12). Their hearts resound with the words from Hebrews: "Let us approach with a true heart . . . Let us hold fast to the confession of our hope without wavering, for he who has promised is faithful. . . . And let us consider how to provoke one another to love and good deeds" (10:22–24). Their hearts were waiting for the final sign of approval from the one who stood in the place of Christ. With his approval words from later in Hebrews would be theirs:

Therefore, since we are surrounded by so great a cloud of witnesses, let us also lay aside every weight and the sin that clings so closely, and let us run with perseverance the race that is set before us [*ad propositum nobis certamen*], looking to Jesus the pioneer and perfecter of our faith, who for the sake of the joy that was set before him endured the cross, disregarding its shame, and has taken his seat at the right hand of the throne of God. (12:1–2)

This passage from Hebrews summarizes the Spiritual Exercises. In the Call [*vocatio*] of the King they had heard Jesus call [*vocat*] them, "Whoever wishes to come with me must labor [*laborare*] with me, so that through following [*sequitur*] me in the pain [*labore*] . . . [you] may follow [*sequatur*] me also in the glory" [95]. Now they hear in their minds the voice of the vicar of Christ: "Press on, follow your call [*vocationem sequimini*]; work [*laborate*] with all your heart." The words of Pope Paul III confirm the words of Jesus; the pope authorizes them to do what Jesus calls them to do.

One day a scribe said to Jesus, "I will follow you wherever you go" (Matt. 8:19). He was enthusiastic, but inexperienced in following Jesus, who explained to him: "Foxes have holes, and birds of the air have nests; but the Son of Man has nowhere to lay his head" (Matt. 8:20). Ignatius and his companions are more experienced in following Jesus; they know what being with him demands. Yet they long to hear the vicar of Christ say to them: "Follow your call wherever the Holy Spirit leads you." They have been following for years, like Moses and the people who year after year followed the cloud God sent to lead them through the desert: "Whenever the cloud lifted from over the tent, then the Israelites would set out; and in the place where the cloud settled down, there the Israelites would camp. At the command of the Lord the Israelites would set out, and at the command of the Lord they would camp" (Num. 9:17–18).

"*Spiritu Sancto . . . impellente,*" *Cum ex plurium* says near the beginning. "With the Holy Spirit impelling" them, they had set out on a common enterprise, and because the Holy Spirit was with them, they thought they knew where they were going. They thought they were going to Jerusalem. Experience taught them, however, that just as "the wind blows where it chooses" (John 3:8), so does the Spirit. "With the Holy Spirit impelling," they came together again in a Deliberation that changed their lives. Not knowing what the results would be, they abandoned their ideas and wishes and desires to the Spirit, and the Formula of the Institute was the result. Now they are ready to set out again like Abraham, "not knowing where he was going" (Heb. 11:8); and as Gregory of Nyssa says of Abraham, they are convinced they are going to get there precisely because they do not know the way.[4]

"Follow your call wherever the Holy Spirit leads you." A challenge and a battle cry, a quiet counsel, a secret whisper. Dangerous. Only those solemnly declared free of heresy would have the courage to enclose their way of living [*viuendi formula*] between two startling statements about the Holy Spirit. They are not Alumbrados, *illuminati* [enlightened ones], hunted down by the Inquisition, who claim to be directly under the influence of the Holy Spirit, and who recognize no authority other than the Spirit.[5] Nonetheless, near the beginning of *Cum ex plurium* they place the words, "with the Holy Spirit impelling you [*Spiritu Sancto . . . impellente*]," and near the end, "follow . . . wherever the Holy Spirit leads you [*quo vos ducit Spiritus Sanctus*]." They are not courting danger; they are rather expressing a conviction based on their faith experience. With the Holy Spirit impelling them, they have arrived at this point of their lives where they wish to bind themselves together forever in the service of Christ and of his vicar. They cannot imagine themselves without the impelling power of the Spirit, nor can they imagine where that Spirit might lead them. Until now they have waited and listened and followed; they will wait and listen and follow in the future. And those who follow them will wait and listen and follow the impulse of the Spirit wherever the Spirit might lead them. "The wind blows where it chooses," and so does the Spirit. Their plans are always open to change, their projects always subordinate to the impelling power of the Spirit. What they conceive as important one day may not be important the next. What is always important is to respond to the movement of the Spirit.

This hoped for, suggested, expected command of the pope reveals how the companions envision their Society after the pattern of La Storta. At the side of Jesus, Creator and Lord, driven into the wilderness by the Spirit (Mark 1:12), they expect the impelling Spirit to drive them, too, into that vast desert where good and evil struggle and evil falls, where the Spirit breathes and dry bones rise again to take on new life (Ezek. 37). In that vast openness anything can happen. Their call is to listen to the Spirit and allow themselves to be swept along by the Spirit's impelling power. They cannot envision what their Society might become. They set no limits, for the impelling Spirit is infinitely creative. They only know that the Holy Spirit is the Spirit of Jesus, and Jesus is the head of the Company of Jesus in the service of God the Father.

The two phrases "with the Holy Spirit impelling you" and "follow your vocation wherever the Holy Spirit leads you" are the bedrock of the spirituality of the companions and of all who follow them. The two phrases summarize both the Spiritual Exercises and the Formula of the Institute. The ancient search for God alone takes a new form. Openness to the Spirit will lead the Society into new ventures, some dreamed of, some not even imagined by the companions. "Work with all your heart in the vineyard of the Lord" will take on new meanings and a variety of shapes, some familiar, some unfamiliar to Ignatius and his companions: missions to India and Japan and Latin America, the opening of schools, the challenge of changing the Julian calendar, the exploration of new worlds, research into the wonders of science and theater and dance, enlisting into service the power of music, entering into the simplicity of life in an Eskimo village, taking a stand on the clash of cultures in China, sharing with workers the harsh encounters of labor and management, operating radio and television stations, standing in the eye of the storm of race relations, creating camps for refugees, tasting the bitterness of apartheid, writing books on every subject under the sun, succoring the victims of AIDS, protesting injustice, serving on the battlefield, pilgrimaging for peace: *wherever the Holy Spirit leads you.*

Listening to the Spirit, welcoming the impelling movement of the Spirit, following the Spirit wherever it leads, without these the Society of Jesus will wither, without these the Society of Jesus will die. In the centuries that follow Ignatius and his companions, the Society will make mistakes, for not listening to the Spirit, for listening only to human reason, for refusing to risk, for being afraid. Human weakness, however, does not daunt the Holy Spirit. The Holy Spirit impels through all ages, impels the weak as well as the strong, and in their generosity born of grace the members of the Society follow their call and labor diligently in the vineyard of the Lord. The vineyard is immense. They follow their call to whatever part of the vineyard the Holy Spirit leads them. They follow old paths and follow new paths; they follow into excitement and follow into weariness; they follow into life and follow into death.

They follow the Spirit, and the Lord Jesus is at their side [*Domino nostro Jesu Christo vobis fauente*]. On the way to Rome, Ignatius had heard the Father say to him, "I shall be propitious to you [*vobis*] in Rome," and he told Laynez afterward, "I do not know what awaits us; perhaps we shall be crucified in Rome."[6] To carry the cross with Jesus, to be crucified with him, that is the Father's gift to the companions of Jesus. With the Holy Spirit impelling them, and with Jesus at their side, they wish for nothing else.

EPILOGUE

Impelling Spirit

"With the Holy Spirit impelling them," Ignatius and his companions had vowed to go to Jerusalem; if unable to go, they would offer themselves to the pope to go wherever he might send them. Frustrated in finding passage to Jerusalem, the first companions had heard the head of the Church say to them, "Why do you desire so much to go to Jerusalem? Italy is a genuine Jerusalem, if you want to produce fruit for the Church of God" [B 11]. They knew that no passage to Jerusalem simply meant a call from the Spirit to greater creativity. Their crusader spirit, transformed by grace, needed a new outlet for its energy. Their desire to convert to Christ even the Saracens, and to give their lives in the process, needed a new direction. Columbus had already pointed the way by opening a path to a world unknown to Francis and Dominic, but they had not recognized it, unaware that a paradigm shift was taking place in the secular world, and a new paradigm needed to come to birth in the religious world. The world of the companions, which had centered on Jerusalem and the empty tomb of Jesus, had already found a new focus in a wider world that did not know Christ. La Storta invited them beyond the earthly footsteps of Jesus, the Jesus of a particular time and place, to the Jesus beyond history who is Lord of history, the Jesus who walks in every person who walks the earth. When Paul III began to scatter the companions, they did not know that they were about to found the Company of Jesus; they knew only that every discernment leaves itself open to further discernment. In the Deliberation of the First Fathers the Spirit opens to them a whole new world and impels them to express in the Formula of the Institute the new paradigm, and in *Cum ex plurium* all their dreams.

The Deliberation reveals in the companions men of quiet reflection. They are not drinking buddies or political cronies or *literati* who gather together in coffee houses to discuss art and literature and politics. They are reflective men of prayer who are truly friends *in the Lord,* as Ignatius called them [*EI* 119]. The foundation of their friendship is their personal surrender to God in Jesus Christ. Friends *in the Lord* are also friends *in the Church.* They passionately love God's people. It is to the whole Christ that Ignatius and his companions dedicate themselves, to Christ living in his mystical body, to Christ carrying his cross in people of the present moment.[1] These friends in the Lord who are men of the Church begin their deliberation boldly, conscious that the Holy Spirit is at work in them, both in their personal lives and in their life as a Company. This consciousness is not at all surprising in members of a Company who are convinced that Jesus is the head and founder of the Company, and that all life and direction in the Company have their source in him.

The first companions begin their deliberation, each with his own opinion, but when they find themselves divided, they are daring enough "to cast all [their] concerns on the Lord, hoping in him" [*D* 1] and to waste no further time and energy on divisions but to focus on their common desire to find and fulfill the will of God. The documents the companions produce make clear that the Society is not the work of one man. It is the fruit of the Spirit at work in several men, men of different characters and personalities, of different languages and cultures, of different opinions and ideas, men who dare to trust the Spirit at work in them and who dare, therefore, to trust the Spirit at work in one another. The Company of Jesus is born of the Spirit and of those men who freely choose to call themselves the Company of Jesus before they even think of founding a new religious institute; every member of the Society, through the impelling Spirit within him, partakes in the formation of the Company. Through their deliberations the Formula of the Institute comes into being, and finally *Cum ex plurium.*

Tommaso Badia, the pope's theologian, finds the Formula of the companions "good and holy" [*CEP* 1], the work of the Holy Spirit. Paul III accepts Badia's judgment and in approving the Formula orally praises the Society "with a prophetic spirit" [*PSH* 89]. From the hands of Cardinal Contarini *Cum ex plurium* goes into the hands of Cardinal Girolamo Ghinucci so that he might "draw up a brief or a bull" [*C* 21 {9}], "whichever seemed better" [*C* 22] for the solemn approbation of the Society. Although as prefect of the Signatura for Briefs he can draw up a brief and as auditor of the Camera he can pursue a course for issuing a bull,[2] he chooses to do neither. "The wind blows where it chooses," and the Holy Spirit is full of surprises. Preferring to exercise caution, Ghinucci sends *Cum ex plurium* to the chancery, the usual channel for promulgating a bull.[3] The ensuing delay and the events that follow manifest "the singular wisdom of Divine Providence."[4] *Cum ex plurium* comes to the attention of Bartolomeo Guidiccioni, newly created cardinal and newly appointed vicar-general of Rome, who has authored two treatises opposing the establishment of any new religious orders.[5] Guidiccioni proves himself a strong adversary, but he cannot stand up against a campaign of prayer that Ignatius launches. Laynez informs us that those opposing the Society are "changed by the Holy Spirit,"[6] and Polanco points to a classic example of discernment and the action of the impelling Spirit when he reports that Guidiccioni, "overcoming his own reasons by internal impulses and movements" [*PCh* 8], reverses himself graciously.[7] After a long year of delay, Paul III solemnly approves the Society through the bull *Regimini militantis ecclesiae* of September 27, 1540. *Cum ex plurium* dies as a proposed papal letter, but it is buried in the new bull and comes to life in the new bull. Its substance is there, although some of the words are missing or have been changed in order to satisfy curial style.

Along with *Cum ex plurium*, containing the first draft of the Formula of the Institute, the most precious documents of the Society of Jesus for illumining its founding and the working of the Holy Spirit within its founders are the Deliberation of the First Fathers and the accounts of the reflections and decisions immediately following that deliberation. They provide a gold mine, an inexhaustible mother lode of wisdom and enthusiasm and spirituality, for the Society of Jesus even as the twentieth century is coming to an end. The first companions are bold, daring, innovative, creative, passionate, and filled with a sense of urgency. The challenge to the twenty-first century is sharp and clear.

The challenge is to attitudes, mind-sets, dispositions of mind and heart. The early companions were boldly innovative and creative because their conviction that the Holy Spirit was impelling them was not limited to the founding experience. *Cum ex plurium* breathes a conviction that the presence of the Holy Spirit as an impelling force is an abiding presence, that the Spirit impels each member of the Company and the Company itself each and every day as long as the Company exists. The implications for the twenty-first century are immense, for it means that the Society, through the power of the Spirit, refounds itself everyday, reaffirms its roots and its purpose [*propositum*]. The Company remains the work of the Spirit and of the Company, and as such it remains the responsibility of the whole Company. The Company comes into being through discernment, by being open to and trusting in the movements of the impelling Spirit, and only through discernment can it fulfill its purpose [*propositum*]. Discernment, in turn, takes place only in an atmosphere of prayer and of trust, of daring to trust in God and to trust in one another, of daring to trust that the Spirit reveals the direction to go and guides the Company along the right path.

Daring to listen to the impelling Spirit suggests openness to a twofold movement, an interior movement toward unity within, among the members themselves, and an exterior movement to go and to serve. Companionship in service in mission is the heart of *Cum ex plurium.*

First, regarding companionship: *Cum ex plurium*'s conviction of the presence of the impelling Spirit challenges today's companions to dare to acknowledge that all the issues that divide the members of the Society of Jesus at the end of the twentieth century are unimportant beside the commitment of today's companions to seek and find the will of God. Diversity is not a handicap, but an advantage. Differences of opinion do not destroy unity; they enhance it, complementing one another and providing a rich treasury for the entire group. If in unity there is strength, unity in diversity provides much more strength than unity in conformity.

Cum ex plurium's conviction of the presence of the impelling Spirit invites, indeed demands of the Society of the present and of the future to set aside fear, fear of one another, fear of the world, fear of being without all the "supports" the world can give, fear of the future, fear of change. The presence of the impelling Spirit demands boldness in trusting one another and the action of the Spirit within each one, trusting even in disagreement, confident that disagreement can lead to further enlightenment. The call is to listen, listen to the Spirit within, listen to one another, listen to events outside, listen to the sounds and signs of the times, listen to the needs of God's people and God's world.

Listening to the impelling Spirit requires that the members of the Society be bold, set aside the wisdom of the world, and let the Spirit do with the Society what the Spirit wants to do. As the Society moves toward smaller communities designed for a more creative fostering of friendship in diversity, *Cum ex plurium* challenges today's companions to recall that they are not monks pledged to stability of place, but primarily members of one worldwide community pledged to availability for service. Availability for service does not call for iciness and isolation. As the Society moves toward an easier crossing of province boundaries, both the Deliberation of the First Fathers and *Cum ex plurium* challenge today's companions to greater creativity in fostering that kind of companionship that endures separation. The more mobile the membership, the deeper the need. Companionship cannot be left entirely to chance.

Second, regarding service in mission: service abides, and mission abides, but both are transient. As the years passed, Ignatius recognized that a member of the Company could serve both Christ and his vicar by residing in one place, and even later, the Society *missioned* some of its members to reside in a place. In the Society of Jesus residing can be mission, because no matter how long a member of the Company resides in a place, his stay is always transient. The contrast with monasticism is startling and profound. The monk seeks God in and through stability of place. Even the monk on the move searches for a place in which to seek God in stability. Stability of place and service in mission are two contrasting forms of stability of vocation, two contrasting forms of the unending search for God.

The relevance to the twenty-first century is stunning. In a world of profound political and economic turmoil and upheaval, in a world filled with refugees, stability is a desired goal and longed-for blessing: political stability, economic stability, family stability, a stable nation, a stable home, a stable job. Security is highly prized: national security, economic security, family security, personal security. In contrast, neither commitment to stability of place nor commitment to service in mission seeks stability and security; they both seek detachment, freedom from, in order to have freedom for. Neither monks nor companions of the twenty-first century can afford to esteem worldly values, follow worldly goals, or use worldly means.

Daring to listen to the impelling Spirit also means that the Society, from within the framework of the Church, always needs to dare to be innovative and creative in probing its relationship with the Church and with its visible head, never more so than now as the twentieth century moves into the twenty-first, in order to understand to what the Spirit calls the Society, for the Society does not exist apart from the Church, and exists only for the sake of the Church. The Society needs to foster that relationship by loving and serving the Church, but it need not be loved by everyone in the Church. Cheering crowds are not a prerequisite for the work of the Society any more than they were a prerequisite for the work of Jesus. The Spirit creates freedom, joy, spontaneity, creativity, enthusiasm, and generosity. When these are lacking, the Society knows, like all other sinners, that it is in need of healing, of conversion, of the return of the life-giving and impelling Spirit. It needs to be reinserted by the Spirit into the life of the Church.

Within the Church the Society finds itself healthiest, most fully alive and filled with joy, when it finds itself at home among the marginalized, among the poor of Christ, among the *anawim*, the poor beloved of God. The *least Society*, a term dear to Ignatius, is least in the weakness of its foundation (the companions who form it generation after generation) and by reason of the humility demanded in it, the last of all and the servant of all.[8] The Society is called not to pride and arrogance but to humiliation with Christ humiliated. It is alive in the Spirit when it hears and embodies the beatitudes, when it ranks itself among the lowly and becomes an advocate of the lowly. The Society finds its place in the Church of the third millenium whenever and wherever its members freely embrace poverty, that kind of poverty that authenticates mission, that bears the mark of the Spirit.

The first companions were simple and straightforward in their poverty: nothing subtle about it, they simply had nothing. Time proved that poverty is more subtle, that poverty requires profound and attentive discernment, careful listening to the Spirit, setting aside preconceptions and prior convictions. *Cum ex plurium* affirms that the members of the Company, with the Holy Spirit impelling them, should dare to conspire together so that they may have the courage and the generosity and the power to reject worldly norms. The Gospel insists that the insecure are blessed, the hungry are blessed, the persecuted are blessed. The world needs the witness that some of its most precious goals are not final. The Cistercians whom Innocent III missioned to evangelize the Albigensians in the early thirteenth century learned that the pomp and display of papal legates on horseback availed them not at all, that they needed to abandon their horses, walk barefoot, and beg their food. The Company of Jesus, reaching beyond contemporary economics, has its own definition of success, to be the least. *Cum ex plurium* challenges the members of the Company, with the Holy Spirit impelling them, to dare to conspire together, to breathe together in easy, gentle inhalations and exhalations of trust, in order to allow and enable Gospel poverty to authenticate their service and their mission. The attractions, the allurements, the enticements of the world of the twenty-first century are no less snares than were the allurements of the first or the fifth or the thirteenth or the sixteenth century. No one can convert the world by adopting and employing the world's own norms. Jesus made that clear long ago.

Poverty is not the only enigma in the Society. The path to God is clear, the Formula containing the Society's purpose and aim [*propositum*]. But where is God? And how does the Society walk its path to God in a particular time and place? By reading the signs of the times, by adapting to the changing needs of God's people. Reading the signs of the times, however, means more than noticing and meeting the needs of the day. Limitations are also signs of the times, the Spirit's invitation to bolder innovations. The increasing age and the decreasing numbers of today's companions are a challenge to the inventive spirit, not a cause for lamentation. Gideon's three hundred imaginative warriors were more effective than his thirty thousand run-of-the-mill soldiers, for the Spirit of God was with them (Judg. 7). The ability to risk revealed in the Deliberation and in *Cum ex plurium* suggests that today's companions need to dare to conspire together in more things than one. The Holy Spirit urges today's companions to dare to listen together to what the Spirit is impelling each one and to what the Spirit is impelling the Company, to listen to the young if they are leaders, to listen to the old if they are wise. The Spirit invites today's companions neither to defend the established nor to despise the established but to notice where multiple experiences converge, and to be bold in exploiting that convergence, rejoicing in the common desire to follow Christ wherever he leads.

The documents of the Society are not the exclusive property of the Society of Jesus; they belong to the whole Church. The faith of the companions is not a faith that sets them outside the Christian community, as though they share a secret that is not a part of Christian revelation. Their faith is in the Good News of Jesus, a faith they share with others, and it is a living faith: they believe in a practical way the doctrine of the indwelling Spirit, and they believe in a practical way that God is at work in human history. The Spirit lives within, and impels from within, and all are called to dare to listen to the movements of the Spirit within the human heart. The Deliberation calls, *Cum ex plurium* calls, the Gospel itself calls the companions of the twenty-first century to dare to listen to the Spirit at work in people everywhere. They call the companions to listen together even more energetically with those the Spirit has called to labor with them, coworkers of every kind. They are all companions together, and they need to breathe together, to recognize their common love for the Church, their common love for the head of the Church. Strength that is united together is far more powerful than strength that is dispersed. Breathing together, letting the Spirit speak within them, listening together, the companions and their coworkers discover that they and their coworkers agree more richly and more profoundly than they disagree. The disagreements are not worth a puff of air; agreements are of the Spirit.

The exhortation that the first companions put in the mouth of the pope and addressed to themselves in *Cum ex plurium* is an exhortation to the Society of every time and place, and to every person of good will of every time and place: *"**Agite, igitur:** Get moving! Follow the Spirit wherever the Spirit leads you."* The Spirit leads where no human being has ever gone; the Spirit leads into darkness; the Spirit leads into light; the Spirit leads into the unknown; the Spirit leads wherever the children of God are in deeper need. La Storta is the Society's never-ending experience. At the side of Christ carrying his cross in the service of the Father, the companions of Jesus are called to follow the Spirit, to move forward when the Spirit moves forward, to turn when the Spirit turns, to stop when the Spirit stops, to wait when the Spirit waits, to move on when the Spirit moves on. The Spirit leads even into death, but in the Spirit there is no death: in the Spirit death is life.

Abbreviations

MHSI - Monumenta Historica Societatis Iesu

A	Acta P. Ignatii [Autobiography of Ignatius], FN 1:354-507
B	Bobadilla, Autobiographia, FN 3:323-31
C	Constitutiones et Regulae Societatis Iesu
CEP	Cum ex plurium [Prima Societatis Iesu instituti summa], C 14-21 [1-8]
D	Deliberatio primorum patrum, C 1-7 [1-9]
DS	Determinationes Societatis, C 9-14
EB	Epistolae PP. Paschasii Broëti, Claudii Jaji, Joannis Codurii et Simonis Rodericii, S.J.
EI	Epistolae et instructiones Ignatii
EM	Epistolae Mixtae ex variis Europae locis, 1537-1556
EX	Epistolae S. Francisci Xaverii aliaque eius scripta
F	Favre, Memoriale, FN 1:26-49
FD	Fontes documentales
FN	Fontes narrativi
IJ	Ignatius to John of Portugal [Narratio de processibus et carceribus], FN 1:51-54
IR	Ignatius to Isabel Roser [Persecutionis anni 1538 descriptio ignatiana], FN 1:6-14
L	Laynez to Polanco [Epistola Patris Laynez de P. Ignatio, 6 junii 1547], FN 1:70-145
MB	Bobadillae Monumenta
MF	Fabri Monumenta
ML	Lainii Monumenta

MN	*Epistolae et Monumenta P. Hieronymi Nadal*
MS	*Epistolae P. Alphonsi Salmeronis*
MX	*Monumenta Xaveriana*
PCh	Polanco, *Chronicon Societatis Iesu*
PI	Polanco, *Informatio de Instituto Societatis Iesu, FN* 2:305-11
PSH	*Summarium hispanum Polanci, FN* 1:151-256
PSI	*Summarium italicum Polanci, FN* 1:261-98
PV	Polanco, *De vita P. Ignatii et de Societatis Iesu initiis, FN* 2:511-97
R	Rodrigues, *Commentarium, FN* 3:8-135
Scripta de	*Scripta de sancto Ignatio de Loyola*

Other Abbreviations

See Bibliography for complete bibliographical data.

ACW	Ancient Christian Writers
AHSI	*Archivum Historicum Societatis Iesu*
ARSI	Archivum Romanum Societatis Iesu
BAC	Bibliotheca de autores cristianos
BRT	*Bullarium Romanum*, Turin edition
Bull. Franc.	*Bullarium Franciscanum*
CCL	Corpus Christianorum, Series Latina
CE	*The Catholic Encyclopedia*
1 Cel.	Thomas of Celano, *Vita prima S. Francisci*
CIC	*Corpus Iuris Canonici*
CIS	*Centrum Ignatianum Spiritualitatis* (periodical)
CIS	Centrum Ignatianum Spiritualitatis (publisher)
CLS	Canon Law Studies
COD	*Conciliorum Oecumenicorum Decreta*
CSEL	Corpus scriptorum ecclesiasticorum Latinorum
Coll. Cist.	*Collectanea Cisterciensia*
CS	Cistercian Studies series
CT	*Concilium Tridentinum*
CWS	Classics of Western Spirituality
DDC	*Dictionnaire de droit canonique*

Diego	Luis de Diego, S.J., *La opción sacerdotal de Ignacio de Loyola*
DIP	*Dizionario degli istituti di perfezione*
DSAM	*Dictionnaire de spiritualité ascétique et mystique*
DTC	*Dictionnaire de théologie catholique*
E.T.	English Translation
IHSI	Institutum Historicum Societatis Iesu
Koudelka	*Monumenta diplomatica S. Dominici*, ed., V. J. Koudelka
LM	*Legenda maior S. Francisci*
LTS	*Legenda trium sociorum*
MGH, SS	*Monumenta Germaniae Historica, Scriptores*
MHSI	Monumenta Historica Societatis Iesu
MOPH	Monumenta Ordinis Fratrum Praedicatorum Historica
NCE	*The New Catholic Encyclopedia*
NRSV	*New Revised Standard Version Bible*
ODCC	*Oxford Dictionary of the Christian Church*
OED	*Oxford English Dictionary*
OLD	*Oxford Latin Dictionary*, 1968 ed.
Olin	John C. Olin, *The Catholic Reformation: Savanarola to Ignatius*
Pastor	Ludwig F. von Pastor, *The History of the Popes*, vol. 11
PATC	*Les plus anciens textes de Cîteaux*, ed., Bouton & Van Damme
PG	*Patrologia Graeca*
PL	*Patrologia Latina*
PUG	Pontificia Università Gregoriana
RAM	*Revue d'ascétique et de mystique*
RB	*Regula Benedicti, Rule of Benedict*
RB 80	*RB 1980: The Rule of St. Benedict in Latin and English*, ed., Timothy Fry
RM	*Regula Magistri, Rule of the Master*
SC	Sources chrétiennes
SCH	Studies in Church History
Schroeder	H. J. Schroeder, *Disciplinary Decrees of the General Councils*
Schur.	Georg Schurhammer, S.J., *Francis Xavier, His Life and Times*, vol. 1
TV	Pietro Tacchi Venturi, S.J., *Storia della Compagnia di Gesù in Italia*

Endnotes

Preface

1. Augusto Coemans, Carlo Martini, and Mario Gioia, *Introducción al estudio de la Fórmula del Instituto S.I.* (Rome: CIS, 1974).

2. Antonio M. de Aldama, *Notas para un comentario a: La Fórmula del Instituto de la Compañía de Jesús* (Rome: CIS, 1981), 13-23 [Spanish text of 1550 Formula]; E.T., *The Formula of the Institute: Notes for a Commentary* (St. Louis: Institute of Jesuit Sources, 1990), 2-23 [Formula of 1539 and Formula of 1550 on facing pages].

3. Another who does the same is Pedro de Leturia, S.J., *Estudios ignacianos*, 2 vols. (Rome: Institutum Historicum S.I., 1957), 1:24.

4. Dominique Bertrand, S.J., *Un corps pour l'Esprit: Essai sur l'expérience communautaire d'après les Constitutions de la Compagnie de Jésus* (Paris: Desclée de Brouwer, 1974), 57-58.

Introduction

1. MHSI, vol. 63, *Constitutiones Societatis Jesu, Tomus Primus: Monumenta Constitutionum Praevia* [C 14-21]. C, followed by page numbers, with paragraph numbers in brackets when needed, refers to vol. 1 of the four volumes of *Constitutiones et Regulae Societatis Iesu, MHSI* (Rome, 1934-48). Vol. 1 contains early documents pertaining to the Society of Jesus.

2. D, followed by paragraph numbers, refers to *Deliberatio primorum patrum*, C 1-7 [1-9]. The translation of each individual passage is my own. The following English translations of the entire *Deliberatio primorum patrum* are available: Dominic Maruca, S.J., "The Deliberation of Our First Fathers," *Woodstock Letters* 95

(1966): 325-33; John C. Futrell, S.J., *Making an Apostolic Community of Love* (St. Louis: Institute of Jesuit Sources, 1970), Appendix 1, "The Deliberation of the First Fathers," 188-94; Jules J. Toner, S.J., "The Deliberation That Started the Jesuits. A Commentary on the *Deliberatio primorum patrum*, Newly Translated with a Historical Introduction," *Studies in the Spirituality of Jesuits* 6 (1974): 179-212. For sketches of the first companions who took part in the Deliberation, see chap. 1.

3. Biblical quotations are from the *New Revised Standard Version* [*NRSV*] unless otherwise indicated.

4. The bracketed space is blank; the *Monumenta* editors suggest the possibility of *turca* or *ad turcas*, *C* 3 n. 6.

5. Bobadilla here uses *pronomina* in the general sense of words used to designate persons or objects without naming them. Five of the companions signed the document with both Christian and family names, four with Christian names only, and Bobadilla with his nickname. His name is Nicolás Alonso y Perez. From the village of Bobadilla in Spain, he is called de Bobadilla or simply Bobadilla. Del Camino is sometimes added to distinguish the village from others of the same name. Hence his full name is Nicolás Alonso y Perez de Bobadilla del Camino. See *MB* vi and *B* 1. *MB*, with page number, refers to *Bobadillae Monumenta*, MHSI (Madrid: 1913); *B*, with paragraph number, refers to a fragment of *Nicolai Bobadilla autobiographia*, *FN* 3:323-31 [1-29]. Bobadilla's complete *Autobiographia* is in *MB* 613-33.

6. If Bobadilla's account is correct, he gives us new information about the opening date of the Deliberation of the First Fathers. The first words of the Deliberation indicate that they began toward the end of Lent [*D* 1], and the final paragraph says they met from the middle of Lent to the feast of John the Baptist (June 24) [*D* 9]. That year Ash Wednesday was on February 19, and Easter on April 6. If the companions took two weeks to make their determination regarding the vow of obedience, the Deliberation began March 31 or April 1, Monday or Tuesday of Holy Week. If it began more toward the middle of Lent, Bobadilla may have been mistaken about the amount of time they took to decide on obedience, or on the interval between the decision to form a group bound by obedience and the ritual acting out of that decision. The importance of Bobadilla's contribution, however, lies not in the matter of the date but in providing the context for the vow document dated April 15, 1539.

7. *DS*, with paragraph number, refers to *Determinationes Societatis*, *C* 9-14. An excellent brief commentary on this latter document

from the point of view of community is to be found in Javier Osuna, S.J., *Friends in the Lord*, trans. Nicholas King, S.J., Way Series 3 (London, 1974), 113-19.

8. Although commonly called "the Five Chapters" in Jesuit writings, the five brief divisions are the determinations the companions reached in deciding how they wanted to live. They are like the decrees of a general congregation today or of a general chapter in a monastic community; they are not chapters as in a book. Each is only one paragraph in length. A concluding statement brings the number to six paragraphs. A later system assigned a number to each of the six paragraphs, creating the impression of six decrees. *CEP* with paragraph numbers refers to *Cum ex plurium*, otherwise known as *Prima Societatis Jesu instituti summa*, *C* 14-21.

9. For a sketch of Contarini, see the beginning of chap. 2; for one of Badia, see the beginning of chap. 19.

10. Antonio M. de Aldama, "Origine e storia della Formula dell' Istituto," in *La Formula dell'Istituto, S.J.* (Rome: CIS, 1977), 16; E.T., "Origin and History of the Formula of the Institute," in *The Formula of the Institute* (Rome: CIS, 1982), 18.

11. For an English translation of *Solet annuere* and the Rule of Francis, see *Francis and Clare: The Complete Works*, trans. Regis J. Armstrong, O.F.M.Cap., and Ignatius C. Brady, O.F.M., CWS (New York: Paulist Press, 1982), 136-45.

12. Cardinal Girolamo Ghinucci (+1541), for years prefect of the Signatura of Briefs and auditor of the Camera, was a member of Paul III's council for reform. For details of Ghinucci's life, see Ciaconius-Oldoinus, *Vitae et res gestae pontificum romanorum usque ad Clementem IX*, vol. 3 (Rome 1677), 569-70; R. Aubert, "Ghinucci," *Dictionnaire d'histoire et de géographie ecclésiastiques*, vol. 20 (Paris: Letouzey & Ané, 1984), 1177-79; Pietro Tacchi Venturi S.J., *Storia della Compagnia di Gesù in Italia, narrata col susidio di fonti inedite*, 2d ed. (Rome: La Civiltà Cattolica, 1950-51), 2/1:276 (henceforth called TV with volume, part and page number). The first edition was published in 1910, and the second edition of vol. 1 was first published in 1931.

13. *L*, with a paragraph number, refers to *Epistola Patris Laynez de P. Ignatio*, *FN* 1:70-145. *FN*, with volume and page numbers, refers to four volumes containing documents relative to the origins of the Society, *Fontes narrativi de S. Ignatio de Loyola et de Societatis Iesu initiis*, MHSI (Rome 1943-65).

14. *A*, with a paragraph number, refers to *Acta Patris Ignatii*, the Autobiography of Ignatius, narrated by him on different occasions

during 1553-55 to Luis Gonçalves da Câmara, a Portuguese Jesuit, who dictated it to a scribe. In the middle of paragraph 79 da Câmara changes from Spanish to Italian for lack of a Spanish scribe. The text in Spanish/Italian along with a Latin translation is found in *FN* 1:354-507, preceded by editorial notes, *ibid.*, 323-52. The translation of the Autobiography used in this book is that of Parmananda R. Divarkar in *Ignatius of Loyola*, ed. George E. Ganss, S.J., CWS (New York: Paulist Press, 1991).

15. *R*, with a paragraph number, refers to *Simonis Rodrigues commentarium de origine et progressu Societatis Iesu*, *FN* 3:8-135, an account in Latin of the origins and progress of the Society, a letter written from Lisbon on July 25, 1577, (including a draft in Portuguese), by Simão Rodrigues, one of the first companions, at the request of the fourth Father General of the Society, Everard Mercurian. At the age of sixty-seven, the author was somewhat distrustful of "the memory of old men" [*R* 1]. Although he does make a few errors of fact, his narrative is by and large trustworthy.

16. Drawn mostly from *Polanci Complementa*, 2 vols., MHSI (Madrid, 1916-17), 1:vi-vii.

17. *PSH*, followed by paragraph number, refers to *Summarium hispanum Polanci*, *FN* 1:151-256, Polanco's Spanish summary of the origin and progress of the Society. The full title is, *Sumario de las cosas mas notables que a la institución y progreso de la Compañia de Jesús tocan*.

18. Letter of Lattanzio Tolomei to Contarini, September 28, 1539, in Franz Dittrich, *Regesten und Briefe des Cardinals Gasparo Contarini (1483-1542)* (Braunsberg, 1881), 379-80.

19. *Dialogi pro Societate contra haereticos*, *FN* 2:265 [27]. This part of the second dialogue was written in 1563. See *FN* 2:225 [v]. See also *FN* 2:173 [3], an Italian version of an exhortation Nadal gave in Alcalá in 1561. The statement does not appear in the original Spanish but in an Italian version edited by Nadal in 1576.

20. Heinrich Böhmer, *Studien zur Geschichte der Gesellschaft Jesu*, vol. 1 (Bonn, 1914), 248-49.

21. *C* ccvi-ccvii, 4. Limiting ourselves to the introductory sentence of *Cum ex plurium*, we find, for example, "have joined together in one body" [*CEP*] and "our uniting in one" [*C* 162]. Compare also the statement, "You would dedicate your lives to the perpetual service of our Lord Jesus Christ and his vicar on earth" [*CEP*], with "All our intent and desire . . . we have

subjected to Christ our Creator and Lord and his universal vicar" [*C* 160].

22. Aldama, "Origine e storia," 13, 16, 19; E.T., 15, 18, 21.

23. See Georg Schurhammer, S.J., "Zur Frage des Schreibers der fünf Kapitel, approbiert von Paul III," *AHSI* 30 (1961): 264-66. See also, Georg Schurhammer, S.J., *Francis Xavier, His Life and Times*, vol. 1, *Europe, 1506-1541*, trans. M. Joseph Costelloe, S.J. (Rome: The Jesuit Historical Institute, 1973), 467 n. 16 (hereafter Schur. with page number).

24. Jesús Iturrioz, S.J., "Aprobación 'oral' de la 'Compañía de Jesús'," *Manresa* 61 (1989): 375-77.

25. *FD*, followed by a page number, refers to *Fontes documentales de S. Ignatio de Loyola,* MHSI (Rome, 1977), containing documents concerning Ignatius and his family, his youth and his companions after his conversion.

26. *IR*, followed by a paragraph number, refers to a letter Ignatius wrote from Rome to Isabel Roser, a friend and benefactress in Barcelona, on December 19, 1538, *FN* 1:6-14. The editors of this volume of MHSI have given the letter the title: *Persecutionis anni 1538 descriptio ignatiana* [*FN* 1:4]. It is also found in *EI* 137-44 without the paragraph numbers. *EI*, with page number, refers to vol. 1 of the twelve volumes of the letters of Ignatius, *Epistolae et instructiones*, MHSI (Madrid, 1903-11).

27. *Scripta de*, 2:471. *Scripta de*, followed by volume and page number, refers to two volumes of documents about Ignatius, *Scripta de sancto Ignatio de Loyola,* MHSI (Madrid, 1904, 1918).

28. Iturrioz, "Aprobación," 374.

29. Luis González da Câmara, *Memoriale, FN* 1:697 [290]. Cf. Baldesar Castiglione, *The Book of the Courtier* (New York: Horace Liveright, 1929; originally published as *Il Libro del Cortegiano*, Venice, 1528).

30. Benedetto Palmio, S.J., *Autobiographia, FN* 3:164 [11]. For an exposition of life in the palace of Juan Velázquez, see Luis Fernández Martín, S.J., "El hogar donde Iñigo de Loyola se hizo hombre, 1506-1517," *AHSI* 49 (1980): 21-92.

31. *Scripta de*, 2:471.

32. *PV*, followed by a paragraph number, refers to Juan Alonso de Polanco, *De vita P. Ignatii et de Societatis Iesu initiis*, in *FN* 2:511-97. For a more complete account of Ignatius' life as a courtier, see Pedro de Leturia, S.J., *Iñigo de Loyola*, trans. Aloysius J. Owen, S.J. (Syracuse: Le Moyne College Press, 1949; reprint, Chicago: Loyola University Press, 1965), 27-68; Cándido de Dalmases,

Ignatius of Loyola, Founder of the Jesuits, trans. Jerome Aixalá, S.J. (St. Louis: The Institute of Jesuit Sources, 1985), 28-38; and Rogelio García Mateo, S.J., "El mundo caballeresco en la vida de Ignacio de Loyola," *AHSI* 60 (1991): 5-28, especially 13-17.

33. *C* ccvii. For the June 20 date, cf. Favre, *Memoriale, FN* 1:42, 19 n. 44.

34. Iturrioz, "Aprobación," 367-84, esp., 373-75.

35. *EB*, followed by a page number, refers to *Epistolae PP. Paschasii Broëti, Claudii Jaji, Joannis Codurii et Simonis Rodericii, Societatis Jesu*, MHSI (Madrid, 1903).

36. They were present to sign a document on April 15, 1539 [*C* 8], but were not present to sign the document, Decisions about the Company [*Determinationes Societatis*] [*DS* 1-17].

37. *EM*, followed by a page number, refers to the first of five volumes of *Epistolae Mixtae*, MHSI (Madrid, 1898).

38. José Calveras, S.J., "Acerca del copista del autógrafo de los ejercicios," *AHSI* 30 (1961): 244-63. The same person copied the autograph version of the Exercises and *Cum ex plurium.*

39. AA. Arm. I-XVIII, 6461, ff. 145r-148r.

40. Dittrich, *Regesten und Briefe*, 304-5. See also by the same author, *Gasparo Contarini, 1483-1542, eine Monographie* (Braunsberg, 1885), based on the 1881 work; pp. 406-11 deal with the Society.

41. TV 1/2:180-92.

42. *Cum ex plurium*, like the Formula itself, is mainly concerned with the actual life of the existing group; neither concerns itself with how to induct new members into that life, matters later treated in Parts I to V of the Constitutions.

43. James J, *From Here to Eternity* (New York: Charles Scribner's Sons, 1951), 7.

Chapter One: Pope Paul III and His Beloved Sons

1. Broët is really from Amiens. Cf. *FD* 544 n. 1.

2. Cf. F. Claeys-Boúúaert, "Bref," *DDC*, 2:1060-62, "Bulle," *ibid.*, 1126-32; Herbert Thurston, "Bulls and Briefs," *CE*, 3:52-58; L. de Mas Latrie, "Les éléments de la diplomatique pontificale," *Revue des questions historiques* 39 (1886): 415-51 and 41 (1887): 382-435.

3. In addition to the sources indicated in the text and endnotes, the source for information on Paul III is Ludwig F. von Pastor,

The History of the Popes from the Close of the Middle Ages, 40 vols. (London, 1889-1953), 11:10-41. Henceforth Pastor with page number refers to vol. 11. For a summary of Paul III's activities and a sense of the political climate of his day, see Peter Partner, *Renaissance Rome 1500-1559: A Portrait of a Society* (Berkeley: University of California Press, 1976), 33-41. For a recent reappraisal of Paul III's role in history, see Elisabeth G. Gleason, "Who Was the First Counter-Reformation Pope?" *The Catholic Historical Review* 81 (1995): 173-84.

4. Vinzenz Schweitzer, "Kardinal Bartolomeo Guidiccioni," *Römische Quartalschrift* 20 (1906): 40-42.

5. Pastor, 138-39, particularly n. 1. Alessandro Farnese, born in 1520, was the son of the pope's son Pierluigi and was fourteen years old. He held the office of vice-chancellor in the papal curia when the Society was solemnly approved in 1540. Guido Sforza, born in 1518, was the son of the pope's daughter, Costanza, and was sixteen years old. Their grandfather richly endowed them with benefices and bishoprics. On Paul III's endeavors to raise his family's status, see Clare Robertson, *'Il gran cardinale': Alessandro Farnese, Patron of the Arts* (New Haven and London: Yale University Press, 1992), 8-12, which also includes a graph of the Farnese family tree (1390-1643), p. ix, and several portraits of Paul III, his children and grandchildren.

6. A year after Ignatius arrived in Paris, he directed three theology students through the Spiritual Exercises. They abandoned everything and began to beg from door to door, much to the consternation of the academic community. Dr. Ortiz, who was the guardian or patron of one of the students, reported Ignatius to the Inquisition. See Schur., 139.

7. According to Polanco [*PV* 81], Gianpietro Carafa had renounced the archbishopric of Chiete (Theate) to help found the religious order known as the Theatines. Ignatius had met him in Venice and had charitably made some suggestions regarding the new order, which suggestions were not received in good part by Carafa. Ignatius never told the whole story to anyone, but it is clear from what he did say about it that the incident was a weighty one.

8. See also *A* 93, *PSH* 66, 68. Yet Ignatius states that he came to Rome at the end of 1537 because both of his former antagonists were now friendly [*A* 96].

9. Schur., 324-25.

10. *Ibid.*, 336 n. 201.

11. Letter of Ignatius to Juan de Verdolay, from Venice, July 24, 1537 [*EI* 118-22]. The official document in the archives granting permission to make a pilgrimage to Jerusalem is addressed to Pierre Favre, for himself and twelve companions [*FD* 528]: his nine companions from Paris, and three more. A document dated the same day grants permission to be ordained to the seven companions who were not priests (Favre, Jay, and Broët were already ordained) and adds Miguel Landívar just before the name of Ignatius, who is last on the list [*FD* 526]. A third document, dated three days later, grants faculties to Favre, Arias, and Hozes to hear confessions [*MF* 7-8]. The three extra companions, therefore, are Landívar, Arias, and Hozes. Hozes had joined Ignatius in Venice after making the Spiritual Exercises under his direction [*A* 92]. Apparently Antonio Arias and Miguel Landívar, who had known the companions in Paris, had joined them in Venice. *MF*, with page numbers, refers to *Beati Petri Fabri, primi sacerdotis e Societate Jesu, epistolae, memoriale et processus*, MHSI (Madrid, 1914).

12. Pedro Leturia, S.J., "Importancia del año 1538 en el cumplimiento del 'voto de Montmarte,'" *AHSI* 9 (1940): 193.

13. In a letter to Ignatius from Worms, December 27, 1540, Pierre Favre lists the following as his spiritual sons, acquired with no effort on his part: Nicolas de Granvelle, Charles V's prime minister, and his son, Antoine, the bishop of Arras; Berardo Sanctius, the bishop of Aquila; John Morone, the cardinal bishop of Modena; Dr. Moscoso, a theologian friend from Paris who was chaplain to Charles V; Dr. Ortiz; a Scottish bishop by the name of Robert Wauchope; and Tommaso Badia, the Master of the Sacred Palace, the theologian to whom Paul III delegated the task of examining the five decrees of the Formula (see chap. 19) [*MF* 45-46]. For a detailed and thoroughly documented chronology of the lives of Favre and the other eight first companions, see a series of articles by various authors in *AHSI* 59 (1990): 179-344 (*AHSI* 1540-1990 commemorative issue).

14. *MS*, followed by volume and page (and in this instance, paragraph) number, refers to two volumes of *Epistolae P. Alphonsi Salmeronis, Societatis Jesu*, MHSI (Madrid, 1906-7).

15. *ML*, followed by page number, refers to vol. 1 of eight volumes of *Epistolae et acta Patris Jacobi Lainii, secundi praepositi generalis Societatis Jesu*, MHSI (Madrid, 1912-17).

16. *F*, followed by a paragraph number, refers to a fragment of Favre's *Memoriale* dealing with his early life and the beginnings of the Society, in *FN* 1:26-49. The full *Memoriale* is found in *MF* 489-696, with the relevant reference in 498 [19].

17. *PCh*, with volume and paragraph number, refers to one of the six volumes of Polanco's *Chronicon*, MHSI (Madrid, 1894-98); *PCh* without a volume number refers to vol. 1.

18. See Daniel Bartoli, S.J., *History of the Life and Institute of St. Ignatius de Loyola, Founder of the Society of Jesus*, 2 vols. (New York: P. J. Kenedy, 1855; published as *Vita di S. Ignazio*, 1650), 1:288-89 and Schur., 394-96, especially n. 39.

19. Schur., 336 n. 201.

20. Rodrigues does not identify Xavier, but Laynez does [*L* 35]. Rodrigues incorrectly identifies the disease as leprosy, but Laynez correctly calls it *mal francés*, "the French disease." It was given the name syphilis in 1530 from the title of a Latin poem by Fracastoro, "Syphilis sive Morbus Gallicus," after the shepherd hero, Syphilis (Webster's Dictionary). The French, of course, called it the Italian disease.

21. *MX*, followed by volume and page number, refers to two volumes of *Monumenta Xaveriana*, MHSI (Madrid, 1899, 1912). J. Iturrioz, S.J., in "San Francisco de Xabier," *Manresa* 58 (1986): 175-79, shows clearly that the mission was not limited to the lands governed by Portugal.

22. Nadal, *Apologia contra censuram, FN* 2:94 [102].

23. Various letters of Paul III to Codure and Salmerón as well as to the cardinal of Scotland, the king of Scotland, and the rulers and the people of Ireland.

24. Nadal, *Apologia contra censuram, FN* 2:86 [83].

25. *Ibid.*, 105 [124], 94 [102].

26. *Constitutiones anni 1541, C* 34.

27. Nadal, *Apologia contra censuram, FN* 2:105 [124], and n. 170.

28. See, for example, the Theatine brief, *Exponi nobis* (1524), [*BRT* 6:73a]; the Barnabite brief, *Vota, per quae* (1533), [*BRT* 6:160a]; the Theatine brief, *Dudum pro parte* (1533), [*BRT* 6:160b]; the Barnabite bull, *Dudum felicis* (1535), [*BRT* 6:190b]. *BRT*, with volume and page number, refers to *Bullarum, diplomatum et privilegiorum sanctorum Romanorum Pontificum Taurinensis editio*, ed. A. Tomasetti, 25 vols. (Turin, 1857-72).

29. John W. O'Malley, S.J., "Some Distinctive Characteristics of Jesuit Spirituality in the Sixteenth Century," in *Jesuit Spirituality: A Now and Future Resource*, by John W. O'Malley, S.J., John W. Padberg, S.J., Vincent T. O'Keefe, S.J. (Chicago: Loyola University Press, 1990), 8-9.

30. Schur., 119.

31. Most of the details on the University of Paris and the education of the first companions are drawn from Schur., 78-269, *passim*, and Luis de Diego, *La opción sacerdotal de Ignacio de Loyola y sus compañeros [1515-1540]* (CIS, 1975), 110-51 (henceforth referred to as Diego with page number). See also Victoriano Larrañaga, S.J., "Los estudios superiores de San Ignacio en París, Bolonia y Venecia," *Razón y Fe* 153 (1956): 221-42; George E. Ganss, S.J., *Saint Ignatius' Idea of a Jesuit University* (Milwaukee: Marquette University Press, 1954), 11-17; James K. Farge, "The University of Paris in the Time of Ignatius Loyola," in *Ignacio de Loyola y su tiempo. Congreso internacional de historia (9-13 Setiembre 1991)*, ed. Juan Plazaola, S.J. (Bilbao: Mensajero and Universidad de Deusto, 1992), 221-43; and André Ravier, S.J., "The Life of Iñigo de Loyola and his First Companions at the University of Paris (October 1525 - December 1536)," *CIS* 23, no. 2 (1992): 86-94.

32. Pedro Ribadeneira, *De actis patris nostri Ignatii, FN* 2:383.

33. "Et cum fratribus convenirem ad chartusianos, ad sacram synaxim diebus dominicis [*MN* 1:2.4]"; Etienne Pasquier, *Le playdoyer, FN* 3:816. *MN,* followed by volume, page, and paragraph numbers, refers to volumes of the *Monumenta*, MHSI (Madrid-Rome, 1898-1964), containing the works of Jerónimo Nadal, S.J., and going by various titles. See also André Ravier, S.J., "Ignace de Loyola et la Chartreuse de Paris," *Christus* 42 (1995): 230-32.

34. The documents testifying to the degree of Bachelor of Arts for Ignatius and the other companions can be found in *FD* 384-88; for the licentiate, *FD* 389-92; for Ignatius's Master of Arts, *FD* 395-97; for testimony from the university regarding his theological studies at the University of Paris, *FD* 523. Schur., 269 n. 198, indicates where the documents concerning the Master of Arts can be located for most of the other companions. The "certificate" such as Ignatius received for theology was a standard document issued by the University of Paris indicating that the student had completed a minimum of a year and a half of study. Similar documents for some of the others are still extant (Schur., 269 n. 199; Diego, 149 n. 114).

35. Dominique Bertrand, *La politique de S. Ignace de Loyola* (Paris: Éditions du Cerf, 1985), 417-67.

36. The rise of the masters in the twelfth century gave the world a new social category. "This term 'master' had over others such as 'lord' or 'abbot' the advantage of being free from implications of power or temporal responsibilities" (M.-D Chenu, O.P.,

Nature, Man, and Society in the Twelfth Century [University of Chicago, 1968], 252 n. 18).

Chapter Two: Their Choice to Be Poor

1. The information on Contarini comes from Pastor, 144-58. Elisabeth G. Gleason offers a fresh assessment of Contarini's significance in her *Gasparo Contarini: Venice, Rome, and Reform* (Berkeley: University of California Press, 1993), a critical biography that came to our attention after completing research for *Impelling Spirit*.
2. *EI* 123 n. 2 makes Pietro Contarini a nephew of Gasparo Contarini, but Tacchi Venturi points out that they come from two different branches of the Contarini family, TV, 1/2:48-49 n. 1; 2/1:108 n. 5.
3. This conversation took place when the pope returned from Nice after an absence of four months.
4. *FN* 1:9 n. 21 suggests Cardinal Contarini as the friend, qualifying with "perhaps;" Schur., 431 n. 187, says "probably."
5. See *FN* 1:500 n. 1. For a biographical sketch of Dr. Pedro Ortiz and a survey of his relationships with Ignatius, see Luis Fernández, "Iñigo de Loyola y los alumbrados," *Hispania sacra* 35 (1983): 626-30.
6. Schur., 412.
7. *Memoriale seu diarium Patris Ludovici Gonzalez de Camara*, *FN* 1:705 [307]; *PV* 102; TV, 2/1:304-9, 385-87; Schur., 505-7.
8. Schur., 499, spelled Vauchop; Schur., 499 n. 50; Pastor, 109.
9. See TV, 2/1:136 and Schur., 420, both citing *PCh* 6:52 [149] where Polanco says that when Laynez, as vicar after Ignatius' death, called upon Paul IV (Carafa), the pope affirmed his special love for the Society and cited examples of actions he had taken in the city of Rome itself on the Society's behalf, beginning with the time that his cousin was legate of Rome during the absence of Paul III.
10. Bobadilla's correspondence suggests that the list could go on and on [*MB* 6, 10-12, 22].
11. The manuscript in the Vatican has a comma at the end of the introductory clause: "Since from the words of many we have often gathered [*intellexissemus*]," and another at the end of the phrase, "Christ's poor priests [*sacerdotes*]," indicating that the

words between the two commas, *vos sponte pauperes Christi sacerdotes*, form a self-contained unit.

12. Bracketed numbers refer to paragraphs in the Spiritual Exercises. Ignatius wrote the Spiritual Exercises in Spanish. For the Spanish text, see *Sancti Ignatii de Loyola Exercitia Spiritualia*, MHSI (Rome, 1969). The same volume also contains the Latin text of the Spiritual Exercises, *Versio prima A. 1541*, probably translated by Ignatius himself. The English translation of the Spiritual Exercises used in this book is that of George E. Ganss in *Ignatius of Loyola*, ed. George E. Ganss, S.J., CWS (New York: Paulist Press, 1991).

13. The significance of this term will be considered in a later chapter. The letter itself is in *EM* 1:24 n. 1, and is dated August 26, 1539, but the inscription in which the term is used is not included. The original manuscript is found in the Jesuit archives in Rome, *Epp. Ext.* 23, fol. 2v, and reads: Alli molto Veń. in *Xpo Jhu* li fratelli di la Compagnia de' preti peregrini Romae. The equivalent, freely transcribed, is found in *PCh* p. 81 n. 1.

14. For example, the Theatines in 1524, and the Barnabites in 1533, who hoped to establish themselves as models for diocesan priests. Cf. Michel Dortel-Claudot, S.J., *Etat de Vie et Rôle du Prêtre* (Paris: Le Centurion, 1970), 108, and Paul A. Kunkel, *The Theatines in the History of Catholic Reform before the Establishment of Lutheranism* (Washington, D.C.: Catholic University of America Press, 1941), 82. Kunkel writes: "The exemplary life of the Theatines was, in fact, a perfect model for the clerical state" (47). See also H. Jedin, "Did the Council of Trent Create a Prototype of the Priest?" in *Priesthood and Celibacy*, ed. J. Coppens (Milan: Àncora, 1972), 165; and TV, 1/1:66. Regarding the Theatines and Barnabites in general, see Kenneth J. Jorgensen, S.J., "The Theatines," and Richard L. DeMolen, "The First Centenary of the Barnabites (1533-1633)," in *Religious Orders of the Catholic Reformation*, ed. Richard L. DeMolen (New York: Fordham University Press, 1994), 1-29 and 59-96.

15. "*Breve Ssmi Dni Pauli III per li preti reformati del Gesú,*" AA.Arm. I-XVIII, 6461, ff.145r-148r, Vat. Arch. Cf. TV, 1/2:179-80. For later examples of the use of *preti reformati*, see TV, 2/1:359 and 1/2:223-28.

16. The remarks on *pauperes Christi* depend in great part on a section of M. Mollat's lengthy treatment of poverty, "Povertà: Pauperes Christi," *DIP*, 7 (1983): 271-74.

17. *The Historia Occidentalis of Jacques de Vitry: A Critical Edition*, ed. John Frederick Hinnebusch, O.P., Spicilegium Friburgense, vol. 17 (Fribourg: University Press, 1972), chap. 29 (hereafter

referred to as *Historia occidentalis* with chapter number; some authors refer to this work as *Historia orientalis, History of the Orient.* It is the same work but has been variously named). See Michel Mollat, "Hospitalité et assistance au début du XIIIe siècle," in *Poverty in the Middle Ages*, ed. David Flood, Franziskanische Forschungen 27 (Werl: Dietrich-Coelde, 1975), 37-51.

18. See *Harper's Latin Dictionary* (New York: American Book Co., 1907), 1318.

19. The dedicatory letter of the book *Quadripertitum exercitium cellae* addresses itself "to the prior of the poor of Christ [*priori pauperum Christi*] living at Witham" (*PL* 153, 799D). Cf. several letters by Guigo I, 5th prior of La Chartreuse, in which he uses "poor" but not "Christ" (*PL* 153, 594C, 600A and 600B).

20. "For they are the poor of Christ [*pauperes Christi*]: they have no defense through riches or power against their enemies, but place all their hope in God's mercy and Yours" (*Exordium parvum* 12) and, "The little flock voiced its one and only complaint: that it was small in numbers. As I said, the 'poor of Christ [*Christi pauperes*]' came to fear and dread that they might not be able to leave behind heirs to their poverty" (*Exordium Cistercii* 2, "Early Cistercian Documents in Translation," trans. Bede K. Lackner, O.Cist., in Louis J. Lekai, *The Cistercians: Ideals and Reality* [Kent State University Press, 1977], Appendix 1: 443-66; Latin words are added, taken from *Les plus anciens textes de Cîteaux: Sources, textes et notes historiques*, ed. Jean de la Croix Bouton and Jean Baptiste Van Damme, Cîteaux - Commentarii Cistercienses: Studia et Documenta, vol. 2 [Achel, 1974], hereafter referred to as *PATC*). The first quotation stresses dependence on God against power and riches, and the second is all about the little flock.

21. "Pauperum Christi de Clara-Valle servus" (*PL* 182, 619).

22. "Carthusiensium pauperum servus inutilis" (*Ad Patres in synodo I Otrensi congregatos, PL* 153, 600B); "servi et filii Carthusiae pauperes" (*Ad Innocentium papam II, PL* 153, 600A).

23. "Nudum Christum, nudus sequere" (*Ep.* 125.20, *Ad Rusticum monachum, PL* 22, 1085). Bruno, the founder of the Carthusians, quotes Jerome's passage about following the naked Christ (*PL* 152, 485A).

24. The *vita apostolica* [apostolic life] was the norm for every true renewal movement from earliest times, the life the apostles led: poverty, simplicity, prayer, and common life, not the zeal and activity the term connotes in the twentieth century. For the movements in the twelfth century, see Brenda M. Bolton,

"*Paupertas Christi:* Old Wealth and New Poverty in the Twelfth Century," in *Renaissance and Renewal in Christian History*, ed. Derek Baker, SCH 14 (Oxford: Blackwell, 1977), 95-103. The author suggests that these movements were a reaction to a new tolerance for the activities of merchants; a century earlier the common view was that merchants rarely, if ever, were able to please God. For a good understanding of the historical development of the concept of *vita apostolica*, see Henri Holstein, S.J., "The History of the Development of the Word 'Apostolic'," in *Apostolic Life*, trans. Ronald Halstead (Westminster, MD: Newman Press, 1958), 31-49. See also M.-H. Vicaire, O.P. *L'imitation des apôtres: Moines, chanoines, mendiants (IVe-XIIIe siècles)* (Paris, 1963), E.T. by William DeNaple, *The Apostolic Life* (Chicago, 1966); Simon Tugwell, O.P., *The Way of the Preacher* (Springfield, IL: Templegate, 1979), Appendix 2: The Apostolic Life, 111-16.

25. See among others, Brenda Bolton, *The Medieval Reformation: Foundations of Medieval History* (Baltimore: E. Arnold, 1983), 55-66.

26. Michel Mollat, "Pauvreté Chrétienne, Moyen Âge," *DSAM* 12 (1984): 652.

27. *Legenda maior* 7.11 in *Analecta Franciscana*, vol. 10 (Quaracchi: Collegium S. Bonaventurae, 1926-41), 555-652, hereafter referred to as *LM*, with chapter and paragraph number; see also *pauperem Christi* (*LM* 7.7). Francis tells an aspirant, "If you want to join the poor of Christ [*Christi pauperibus*], give your goods to the poor" (*LM* 7.3). An E.T. of *LM* is found in *Bonaventure: The Soul's Journey into God, The Tree of Life, The Life of St. Francis*, trans. Ewert Cousins, CWS (New York: Paulist Press, 1978), 177-327.

28. In Latin, "omnia propter Christum relinquere et in paupertate ei serviendo ipsum predicare," *Tractatus de approbatione Ordinis F. Praedicatorum*, ed. Käpelli, O.P., *Archivum Fratrum Praedicatorum* 6 (1936): 145. Bishop Fulk, who first established Dominic and his companions in his diocese, described them as men "who have committed themselves to go about on foot in evangelical poverty [*in paupertate euuangelica*] after the manner of religious and to preach the word of evangelical truth" (*Monumenta diplomatica S. Dominici*, ed. V. J. Koudelka, MOPH 25 [Rome, 1966], no. 63, hereafter referred to as Koudelka with document number).

29. Cajetan Esser, O.F.M., *Origins of the Franciscan Order* (Chicago: Franciscan Herald Press, 1970), 228.

30. Francis refused to accept anything more than the diaconate (John Moorman, *A History of the Franciscan Order from Its Origin to the Year 1517* [Oxford: Clarendon Press, 1968], 54).

31. Monks owned no personal property, but the monastery could and did, sometimes becoming very wealthy even contrary to the wishes of the monks. At their foundation new religious orders generally had some property, often a church, to which they could relate. The Franciscans apparently began with nothing, but at least they were related to a locality. The foundational documents indicate that the Society of Jesus began without property of any kind, without house or church or land, without indication of any locality to which they belonged other than the whole wide world.

32. The words evoke the opening lines of *The Ascent of Mount Carmel*, written by St. John of the Cross many years later: "One dark night, // Fired with love's urgent longings // -Ah, the sheer grace!- // I went out unseen, // My house being now all stilled" (*The Collected Works of St. John of the Cross*, trans. Kieran Kavanaugh, O.C.D., and Otilio Rodrigues, O.C.D. [Washington, D.C: ICS Publications, 1973], 68).

33. Early converts to Christianity set aside their "worldly" garments for white ones to express their new life in the risen Lord. Would-be monks exchanged their clothes for the rough habit of the order, symbol of the new life to which they were called (*RB 1980, The Rule of St. Benedict in Latin and English with Notes*, ed. T. Fry, O.S.B. [Collegeville: The Liturgical Press, 1981], 58.26-27, pp. 270-71; cf. footnote on 55.1, p. 260; hereafter referred to as *RB 80*). For an excellent study of the transformation of Ignatius's chivalrous ideals, see Juan Manuel Cacho Blecua, "Del gentilhombre mundano al caballero 'a lo divino': Los ideales caballerescos de Ignacio de Loyola," in *Ignacio de Loyola y su tiempo*, 129-59. See also, García Mateo, "El mundo caballeresco," 18-24.

34. The event at Montserrat took place in 1522, the narrative of the event some thirty years later; meantime, from about 1546, Ignatius had spent some time polishing a passage intended to challenge applicants to the Society, a passage reflecting his own mature appreciation of the events at Montserrat. In it he speaks not of the armor of Christ but of the livery [*librea*] of Christ, the uniform issued by a feudal lord to his retainers: "They must diligently observe . . . how much it helps . . . to abhor wholly and not in part what the world loves and embraces, and to accept and desire with their whole strength whatsoever Christ our Lord loved and embraced . . . to be clothed with the same garment [*vestidura*] and with the livery [*librea*] of their Lord for His love and reverence; insomuch that if it could be done without offence of the divine Majesty and without sin on the part of their

neighbor, they would wish to suffer reproaches [*ingiurias* (sic)], slanders [*falsos testimonios*] and injuries [*afrentas*], and to be treated and accounted as fools (without at the same time giving any occasion for it), because they desire to imitate and resemble in some sort their Creator and Lord Jesus Christ, and to be clothed with His garments [*vestidura*] and livery [*librea*]; since He clothed Himself with the same . . . and gave us an example, that . . . we may seek to imitate and follow Him, seeing He is the true way that leads men to life" (*Exam. Gen.*, Textus A, ca 1550, C 2:84-86; E.T. from *Summary of the Constitutions; Common Rules; Rules of Modesty, and an Epistle on Obedience* [Roehampton, 1926], 5-7).

35. Tacchi Venturi eliminates Ignatius, Favre, and Rodrigues as possible recipients of the letter (TV, 1/2:43 n. 1); for various reasons Schurhammer argues in favor of Jean Codure (Schur., 360-61 n. 194).

36. For some reason Tacchi Venturi omitted this one sentence which draws on St. Jerome (*Ep.* 125.20, *Ad Rusticum monachum*, PL 22, 1085). Schurhammer retrieved it from ARSI: *Inst. 110*, 203-v, Schur., 354-55 n. 131.

37. TV, 1/2:44. The letter is not found in MHSI.

38. Both Francis and Dominic were moved by the missionary discourse. Some sources refer to Matt. 10, some to Luke 10. For Francis, see Celano, *Vita prima* 22-23 (in *Analecta Franciscana*, vol. 10, 1-117); *Legenda trium sociorum* 25 (ed. Th. Desbonnets, *Archivum Franciscanum Historicum* 67 [1974]: 38-144, hereafter referred to as *LTS*, with paragraph number); *LM* 3.1. For Dominic, see Vicaire, "L'imitation des apôtres," 74, and "L'ordre de saint Dominique en 1215," *Archivum Fratrum Praedicatorum* 54 (1984): 20. How Francis and Dominic responded to the Gospel each heard may well have been key, on the conscious or subconscious level, in whatever stimulated Ignatius to ask, "What if I should do what St. Francis did, and what St. Dominic did?" [*A* 7]. Cf. Günter Switek, S.J. "In Armut predigen: Die Jesuiten als unbezahlte Wanderapostel," in *Ignatius von Loyola und die Gesellschaft Jesu 1491-1556*, ed. Andreas Falkner, S.J. and Paul Imhof, S.J. (Würzburg: Echter, 1990), 163-65.

39. They retained enough money to pay passage [*viaticum*] for the pilgrimage to Jerusalem [*R* 13]. Favre also indicates that "on the designated day they would leave their parents and nets, except for their viaticum" [*F* 15].

40. See the remark in Diego, 181: "It was an extremely difficult journey, performed in the utmost poverty [*Fue un viaje extremamente difícil y realizado en absoluta pobreza*]."

41. Rodrigues goes on at considerable length about how weak they became after not having any food for two or three days [*R* 49], how they forded a river up to their necks because they could not pay the ferryman, how they ate pine nuts in a forest, "a lot of work, little harvest, much time lost" [*R* 50], how later on they slept in a filthy bed [*R* 51], how they pawned a breviary to pay for a boat ride, then begged enough to buy it back [*R* 53-55], etc. This pilgrimage was not an extended picnic with a few ants in the jelly and sand in the peanut butter sandwiches.

42. To be poor with Christ poor [*con xpo pobre*] [167] is not original with Ignatius, but part of the Christian tradition, for example, "poor with the poor Christ [*cum paupere Christo pauperes*]," in the Cistercian *Exordium parvum* 15.

Chapter Three: Their Choice to Be Priests

1. A. Duval, O.P., "The Council of Trent and Holy Orders," in *The Sacrament of Holy Orders: Some Papers and Discussions concerning Holy Orders at a Session of the Centre de Pastorale Liturgique, 1955* (Collegeville: The Liturgical Press, 1962), 221.

2. Louis Trichet provides a history of the tonsure in *La tonsure: Vie et mort d'une pratique ecclésiastique* (Paris: Éditions du Cerf, 1990). From the thirteenth to the eighteenth centuries the tonsure had three purposes: (1) to distinguish clerics from lay, (2) to symbolize their dignity as men of the Church, and (3) to assure their protection, pp. 147-55.

3. That Ignatius received the tonsure is argued from the fact that he is called a cleric in the document granting him permission to make a pilgrimage to Jerusalem [*FD* 290]; that he received it as a boy is likely and in accordance with the spirit of the times (cf. Leturia, *Iñigo de Loyola*, 20). Dalmases is uncertain (*Ignatius of Loyola*, 28).

4. Cf. a series of documents on the matter from Azpeitia and Pamplona in 1515 [*FD* 229-46].

5. Diego, 22 n. 10, gives brief excerpts from the bull *Romanum decet* of Alexander VI dated July 27, 1493 (AS Vat. Reg. Vat. 869, fol. 137-138 v, and Reg. Vat. 871 fol. 117v-120). The documents from Azpeitia and Pamplona relative to the judicial process concerning Ignatius and his brother refer to the same bull [*FD* 229-46].

6. See, among others, Jedin, "Did the Council of Trent," 153-80.

7. Yves M. J. Congar, O.P., *Lay People in the Church* (Westminster, MD: Newman, 1965), 3-8.

8. Jean Leclercq, "The Priesthood in the Patristic and Medieval Church," in *The Christian Priesthood*, ed. Nicholas Lash and Joseph Rhymer (Denville, NJ: Dimension Books, 1970), 53-75. Leclercq's chapter briefly covers the patristic period and devotes itself mainly to the middle ages. His main source of information is *Prêtres d'hier et d'aujourd'hui*, Coll. Unam Sanctam, under direction of Y. Congar (Paris, 1954).

9. Michel Meslin, "Ecclesiastical Institutions and Clericalization from 100 to 500 A.D.," in *Sacralization and Secularization*, ed. Roger Aubert, Concilium 47 (New York: Paulist Press, 1969), 39-54; Jedin, "Did the Council of Trent," 154. For priesthood in the eighth through the thirteenth centuries, see Edward Schillebeeckx, *The Church with a Human Face: A New and Expanded Theology of Ministry* (New York: Crossroad, 1985), 161-94. For the development and evolution of the gap between clergy and laity, see Leopold Desjardins, C.SS.R., "Le renouveau de l'idée de sacerdoce universel à la fin du Moyen Âge," in *Le prêtre, hier, aujourd'hui, demain* (Montreal: Fides, 1970), 128-41.

10. Ét. Magnin, "Immunités ecclésiastiques," *DTC*, 7/1:1218-62; A. Boudinhon, "Immunity," *CE*, 7:690a-92b. An entertaining account of the situation in the 14th c. is found in Barbara W. Tuchman, *A Distant Mirror: The Calamitous 14th Century* (New York: Ballantine, 1978), 25, who describes the conflict over taxation between Philip the Fair of France and Pope Boniface VIII. Tuchman indicates that the clergy were not the only ones exempt from certain taxes; the nobility also were, p. 15. According to the accepted system, the clergy prayed, the nobles protected, and the people provided, but down the ages the peasant experience has often been that the clergy preyed, the nobles preyed, and the people prayed and paid. The power of Church and government over against the weakness and need of the people is perhaps best seen in the central plaza of any large Latin American city, where the city hall or seat of government stands on one side and next to it or on another side stands the cathedral and the bishop's palace.

11. Leona C. Gabel, *Benefit of Clergy in England in the Later Middle Ages*, Smith College Studies in History, vol. 14, nos. 1-4, (Northhampton, Mass. 1928), 85-87; R. L. Burtrell, "Benefit of Clergy," *CE*, 2:476b-77a; R. Genestal, *Le Privilegium Fori en France du Décret de Gratien à la fin du XIVe siècle*, 2 vols. (Paris: Leroux, 1921). Genestal says that from the 5th c. secular priests bor-

rowed the tonsure from monks, and that the Decretals of Gregory IX established tonsure as the base of clerical privilege, 1:3-4. He also indicates that the tonsure was not to be given to illiterates, 1:5 n. 2, which, of course, suggests that it was so being given. Not *all* of the clergy by any means were well educated. For a detailed account of the situations in Spain, France, and Italy in the time of Ignatius, see Diego, 21-55, 89-119, 163-79. For a summary of sixteenth-century conditions in Spain, see Luis de Diego, S.J., "Ignacio de Loyola sacerdote: de ayer a hoy," *Manresa* 63 (1991): 89-90.

12. Congar, *Lay People*, 6-10, and especially the original French edition, p. 23 n. 10. Priesthood as a much more common practice for monks developed later, and so did preaching as a function of a monk. For the nature of the monastic priesthood, see Adalbert de Vogüé, "Priest and Monastic Community in Antiquity," *Cistercian Studies* 22 (1987): 17-24; Jean Leclercq, "On Monastic Priesthood according to the Ancient Medieval Tradition," *Studia Monastica* 3 (1961): 137-55, and also, "The Priesthood for Monks," *Monastic Studies* 3 (1965): 53-85; O. Rousseau, O.S.B., "Priesthood and Monasticism," in *Sacrament of Orders*, 168-80. To be a priest or a preacher is not a part of, although not opposed to, the monastic vocation. In ancient times monks were called to preach only as a temporary activity within the monastic structure. Priesthood was either a reward for virtue, an ascetical priesthood, or designed to meet the needs of the other monks, a contemplative priesthood arising from contemplation and oriented toward contemplation.

13. The big difference between Waldo and Ignatius was the big difference between Waldo and Francis. Like Francis, Ignatius accepted church authority and Waldo did not. For Waldo and the Waldensians, see among others: three works by Brenda Bolton: *The Medieval Reformation*, 55-62, "*Paupertas Christi*," 95-103, and "Tradition and Temerity: Papal Attitudes to Deviants, 1159-1216," in *Schism, Heresy and Religious Protest*, ed. Derek Baker, SCH 9 (Cambridge, 1972), 79-91; B. Marthaler, O.F.M. Conv., "Forerunners of the Franciscans: The Waldenses," *Franciscan Studies* 18 (1958): 133-42; Christine Thouzellier, "Hérésie et Pauvreté à la fin du XIIe et au début du XIIIe siècle," in *Études sur l'histoire de la pauvreté*, ed. M. Mollat (Paris, 1974), 371-88.

14. The mystique of Francis's betrothal to Lady Poverty is a later development not to be found in the early sources. Francis was not so much concerned with poverty for its own sake as he was with imitating Christ. Cf. Esser, *Origins*, 228-40, esp. 233-34.

Much of the material in the preceding note on Waldo is pertinent also to Francis. In 1209 or 1210 Innocent III made the Franciscans (basically laymen) able to preach by requiring them to receive small tonsures, which either made them clerics or made them look like clerics (*LTS* 51-52; *LM* 3.10). Whether or not the small tonsures were bestowed according to the proper ritual, they did have the effect of connecting the friars with the Church hierarchy, making it easier for them to preach penance everywhere (Laurentio C. Landini, O.F.M., *The Causes of the Clericalization of the Order of Friars Minor: 1209-1260 in the Light of Early Franciscan Sources* [Chicago, 1968], xxii-xxiv, and 30-32). Although the friars began by preaching repentance, for they were interested in changing people's lives, before long they were able to preach doctrine as well (Atanasio Matanić, O.F.M., "Papa Innocenzo III di fronte a San Domenico e San Francesco," *Antonianum* 35 [1960]: 519 n. 4).

15. Jedin, "Did the Council of Trent," 156-57. For a brief description of the historical development of benefices, see Donald E. Heintschel, *The Mediaeval Concept of an Ecclesiastical Office* (Washington, DC: Catholic University of America Press, 1956) 6-10. For more details, see G. Mollat, "Bénéfices écclésiastiques en occident," *DDC*, 2: 406-49. In the apostolic era the clergy were generally poor and supported themselves by working. By the sixth century bishops were required to provide them with a stipend or salary. For a thorough treatment of sixteenth-century practices of income from or inheritance of Church benefices, simony, nepotism and other property-related abuses, see Barbara McClung Hallman, *Italian Cardinals, Reform, and the Church as Property* (Berkeley and Los Angeles: University of California Press, 1985). A fascinating little *History of Benefices* written about 1600 by Paolo Sarpi, a Venetian friar, was not published until 1675. It can be found in *Sarpi: History of Benefices and Selections from History of the Council of Trent*, ed. Peter Burke (New York: Washington Square Press, 1967).

16. Cf. Lateran Council I (1123), canon 4 (*COD*, 166), and Lateran Council III (1179), canon 3 (*COD*, 188). (E.T. and commentary in H. J. Schroeder, *Disciplinary Decrees of the General Councils* [St. Louis: Herder Book Co., 1937], 182-84 and 216-18, hereafter referred to as Schroeder with page number. Note that the numbering systems are different, so that Lateran I, canon 4 in *COD* is called canon 7 in Schroeder.) On *cura animarum* see the reflections of José Maria Diaz Moreno, *La regulación juridica de la cura de almas en los canonistas hispanicos de los siglos xvi-xvii*, Biblioteca Teologica Granadina 14 (Granada, 1972), 102-9. The description

of *cura animarum* is based on that of Alvaro Pelayo [Pelagius] (+1349), *De Planctu Ecclesiae*, Lib. I, cap. 70 (Biblioth. Max. Pontificia, Io. Th. Rocaberti, Tomus III, Romae 1698, 258), cited by Diaz Moreno, p. 50. In the early Middle Ages only a few monasteries owned and served parish churches. As the number of monks engaged in *cura animarum* gradually increased, their activity was in time perceived as a threat to the rights of diocesan priests and the control of bishops over their dioceses. Giles Constable describes the situation in detail in a study entitled, "Monasteries, Rural Churches and the *Cura animarum* in the Early Middle Ages," in *Monks, Hermits and Crusaders in Medieval Europe* (London: Variorum Reprints, 1988), 349-89. Bede Lackner, in his "Early Cîteaux and the Care of Souls," in *Noble Piety and Reformed Monasticism*, ed. E. Rozanne Elder, Studies in Medieval Cistercian History 7 (Kalamazoo: 1981), 52-67, offers an interesting picture "in reverse," by spelling out the *cura animarum* 12th century monks were to abstain from, namely, the care of persons living outside the monastery. A good discussion of *cura animarum* is found in G. Fransen, "The Tradition in Medieval Canon Law," in *Sacrament of Holy Orders*, 202-18, especially 211-12 which illustrates the complexity of the concept.

17. Cf. Jedin, "Did the Council of Trent," 156-57. Distinction was made between higher and lower clergy, cf. *ibid.*, 155; Diego, 33. Regarding the wealth of the higher clergy, remember that this was the day of simony and multiple benefices. Diego, 44-46, enlarges on the wealth of the clergy. What he writes of Spain is true of other countries as well. See also Fliché-Martin, *Histoire de l'Eglise depuis les origines jusqu'à nos jours*, vol. 15, *L'Eglise et la Renaissance (1449-1517)* (Paris, 1951), 314-18. Although written of a different age, what Tuchman writes is true of Ignatius's day: "Between the prelacy and the poor half-educated priest living on a crumb and a pittance there was little in common" (*Distant Mirrors*, 14). Yet Ignatius and his companions worked and dined with high and low alike. For a treatment of clerical education, see Luis Sala Balust and Francisco Martin Hernandez, *La formación sacerdotal en la iglesia* (Barcelona: Flors, 1966); also Diego, 165. For the poor education of the clergy, see Olivier de la Brosse, *Latran V et Trente*, Histoire des conciles oecuméniques, vol. 10 (Paris: Éditions de l'Orante, 1975), 18-20; for the sad state of the clergy from moral, economic, and educational points of view, see Fliché-Martin, *Histoire*, 15:330-37.

18. Regarding "office," see John W. O'Malley, S.J., "Priesthood, Ministry, and Religious Life: Some Historical and Historiographical

Considerations," *Theological Studies* 49 (1988): 232; also Heintschel, *Mediaeval Concept.*

19. Edward L. Cutts, *Scenes and Characters of the Middle Ages* (London: Virtue & Co., 1872), 207. The Council of Trent would deplore the situation in these words: "There are so many untrained and uneducated priests that their number seems almost infinite" (*CT*, 6:596 [7]).

20. Decrees 13-14 of Lateran Council III (1179) (*COD*, 194-95) railed against the practice but without success. Dioceses were without resident bishops and parishes without resident pastors. Abuses regarding benefices are brought up again in Lateran V (1514) (*COD*, 599; Schroeder, 497), and are outlined in detail in John C. Olin, ed., "The *Consilium de emendanda ecclesia, 1537*," trans. John Higgins and John Olin, in *The Catholic Reformation: Savonarola to Ignatius Loyola, Reform in the Church 1495-1540* (New York: Harper & Row, 1969), 188-91 (henceforth simply called Olin with page number), reprinted in John C. Olin, *Catholic Reform from Cardinal Ximenes to the Council of Trent, 1495-1563: An Essay with Illustrative Documents and a Brief Study of St. Ignatius Loyola* (New York: Fordham University Press, 1990), 65-79. No wonder the Council of Trent would need to issue a lengthy decree enjoining the obligation of residence on bishops and priests (*De residentia, COD*, 657-59).

21. Decree 7 of Lateran III (1179) (*COD*, 190-91) complains about charging for everything, and not just on the part of parish priests; cf. Lateran IV (1215), decree 66 (*COD*, 241).

22. Alfonso de Valdés, *Diálogo de las cosas ocurridas en Roma* (Madrid: Espasa, 1969), 66. This marvelous passage from the secretary of Charles V (1500-1558) is quoted by Diego, 45 n. 112.

23. At the same time there was also profound piety. Cf., among others, Fliché-Martin, *Histoire*, 15:318-30.

24. Concubinage was a problem that would not go away. Cf. Lateran Council III (1179), decree 11 (*COD*, 193-94); Lateran IV (1215), decree 14 (*COD*, 218); Lateran V, the bull of May 5, 1514, III, 3 (*COD*, 598-99). E.T. found in Schroeder, 496, and in Olin, "The reform bull, *Supernae dispositionis arbitrio*, 1514," 63. See also, "Giberti's *Constitutions*, after 1527," *ibid.*, 144-45.

25. Beltrán Ibáñez de Oñaz, Ignatius's father, ceded the family house and the patronage of the parish church to Martín on the occasion of his marriage to Madalena de Araoz, September 11, 1498 (*Informatio de Martino García de Oñaz*, in *FD* 195-201). Beltrán did not die until 1507. The family tree is inserted in *FD* 816.

26. For sons of princes, see de la Brosse, *Latran V et Trente*, 17-18; Diego, 42, lists some bastard sons of kings and princes who had an ecclesiastical career. Diego notes that sons of clerics were forbidden to succeed to their fathers' benefices, a law frequently broken. The fact that the councils (Lateran II in 1139, decree 21, *COD*, 178, and Lateran IV in 1215, decree 31, *COD*, 225) decreed against it suggests that it was being done.

27. The editors of the *Monumenta* edition of the *Spiritual Exercises* note that Ignatius composed the rules for election at Manresa, "at least in a sketchy sort of way [*modo saltem imperfecto*]," p. 31. Annotation 16, which refers to an inordinate affection for an office or benefice, was probably not added until Paris, p. 32.

28. Diego, 67, develops this point somewhat with a couple of quotations from Nadal.

29. *Anima* [soul] meant the whole person; even today we hear "Not a soul was there" or "A town of some 1500 souls."

30. Diego, 66-85, leads us step by step through the years from Manresa to Paris inclusive as Ignatius tries to live out his vocation, but he finds no decisive moment of choosing priesthood. Cf. Diego, "Ignacio de Loyola sacerdote," 91-92.

31. *Adhortationes in librum examinis* (1539), *FN* 2:137-38. To oversimplify: Conventual Franciscans and Observant Franciscans worked with people, but the Observants also tended toward a more eremitical way of life.

32. In spite of the corruption in the Church many movements pointed toward reform. Gian Matteo Giberti, bishop of Verona, was an outstanding pastor of souls with deep concern for his clergy (cf. Olin, 133-35). Diego, 173, notes that he was the bishop of Verona while Broët and Bobadilla were working there (see *L* 41). Cf. also Paul Broutin, S.J., *L'Évêque dans la tradition pastorale du XVIe siècle*, French adaptation of "Das Bischofsideal der katolischen Reformation" by Hubert Jedin (Bruges: Desclée de Brouwer, 1953), 44-51. Diego, 51-52, lists a number of praiseworthy bishops in Spain. In France the Council of Paris (Sens) was in session even as Ignatius entered Paris. The bishops showed much concern about the clergy, although many of their efforts were ineffective (Diego, 89-95).

33. Juan de Avila, born shortly after Ignatius, worked tirelessly for the formation of priests (Diego, 52-53). At the same time Josse Clichtove in France tried, not wholly successfully, to elaborate a spirituality for diocesan priests (Diego, 101-10; Schillebeeckx, *Church*, 195-97). Gaetano da Thiene, later canonized, was

cofounder of the Theatines, priests who worked hard for the renewal of the diocesan clergy (Diego, 176-77; Olin, 128-29; Jorgensen, "Theatines," 1-3; F. Andreu, "Gaetano Thiene, Santo", *DIP*, 4 [1977]: 1010-14. For a more complete life of Gaetano, see Pio Paschini, *S. Gaetano Thiene, Gian Pietro Carafa, e le origini dei Chierici Regolari Teatini* [Rome, 1926]). Duval, "Council of Trent," has some good pages on "true pastors," 222-26. On p. 223 he indicates that Gaetano called himself "poor priest." Gaetano, however, did not use the term *pauper sacerdos* but *misero prete* or *miser presbiter*. See F. Andreu, *Le lettere di San Gaetano de Thiene*, Studi e testi 177 (Rome, 1954), where *misero prete* is found on pp. 31, 34, 38, and 51, and *miser presbiter* on pp. 57, 62, and 67.

34. Diego, 110-17, 135-43.

35. According to the editors of the *Monumenta* edition of the *Spiritual Exercises*, p. 32.

36. *Ibid.* The editors suggest the addition at this time of Rules 3-5 [316-18] for the first week.

37. Schur., 155-58. The document attesting his nobility is found in *MX* 2:37-39.

38. Schur., 158. *EX* 1:12-14 give evidence of some letters that have been lost. *EX*, with volume and page numbers, refers to *Epistolae S. Francisci Xaverii aliaque eius scripta* (Rome: MHSI, 1944-45).

39. Schur., 270.

40. See Schillebeeckx: ". . . originally the Franciscan movement was not a priestly movement but a lay movement (although it soon allowed itself to be clericalized)" (*Church*, 180). Dominic, too, saw that priesthood was for ministry. The ministry of Francis and Dominic did not derive from office (see O'Malley, "Priesthood, Ministry," 231-32).

41. On *presbuteroi* in the Post-Apostolic Fathers and the Early Church, see Kittel, *TDNT*, 6: 672-80. On priesthood in Hebrews, cf. A. Gelin, P.S.S., "The Priesthood of Christ in the Epistle to the Hebrews," in *Sacrament of Holy Orders*, 30-43 (See also the chapter on Hebrews in Edward Schillebeeckx, *Christ: The Experience of Jesus as Lord* [New York: Seabury Press, 1980], 237-93; Part Two of Albert Vanhoye, S.J., *Old Testament Priests and the New Priest* [Petersham, MA: St. Bede's Publications, 1980], 61-238; Kenan B. Osborne, O.F.M., *Priesthood: A History of the Ordained Ministry in the Roman Catholic Church* [New York: Paulist Press, 1988], esp. 3-29, 44-53, 204-12). On *sacerdos* as applied to bishops and priests, see P. M. Gy, O.P., "Notes on the

Early Terminology of Christian Priesthood," in *Sacrament of Holy Orders*, 98-115. Schillebeeckx has a brief account of the "sacerdotalizing" of ministry (*Church*, 144-45).

42. I use the word *stimulus* rather than *argument* because it set me thinking along this line. We are dealing here with speculation, not argumentation.

43. TV, 1/2:225.

44. This fact is confirmed by the next phrase in the will, "that is, those called and named reformed [*cioè di quelli chiamati et nominati riformati*]." Faustina was apparently anxious to give her home not merely to priests, or to poor priests, but to priests who were engaged in ministry.

45. Gelasius I (429-96) had set down the principle in his theory of the two powers; Boniface VIII proclaimed it again in the bull *Unam Sanctam* (1302), probably the high-water mark of the power approach (in the secular sense) to spiritual authority. E.T. of *Unam Sanctam* is found in G. R. Elton, *Renaissance and Reformation 1300-1648*, 3d ed. (New York: Macmillan, 1976), 3-5.

46. Heintschel, *Mediaeval Concept*, 75-98. See also Stanley Chodorow, *Christian Political Theory and Church Politics in the Mid-Twelfth Century: The Ecclesiology of Gratian's Decretum* (Berkeley: University of California Press, 1972), 154-86.

47. Cf. Schillebeeckx, *Church*, 175.

48. Lateran Council IV (1215), canon 21, decreed that all those who have reached the age of discretion are to confess their sins at least once a year to their parish priest [*proprio sacerdoti*] and to receive the Eucharist at least at Easter (*COD*, 221; Schroeder, 259-63 with background commentary). On the duties of pastors, see J. Gaudemet, *Le Gouvernement de l'église à l'époque classique*, 2e partie: *Le gouvernement local*, tome 8, vol. 2 of *Histoire de Droit et des Institutions de l'Église en Occident* (Paris: Editions Cujas, 1979), 257-60, and on *proprio sacerdoti*, *ibid.*, 236-40. For a good historical synopsis of the development of parochial rights before the Council of Trent, see Bernard M. Kelly, *The Functions Reserved to Pastors*, CLS no. 250 (Washington, D.C.: Catholic University of America Press, 1947), 3-27.

49. Schillebeeckx points out that the term *corpus mysticum* originally meant the Eucharistic body of Christ, and adds: "Thus whereas formerly it had been said that a minister needed to be ordained to preside over the church community (= *corpus verum*), the terminology now became that of presiding over the *corpus mysticum*, i.e., of celebrating the eucharist" (*Church*, 194).

See the masterful study by Henri de Lubac, *Corpus Mysticum: L'Eucharistie et l'Église au Moyen Age*, 2d ed. (Paris: Aubier, 1949), 373pp. A brief summary of St. Thomas's position, with emphasis on *sacerdotium* as sacred power, is presented by Brian E. Daley, S.J., "The Ministry of Disciples: Historical Reflections on the Role of Religious Priests," *Theological Studies* 48 (1987): 614.

50. Suppl. q. 36 a. 2 ad 1um. Thomas maintains that less education is required for those who do not have the care of souls than for those who do. Presiding over the liturgy is less demanding than having responsibility for the spiritual welfare of a flock. Dominic and Ignatius, however, tended to break out of theological categories. Both avoided *cura animarum* and both demanded a high degree of education for their men. Both thought ministry more important than power. For Dominic's attitude toward *cura animarum*, see Jean Pierre Renard, *La formation et la désignation des prédicateurs au début de l'Ordre des Prêcheurs (1215-1237)* (Fribourg: St Canisius, 1977), 63, and 194 n. 11.

51. By this time increasing numbers of monks were being ordained to the priesthood.

52. Schillebeeckx, *Church*, 174-79; M.-H. Vicaire, "Sacerdoce et prédication aux origines de l'Ordre des Prêcheurs," *Rev. Sc. ph. th.* 64 (1980): 244-45, re conflict between monks and secular clergy; Caroline Walker Bynum, *Docere Verbo et Exemplo: An Aspect of Twelfth-Century Spirituality* (Missoula: Scholars Press, 1979), 3, on polemical exchanges between monks and regular canons; regarding canons in general, *ibid.*, 2-3, 19-21; C. H. Lawrence, *Medieval Monasticism: Forms of Religious Life in Western Europe in the Middle Ages*, 2d ed. (London: Longman, 1989), 163-69; see also C. W. Bynum, "The Spirituality of Regular Canons in the Twelfth Century," in *Jesus as Mother: Studies in the Spirituality of the High Middle Ages* (Berkeley: University of California Press, 1982), 22-58; Grover Zinn, "The Regular Canons," in *Christian Spirituality I: Origins to the Twelfth Century*, ed. B. McGinn, J. Meyendorff, and J. Leclercq (New York: Crossroad, 1985), 218-28.

53. Schillebeeckx, *Church*, 179-87; Lawrence, *Medieval Monasticism*, 261-63; Gaudemet, *Gouvernement de l'église*, 289-92; Ralph V. Shuhler, *Privileges of Regulars to Absolve and Dispense*, CLS no. 186 (Washington, D.C.: Catholic University of America Press, 1943), 9-15.

54. Vatican II's decree on the priesthood, *Presbyterorum ordinis*, prefers *presbyter* to *sacerdos* and emphasizes ministry rather than power. The companions sound more like Thomas even as they act like Vatican II.

55. Consider their work before ordination in Venice described in *L* 35; *PSH* 65-66; *R* 42-48. For a detailed account of their ministry in Venice, see Severin Leitner, S.J., "In Oberitalien: Aufbruch zum priestlichen Dienst," in *Ignatius von Loyola*, 131-37.

56. Broët was ordained a priest on March 12, 1524 (Schur., 262 n. 115 refers to Prat, *Mémoires Broët*, 557-60), Jay on March 28, 1528 (Schur., 260 n. 99 indicates that the text of the document attesting his ordination is found in ARSI: *Epp. NN. 89*, n. 3), Favre on May 30, 1534 [*MF* 3]. In his letter to Juan de Verdolay Ignatius says that "on the feast of John the Baptist we finished receiving all the orders, including the priesthood; there were seven of us ordained" [*EI* 120]. The dimissorial letter [*FD* 526-27] from Cardinal Pucci names eight, including Miguel Landívar, who apparently was not ordained [cf. *FD* 530 n. 4]. When Ignatius said "seven" he evidently referred to the fact that seven of them received "all the orders" on the same series of days, not indicating that Salmerón's ordination to the *priesthood* had to be postponed until October because he was too young [*FD* 531 n. 6].

57. Given at Rome, April 27, 1537, under the seal of the Office of the Penitentiary. This document is an excellent example of the paradox of Roman practice. It takes for granted that many bishops lived outside their own dioceses. Moreover, just about anybody, qualified or unqualified, could receive papers from Rome to be ordained (for a fee, of course), even those refused papers by their own bishop. Cf. Diego, 164 n. 2, who refers to Pelliccia, G., *La preparazione ed ammissione dei chierici ai santi ordini nella Roma del secolo XVI* (Roma: Pia Società San Paolo, 1946), 25. On the other hand, corruption was not so blind as to be unable to recognize virtue and competence nor so greedy as to demand a fee from those unable to pay. The laxity of the system worked to the advantage of the companions, who did not have to spend all the time and energy required to receive papers from their respective bishops.

58. Negusanti was bishop of Arbe, an island off the coast of Dalmatia; he normally lived in Venice and was "known as a pious and learned prelate, skilled in canon law and in Latin, Greek, and Hebrew" (Schur., 342). The ordinations cost the companions nothing, either in Rome or in Venice [*EI* 121]. Not all absentee bishops were lax of morals.

59. Ignatius [*A* 93] and Rodrigues [*R* 60] indicate they also took vows of chastity, as does Polanco [*PSH* 70]; [*PSI* 10]; and Nadal explicitly says, "and they took vows of chastity, not that only which is attached to holy orders, but of poverty and chastity

expressed into the hands of the Most Reverend Legate Veralli" (*Apologia contra censuram, FN* 2:83 [78]).

60. M. J. Dlouhy, "Ordination, Title of," *NCE*, 10:726b-27a; F. Claeys-Boúúaert, "Clerc," *DDC*, 3:831. The Council of Chalcedon (451) had already stated that no one is to be ordained a priest or deacon without a title, canon 6 (*COD*, 66). E.T. and brief history in Schroeder, 95-96. See also Schillebeeckx, *Church*, 154-56. Lateran Council III (1179) says that a bishop who ordains a priest without a title should provide for his needs (decree 5, *COD*, 190). For the significance of the concept of title as found in the above conciliary decrees, see Heintschel, *Mediaeval Concept*, 39-40 and 80-81. See also Fransen, "Tradition in Medieval Canon Law," 205-6.

61. "Regionary clerics" were ordained without title, i.e., a right to material support, and bishops used them to fill in here and there. These untitled priests often wandered about seeking means of survival, and many abuses existed. Alexander III tried at Lateran III to eliminate the practice. The Council of Trent finally managed to establish the necessity of a title for ordination (Session XXI, ch. 2). See William H. W. Fanning, "Cleric," *CE*, 4:49b, and Joseph N. Gignac, "Alimentation," *CE*, 1:312b.

62. The term used by Laynez [*L* 39]. Negusanti uses *ad titulum* in place of *sub titulo* [*FD* 532], as does Laynez.

63. The Friars Minor of the Strict Observance were described in 1532 as "sub voluntariae paupertatis habitu militantes" [*BRT* 6:156a], as were also the Jesuati in 1533 [*BRT* 6:158b].

64. Contemporary discussions of the title of poverty indicate that it means that the religious community will support the one ordained. Perhaps that is true today, but I think that what it meant originally was that the bishop was not responsible for his support. The community was directly responsible for his person, but the economic support of all of them was from the lay community surrounding them.

65. Nikolaus Nilles, S.J., "Asterisken zur Geschichte der Ordination des heiligen Ignatius von Loyola und seiner Gefährten," *Zeitschrift für katholische Theologie* 15 (1891): 146-59. Those outside a religious order needed a dispensation to be ordained under the title of poverty.

66. Diego, 184-85, calls this title "that which the companions judged would be able to support them in a dignified manner, living off what they received for their services, after the manner of alms."

67. Their attitude and intent is clearly revealed a year later when Favre and Laynez were called to Rome and Ignatius went with them [*F* 17]. "The two began immediately to teach *gratis* at the Sapienza" [*IR* 2].

68. Favre's ordination in 1534, differing somewhat juridically, was not all that different in spirit. Favre could have been ordained *sub titulo sufficientis scientiae*, opening the door to an academic career and emoluments. Instead, he was ordained *ad titulum sui patrimonii* "and he was content with that," a rather small patrimony [*MF* 2]. Two and a half months later he negated the patrimony by taking a vow of poverty at Montmartre along with the other companions.

69. "Qui verbum Domini gratis et fideliter proponentes, intendendo profectibus animarum ipsum Dominum solum secuti paupertatis titulum pretulerunt" (Koudelka, no. 86; cf. no. 101). This formula appears regularly in bulls recommending the Dominicans, indicating their profession rather than a transient choice. The pope here confirmed the title of poverty, which took the place of any benefice (M.-H. Vicaire, O.P., "Fondation, approbation, confirmation de l'Ordre des Prêcheurs," *Revue d'Histoire Ecclesiastique* 47 [1952]: 602-3). Honorius also speaks of their preaching "in the lowliness of voluntary poverty [*in abiectione voluntarie paupertatis*]" (Koudelka, nos. 109, 111, 122, 140).

70. This document is addressed to Ignatius alone. The editor indicates that the same codex contains similar faculties granted to Bobadilla, Laynez, Favre, Broët, Codure, and Jay. He mentions that Salmerón was not yet old enough to be ordained a priest. Apparently the documents for Xavier and Rodrigues have not been preserved or have not been located.

71. For the more universal mission of the mendicants, see Vicaire, "Sacerdoce et prédication," 246-49; Renard, *Formation et désignation*, 65-72; Schillebeeckx, *Church*, 182-85; Rosalind B. Brooke, *The Coming of the Friars* (New York: Barnes & Noble, 1975), 106-11; Shuhler, *Privileges*, 8-23.

72. With regard to monastic practices in mendicant life, for the Franciscans, see *The Later Rule* 3.1 in *Francis and Clare*, 139, and Esser, *Origins*, 104-7; 175-77. For the Dominicans, see the Constitutions of the Friars Preachers. The most available edition is found in Raymond Creytens, O.P., "Les Constitutions des Frères Prêcheurs dans la rédaction de S. Raymond de Peñafort," *Archivum Fratrum Praedicatorum* 18 (1948):

5-68. See also Vicaire, *St. Dominic and His Times* (New York: McGraw-Hill, 1964), 208-9; William A. Hinnebusch, O.P., *The History of the Dominican Order*, vol. 1 (Staten Island: Alba House, 1965), 349-53.

73. Michel Dortel-Claudot, S.J., *Le genre de vie extérieur de la Compagnie de Jésus* (Rome: Univ. Greg., 1971), 16 n. 13.

74. In 1539 there had as yet been no thought of lay brothers, an idea that was to come a few years later.

Chapter Four: Their Choice to Join into One Body

1. 1 Celano 30.

2. Spain and France were at war, and Xavier's brothers had fought for the French king against Ignatius and the Spanish crown at Pamplona. Imagine a gathering of the same nature and for the same purpose during the 1991 war in the Persian Gulf, say of two Israelis, three Americans, four Iraqis, and one Iranian.

3. Similar phrases elsewhere consistently describe the companions as hailing from various parts of the world rather than as deliberately coming together from various parts of the world [*D* 1, 3; *C* 25 {2}; 160 {1}; 374 {2}; *C* 2:562-63].

4. Besides the sources in the text or endnotes, the source of information on the companions is Schur., 78-263, *passim.*

5. Francisco Rodrigues, S.J., *História da Companhia de Jesus da Assistência de Portugal*, vol. 1 (Porto, 1931), 41-44.

6. *MN* 1:2.4; Étienne Pasquier, *Le plaidoyer*, *FN* 3:816. This group included more than the companions. Cf. Ravier, "Ignace . . . Chartreuse," 231-32. For a more detailed narrative of the Parisian period of the first companions, written from the perspective of discovering "the impact of facts, events and situations on the 'mens Ignatiana'," see Ravier, "Life of Iñigo . . . Paris," 88-102. See also, Carlos García Hirschfeld, S.J., "Origen de la comunidad en la Compañía de Jesús: Una experiencia humana y religiosa en un grupo de universitarios del s. XVI," *Manresa* 63 (1991): 398-403.

7. Jay may very well have been with them also in 1535 [*R* 15 n. 12, in *FN* 3:25].

8. *Conuenisse in vnum* equals *inuicem vnire et congregare.* We might have expected, "deigned to gather us together and unite us," but the companions expressed their experience that God had

united them, gifted them with friendship [*inuicem vnire*], and then formed them into a body [*congregare*]. Other translations differ. Maruca, "Deliberation," 328, has: "assemble and bind us to one another" and "what God has united and bound together." Toner, "Deliberation," 192, has: "gather us together and unite us" and "what God has gathered and united." Futrell, *Apostolic Community*, 189-90, however, has: "unite us to one another and bring us together" and "God's union and bringing together."

9. Cf. García Hirschfeld, "Origen de la comunidad," 404–5.

Chapter Five: The Impelling Action of the Holy Spirit

1. See Luis Gonzalez, S.J., "La deliberación de los primeros compañeros," *Manresa* 61 (1989): 245, who notes that the companions paid attention not only to reason but to the movements of the spirits.

2. Other translators place a different emphasis on "*ut niteretur in inueniendo*," which we translate "as to rely on finding." Both Maruca and Futrell render the phrase: "that he make every effort to find," and Toner: "in order to strive for peace and joy." There is an enormous difference, however, between *relying* on finding joy and peace in the Holy Spirit and *striving* to find joy and peace. (Maruca, "Deliberation," 330; Futrell, *Apostolic Community*, 191; Toner, "Deliberation," 197.)

3. *Exhortationes in Hispania* (1554), *FN* 1:312 [14].

4. *Adhort. Complut.*, *FN* 2:173-74 [3].

5. At present I have an article in preparation treating this matter in minute detail.

6. Cf. *OED*, 871ab; *Harper's Latin Dictionary*, 436b. In Osuna's *Friends in the Lord*, 120 n. 350, Nicholas King translates the phrase from *CEP*: "they agreed among themselves to work for a single purpose."

Chapter Six: Free to Serve

1. Three years later, in 1542, Favre would write in his *Memoriale* of their determination "to abandon relatives and nets [*relinquere parentes, et retia*]" [*F* 15], a clear reference to the Latin Vulgate

Matt. 4:22: "*relictis retibus et patre* [they . . . left their nets and father (Douay-Rheims)]."

2. Cf. articles in *RAM* 41 (1965): 233-432, all devoted to "La notion de 'mépris du monde' dans la tradition spirituelle occidentale." See also the excellent article by Michael Casey, O.C.S.O., "Strangers to Worldly Ways: RB 4.20," *Tjurunga* [An Australasian Benedictine Review], no. 29 (1985): 37-46, and Aquinata Böckmann, O.S.B., "Openness to the World and Separation from the World according to RB," *American Benedictine Review* 37 (1986): 304-22.

3. We need constantly to be reminded that *despise* comes from the Latin *despicere*, which means primarily *to regard from above* and has a transferred meaning of *look down upon* or *despise*.

4. For the early Christian meaning of world [*mundus* or *saeculum*], see L. Th. A. Lorié, S.J., *Spiritual Terminology in the Latin Translations of the Vita Antonii with reference to fourth and fifth century monastic literature* (Nijmegen: Dekker & van de Vegt, 1955), 60-62.

5. "Qui contemptis atque desertis mundi huius illecebris, in communem vitam castissimam sanctissimamque congregati . . ." (*De mor. eccl. cath.* 1.31.67, *PL* 32, 1338).

6. For example, Gregory the Great says of Benedict: "Despectis itaque litterarum studiis, relicta domo rebusque patris, soli Deo placere desiderans, sanctae conuersationis habitum quaesiuit" (*Dialogues*, vol. 2, SC 260, 126). Also: "Nullis ulterius saeculi laqueis inretitus, securus pergat et solus ad Dominum" (*La Règle du Maître*, vol. 2, SC 106, 400); and from the *Life of Bruno*: "Deliberaverunt ipse et sex alii probi viri secum abrenuntiare mundo et pompis ejus, et . . . relictis omnibus divitiis et deliciis et honoribus hujus mundi, accipere singuli cruces suas, et nudi nudum Christum sequi per arctam viam, quae ducit ad vitam" (*Vita antiquior*, *PL* 152:485A).

7. "Ecce hujus saeculi divitiis spretis, coeperunt novi milites Christi cum paupere Christo pauperes, inter se tractare quo ingenio quove artificio seu quo exercitio, in hac vita se hospitesque divites et pauperes supervenientes, quos ut Christum suscipere praecipit regula, sustentarent" (*Exordium parvum* 15).

8. "Cum dilecti filii Frater Franciscus et Socii ejus . . . abjectis vanitatibus hujus Mundi, elegerint vitae viam a Romana Ecclesia merito approbatam; ac serendo semina Verbi Dei Apostolorum exemplo diversas circumeant mansiones . . ." (*Bullarium Franciscanum Romanorum Pontificum*, vol. 1 [Rome, 1759], no. 2).

Ferdinand M. Delorme, O.F.M., presents a slightly different version in *Archivum Franciscanum Historicum* 12 (1919): 591-92.

9. 1 Celano 37. Or, in the words of the author of the *Legenda trium sociorum*, "Many brilliant scholars, both men of the world and beneficed clergy, having spurned the allurements [*illecebris*] of the flesh, and having totally abandoned a life of sin and the pursuit of secular longings, entered the . . . order of little [brothers]" (*LTS* 73).

10. 1 Celano 71.

11. J. J. Muzas, "Vicar of Christ," *NCE*, 14 (1967): 641a.

12. Irénée de Lyon, *Contre les hérésies*, bk. 4, vol. 2, SC 100 (Paris: Editions du Cerf, 1965), 540-41. The entire passage extends from p. 534 to p. 541. Everyone quotes Irenaeus: "The glory of God is the human person fully alive." But then if the glory of the human person is in serving God, in serving God the human person becomes fully alive.

13. García M. Colombás, "The Ancient Concept of the Monastic Life," *Monastic Studies* 2 (1964): 80. The original article, entitled "El concepto de monje y vida monástica hasta fines del siglo V" (*Studia Monastica* 1 [1959]: 281), gives abundant references in the footnotes to Augustine, Jerome, Cassian, and others. See also Lorié, *Spiritual Terminology*, 93-94; Christine Mohrmann, "La langue de saint Benoît, in *Études sur le latin des chrétiens*, vol. 2 (Rome, 1961), 336-37.

14. See *RB 80*, 165 n. 45; Mohrmann, "Langue," 336-40; García M. Colombás, *La regla de San Benito*, BAC 406 (Madrid, 1979), 204-10; André Borias, "Christ and the Monk," *Monastic Studies* 10 (1974): 98-99.

15. The role of the pope will be increasingly nuanced in later documents evolving from *Cum ex plurium*. For example, the final version of the Formula of the Institute in 1550 removes any ambiguity about the object of service by using words that clearly indicate the pope's relation to the whole Church: "to serve the Lord alone and the Church, his spouse, under the Roman pontiff, the vicar of Christ on earth" [*C* 375 {3}].

16. *Adhortationes* 1559, *FN* 2:133. What happened at La Storta has been examined by others, and there is no need to repeat those studies here. Schur., 410 n. 20, lists the main sources in chronological order: Ignatius in 1544 (reference in his spiritual diary in *C* 104), Nadal in 1554 (*FN* 1:313), Ignatius in 1555 (*A* 96), Nadal in 1557 (*FN* 2:9-10), Laynez in 1559 (*ibid.* 133), Nadal in 1561 (*ibid.* 158), Nadal in 1563 (*ibid.* 259-60), Polanco in 1564

(*PI* 9) Ribadeneira in 1566 (*FN* 2:377), the anonymous author about 1567 (*ibid.* 443), Ribadeneira in 1572 (*Vita* 2.11), Canisius about 1572 (*Scripta de*, 1:715), Polanco in 1574 (*PV* 95, 112). (*PI*, with paragraph number, refers to Polanco's *Informatio de instituto Societatis Iesu*, *FN* 2:304-11, a selection from *Polanci Complementa*, 1:504-10.) Hugo Rahner has analyzed all the texts in *The Vision of Ignatius in the Chapel of La Storta* (Rome: CIS, 1979), which translates the better part of what is contained in the original articles in *Zeitschrift für Aszese und Mystik* 10 (1935): 17-35, 124-39, 202-20, 265-82. Theodor Baumann has written a well-researched historical commentary, "Die Berichte über die Vision des Heiligen Ignatius bei La Storta," *AHSI* 27 (1958): 181-208. See also various authors in *The Vision of La Storta*, *CIS* 19, no. 1 (1988); Diego, "Ignacio de Loyola sacerdote," 92-93.

17. *Totum* (Latin) or *todo* (Spanish) [all, everything] runs through the five decrees of the Formula like a drumbeat; it is as characteristic of Ignatius as is *magis* [more].

18. The Latin here is *se totum divino mancipavit obsequio*. *Mancipare* derives from *manus* [hand] and *capere* [to take], and suggests the idea of handing over property, disposing of it, selling it, alienating it, and is frequently connected with the idea of slavery. Ignatius has gotten rid of himself, bound himself over to God. *Obsequium* means not only obedience and allegiance but compliance, a spirit of pliant yielding. He is totally available to God, wholly at the disposal of the divine will.

19. There are many "primary" texts, but the major ones written by the companions in chronological order are *F* 15, *L* 30, 36, *A* 85, *R* 12-18, and *B* 5, 11, as well as *MB* 602 or *FN* 3:320-21. Nadal has also touched on the subject a number of times: *FN* 2:79, 82, 92, 253, *MN* 5:626-27, as has Polanco: *PSH* 55, 57, 65, 69; *PSI* 7; *PI* 9; *PV* 69, 85-86; *PCh* 3, 7. (*PSI*, with paragraph number, refers to an Italian version of *PSH*, *FN* 1:256-98.) For further details on Montmartre, see Pedro de Leturia, S.J., *Estudios Ignacianos*, 2 vols. (Rome: IHSI, 1957): "Jerusalén y Roma en los designios de San Ignacio de Loyola," 1:181-200; "Importancia del año 1538 en el cumplimiento del 'voto de Montmartre'," 1:201-21; "La primera misa de San Ignacio de Loyola y sus relaciones con la fundación de la Compañía," 1:223-35; "El voto de San Ignacio en Montmartre," 2:405-10. See also *The Montmartre Vows: History and Spirituality*, *CIS* 16 no. 2 (1985); José M. García Maderiaga, S.J., "Contenido de la cláusula papal del voto de Montmarte," *Manresa* 48 (1976): 231-45; Günter Switek, S.J., "Die Gelübde des hl. Ignatius und seiner Gefährten auf dem

Montmartre: Zur Aktualität ihrer Mystik und missionarischen Dynamik," *Geist und Leben* 65 (1992): 245-57; Johannes G. Gerhartz, S.J., "Von Jerusalem nach Rom: Der Weg des Ignatius zu seiner Kirchlichkeit," in *Ignatius von Loyola*, 99-102; and Anton Witwer, S.J., "The Missionary Focus of the Vows in the Ignatian Charism," *CIS* 24, no. 1 (1993): 42-43.

20. Rodrigues agrees: "The Fathers immediately made clear that they were not bound by the vow of poverty while engaged in their studies in Paris, and that they could take what was necessary for the pilgrimage to Jerusalem" [*R* 13].

21. Manuel Ruiz Jurado suggests that the chapel of the vows probably contained a picture of Mary, *la Pietà*, "a votive offering of Abbot Guillaume Lévêque (1410) now kept in the Louvre" ("What Exactly Happened at Montmartre on August 15, 1534?" in *The Montmartre Vows*, 17).

22. In these pages all Latin quotations from scripture are from the Latin Vulgate, all English quotations from *NRSV* unless otherwise indicated. *NRSV* translates from Greek originals, whereas the English version known as Douay-Rheims, sometimes referred to here, translates from the Latin Vulgate. (Note on versions of Scripture: The Latin Vulgate is St. Jerome's fourth-century translation of the Old and the New Testaments from the best manuscripts available to him. Since the Vulgate was in common use during the time of Ignatius and his companions, it seems proper to refer to the Vulgate as a text familiar to them. The Douay-Rheims version is an English translation of the Latin Vulgate, commonly used by English speaking Catholics until the middle of this century. The Vulgate and its Douay-Rheims version in English may differ substantially or in some interesting ways from more modern translations based on better manuscripts than those available to Jerome.)

23. This part, although told in Spanish, is written in Italian. In his preface to Ignatius's account da Câmara indicates that he did not have a Spanish scribe at this time [*A* 5*].

24. Cf. Ruiz Jurado, "Montmartre," 26-35. Ruiz Jurado discusses the content of the oblation at Montmartre on pages 27 to 34. "All the eyewitness accounts are at one," he writes, "in that at Montmartre the companions vowed to devote themselves to the service of the Lord in poverty and to make a pilgrimage to Jerusalem . . ." (p. 27). Regarding chastity, he indicates that some sources are affirmative and some are silent. Mentioning chastity in connection with Paris are Polanco [*PSI* 6], [*PI* 9];

Nadal (*Dialogi pro Societate*, *FN* 2:253 [17]); Rodrigues [*R* 13]; "and also Manare who reports the tradition he had received, which is considered trustworthy." (See also the remarks Manare makes regarding Ribadeneira's life of Ignatius, *Censura Patris Oliverii Manarei*, *FN* 4:990.) Those not mentioning chastity are Favre [*MF* 15], although it is implied (see above); Laynez [*L* 30, 36]; Polanco [*PSH* 55-57, 65], [*PV* 69]; Ignatius [*A* 85]; and Bobadilla [*MB* 5]. Any argument from silence denying a vow of chastity would not be convincing, especially when Polanco is not silent elsewhere. The silence simply indicates that the writers were not trying to answer that particular question. There is also silence regarding poverty, in the sense that Ignatius and Favre do not mention it.

25. Rodrigues gives more details about poverty than any of the others: "They vowed besides that they would never accept anything for celebrating Mass . . . they wanted to rid themselves voluntarily even of legitimate things, so that, as far as possible, they could avoid the malicious lies of heretics and give them no grounds for saying that they did something out of a pretext of piety in order to gain much profit and make themselves richer and wealthier" [*R* 13].

26. Reading Ignatius [*A* 85] or Laynez [*L* 36], one gets the impression that the companions had decided to stay in Jerusalem if they could. Favre [*F* 15], however, writes as if they intended to return in order to present themselves to the pope. Nadal's accounts (*Apologia contra censuram*, *FN* 2:82 [76]; *Dialogi pro Societate*, *FN* 2:253 [17]) agree with those of Ignatius and Laynez. Polanco, on the other hand, mentions a new discernment to be made in Jerusalem [*PSH* 57], [*PSI* 7], [*PV* 69], although he also writes in one instance: "Their intent was that after visiting the holy places they would go amongst the unbelievers and spend their lives on their behalf, if God would be served, or meet death for the divine glory; since it had not turned out that way the first time, Father Ignatius was going to try it a second time" [*PI* 9].

27. The three companions who were welcomed into the group after Ignatius left Paris joined the other six in renewing those vows each year on August 15 while the group was in Paris.

28. Bobadilla's narrative is neither as prolix nor as colorful as that of Rodrigues. At the age of eighty his memory is inexact with regard to dates and numbers. See *FN* 3:322.

29. Father General Kolvenbach has pointed out the harmony in that liturgy and the movement of the Exercises: after the elec-

tion when the exercitant has chosen to be conformed entirely with Christ, Ignatius invites to the contemplation of the Eucharist and the passion of Jesus, his longing to give himself totally to the Father and to his brothers and sisters in total self-surrender ("On the 450th Anniversary of the Vow of Montmartre," *The Montmartre Vows*, 10).

30. See José M. García Madariaga, S.J., "La oblación del grupo Ignaciano al Papa en 1538," *Manresa* 48 (1976): 25-39; J. Iturrioz, S.J., "El peregrino de París a Roma: El año 1537 de San Ignacio; Recuerdo a los 450 años," *Manresa* 60 (1988): 21-43.

31. Aldama, "Origine," 9-11. E.T., "Origin," 11-13.

32. *Monumenta Brasiliae*, vol. 1, MHSI (Rome: 1956), 87-97. He also wrote twice to the companions themselves, but those letters have been lost (*ibid.*, 97).

33. If we are dealing with an event rather than an experience, the event obviously took place some time between the governor's decision on November 18 and the writing of the letter of November 23, 1538.

34. Favre's response was first published in *EI* 132-34, only its existence indicated in *MF* 14, but the part on the missions appears again in *Monumenta Brasiliae*, 1:98-101, along with a Portuguese translation of that part of the letter. A complete E.T. of the letter to Gouveia is found in Olin, *Catholic Reform*, 80-82.

35. The vocabulary of this paragraph is rich and finds multiple echoes in *Cum ex plurium*. "Rejoice" [*gauderet*] here finds an echo in *Cum ex plurium*'s "began to rejoice" [*gaudebamus*]; in both cases the pope is the subject of the verb. "What we had determined to do" translates *nostris propositis*, which echoes *propositum*, an important word in *Cum ex plurium*. The meaning of *propositum* will be the subject of reflection at that point where the word appears in *Cum ex plurium*. (See chapters 19 through 21.) Suffice it to say that in offering themselves the companions are manifesting their determination to enter into a contract with the pope and with the Church. When Steidle discusses monastic profession he indicates that even in its earliest form it was viewed as "a covenant [*Vertrag*] with God." (Basilius Steidle, O.S.B., *Die Regel St. Benedikts: eingeleitet, übersetzt und aus dem alten Mönchtum erklärt* [Beuron, 1952], 282; E.T., *The Rule of St. Benedict: A Commentary*, trans. Urban J. Schnitzhofer, O.S.B. [Canon City, CO, 1967], "a contract with God," 247). Steidle also talks about this covenant as a "renunciation." Favre has just spoken of "holocaust," which is the same idea. Bertrand speaks of the pact [*contrat*] the companions had with the Church (*Un corps pour*

l'Esprit, 22). Bertrand calls the institute the "fundamental contract [*contrat*] amongst the companions, on the one hand, and between themselves and the Holy See on the other" (p. 57). See also Bertrand's article, "La Compagnie de Jésus et son Institut", *Vie Consacrée* 55 (1983): 292-309. On p. 293 he says "institut . . . est alliance avec l'Eglise hiérarchique qui donne vie" and a bit farther on he speaks of "alliance fondatrice."

36. The letter, some months after the judgment of November 18, 1538, seems to speak of an event, but there is no indication of how to date that event. By that time it was certainly clear the pope understood them to be at his disposal. If the offering of themselves took place between November 18 and 23 of 1538, it seems odd that Bobadilla made no mention of this event in a letter he wrote to Duke Ercole II on November 26, 1538 [*MB* 12-14].

37. Cf. Witwer, "Missionary Focus," 44-45, and José María García Madariaga, S.J., "La oblación al Papa según las Deliberaciones de 1539," *Manresa* 49 (1977): 55-68, where the author discusses the problem of the "two obediences," that to the pope and that to the superior, a problem that does not concern us here. In another article by the same author, "La oblación del grupo," 33-34, the author quotes a line from Rodrigues that he maintains refers to the oblation of 1538: "Now that they had a quiet and opportune time [after the period of persecutions] the companions decided to inform the Pontiff of the life they wished to establish in God's honor and the service [*obsequium*] of the Apostolic See" [*R* 91]. Since Rodrigues then discusses the Deliberations of 1539, I am inclined to the opinion that the above sentence refers rather to the written declaration to the pope, namely the five decrees of the Formula. Whatever the case, the passage speaks of dedication that is: (1) total: a *life*, not just an *effort*, (2) service that is worship: a life in honor of God and in the service of the Apostolic See.

38. There is a blank space here and the editors suggest the possibility of *turca* or *ad turcas* [*D* 3 n. 6].

39. Father General Kolvenbach has some stirring reflections on the use and meaning of the word *discurrir* in the Constitutions (Peter-Hans Kolvenbach, S.J., "A Certain Pathway to God ['Via quaedam ad Deum']," *CIS* 22, no. 3 (1991): 29-31). Cf. José M. Rambla, S.J., "Del 'pobre peregrino Iñigo' a Ignacio 'el peregrino': De la peregrinación a la misión," *Vida religiosa* 70 (1991): 253-54.

40. This passage can be read to refer to any of three different moments: (1) Montmartre in 1534, (2) an oblation to the pope

in 1538, (3) the solemn profession of the companions in 1541. The editors of the *Monumenta* argue for Montmartre [*C* 1:cxxiii-cxxv]; García Madariaga favors 1538 ("La oblación del grupo," 29-33). Since we are concerned only with the dedication of the first companions, it makes little difference whether this passage refers to Montmartre or the oblation of 1538. For obedience to the pope as the first principle and foundation of the Society, see Burkhart Schneider, S.J., "*Nuestro principio y principal fundamento*: zum historischen Verständnis des Papstgehorsamsgelübdes," *AHSI* 25 (1956): 488-513, esp., 510-13. John W. O'Malley, S.J., discusses a more contemporary understanding of Ignatius's phrase in "How the Jesuits Changed: 1540-56," *America* 165, no. 2 (1991): 28-32.

41. Schur, 439-40, suggests this possibility.

Chapter Seven: Workers in the Vineyard

1. *Reg.* 190 (*Leg.* 14), cited by Adalbert de Vogüé, *La Règle de Saint Benoît*, vol. 1, SC 181 (Paris: Éditions du Cerf, 1972), 425 n. 49. E.T., "If one of the brothers has a grievance . . . brothers of proven life and faith [*probatae fratres conversationis et fidei*] must hear the case and bear judgement" (Armand Veilleux, O.C.S.O., trans., *Pachomian Koinonia*, vol. 2, *Pachomian Chronicles and Rules*, Cistercian Studies Series 46 [Kalamazoo, MI: 1981], p. 183, par. 14). See also *Reg.* 52 (*Praec.* 53) and *Reg.* 53 (*Praec.* 54), E.T. *ibid.*, pp. 154-55, par. 53-54.

2. G. G. Meersseman, O.P., *Dossier de l'Ordre de la Pénitence au XIIIe siècle*, Spicilegium Friburgense, vol. 7 (Fribourg: Editions universitaires, 1961), 282. "Vestri . . . moris erit, singulis diebus dominicis ad audiendum dei verbum in loco idoneo convenire, ubi aliquis vel aliqui *fratrum probate fidei* [emphasis added] et experte religionis, qui 'potentes sint in opere ac sermone' (Luc 24,19), licentia diocesani episcopi verbum exhortationis proponent [It will be your custom . . . to assemble every Sunday in a suitable place to hear the word of God, and there, one or more of the brethren of proven faith and experience in religion and powerful in deed and word, with permission of the bishop of the diocese, might propose a word of exhortation]."

3. *Supernae dispositionis arbitrio:* "Circumspectos nihilo minus ac probatae fidei viros nuntios nostros . . ." (*COD*, 586).

4. In Latin, "viris probis et fidedignis"; *Processus remissorialis Minorissensis* (1606), *Scripta de*, 2:708. Elsewhere in the same

process we find the phrases "probi viri et honeste mulieres" (709), "quamplurimis personis fide dignis" (698), "multis personis fidedignis" (704), "multis personis fidedignis," and "personis quidem uirtuosis et fidedignis" (713).

5. Douay-Rheims translation of Vulgate: 2 Cor. 13:5: "Vosmetipsos tentate, si estis in fide: ipsi vos probate." Heb. 11:39 reads: "Et hi omnes testimonio fidei probati non acceperunt repromissioncm."

6. TV, 2/1:135-36.

7. A priest of the diocese of Pistoia, he had been consecrated bishop of Bertinoro in 1537 and named governor of Rome in March 1538. See *FD* 545 n. 9 and Schur., 423 n. 123.

8. Francis Picalques, a sixty-year-old priest from Manresa, mentions all of these activities in his testimony: *Processus remissorialis Minorissensis*, in *Scripta de*, 2:706. Picalques bases his testimony on what he had heard from many other people, but especially from three women, Angela Amigant, Anna Canyelles, and Agnes Clauera (*ibid.*, 705-6). During the investigation many others corroborated that testimony.

9. *Ibid.*, 746.

10. In his study of Ignatius, for example, Dalmases mentions his works of charity for the poor and the sick but pays so much attention to his interior development that the reader may not integrate Ignatius's apostolic activity into the full image of the man (Dalmases, *Ignatius of Loyola*, 55-64). For a different perspective, see Jean Sainsaulieu, "L'ermite de Manrèse," *Christus* 39 (1992): 476-83.

11. *Dialogus II* (1562-1565), *MN* 5:661 [41]. See my own *Contemplation in Action: A Study in Ignatian Prayer* (Spokane: Gonzaga University, 1957), 23-45.

12. Olin, 152, "The Capuchin Constitutions of 1536," trans. Mark Stier, O.F.M.Cap. For the original Italian text, see *Liber Memorialis O.F.M. Capuccinorum* (1528-1928), Suppl. vol. 44 Analectorum Ordinis (Rome, 1928), 356.

13. Some months after the events of 1539 that are the subject of this book Rodrigues had an experience in prayer in which he saw "a barren vineyard running wild in a strangulation of roots and weeds, unattended, with its vines unpruned and withering away . . . an image of the state of the Church at the time" [*R* 103]. He also saw the Society as a vine (not a vineyard) "adorned with many green leaves which were very large and

delightful. From it came forth very long shoots or vine branches with beautiful and abundant clusters of grapes which had nonetheless not yet reached maturity . . . the condition of this yet recent Society" [R 103].

Chapter Eight: Planting and Tending the Vineyard

1. For further details see, for example, Hervé Martin, *Le métier de prédicateur en France septentrionale à la fin du Moyen Age (1350-1520)* (Paris: Editions du Cerf, 1988), 131-43.
2. Sanchez de Arévalo, "Sermo in dominica passionis Domini in quadragesima" (BAV cod. Vat. lat. 4881, fol. 234r): "non . . . praedicatoribus sed rapacissimis quaestoribus," cited by John O'Malley, *Praise and Blame in Renaissance Rome: Rhetoric, Doctrine, and Reform in the Sacred Orators of the Papal Court, c. 1450-1521* (Durham: Duke University Press, 1979), 226 n. 121. O'Malley's examination of the themes of the preachers at the papal court provides important insights into the felt need for reform in a Church in many ways paralysed at the top.
3. *Handbook of Church History*, ed. Hubert Jedin and John Dolan (New York: Herder and Herder, 1970), 4:575, referring in nn. 30-31 to F. W. Oediger, *Über die Bildung der Geistlichen im späten Mittelalter* (Leiden and Cologne, 1953), 115 n. 5 and 116 n. 1.
4. "Qua fronte docebit, quod et docuit et exhibuit Christus . . ." (Desiderius Erasmus, *Opera Omnia* [Amsterdam-Oxford: North-Holland Publishing Co., 1981], II-5, 184, line 517. E.T. in "Erasmus' *Sileni Alcibiadis, 1515*," trans. Margaret Mann Phillips, in Olin, 85).
5. "Episcopus ad confligendum armis ac bombardis affatim instructus est, sed idem ad docendum, ad exhortandum, ad consolandum mutus est. Armatus est iaculis ac balistis, diuinis scripturis prorsus inermis est" (Erasmus, *ibid.*, II-5, 189, lines 624-26. E.T., Olin, 88).
6. Session XI, Dec. 19, 1516, *COD*, 610-14. The pertinent part of this decree is found in E.T. in Schroeder, 505-6. Our "exemplary life" translates *vitae exemplaritate* (*COD*, 612, line 33), which Schroeder translates as "exemplariness of life" (505, par. 1).
7. In Latin, *nudos ac mendicos*. Philip Labbeus and Gabriel Cossartius, *Sacrosancta Concilia ad regiam editionem exacta* (Venice, 1728-1733), XIX, cap. 4, 1185, cited by Diego, 90 n. 9.

8. *Ibid.*, XIX, cap. 35, 1198, cited by Diego, 93 n. 22.
9. *Constitutions*, Book III, "Preaching the Divine Word," trans. James F. Brady, Jr., in Olin, 145-46.
10. In Italian, "vita et fama et della catholica opinione." Gianpietro Carafa, "Memorial to Pope Clement VII (1532)," in *Reform Thought in Sixteenth-Century Italy*, trans. Elisabeth G. Gleason (Chico: Scholars Press, 1981), 61. The original Italian phrase is found in *CT*, 12:69, line 18; the document carries a Latin title, "De Lutheranorum haeresi reprimenda et ecclesia reformanda" (*CT*, 12:67).
11. The Italian is "et nella vita et nella dottrina"; *CT*, 12:69, line 41; Gleason, *Reform Thought*, 62.
12. Olin, 172-73, "The Capuchin Constitutions of 1536," chap. 9, no. 110. The original Italian text reads: "Ne se li dia tale officio se non vederanno che siano di vita sancta et exemplare, claro et maturo iudicio, forte et ardente volunta, che la scientia et eloquentia senza charita non edifica, imo molte volte destruge" (*Liber Memorialis Ordinis*, 401). On the style of preaching and other activities the early Capuchins engaged in, see Elisabeth G. Gleason, "The Capuchins," in *Religious Orders of the Catholic Reformation*, 41-47.
13. *Consilium de emendanda ecclesia*, in *CT*, 12:140; E.T. in Olin, 193-94.
14. The letter from Ignatius is to Juan de Verdolay, July 24, 1537. For an account of those who often attended discussions and disputations at the pope's table, cf. TV, 2/1:83-84.
15. The document is signed by Cardinal Ghinucci, April 30, 1537, and is in favor of Favre, Antonio Arias, and Hozes [*MF* 7-8]. For some reason Tacchi Venturi names instead Favre, Jay, and Broët (TV, 2/1:1 85).
16. The phrase in *Acta canonizationis*, ed. A. Walz, in *Monumenta Historica Sancti Patris Nostri Dominici*, MOPH 16 (Rome, 1935), 179, is *tam verbo quam exemplo*. The idea is applied to the canons regular of the twelfth century by Bynum, *Docere Verbo et Exemplo*. She sees the regular canons as differing from monks, not by reason of particular activities, but by their "attitudes and assumptions: canons approach the religious life with a feeling of obligation to edify others" (p. 21). Innocent III uses *verbo et exemplo* in *PL* 215, 361D, but also other phrases with the same meaning, e.g., *in opere et sermone* (Lk. 24:19), *PL* 215, 359B, *verbis vel actibus*, *PL* 215, 360B, and *exemplum operis et documentum sermonis* in *PL* 215, 1025B. Lateran IV (1215) provides that where there are mixed rites and languages suitable men should teach the people *verbo*

... *et exemplo* (Canon 9), and that bishops should provide preachers everywhere who can edify people *uerbo . . . et exemplo* (Canon 10), *COD*, 215; for E.T., see Schroeder, 250-51 (canon 9), 252 (canon 10). Jacques de Vitry, who lived at the same time as Dominic and Francis, indicates that the *Humiliati* are examples of humility *in omnibus uerbis et operibus* (*Historia occidentalis* 28); and he portrays the Franciscans as converting people *praedicatione [et] exemplo* (*ibid.*, 32). Much as Francis preached, he was even more insistent upon good example: "For myself, I wish to have this privilege from the Lord that I have no privilege from man, unless it be to do reverence to all and through obedience to the holy Rule, by example more than by word [*exemplo plus quam verbo*], to convert the whole world" (*Scripta Leonis, Rufini et Angeli, sociorum S. Francisci: The Writings of Leo, Rufino and Angelo, Companions of St. Francis*, ed. Rosalind B. Brooke [Oxford: Clarendon Press, 1970], 288-89, par. 115). It was also said of Francis that he taught "more by deeds than by words [*magis operibus quam verbis*]" (*ibid.*, 236, par. 85).

17. Simon Tugwell, O.P., makes the point that preaching was one possibility for Francis while for Dominic it was essential (*Early Dominicans: Selected Writings*, ed. Simon Tugwell, O.P., CWS [New York: Paulist Press, 1982] 44 n. 92).

18. *LM* 2.1. Francis's call to repair the church is also found in *LTS* 13, and *2 Celano* 10.

19. *LM* 2.4; *LTS* 20.

20. When speaking of the missionary inspiration of either Francis or Dominic, some of the sources refer to the missionary discourse in Luke 10, which begins in much the same way. Luke's narrative is about the sending of the seventy-two disciples rather than the sending of the twelve apostles, as in Matthew 10.

21. 1 Celano 22. See also *LTS* 25 and *LM* 3.1. The date when the event took place is not absolutely clear. It is put at 1206, the same year Dominic began preaching, by Moorman, *A History*, 8, but in n. 5 the author indicates the preferences of other authors. It is placed in 1208 in *Francis and Clare*, 4, and also in Tugwell, *Early Dominicans*, 18.

22. Tugwell argues that Francis's approach to poverty and preaching is ascetical, poverty in imitation of Jesus and the apostles, and preaching as a part of that imitation as well, whereas for Dominic preaching was seen as something needed at the time, and preaching like the apostles demanded living like the apostles (*Early Dominicans*, 18-19).

23. Thomas of Spalato, *Historia pontificum Salonitanorum et Spalatinorum*, MGH, SS 29, p. 580.
24. Esser, *Origins*, 218. The manner of preaching of the early Franciscans is much disputed (*ibid.*, 257 n. 88).
25. A somewhat free translation of Jacques de Vitry's *Historia occidentalis* (c.1220), a passage of chap. 32, "De ordine et predicatione fratrum minorum."
26. Pierre Mandonnet, O.P., *Saint Dominique, l'idée, l'homme et l'oeuvre*, 2 vols. (Paris: Desclée de Brouwer & Cie., 1937), 1:119; E.T., *St. Dominic and His Work*, trans. Sister Mary Benedicta Larkin, O.P. (St. Louis: Herder, 1945), 385.
27. ". . . ceteris omissis, predicationi ardentius insudarent et, ut possent ora obstruere malignorum, in humilitate procedentes, exemplo Pii Magistri facerent et docerent, irent pedites absque auro et argento, per omnia formam apostolicam imitantes" (*Petri Vallium Sarnaii monachi Hystoria Albigensis*, ed. Pascal Guébin et Ernest Lyon, vol. 1 [Paris: Librairie de la société de l'histoire de France, 1926], 23). For a concrete description of all that was entailed, see M.-H. Vicaire, "Rencontre à Pamiers des courants vaudois et dominicain (1207)," in *Vaudois languedociens et Pauvres Catholiques*, Cahiers de Fanjeaux 2 (Toulouse: E. Privat, 1967), 163-94, especially 185-92.
28. Vicaire, *Saint Dominic*, 89-95. See also Allan White, O.P., "The Foundation of the Order of Preachers and its Historical Setting," in Tugwell, *The Way of the Preacher*, Appendix One, 97-110.
29. *COD*, 215; Schroeder, Canon 10, 252.
30. Jean Longère, *La Prédication Médiévale* (Paris: Études Augustiniennes, 1983), 83-84.
31. See Koudelka, no. 63, decree by Fulk, bishop of Toulouse: "instituimus predicatores in episcopatu nostro fratrem Dominicum et socios eius, qui, in paupertate euuangelica, pedites religiose proposuerunt incedere et veritatis euuangelice verbum predicare." Fulk was a Cistercian before his appointment as bishop. See Lekai, *Cistercians*, 56.
32. Later Ignatius will make that specific quotation from Matthew in the Constitutions, Part VI [565].
33. Vicaire, "L'Ordre," 25-26.
34. Cf. the remarks of Vicaire, in *L'imitation des apôtres*, 76-77.
35. Cf. *The Earlier Rule* [regula non bullata], 7.7-8, 9.3, and *The Testament*, 20-22, in *Francis and Clare*, 115 and 155.

36. *Apologia contra censuram, FN* 2:84 [80]. A confusion of tongues is not uncommon for those lacking genuine fluency in languages. For Ignatius, Basque was his first and native language, a tongue totally unrelated to the Romance languages. His Spanish has a sort of Basque twist to it. Leturia remarks: "But the principal key to his peculiar style lies in the Basque which explains his continual ellipses, his substantival infinitives, his incorrect use of reflexives, his strange use or omission of articles and pronouns, his hyperbaton, and almost word for word translation of some phrases" (*Iñigo*, 25. Leturia's reference is: Placido Mujica, S.J., "Reminiscencias de la lengua vasca en el 'Diario' de San Ignacio," RIEV 27 [1936]: 53-62). Ignatius spent seven years in Paris where he had to speak French and Latin, then went to Italy where he had to learn Italian. Perhaps it was even necessary to learn some Catalan while in Barcelona. He was not a linguist, but he managed to communicate successfully in a variety of tongues. In his superb study of first-generation Jesuit ministries, John W. O'Malley, S.J., describes some sixteenth-century preaching practices and customs the early companions encountered in Italy (*The First Jesuits* [Cambridge: Harvard University Press, 1993], 92-93).

37. Dr. Arze may very well have been one of those who had spoken favorably to Paul III about the companions. The quotation is from Mark 1:22, after Jesus' first sermon in Capharnaum, and in Matt. 7:29, after the Sermon on the Mount.

38. The contrast between Ignatius's contemporary but laconic report and Rodrigues's enthusiastic account as he recalled it forty years later is striking, but as usual we pick up bits of information from Rodrigues that Ignatius passes over in silence. In their original plan to present themselves to the pope, Rodrigues tells us, they had intended that they "would ask for unrestricted faculties to preach [*liberam ubique terrarum ad concionandum . . . facultatem*], hear confessions, and celebrate the Eucharist anywhere in the world" [*R* 14]. Whether or not this is what they intended to ask for, this is what they received. They also wanted to communicate to the pope that they were ready "to proclaim the Gospel of Christ throughout the whole world [*ad annuntiandum Christi evangelium . . . per totum terrarum orbem*" [*R* 14]. If this is what they asked, they were certainly heard and understood.

39. Some evidence suggests that Gianpietro Carafa influenced his cousin Vincenzo to grant the faculties. See chap. 2, n. 10. Although Gianpietro and Ignatius did not agree on everything, he was profoundly impressed by the companions' lives, their

talents, and their qualifications. Recall in contrast the vigorous attack Gianpietro made on the granting of faculties to those who were not well qualified.

40. Gérard Gilles Meersseman, "Eremitismo e predicazione itinerante dei secoli XI e XII," in *L'Eremitismo in Occidente nei Secoli XI e XII* (Milan: Vita e Pensiero, 1965), 164-79; Renard, *Formation*, 41-44; Mandonnet, *St. Dominic*, 140-44. For examples of preaching privileges in an earlier age (6th - 9th centuries), see Shuhler, *Privileges*, 6.

41. Meersseman, "Eremitismo," 171.

42. Whether the *license to preach* for Wedericus extended *everywhere* is not immediately clear, for he limited himself to the provinces of Flanders and Brabant: "qui *apostolicae auctoritatis licentia* Flandriam et Brabantia provincias circuibat" (Meersseman, "Eremitismo," 172; Renard, *Formation*, 42). Both cite *Chronicon Affligemense* in *MGH, SS* 9.

43. The Latin is "licentiam praedicandi ubique poenitentiam." *LTS* 51. Cf. *LM* 3.10. That Francis missioned the other friars is narrated *ibid.*, 59. Cf. Jacques de Vitry's comment: "The Lord pope confirmed their rule and authorized them to preach in whatever churches they came to, after first obtaining permission from the local prelate out of courtesy" (trans. from *Historia occidentalis* 32).

44. Vicaire, "Sacerdoce et prédication," 246-49; Renard, *Formation*, 44-47. Vicaire's analysis of Dominic's understanding of the Gospel ideal described in Matt. 10 and Luke 10 reveals the life purpose of Dominic and his companions (and that of Ignatius and his companions three hundred years later): (1) a personal mission (a call and a mandate): each has been called, each has been sent; (2) a ministry [*officium*], flowing from the mandate: the preaching of the good news of the kingdom; (3) total poverty; (4) the necessity to travel [*itinérance*—a stronger word in French than *mobility* in English]; and (5) common life: going two by two (Vicaire, *The Apostolic Life*, 98-102).

45. Schur., 421, supposes that they began to preach on May 5, which would have been the first Sunday after the faculties were granted, and that may well be true, for they certainly were eager.

46. That is how far the pendulum had swung. What had begun more or less as a prerogative of the bishop and extended gradually to the diocesan priests who were an extension of his presence had gradually been taken over by the religious orders. (For the history of preaching, see Longère, *Prédication*, for the relation between priesthood and preaching, see Renard, *Formation*, 37-

41.) In Jerome's day he would say, "The monk's job is not teaching but weeping [*Monachus autem non doctoris habet, sed plangentis officium*]" (*Contra Vigilantium*, 15; *PL* 23, 367A). But later, especially with the coming of the mendicants, the monks and friars became the preachers. (On the relation between priesthood and preaching in the Order of Preachers, see Vicaire, "Sacerdoce et prédication," 241-54.) The monasteries were, after all, the centers of learning at that time, and with their emphasis on preaching the mendicants had insisted on a better education than that normally provided for the diocesan clergy.

47. More than a year before ordination Ignatius wrote a letter to Jaime Cazador, archdeacon of Barcelona, from Venice, February 12, 1536: "I share the desire you manifest to see me there and preaching in public; not that I desire within me the glory of doing what others cannot do, or of attaining what others cannot achieve; but more to preach, as a less important person, on things that are less weighty and more easily understood" [*EI* 95].

48. Étienne Delaruelle, "Les ermites et la spiritualité populaire," in *L'Eremitismo in Occidente*, 216-17.

49. See Meersseman, *Dossier*, who provides an appendix, 276-89, containing the *propositum* of the *Humiliati* (1201), that of the Poor Catholics (1208) and of the penitents they directed (1212), and the first and second *proposita* of the Poor Lombards (1210, 1212). The language of exhortation is found in each of them. See also Chenu, *Nature, Man, and Society*, 260-61; Renard, *Formation*, 53-55; Bolton, *Medieval Reformation*, 97-99. The document referenced here generally (with the one exception of the salutation) uses masculine terms; if these terms should be translated as gender-inclusive—i.e., if women could preach the *verbum exhortationis*—is an intriguing question that cannot be answered on the basis of this document.

50. Anonymous, *Vita sancti Guidonis* (*Acta sanctorum*, September, IV, 42). Chenu has some amusing quotations that fill out the picture of that time: "A merchant is rarely or never able to please God" (*Decretum* 1.88.11); "What hope have merchants got? Not much, for they acquire almost all they have by fraud, lying, and greed" (Honorius of Autun, *Elucidarium* 2.18, "De variis laicorum statibus"). All cited by Chenu, *Nature, Man, and Society*, 224 n. 45. The waning years of the twentieth century are witnessing a renewal of the debate whether business and ethics are compatible.

51. Jacques Le Goff, *Your Money or Your Life: Economy and Religion in the Middle Ages* (New York: Zone Books, 1988), 54-56.

52. Bolton comments: "Deviants of all kinds struck a note of simplicity beside the opulence of the hierarchical and elitist prelates" ("Tradition and Temerity," 81).

53. For the situation in the monasteries, see Bernard Bligny, "Monachisme et pauvreté au XIIe siècle," in *La povertà del secolo XII e Francesco d'Assisi: Assisi, 17-19 ottobre 1974* (Assisi: Atti del II Convegno Internationale, 1975), 99-147.

54. The poverty of the *Humiliati* seems to have been relative to the position of each member in society. See Brenda M. Bolton, "The Poverty of the *Humiliati*," in *Poverty in the Middle Ages*, ed. David Flood, Franziskanische Forschungen 27 (Werl: Dietrich-Coelde, 1975), 52-59.

55. Bolton, "Tradition and Temerity," 85; "Innocent III's Treatment of the *Humiliati*," in *Popular Belief and Practice*, ed. G. J. Cuming and Derek Baker, SCH 8 (Cambridge: University Press, 1972), 75 n. 4. See her *Medieval Reformation*, especially chap. 3 on lay religious movements, 55-66, and chap. 6 on the reaction of Church and papacy, 94-111.

56. See Thouzellier re the Waldensians, "Hérésie et pauvreté," 371-88. For the apostolic life [*vita apostolica*] as a reaction to the religious crisis of the twelfth century, see Bolton, *Medieval Reformation*, 19-21. For meaning of *vita apostolica*, cf. chap. 2, n. 25.

57. In Latin, "nisi rogantibus sacerdotibus"; Bolton, "Tradition and Temerity," 84-85; for the Latin phrase Bolton refers in n. 4 to *Chronicon Universale Anonymi Laudunensis*, p. 29 (ed. A. Cartellieri & W. Stechèle, Paris 1909). It is also to be found in *MGH, SS* 26, 449. The *Chronicon* covers events from 1066 to 1219. Among other events of history it includes a synopsis of the Waldensian story. The Latin phrase, however, has a longer history, and appears in a document that comes from southern Gaul and dates back to the second half of the fifth century: "A layman should not presume to teach in the presence of clerics unless they approve of it [*Laicus, praesentibus clericis, nisi ipsis probantibus, docere non audeat*]," which suggests that what the law forbade had been going on (*Statuta ecclesiae antiqua*, canon 38, in *Concilia Galliae (A. 314 - A. 506)*, ed. C. Munier, CCL 148 [Turnhout: Brepols, 1963], 172, where variant readings for *probantibus* are noted: *rogantibus, prouocantibus*). As Schillebeeckx points out, "Origen and Jerome had already said that earlier" (*Church*, 188). Law, however, does not necessarily eliminate practice. That women were accepted as preachers and teachers at the very beginnings of the Christian missionary movement

(as portrayed in New Testament writings and contemporary apocalyptic literature) is shown by Elisabeth Schüssler Fiorenza, *In Memory of Her: A Feminist Theological Reconstruction of Christian Origins* (New York: Crossroad, 1984), 169-74, 183-84, 334.

58. See Meersseman, *Dossier*, 282-89; Chenu, *Nature, Man, and Society*, 260-61; Bolton, *Medieval Reformation*, 57-60, 98-99. A good treatment of this whole subject is found in Renard, *Formation*, 49-57, 183-90.

59. Bull of Innocent III, entitled *Incumbit nobis*, quoted in Latin by Meersseman, *Dossier*, 282. See Bolton, "Innocent III's Treatment of the *Humiliati*," 73-82, but especially 77, and by the same author, *Medieval Reformation*, 63-66. See also *Historia occidentalis* 28, "De religione et regula humiliatorum."

60. See n. 16 above.

61. Thouzellier describes Waldo as *non missus* [not sent] ("Hérésie et pauvreté," 379).

62. In Latin, "apostolicae sedi in omnibus obedientes"; the phrase is found in the *Chronicon Urspergense*, attributed to the Premonstratensian, Burchard of Ursperg (+1230), under the year 1212 (*MGH, SS* 23, 376). Burchard was an eyewitness of the Franciscan movement from the beginning, and his testimony is singularly valuable (Esser, *Origins*, 8). Cf. Marthaler, "Forerunners," 138-40.

63. Testimony of a seventy-two year old widow, Domenja de Vgarte, sixty-nine year old Françisco de Çuola, and María de Vlaçia, seventy-five year old widow of Miguel de Ybarguen, in *Processus Azpeitianus, Scripta de*, 2:184, 208, 217.

64. *Processus remissorialis Minorissensis (1606), Scripta de*, 2:746, testimony of an eyewitness, ninety-six year old Margarita Capdepós, widow.

65. James Dallen, *The Reconciling Community: The Rite of Penance* (New York: Pueblo Publishing Co., 1986), 156-57. The entire section, "Penance on the Eve of the Reformation," 156-62, plus accompanying footnotes, 165-67, is pertinent here. Cf. O'Malley, *First Jesuits*, 136. For an overview of the general historical evolution of confessional privileges among religious from their origins to the Council of Trent, see Shuler, *Privileges*, 1-23; for a good understanding of the development of parochial rights during that same period insofar as the sacrament of penance is concerned, see Kelly, *Functions Reserved*, 11-15.

66. Dallen, *Reconciling Community*, 157-62. "In many respects, the bewildering maze of distinctions, circumstances, jurisdiction, reservation, and casuistry made the system a mass of legalism

and ritualism, but the system also focused on the conscience of the individual and the individual's realization of guilt, desire for forgiveness, and purpose of amendment" (160).

67. *Memoriale. CT*, 12:69; Gleason, *Reform Thought*, 62.
68. "The Theatine Rule of 1526," trans. John Olin, in Olin, 131.
69. Canon 21 of Lateran IV (1215) had required that the faithful confess their sins at least once a year and receive the Eucharist at least at Easter (*COD*, 221; Schroeder, 259-63).
70. *Memoriale. CT*, 12:69-70; Gleason, *Reform Thought*, 63.
71. Olin, 168, "The Capuchin Constitutions of 1536," chap. 7, no. 90. For original Italian, see *Liber Memorialis*, 391-92.
72. Shuler, *Privileges*, 9-22, 70-75.
73. "They refreshed themselves daily with the sacrament of confession and communion" [*PV* 84]. Cf. O'Malley, *First Jesuits*, 137-39. The Constitutions of the Capuchins prescribe that the friars themselves are to confess at least twice a week and receive Holy Communion every fortnight or oftener, every Sunday during Advent and Lent ("Capuchin Constitutions," in Olin, 168-69).
74. *Devotio Moderna: Basic Writings*, trans. John Van Engen, CWS (New York: Paulist Press, 1988), 50. See also 29-30.
75. M. Smits Van Waesberghe, S.J., "Origine et développement des exercices spirituels avant Saint Ignace," *RAM* 33 (1957): 264-72. The author begins with St. Benedict (+547) and works his way through the Cistercians, St. Gertrude, the Franciscans, and the *devotio moderna* to the Benedictine Garcia Ximenes de Cisneros (+1510). A good discussion of the possible influence of Cisneros is found in Arturo Codina, S.J., 'Los 'Ejercicios' de san Ignacio y el 'Ejercitatorio' de Cisneros," *Razon y fe* 48 (1917): 286-99, 426-36; 49 (1917) 16-29; Terence W. O'Reilly, "The Exercises of Saint Ignatius Loyola and the Exercitatorio de la vida spiritual," *Studia Monastica* 16 (1974): 301-23; Manuel Ruiz Jurado, S.J., "¿Influyó en S. Ignacio el Ejercitatorio de Cisneros?" *Manresa* 51 (1979): 65-75. Leturia touches on the same subject in *Iñigo de Loyola*, 150-53, and in a brief section of "Génesis de los ejercicios de San Ignacio y su influjo en la fundación de la Compañía de Jesús (1521-1540)," in *Estudios Ignacianos*, 2:10-13. Gertrude's work and that of Ignatius share at least the same title: Gertrud the Great of Helfta, *Spiritual Exercises* (Kalamazoo: Cistercian Publications, 1989).
76. Cf. Mark Rotsaert, S.J., "L'originalité des Exercices Spirituels d'Ignace de Loyola sur l'arrière-fond des renouveaux spirituels en Castille au début du seizième siècle," in *Ignacio de Loyola y su*

tiempo, 329-41. Heinrich Bacht, S.J., "Early Monastic Elements in Ignatian Spirituality: Toward Clarifying Some Fundamental Concepts of the Exercises," in *Ignatius of Loyola, His Personality and Spiritual Heritage, 1556-1956*, (St. Louis: Institute of Jesuit Sources, 1977), 200-36; Hugo Rahner, S.J., "The Discernment of Spirits," chap. 4 in *Ignatius the Theologian* (New York: Herder and Herder, 1968), 136-80; Joseph T. Lienhard, S.J., "On 'Discernment of Spirits' in the Early Church," *Theological Studies* 41 (1980) 505-29. Pope Leo the Great refers to "the forty days' exercise [*quadraginta . . . dierum exercitatio*]" of Lent (De quadragesima sermo IV, SC 49, 44).

77. *Processus remissorialis Minorissensis, Scripta de*, 2:709, testimony from the hearings for Ignatius's canonization that took place at Manresa, September 4–18, 1606.

78. See notes 8-11 supplied by the editors, *FN* 1:170-71. Polanco does not clearly distinguish where Ignatius found his companions, but the editors do.

79. Ignacio Iparraguirre, S.J., *Historia de los Ejercicios espirituales de San Ignacio*, vol. 1, *Práctica de los Ejercicios de San Ignacio de Loyola en vida de su autor* (Bilbao, 1946), 1.

80. *FN* 1:179 n. 47.

81. *FN* 1:33 n. 15. Dr. Ortiz may have had some responsibility regarding these two, for he became incensed at Ignatius because of the changes he saw in them [*PSH* 68].

82. Iparraguirre, *Práctica*, 1:2; *FN* 1:181 n. 55.

83. It is also from this passage that we learn the name of Estevan.

84. Iparraguirre, *Práctica*, 1:290 *1053.

85. *Dialogi pro Societate contra haereticos*, (1563) *FN* 2:257 [21].

Chapter Nine: Tending the Weakest Vines

1. E. Nasalli-Rocca, "Hospitals," *NCE*, 7:159a-60b. On hospitality in the monastic tradition, see among others: Adalbert de Vogüé, "The Meaning of Benedictine Hospitality," *Cistercian Studies* 21 (1986): 186-94; Terrence Kardong, "To Receive All as Christ," *Cistercian Studies* 19 (1984): 195-207; Michel Mollat, "Les moines et les pauvres (XIe-XIIe siècles)," in *Il monachesimo e la riforma ecclesiastica (1049-1122)* (Milan: Vita e pensiero, 1971), 193-215. For the 13th century, see Mollat, "Hospitalité et assistance," 37-51.

2. *FN* 1:490 n. 1.

3. Schur., 308; reference: Cassiano da Langasco, O.F.M.Cap., *Gli Ospedali degli Incurabili* (Genova, 1938), 46-48, 55-57.

4. Good sources include, "Peregrinatio," *DIP*, 6 (1980): 1424-36; "Pèlerinages," *DSAM*, 12/1 (1984): 888-940; Jean Leclercq, "Monachisme et pérégrination," in *Aux sources de la spiritualité occidentale* (Paris: Editions du Cerf, 1964), 35-90; Jonathan Sumption, *Pilgrimage: An Image of Mediaeval Religion* (London: Faber & Faber, 1975), 391pp.; Thomas Merton, "From Pilgrimage to Crusade," in *Mystics & Zen Masters* (New York: Dell, 1967), 91-112; Giles Constable, "Monachisme et pèlerinage au Moyen Âge," *Revue Historique* 101 (1977): 3-27; García M. Colombás, O.S.B., *El monacato primitivo*, vol. 2, *La espiritualidad*, BAC 376 (Madrid, 1975), 129-33; Marie-Humbert Vicaire, "Les trois itinérances du pèlerinage aux XIIIe et XIVe siècles," in *Le Pèlerinage*, Cahiers de Fanjeaux 15 - Collection d'Histoire religieuse du Languedoc au XIIIe et au début du XIVe siècles (Toulouse: E. Privat, 1980), 17-41.

5. Leclercq points out that the French and German languages generally use two different words, *pèlerinage* and *Wallfahrt* respectively for visiting shrines, and *pérégrination* and *Pilgerfahrt* for going into exile ("Monachisme et pérégrination," 42). They also use the latter words for the third meaning.

6. After his enlightenment at Bodh Gaya, the Buddha went about preaching in various places, like the Deer Park in Benares. See Paul Rietsch, "Pèlerinages bouddhistes," *DSAM*, 12:893.

7. Vicaire, "Trois itinérances," 18-19.

8. Antoine Guillaumont, "Le dépaysement comme forme d'ascèse dans le monachisme," in *Aux origines du monachisme chrétien* (Bégrolles en Mauge, Maine & Loire: Abbaye de Bellefontaine, 1979), 90. Guillaumont notes that a number of monastic terms seem to have a military origin.

9. Alfred Ernout et Antoine Meillet, *Dictionnaire étymologique de la langue Latine* (Paris: Klincksieck, 1959), 402-3.

10. See among many others, Merton, "Pilgrimage to Crusade," 92-94. The paradigm for pilgrim stories is that of Egeria in the early fifth century. For a translation, see G. Gingras, *Egeria: Diary of a Pilgrimage* (New York: Newman Press, 1970). For an analysis, see George E. Saint-Laurent, "The Pilgrimage of Egeria," *Word and Spirit* 6 (1984): 24-40.

11. See Sumption, *Pilgrimage*, on the penitential pilgrimage, 98-113. He describes the journey itself, 168-210.

12. *Historia Hierosolymitana*, LXXXII, pp. 1096-7 (cited by Sumption, *Pilgrimage*, 112).
13. Cf. Sumption, *Pilgrimage*, 168-210 *passim*, where the author describes the pilgrimage journey of the Middle Ages; also, Merton, "Pilgrimage," 98-99, although Merton limits his remarks to pilgrimages performed as a canonical penance.
14. Henri Gilles, "Lex peregrinorum," in *Le Pèlerinage*, 161-89.
15. The Greek for *strangers and exiles* is *xenoi kai parepidēmoi*; the Latin Vulgate has *peregrini et hospites*; the Douay-Rheims version reads *pilgrims and strangers*. The two words seem somewhat interchangeable.
16. *Paroikos kai parepidēmos*. We now have three Greek words meaning more or less the same thing: *xenos, paroikos,* and *parepidēmos*. We shall see more of *xenos* in the text; it survives in English in such words as *xenophobia*, fear of strangers. *Parish* and *parochial* are drawn from *paroikos*. Clement of Rome wrote a letter "from the Church of God which sojourns [*paroikousa*] in Rome to the Church of God which sojourns [*paroikousei*] in Corinth," that is, from those who were strangers or exiles in Rome to those who were strangers or exiles in Corinth (Clément de Rome, *Epître aux Corinthiens*, SC 167 [Paris: Editions du Cerf, 1971], E.T. by Robert M. Grant and Holt H. Graham, *The Apostolic Fathers* [New York: Thomas Nelson & Sons, 1965], 15.) The word came to be used to designate a territorial entity, first the diocese and then the local church, or even a political district, but that fact takes away nothing from the alien condition of those who reside there. *Parepidēmos* did not make its way into the English language.
17. Guillaumont, "Perspectives actuelles sur les origines du monachisme," in *Aux origines*, 224. For a longer treatment of *xeniteia*, see Guillaumont's article, "Le dépaysement," *ibid.*, 89-116, and Colombás, *Monacato primitivo*, 2:129-33.
18. Guillaumont, "Dépaysement," 102; see also Leclercq, "Monachisme et pérégrination," 51.
19. Guillaumont, "Perspectives actuelles," 218. See also Mark Sheridan, O.S.B., "Monastic Terminology," in *RB 80*, Appendix 1, 305-11.
20. Guillaumont, "Le dépaysement," 104.
21. In Latin, "stabilitas in peregrinatione"; cf. Leclercq, "Monachisme et pérégrination," a section on "Pérégrination et solitude," 44-52.
22. Leclercq, *ibid.*, a section on "Pérégrination et prédication," 53-64.

23. After Arab armies conquered Jerusalem in 638, the city remained for the most part closed to the West until the eleventh century; this fact no doubt affected the significance of Jerusalem as symbol. (See Thomas Renna, "The Idea of Jerusalem: Monastic to Scholastic," in *From Cloister to Classroom: Monastic and Scholastic Approaches to Truth* [Kalamazoo: Cistercian Publications, 1986], 96-109, especially 106.) On this same theme of going on pilgrimage to Jerusalem, see also Jean Leclercq, *The Love of Learning and the Desire for God: A Study of Monastic Culture* (New York: Fordham University Press, 1961), 58-61. St. Jerome had already said enigmatically: "What is to be praised is not having been to Jerusalem, but having lived well in Jerusalem [*Non Hierosolymis fuisse, sed Hierosolymis bene uixisse laudandum est*]" (*Ep.* 58.2, CSEL 54, 529). Bernard of Clairvaux interprets Jerome: "The purpose of monks is to search, not for the earthly Jerusalem, but the celestial one, and that not by advancing with their feet but by making progress with their heart" (*Ep.* 399, Leclercq/Rochais, eds., *Sancti Bernardi Opera*, 8:379-80). A contemporary Coptic hermit, Abûnâ Mattâ al-Maskîn, when asked about pilgrimages to holy places, replied: "Jerusalem the Holy is right here, in and around these caves, for what else is my cave, but the place where my Savior Christ was born, what else is my cave, but the place where my Savior Christ was taken to rest, what else is my cave, but the place from where he most gloriously rose again from the dead. Jerusalem is here, right here, and all the spiritual riches of the Holy City are found in this wâdî" (Otto Meinardus, "The hermits of Wâdî Rayân," *Studia Orientalia Christiana, Collectanea*, 11 [Cairo, 1966], 308.

24. In Latin, "peregrinatio in stabilitate"; Leclercq, "Monachisme et pérégrination," 86-87.

25. For this brief section I have drawn freely on Vicaire, "Trois itinérances."

26. Ched Myers, *Binding the Strong Man: A Political Reading of Mark's Story of Jesus* (Maryknoll, N.Y.: Orbis Books, 1988), 213.

27. See n. 42 of the preceding chapter.

28. *Bull. Franc.*, vol. 1, no. 2. "Stopping place" translates *mansio*, a day's journey. For a treatment of the itinerant preaching of Francis and his companions comparable to Vicaire's sketch of the preaching of St. Dominic, see Esser, *Origins*, 54-58, 217-28, plus notes on 111-13, 257-61. Esser comments that the author of the *Vita Aegidii* (chaps. 3-5) describes the wanderings of Blessed Giles as real preaching journeys, but then the author

"transforms these preaching journeys into pilgrimages, since this seems to him to be more in keeping with the idea of the life of a saint" (57-58). What Esser really objects to is transforming the preaching journeys into visits to holy places: St. James of Compostella, the shrines of St. Michael on Monte Gargano and St. Nicholas at Bari, the Holy Land. (See *Vita beati fratris Egidii* [*The Life of Blessed Brother Giles*], chaps. 3-6, in *Scripta Leonis*, 322-26.) The journeys of itinerant preachers had been called *pilgrimages* for a long time before Francis and Dominic came on the scene. Cf. Delaruelle, "Les ermites," 224-25. Like Abraham, Bro. Giles abandoned all things and went into exile, and this for the sake of preaching the Gospel.

29. Esser, *Origins*, 55. "Our conclusion is that, in the first decades of the Order's existence, the Friars Minor, as true religious and yet free from all ties of monastic stability, went through the world on apostolic journeyings and that in such a 'life according to the Gospel' (Lk. 9 and 10) they followed the example of Christ and his Apostles" (*ibid.*, 58).

30. Cf. John C. Olin, "The Idea of Pilgrimage in the Experience of Ignatius Loyola," *Church History* 48 (1979): 387-97. Olin is also interested in whether and to what extent the Society of Jesus reflects or embodies the idea of pilgrimage.

31. At Montmartre they vowed to go to Jerusalem, but they also vowed poverty and chastity. At the ordinations in Venice they again vowed poverty and chastity [*PSH* 70; *PSI* 10; *A* 93; *R* 60]. See also Iturrioz, "El peregrino," 21-43.

32. In 1524 Ignatius signed the first of his many extant letters, "The poor pilgrim [*El pobre peregrino*]" [*EI* 73]. Cf. Rambla, "Pobre peregrino," 244-57. See also Michel Mollat du Jourdin, "Saint Ignace et les pèlerinages de son temps," in *Ignacio de Loyola y su tiempo*, 161-78; and especially Father General Kolvenbach's reflections on "pilgrim," "pilgrimage," and "mission" in "A Certain Pathway to God," 31-44.

33. Commenting on this passage from Laynez, Jean Leclercq points out that according to the Rule of Benedict the monk "will not have even his own body at his disposal" [*RB* 58.25]. Leclercq sees Ignatius's departure as "flight", after the manner of Abraham and others who went into voluntary exile. He continues: "Those fugitives for God had left their home, sometimes their monastery, in order to lead, far from home, far from all the facilities to which they were accustomed, an existence entirely devoted to more intense prayer and more austere

mortification. The phrase 'to enter upon the life of penitence', applies exactly to all those exiles for Christ. *Peregrinari pro Christo* meant to become a voluntary penitent" ("Saint Ignatius at Montserrat," in *Aspects of Monasticism* [Kalamazoo: Cistercian Publications, 1978), 297-98; article first published in *Christus* 13 [1966] 161-73).

34. See Gregory of Nyssa's comment on Abraham: "Because he did not know whither he went . . . he knew he was going right, for then he was certain that he was not being led by the light of his own mind, but by the will of God" (*Contra Eunomium* 22; *PG* 44, 940, B.D., cited by Jean Daniélou, *Advent*, trans. Rosemary Sheed [New York: Sheed & Ward, 1951], 26-27.)

35. In Italian, "preti peregrini"; ARSI, *Epp. Ext. 23*, fol.2v.

36. "Preti peligrini." *EX* with volume and page number refers to two volumes entitled, *Epistolae S. Francisci Xaverii aliaque eius scripta*, MHSI (Rome, 1944-45).

37. See above, n. 29, what Esser says about the Franciscans. In 1554 Nadal said: "Note the kinds of houses and dwellings in the Society. There is the house of probation, the college, the professed house, and pilgrimage, and by this last the whole world becomes our dwelling" (*Exhort. 1554 in Hispania, MN* 5:54 [38]). In another passage, after saying the same thing in more detail, Nadal writes: "They see that they could not build or obtain so many houses as to be able to carry on the fight from close at hand. And so they regard as the quietest and most pleasant habitation always to be on pilgrimage, wandering over the whole earth, having no proper dwelling anywhere, always poor, always beggars, as long as in some way at least they strive to imitate Christ Jesus, who had no place to lay his head [Matt. 8:20; Luke 9:58] and spent the whole time of his preaching in wandering about [pilgrimaging]" (*Dialogus II, MN* 5:774 [188]). John W. O'Malley, S.J., brings out the significance of these passages (and others) for the life of the Society in his provocative article, "To Travel to Any Part of the World: Jerónimo Nadal and the Jesuit Vocation," *Studies in the Spirituality of Jesuits* 16 (March, 1984): 1-20. Cf. the final paragraph of Jean Leclercq's article on Ignatius at Montserrat: "Thus there are two very different forms of life based on solitude and asceticism. Both lead alike to the singular love of God and man. The hermit takes one, the Jesuit takes another" ("Ignatius," 307).

38. Cf. Rambla, "Pobre peregrino," 253-55; Kolvenbach, "A Certain Pathway to God," 42-44; José Rambla, S.J., "Del 'peregrino' a la 'minima' Compañía de Jesús," *Manresa* 54 (1982): 5-23. Rambla

suggests three fundamental characteristics of the pilgrim lifestyle: (1) renouncing worldly goods and embracing poverty, (2) abhorring what the world loves and embraces, (3) total confidence in God. Like Olin, "The Idea of Pilgrimage," he is interested in the way the pilgrim lifestyle affects the whole Society of Jesus. That the early Jesuits *did* travel is amply verified in an article by Mario Scaduto, S.J., "La strada e i primi Gesuiti," *AHSI* 40 (1971): 323-90.

39. Antonio M. de Aldama, "Peculiarem curam circa puerorum eruditionem," *Recherches Ignatiennes* 4, no. 5 (1977): 5. An E.T. of Augustine's text can be found in *St. Augustine: The First Catechetical Instruction [De Catechizandis Rudibus]*, trans. Joseph P. Christopher, ACW 2 (Westminster, MD: Newman Press, 1962). A critical edition of the Latin text can be found in *Aurelii Augustini Opera*, pt. 13, 2, CCL 46 (Turnhout: Brepols, 1969), 115-78.

40. *OLD*, 1665a-c.

41. John Boswell, *The Kindness of Strangers: The Abandonment of Children in Western Europe from Late Antiquity to the Renaissance* (New York: Pantheon Books, 1988). The author discusses on 22-39 the ambiguities in the term, *pueri* [children], which can include children, slaves, servants, and the objects of romantic desires. All but the last share an absence of power.

42. Cf. TV, 1/1:323, 329.

43. *Supernae maiestatis*, bull of Leo X, December 19, 1516, *COD*, 611, 18-28; 612, 17-20.

44. Gian Pietro Giussano, *Istoria della vita, virtu, morte e miracoli di Carlo Borromeo* (Milan, 1610), 50, cited by TV, 1/1:322. (E.T. of passage my own. Book trans. into English with pref. by H. E. Manning, 2 vols. [London, 1884]).

45. Session IX, 1514. Reform bull, *Supernae dispositionis arbitrio* (*COD*, 597; E.T., Olin, 62).

46. The work of the early Jesuits in Rome provided the stimulus to the catechetical movement that produced schools of Christian Doctrine [*Dottrina Cristiana*] twenty years later. Cf. Gerardo Franza, S.S.P., *Il catechismo a Roma dal Concilio di Trento a Pio VI nello zelo dell' Arciconfraternità della Dottrina Cristiana* (Rome: PUG, 1958), 44-48. See also, TV, 1/1:335-69, a chapter on the catechism in the 1500's. For Germany, see Ottone Braunsberger, S.J., *Entstehung und erste Entwicklung der Katechismen des sel. Petrus Canisius* (Freiburg i. B., 1893), 8, cited by TV, 1/1:337 n. 2. Luther, too, was concerned about teaching and preaching. His small and large catechism were published in 1529. See Jos.

E. Vercruysse, "Luther as Reformer within Christendom," *Studia Missionalia* 34 (1985), 363-64. See also André Ravier, S.J., *Ignatius of Loyola and the Founding of the Society of Jesus* (San Francisco: Ignatius Press, 1987), 50-53; Medard Kehl, S.J., "Seelsorge für 'Kinder und einfache Menschen'," in *Ignatianisch, Eigenart und Methode der Gesellschaft Jesu*, ed. M. Sievernich, S.J. and G. Switek, S.J. (Freiburg: Herder, 1990), 557-68; O'Malley, *First Jesuits*, 116-17.

47. Later they institutionalized some of these works. In 1541 Ignatius brought about the establishment of an orphanage for boys and girls. The boys are still cared for by the Somaschi Fathers, but the orphanage for girls moved to another part of town (*FN* 1:126 n. 34). 1543 saw the establishment of the House of Martha for prostitutes (*FN* 1:198 n. 5) and two houses for Jewish catechumens (*FN* 1:126 n. 35). The house for girls in danger of prostitution was established in 1546 (*FN* 1:198 n. 3). For a description of the House of Martha, see Charles Chauvin, "La maison Sainte-Marthe: Ignace et les prostituées de Rome," *Christus* 38 (1991): 117-26. For a possible connection between the problem of abandoned children and the establishment of the house for fallen women and another for young girls in danger of falling, see Boswell, *Kindness of Strangers*, 3-4.

48. Testimony given at the hearings in Manresa prior to the canonization of Ignatius: *Processus remissorialis Minorissensis*, 4-18 Septembris, 1606, in *Scripta de*, 2:746. For abundant second-generation corroboration of the elderly woman's testimony, see pp. 706, 708, 711, 717, 723, 730, 733, 738, 744. In an excellent article on Ignatius and catechism André Ravier states that regarding catechism classes for the children of Manresa and Barcelona we have nothing more than oral traditions "which can scarcely be vouched for" (André Ravier, S.J., "St. Ignatius and the Catechism," *CIS* 18, no. 2 [1987]:84). His statement is not entirely gratuitous, for much, but not all, of the testimony is hearsay. That this testimony should be rejected out of hand as merely uncorroborated hearsay, however, does seem somewhat gratuitous for three reasons: (1) many of the oral traditions confirm, and none of them contradict, what Ignatius himself tells us in his autobiography, so that it seems reasonable to accept as fact even what he does not tell us himself; (2) at least one of those who testified in Manresa is not in the "oral tradition" but is an eyewitness, and there is no reason to doubt her youthful memories, nor is there any contradiction between her testimony and that of the other witnesses; (3) the theme of teaching Christian doctrine recurs consistently in the

witnesses' testimony and without contradiction and confusion, so that it seems worthy of belief.

49. Most of these details are in Ignatius's own account [*A* 87-88]; the rest are supplied by Polanco [*PV* 74], [*PSH* 58].

50. For the story of Ignatius as catechist up to 1539, see Cecilio Gómez Rodeles, S.J., *La Compañía de Jesús catequista: legislación, doctrineros, centros catequísticas* (Madrid: Horno, 1913), 3-12. See also André Ravier, S.J., "Saint Ignace enseignait le catéchisme...," *Lumen vitae* 45 (1990): 165-72.

51. For Rome, see also *PCh* 4, *PSH* 80, *PSI* 12. Xavier's experience teaching Christian doctrine in Rome and elsewhere bore much fruit in India. He established a school in Goa in 1542, and Ignatius adapted the idea to Europe, the first small step toward the apostolate of Jesuit education. Cf. Allan P. Farrell, S.J., *The Jesuit Code of Liberal Education* (Milwaukee: Bruce, 1938), 16.

52. See also *PV* 100. Cf. Dieter B. Scholz, S.J., "Für die Armen und Flüchtenden da sein: Praktische Nächstenliebe in Rom (1538)," in *Ignatius von Loyola*, 175-76, who masterfully brings out the implications for today, 176-84.

53. Of a later period in Ethiopia: "They taught Christian *life* and doctrine" [*PSI* 34]. [Emphasis added.]

54. Polanco indicates that several schoolmasters brought their students to the companions for the purpose of learning Christian doctrine, whether before or after the governor's decree, he does not say [*PSH* 80, *PV* 98].

55. With that as guide we can conclude that Ignatius and his companions taught far more than that minimum. Further evidence of what they taught comes from a later date and concerns a later date, so that it does not seem pertinent to introduce it here. Aldama, "Peculiarem curam," 5, refers to some norms *De mostrar muchahos* [On teaching children] set down by Ignatius [*C* 43-45] and on p. 7 to an instruction entitled *Para instruir mochachos y otras personas rudes por diversos modos* [On various ways of teaching children and other uninitiated persons] in *Mon. Paed.* Ia ed. 648-49. For a summary in Italian of Ignatius's method of teaching, see *De doctrina Christiana* [On Christian doctrine], [*EI* 12:666-73]. A Spanish translation has been published by M. A. Fiorito, S.J., and J. L. Lazzarini, S.J., "Una predicación sobre la doctrina cristiana por san Ignacio de Loyola," *Boletín de espiritualidad* 36 (1974): 9-23. The precise content, however, of the Christian doctrine they taught as their system of teaching developed over the years requires further study.

56. Ignatius did not write these norms explicitly into the Constitutions, but he inserted into the vow formula special concern for teaching children. He states that this work is particularly recommended for the singular service it renders God and because of the danger of forgetting and discarding it for more conspicuous works [Part V, c.3 B {528}]. Cf. Ravier, "Saint Ignace enseignait," 168-69.

57. Ravier gives an excellent analysis of what he calls the *mens ignatiana* [Ignatian mind] regarding the teaching of Christian doctrine ("St. Ignatius and the Catechism," 92-94). His study covers the whole of Ignatius's life, whereas the present work limits itself to the period up to 1539 when the first draft of the Formula of the Institute was written.

58. In spite of their emphasis on the teaching of children and others in the Deliberations immediately preceding the writing of *Cum ex plurium*, the Companions did not include it in the three experiments they chose for admission to the Society: a month in making the Spiritual Exercises, a month serving in a hospital, a month on pilgrimage begging from door to door. Later, when Ignatius wrote the *General Examen* in 1546 he included teaching Christian doctrine as one of six experiments; the other two additions were low and humble duties around the house and preaching or hearing confessions for novice priests [*C* 2:52-57].

59. *Apologia contra censuram FN* 2:84-85 [81].

60. In 1547 Polanco, who was not an eyewitness but had plenty of eyewitnesses at hand, summarized their activities in Rome in those early days before he himself came on the scene: "Finally they all returned to Rome in the following summer of 1538, and they began almost all together to preach in different churches in Rome (where up to that time two had been lecturing at the Sapienza, one on Scripture, that is to say, Master Pierre Favre, and the other on scholastic theology, that is, Master Diego Laynez, who had come there earlier with Master Ignatius), exhorting people to live a good life and to the frequent reception of the sacraments and to good works, some in Italian, some in French, some in Spanish, to people of these nationalities, and teaching Christian doctrine to the children and simple folk, hearing the confessions of a large number of people, and helping others, including leading persons of the papal court, in exercises and spiritual conversations, and assisting the poor in the hospitals and outside of them in their bodily needs; and since there was great need that year they gathered them into their house, nourishing them with both corporal and

spiritual food, more than 300 or 400 people who were dying of hunger and cold on the streets, and this caused great edification in Rome" [*PSI* 12].

Chapter Ten: Stewardship of the Vineyard

1. *OLD*, 1191c-92a.
2. See, for example, John Olin's essay, "Catholic Reform from Cardinal Ximenes to the Council of Trent," in *Catholic Reform*, 1-43. Tacchi Venturi has a chapter on the Protestant Reformation in Italy as background for the work of the early Society (TV, 1/1:431-84). For surviving popular medieval heresies and the Reformation, see G. H. Williams, *The Radical Reformation* (London, 1962).
3. *CT*, 12:67; Gleason, *Reform Thought*, 58. Carafa explicitly mentions the Franciscan Girolamo Galateo, who was tried and condemned to death in 1530 at Carafa's instigation, but was still in prison. He also names Bartholomeo Fonzio, another Franciscan he suspected of heresy in 1529, who fled to Germany and became a Lutheran. A third Franciscan he names is Alessandro Pagliarino of Pieve di Sacco, in prison at the time of Carafa's writing. For further details, see *CT*, 12:67-68; Gleason, *Reform Thought*, 58-59, plus more extensive notes accompanying text.
4. *Religious Reformers: Christianity and other Religions*, Studia Missionalia 34 (Rome: Gregorian Univ. Press, 1985), contains four studies of interest to this work: Cornelio del Zotto, "San Francesco d'Assisi, riformatore nella Chiesa cattolica," 257-320; Cándido de Dalmases, "San Ignacio de Loyola y la Contrarreforma," 321-50; Jos E. Vercruysse, "Luther as Reformer within Christendom," 351-72; Stefan Scheld, "Calvin als Reformer abendländischen Christentums," 373-407. On the religious climate and renewal movements in Castile at the beginning of the sixteenth century, see Mark Rotsaert, *Ignace de Loyola et les renouveaux spirituels en Castille au début du XVIe siècle* (Rome: CIS, 1982); on the *Alumbrados* in Spain, see Alastair Hamilton, *Heresy and Mysticism in Sixteenth-Century Spain: The Alumbrados* (Toronto: University of Toronto Press, 1992). For Ignatius's conversion in the context of the *Alumbrados*, see Piet Penning de Vries, S.J., "Protestants and Other Spirituals: Ignatius's Vision and Why He Took This Position," *AHSI* 40 (1971): 463-83. For his years in Paris, see John C. Olin, "Erasmus and St. Ignatius Loyola," in *Six Essays on Erasmus* (New York: Fordham Univ. Press, 1979), 79-92.

5. Entitled by the editor, *Narratio S. Ignatii de processibus et carceribus quos passus est, FN* 1:50-54. It is also found in *EI* 296-98. For brevity's sake, the letter will be referred to as *IJ* (Ignatius to John), followed by the paragraph number.

6. The official proceedings are in *Processus Complutenses de sancti Ignatii sociorumque vita et doctrina, FD* 319-49. Four depositions were taken on November 19, 1526, and on November 21, 1526, Figueroa handed down his decision in which he condemned nothing but told the defendants to dress in ordinary garb. Three depositions were taken on March 6, 1527, one on May 10, 1527, three on May 14, 1527. On May 18, 1527, Figueroa interviewed Ignatius himself. Three more depositions were taken on May 21, 1527, and final judgment handed down on June 1, 1527. Nothing was said about erroneous doctrine but Ignatius and his companions at the time were forbidden to teach for a period of three years. Cf. Rafael Mª Sanz de Diego, S.J., "Ignacio de Loyola en Alcalá de Henares (1526-1527): Andanzas de un universitario atípico," in *Ignacio de Loyola y su tiempo*, 890-96. John E. Longhurst has written an informative article on the contacts Ignatius had with the illuminists in Alcalá and how profoundly he differed from them ("Saint Ignatius at Alcalá, 1526-1527," *AHSI* 26 [1957]: 252-56). See also Luis Fernández, "Iñigo de Loyola y los alumbrados," *Hispania sacra* 35 (1983): 585-680.

7. The names of the judges mentioned in *A* 68 are correct but the duties attributed to them have been confused. Their decision was based on canonical and administrative grounds rather than theological and spiritual grounds. See Benigno Hernández Montés, S.J., "Identidad de los personajes que juzgaron a San Ignacio en Salamanca: Problemas históricos suscitados por las primeras fuentes," *AHSI* 52 (1983): 3-51. Bernardino Llorca, S.J., makes the point that Ignatius was not tried by the Spanish Inquisition, as is often stated. The Inquisition did, indeed, begin an investigation, but after finding nothing they turned the matter over to local diocesan authorities (*La inquisición española y los Alumbrados (1509-1667)*, Biblioteca Salmanticensis 32 [Salamanca: Universidad Pontificia, 1980], 86-92).

8. The sentence ends clumsily because Ignatius begins with *yo* [I] as subject, but finishes with a verb in the plural.

9. In his testimony in the judicial process in Rome in 1538 Ortiz states: "As for Master Ignatius . . . in Paris I had an inquiry made into his life and morals and faith because of the unusual change I had seen in a relative of mine, Master de Peralta, and

in a doctor of theology by the name of de Castro, who had had some dealings with him, so he was put under some stress because of me" [*FD* 548]. Dr. Matthieu Ory (Ori) was the inquisitor of Paris in 1529, the date of this incident, having been appointed by Pope Clement VII in 1528 (John C. Olin, ed., *The Autobiography of St. Ignatius Loyola*, 78 n. 8). For Ory's opinion of Ignatius and his companions, see below the testimony about their Paris days that he gives during the same judicial process in Rome.

10. Ignatius did not name the inquisitor; we learn Liévin's name from his successor, Thomas Laurency, O.P. [*FD* 524].

11. Schur., 250.

12. Lorenzo García, a fellow student of the companions in Paris [*FD* 524-25], joined the company in Italy. His name appears with those of the companions in Rome in a document dated May 3, 1538, granting all of them faculties to preach and administer the sacraments wherever they are [*FD* 537-39]. As we shall see, he later became a source of trouble [*R* 84 n. 13, *FD* 540-41]. Cáceres came to Rome the following year where he took part in the Deliberation of the First Fathers and signed his name as Caçres to the document called *Determinationes Societatis* [*DS* 13]. He returned to Paris to study, but broke off his relationship with the companions in 1541 or 1542 [*FD* 525 n. 3].

13. De' Dotti is variously called de Doctis, de Dotti, and de Dottis [*FN* 1:11 n. 30]. Always a friend of the Society, de' Dotti received permission from the pope in 1546 to enter the Society with a view to solemn profession, but for some reason he did not follow through. While he was governor of Loreto he was given the simple vows of the Society in 1556 and was allowed by Ignatius to carry on his work in Loreto (*FN* 1:11 n. 30; *FD* 535 n. 1).

14. The main source for this segment is the letter Ignatius wrote to Isabel Roser from Rome on December 19, 1538, one month after the final judgment [*FN* 1:6-14]. Ignatius's own story, as dictated to da Câmara some fifteen years after the event, fills out some of the details. We also have some documents and testimonies from the proceedings, collected from the state archives in Rome and edited by Marcello Del Piazzo, director of the state archives, and Cándido de Dalmases, S.J., "Il processo sull'ortodossia di S. Ignazio e dei suoi compagni svoltosi a Roma nel 1538," *AHSI* 38 (1969): 431-53, and again by Dalmases in 1977, *Processus Romanus de S. Ignatii sociorumque orthodoxia* [*FD* 542-58].

15. Ignatius is more specific in his account to da Câmara: "Then the persecutions began. Miguel [Landívar] began to give trouble and to speak badly of the pilgrim, who caused him to be summoned before the governor. He first showed the governor a letter of Miguel's, in which he praised the pilgrim very much. The governor examined Miguel, and ended by banishing him from Rome" [*A* 98]. Ignatius pleaded to no avail on behalf of Miguel [*PSH* 84; *PV* 104] and asked that his accusers not be punished (Nadal, *Apologia contra censuram*, [*FN* 2:91 {96}]). Miguel Landívar was Xavier's servant in Paris [*R* 86]. According to Rodrigues he followed the companions to Venice and asked to be admitted among their number but was refused. He must have made the journey to Rome with them, for the dimissorial letters granting the rest of the companions who were not priests permission to be ordained includes his name with the others [*FD* 526-27]. This document is quoted in the ordination document and still retains his name [*FD* 529-32]. Nowhere does Ignatius name the second person, but Favre mentions in connection with Miguel the same Lorenzo García who had testified on their behalf in Paris and joined them in Rome. Upon being summoned he simply fled from Rome, for a few days later, on May 11, he testified before a notary in the town of Otriculi that he knew nothing against Ignatius or his companions regarding the faith or the Church's teaching, that any adverse remarks he had made were in jest [*FD* 540-41]. From Paris García later sent a letter with Cáceres begging to be readmitted to the company as a cook [*EM* 15-16]. Still later in Perpignan he begged Pierre Favre in tears and on his knees to forgive him, and expressed again his longing to be readmitted (letter of Favre to Ignatius, March 22, 1542 [*MF* 156-57]).

16. In the account to da Câmara, Ignatius is less reluctant to name names, and he identifies two of the three: "Mudarra and Barreda then began their persecution, saying that the pilgrim and his companions were fugitives from Spain, from Paris, and from Venice" [*A* 98]. Favre names Matthaeo Pascual with Landívar and García [*MF* 157], whereas Ribadeneira names Pedro de Castilla along with Mudarra and Barreda, *De Actis P. Ignatii* [*FN* 2:373 {77}]. Schur., 437 n. 224, narrates the fate of the three accusers, Mudarra, Barrera [Barreda], and Castilla, and gives all the references. Luis Fernández Martín, S.J., fills out the biography of Mudarra and Ignatius's further relationships with him ("Francisco Mudarra, difamador y protegido de san Ignacio, 1538-1555," *AHSI* 62 [1993]: 161-73).

17. Time did not dull the depths of the feelings Ignatius experienced at that time, for in his account to da Câmara he uses even stronger language: "The legate ordered silence to be imposed on the whole affair, but the pilgrim did not accept that, saying that he wanted a definite sentence. This did not please the legate nor the governor nor even those who at first favored the pilgrim" [*A* 98].
18. Schur., 430.
19. The editor of the letter to Isabel suggests Cardinal Contarini [*IR* 5 n. 21] in view of a letter Ignatius wrote to Pietro Contarini on December 2, 1538, thanking him for writing to him and also for writing to Cardinal Contarini to bring his influence to bear on their behalf [*EI* 134].
20. As Ignatius indicates, the Company carried on theological discussions every two weeks during the pope's dinner [*IR* 6]; of the other companions Favre and Laynez were best known to him since they had been in Rome longer.
21. Frascati [*A* 98].
22. See Dalmases, *Ignatius of Loyola*, 160.
23. The sources give no indication of any trouble in Vicenza; the words of the bishop must have been words of praise. For Figueroa, de' Dotti, and Ory, see earlier segments of this chapter.
24. Del Piazzo and Dalmases, "Il processo," 437-38 n. 45. Ory's testimony, for example is found in a different register, in a box that contains fragments of a third register.
25. Later on he thought about entering the Society, but was dissuaded by reason of his advanced age (*FD* 550 n. 1).
26. *FD* 554 n. 1.
27. In Spanish, "mi señor en el Señor nuestro"; for a discussion of this phrase, see Bertrand, *La Politique*, 427-38; cf. above, pp. 44-45.
28. See O'Malley, *Praise and Blame*, 186-87.
29. A good summary of the situation is found in Diego, 96-97. See also above, chap. 3, pp. 67-68.
30. "Colet's Convocation Sermon, 1512," trans. Frederic Seebohm, in Olin, 33-34.
31. Testimony of Father Raphael Scosi, among others, at the investigation in Manresa into Ignatius's sanctity in September 1606. Scosi testified that he had heard his grandmother say that Ignatius "went through the town begging alms from door to door, and meeting the needs of other poor people and beggars

from what he received" [*Scripta de*, 2:744]. As he boarded ship in Barcelona to go to Gaeta Ignatius left on a bench the little he still had from what he had begged [*A* 36]; on his way from Rome to Venice (when he was going to the Holy Land) he gave away almost all of the alms he had received in Rome to make the trip to Jerusalem [*A* 40]; on his return from Jerusalem he received alms in Venice but gave everything away [*A* 50]; in Paris part of what he begged he gave to others [*PSH* 47]; he did the same in Azpeitia when he went home from Paris on the way to Venice [*Scripta de*, 2:173-245, *passim*].

32. "Giberti's *Constitutions*, after 1527," in Olin, 137-41. Cf. chap. 3, n. 24.
33. "Colet's Convocation Sermon, 1512," in Olin, 33.
34. See also the testimony of Ferdinando Diez, a Spanish priest working in Rome [*FD* 553].
35. Gleason, *Reform Thought*, 71.
36. "The *Consilium de emendanda ecclesia*, 1537," in Olin, 193.

Concluding Reflection

1. The list appears, with notable exceptions, to be close to the catalog of duties outlined for bishops in a study of the history of canon law in medieval times. See Jean Gaudemet, *Gouvernement de l'église*, 122-27. Gaudemet discusses the bishop as teacher, preacher, educator, provider for the poor, ruler. Nadal points out that the Society uses "all the ecclesiastical means there are except for two that belong to bishops, to confirm and ordain, and to hold ecclesiastical jurisdiction; but they are not necessary" ("Plática Cuarta en Coimbra," in *Pláticas espirituales del P. Jerónimo Nadal, S.I., en Coimbra (1561)*, ed. Miguel Nicolau, S.J. [Granada: Facultad Teológica de la Compañía de Jesús, 1945], 76 [15]).

Chapter Eleven: The Ancient Christian Way of Living

1. *Richard III*, act 3, sc. 5, line 31. The word *intercourse* has a similar ambiguity in our day: conversation, association, copulation.
2. Dortel-Claudot, *Le genre de vie extérieur*, 54. Much of the book is about the meaning of the term *honestus sacerdos*. See also by the same author, *Mode de vie. Niveau de vie et pauvreté de la Compagnie de Jésus* (Rome: CIS, 1973), 39.

3. Jean Gribomont, "Monasticism and Asceticism: Eastern Christianity," in *Christian Spirituality I: Origins to the Twelfth Century*, ed. Bernard McGinn, John Meyendorff, Jean Leclercq (New York: Crossroad, 1985), 89.

4. *RB 80*, 459. Athanasius, for example, in his *Life of Antony*, uses the term *politeia* for moral conduct, just as Phil. 3:20 uses the related word, *politeuma*. Evagrius of Antioch translated the *Life* into Latin, as did another translator whose name is not known. Both translations render *politeia* as *conversatio*. In view of the moral aspect of *conversatio*, it is not surprising that Evagrius also translates *askēsis*, the ascetic way of life, by the same word, *conversatio*. In like manner, the Vulgate translates *politeuma* of Phil. 3:20 as *conversatio*.

5. *Leg.* 14. See above, chap. 7, n. 1.

6. Irene Nowell, O.S.B., "Turning and Being Turned to the Lord: Biblical Foundations of *Conversatio* in the RB," *Benedictines* 36, no. 2 (Fall-Winter 1981): 17.

7. In the context, the reference is to Cassian, Athanasius, Jerome, and others who also used *conversatio* in the sense of a holy way of living. Cf. Lorié, *Spiritual Terminology*, 94-95.

8. "But as we progress in this way of life [*conversationis*] and in faith [*et fidei*], we shall run on the path of God's commandments" [Prol. 49]. *RB* Prol. 21 also connects faith and action, but the word *conversatio* is not used: "Succinctis ergo fide vel observantia bonorum actuum lumbis nostris [Clothed then with faith and the performance of good works]."

9. Ambrose Wathen, "*Conversatio* and Stability in the Rule of Benedict," *Monastic Studies* 11 (1975): 39.

10. Cf. Nowell, "Turning," 16-29. For a good understanding of *conversatio* in monastic history and practice and for a discussion on the difference between *conversatio* and *conversio*, see Lorié, *Spiritual Terminology*, 82-85; Mohrmann, "Langue de saint Benoît," 341-45; Eoin de Bhaldraithe, O.Cist., "Conversatio: St. Benedict Recovers Early Christian Terminology," *Regulae Benedicti Studia Annuarium Internationale* 13 (1984): 3-15; Wathen, "*Conversatio*," 1-44; Claude Peifer, O.S.B., "Monastic Formation and Profession," in *RB 80*, Appendix 5, 457-66; Michael Casey, O.C.S.O., "The Benedictine Promises," *Tjurunga* [an Australasian Benedictine Review], no. 24 (1983): 17-34, especially 22-27; and an article by Thomas Merton, "Conversion of Life," in *The Monastic Journey*, ed. Patrick Hart (Kansas City: Sheed Andrews and McMeel, 1977), 107-20 (originally published in *Cistercian Studies* 1 [1966]: 130-44).

11. *LTS* 58; 66.
12. 1 Celano 27.
13. Cf. Esser, *Origins*, 26, and n. 30 on 45-46. Esser points out that *Sacrum commercium*, an early Franciscan work, uses *sancta conversatio* in reference to the religious life in the early Church (28, 42, 48, 50), and refers to the founders of the existing religious orders as *sanctae conversationis institutores*.
14. *Acta canonizationis*, 123, 135.
15. Stephanus de Salaniaco et Bernardus Guidonis, *De quatuor in quibus Deus Praedicatorum ordinem insignivit*, ed. Thomas Kaeppeli, O.P., MOPH 22 (Rome: Institutum Historicum Fratrum Praedicatorum, 1949), 9.

Chapter Twelve: *Ecclesia semper reformanda*

1. Le Goff, *Your Money*, 13. See also Jean-Claude Schmitt, *Prêcher d'exemples* (Paris: Stock, 1985), 10.
2. Leturia, *Iñigo*, 94-95.
3. O'Malley, *Praise and Blame*, 193-94.
4. Nelson H. Minnich, S.J., "Concepts of Reform Proposed at the Fifth Lateran Council," *Arch. Hist. Pont.* 7 (1969): 181-82. Archbishop Marcellus, too, insisted on law, but law was not enough; for him law that was obeyed was what was needed. That itself would be a change indeed, but wherein lay the motive to obey?
5. *COD*, 612.
6. Diego, 101-10.
7. History owes the phrase, "*reformatio tam in capite, quam in membris*," to William Duranti (or Durandus), the Younger, bishop of Mende, who wrote in his book entitled *Tractatus de modo generalis concilii celebrandi* (Paris: Clousier, 1671; reprint, London: Gregg Press, 1964) and presented to the Council of Vienne in 1311: "reformarentur illa quae sunt in ecclesia Dei corrigenda & reformanda, tam in capite, quam in membris" (titulus I, pars I).
8. Hubert Jedin, *A History of the Council of Trent*, 2 vols. (London: Thomas Nelson and Sons, 1957-61), 1:289, 349. He not only practiced nepotism, he wanted his children and his grandchildren to marry into the ruling houses of Italy. For a good understanding of Paul III's practice of nepotism and its role in sixteenth-century Italian society, see Gleason, "First Counter-Reformation Pope," 183-84.

9. *CT*, 4:451, citing Barber, *Acta consist.*, XXXVI. I, f. 216.
10. *Gasparis Contareni cardinalis opera* (Paris, 1571; reprint, 1968), bk. 2, 421B; Olin, 101.
11. Jedin, *History*, 1:419.
12. Olin, 183; see also Jedin, *History*, 1:423-24, and Olin, "Catholic Reform," 20.
13. Olin, 133 n. 1 credits the phrase to Wilhelm Schenk, *Reginald Pole, Cardinal of England* (London, 1950), 54.
14. Jedin, *History*, 1:423 n. 4. A brief discussion of the commission and some of its adversaries is found in 1:423-26. See also Gleason, *Gasparo Contarini*, 140-43, and her "First Counter-Reformation Pope," in which she looks anew at Paul III's commitment to Church reform (179-81).
15. "Oratio R^{mi} Jacobi Sadoleti," *CT*, 12:117.
16. "Hieronymi Aleandri de convocando concilio sententia" (1537), *CT*, 12:127-28.
17. The Latin title is *Consilium de emendanda ecclesia*. For an English translation of the entire document plus an explanatory introduction, see Olin, 182-97. (Reprinted in John C. Olin, *Catholic Reform*, 65-79.) The Latin original is found in *CT*, 12:134-45. For an in-depth discussion of the commission's report and the way it was received, see Gleason, *Gasparo Contarini*, 143-57.
18. "That ... Spirit of God ... has determined to rebuild through you the Church of Christ, tottering, nay, in fact collapsed ... and to raise it up to its original height and restore it to its pristine beauty" (*CT*, 12:134; Olin, 186).
19. *LM* 2.1; *LTS* 13.
20. *CT*, 12:136; Olin, 188.
21. *CT*, 12:138; Olin, 191. Other abuses amongst prelates are found in *CT*, 12:136-39.
22. *CT*, 12:139; Olin, 193.
23. 1.18.4. *The Imitation of Christ*, trans. Joseph N. Tylenda, S.J. (Wilmington: Michael Glazier, 1984) 52-53; Latin text from *Thomae Hemerken a Kempis opera omnia*, ed. M. J. Pohl, vol. 2, *Thomae Hemerken a Kempis de imitatione Christi* (Fribourg, 1904) 31.
24. See *Acta canonizationis* 3 and 7, pp. 178-79.
25. For example: *Scripta Leonis*, paragraph, page: 2, 90; 38, 156; 61, 194; 79, 226; 85, 236; 87, 238; 92, 250.
26. For example: 1 Celano 31, 34; *LTS* 36; *Testamentum* 21; *Epistola ad fideles* 2.53.

27. As I write these words, November 16, 1989, the feast of the martyrdom of the Jesuit Latin American martyrs, Roch Gonzalez and his companions, word comes from El Salvador that six Jesuits and two lay persons have been tortured and martyred at the Jesuit university in San Salvador. Their *example* illustrates most clearly exactly what I am trying to say. The tradition continues, the vast cloud of witnesses, from Abel and the prophets, through Jesus to an unending line of which today's El Salvadoran witnesses share a tiny part; more are to come.

28. This sentence is almost a direct quotation from Gerhart B. Ladner, *Images and Ideas in the Middle Ages: Selected Studies in History and Art*, vol. 2, Storia e Letteratura: Raccolta di Studi e Testi, 156 (Rome: 1983), 520.

29. *Ibid.*, 519-20.

30. *Lauda Sion.* E.T. from *New St. Joseph Sunday Missal* (New York: Catholic Book Publishing Company, 1974), 368.

31. See John W. O'Malley's discussion of various approaches to renewal, *Tradition and Transition: Historical Perspectives on Vatican II*, Theology and Life Series 26 (Wilmington: Michael Glazier, 1989), 65-73.

32. O'Malley points out that Constitution 50 of Lateran IV (1215) is "the first unmistakably clear conciliar statement" that a change in the times might require a change in discipline (*Tradition and Transition*, 53).

33. A good example of the Church's evolving consciousness of Christ, for example, is seen in Jaroslav Pelikan, *Jesus through the Centuries: His Place in the History of Culture* (New Haven: Yale University Press, 1985).

34. For the meaning of reform and how it works in the Church from Hubert Jedin's point of view, see Giuseppe Alberigo, "'Réforme' en tant que critère de l'Histoire de l'Église," *Revue d'Histoire Ecclésiastique* 76 (1981): 72-81.

35. Vatican II is a special problem for many different philosophies of history were at work, nor has its practice been "explicitly related . . . to an adequate contemporary philosophy of history" (O'Malley, *Tradition and Transition*, 73).

36. Two books on the Reformation that are easy to read are: (1) Anthony E. Gilles, *The People of Anguish: The Story behind the Reformation* (Cincinnati: St. Anthony Messenger Press, 1987), xvi-194; (2) Owen Chadwick, *The Reformation* (Baltimore: Penguin, 1964), 463pp. For the life of faith and piety of the late

medieval church, see Erwin Iserloh, "The Inner Life of the Church," in *Handbook of Church History*, ed. Hubert Jedin and John Dolan, vol. 4, *From the High Middle Ages to the Eve of the Reformation* (New York: Herder & Herder, 1970), especially pages 566-85 on the urban parish. For signs of faith and piety in ordinary aspects of life in an ordinary part of the country, see A. N. Galpern, "The Legacy of Late Medieval Religion in Sixteenth Century Champagne," in *Studies in Medieval and Reformation Thought*, ed. Heiko A. Oberman, vol. 10, *The Pursuit of Holiness in Late Medieval and Renaissance Religion*, ed. Charles Trinkaus with Heiko A. Oberman (Leiden: Brill, 1974), 141-76.

37. Some of the abuses amongst prelates are indicated in Carafa's *Memorial* to Clement VII. To his remarks about bishops, Carafa adds some about priests, especially their reading of heretical books (*CT*, 12:71-73; Gleason, *Reform Thought*, 67-71).

38. Henry Outram Evennett, "The New Orders," in *The New Cambridge Modern History*, ed. G. R. Elton, vol. 2, *The Reformation 1520-1559* (Cambridge: University Press, 1958), chap. 9, 275-300 (Capuchins, 278-85; Theatines, 285-87) and especially *Religious Orders of the Catholic Reformation*, a collection of essays by various authors, edited by Richard L. DeMolen (New York: Fordham University Press, 1994), which came to our attention when this book was already at the publisher (Theatines, 1-29; Capuchins, 31-57; Barnabites, 59-96; Ursulines, 99-136).

39. Carafa has some bitter things to say in his *Memorial* (*CT*, 12:73-77; Gleason, *Reform Thought*, 71-80). Carafa's own Rule for the Theatines, drawn up in 1526, is found with a brief introduction in Olin, 128-32. The Capuchin Constitutions of 1536, with suitable introduction, are found *ibid.*, 148-81. Concerning reform efforts of the Benedictines, see Philibert Schmitz, *Histoire de l'Ordre de Saint-Benoît*, 7 vols. (Maredsous: Éditions de l'Abbaye, 1948), 3:175-269; also *RB 80*, 131-34; David Knowles, *Christian Monasticism*, World University Library (London: Weidenfeld and Nicolson, 1969), 135-41. For the Cistercians, see Lekai, *Cistercians*, 109-25, 417-19; for the Franciscans, see Moorman, *History*, 441-585. For an overview of the better aspects of religious life in a time badly in need of reform, see François Vandenbroucke, "The Heirs of the Middle Ages," in *The Spirituality of the Middle Ages*, vol. 2 of *A History of Christian Spirituality*, ed. Louis Bouyer et al. (New York: Seabury Press, 1968), 447-80.

40. For some excellent extracts from preachers, see O'Malley, *Praise and Blame*, 211-26.

41. Olin, 140. Excerpts from Giberti's Constitutions are to be found in Olin, 136-48. Much of the Constitutions has to do with good example, explicitly mentioned in chapter 16 (Olin, 138).
42. *CT*, 12:73; Gleason, *Reform Thought*, 71.
43. John W. O'Malley, S.J., *Giles of Viterbo on Church and Reform: A Study in Renaissance Thought* (Leiden: Brill, 1968), 142-43.
44. O'Malley, *Praise and Blame*, 214 n. 75, quoting Brandolini's "Oratio ad Lateranense concilium," BAV cod. Ottob. lat. 813, fols. 56v-57r. Similar ideas were also operative in the twelfth and thirteenth centuries. Cf. Adriaan H. Bredero's reflections on *antiquitas* and *tempus modernum* (*Christendom and Christianity in the Middle Ages: The Relations between Religion, Church, and Society*, trans. Reinder Bruinsma [Grand Rapids: Eerdmans, 1994], 57-62).
45. Bishop Simon Begnius of Modrus in Dalmatia. The original Latin is in Minnich, "Concepts of Reform," 187 n. 82, who cites *Mansi*, vol. 32, 799D, an excellent article for understanding what the fathers at Lateran V meant by reform.
46. Robert F. McNally, S.J., "Pope Adrian VI (1522-23) and Church Reform," *Archivum Historiae Pontificiae* 7 (1969): 258.
47. 1 Tim. 4:12. The text in the Latin Vulgate reads: "Nemo adolescentiam tuam contemnat: sed *exemplum* esto fidelium in verbo, in *conversatione*, in caritate, in fide, in castitate [emphasis added]."
48. De Bhaldraithe, "Conversatio," 10. The author has made an analysis of all the texts in the New Testament dealing with *conversatio*. The analysis of 1 Tim. 4:12 is on p. 7.
49. *De Ordinatione Presbyteri, Pontificale Romanum*, passim. In 1294 William Duranti the Elder, bishop of Mende and known as "the Speculator" (uncle of William the Younger of "reform in head and members" fame), revised the Roman Pontifical. That revision prevailed during the later Middle Ages and was the model for the official text of Innocent VIII in 1485. The text of 1485 remained substantially the same until Vatican II. See Michel Andrieu, *Le Pontifical romain au moyen-âge*, vol. 1, Studi e Testi 86 (Vatican City: Biblioteca Apostolica Vaticana, 1938), v; Marc Dykmans, S.J., *Le Pontifical romain révisé au XVe siècle*, Studi e Testi 311 (Vatican City: Biblioteca Apostolica Vaticana, 1985), esp. 5-15, 149-57; J. H. Crehan, S.J., "Medieval Ordinations," in *The Study of the Liturgy*, ed. Cheslyn Jones, Geoffrey Wainwright, Edward Yarnold, S.J. (New York: Oxford University Press, 1978), 320-31.

Concluding Reflection

1. Guillaumont, "Perspectives actuelles," 222-26.
2. In Part VI of the Constitutions, in speaking of chastity, Ignatius will talk about imitating angelic purity, in other words, seeking again the undivided heart. For further elucidation on this point, see my own study, "Living and Dying in the Society of Jesus, or Endeavoring to Imitate Angelic Purity," *Studies in the Spirituality of Jesuits* 12 (May 1980): 1-63.
3. *FN* 3:321.

Chapter Thirteen: Prophetic Commitment

1. Also to be rejected in the context: *vestra pietas* as a title after the manner of "Your Holiness". See Niermeyer, *Lexicon*, 906b. If *pietas* and *religio* are taken as titles in *Cum ex plurium*, the pope would simply be saying, "You are pleasing to us." Since the letter addresses itself to ten people, the likelihood of one title for all is improbable.
2. Cf. 1 Tim. 4:8, where *eusebeia* is translated by *pietas* in the Vulgate.
3. "Piety is also normally understood as the worship of God, what the Greeks call *eusebeia*; by the custom of ordinary people this name is also given to the works of mercy" (Augustine, *De civitate Dei* [The City of God] 10.1.3, *PL* 41, 279).
4. In the single use of *pietas* in the Rule of Benedict God is the possessor of pietas: "See how the Lord in his love [*pietate*] shows us the way of life" (*RB* Prol. 20). Similarly, the Cistercian *Exordium parvum* speaks of "those whom the divine goodness has set over our diocese" (*EP* 13). For further examples, see under *pietas*, Blaise, *Dictionnaire*, 624-25.
5. "Deus misericordiae et pietatis magister" (Fastidius, *De vita christiana* 8, *PL* 40, 1038).
6. Marc-François Lacan, "Piety," in *Dictionary of Biblical Theology*, ed. Xavier Léon-Dufour, 2d ed. (New York: Seabury Press, 1973), 429a-30b; P. van Imschoot, "Grace," in *Encyclopedic Dictionary of the Bible*, ed. Louis F. Hartman, C.SS.R., 2d ed. (New York: McGraw-Hill, 1963), 897a-903a.
7. For a fuller history of the meaning of *religio*, see: J. Gribomont and J.-M.-R. Tillard, "Religio (Religiosus)," *DIP*, 7 (1983): 1628-36; Grégoire, R., "'Religiosus', Etude sur le vocabulaire de la

vie religieuse," *Studi medievali* 10 (1969) [= Melanges Ermini, vol. 2, Soleto 1970]: 415-30; Ernst Feil, *Religio: Die Geschichte eines neuzeitlichen Grundbegriffs vom Frühchristentum bis zur Reformation* (Göttingen: Vandenhoeck & Ruprecht, 1986).

8. Cicero (106-43 B.C.) says that "those who . . . went over again [*relegerent*] whatever pertained to the cult of the gods were called religious people, from *relegendo*" (*De natura deorum* 2.2.72, ed. Joseph B. Mayor, vol. 2 [Cambridge University Press, 1883], 27).

9. Massurius Sabinus, a jurist of the first century of the Christian era, says that a thing is called religious [*religiosum*], "on account of some holiness that is remote and far removed from us; the word comes from '*relinquendo*'" (from Sabinus's commentary *De indigenis* as quoted by Aulus Gellius, *Noctes Atticae* 4.9.8, ed. P. K. Marshall, vol. 1 [Oxford: Clarendon Press, 1968], 174).

10. *Div. inst.* 4.28, CSEL 19, 391.

11. *De quantitate animae* 80, *PL* 32, 1080. Augustine is aware of Cicero's position and gives it a kinder interpretation than does Lactantius. St. Thomas embraces Cicero, Augustine, and Lactantius together: "Whether religion comes from frequent rereading or from repeated choosing of that which has been lost through negligence, or from rebinding, religion implies a relationship to God" (*Summa theologica*, 2a 2ae q. 81 a.1).

12. In the Vulgate *religio* signifies both ritual [*latreia* = worship/service] (Ex. 12:26) and the law [*nomos*] regulating the ritual (Ex. 12:43).

13. The Greek word is *thrēskeia* [*religio* (Lat.), religion]. For *thrēskeia*, see K. L. Schmidt, Kittel 3:155-59.

14. Language limiting *religious life* to those living under a rule approved by the Church is seriously challenged today by those who maintain, as did the early Christians, that every Christian is called to the religious life, that is, the ascetical life.

15. See *Admonitio ad omnes regni ordines* (a. 823-25): "so that holy religion [*sancta religio*] might be observed in the monasteries]" (*MGH, Capitularia Regum Francorum*, vol. 1, chap. 4, p. 303); "what pertains to the way of life [*religionem*] of canons, monks, and nuns" (*ibid.*, chap. 10, p. 305).

16. Guiges Ier, *Coutumes de Chartreuse.*

17. *EP* 11.

18. Religious orders (Schroeder, 255); religious rules and foundations (James M. Powell, "The Papacy and the Early Franciscans," *Franciscan Studies* 36 [1976]: 249); for Latin text, see *COD*, 218.

19. Religious fervor: *Religionis zelus* (1528), *BRT* 6:113a; religious life: *Sacrae religionis sinceritas* (1533), *BRT* 6:158b; *Vota per quae* (1533), *BRT* 6:160a; religious order: Fifth Lateran Council, Session XI (1516), *COD*, 621, line 43; *In suprema militantis* (1532), *BRT* 6:156b.

20. Other examples of *religio* as religious order or institute: *D* 7, *R* 92, *R* 101, *FN* 3:321.

Chapter Fourteen:
Vite institutum: A Way that Leads to God

1. An alternate form of *vitae*.
2. For examples, see *OED*, 8:353a.
3. For various passages in which Evagrius uses *institutum* to translate *askēsis*, see Lorié, *Spiritual Terminology*, 81-82.
4. Chapter 7, *PL* 73, 131B.
5. Jean Cassien, *Institutions cénobitiques*, SC 109 (Paris: Editions du Cerf, 1965), praef.3, 7, 9.; I.1.1; 2.2; 2.4. II.3.3; 3.5; III.1; IV.9; 10; 19.1.
6. Cassian's work was widely diffused, and his writings were very influential. When the Rule of Benedict mentions "the *Conferences* of the Fathers, their *Institutes* and their *Lives* [*Collationes Patrum et Instituta et Vitas*] [*RB* 73.5]", it is commonly accepted that reference is being made to the *Conferences* of Cassian, his *Institutes*, and possibly the brief lives found in the *Conferences*. See *RB 80*, 297n.
7. Concilium Vernense, an. 755, and Concilium Romanum, an. 769, *MGH*, *Concilia*, vol. 2, 54 and 83.
8. For example, St. Ubald (+1160) "having been educated [*institutus*] well in letters," joined "an institute [*institutum*] of canons regular of St. Augustine" (*Breviarium Romanum*, 2 noct., lect. 4, 16 maii).
9. *Vita tertia* [Brunonis], *PL* 152, 537A.
10. *Exordium Cistercii* 2; E.T., Lekai, *Cistercians*, 444.
11. *Exordium parvum* 15. This is an important chapter, inasmuch as these *instituta* are deemed to contain the early *propositum* the monks presented first to the papal legate and then to Pope Paschal II in order to secure approbation of their renewal efforts. Cf. *PATC*, 79 n. 1. See also M. N. Bouchard, "Les 'Instituta' des moines cisterciens venant de Molesme," *Coll. Cist.* 50 (1988): 289-306, esp. 289.

12. When narrating the story of the oral approbation of the Society, Rodrigues reports that Contarini told Paul III how the companions desired to open their way of life [*vitae institutum*] to others. Paul III responded by saying how pleased he was with the companions and how acceptable their way of life [*vitae institutum*] was to him [*R* 92].
13. Pedro Leturia, who edited the letter to Isabel for the *Monumenta*, *FN* 1:6*, suggests three of the four or five: Pietro Codacio or Codazzo, Bartolomeo Ferrão, and Francisco Estrada [*FN* 1:13 n. 37].
14. *Memoriale*, *FN* 1:705 [307].
15. Schur., 505-7, gives a good sketch of Codacio complete with references. A canon in Lodi, he came to Rome early in his career. Although the Holy See had given him the church of Santa Maria della Strada, he managed to have it granted to the Society instead (*Bulla secunda Pauli III*, 1541 [*Sacrosancte Romane Ecclesie*], *C* 70-77).
16. Schur., 467 n. 16, and a longer discussion by the same author, "Zur Frage," 264-66.
17. Da Câmara, *Memoriale*, *FN* 1:602-3 [126]; Schur., 450.
18. *FN* 1:244 n. 1.
19. Polanco writes about Estrada in *PSH* 152-60, *PV* 96, and *PCh* 10.
20. For Miguel Landívar, see chap. 10, n. 15; for Lorenzo García, *ibid.*, nn. 12 and 15.
21. Salmerón in a letter to Laynez's father, Juan, *EI* 154.
22. The Latin translation of the Spanish text has *vitae institutum* [*FN* 1:121 {42}].
23. If we were to reach into the first months after the oral confirmation of the Society in September 1539 we would find such stalwarts as Juan Jerónimo Doménech and Paolo de Achille, who were already priests, and Elpidio Ugoleto and Giovanni Battista Viola [*PCh* 12]. Favre and Laynez recruited all of them in Parma. Another Favre mentions in a letter to Xavier was Esbrando, whom he wanted Ignatius to direct in the Exercises [*MF* 19]. The oral approbation of 1539 did not lessen the dilemma of attracting young men to the Society. When Broët and Rodrigues went to Siena, the latter began teaching some of the youth of that city. In their eagerness to serve God some took off for Rome to join the Society without consulting their parents. The unhappy parents intercepted them halfway to Rome, but the young people tried it again, and this time they

made it to Rome where some of them were admitted into the Society [R 97].

Chapter Fifteen: Companionship in Christ

1. "The Early Dominican Constitutions," in Tugwell, *Early Dominicans*, 456; Latin text in *Constitutiones antiquae ordinis fratrum Praedicatorum*, ed. Heribert C. Scheeben in *Die Konstitutionen des Predigerordens unter Jordan von Sachsen* (Cologne: Albertus-Magnus-Verlag, 1939), Prol. 1.49.

2. For the English, see Lekai, *Cistercians*, 461-62; for the Latin, see *PATC*, 132.

3. These terms are not particularly religious, nor were they part of the established vocabulary of religious orders at this time. Benedict uses neither *socius* nor *societas*, but he does use *sociare* [to join, to associate with, to unite] [*RB* 43.11; 53.4; 53.23; 60.8; 61.6], and *sociandus* [to be made a companion] [61.8] in the sense of entering into some activity or state with someone else. The words have no special significance in Cistercian and Carthusian sources.

4. Cf. Feliciano Delgado, S.J., "Compañía de Jesús. Análisis filológico del término," *Manresa* 61 (1989): 249-56.

5. On the recipient of the letter, see *EI* 114 n. 1. For further details, see Georges Bottereau, S.J., "La 'lettre' d'Ignace de Loyola à Gian Pietro Carafa," *AHSI* 44 (1975): 139-52, who finds in this letter the essence of the Exercises and the germ of the future Constitutions. The manuscript contains many corrections in Ignatius's hand.

6. "Questa povera compagnia sarà perpetua, se a Dio piace" (*Barb. lat.* 5697, f. 58, 1532, cited by F. Andreu, "Chierici regolari teatini," *DIP*, 2 [1975]: 979).

7. In the Deliberation of the First Fathers, Ignatius and his companions have to face the fact that they are being divided and scattered abroad to those places "where [the pope] judged they could bear more fruit" [*D* 3]. Should the physical separation [*corporum diuisio*] shatter their unity? Some years later in the *Constituciones circa missiones* Ignatius writes of "our intention and desire to be scattered [*esparzidos*] through various different regions" [*C* 160].

8. *The Golden Legend of Jacobus de Voragine*, trans. Granger Ryan and Helmut Ripperger (New York: Longmans, Green and Co., 1941), 416.

9. *LTS*, Rubric, 89.
10. *LTS* 13, 9, 32, 29.
11. 1.14, 25.
12. Andreu, "Teatini," 978-99; for a fuller treatment of the Theatines, see Paschini, *Gaetano Thiene*. See also Kunkel, *Theatines in History*; and especially Jorgensen, "The Theatines," 1-29.
13. Paschini, *Gaetano Thiene*, 57, 71.
14. Twice in a letter to the duke of Ferrara on July 4, 1539 (shortly after the the Deliberation ended), Bobadilla refers to the Society: (1) various people have requested that "for the love of God two of our Company [*Compañía*] be sent to the city of Siena [*MB* 16];" and (2) "the Company [*Compañía*] is eager to serve Your Excellency" [*MB* 16].
15. Favre is one of the candidates for the scribe who wrote the Deliberation of the First Fathers [*C* xxxvii-xxxviii].
16. As usual, Laynez summarizes lengthy material in a very terse and concise fashion. For him, the whole of the Deliberation of the First Fathers concerned "things respecting our vocation [*cosas que tocaban a nuestra vocación*] . . . and without anyone's dissenting we decided first of all that it would be good to try to establish a company [*compañía*] that would last, and not simply to be concerned with our individual selves" [*L* 49].
17. In his letter of 1547 to Polanco about the "origins of the Society [*principios de la Compañía*]" [*L* 1], Laynez uses the word *compañía* only sparingly in discussing events before the confirmation of the Society. For the most part he bears witness to their companionship by consistently using the first person plural when talking about the companions. Rodrigues uses *socius* or *socii* almost every paragraph in his *Commentarium*. Bobadilla also frequently uses *socius* or *socii* in his Autobiography. He recalls the early days of his life in Paris, frequenting the Carthusian church on Sundays and feasts along with others, including some "companions and brothers of the Society of Jesus [*alii socii et fratres Societatis Iesu*]" [*B* 5]. Although this obviously refers to the others who, with him, would eventually become the Society of Jesus, it is significant that he uses the words "companions and brothers." What is important to Bobadilla is the communion existing within the group.
18. Bobadilla bears witness that while they were waiting in Rome to go to Jerusalem "four of the companions [*quatuor ex sociis*]" [*B* 11] carried on disputations in the presence of the pope. When Paul III said that Rome would make a good Jerusalem for

them, they brought these words back "to the other companions [*aliis sociis*]" [*B* 11], and started thinking "about founding a religious order [*de religione instituenda*] for up to that time they always intended and spoke of fulfilling their vow of pilgrimaging to Jerusalem" [*B* 11]. They began, in fact, "all together to reflect on being united in one body [*de unione in unum corpus*] and about establishing a religious order [*et de religione instituenda*]" [*B* 12]. Fifty years later Bobadilla is clear on what the Deliberation of the First Fathers was all about: (1) union: or being united in one body [*de unione in unum corpus*] is little different from forming ourselves into one body [*reducendo nos in vnum corpus*]; (2) obedience: as he puts it, becoming a religious order [*de religione instituenda*]. Their desire must have burnt itself deeply into his heart and mind.

19. Schur., 108-10.
20. A year later, in the solemn bull of confirmation, *Regimini militantis ecclesiae*, the language was changed slightly: "ad perficiendam et conseruandam eorum Societatis in Christo vnionem" [*C* 26 {2}]. Either the one who rewrote the document did not understand the companions' experience of union already granted by God, in which case the phrase could be translated: "to achieve and preserve the union in Christ of their Society," or he did understand it and wishes to say that now it seems more important to bring that union to perfection first, to live it to the full, and then to preserve it, to maintain for the future that same high level of union.
21. When Nadal comments on this passage of the Deliberation, he reverses the order of the words and has *congregationem et societatem* instead of *unionem et congregationem*. Nevertheless, for him the basic significance of *societas* is "union" [*Apologia contra censuram, FN* 2:93 {99}].
22. Iturrioz has listed a number of those dating from the time of Paul III and later in the sixteenth century (J. Iturrioz, S.J., "Compañía de Jesús: Sentido historico y ascético de este nombre," *Manresa* 27 [1955]: 43-53). The author does not always indicate which ones precede the founding of the Society of Jesus.
23. Cf. García Hirschfeld, S.J., "Origen de la comunidad," 404-5.
24. Edward J. Malatesta and George E. Ganss, "Selections from *The Spiritual Diary*," in Ganss, *Ignatius of Loyola*, [66], 248; Latin text: *C* 104.
25. See Niermeyer, *Lexicon*, 246a.
26. Canon 488 $2.^0$ of the 1917 code made a distinction between an order in which solemn vows were taken and a congregation in

which simple vows were taken. Canon 1308 §2 defined, "A vow is solemn if it is recognized as such by the Church; otherwise it is simple." The distinction was mainly in the effects: a solemn vow might render an action invalid, while a simple vow might render the same action valid but illicit. Canon 607 of the 1983 code makes no such distinctions.

27. Cicero, *Ep. ad Quintum Fratrem* 1.1.6.
28. Recall what was said above about Jesus as head of the Society. It was Jesus who proposed their end to the companions and was at work in them at all times bringing it about.
29. On the terminology of decrees or chapters, see note 8 of Introduction.
30. TV, 2/1:181; also 271.
31. *Exhort. 1554 in Hispania, MN* 5:40 [13].
32. Aldama, *Notas para un comentario,* 27-29; E.T., 25-27.
33. *Ibid.,* 13-23. This is a translation of the final text of 1550, but the changes do not affect the point made here.
34. *Obedientie* is a variant of *obedientiae.*
35. These remarks on obedience are drawn from Catherine Cappelle, *Le voeu d'obéissance des origines au xiie siècle,* Librairie Générale de Droit et de Jurisprudence (Paris: Pichon et Durand-Auzias, 1959), 240.
36. Here *religio* and *obedientia* are synonyms, much as *sub regula* [under a rule] and *sub abbate* [under an abbot] were synonyms. The phrase in the next objection, "to live under obedience [*viuere sub obedientia*]" [*D* 7], means "to live under a rule in a religious institute." In earliest times, to live under a rule or to live under an abbot was identical: the abbot was the rule, that is, the abbot communicated to the monks the tradition coming down from the apostles and the early Christian community, and the members of the community lived in obedience to the abbot who embodied the rule. Although *sub regula vel abbate* in the Rule of the Master [*RM* 1:2] and the Rule of Benedict [*RB* 1:2] no longer implies an oral, but a written rule, there is still obedience to the rule and obedience to the abbot (Cf. Adalbert de Vogüé, "*Sub regula uel abbate:* A Study of the Theological Significance of the Ancient Monastic Rule," in *Rule and Life,* CS 12 [Kalamazoo: Cistercian Publications, 1971], 23-29. Sometimes, as here, *vel* is the equivalent of *et*). The commitment to live by the rule and obey the abbot did not take the shape of a vow for some centuries. (See chap. 17.) Even today those in the Bene-

dictine tradition promise "stability, fidelity to monastic life [*conversatio morum*], and obedience." Poverty and chastity are assumed as part of the monastic way of life (For a full discussion, see Claude Peifer, O.S.B., "Monastic Formation and Profession," in *RB 80*, 457-66). In similar manner, the Dominican formula explicitly mentions only obedience, subsuming everything else under that one title (See *Constitutiones antiquae* 1.16.1). The religious life cannot do without obedience.

37. Cf. *RB* 71.2, 5.11, 15.

Chapter Sixteen: The Meaning of *viuendi formula*

1. Drawn mainly from Pastor, *passim*, and from Jedin, *History of the Council of Trent*, vol. 1, *passim*.
2. Vicaire, *Saint Dominic*, 195. For the example of the Trinitarians, see *BRT* 3:134a.
3. Again, in 1532 Clement VII said that he approved the Capuchins "after mature consultation with cardinals and others who were well informed about the order, and with the unanimous consent of the cardinals" [*BRT* 6:156b]. Later in the century, in 1586, Sixtus V would approve the Camillians after consultation with the cardinals [*BRT* 8:669h].
4. Chap. 19 will treat of the delegate and his response.
5. *Lexicon*, 445b-46a. For examples of this use of *forma*, see *Consuetudines Cartusiae* 15.1, 29.2, 43.2.
6. The treatise is attributed to Firmicius Maternus (+after 360), a rhetorician, probably of Sicilian origin and converted to Christianity in adult life (*ODCC*, 514a): *I. Firmici Materni Consultationes Zacchaei et Apollonii*, ed. Germanus Morin, O.S.B., Florilegium Patristicum 39 (Bonn: Hanstein, 1935). This ancient treatise also uses other terms found in *Cum ex plurium*, like *conversatio, religio, institutum, propositum*. For E.T. of bk. 3, see "The Discussions of Zacchaeus and Apollonius, III, 1-6," *Monastic Studies* 12 (1976): 271-87.
7. Meersseman, *Dossier: vita* (128, 129, 243, 291, 293, 294, 297, 302), *forma vite* (303, 305), *vite forma* (156, 291), *vite formula* (138), *vivendi forma* (154, 156, 282, 290), *vivendi modus* (129), *modus vivendi* (293), *vivendi modus et formula* (155), *forma sive dogma vivendi* (295), *regula seu vivendi formula* (156, 295), *dogma seu forma Vite* (290). Alternative forms of the idea appear elsewhere, such as *forma sanctae conversationis* (*LTS* 34), and *conversationis*

vestrae formula (Bruno Secondin, O. Carm., ed., *La Regola del Carmelo oggi* [Rome: Institutum Carmelitanum, 1983], 25).

8. Carlo Cicconetti, O. Carm., *La Regola del Carmelo: Origine, natura, significato* (Rome: Institutum Carmelitanum, 1973), 115-23.

9. Meersseman, *Dossier*, 282.

10. In the Franciscan sources one finds, for example: *vita* (*Earlier Rule*, Prologue), *vita et regula* (*LTS* 29), *vitae forma et regula* (1Cel 32), *vivere secundum formam sancti Evangelii* (*Testamentum* 14, *LTS* 29, *Scripta Leonis* 4), *vivendi modus* (*LM* 3.8), *vivendi regula* (*LM* 3.9), *forma evangelicae vitae* (*LM* 3.9), *forma evangelica in vivendo* (*LM* 3.1), *formula vitae* (*LM* 3.8), *forma sanctae conversationis* (*LTS* 34), *vivere secundum formam primitive ecclesie* (*Lettres de Jacques de Vitry*, éd. critique par R. B. C. Huygens [Leiden: Brill, 1960], 75, 131).

11. Shortly before Lateran IV, when the Carmelites were getting a start in the Holy Land near Mount Carmel, Albert, the Patriarch of Jerusalem, wrote for them a form of living [*vitae formulam*] based on their own traditional patterns, a norm on which they could model their lives (Cicconetti, *Regola del Carmelo*, 115-26. For the Carmelites, see also Secondin, *Regola del Carmelo oggi*; Elias Friedman, *The Latin Hermits of Mount Carmel: A Study in Carmelite Origins* [Rome: Teresianum, 1979]; *The Rule of St. Albert*, ed. Bede Edwards, O.D.C. [Aylesford and Kensington, 1973]).

12. F. Andreu, "Chierici regolari Teatini," *DIP*, 2 (1975): 979.

13. When Polanco tells the same story in Latin in 1574, he writes: "Before they, who from a variety of nations had been united by the Lord in one spirit and one calling [*vocatione*], were scattered to various places, they began to discuss the form of living [*vivendi formula*] they ought to follow" [*PV* 107].

14. Cf. Bertrand, *Un corps pour l'Esprit*, 22, 57.

Chapter Seventeen: The Evangelical Counsels

1. See Meersseman, *Dossier*, 283, 284, 288.

2. *Testamentum sancti Francisci* 14, *Francis and Clare*, 155; Latin original, *François d'Assise: Écrits*, ed. T. Desbonnets and others, SC no 285 (Paris: Editions du Cerf, 1981), 206. See also n. 11 of the preceding chapter. As Esser comments: "The Gospel is the

Rule of the Friars Minor, their way of life, their form of life, but also their norm of life" (*Origins*, 213). Esser discusses the meaning of *vivere secundum formam s. evangelii*, 208-17.

3. *Historia occidentalis* 32.

4. Summa eius intentio, praecipuum desiderium, supremumque propositum eius erat sanctum Evangelium in omnibus et per omnia observare, ac perfecte omni vigilantia, omni studio, toto desiderio mentis, toto cordis fervore, "Domini nostri Iesu Christi doctrinam sequi et vestigia" imitari (1 Celano 84).

5. *Francis and Clare*, 108. Latin original: Haec est vita evangelii Jesu Christi, *Écrits*, 122. Cf. Esser, *Origins*, 213.

6. For a study of the meaning of "This is the life of the Gospel of Jesus Christ," and "The rule and life of these brothers is this," see Dino Dozzi, *Il vangelo nella regola non bollata di Francesco d'Assisi*, 2d ed., Bibliotheca Seraphico-Capuccina 36 (Rome: Istituto storico dei Cappucini, 1989), 49-50, 131-37.

7. Laurentius Casutt, O.F.M.Cap., *Die älteste franziskanische Lebensform: Untersuchungen zur Regula prima sine bulla* (Graz, 1955), 77-78.

8. *Francis and Clare*, 109; Latin original, *Écrits*, 122. In a bull of 1198, *Operante divinae dispositionis*, Innocent III affirmed the Rule of the Brothers of the Holy Trinity for the Redemption of Captives, who "live under obedience [*sub obedientia*] to the superior of their house . . . in chastity [*in castitate*], and without anything of their own [*et sine proprio*]" [*BRT* 3:134a]. Esser raises the question whether by the insertion Francis's broader evangelical outlook "may not have been narrowed to the threefold evangelical counsels, which were then becoming standard" (*Origins*, 256 n. 58; see also 192-93 n. 76). What follows is not an attempt to solve this problem, but may help to place it in perspective.

9. Dozzi, *Il vangelo*, 134-36.

10. *Francis and Clare*, 137; Latin original, *Écrits*, 181. "Without anything of their own [*sine proprio*]" does not have the same meaning in the Franciscan Rule as in the Trinitarian bull (see above, n. 8). The bull explicitly states that one third of the income of the Trinitarians, whatever the legitimate source, is for works of charity, one third for their sustenance, and one third for the redemption of captives [*BRT* 3:134ab]. Francis wanted his brothers to have nothing except what they received from begging or a little manual work (*Earlier Rule* 8, *Later Rule* 5, 6; *Testament* 20-22).

11. Vatican II restored the old approach, but it did not abandon the new terminology: "Since the final norm of the religious life [*vitae religiosae ultima norma*] is the following of Christ as it is put before us in the Gospel [*Christi sequela in Evangelio proposita*], this must be taken by all institutes as the supreme rule [*suprema regula*].... Before all else, religious life is ordered to the following of Christ by its members and to their becoming united with God by the profession of the evangelical counsels [*consiliorum evangelicorum*]" (*Perfectae caritatis*, 2a, 2e; E.T., "Decree on the Up-to-date Renewal of Religious Life," in *Vatican Council II: The Conciliar and Post Conciliar Documents*, ed. Austin Flannery, O.P. [Collegeville: Liturgical Press, 1975], 612, 613). Vatican II presents a refinement of the classical doctrine of St. Thomas Aquinas. Although the "popular" position of the earlier part of the twentieth century did not deny the universal call to holiness addressed to all Christians, it emphasized that following the counsels was better and appealed to the generosity of young people to follow a way that was harder. The dogmatic constitution on the Church, *Lumen Gentium*, lays much more stress on the beatitudes and on the call to all Christians to be perfect as their heavenly Father is perfect (Mt. 5). In discussing the evangelical counsels, *Lumen Gentium* and the other documents of Vatican II say nothing about the Council of Trent's position in 1563 that virginity is better than marriage [Session XXIV, Canon 10 on matrimony, *COD*, 731], but they do speak of the witness given through the practice of the evangelical counsels to the holiness to which all Christians are called.

12. *Vita Antonii* 2. For an insightful analysis of the place of Scripture in fourth-century Christian Egypt, see Douglas Burton-Christie, *The Word in the Desert: Scripture and the Quest for Holiness in Early Christian Monasticism* (New York: Oxford University Press, 1993), especially 107-77.

13. Adalbert de Vogüé, O.S.B., "Les critères du discernement des vocations dans la tradition monastique ancienne," *Collectanea Cisterciensia* 51 (1989): 113.

14. The eastern monks called submission *hypotagē* and renunciation *apotagē*. See Armand Veilleux, O.C.S.O., "Asceticism in Pachomian Cenobitism," in *The Continuing Quest for God: Monastic Spirituality in Tradition and Transition*, ed. William Skudlarek, O.S.B. (Collegeville: Liturgical Press, 1982), 77.

15. "The monastic way of life was conceived as a response to the precepts of Scripture and was oriented toward the progressive assimilation of the truths of Scripture" (Ansgar Kristensen, O.S.B., and Mark Sheridan, O.S.B., "The Role and Interpreta-

tion of Scripture in the Rule of Benedict," in *RB 80*, Appendix 6, 467). "Precepts" here is used in the sense in which it is used in *RB* 2.4, "the Lord's instructions [*praeceptum Domini*]". In that sense, the "counsels" would be included amongst the "precepts" of the Lord.

16. Adalbert de Vogüé, "The Evangelical Counsels in the Master and Saint Benedict," *Cistercian Studies* 15 (1980): 4; Mary Collins, O.S.B., "Rule and Gospel: The Meaning of Benedictine Vowing," *Benedictines* 35, no. 2 (Fall-Winter 1980): 30-33.

17. De Vogüé, "Evangelical Counsels," 12-13.

18. For a reflection on how the monastic life includes the reality of the counsels even though approaching them obliquely, see de Vogüé, "The Evangelical Counsels," 3-16; for the monastic life in terms of the Gospel, see Collins, "Rule and Gospel," 27-46; for an overview of the historical development of monastic commitment, see, among others, Cornelius Justice, "Evolution of the Teaching on Commitment by Monastic Vow from New Testament Times to the Ninth Century," *Cistercian Studies* 12 (1977): 18-40; Steidle, Excursus on "History of Monastic Profession," in *Rule of St. Benedict*, 247-57; Peifer, "Monastic Formation and Profession," in *RB 80*, 437-66.

19. Among others, for example, the following authors mention Odo's triad, but that is all: J.-M.-R. Tillard, "Consigli evangelici," *DIP*, 2 (1975): 1653; G. Rocca, "Professione," *DIP*, 7 (1983): 940; Ludwig Hertling, S.J., "Die professio der Kleriker und die Entstehung der drei Gelübde," *Zeitschrift für Katholische Theologie* 56 (1932): 171.

20. *PL* 196, 1399B. A profession formula from St. Victor's uses identical terminology (*Antiquae consuetudines canonicorum regularium insignis monasterii S. Victoris Parisiensis*, ed. E. Martène, *De antiquis*, vol. 3, appendix, col. 810-11). Odo was named prior of the abbey of St. Victor in Paris in 1133, and he held that office until elected the first abbot of the new foundation of St. Genevieve in 1148. (Robert-Henri Bautier, "Les origines et les premiers développements de l'abbaye Saint-Victor de Paris." In *L'Abbaye parisienne de Saint-Victor au moyen age:* Communications présentées au XIIIe Colloque d'Humanisme médiéval de Paris [1986-1988], ed. Jean Longère, pp. 44, 49-50. Bibliotheca Victorina 1 [Turnhout: Brepols, 1991].) It is safe to assume, therefore, that the actual formula of profession in use at St. Genevieve's in 1148 was identical to that used at St. Victor's. Nonetheless, Hertling, "Die professio," 172, argues that the Victorine formula comes later, otherwise it

would have been known to Hugh of St. Victor (+1141), or at least to Peter Comestor (+ca. 1178), who uses a different triad, "shared fraternal love [*communi dilectione fraterna*], shared goods [*communi substantia*], shared obedience [*communi obedientia*]" (*PL* 198, 1842C). Peter, however, is talking about the law of common life [*vitae communis*], which is at the heart of the Rule of Augustine, and is comparing his community to the apostolic community in Acts. Note that fraternal charity is an element of chaste love in both Peter's celibate community and the noncelibate community of Acts.

21. Luc Verheijen, *La Règle de Saint Augustin*, vol. 1, *Tradition Manuscrite* (Paris: Études Augustiniennes, 1967), 417.
22. *PL* 196, 1399B-1400A.
23. *Ibid.*, 1401A.
24. *Ibid.*, 1401D-1402B.
25. Cf. the remarks of de Vogüé, "The Evangelical Counsels," 12-13.
26. *PL* 196, 1402C-1403A.
27. Dom Ursmer Berlière, "Innocent III et la réorganisation des monastères bénédictins," *Revue bénédictine* 32 (1920): 22-42, 145-59, esp. p. 35. See also Aloisio di Paolo, *Innocenzo III e gli ordini religiosi* [dissertation excerpt] (Rome: PUG, 1957); Brenda M. Bolton, "*Via ascetica*: A Papal Quandary," in *Monks, Hermits and the Ascetic Tradition*, ed. W. J. Sheils, SCH 22 (London: Blackwell, 1985), 161-91.
28. The entire letter is in *PL* 214, 1064-66. Innocent wrote a somewhat similar letter to Montecassino (*PL* 217, 249-53). See also Berlière, "Innocent III," 39-40.
29. For example, P. Séjourné, "Voeux de religion," *DTC*, 15/2 (1950): 3271-72; P. F. Mulhern, "Vows," *NCE*, 14 (1967): 757a; Tillard, "Consigli," 1652.
30. "Nec aestimet abbas, quod super habenda proprietate possit cum aliquo monacho dispensare, quia abdicatio proprietatis, sicut et custodia castitatis, adeo est annexa regulae monachali, ut contra eam nec summus Pontifex possit licentiam indulgere" (*Decretales* 3.35, De statu monachorum et canonicorum regularium, chap. 6, in *Corpus iuris canonici*, ed. Friedberg [Leipzig: Tauchnitz, 1922], 2:600).
31. See above, chap. 8, pp. 151-52; also, Bolton, *Medieval Reformation*, chap. 3, on "Lay religious movements," 55-66, and chap. 6, "Reaction of Church and papacy," 94-111.

32. 2a 2ae q. 186 a.3.
33. The bull is *In divini timore*, *Bull. Franc.* 1:316D, as quoted by Tillard, "Consigli," 1653.
34. Tillard translates this passage into Italian as: "Questa Regola (di Benedetto) vincola le suore soltanto all'obbedienza, alla renuncia della proprietà privata e alla castità perpetua, che costituiscono i valori essenziali di ogni forma di vita religiosa" (he provides the Latin text for part of his quotation: "nisi ad obedientiam, abdicationem proprii ac perpetuam castitatem quae substantialia cujuslibet religionis existunt). He makes no mention of a variant reading to justify substituting *substantialia* for *sub alia*. The reference he provides is: "cf L. Oliger, *De origine regularum Ordinis s. Clarae*, in ArchFrancHist 5 [1912] 203-4; *Bull-Franc.* I, p. 316)." Oliger has a variant reading, but it is *quae sub alia cuiuslibet Religione existunt.* The other reference is the same as our own. Mandonnet also has *substantialia* in his reading (*Saint Dominique*, 2:180 n. 59) and refers to Sbaralea I, 316, but this is just another way of writing *Bull. Franc.* 1:316D, for Sbaralea is the editor of *Bull. Franc.* Mandonnet gives no variant reading as a ground for substituting *substantialia* for *sub alia*.
35. The abbess was concerned about their obligation, as followers of Francis and Clare, to observe a rule based on that of St. Benedict which Hugolino Conti, their cardinal protector had given them in 1219. Innocent IV is telling her that the Rule of Benedict makes their order legitimate. See below in chap. 18, pp. 324-25, the norms of Canon 13 of Lateran IV (1215) that any religious order coming into existence must adopt one of the pre-existing rules. Not long after Conti became Pope Gregory IX, he appointed his nephew, Raynaldo Conti, cardinal protector in his place and, later on, his successor as cardinal of Ostia. In his letter Innocent IV explains what his "predecessor [Gregory IX], with the cardinal of Ostia [Raynaldo Conti] present and listening," said regarding the obligation of the Poor Clares to follow the Benedictine Rule. The clause, *quae sub alia*, etc., may be part of what Gregory said, or it may be Innocent's own remark. The sentence continues, "et in quibus consistit meritum consequendi perpetuae felicitatis effectum" (*Bull. Franc.* 1:316D-17A).
36. Capuchins: *Religionis zelus*, 1528: "Regulam beati Francisci observare" (*BRT* 6:113b); Franciscans of the Strict Observance: *In suprema*, 1532: "Regulam B. Francisci" (*BRT* 6:156a); Somaschi: *Iniunctum nobis*, 1568: "sub Regula S. Augustini" (*BRT* 7:730b).

37. Third Order Franciscans: *Inter cetera*, 1521 (*BRT* 5:767a); Theatines: *Exponi nobis*, 1524 (*BRT* 6:73a,b); Barnabites: *Dudum felicis*, 1535 (*BRT* 6:191a,b); Camillians: *Ex omnibus*, 1586: "sub paupertate, castitate et obedientia, ita tamen ut voto adstricti non sint" (*BRT* 8:669b). Notice that *substantialia* [substantial] substitutes for what Thomas had called *essentialia* [essential] (2a 2ae q. 186 a.2, ad 3).

38. Cassian's first conference, "The Goal or Objective of the Monk," written centuries before Ignatius, is a good commentary on all that is meant by "work against their human sensitivies, etc." See *Cassian: Conferences*, trans. Colm Luibheid, CWS (New York: Paulist Press, 1985), 37-59.

39. Even at Manresa Ignatius seems to have been spontaneously Thomistic. Although St. Thomas distinguished between precepts and counsels, he placed Christian perfection in the fulfillment of the *precept* of charity (2a 2ae q. 184 a.3): to love God with one's whole heart and to love one's neighbor as oneself. This precept has no limits. It demands the whole of a person, and it demands it from every Christian. The purpose of other precepts is to remove whatever is contrary to charity, obstacles that make charity impossible. The purpose of the counsels, such as voluntary poverty, celibacy for the sake of the kingdom, obedience, fasting and other forms of mortification, is to remove obstacles to charity that do not make charity impossible, e.g., engaging in commerce or marriage. For a brief exposé of Thomas's teaching on the vows, see Witwer, "Missionary Focus of Vows," 40-42.

40. According to Calveras/Dalmases, Ignatius wrote these two annotations in Italy after he had left Paris ("Introductio generalis," *Exercitia Spiritualia*, 32).

41. The magnanimity that Ignatius seeks in the fifth annotation [5] is to be tempered by quiet waiting. The exercitant has already found God, (or God has already found the exercitant!), and the initiative belongs to God.

42. Cassian cautions against confusing the means with the end in *Conference* 1.7 (*Cassian: Conferences*, 42).

43. In 1539, the year of *Cum ex plurium*, Ignatius had probably not yet written two other passages, one that we ought to praise religious orders [356], and the other that we ought to praise religious vows [357], nor do they add anything of substance to the above (Calveras/Dalmases, *Exercitia Spiritualia*, 33).

44. Leturia, *Iñigo de Loyola*, 134.

45. Compare the language concerning poverty, chastity, and obedience in the whole of *Cum ex plurium* with the express mention of the "three substantial vows of religion" in the apostolic letters approving other orders founded in the sixteenth century, n. 37 above.

46. St. Thomas Aquinas considers the general question whether a religious is bound to all of the counsels. In replying in the negative he describes the religious state as "a certain discipline or exercise of arriving at perfection" and wisely says that different persons arrive at the goal through different exercises. They do not have to be perfect but to tend toward perfection. Nor do they have to do everything (2a 2ae q. 186 a.2).

47. The next year, 1540, the solemn bull of approbation, *Regimini militantis ecclesiae*, begins in the same way, changing only "the Lord alone and his vicar on earth" to "the Lord alone and the Roman Pontiff, his vicar on earth." It was not until *Exposcit debitum* in 1550 that "after a solemn vow of perpetual chastity" was changed to "after a solemn vow of perpetual chastity, poverty and obedience."

48. For a contemporary understanding of Ignatius's attitude and decision see Robert Taft, S.J., *The Liturgy of the Hours in East and West: The Origins of the Divine Office and Its Meaning for Today* (Collegeville: Liturgical Press, 1986), 301-6. Cf. Klaus Schatz, S.J., "Ordensleben: Die evangelischen Räte im Zeitalter der Reformation," in *Ignatius von Loyola*, 109-20, and Witwer, "Missionary Focus of Vows," 46.

49. The Council of Vienne (1311-12), indeed, raises the question whether the Franciscan rule binds a friar to the fulfillment of all the evangelical counsels or to those only that are mentioned in the rule [*COD*, 369]. The answer, "one vowing to keep the rule is not bound by force of this vow to keep the evangelical counsels not found in the rule," while true in its own limited way, misses the whole point of Francis's Rule, which is to set one on the path of the Gospel, "to follow the teaching and the footsteps of our Lord Jesus Christ." For Francis the Gospel is the rule.

Chapter Eighteen:
The Normative Teaching of the Fathers

1. A good analysis of *canon*, its roots and its uses, can be found in the introductory remarks of Schroeder, 1-4.

2. Blaise, *Dictionnaire*, 736a. Kings also have issued various "Pragmatic Sanctions" throughout history, decrees proclaiming a variety of matters, not necessarily penalties.
3. For example, in *Constitutiones* 8 and 14 of Lateran IV (1215) [*COD*, 213, 218]; twice in the decree of Julius II in 1512 condemning the Council of Pisa [*COD*, 571 and 572].
4. *Fulgens sicut stella*, *BRT* 4:340b; the passage is somewhat abbreviated in *Summi Magistri dignatio* (1336), *BRT* 4:373a.
5. The Latin text of the rule is in the appendix to Kunkel, *Theatines*, 166-67; E.T. in Olin, 130-32.
6. With regard to chastity, see chap. 3, n. 24. The same chapter refers to decrees on the care of souls [*cura animarum*], nn. 16 and 48; decrees on clerical cupidity, benefices and other sources of clerical income, nn. 20 and 21; clerical dress is indirectly addressed in the section on Ignatius the cleric, p. 66. For the proper training of clerics, which was a major concern of Lateran V, see chap. 3, n. 17, and also chap. 8, p. 141. The norms for preaching set down by Lateran IV have been indicated in this latter chapter on p. 146 and in nn. 16 and 29.
7. H. Leclercq, "Lateran Councils," *CE*, 9:18a. *Regimini militantis ecclesiae*, the bull solemnly approving the Society in 1540, provides an example of referring to Lateran IV as *the* general council without specifying its name: "in spite of any constitutions of the general council and of Pope Gregory X of happy memory, our predecessor, or of any other constitutions or apostolic determinations, or of anything else whatsoever to the contrary" [*C* 31 {10}]. Gregory X presided over the Second Council of Lyons (1274), which reasserted the decree of Lateran IV (1215) regarding new religious orders. In the second session of the Fifth Lateran Council Julius II states that the decrees of Lateran V have the same force and validity as those of other general councils, "especially the Lateran" [*COD*, 572], probably referring to Lateran IV [*COD*, 572 n. 1].
8. Raymond Hostie, S.J., *Vie et mort des ordres religieux: Approches psychosociologiques*, Bibliothèque d'études psychoreligieuses (Paris: Desclée De Brouwer, 1972), 37.
9. See Bolton, "Tradition and Temerity," esp. 79 and 90; "Innocent III's Treatment of the Humiliati," esp. 81-82; also her *Medieval Reformation*, 108; Mandonnet, *St. Dominic*, 442; J. Dubois, "Institutio," *DIP*, 4 (1977): 1727, who says the bishops were disturbed.

10. M. Maccarrone, "Riforma e sviluppo della vita religiosa con Innocenzo III," *Revista di Storia della Chiesa in Italia* 16 (1962) 29-72, and "Lateranense IV, Concilio," *DIP*, 5 (1978): 490-92; Powell, "Papacy and Early Franciscans," while not rejecting Maccarrone's position, qualifies it to make Innocent more conservative than Maccarrone presents him.
11. Lekai, *Cistercians*, 26-29.
12. J. Dubois, "Les ordres religieux au XIIe siècle selon la curie romaine," *Revue bénédictine* 78 (1968): 283-309, esp. 308-9; cf. Lekai, *Cistercians*, 30.
13. Vicaire, "L'Ordre," 9; Luigi Prosdocimi, "A proposito della terminologia e della natura giuridica delle norme monastiche e canonicali nei secoli XI et XII," in *La vita comune del clero nei secoli XI e XII* (Milan: Vita e Pensiero, 1962), 2:1-8.
14. See above chap. 13, p. 244.
15. Esser, *Origins*, 43 n. 8, gives examples of popular usage at the time. He notes, however, that in official Church usage *religio* was more widely employed.
16. J. Dubois, "Ordo," *DIP*, 6 (1980): 806-20, esp. 809-11.
17. A rule was considered approved either because it had received the approbation of a proper authority, or because it had stood the test of time in the life of the Church. See J. Torres, "Documenti pontifici di approvazione," *DIP*, 3 (1973:) 752. The entire article, 751-77, provides a much more detailed and nuanced presentation of the whole history of approving rules. See also: Clement Raymond Orth, O.M.C., *The Approbation of Religious Institutes*, Canon Law Studies no. 71 (Washington, D.C.: Catholic University of America Press, 1931); Theodore Baa, T.O.R., *The Ecclesiastical Approbation of a Religious Institute*, Angelicum dissertation (Rome, 1961).
18. Cicconetti, *Regola del Carmelo*, 52-56, 118-19.
19. A. Linage Conde, "Militari, Ordini," *DIP*, 5 (1978) 1287-99, esp. 1291; G. Escudero, *El voto solemne de pobreza: Su historia, su naturaleza y su problemática actual* (Madrid: Editorial Coculsa, 1955), 86-88; Lawrence, *Medieval Monasticism*, 206-15.
20. Maccarrone, "Riforma e sviluppo," 44-55.
21. Maccarrone, "Lateranense IV," 492.
22. The translation of this canon that appears in H. J. Schroeder's *Disciplinary Decrees of the General Councils* shows how some important terms have been misunderstood: "Lest too great a diversity

of religious orders [*religionum*] lead to grave confusion in the Church of God, we strictly forbid anyone in the future to found a new order [*religionem*], but whoever should wish to enter an order [*religionem*], let him choose one already approved. Similarly, he who would wish to found a new monastery [*religiosam domum*], must accept a rule [*regulam et institutionem*] already approved [*de religionibus approbatis*]" (p. 255). The Latin inserts [*COD*, 218] are not part of Schroeder's text.

23. Dubois, "Les ordres religieux," 283-309, esp. 308-9.

24. Considerable confusion has been generated by the inattention of authors to the meaning of *institutio*. Mandonnet deplores the confusion and defines the terms clearly through a study of the way the Church used the terms after Lateran IV, distinguishing between *regula et institutio* found in Canon 13 and *regula et institutiones* found in profession formulas. *Institutio* in Canon 13 refers to the fundamental organization of the religious house; *institutiones* in the formulas of profession refers to the constitutions. No new group was ever required to adopt already approved constitutions (*Saint Dominique, l'idée, l'homme et l'oeuvre/ St. Dominic and His Work* [1937/1945], 2:178-79 n. 58; E.T., 443 n. 45). Note that the English translation of Vicaire's later work, *Histoire de Saint Dominique*, refers to that footnote but incorrectly places it in vol. 1 rather than in vol. 2. Unhappily, moreover, it renders *institutionem* in Canon 13 as *constitutions*, thereby undoing the work of the French original (*St. Dominic and His Times* [1964], 198). Vicaire's original French text reads "De la même façon, qui veut désormais fonder une maison religieuse prenne la règle et l'institution d'une société religieuse approuvée" (*Histoire de Saint Dominique* [Paris: Editions du Cerf, 1957], 2:24). Unhappily, again, in J. Leclercq, O.S.B., "Qu'est-ce que vivre 'selon une règle'?", where the text refers to *regula et institutiones* of Canon 13, the plural, *institutiones*, might engender some confusion (*Coll. Cist.* 32 [1970]: 157-58).

25. The final sentence in Canon 13, omitted above as less relevant, deserves a brief comment. The text reads: "We also forbid a monk to belong to a variety of monasteries, nor should an abbot preside over several monasteries" (*COD*, 218). That made eminent sense in a monastic world committed to stability of place. Imagine the mind-stretching everyone in the Church had to undergo to accept the unheard-of reality of the upstart Franciscans and Dominicans, who would move from house to house freely, and would soon have provincials governing a variety of houses spread all over the world.

26. See above, chap. 17, pp. 308-9.
27. *Bull. Franc.* 1:315-17.
28. *Clare of Assisi: Early Documents*, ed. Regis J. Armstrong, O.F.M.Cap. (New York: Paulist Press, 1988), 88-89. Latin text from *Bull Franc.* 1:264, quoted by Mandonnet, *Saint Dominique*, 180 n. 59.
29. Maccarrone, "Lateranense IV," 495.
30. Richard W. Emery, "The Second Council of Lyons and the Mendicant Orders," *The Catholic Historical Review* 39 (1953): 258.
31. *Const.* 23, *COD*, 302-3. Of those orders that had papal approval, Rome suppressed only the Friars of the Sack and the Friars of the Blessed Mary (Pied Friars). The Order of the Holy Cross, known today as the Crosiers, apparently evolved into an order of canons regular, which allowed them to escape suppression. After much struggle on the part of the Servites, Honorius IV issued bulls in 1286 and 1287 allowing them to continue. The same pope issued bulls in 1286 favoring the Augustinians, the Carmelites, and Williamites. He took a sharp stand, however, against the Apostolic Friars, who had not been approved. As for other orders, approved and unapproved, they gradually disappeared from history (Emery, "Second Council," 257-71).
32. *COD*, 303.
33. Torres, "Documenti pontifici," 754.
34. M. Conti, "Regola Francescana," *DIP*, 7 (1983): 1483.
35. Cf. Hostie, *Vie et mort*, 168.
36. *Ibid.*, 169.
37. P. Bianchini, "Chierici Regolari Somaschi," *DIP*, 2 (1975): 975-76.
38. Estanilao Olivares, S.J., "Aportación de la Compañía de Jesús a la vida religiosa en su época," *Manresa* 56 (1984): 232-33. See also Jean Beyer, S.J., "Novità della Compagnia di Gesù nelle strutture degli ordini religiosi," *Vita consacrata* 27 (1991): 735-39.
39. See above, chap. 16.
40. José Luis Urrutia, S.J., "Regimen de las ordenes religiosas a mediados del s. XVI y aportación de San Ignacio," *Miscelánea Comillas* 36 (1961): 140-41. See also Schatz, "Ordensleben," 113-14, and Rafael Mª Sanz de Diego, S.J., "La novedad de Ignacio de Loyola ante un mundo nuevo," in *Ignacio de Loyola y su tiempo*, 922-25.
41. The Council of Trent will use the term *clerks regular* [clergy with a rule] to distinguish religious clergy from diocesan clergy

(*COD*, 665, lines 19-20; 756, line 35). Trent will refer to the Society's members as "secular clergy of the Society of Jesus," and protocol will list Jay, Laynez, and Salmerón with the theologians of the secular clergy (*CT*, 5:162, 255; 7/1:241, 244).

42. *CIC, Decretum Gratiani* 2.18.2.10 (Friedberg 1:832); *COD*, 65, lines 16-20.

43. *CIC*, Extravag. Joann. XXII, tit. 7, "De religiosis domibus" (Friedberg 2:1213-14). See what is said above about the practice of the Church, pp. 325-26.

Chapter Nineteen: The Meaning of *propositum* in Christian Tradition

1. The title had first been given to St. Dominic when he was named to the post in 1218, and a Dominican has held it ever since (Reginald Walsh, "Master of the Sacred Palace," *CE*, 10:39). P. C. Van Lierde softens the statement concerning Dominic to "is thought to have been the first to be so appointed," in a brief article, "Master of the Sacred Palace" *NCE*, 9:437b. Mandonnet says that when the popes moved to Avignon in the beginning of the 14th c. they instituted a school of theology in the palace. The office was entrusted to a Dominican, and he was given the title, Master of the Sacred Palace (*St. Dominic*, 79). A detailed examination of sources for this title is found in Dr. Berthold Altaner, *Der hl. Dominikus: Untersuchungen und Texte* (Breslau: G. P. Aderholz, 1922), 201-7.

2. Pastor, 203. Cf. Innocentius Taurisano, O.P., *Hierarchia Ordinis Praedicatorum* (Rome: Manuzio, 1916), 51-52. Modena's Latin name is Mutinensis de Abbatiis [Abadia].

3. Pastor, 155, 161-62, 169.

4. TV, 2/1:269 n. 4; letter of Cardinal Aleandro to Msgr. Nicolò Ardinghelli and found in Cortese, *Opera* I, 55ff.

5. Pastor, 204. G. Alberigo provides a good summary of Badia's life in "Badia," *Dizionario Biografico degli Italiani*, ed. A. M. Ghisaberti, vol. 5 (Rome: Istituto della Enciclopedia italiana, 1963), 74b-76b.

6. Bartoli, *History*, 1:318 (*Vita*, l.2, c. 45, p. 178). Although the editors of the Monumenta do not challenge the historicity of Bartoli's statement, they do add the qualifying phrase, "if we can believe him in this matter" [*C* ccvi, 3].

7. TV, 2/1:270 n. 3; cf. Schur., 468.

8. On May 6, 1220, Pope Honorius III wrote to the archbishop of Barcelona commending the Dominicans and asking him to promote the order in his archdiocese. He refers to their "good intent and needed ministry [*pium propositum et necessarium ministerium*]" (Koudelka, no. 122). In a letter of January 18, 1221, he uses "holy intent and needed ministry [*sanctum propositum et necessarium ministerium*]" (Koudelka, no. 140). *Pium* and *sanctum* are more or less synonymous.

9. Justice, "Evolution of Teaching," 20. North American sports fans can gain some sense of the meaning of *propositum* from the "letter of intent" sent by a high school athlete to one of the colleges or universities that has recruited the athlete, accepting a scholarship offered and committing the athlete to enroll in the sports program at that school.

10. Caesar, *De bello civili* 1.83; Cicero, *Epistulae ad Brutum* 19.2 (1.ii.2); Phaedrus, *Fab. Aesop.* 3, prol. 15; Velleius, *Hist. rom.* 2.2.2; Seneca, *Ep.* 68.3.

11. For a detailed treatment of the term *propositum* in various periods of Christian tradition, see: Hertling, "Die professio," 148-74; Lorié, *Spiritual Terminology*, 74-86, 98-101; Capelle, *Voeu d'Obéissance, passim*; J. Campos, "El 'propositum' monástico en la tradición patrística," *La Ciudad de Dios* 181 (1968): 535-47; Cicconetti, *Regola del Carmelo*, 58-83, 93-107; Germain Lesage, "Sacred Bonds in the Consecrated Life," *The Way*, Supplement no. 37 (Spring 1980): 78-96. This is an abridgement of the original Latin, "Evolutio et momentum vinculi sacri in professione vitae consecratae," *Periodica de re morali canonica liturgica* 67 (1978): 413-45.

12. *Ep.* 55.21, *Ep.* 72.3, CSEL 3, 639, 778.

13. *Ep.* 55.20, CSEL 3, 638.

14. Sermo 56, *PL* 17, 720A (sermon ascribed to Ambrose).

15. *De virginibus* 3.1.1.

16. René Metz, *La consécration des vierges dans l'église romaine* (Paris: Presses universitaires de France, 1954). See especially 138-44, 431-36.

17. *Ordo consecrationis virginum* (*Pontificale Romanum*), editio typica (Vatican City, 1970), no. 24.

18. Seneca, *De beneficiis* 6.7.4; Quintilian, *Declamationes* 255.

19. *Propositum continentiae*: Cyprian, *Ep.* 55.20; Augustine, *De bono viduitatis* 8.11; *Decretum Gratiani* 1.30.15 (quoting Council of Granga). *Propositum virginitatis*: Ambrose, *sermo* 56; Leo the Great, *Ep.* 12.11 and *Ep.* 167.15. *Propositum castitatis*: *Cons. Zacch.*

& *Apol.* 3.3. *Propositum virginale:* Innocent I, *Ep.* Victricio; Council of Tours (567) quoting Innocent I; *Decretum Gratiani* 2.27.1.2, 9 in each instance quoting Innocent I. *Propositum viduitatis:* Innocent I, *Ep.* Victricio; *Decretum Gratiani* 2.27.1.9. *Propositum vidualis castitatis:* Augustine, *De bono viduitatis* 8.11. *Propositum monachi:* Leo the Great, *Ep.* 167.14 (included in *Decr. Gratiani* 2.20.3.1). *Propositum monachorum:* 4th Council of Toledo (631), c. 49 (included in *Decr. Gratiani* 2.19.1.1). *Propositum canonicorum:* Urban II, bull *Potestatem ligandi* (1092), *BRT* 2:131a.

20. *Propositum serviendi Deo* [serving God]: Augustine, *Vita* auctore Possidio, cap. 2. *Propositum paupertatis* [poverty]: Augustine, *sermo* 356.3. *Propositum religionis* [religion]: 10th Council of Toledo (656); *Decretum Gratiani* 2.20.1.16; 2.27.1.2, 19; Meersseman, *Dossier,* 47. *Intrandi monasterium propositum* [entering a monastery]: *Decretal. Gregor.* IX 3.32.16. *Propositum penitentie* [penance]: Meersseman, *Dossier,* 255. *Peregrinationis propositum* [pilgrimage]: *Decretal. Gregor.* IX 3.34.7.

21. *Ep.* 2 to Victricius of Rouen, *PL* 20, 479-80.

22. *Sermo* 355, *PL* 39, 1573; *De bono viduitatis* 9.12, CSEL 41, 317-18.

23. *Decretum Gratiani* 2.27.1.1-19 (Friedberg 1:1047-54).

24. Peter Brown, *The Body and Society: Men, Women, and Sexual Renunciation in Early Christianity* (New York: Columbia University Press, 1988), 259-84.

25. Lesage, "Sacred Bonds," 79.

26. See, for example, St. Jerome, *Ep.* 22.14 and 18, CSEL 54, 162 and 167.

27. Lorié, *Spiritual Terminology,* 2.

28. *PG* 26, 851. References are to the Latin text of Evagrius, printed below the Greek text of the 1698 Benedictine edition by Bernard de Montfaucon in *PG* 26, 835-976. Cf. Lorié, *Spiritual Terminology,* 74, 80-81.

29. *PG* 26, 847 and 867.

30. See Campos, "Propositum monástico," 540-41.

31. *La Règle du Maître,* ed. Adalbert de Vogüé, 2 vols., SC 105 and 106 (Paris: Editions du Cerf, 1964).

32. Guiges Ier, Prieur de Chartreuse, *Coutumes de Chartreuse.*

33. See chap. 21.

34. Meersseman, *Dossier,* 276-89; see also 47, 54, 92-112, 255, 292.

35. *Ibid.,* 276, introduction; 281, no. 13.

36. *Ibid.*, 282, no. 17.
37. See above, chap. 16.
38. *Dialogi*, bk.1, *PL* 188, 1156b.
39. *Rule of St. Albert*, Prologue, 78-79.
40. See Campos, "Propositum monástico," a philological presentation of the changes in meaning *propositum* undergoes when shifting synonyms, moving from the determination [*intentio*] or resolve [*voluntas*] to live in a particular manner, to living that way [*conversatio*], and finally to the way of living itself [*institutum*]. That *propositum* becomes *institutum*, that an inspiration becomes an institution, does not mean that the *propositum* loses its charismatic nature and ceases to be an inspiration. A vocation from God, even when it is institutionalized, is by its nature a charism and always retains its inspired and inspiring character. See Bertrand, *Un corps pour l'Esprit*, 10-13, where the author discusses the charism of the Exercises and the institutional nature of the Constitutions.

Chapter Twenty: The *propositum* of Ignatius

1. Calveras/Dalmases, *Exercitia Spiritualia*, 30-33.
2. Antonio T. de Nicolas, *Powers of Imagining: Ignatius de Loyola* (Albany: State University of New York Press, 1986), 166.
3. Leturia explains why Ignatius and Martín do not share the same name: "It was customary during this period for brothers to apportion among themselves the various names occurring in the family genealogy. Ignatius' eldest brother was called *Juan Perez de Loyola* after an ancestor of that name who lived around 1280. His elder brother was named *Martin Garcia de Oñaz* after Lope Garcia who lived around 1260. Finally, Ignatius along with his priest brother Pero used the name *Lopez* which had been in the family since 1221. They combined it with the title of the family estate which has been immortalized by history: both are *Lopez de Loyola*" (*Iñigo*, ix). Ignatius, therefore, was known as *Iñigo Lopez de Loyola*.
4. *Epistulae ad Atticum* 14.1.2.
5. E.T., Ganss, *Ignatius*, 334.
6. Polanco says the conversation was in Latin [*PSH* 85].
7. The main source for this section is Ignatius's autobiographical dictation to Luis Gonçalves da Câmara in the years 1553 to

1555 following Nadal's insistence that the whole Society needed to know how God had dealt with the founder.

8. *Exhort. 1554 in Hispania, MN* 5:37 [4-5]; *Annot. in Examen* (1557), *MN* 5:135-36 [4]; *Exhort. 1 Complut., MN* 5:226-29 [8-8*]; *Exhort. 2 Compl., MN* 5:262-63 [33-33*]; *Exhort. Colonienses, MN* 5:780 [4]. See Richard Ward Dunphy, S.J., *Placed with Jesus Bearing His Cross: A Study of Jesuit Identity in the Light of St. Ignatius Loyola's Life of Grace, as Based upon the First Jesuits' Understanding of Their Relationship to Their Founder* (Rome: PUG, 1983), esp. 32-57; Conwell, *Contemplation in Action*, 16-45; Miguel Nicolau, S.J., *Jerónimo Nadal, S.I. (1507-1580) Sus obras y doctrinas espirituales* (Madrid, 1949), 148-51, and appendix two, "Pláticas de renovación en Roma el año 1557," 490-91; Miguel Nicolau, S.J., ed., *Pláticas espirituales del P. Jerónimo Nadal, S.I., en Coimbra (1561)* (Granada, 1945), 62-70.

9. The urge to go to Jerusalem must have come from reading the *Life of Christ*, the urge to imitate the saints from reading the *Lives of the Saints*. The latter contains little about going to Jerusalem. One of the saints Ignatius admired was Humphrey or Onfroy [*Onuphrius*], whom we shall meet again below, a desert monk who ate nothing but vegetables.

10. Martín was the head of the household and the only brother at home. For the whereabouts of the other brothers, see Dalmases, *Ignatius of Loyola*, 12-14.

11. When Laynez describes this period in which Ignatius experienced movements of various spirits, he sometimes uses synonyms for *propositum*, saying that God gave Ignatius a "clear intention [*intención*] and good will [*voluntad*]." He tells how Ignatius took from the lives of the saints "what appealed to him for his purpose [*propósito*]," that "he made a resolution [*propósito*] to lead a very austere life," and "he decided [*determinó*] . . . to leave his house, totally renounce his land and his people and his own body, and enter on the way of penance [*vía de penitencia*]" [*L* 4].

12. See the editorial remarks in *FN* 1:380 n. 2.

13. As the editors of the *Monumenta* point out, Laynez does not indicate what is deficient in the devotion of Ignatius for Our Lady. The deficiency may be in his attitude, reflected in the incident where he wonders if he should kill the Moor who slighted Our Lady [*A* 15-16], or in making the vow to Mary rather than to God [*FN* 1:76 n. 9]. Perhaps Laynez means the vow was made out of fear, lacking full maturity. Even though Ignatius might be inexact in his theology, he is spontaneously

in harmony with an ancient way of dedicating oneself to Christ. At this point Ignatius lacks any institutional or ecclesiastical manifestation of what has taken place within him. He is acting on his own.

14. Hugo Rahner, S.J., *The Spirituality of St. Ignatius Loyola: An Account of Its Historical Development*, trans. Francis John Smith, S.J. (Chicago: Loyola University Press, 1953), 47. Or, in the words of Franceso Rossi de Gasperis, S.J., "Ignatius acquired a sense of the Church through the solitude of being a hermit, and not viceversa" ("Ignatius of Loyola: The Man of the Experience of God," *CIS* 24, no. 3 [1993]: 47).

15. The *Vita sancti Onuphrii* [Life of St. Humphrey] is found in *PL* 73, 211-22. For a contemporary E.T., see Tim Vivian, trans., *Paphnutius: Histories of the Monks of Upper Egypt and the Life of Onnophrius* (Kalamazoo: Cistercian Publications, 1993), 143-66. See Leturia, *Iñigo*, Appendix 1, no. 7, 174-75, for a brief description of Onuphrius drawn from the *Flos Sanctorum*, 230-33. In Leturia's bibliography we find the note after *Flos Sanctorum*: "Prologues by Fray Gauberto, M. Vagad. Copy existing in Archives of Loyola, printed probably at Saragossa between 1490 and 1510" (*ibid.*, 185). The story of the holy hermit is not found in the *Golden Legend of Jacobus de Voragine*, translated and adapted from the Latin by Ryan and Ripperger, even though it is from de Voragine's *Golden Legend* that the *Flos Sanctorum* is drawn. The Ryan-Ripperger translation is based on Graesse's Latin edition of the *Legenda aurea* published in Leipzig in 1850. It omits an appendix found in Graesse "containing certain legends superadded by others," but that of Humphrey is not amongst them (*Golden Legend*, xvi). Not only was the *Legenda* a much copied manuscript in the Middle Ages, but in the fifteenth century it outnumbered the editions of the Bible and was often one of the first books printed (See *Legenda Aurea: Sept siècles de diffusion* [Montréal: Bellarmin, 1986], 13). Vernacular translations often reflected local or regional interests (*ibid.*, 14). The story of Humphrey is found in a thirteenth century Alsatian manuscript containing additional stories (*ibid.*, 248-51).

16. The Latin translation dating from about 1560 [*FN* 1:335] renders *buena intención* by *instituto pio* [*FN* 1:425]. Note that we now have four Spanish words from Ignatius, *deseo, propósito, determinación, intención*, and a Latin word from his translator, *institutum*, with much identical meanings.

17. Laynez notes how Ignatius began with great austerities and considered becoming a Carthusian, "but then seeing that he

was called to help others, he said that he had then very quickly desired to be a Conventual rather than an Observant so as to be more able to help souls" (*Adhortationes in Librum Examinis 1559, FN* 2:137-38). Concerning Ignatius's attraction to the Carthusians, see Alain Saint-Saëns, "Ignace de Loyola devant l'érémitisme: La dimension cartusienne," *Mélanges de l'École française de Rome, Italie et Méditerranée* 102 (1990): 191-209.

18. It is a fitting move in a pilgrimage that brings him from the mud flats or alluvial lands of Loyola (*loi* [mud] and *ola*, either a locative suffix or an indication of abundance) to the mud flats or fertile fields of Lutetia (*lutum* [mud]), the Latin name for Paris. Both become, indeed, fertile fields for the Society of Jesus. See Leturia, *Iñigo*, 1.

19. *FN* 1:170 n. 8.

20. Immediately before this point in the narrative the language changes from Spanish to Italian.

21. Cf. Guillaumont, "Perspectives actuelles sur les origines du monachisme," in *Aux origines*, 215-27.

22. Technically Ignatius is a cleric at this time, since he received the tonsure as a boy, a victim of the confused vision of ecclesiastical life in his day. Until his ordination he makes no pretense to be anything other than a layman, for, except for a technicality, that is what he is in his heart. Cf. José M. Rambla, S.J., "Ignacio de Loyola y la vocación laical," *Manresa* 67 (1995): 5-7.

Chapter Twenty-One: Companions with the Same *propositum*

1. Guigo the Carthusian, *Vita sancti Hugonis, episcopi gratianopolitani*, *PL* 153, 769C.

2. *Vita antiquior*, *PL* 152, 485AB: "Deliberaverunt ipse et sex alii probi viri secum abrenuntiare mundo et pompis ejus, et ad perpetuam poenitentiam peragendam eremi deserta competentia quaerere, et ibidem, relictis omnibus divitiis et deliciis et honoribus hujus mundi, accipere singuli cruces suas, et nudi nudum Christum sequi per arctam viam, quae ducit ad vitam. . . . Sancto spiritu inspirante, proposuerunt ad memoratum sanctum episcopum simul accedere . . . ut . . . sanctum et salubre propositum possent effectui mancipare."

3. *MN* 1:4, p. 2 (*Chronicon*); see also recollections of Etienne Pasquier, *FN* 3:816. Cf. Ravier, "Ignace . . . Chartreuse de Paris," 230-32.

4. Franciscus a Puteo, *Vita altera*, *PL* 152, 504D-5A. The work is called *altera* [second] because it is second to the 13th century life called *Vita antiquior*. A third life [*Vita tertia*], of the late 16th century, uses almost the same language: "The holy bishop, seeing their constancy and the unchanging determination [*propositum*] to persevere, said to them: Dearly beloved, I heartily approve of your holy desire [*desiderium*]" (*PL* 152, 534D-35A).

5. A. Ravier, S.J., *Saint Bruno le Chartreux* (Paris: Lethielleux, 1981), 79.

6. *Vita tertia*, *PL* 152, 537A.

7. *Vita altera*, *PL* 152, 509A.

8. *Vita antiquior*, *PL* 152, 489A.

9. *Exordium Cistercii* 1; Latin text, *PATC*, 111; E.T. in Lekai, *Cistercians*, 443.

10. *Exordium parvum* 2, letter of the legate Hugh.

11. *Exordium Cistercii* 1: "Viginti et unus monachi . . . egressi, communi consilio, communi perficere nituntur assensu quod uno spiritu conceperunt. . . . Tandem desiderio potiti . . . Sed milites Christi loci asperitatem ab arto proposito quod jam animo conceperunt non discedere judicantes, ut vere sibi divinitus praeparatum, tam gratum habuere locum quam carum propositum." Latin text, *PATC*, 111; E.T. in Lekai, *Cistercians*, 443.

12. Lekai, *Cistercians*, 458; Latin text: *PATC*, 77.

13. See 1C 25, *LTS* 28-32.

14. Celano uses *convenire* and *congregare* in the same way Ignatius and his companions will use them three hundred years later, in the sense of *convene for a purpose*, e.g., *convenire*, 1C 27, line 11; *congregare*, 30, 5; *convenirent*, 30, 7; *convenientibus in unum*, 30, 7; *uno convenisse desiderio*, 30, 8.

15. This section is drawn mainly from two works of Vicaire, *St. Dominic*, 162-63, 168-71, 191, 201-4, and "L'Ordre," 5, 13, 24. Jordan of Saxony's *Libellus de principiis ordinis praedicatorum*, MOPH 16 (Rome, 1935) is referred to in the text as *Lib*. For a more detailed description of Dominican beginnings, see the first chapter of Benedict M. Ashley, O.P., *The Dominicans*, A Michael Glazier Book (Collegeville: Liturgical Press, 1990), and Allan White, O.P., "The Foundation of the Order of Preachers and its Historical Setting," in Tugwell, *Way of the Preacher*, 97-110.

16. Mandonnet, *St. Dominic*, 28.

17. Koudelka, no. 63: "Instituimus predicatores in episcopatu nostro fratrem Dominicum et socios eius, qui in paupertate euuangelica pedites religiose proposuerunt incedere et veritatis euuangelice verbum predicare."
18. Salaniaco, *De quatuor*, 9.
19. By this time Dominic had about fifteen companions, *ibid.*, 150-57.
20. Koudelka, no. 77.
21. The pope's actions were encouraging. The following year, 1218, Honorius wrote to all the archbishops, bishops, abbots, priors, and prelates of the Church urging them to provide support to the friars "in their praiseworthy endeavor [*in eorum proposito laudabili*]" (Koudelka, no. 86; cf. Koudelka, nos. 91 and 101 for similar letters).
22. Ignatius himself is less eloquent: "At this time he associated with [*conversava*] Master Pierre Favre and Master Francis Xavier, whom he later won for God's service [*servitio*] by means of the Exercises" [*A* 82].
23. Pedro de Ribadeneira, S.J., *Vita Ignatii Loyolae* 2.4.21, in *FN* 4:233.
24. *Vita sancti Onuphrii* 5, *PL* 73, 213-14.
25. In Spanish, *confirmamos*; the Latin translation (1593) of his Spanish letter (cf. *FN* 1:68-69) renders *confirmamos* as: "*in bono proposito perseverabamus* [we persevered in our good resolve (or, manner of life)]."
26. Polanco, who relies on Laynez, says that the companions had various elements for maintaining their way of life [*propósito*] [*PSH* 55]. Later he calls each of these *ratio*, and adds a new *ratio*: the election and providence of the Divine Goodness [*PV* 69-72]. Divine Goodness [*bonitas*] is a constant theme in Bruno the Carthusian and also in Ignatius.
27. Polanco says that before the companions scattered they started talking about a permanent society that others could join "who might want to follow God according to the way of life [*vitae rationem*] instituted [*institutam*] by themselves," and so "they began to work out the way of living [*vivendi formula*] that they ought to follow" [*PCh* 70].

Chapter Twenty-Two: The Summary of the Rule: The Formula of the Institute

1. See above, chap. 18, pp. 323-24.

2. See above, chap. 16; see also Cicconetti, *Regola del Carmelo*, 58-66, 115-18; for texts, see Meersseman, *Dossier*, 128-56, 282-307, who also has written on penitents, "I penitenti nei secoli XI e XII," in *I laici nella "Societas Christiana" dei secoli XI e XII*, Miscellanea del Centro di Studi Medioevali, vol. 5 (Milan: Vita e Pensiero, 1968), 306-39.

3. See above, chap. 17, p. 301. Thomas of Celano presents Francis as writing a way of life and a rule [*vitae formam et regulam*], 1 Celano 32. Cf. Esser, *Origins*, 92. In the *Legenda Trium Sociorum* Francis says to his earliest companions: "Brothers, this is our life [*vita*] and our rule [*regula*] and that of all who wish to join our society." [*LTS* 29].

4. The bull of Honorius III, *Solet annuere*, which introduces the *Regula bullata*. For E.T., see *Francis and Clare*, 137.

5. Esser, *Origins*, 19-29.

6. Jordan of Saxony, *Libellus* 41-42.

7. Selections of Premonstratensian and Dominican parallel texts are in Tugwell, *Early Dominicans*, 456-65.

8. Bull *Religiosam vitam* of December 22, 1216: Koudelka, no. 77; see also *BRT* 3:309-11.

9. Cf. Vicaire, "L'ordre," 33-34.

10. *Acta canonizationis, passim;* cf., Mandonnet, *Saint Dominique*, 2:215-18, 266; also Gerardus de Fracheto, *Vitae fratrum ordinis Praedicatorum*, MOPH 1, p. 138.

11. Mandonnet, *Saint Dominique*, 2:266.

12. Maccarrone, "Lateranense IV," 494.

13. M. Gioia, in referring to this statement from the Formula, notes: "In the complexus of Jesuit legislation the term *regula*—in a sense analagous to that of the rule of Benedict—depends wholly on the above text" ("Regola della Compagnia di Gesù," *DIP*, 7 [1983]: 1464).

14. In reference to *Regimini militantis ecclesiae*, the papal bull of 1540 giving solemn approval to the Society, Torres indicates that "the institute approved by the pontiff was not exactly a rule of the ancient kind, but a kind of constitutional codex or 'fundamental law' in the modern sense, drawn up in the manner of an ancient rule" ("Approvazione," 765). Bertrand puts it thus: "That which, in the Company, enjoys the role of the great rules of the past, is the 'formula'" ("La Compagnie de Jésus et son 'institut,'" 293).

15. The translation assumes that the Formula, the rule of the Society, addresses itself to the members of the Company. Other

16. The final version of 1550 changes the text to read "after a solemn vow of perpetual chastity, poverty, and obedience." The change deprives chastity of its own special context of mission and service. On the other hand, it has the advantage of making mission and service the context of all three vows.
17. See above, chap. 17, n. 40.
18. See my study, "Living and Dying," 1-63.
19. For the broader social and religious sixteenth-century context, see Francisco de Borja Medina, S.J., "Ignacio de Loyola y la 'limpieza de sangre'," in *Ignacio y su tiempo*, 579-615.
20. Although later legislation based on experience allows for some communal ownership (the first house the Society owned was in Lisbon in 1542), the spirit animating Ignatius and his companions in the beginning is to own nothing at all. The same was true of the Franciscans in their earliest years. They had someone in charge of the whole group, but no local superior, for they belonged in no place and had no monastery (Esser, *Origins*, 54-57, 111 n. 3, 112 n. 6, and his conclusion on 110, #1). The Dominican bull of confirmation mentions property, a real place where the community lives (*Religiosam vitam*, Koudelka, no. 77). The Theatine brief states that they will live together in common [*BRT* 6:73b]. The Barnabites are to live in the diocese of Milan [*BRT* 6:160a], and later the Somaschi brief names a variety of places where they live [*BRT* 7:729b]. These orders eventually choose to follow the Rule of Augustine in some form.
21. Aldama, "Origin and History," 14, 16.

Chapter Twenty-Three: Papal Approval and Commissioning

1. *Adv. Haereses* 4.20.7: "gloria enim Dei, vivens homo, vita autem hominis visio Dei" (SC 100, 648-49).
2. *Constitutiones anni 1541*, C 33-48, minutes of a meeting of the six companions written by Codure.

3. *Forma de la Compañía y oblación, FN* 1:16-22.
4. A free rendering of Gregory's thought; see above, chap. 9, n. 34.
5. Cf. Thomas K. Connolly, O.P., "Alumbrados (Illuminati)," *NCE*, 1:356; Rotsaert, *Renouveaux spirituels*, 81-85, 113-27.
6. *Adhortationes in librum Examinis, FN* 2:133 [7].

Epilogue: Impelling Spirit

1. Jerónimo Nadal, *Adhortationes in Collegio Romano* in *FN* 2:10 [24].
2. In 1536 Paul III instituted the way of the Camera [*via de camera*] to avoid delays typical of the way of the chancery [*via de cancellaria*] (Herbert Thurston, "Bulls and Briefs," *CE* 3:57b; F. Claeys Boúúaert, "Bulle," *DDC* 2:1130).
3. Letter of Lattanzio Tolomei, Ghinucci's nephew and Siena's ambassador to the Holy See, to Cardinal Contarini, in Dittrich, *Regesten und Briefe*, 379.
4. Jerónimo Nadal, *Apologia*, in *FN* 2:95 [104].
5. For *De concilio universali*, see Pastor, 95; Schweitzer, "Guidiccioni," 51. A fragment of the text is in TV, 1/2:207-8. For *De ecclesia et emendatione ministrorum eorumque abusuum per generale concilium facienda*, see the pertinent part of the text in TV, 1/2:208-14. The full text is in *CT*, 12:226-56 (the part about religious, 250-53); cf. also *CT*, 4:271.
6. *Adhortationes 1559*, in *FN* 2:135 [10].
7. I am preparing an article to refute the contention that Ghinucci was a bitter adversary of the Society's confirmation (cf. *FN* 2:696 n. 1), and another to sort out fact from fiction in the story of Guidiccioni's opposition.
8. Cf. Laynez, *Adhortationes, FN* 2:131-32; Nadal, *Exhortationes (1554), FN* 1:311-12.

Select Bibliography

As it is impossible to list all the sources and works used and consulted in this study we shall limit ourselves to those that have proven to be most helpful and/or used most often. The notes contain full references for sources, books, and articles cited occasionally.

Bibliographical Works

Iparraguirre, Ignacio, S.J. *Orientaciones bibliográficas sobre san Ignacio de Loyola.* Subsidia ad historiam Societatis Iesu, no. 1. 2d ed. Rome: Institutum Historicum S.I., 1965.

Ruiz Jurado, Manuel, S.J. *Orientaciones bibliográficas sobre san Ignacio de Loyola.* Vol. 2, *1965-1976*; vol. 3, *1977-1989.* Subsidia ad historiam Societatis Iesu, no. 8 and no. 10. Rome: Institutum Historicum S.I., 1977, 1990.

Polgár, László, S.J. *Bibliographie sur l'histoire de la Compagnie de Jésus, 1901-1980.* Vol. 1, *Toute la Compagnie.* Rome: Institutum Historicum S.I., 1981.

Polgár, László, S.J. "Bibliographie sur l'histoire de la Compagnie de Jésus." In *Archivum Historicum Societatis Iesu,* vols. 51-63 (1982-1994).

Primary Sources: MHSI

Bobadillae Monumenta. Edited by D. Restrepo, S.J. 1 vol. Madrid, 1913.

Chronicon Societatis Iesu, auctore Joanne Alphonso de Polanco, S.J. Edited by J. M. Velez, S.J., and V. Agusti, S.J. 6 vols. Madrid, 1894-98.

Constitutiones et Regulae Societatis Iesu. Edited by A. Codina, S.J., and D. Fernández Zapico, S.J. 4 vols. Rome, 1934-48.

Epistolae et Monumenta P. Hieronymi Nadal. Edited by F. Cervós, S.J., and M. Nicolau, S.J. 6 vols. Vol. 1-4, Madrid, 1898-1905. Vols. 5-6, Rome, 1962-64.

Epistolae Mixtae ex variis Europae locis, 1537-1556. Edited by V. Agusti, S.J. 5 vols. Madrid, 1898-1901.

Epistolae P. Alphonsi Salmeronis. Edited by R. Vidurre, S.J., and F. Cervós, S.J. 2 vols. Madrid, 1906-7.

Epistolae PP. Paschasii Broet, Claudii Jaji, Joannis Codurii et Simonis Rodericii S.J. Edited by F. Cervós, S.J. 1 vol. Madrid, 1903.

Epistolae S. Francisci Xaverii. Edited by G. Schurhammer, S.J., and J. Wicki, S.J. 2 vols. Rome, 1944-45.

Fabri Monumenta. Edited by F. Lirola, S.J. 1 vol. Madrid, 1914.

Fontes documentales de S. Ignatio de Loyola: Documenta de S. Ignatii familia et patria, iuventute, primis sociis. Edited by C. de Dalmases, S.J. 1 vol. Rome, 1977.

Fontes narrativi de S. Ignacio de Loyola et de Societatis Iesu initiis. Edited by D. Fernández Zapico, S.J., C. de Dalmases, S.J., and P. Leturia, S.J. 4 vols. Rome, 1943-65.

Lainii Monumenta. Edited by E. Astudillo, S.J. 8 vols. Madrid, 1912-17.

Monumenta Brasiliae. Edited by S. Leite, S.J. 5 vols. Rome, 1956-68.

Monumenta Xaveriana. Edited by M. Lecina, S.J., D. Restrepo, S.J. 2 vols. Madrid, 1899, 1912.

Sancti Ignatii de Loyola Exercitia Spiritualia. Textuum antiquissimorum nova editio. Lexicon textus hispani. Edited by J. Calveras, S.J., and C. de Dalmases, S.J. 1 vol. Rome, 1969.

Sancti Ignatii de Loyola Societatis Jesu Fundatoris Epistolae et Instructiones. Edited by M. Lecina, S.J., V. Agusti, S.J., and D. Restrepo, S.J. 12 vols. Madrid, 1903-11.

Scripta de Sancto Ignatio de Loyola. Edited by L. M. Ortiz, V. Agustí, M. Lecina, A. Macia, A. Codina, D. Fernández, D. Restrepo. 2 vols. Madrid, 1904, 1918.

Other Primary Sources

Society of Jesus (other than MHSI)

Institutum Societatis Iesu. Vol. 1, *Bullarium et Compendium Privilegiorum.* Florence, 1892.

Nicolau, Miguel, S.J., ed. *Pláticas espirituales del P. Jerónimo Nadal, S.I., en Coimbra (1561)*. Granada: Facultad Teológica de la Compañía de Jesús, 1945.

Church History

Bullarum, diplomatum et privilegiorum sanctorum Romanorum Pontificum Taurinensis editio. Edited by A. Tomasetti. 25 vols. Turin, 1857-72.

Ciaconius, Alphonsus, O.P. *Vitae et res gestae pontificum romanorum usque ad Clementem IX*. Revised by Augustinus Oldoinus, S.J. Vol. 3. Rome, 1677.

Concilium Oecumenicorum Decreta. Edited by Joseph Alberigo and others. Basel: Herder, 1962.

Concilium Tridentinum. Diariorum, Actorum, Epistularum, Tractatuum nova collectio. Edited by St. Ehses and Görres Gesellschaft. 13 vols. Freiburg-im-Breisgau: Herder, 1901-67.

Corpus Iuris Canonici. Edited by E. Friedberg. 2 vols. Leipzig: Tauchnitz, 1922.

Dittrich, Franz, ed. *Regesten und Briefe des Cardinals Gasparo Contarini (1483-1542)*. Braunsberg, 1881.

Dossier de l'Ordre de la Pénitence au XIIIe siècle. Edited by G. G. Meersseman, O.P. Spicilegium Friburgense, vol. 7. Fribourg: Editions universitaires, 1961.

Jacques de Vitry. *Lettres de Jacques de Vitry*. Edited by R. B. C. Huygens. Leiden: Brill, 1960.

Jacques de Vitry. *The Historia Occidentalis of Jacques de Vitry: A Critical Edition*. Edited by John Frederick Hinnebusch, O.P. Spicilegium Friburgense, vol. 17. Fribourg: University Press, 1972.

Monastic Sources

Benedict, Saint. *La Règle de saint Benoît*. Edited and translated by Adalbert de Vogüé and Jean Neufville. 6 vols. SC 181-186. Paris: Editions du Cerf, 1971-72.

Bouton, Jean de la Croix, O.C.S.O., and Jean Baptiste Van Damme, O.C.S.O., eds. *Les plus anciens textes de Cîteaux: Sources, textes et notes historiques*. Cîteaux - Commentarii Cistercienses. Studia et Documenta, vol. 2. Achel: Abbaye Cistercienne, 1974. Reimpression, 1985.

Cassian, John. *Jean Cassien: Les Conférences*. Edited and translated by E. Pichery. 3 vols. SC 42, 54, 64. Paris: Editions du Cerf, 1955, 1958, 1959.

———. *Jean Cassien: Les Institutions cénobitiques*. Edited and translated by J. C. Guy. SC 109. Paris: Editions du Cerf, 1965.

Guigo I. *Guiges 1ᵉʳ, prieur de Chartreuse: Coutumes de Chartreuse*. Edited and translated by a Carthusian. SC 313. Paris: Editions du Cerf, 1984.

La Règle du Maître. Edited and translated by Adalbert de Vogüé. 2 vols. SC 105, 106. Paris: Editions du Cerf, 1964.

Vita antiquior, altera, tertia [Sancti Brunonis, Carthusiorum institutoris]. PL 152, 481-552.

Vita Sancti Onuphrii, eremitae. PL 73, 211-22.

Dominican Sources

Acta canonizationis S. Dominici. Edited by A. Walz in *Monumenta Historica Sancti Patris Nostri Dominici*, 91-194. MOPH 16. Rome: Institutum Historicum Fratrum Praedicatorum, 1935.

Constitutiones antiquae ordinis fratrum Praedicatorum. Edited by Heribert C. Scheeben in *Die Konstitutionen des Predigerordens unter Jordan von Sachsen*, 48-80. Quellen und Forschungen 38. Cologne-Leipzig: Albertus Magnus Verlag, 1939.

Jordan of Saxony, Bl. *Libellus de principiis ordinis praedicatorum*. Edited by H.-C. Scheeben in *Monumenta Historica Sancti Patris Nostri Dominici*, 25-88. MOPH 16. Rome: Institutum Historicum Fratrum Praedicatorum, 1935.

Monumenta diplomatica S. Dominici. Edited by Vladimir J. Koudelka, O.P. MOPH 25. Rome: Institutum Historicum Fratrum Praedicatorum, 1966.

Stephen of Salagnac and Bernard Gui. *De quatuor in quibus Deus Praedicatorum ordinem insignivit*. Edited by Thomas Kaeppeli, O.P. MOPH 22. Rome: Institutum Historicum Fratrum Praedicatorum, 1949.

Franciscan Sources

Bonaventure, Saint. *Legenda maior S. Francisci*. Edited by the fathers of the Collegium S. Bonaventurae in *Analecta Franciscana*, vol.10: *Legendae S. Francisci Assisiensis saeculis XIII et XIV conscriptae*, 555-652. Quaracchi: Collegium S. Bonaventurae, 1926-41.

Bullarium Franciscanum Romanorum Pontificum. Vol. 1, *Ab Honorio III ad Innocentium IIII*. Edited by J. H. Sbaralea. Rome, 1759.

Clare of Assisi, Saint. *Claire d'Assise: Ecrits*. Edited and translated by Marie-France Becker, Jean-François Godet, and Thaddée Matura. SC 325. Paris: Editions du Cerf, 1985.

Francis of Assisi, Saint. *François d'Assise: Ecrits.* Edited by Théophile Desbonnets, Jean-François Godet, Thaddée Matura, and Damien Vorreux. SC 285. Paris: Editions du Cerf, 1981.

Legenda trium sociorum. Edited by Théophile Desbonnets, O.F.M. *Archivum Franciscanum Historicum* 67 (1974): 38-144.

Primigeniae Legislationis Ordinis Fratrum Minorum Capuccinorum textus originales seu Constitutiones anno 1536 ordinatae et anno 1552 recognitae. Original Italian text edited by Edouard d'Alençon in *Liber Memorialis O.F.M. Capuccinorum* (1528-1928), 356-419. Suppl. vol. 44 Analectorum Ordinis. Rome: Curia generalis, 1928.

Scripta Leonis, Rufini et Angeli, sociorum S. Francisci: The Writings of Leo, Rufino and Angelo, Companions of St. Francis. Edited and translated by Rosalind B. Brooke. Oxford: Clarendon Press, 1970.

Thomas of Celano, O.F.M. *Vita prima S. Francisci Assisiensis.* Edited by the fathers of the Collegium S. Bonaventurae in *Analecta Franciscana*, vol. 10: *Legendae S. Francisci Assisiensis saeculis XIII et XIV conscriptae*, 1-117. Quaracchi: Collegium S. Bonaventurae, 1926-41.

Sources in English Translation

Bonaventure: The Soul's Journey into God, The Tree of Life, The Life of St. Francis. Translated by Ewert Cousins. CWS. New York: Paulist Press, 1978.

Clare of Assisi: Early Documents. Edited and translated by Regis J. Armstrong, O.F.M.Cap. New York: Paulist Press, 1988.

Early Dominicans: Selected Writings. Edited by Simon Tugwell, O.P. CWS. New York: Paulist Press, 1982.

Francis and Clare: The Complete Works. Translated by Regis J. Armstrong, O.F.M.Cap., and Ignatius C. Brady, O.F.M. CWS. New York: Paulist Press, 1982.

Gleason, Elisabeth G., ed. and trans. *Reform Thought in Sixteenth-Century Italy.* The American Academy of Religion: Texts and Translation series, no. 4. Chico: Scholars Press, 1981.

The Golden Legend of Jacobus de Voragine. Translated and adapted from the Latin by Granger Ryan and Helmut Ripperger. New York: Longmans, Green and Co., 1941.

Ignatius of Loyola, Saint. *The Constitutions of the Society of Jesus.* Translated, with an introduction and a commentary, by George E. Ganss, S.J. St. Louis: Institute of Jesuit Sources, 1970.

———. *The Autobiography of St. Ignatius Loyola.* Translated by Joseph F. O'Callaghan, edited by John C. Olin. New York: Harper & Row, 1974.

———. *A Pilgrim's Journey: the Autobiography of Ignatius of Loyola.* Translated by by Joseph N. Tylenda, S.J. Wilmington: Glazier, 1985.

———. *St. Ignatius' Own Story as Told to Luis González de Camara. With a sampling of his letters.* Translated by William J. Young, S.J. Henry Regnery Company, 1956. Reprint. Chicago: Loyola University Press, 1980.

———. *Ignatius of Loyola: The Spiritual Exercises and Selected Works.* Edited by George E. Ganss, S.J., with the collaboration of Parmananda R. Divarkar, S.J., Edward J. Malatesta, S.J., and Martin E. Palmer, S.J. CWS. New York: Paulist Press, 1991.

———. *Letters and Instructions of St. Ignatius Loyola.* Vol. 1, 1524-1547. Translated by D. F. O'Leary, edited by A. Goodier, S.J. St. Louis: Herder, 1914.

———. *Letters of St. Ignatius of Loyola.* Selected and translated by William J. Young, S.J. Chicago: Loyola University Press, 1959.

John Cassian: Conferences. Translated by Colm Luibheid. CWS. New York: Paulist Press, 1985.

Lackner, Bede K., O.Cist., trans. "Early Cistercian Documents in Translation." In Louis J. Lekai, O.Cist., *The Cistercians: Ideals and Reality,* 443-66. Kent State University Press, 1977.

Olin, John C., ed. *The Catholic Reformation: Savonarola to Ignatius Loyola, Reform in the Church 1495-1540.* New York: Harper & Row, 1969.

Pachomian Koinonia. Vol. 2, *Pachomian Chronicles and Rules.* Translated by Armand Veilleux, O.C.S.O. Cistercian Studies Series 46. Kalamazoo: Cistercian Publications, 1981.

RB 1980: The Rule of St. Benedict in Latin and English with Notes. Edited by T. Fry, O.S.B. Collegeville: The Liturgical Press, 1981.

Summary of the Constitutions; Common Rules; Rules of Modesty, and an Epistle on Obedience. Roehampton, 1926.

Vatican Council II: The Conciliar and Post Conciliar Documents. Edited by Austin Flannery, O.P. Collegeville: Liturgical Press, 1975.

Secondary Sources: Books

Aldama, Antonio M. de, S.J. *Repartiéndose en la viña de Cristo: Comentario a la séptima parte de las Constituciones de la Compañía de Jesús.* Rome: CIS, 1973.

———. *Notas para un comentario a: La Fórmula del Instituto de la Compañía de Jesús*. Rome: CIS, 1981. Translated by Ignacio Echániz, S.J., under the title *The Formula of the Institute: Notes for a Commentary*. St. Louis: Institute of Jesuit Sources, 1990.

Andreu, F. *Le lettere di San Gaetano de Thiene*. Studi e Testi 177. Rome, 1954.

Andrieu, Michel. *Le Pontifical romain au moyen-âge*, vol. 1. Studi e Testi 86. Vatican City: Biblioteca Apostolica Vaticana, 1938.

Aubenas, Roger and Robert Ricard. *L'Église et la Renaissance (1449-1517)*. Vol. 15 of *Histoire de l'Église depuis les origines jusqu'à nos jours*, edited by A. Fliché and V. Martin. Paris: Bloud et Gay, 1951.

Baa, Theodore, T.O.R. *The Ecclesiastical Approbation of a Religious Institute*. Angelicum dissertation. Rome, 1961.

Bangert, William V., S.J. *Claude Jay and Alfonso Salmerón: Two Early Jesuits*. Chicago: Loyola University Press, 1985.

Bartoli, Daniel, S.J. *History of the Life and Institute of St. Ignatius de Loyola, Founder of the Society of Jesus*. 2 vols. New York: P. J. Kenedy, 1855. Originally published in 1650 as *Vita di S. Ignazio*.

Bertrand, Dominique, S.J. *Un corps pour l'Esprit: Essai sur l'expérience communautaire d'après les Constitutions de la Compagnie de Jésus*. Collection Christus, no 38. Paris: Desclée de Brouwer, 1974.

———. *La politique de S. Ignace de Loyola: L'analyse sociale*. Paris: Editions du Cerf, 1985.

Blaise, Albert. *Dictionnaire latin-français des auteurs chrétiens*. Turnhout: Brepols, 1954.

———. *Lexicon Latinitatis Medii Aevi: Dictionnaire latin-français des auteurs du Moyen-Age*. Turnhout: Brepols, 1975.

Boehmer, Heinrich. *Studien zur Geschichte der Gesellschaft Jesu*, vol. 1. Bonn, 1914.

Bolton, Brenda. *The Medieval Reformation: Foundations of Medieval History*. Baltimore: Edward Arnold, 1983.

Boswell, John. *The Kindness of Strangers: The Abandonment of Children in Western Europe from Late Antiquity to the Renaissance*. New York: Pantheon Books, 1988.

Brooke, Rosalind B. *The Coming of the Friars*. New York: Barnes & Noble, 1975.

Broutin, Paul, S.J. *L'Évêque dans la tradition pastorale du XVIe siècle*. French adaptation of "Das Bischofsideal der katolischen Reformation" by Hubert Jedin. Museum Lessianum - Section historique, no. 16. Bruges: Desclée de Brouwer, 1953. [Originally published in *Sacramentum Ordinis*. (Breslau, 1942).]

Brown, Peter. *The Body and Society: Men, Women, and Sexual Renunciation in Early Christianity*. New York: Columbia University Press, 1988.

Burke, Peter, ed. *Sarpi: History of Benefices and Selections from History of the Council of Trent*. New York: Washington Square Press, 1967.

Bynum, Caroline Walker. *Docere Verbo et Exemplo: An Aspect of Twelfth-Century Spirituality*. Missoula: Scholars Press, 1979.

Cameron, Euan. *The Reformation of the Heretics: The Waldenses of the Alps, 1480-1580*. Oxford: Clarendon Press, 1984.

Cappelle, Catherine. *Le voeu d'obéissance des origines au xiie siècle*. Librairie Générale de Droit et de Jurisprudence. Paris: R. Pichon et R. Durand-Auzias, 1959.

Castiglione, Baldesar. *The Book of the Courtier*. New York: Horace Liveright, 1929. Originally published as *Il Libro del Cortegiano* (Venice, 1528).

Casutt, Laurentius, O.F.M.Cap. *Die älteste franziskanische Lebensform: Untersuchungen zur Regula prima sine bulla*. Graz: Verlag Styria, 1955.

The Catholic Encyclopedia (CE). Edited by C. Herbermann and others. 16 vols. New York: Robert Appleton, 1907-14.

Chenu, M.-D., O.P. *Nature, Man, and Society in the Twelfth Century: Essays on New Theological Perspectives in the Latin West*. Edited and translated by Jerome Taylor and Lester K. Little. Chicago: University of Chicago Press, 1968. Originally published as *La théologie au douzième siècle* (Paris: Vrin, 1957).

Cicconetti, Carlo, O. Carm. *La Regola del Carmelo: Origine, natura, significato*. Rome: Institutum Carmelitanum, 1973.

Coemans, Augusto, S.J., Carlo Martini, and Mario Gioia. *Introducción al estudio de la Fórmula del Instituto S.I.* Rome: CIS, 1974.

Colombás, García M., O.S.B. *El monacato primitivo*. Vol. 2, *La espiritualidad*. BAC 376. Madrid: La Editorial Católica, 1975.

———. *La regla de San Benito*. BAC 406. Madrid: La Editorial Católica, 1979.

Congar, Yves M. J., O.P. *Lay People in the Church: A Study for a Theology of Laity*. Translated by Donald Attwater. London: Geoffrey Chapman, 1957. Reprint. Westminster: Newman, 1965. Originally published as *Jalons pour une théologie du laïcat*. Unam Sanctam 23 (Paris: Editions du Cerf, 1954).

Conwell, Joseph F., S.J. *Contemplation in Action: A Study in Ignatian Prayer*. Spokane, Washington: Gonzaga University, 1957.

Dallen, James. *The Reconciling Community: The Rite of Penance.* New York: Pueblo Publishing Co., 1986.

Dalmases, Cándido de, S.J. *Ignatius of Loyola, Founder of the Jesuits: His Life and Works.* Translated by Jerome Aixalá, S.J. St. Louis: The Institute of Jesuit Sources, 1985.

de la Brosse, Olivier, O.P., et al. *Latran V et Trente.* Histoire des conciles oecuméniques, vol. 10. Paris: Editions de l'Orante, 1975.

DeMolen, Richard L., ed. *Religious Orders of the Catholic Reformation* (In Honor of John C. Olin on His Seventy-Fifth Birthday). New York: Fordham University Press, 1994.

De Nicolas, Antonio T. *Powers of Imagining: Ignatius de Loyola. A Philosophical Hermeneutic of Imagining through the Collected Works of Ignatius de Loyola with a Translation of These Works.* Albany: State University of New York Press, 1986.

de Vogüé, Adalbert, O.S.B. *The Rule of Saint Benedict: A Doctrinal and Spiritual Commentary.* Translated by J. B. Hasbrouck. Kalamazoo: Cistercian Publications, 1983. Originally published as *La Règle de saint Benoît,* vol. 7 (Paris: Editions du Cerf, 1977).

Diaz Moreno, José Maria, S.J. *La regulación juridica de la cura de almas en los canonistas hispanicos de los siglos xvi-xvii.* Biblioteca Teologica Granadina 14. Granada: Facultad de Teologia, 1972.

Dictionnaire d'histoire et de géographie ecclésiastiques (DHGE). Edited by A. Baudrillart and others. Paris: Letouzey & Ané, 1912—.

Dictionnaire de droit canonique (DDC). Edited by R. Naz. 7 vols. Paris: Letouzey et Ané, 1935-65.

Dictionnaire de spiritualité ascétique et mystique, doctrine et histoire (DSAM). Edited by M. Viller, S.J., and others. Paris: Beauchesne, 1937—.

Dictionnaire de théologie catholique (DTC). Edited by A. Vacant and others. 15 vols. Paris: Letouzey et Ané, 1903-50.

Diego, Luis de, S.J. *La opción sacerdotal de Ignacio de Loyola y sus compañeros [1515-1540]: Estudio histórico e interpretación teológico-espiritual.* Rome: CIS, 1975.

Dittrich, Franz. *Gasparo Contarini, 1483-1542, eine Monographie.* Braunsberg, 1885.

Dizionario degli istituti di perfezione (DIP). Edited by G. Pellicia and G. Rocca. Rome: Edizioni Paoline, 1974—.

Dortel-Claudot, Michel, S.J. *Etat de vie et rôle du prêtre.* Paris: Le Centurion, 1970.

———. *Le genre de vie extérieur de la Compagnie de Jésus.* Rome: Presses de l'Université Grégorienne, 1971.

———. *Mode de vie. Niveau de vie et pauvreté de la Compagnie de Jésus*. Rome: CIS, 1973.

Dozzi, Dino. *Il vangelo nella regola non bollata di Francesco d'Assisi*. 2d ed. Bibliotheca Seraphico-Capuccina 36. Rome: Istituto storico dei Cappucini, 1989.

Dunphy, Richard Ward S.J. *Placed with Jesus Bearing His Cross: A Study of Jesuit Identity in the Light of St. Ignatius Loyola's Life of Grace, as Based upon the First Jesuits' Understanding of Their Relationship to Their Founder*. Rome: Pontificia Universitas Gregoriana, 1983.

Dykmans, Marc, S.J. *Le pontifical romain révisé au XVe siècle*. Studi e Testi 311. Vatican City: Biblioteca Apostolica Vaticana, 1985.

Edwards, Bede, O.D.C., ed. *The Rule of Saint Albert*. Vinea Carmeli 1. Aylesford and Kensington, 1973.

Ellebracht, Marie Pierre. *Remarks on the Vocabulary of the Ancient Orations in the Missale Romanum*. 2d ed. Nijmegen: Dekker & Van de Vegt, 1966.

Elton, G. R. *Renaissance and Reformation 1300-1648*. 3d ed. New York: Macmillan, 1976.

———, ed. *The Reformation, 1520-1559*. Vol. 2 of *The New Cambridge Modern History*. Cambridge: University Press, 1958.

Escudero, Gerardo, C.M.F. *El voto solemne de pobreza: Su historia, su naturaleza y su problemática actual*. Madrid: Editorial Coculsa, 1955.

Esser, Cajetan, O.F.M. *Origins of the Franciscan Order*. Translated by Aedan Daly and Irina Lynch. Chicago: Franciscan Herald Press, 1970. Originally published as *Anfänge und Ursprüngliche Zielsetzungen des Ordens der Minderbrüder* (Leiden: Brill, 1966).

Falkner, Andreas, S.J., and Paul Imhof, S.J., eds. *Ignatius von Loyola und die Gesellschaft Jesu 1491-1556*. Würzburg: Echter, 1990.

Farrell, Allan P., S.J. *The Jesuit Code of Liberal Education*. Milwaukee: Bruce, 1938.

Fenlon, Dermot. *Heresy and Obedience in Tridentine Italy: Cardinal Pole and the Counter Reformation*. Cambridge: University Press, 1972.

Franza, Gerardo, S.S.P. *Il catechismo a Roma dal Concilio di Trento a Pio VI nello zelo dell' Arciconfraternità della Dottrina Cristiana*. Rome: Pontificia Universitas Gregoriana, 1958.

Futrell, John C., S.J. *Making an Apostolic Community of Love: The Role of the Superior according to St. Ignatius of Loyola*. St. Louis: Institute of Jesuit Sources, 1970.

Ganss, George E., S.J. *Saint Ignatius' Idea of a Jesuit University*. Milwaukee: Marquette University Press, 1954.

Gaudemet, J. *Le Gouvernement de l'église à l'époque classique*, 2e partie: *Le gouvernement local*. Tome 8, vol. 2 of *Histoire du Droit et des Institutions de l'Eglise en Occident*, published under the direction of Gabriel Le Bras et Jean Gaudemet. Paris: Editions Cujas, 1979.

Gimenez Ribes, José M. *Un catecismo para la iglesia universal: Historia de la iniciativa desde su origen hasta el Sínodo Extraordinario de 1985.* Pamplona: Ediciones Universidad de Navarra, 1987.

Gleason, Elisabeth G. *Gasparo Contarini: Venice, Rome, and Reform.* Berkeley: University of California Press, 1993.

Gómez Rodeles, Cecilio, S.J. *La Compañía de Jesús catequista: legislación, doctrineros, centros catequísticas.* Madrid: Horno, 1913.

Granero, Jesús M., S.J. *San Ignacio de Loyola. La mision de su vida.* Madrid: Razon y fe, 1984.

Guillaumont, Antoine. *Aux origines du monachisme chrétien: Pour une phénoménologie du monachisme.* Spiritualité orientale, no. 30. Bégrolles en Mauges (Maine & Loire): Abbaye de Bellefontaine, 1979.

Heintschel, Donald E. *The Mediaeval Concept of an Ecclesiastical Office.* Canon Law Studies no. 363. Washington: Catholic University of America Press, 1956.

Hinnebusch, William A., O.P. *The History of the Dominican Order.* Vol.1, *Origins and Growth to 1500.* Staten Island: Alba House, 1965.

Hostie, Raymond, S.J. *Vie et mort des ordres religieux: Approches psychosociologiques.* Bibliothèque d'études psychoreligieuses. Paris: Desclée De Brouwer, 1972.

Hourlier, Jacques. *L'age classique (1140-1378): Les religieux.* Tome 10 of *Histoire du Droit et des Institutions de l'Eglise en Occident*, published under the direction of Gabriel Le Bras. Paris: Editions Cujas, 1974.

Ignace de Loyola. *Texte autographe des Exercises Spirituels et documents contemporains (1526-1615).* Collection Christus, no. 60. Paris: Desclée de Brouwer, 1986.

Iparraguirre, Ignacio, S.J. *Historia de los Ejercicios espirituales de San Ignacio.* Vol. 1: *Práctica de los Ejercicios de San Ignacio de Loyola en vida de su autor (1522-1556).* Bibliotheca Instituti Historici S.I., vol. 3. Bilbao: El Mensajero—Rome: IHSI, 1946.

Jedin, Hubert. *A History of the Council of Trent.* Translated by Ernest Graf, O.S.B. 2 vols. London: Thomas Nelson and Sons, 1957-61. Originally published as *Geschichte des Konzils von Trient* (Freiburg im Breisgau: Herder, 1949-57).

Jedin, Hubert and John Dolan, eds. *Handbook of Church History*. Vol. 4, *From the High Middle Ages to the Eve of the Reformation*, translated by Anselm Briggs. New York: Herder and Herder, 1970.

Kelly, Bernard M. *The Functions Reserved to Pastors*. Canon Law Studies no. 250. Washington, D.C.: Catholic University of America Press, 1947.

Knowles, David, O.S.B. *Christian Monasticism*. World University Library. London: Weidenfeld and Nicolson, 1969.

Kunkel, Paul A. *The Theatines in the History of Catholic Reform before the Establishment of Lutheranism*. Washington, D.C.: Catholic University of America Press, 1941.

Ladner, Gerhart B. *The Idea of Reform: Its Impact on Christian Thought and Action in the Age of the Fathers*. Cambridge: Harvard University Press, 1959.

———. *Images and Ideas in the Middle Ages: Selected Studies in History and Art*, vol. 2. Storia e Letteratura, Raccolta di Studi e Testi, 156. Rome: Storia e Letteratura, 1983.

Landini, Laurentio C., O.F.M. *The Causes of the Clericalization of the Order of Friars Minor: 1209-1260 in the Light of Early Franciscan Sources*. Chicago: Franciscan Herald Press, 1968.

Lawrence, C. H. *Medieval Monasticism: Forms of Religious Life in Western Europe in the Middle Ages*, 2d ed. London: Longman, 1989.

Le Goff, Jacques. *Your Money or Your Life: Economy and Religion in the Middle Ages*. New York: Zone Books, 1988.

Lecler, Joseph, S.J. *Vienne*. Histoire des conciles oecuméniques, vol. 8. Paris: Editions de l'Orante, 1964.

Leclercq, Jean, O.S.B. *The Love of Learning and the Desire for God: A Study of Monastic Culture*. Translated by Catharine Misrahi. New York: Fordham University Press, 1961. Originally published as *L'amour des lettres et le désir de Dieu: Initiation aux auteurs monastiques du moyen-âge*. (Paris: Editions du Cerf, 1957).

———. *Etudes sur le vocabulaire monastique du moyen âge*. Studia Anselmiana 48. Rome: Herder, 1961.

———. *Otia Monastica: Etudes sur le vocabulaire de la contemplation au moyen âge*. Studia Anselmiana 51. Rome: Herder, 1963.

———. *Aux sources de la spiritualité occidentale. Étapes et constantes*. Tradition et spiritualité 4. Paris: Editions du Cerf, 1964.

Leclercq, Jean, O.S.B., François Vandenbroucke, and Louis Bouyer. *The Spirituality of the Middle Ages*. Vol. 2 of *A History of Christian Spirituality*. Translated by the Benedictines of Holme Eden Abbey, Carlisle. New York: Seabury Press, 1968. Originally published as *La Spiritualité du Moyen Age* (Paris: Editions Montaigne, 1961).

Legenda Aurea: Sept siècles de diffusion. Actes du colloque international sur la *Legenda aurea*: texte latin et branches vernaculaires à l'Université du Québec à Montréal, 11-12 mai 1983. Ouvrage publié sous la direction de Brenda Dunn-Lardeau. Montréal: Bellarmin, 1986.

Lekai, Louis J., O.Cist. *The Cistercians: Ideals and Reality.* Kent State University Press, 1977.

Leturia, Pedro de, S.J. *Estudios ignacianos.* Edited by Ignacio Iparraguirre, S.J. 2 vols. Bibliotheca Instituti Historici S.I., vol. 10, 11. Rome: IHSI, 1957.

———. S.J. *Iñigo de Loyola.* Translated by Aloysius J. Owen, S.J. Syracuse: Le Moyne College Press, 1949. Reprint. Chicago: Loyola University Press, 1965.

Llorca, Bernardino, S.J. *La inquisición española y los Alumbrados (1509-1667).* Biblioteca Salmanticensis, Estudios 32. Salamanca: Universidad Pontificia, 1980.

Longère, Jean. *La Prédication Médiévale.* Paris: Études Augustiniennes, 1983.

Lorié, L. Th. A., S.J. *Spiritual Terminology in the Latin Translations of the Vita Antonii with reference to fourth and fifth century monastic literature.* Latinitas Christianorum Primaeva, vol. 11. Nijmegen: Dekker & van de Vegt, 1955.

Mandonnet, Pierre, O. P. *St. Dominic and His Work.* Translated by Sister Mary Benedicta Larkin, O.P. [Five technical studies omitted]. St. Louis: Herder Book Co., 1945. Originally published as *Saint Dominique, l'idée, l'homme et l'oeuvre.* Augmenté de notes et d'études critiques par M.-H. Vicaire, O.P. 2 vols. Paris: Desclée de Brouwer & Cie, 1937.

Martin, Hervé. *Le métier de prédicateur en France septentrionale à la fin du Moyen Age (1350-1520).* Paris: Editions du Cerf, 1988.

Metz, René. *La consécration des vierges dans l'église romaine.* Paris: Presses universitaires de France, 1954.

Mohrmann, Christine. *Études sur le Latin des Chrétiens.* Vol. 2, *Latin chrétien et médiéval.* Rome: Storia e Letteratura, 1961.

Moorman, John. *A History of the Franciscan Order from Its Origin to the Year 1517.* Oxford: Clarendon Press, 1968.

New Catholic Encyclopedia (NCE). Edited by W. J. McDonald and others at the Catholic University of America. 16 vols. New York: McGraw-Hill Book Company, 1967.

Nicolau, Miguel, S.J. *Jerónimo Nadal, S.I. (1507-1580): Sus obras y doctrinas espirituales.* Madrid: Editorial Urania, 1949.

Niermeyer, J. F. *Mediae Latinitatis Lexicon Minus: A Medieval Latin—French/English Dictionary.* Leiden: Brill, 1976. Photoprinted, 1984.

O'Malley, John W., S.J. *Giles of Viterbo on Church and Reform: A Study in Renaissance Thought.* Leiden: Brill, 1968.

———. *Praise and Blame in Renaissance Rome: Rhetoric, Doctrine, and Reform in the Sacred Orators of the Papal Court, c. 1450-1521.* Durham: Duke University Press, 1979.

———. *Tradition and Transition: Historical Perspectives on Vatican II.* Theology and Life Series 26. Wilmington: Michael Glazier, 1989.

———. *The First Jesuits.* Cambridge: Harvard University Press, 1993.

Olin, John C. *Six Essays on Erasmus.* New York: Fordham University Press, 1979.

———. *Catholic Reform from Cardinal Ximenes to the Council of Trent, 1495-1563: An Essay with Illustrative Documents and a Brief Study of St. Ignatius Loyola.* New York: Fordham University Press, 1990.

Orth, Clement Raymond, O.M.C. *The Approbation of Religious Institutes.* Canon Law Studies no. 71. Washington, D.C.: Catholic University of America Press, 1931.

Osborne, Kenan B., O.F.M. *Priesthood: A History of the Ordained Ministry in the Roman Catholic Church.* New York: Paulist Press, 1988.

Osuna, Javier, S.J. *Friends in the Lord.* Translated by Nicholas King, S.J. The Way Series 3. London: The Way, 1974.

The Oxford Dictionary of the Christian Church (ODCC). Edited by F. L. Cross. 2d edition edited by F. L. Cross and E. A. Livingstone. Oxford: University Press, 1974. Reprint, 1985.

Paolo, Aloisio di. *Innocenzo III e gli ordini religiosi.* [Dissertation excerpt.] Rome: Pontificia Universitas Gregoriana, 1957.

Partner, Peter. *Renaissance Rome 1500-1559: A Portrait of a Society.* Berkeley: University of California Press, 1976.

Paschini, Pio. *S. Gaetano Thiene, Gian Pietro Carafa, e le origini dei chierici regolari Teatini.* Rome: Scuola Tipografica Pio X, 1926.

Pastor, Ludwig F. von. *The History of the Popes from the Close of the Middle Ages.* 40 vols. London: Kegan Paul, 1889-1953. Originally published as *Geschichte der Päpste,* 16 vols. (Freiburg 1885-1933).

Plazaola, Juan, S.J., ed. *Ignacio de Loyola y su tiempo. Congreso internacional de historia (9-13 Setiembre 1991).* Bilbao: Mensajero and Universidad de Deusto, 1992.

Rahner, Hugo, S.J. *The Spirituality of St. Ignatius Loyola: An Account of Its Historical Development.* Translated by Francis John Smith, S.J. Chicago: Loyola University Press, 1953.

———. *Ignatius the Theologian.* Translated by Michael Barry. New York: Herder and Herder, 1968.

———. *The Vision of Ignatius in the Chapel of La Storta.* Rome: CIS, 1979. Originally published as articles in *Zeitschrift für Aszese und Mystik* 10 (1935): 17-35, 124-39, 202-20, 265-82.

Ravier André, S.J. *Les Chroniques saint Ignace de Loyola.* Paris: Nouvelle Librairie de France, 1973.

———. *Ignatius of Loyola and the Founding of the Society of Jesus.* Translated by Maura Daly, John Daly and Carson Daly. San Francisco: Ignatius Press, 1987. Originally published as *Ignace de Loyola fonde la Compagnie de Jésus* (Paris: Desclée de Brouwer, 1974).

———. *Saint Bruno le Chartreux.* Paris: Lethielleux, 1981.

Renard, Jean-Pierre. *La formation et la désignation des prédicateurs au début de l'Ordre des Prêcheurs (1215-1237).* Fribourg: Imprimerie St-Canisius, 1977.

Rodrigues, Francisco, S.J. *História da Companhia de Jesus da Assistência de Portugal.* 4 vols. in 7. Porto, 1931-50.

Rotsaert, Marc, S.J. *Ignace de Loyola et les renouveaux spirituels en Castille au début du XVIe siècle.* Rome: CIS, 1982.

Sala Balust, Luis, and Francisco Martin Hernandez. *La formación sacerdotal en la iglesia.* Barcelona: Juan Flors, 1966.

Schillebeeckx, Edward, O.P. *The Church with a Human Face: A New and Expanded Theology of Ministry.* New York: Crossroad, 1985.

Schmitt, Jean-Claude. *Prêcher d'exemples.* Paris: Stock, 1985.

Schmitz, Philibert, O.S.B. *Histoire de l'Ordre de Saint-Benoît.* 7 vols. Maredsous: Éditions de l'Abbaye, 1942-56.

Schroeder, H. J. *Disciplinary Decrees of the General Councils.* St. Louis: Herder Book Co., 1937.

Schurhammer, Georg, S.J. *Francis Xavier, His Life and Times.* Vol. 1, *Europe, 1506-1541.* Translated by M. Joseph Costelloe, S.J. Rome: The Jesuit Historical Institute, 1973. Originally published as *Franz Xaver: Sein Leben und Seine Zeit.* Vol. 1, *Europa, 1506-1541* (Freiburg im Breisgau: Herder, 1955).

Secondin, Bruno, O. Carm., ed. *La Regola del Carmelo oggi.* Rome: Institutum Carmelitanum, 1983.

Shuhler, Ralph V. *Privileges of Regulars to Absolve and Dispense.* Canon Law Studies no. 186. Washington, D.C.: Catholic University of America Press, 1943.

Steidle, Basilius, O.S.B. *The Rule of St. Benedict: A Commentary.* Translated by Urban J. Schnitzhofer. Canon City, CO: Holy Cross Abbey, 1967. Originally published as *Die Regel St. Benedikts. Eingeleitet, übersetzt und aus dem alten Mönchtum erklärt* (Beuron: Kunstverlag, 1952).

Stierli, Josef, S.J. trans. *Dokumente zur Grundung der Gesellschaft Jesu 1539-1541. Geistliche Texte no. 8*, herausgegeben im Auftrag der Provinzialskonferenz der Deutschen Assistenz. Frankfurt/M, 1983.

Sumption, Jonathan. *Pilgrimage: An Image of Mediaeval Religion*. London: Faber & Faber, 1975.

Tacchi Venturi, Pietro, S.J. *Storia della Compagnia di Gesù in Italia, narrata col susidio di fonti inedite*. 2 vols. in 4 parts. 2d ed. Rome: La Civiltà Cattolica, 1950-51.

Trichet, Louis. *La tonsure: Vie et mort d'une pratique ecclésiastique*. Paris: Editions du Cerf, 1990.

Tugwell, Simon, O.P. *The Way of the Preacher*. Springfield, IL: Templegate, 1979.

Verheijen, Luc. *La Règle de Saint Augustin*. Vol. 1, *Tradition Manuscrite*. Paris: Études Augustiniennes, 1967.

Vicaire, M.-H., O.P. *Saint Dominic and His Times*. Translated by Kathleen Pond. New York: McGraw-Hill, 1964. Originally published as *Histoire de Saint Dominique*. 2 vols. (Paris: Editions du Cerf, 1957.)

———. *The Apostolic Life*. Translated by William E. DeNaple. Chicago: The Priory Press, 1966. Originally published as *L'imitation des apôtres: Moines, chanoines, mendiants (IVe-XIIIe siècles)* (Paris: Editions du Cerf, 1963).

Werner, Ernst. *Pauperes Christi: Studien zu sozial-religiösen Bewegungen im Zeitalter des Reformpapsttums*. Leipzig: Koehler-Amelang, 1956

Secondary Sources: Articles

Alberigo, Giuseppe. "'Réforme' en tant que critère de l'Histoire de l'Église." *Revue d'histoire ecclésiastique* 76 (1981): 72-81.

Aldama, Antonio M. de, S.J. "Peculiarem curam circa puerorum eruditionem." *Recherches Ignatiennes* 4, no. 5 (1977): 1-23.

———. "Origine e Storia della Formula dell'Istituto." In *La Formula dell'Istituto, S.J.*, 9-31. Rome: CIS, 1977. English translation: "Origin and History of the Formula of the Institute." In *The Formula of the Institute*, 11-53. Rome: CIS, 1982.

Bacht, Heinrich, S.J. "Early Monastic Elements in Ignatian Spirituality: Toward Clarifying Some Fundamental Concepts of the Exercises." In *Ignatius of Loyola: His Personality and Spiritual Heritage, 1556-1956*, edited by Friedrich Wulf, S.J., 200-236. St. Louis: Institute of Jesuit Sources, 1977. Originally published as *Ignatius von Loyola:*

seine geistliche Gestalt und sein Vermächtnis (1556-1956) (Würzburg: Echter-Verlag, 1956).

Baumann, Theodor, S.J. "Die Berichte über die Vision des Heiligen Ignatius bei La Storta." *AHSI* 27 (1958): 181-208.

———. "Compagnie de Jésus. Origine et sens primitif de ce nom." *Revue d'ascétique et de mystique* 37 (1961): 47-60.

———. "Compagnie de Jésus. La confirmation de ce nom dans la vision de la Storta." *Revue d'ascétique et de mystique* 38 (1962): 52-63.

Berlière, Dom Ursmer, O.S.B. "Innocent III et la réorganisation des monastères bénédictins." *Revue bénédictine* 32 (1920): 22-42, 145-59.

Bertrand, Dominique, S.J. "La Compagnie de Jésus et son 'institut'." *Vie consacrée* 55 (1983): 292-309.

Beyer, Jean, S.J. "Saint Ignace de Loyola chartreux..." *Nouvelle revue théologique* 78 (1956): 937-51.

———. "Novità della Compagnia di Gesù nelle strutture degli ordini religiosi." *Vita consacrata* 27 (1991): 733-44.

Bligny, Bernard. "Monachisme et pauvreté au XIIe siècle." In *La povertà del secolo XII e Francesco d'Assisi: Assisi, 17-19 ottobre 1974*, 99-147. Assisi: Atti del II Convegno Internationale, 1975.

Böckmann, Aquinata, O.S.B. "Openness to the World and Separation from the World according to RB." *American Benedictine Review* 37 (1986): 304-22.

Bolton, Brenda M. "Innocent III's Treatment of the *Humiliati*." In *Popular Belief and Practice*, edited by G. J. Cuming and Derek Baker, 73-82. Studies in Church History 8. Cambridge: University Press, 1972.

———. "Tradition and Temerity: Papal Attitudes to Deviants, 1159-1216." In *Schism, Heresy and Religious Protest*, edited by Derek Baker, 79-91. Studies in Church History 9. Cambridge: University Press, 1972.

———. "The Poverty of the *Humiliati*." In *Poverty in the Middle Ages*, edited by David Flood, 52-59. Franziskanische Forschungen 27. Werl: Dietrich-Coelde, 1975.

———. "*Paupertas Christi:* Old Wealth and New Poverty in the Twelfth Century." In *Renaissance and Renewal in Christian History*, edited by Derek Baker, 95-103. Studies in Church History 14. Oxford: Blackwell, 1977.

———. "*Via ascetica*: A Papal Quandary." In *Monks, Hermits and the Ascetic Tradition*, edited by W. J. Sheils, 161-91. Studies in Church History 22. London: Blackwell, 1985.

Bottereau, Georges, S.J. "La 'lettre' d'Ignace de Loyola a Gian Pietro Carafa." *AHSI* 44 (1975): 139-52.

Brooke, Christopher N. L. "Monk and Canon: Some Patterns in the Religious Life of the Twelfth Century." In *Monks, Hermits,* 109-29. *See* Bolton 1985.

Calveras, José, S.J. "Acerca del copista del autógrafo de los ejercicios." *AHSI* 30 (1961): 244-63.

Campos, J. "El 'propositum' monástico en la tradición patrística." *La Ciudad de Dios* 181 (1968): 535-47.

Casey, Michael, O.C.S.O. "The Benedictine Promises." *Tjurunga* [An Australasian Benedictine Review], no. 24 (1983): 17-34.

———. "Strangers to Worldly Ways: RB 4.20." *Tjurunga* [An Australasian Benedictine Review], no. 29 (1985): 37-46.

Codina, Arturo, S.J. "Los 'Ejercicios' de san Ignacio y el 'Ejercitatorio' de Cisneros." *Razon y fe* 48 (1917): 286-99, 426-36; 49 (1917): 16-29.

Codina, Victor, S.J. "Le thème du chemin chez Ignace de Loyola." *Christus* 16 (1969): 236-41.

Coemans, Augusto, S.J. "La Fórmula del Instituto aprobada por Paulo III and Julio III." In *Introducción al estudio de la Fórmula del Instituto S.I.*, 7-58. Rome: CIS, 1974.

Collins, Mary, O.S.B. "Rule and Gospel: The Meaning of Benedictine Vowing." *Benedictines* 35, no. 2 (Fall-Winter 1980): 27-46.

Colombás, García M., O.S.B. "The Ancient Concept of the Monastic Life." [Slightly condensed.] *Monastic Studies* 2 (1964): 65-117. Originally published as "El concepto de monje y vida monástica hasta fines del siglo V." (*Studia Monastica* 1 [1959]: 257-342).

Constable, Giles. "Monachisme et pèlerinage au Moyen Âge." *Revue Historique* 101 (1977): 3-27.

———. "Renewal and Reform in Religious Life: Concepts and Realities." In *Renaissance and Renewal in the 12th Century*, edited by R. L. Benson and G. Constable, 37-67. Cambridge: Harvard University Press, 1982.

———. "Monasteries, Rural Churches and the *Cura animarum* in the Early Middle Ages." In *Monks, Hermits and Crusaders in Medieval Europe*, 349-89. London: Variorum Reprints, 1988.

Conwell, Joseph F., S.J. "The Kamikaze Factor: Choosing Jesuit Ministries." *Studies in the Spirituality of Jesuits* 11 (November 1979): 1-71.

———. "Living and Dying in the Society of Jesus, or Endeavoring to Imitate Angelic Purity." *Studies in the Spirituality of Jesuits* 12 (May 1980): 1-63.

Crehan, J. H., S.J. "Medieval Ordinations." In *The Study of Liturgy*, edited by Cheslyn Jones and others, 320-31. New York: Oxford University Press, 1978.

Daley, Brian E., S.J. "The Ministry of Disciples: Historical Reflections on the Role of Religious Priests." *Theological Studies* 48 (1987): 605-29.

Dalmases, Cándido de, S.J. "San Ignacio de Loyola y la Contrarreforma." *Studia Missionalia* 34 (1985): 321-50.

de Bhaldraithe, Eoin, O.Cist. "Faith in the RB: Witness to a Primitive Theology." *Regulae Benedicti Studia Annuarium Internationale* 12 (1983): 89-110.

———. "Conversatio: St. Benedict Recovers Early Christian Terminology." *Regulae Benedicti Studia Annuarium Internationale* 13 (1984): 3-15.

de Fontette, Micheline. "*Religionum diversitatem* et la suppression des ordres mendiants." In *1274: Année charnière. Mutations et continuités. Lyon-Paris 30 septembre - 5 octobre 1974*, 223-29. Colloques internationaux CNRS no 558. Paris: Éditions du centre national de la recherche scientifique, 1977.

Delaruelle, Étienne. "Les ermites et la spiritualité populaire." In *L'Eremitismo in Occidente nei Secoli XI e XII. Atti della seconda Settimana internazionale di studio Mendola, 30 agosto - 6 settembre 1962*, 212-41. Miscellanea del Centro di Studi Medioevali, vol. 4. Milan: Vita e Pensiero, 1965.

Del Piazzo, Marcello and Cándido de Dalmases, S.J. "Il processo sul' ortodossia di S. Ignazio e dei suoi compagni svoltosi a Roma nel 1538." *AHSI* 38 (1969): 431-53.

de Mas Latrie, L. "Les éléments de la diplomatique pontificale." *Revue des questions historiques* 39 (1886): 415-51 & 41 (1887): 382-435.

Desjardins, Léopold, C.SS.R. "Le renouveau de l'idée de sacerdoce universel à la fin du Moyen Âge." In *Le prêtre, hier, aujourd'hui, demain. Travaux du congrès de la Société canadienne de Théologie tenu à Ottawa du 24 au 28 août 1969*, 128-41. Montreal: Fides, 1970.

de Vogüé, Adalbert, O.S.B. "*Sub regula uel abbate*: A Study in the Theological Significance of the Ancient Monastic Rules." In *Rule and Life: An Interdisciplinary Symposium*, edited by M. Basil Pennington, 21-63. Cistercian Studies Series 12. Spencer, MA.: Cistercian Publications, 1971.

———. "The Evangelical Counsels in the Master and Saint Benedict." *Cistercian Studies* 15 (1980): 3-16.

———. "The Meaning of Benedictine Hospitality." *Cistercian Studies* 21 (1986): 186-94.

———. "Priest and Monastic Community in Antiquity." *Cistercian Studies* 22 (1987): 17-24.

———. "Les critères du discernement des vocations dan la tradition monastique ancienne." *Collectanea Cisterciensia* 51 (1989): 109-26.

Delgado, Feliciano, S.J. "Compañía de Jesús. Análisis filológico del término." *Manresa* 61 (1989): 249-56.

Diego, Luis de, S.J. "Ignacio de Loyola sacerdote: de ayer a hoy." *Manresa* 63 (1991): 89-102.

Dubois, Jacques, O.S.B. "Les ordres religieux au XIIe siècle selon la curie romaine." *Revue bénédictine* 78 (1968): 283-309.

Dutton, Marsha L. "The Cistercian Source: Aelred, Bonaventure, and Ignatius." In *Goad and Nail*, edited by E. R. Elder, 151-78. Studies in Medieval Cistercian History 10. Kalamazoo: Cistercian Publications, 1985.

Duval, A., O.P. "The Council of Trent and Holy Orders." In *The Sacrament of Holy Orders: Some Papers and Discussions concerning Holy Orders at a Session of the Centre de Pastorale Liturgique, 1955*, 219-58. Collegeville: The Liturgical Press, 1962.

———. "Quelques données et réflexions historiques sur l'engagement religieux." In J. Colette, A. Dumas, F. Dumas, A. Duval, P. Jacquemont, *Engagement et Fidélité*, 69-115. Paris: Editions du Cerf, 1970.

Emery, Richard W. "The Second Council of Lyons and the Mendicant Orders." *The Catholic Historical Review* 39 (1953): 257-71.

Endean, Philip, S.J. "Who Do You Say Ignatius Is? Jesuit Fundamentalism and Beyond." *Studies in the Spirituality of Jesuits* 19 (November 1987): 1-53.

Fernández Martín, Luis, S.J. "El hogar donde Iñigo de Loyola se hizo hombre, 1506-1517." *AHSI* 49 (1980): 21-92.

———. "Iñigo de Loyola y los alumbrados." *Hispania sacra* 35 (1983): 585-680.

———. "Francisco Mudarra, difamador y protegido de san Ignacio, 1538-1555." *AHSI* 62 (1993): 161-73.

Fiorito, M. A., S.J., and J. L. Lazzarini, S.J. "Una predicación sobre la doctrina cristiana por san Ignacio de Loyola." *Boletín de espiritualidad* 36 (1974): 9-23.

Fransen, G. "The Tradition in Medieval Canon Law." In *The Sacrament of Holy Orders*, 202-18. *See* Duval.

García Hirschfeld, Carlos, S.J. "Origen de la comunidad en la Compañía de Jesús: Una experiencia humana y religiosa en un grupo de universitarios del s. XVI." *Manresa* 63 (1991): 393-410.

García Madariaga, José M., S.J. "La oblación del grupo Ignaciano al Papa en 1538." *Manresa* 48 (1976): 25-39.

———. "Contenido de la clausula papal del voto de Montmarte." *Manresa* 48 (1976): 231-45.

———. "La oblación al Papa según las Deliberaciones de 1539." *Manresa* 49 (1977): 55-68.

Gilles, Henri. "Lex peregrinorum." In *Le Pèlerinage*, 161-89. Cahiers de Fanjeaux 15 - Collection d'Histoire religieuse du Languedoc au XIIIe et au début du XIVe siècles. Toulouse: E. Privat, 1980.

Gleason, Elisabeth G. "The Capuchins." In *Religious Orders of the Catholic Reformation*, ed. Richard L. DeMolen, 41-47. New York: Fordham University Press, 1994.

———. "Who Was the First Counter-Reformation Pope?" *The Catholic Historical Review* 81 (1995): 173-84.

Gonzalez, Luis, S.J. "La deliberación de los primeros compañeros." *Manresa* 61 (1989): 231-48.

Granero, Jesús M., S.J. "La pobreza ignaciana." *Manresa* 40 (1968): 149-74.

Grégoire, Réginald. "'Religiosus', Etude sur le vocabulaire de la vie religieuse." *Studi medievali* 10 (1969) [= Melanges Ermini, vol. 2, Soleto 1970]: 415-30.

———. "La place de la pauvreté dans la conception et la pratique de la vie monastique mediévale latine." In *Il monachesimo e la riforma ecclesiastica (1049-1122): Atti della quarta Settimana internazionale di studio Mendola, 23-29 agosto 1968*, 173-92. Miscellanea del Centro di Studi Medioevali, vol. 6. Milan: Vita e Pensiero, 1971.

Hernández Montés, Benigno, S.J. "Identidad de los personajes que juzgaron a San Ignacio en Salamanca: Problemas historicos suscitados por las primeras fuentes." *AHSI* 52 (1983): 3-51.

Hertling, Ludwig, S.J. "Die professio der Kleriker und die Entstehung der drei Gelübde." *Zeitschrift für Katholische Theologie* 56 (1932): 148-74.

Holstein, Henri, S.J. "The History of the Development of the Word 'Apostolic'." In *Apostolic Life*, translated by Ronald Halstead, 31-49. Westminster, MD: Newman Press, 1958. Originally published as *L'Apostolat* (Paris: Editions du Cerf, n.d.).

Iserloh, Erwin. "The Inner Life of the Church." Chapter 58 in *Handbook of Church History*, vol. 4, edited by Hubert Jedin and John Dolan, 566-85. New York: Herder & Herder, 1970.

Iturrioz, Jesús, S.J. "Compañía de Jesús: Sentido historico y ascético de este nombre." *Manresa* 27 (1955): 43-53.

———. "San Francisco de Xabier 'enviado' del Papa Paulo III, Roma, marzo 1540." *Manresa* 58 (1986): 155-79.

———. "'Nuestro antigo y verdadero padre don Ignatio.' Salamanca, 1527. Roma, Bas. de San Pablo, 1541." *Manresa* 58 (1986): 243-65.

———. "El peregrino de París a Roma: El año 1537 de San Ignacio; Recuerdo a los 450 años." *Manresa* 60 (1988): 21-43.

———. "Primer año de San Ignacio en Roma: Primera oblación al Papa. Noviembre 1538. Primera Misa. 25 de diciembre 1538." *Manresa* 60 (1988): 343-66.

———. "Aprobación 'oral' de la 'Compañía de Jesús'." *Manresa* 61 (1989): 367-84.

Jedin, Hubert. "Did the Council of Trent Create a Prototype of the Priest?" In *Priesthood and Celibacy*, edited by J. Coppens, 153-80. Milan: Âncora, 1972.

Jorgensen, Kenneth J., S.J. "The Theatines." In *Religious Orders of the Catholic Reformation*, 1-29. *See* Gleason 1994.

Justice, Cornelius, O.C.S.O. "Evolution of the Teaching on Commitment by Monastic Vow from New Testament Times to the Ninth Century." *Cistercian Studies* 12 (1977): 18-40.

Kalinowski, Michel. "Le compagnon de Jésus et le moine au XVIe siècle." In *Les Jésuites parmi les hommes aux XVIe et XVIIe siècles*, 3-8. Clermont-Ferrand: Faculté des lettres et sciences humaines, 1987.

Kehl, Medard, S.J. "Seelsorge für 'Kinder und einfache Menschen'," in *Ignatianisch: Eigenart und Methode der Gesellschaft Jesu*, edited by M. Sievernich, S.J. and G. Switek, S.J., 557-68. Freiburg: Herder, 1990.

Kolvenbach, Peter-Hans, S.J. "On the 450th Anniversary of the Vow of Montmartre." *CIS* 16, no. 2 (1985): 9-14.

———. "A Certain Pathway to God ('Via quaedam ad Deum')." *CIS* 22, no. 3 (1991): 25-45.

Lackner, Bede, O.Cist. "Early Cîteaux and the Care of Souls." In *Noble Piety and Reformed Monasticism*, edited by E. Rozanne Elder, 52-67. Studies in Medieval Cistercian History 7. Kalamazoo: Cistercian Publications, 1981.

Larrañaga, Victoriano, S.J. "Los estudios superiores de San Ignacio en París, Bolonia y Venecia." *Razón y Fe* 153 (1956): 221-42.

Leclercq, Jean, O.S.B. "On Monastic Priesthood according to the Ancient Medieval Tradition." *Studia Monastica* 3 (1961): 137-55.

———. "The Priesthood for Monks." Translated by monks of Caldey Abbey, South Wales. *Monastic Studies* 3 (1965): 53-85. Originally published as "Le sacerdoce des moines" (*Irénikon* 36 [1963]: 5-40).

———. Saint Ignatius at Montserrat." In *Aspects of Monasticism*, translated by Mary Dodd, 295-308. Cistercian Studies Series 7. Kalamazoo: Cistercian Publications, 1978. Article first published in *Christus* 13 (1966): 161-73.

———. "Pour l'histoire du vocabulaire latin de la pauvreté." In *Melto: Recherches Orientales* 3 (Mélanges Mgr Pierre Dib) 1967, 293-308.

———. "The Intentions of the Founders of the Cistercian Order." In *The Cistercian Spirit: A Symposium*, edited by M. Basil Pennington, O.C.S.O., 88-133. Cistercian Studies Series 3. Shannon: Irish University Press, 1970.

———. "The Priesthood in the Patristic and Medieval Church." In *The Christian Priesthood*, edited by Nicholas Lash and Joseph Rhymer, 53-75. Denville, NJ: Dimension Books, 1970.

———. "Qu'est-ce que vivre 'selon une règle'?" *Collectanea Cisterciensia* 32 (1970): 155-63.

———. "Profession according to the Rule of St. Benedict: An Historical Study." *Cistercian Studies* 5 (1970): 252-77.

———. "Monasticism and One World." *Cistercian Studies* 21 (1986): 277-310.

———. "Monastic and Scholastic Theology in the Reformers of the Fourteenth to Sixteenth Century." In *From Cloister to Classroom: Monastic and Scholastic Approaches to Truth*, edited by E. Rozanne Elder, 178-201. Vol. 3 of *The Spirituality of Western Christendom.* Cistercian Studies Series 90. Kalamazoo: Cistercian Publications, 1986.

Le Goff, Jacques. "Le Dossier des Mendiants." In *1274: Année charnière*, 211-22. *See* de Fontette.

Lekai, Louis, O.Cist. "The Rule and the Early Cistercians." *Cistercian Studies* 5 (1970): 243-51.

Lesage, Germain. "Sacred Bonds in the Consecrated Life." [Abridged.] *The Way*, Supplement no. 37 (Spring 1980): 78-96. Originally published as "Evolutio et momentum vinculi sacri in professione vitae consecratae" (*Periodica de re morali canonica liturgica* 67 [1978]: 413-45).

Leturia, Pedro, S.J. "Importancia del año 1538 en el cumplimiento del 'voto de Montmarte'." *AHSI* 9 (1940): 188-207.

Lienhard, Joseph T., S.J. "On 'Discernment of Spirits' in the Early Church." *Theological Studies* 41 (1980): 505-29.

Longhurst, John E. "Saint Ignatius at Alcalá, 1526-1527." *AHSI* 26 (1957): 252-56.

Maccarrone, Michele. "Riforma e sviluppo della vita religiosa con Innocenzo III." *Revista di Storia della Chiesa in Italia* 16 (1962): 29-72.

Manning, E. "La signification de 'militare-militia-miles' dans la règle de saint Benoît." *Revue bénédictine* 72 (1962): 135-38.

Marthaler, Berard, O.F.M.Conv. "Forerunners of the Franciscans: The Waldenses." *Franciscan Studies* 18 (1958): 133-42.

Maruca, Dominic, S.J. "The Deliberation of Our First Fathers." *Woodstock Letters* 95 (1966): 325-33.

Matanié, Atanasio, O.F.M. "Papa Innocenzo III di fronte a San Domenico e San Francesco." *Antonianum* 35 (1960): 508-27.

McNally, Robert E., S.J. "Pope Adrian VI (1522-23) and Church Reform." *Archivum Historiae Pontificiae* 7 (1969): 253-85.

Meersseman, Gilles Gérard, O.P. "Eremitismo e predicazione itinerante dei secoli XI e XII." In *L'Eremitismo*, 164-81. *See* Delaruelle.

———. "I penitenti nei secoli XI e XII." In *I laici nella "Societas Christiana" dei secoli XI e XII: Atti della terza Settimana internazionale di studio Mendola, 21-27 agosto 1965*, 306-39. Miscellanea del Centro di Studi Medioevali, vol. 5. Milan: Vita e Pensiero, 1968.

Merton, Thomas. "Conversion of Life." In *The Monastic Journey*, edited by Patrick Hart, 107-20. Kansas City: Sheed Andrews and McMeel, 1977. Originally published in *Cistercian Studies* 1 (1966): 130-44.

———. "From Pilgrimage to Crusade." In *Mystics and Zen Masters*, 91-112. New York: Dell, 1967.

Meslin, Michel. "Ecclesiastical Institutions and Clericalization from 100 to 500 A.D." In *Sacralization and Secularization*, edited by Roger Aubert, 39-54. Concilium 47. New York: Paulist Press, 1969.

Minnich, Nelson H., S.J. "Concepts of Reform Proposed at the Fifth Lateran Council." *Archivum Historiae Pontificiae* 7 (1969): 163-251.

Mollat, Michel. "Les moines et les pauvres: XIe-XIIe siècles." In *Il monachesimo e la riforma*, 193-215. *See* Grégoire 1971.

———. "Hospitalité et assistance au début du XIIIe siècle." In *Poverty in the Middle Ages*, 37-51. *See* Bolton 1975.

The Montmartre Vows: History and Spirituality. CIS 16, no. 2 (1985).

Nicolau, Miguel, S.J. "Notas de la espiritualidad jesuitica." *Manresa* 25 (1953): 259-88.

Nilles, Nikolaus, S.J. "Asterisken zur Geschichte der Ordination des heiligen Ignatius von Loyola und seiner Gefährten." *Zeitschrift für katholische Theologie* 15 (1891): 146-59.

Nowell, Irene, O.S.B. "Turning and Being Turned to the Lord: Biblical Foundations of *Conversatio* in the RB." *Benedictines* 36, no. 2 (Fall-Winter 1981): 16-29.

O'Malley, John W., S.J. "Jesuits, Ignatius and the Counter Reformation: Some Recent Studies and Their Implications for Today." *Studies in the Spirituality of Jesuits* 14 (January 1982): 1-28.

———. "To Travel to Any Part of the World: Jerónimo Nadal and the Jesuit Vocation." *Studies in the Spirituality of Jesuits* 16 (March 1984): 1-20.

———. "Priesthood, Ministry, and Religious Life: Some Historical and Historiographical Considerations." *Theological Studies* 49 (1988): 223-57.

———. "Some Distinctive Characteristics of Jesuit Spirituality in the Sixteenth Century." In *Jesuit Spirituality: A Now and Future Resource*, by John W. O'Malley, S.J., John W. Padberg, S.J., Vincent T. O'Keefe, S.J., 1-20. Chicago: Loyola University Press, 1990.

———. "How the Jesuits Changed: 1540-56." *America* 165, no. 2 (1991): 28-32.

O'Reilly, Terence W. "The Exercises of Saint Ignatius Loyola and the Exercitatorio de la vida espiritual." *Studia Monastica* 16 (1974): 301-23.

Olin, John C. "The Idea of Pilgrimage in the Experience of Ignatius Loyola." *Church History* 48 (1979): 387-97.

———. "Catholic Reform from Cardinal Ximenes to the Council of Trent." In *Catholic Reform*, 1-43.

Olivares, Estanilao, S.J. "Aportación de la Compañía de Jesús a la vida religiosa en su época." *Manresa* 56 (1984): 229-59, 345-64.

Olphe-Galliard, M., S.J. "La vie commune et l'apostolat dans la Compagnie de Jésus." In *La Vie commune*, 61-76. Problèmes de la religieuse d'aujourd'hui. Paris: Editions du Cerf, 1956.

Orsy, Ladislas, S.J. "Bishops, Presbyters and Priesthood in Gratians's Decretum." *Gregorianum* 44 (1963): 788-826.

Osuna, Javier, S.J. "La vida de comunidad en la primitiva Compañía hasta 1540 y las Constituciones." *Boletín del Centro de Espiritualidad*, no. 11 (June 1971): 29-38.

Peifer, Claude, O.S.B. "Monastic Formation and Profession." In *RB 1980*, Appendix 5, 437-66.

Penning de Vries, Piet, S.J. "Protestants and Other Spirituals: Ignatius' Vision and Why He Took This Position." *AHSI* 40 (1971): 463-83.

Pieris, Aloysius, S.J. "The Religious Vows and the Reign of God." *The Way*, Supplement no. 65 (Summer 1989): 3-15.

Powell, James M. "The Papacy and the Early Franciscans." *Franciscan Studies* 36 (1976): 248-62.

Rambla, José, S.J. "Del 'peregrino' a la 'minima' Compañía de Jesús." *Manresa* 54 (1982): 5-23.

―――. "Del 'pobre peregrino Iñigo' a Ignacio 'el peregrino': De la peregrinación a la misión." *Vida religiosa* 70 (1991): 244-57.

―――. "Ignacio de Loyola y la vocación laical." *Manresa* 67 (1995): 5-19.

Ravier, André, S.J. "St. Ignatius and the Catechism." *CIS* 18, no. 2 (1987): 83-94.

―――. "Saint Ignace enseignait le catéchisme..." *Lumen vitae* 45 (1990): 165-75.

―――. "The Life of Iñigo de Loyola and his First Companions at the University of Paris (October 1525 -December 1536)." *CIS* 23, no. 2 (1992): 86-102.

―――. "Ignace de Loyola et la Chartreuse de Paris." *Christus* 42 (1995): 228-35

Religious Reformers: Christianity and other Religions. Studia Missionalia 34. Rome: Gregorian University Press, 1985.

Renna, Thomas. "The Idea of Jerusalem: Monastic to Scholastic." In *From Cloister to Classroom*, 96-109. *See* Leclercq 1986.

Rossi de Gasperis, Francesco, S.J. "Ignatius of Loyola: The Man of the Experience of God." *CIS* 24, no. 3 (1993): 27-54.

Ruiz-Jurado, Manuel, S.J. "Cronología de la vida del P. Jerónimo Nadal, S.I. (1507-1580)." *AHSI* 48 (1979): 248-76.

―――. "¿Influyo en S. Ignacio el Ejercitatorio de Cisneros?" *Manresa* 51 (1979): 65-75.

―――. "What Exactly Happened at Montmartre on August 15, 1534?" *CIS* 16, no. 2 (1985): 15-35.

Saint-Saëns, Alain. "Ignace de Loyola devant l'érémitisme: La dimension cartusienne." *Mélanges de l'École française de Rome. Italie et Méditerranée* 102 (1990): 191-209.

Scaduto, Mario, S.J. "La strada e i primi Gesuiti." *AHSI* 40 (1971): 323-90.

Schneider, Burkhart, S.J. "Nuestro principio y principal fundamento: zum historischen Verständnis des Papstgehorsamsgelübdes." *AHSI* 25 (1956): 488-513.

Schurhammer, Georg, S.J. "Zur Frage des Schreibers der fünf Kapitel, approbiert von Paul III." *AHSI* 30 (1961): 264-66.

Schweitzer, Vinzenz. "Kardinal Bartolomeo Guidiccioni." *Römische Quartalschrift* 20 (1906): 27-53, 142-61, 189-204.

Smits Van Waesberghe, M., S.J. "Origine et développement des exercices spirituels avant Saint Ignace." *Revue d'ascétique et de mystique* 33 (1957): 264-72.

Switek, Günter, S.J. "Die Gelübde des hl. Ignatius und seiner Gefährten auf dem Montmartre: Zur Aktualität ihrer Mystik und missionarischen Dynamik." *Geist und Leben* 65 (1992): 245-57.

Thouzellier, Christine. "Hérésie et pauvreté à la fin du XIIe et au début du XIIIe siècle." In *Études sur l'histoire de la pauvreté*, edited by Michel Mollat, 371-88. Paris: Publications de la Sorbonne, 1974.

Toner, Jules J., S.J. "The Deliberation That Started the Jesuits: A Commentary on the *Deliberatio primorum patrum*. Newly Translated with a Historical Introduction." *Studies in the Spirituality of Jesuits* 6 (1974): 179-212.

Urrutia, José Luis, S.J. "Regimen de las ordenes religiosas a mediados del s. XVI y aportación de San Ignacio." *Miscelánea Comillas* 36 (1961): 91-142.

Veilleux, Armand, O.C.S.O. "Creativeness and Fidelity to Tradition." *Cistercian Studies* 3 (1968): 98-103.

———. "The Interpretation of a Monastic Rule." In *The Cistercian Spirit*, 48-65. *See* Leclercq 1970.

———. "The Evolution of the Religious Life in its Historical and Spiritual Context." *Cistercian Studies* 6 (1971): 8-34.

———. "Citeaux in Search of Its Identity: 1955-1975." *Monastic Exchange* 9 (1977): 9-15.

———. "Asceticism in Pachomian Cenobitism." In *The Continuing Quest for God: Monastic Spirituality in Tradition and Transition*, edited by William Skudlarek, O.S.B., 67-79. Collegeville: Liturgical Press, 1982.

Vercruysse, Jos. E. "Luther as Reformer within Christendom." *Studia Missionalia* 34 (1985): 351-71.

Vicaire, M.-H., O.P. "Fondation, approbation, confirmation de l'Ordre des Prêcheurs." *Revue d'histoire ecclesiastique* 47 (1952): 123-41; 586-603.

———. "La bulle de confirmation des Prêcheurs." *Revue d'histoire ecclesiastique* 47 (1952): 176-92.

———. "Rencontre à Pamiers des courants vaudois et dominicain (1207)." In *Vaudois languedociens et Pauvres Catholiques*, 163-94. Cahiers de Fanjeaux 2 - Collection d'Histoire religieuse du Languedoc au XIIIe et au début du XIVe siècles. Toulouse: E. Privat, 1967.

———. "Les trois itinérances du pèlerinage aux XIIIe et XIVe siècles." In *Le Pèlerinage*, 17-41. *See* Gilles.

———. "Sacerdoce et prédication aux origines de l'Ordre des Prêcheurs." *Revue des Sciences philosophiques et théologiques* 64 (1980): 241-54.

———. "L'Ordre de Saint Dominique en 1215." *Archivum Fratrum Praedicatorum* 54 (1984): 5-38.

The Vision of La Storta: History and Spirituality. *CIS* 19, no. 1 (1988).

Waddell, Chrysogonus, O.C.S.O. "Prelude to a Feast of Freedom: Notes on the Roman Privilege *Desiderium quod* of October 19, 1100." *Cîteaux Commentarii Cistercienses* 33 (1982): 247-303.

Ware, Archimandrite Kallistos. "Silence in Prayer: The Meaning of Hesychia." In *One Yet Two: Monastic Tradition East and West*, edited by M. Basil Pennington, 22-47. Cistercian Studies Series 29. Kalamazoo: Cistercian Publications, 1976.

Wathen, Ambrose, O.S.B. "*Conversatio* and Stability in the Rule of Benedict." *Monastic Studies* 11 (1975): 1-44.

White, Allan, O.P. "The Foundation of the Order of Preachers and its Historical Setting." In Simon Tugwell, *The Way of the Preacher*, Appendix One, 97-110. Springfield, IL: Templegate, 1979.

Witwer, Anton, S.J. "The Missionary Focus of the Vows in the Ignatian Charism." *CIS* 24, no. 1 (1993): 39-53.

Index

Abraham
  as exemplar, 206, 358–59, 408
  paradigm for exile, 168–73,
    481 nn. 28 and 33, 482 n. 34
Abuses in Church, 155, 202, 222,
  446 n. 15, 448 n. 20
Achille, Paolo de, 502 n. 23
Admission into Society, 251–53,
  279, 313, 317, 502 n. 23
  required experiences for, 165,
    176, 180, 205–6, 486 n. 58
Adrian VI, Pope, 226
Aggiornamento, updating, xv,
  224, 331–32, 420, 496
  nn. 32 and 35
Agite igitur, get moving, 406–7,
  421
Agnes of Prague, 325
Albert, Patriarch of Jerusalem,
  350, 508 n. 11
Albigensians, 145, 419
Alcalá. *See* Ignatius de Loyola,
  activities at or in, Alcalá.
Aldama, Antonio de, 21, 118,
  177, 485 n. 55
  on the Formula of the Institute,
    xx, 18, 280
Aleandro, Cardinal Girolamo,
  221–22, 340

Alexander III, Pope, 152, 454
  n. 61
Alexander VI, Pope, 35, 65
Alumbrados, 153, 184, 186, 408
Ambrose, Saint, 343
Amerimnos, free from care, 231
Anachorēsis, withdrawal, 231, 366
Ancient Christian way of living.
  See *Conversatio.*
Andrés de Loyola, 68
Angelic purity, 386–89, 391, 499
  n. 2
Antony, Saint, 98, 321, 347–48,
  361–62
Apostles, 61–62, 232. See also
  Vita apostolica.
  imitating example of, 99,
    171, 175, 182
Apostolic letter, xxi–xxii, 18–20,
  34, 401
Apotagē, renunciation, 231, 510
  n. 14
Apotaxis, renunciation, 231, 366
Approval, papal, 235, 309,
  322–26, 329, 373–74, 382–83
  companions' request for, xx
    17–18, 29, 88, 212, 254,
    287–88, 298, 328–29, 332,
    369, 379. See also *Vivendi*

formula, examining and approving.
  of the Formula of the Institute, xv, xvii, xxi–xxii, xxxi, 18–20, 380, 401–5, 415. See also *Exposcit; Regimini.*
Approved rule, 282, 322–28, 381–83, 500 n. 14, 517 n. 17
Aquaviva, Claude, 115, 117, 175, 388–89
Aránzazu, 166, 173, 313, 359
Araoz, Antonio de, 19, 45, 253
Arévalo, xxix, 24
Arias, Antonio, 434 n. 11, 468 n. 15
Arze, Dr. Jerónimo, 147, 471 n. 37
Askēsis, ascetic life, 214, 243–44, 249, 347, 361, 493 n. 4, 500 n. 14
Athanasius, Saint, 347, 493 nn. 4 and 7
Augustine, Saint, 57, 98–99, 177, 243, 345, 500 n. 11. *See also* Rule of Augustine.
Availability for mission, 174–75, 417. *See also* Missionary journeys; Service of Christ and his vicar.
  in the Formula, 279, 388–89, 392
  heart of the oblation, 119–20, 123–25, 271
  as reflected in Montmartre accounts, 109–16, 471 n. 38
Avarice, 199–200, 227–28, 316, 391. *See also* Clergy, greed of higher.
Azpeitia, 68, 153, 173

Badia, Tommaso, xxxi, 221, 340–41, 434 n. 13
  finds the Formula "good and holy," 18, 381, 395, 415

Bandini, Archbishop Francesco, 53
Barcelona. *See* Ignatius de Loyola, activities at or in, Barcelona.
Barnabites, xxx, 92, 94, 206, 297, 326–27, 438 n. 14, 530 n. 20
Barreda, 490 n. 16
Bartoli, Daniel, 341
Bassano, 41, 61, 265
Begging alms, 145, 260. *See also* Stipends.
  companions' practice of, 63, 77, 79, 117, 143, 146, 265, 327
  practice of Ignatius, 136–37, 153, 164, 178–79, 200, 360–361, 491 n. 31
"Beloved Sons," 34–35, 42, 45
Beltrán, Ignatius's nephew, 94
Beltrán de Loyola, Ignatius's father, 24, 448 n. 25
Benedict, Saint, 215, 230, 243, 281, 284, 318, 321, 458 n. 6, 503 n. 3. *See also* Rule of Benedict.
Benedict XII, Pope, 320
Benefices, 35, 67, 74, 77, 199, 446 n. 15, 447 n. 17, 448 n. 20, 449 n. 26. See also *Cura animarum.*
  the companions and, 43–44, 71–72, 143, 392
Bernard of Clairvaux, Saint, 56, 320, 480 n. 23
Bernard Prim, 152
Bertrand, Dominique, 44, 463–64 n. 35, 523 n. 40, 529 n. 14
Biblical images, 82, 97–98, 100–101, 108–9, 137–39, 457 n. 1
Biel, Gabriel, 39
Bios angelikos, angelic life, 232

Bishops, 140, 449 n. 32
  absentee, 177, 222, 448 n. 20, 453 nn. 57–58
  the companions and, 135, 205, 492 n. 1
Bobadilla, Nicolás de, xxx–xxxii, 37, 42, 84–86, 117, 375, 428 n. 5, 462 n. 28
  on Deliberation, 17, 180, 428 n. 6, 505 n. 18
  ministry of, 134, 140, 185, 229
  on Montmartre vows, 114–16, 388–89
  on pilgrimaging in religion, 115–17, 175, 388–89
  use of *compañía* and *socius* by, 504 nn. 14 and 17–18
Böhmer, Heinrich, 21
Bologna, xxxi, 40, 42, 179, 185
Bolton, Brenda, 439–40 n. 24, 474 n. 52
Bonaventure, Saint, 57
Boniface VIII, Pope, 444 n. 10, 451 n. 45
Borgia, Francis, Saint, 69, 114–15, 359
Borromeo, Cardinal Charles, Saint, 177
Boswell, John, 483 n. 41
Bottereau, Georges, 503 n. 5
Brandolini, Raphael, 226
Broët, Paschase, xxx–xxxii, 25, 40, 42, 85–87, 135, 160, 193, 229, 375, 453 n. 56
  ministry of, 40, 53, 134–35, 165
"Brothers of proven faith," 133, 214, 465 nn. 1–2
Bruno, Saint, 249, 367–69, 528 n. 26
Bulls and briefs, papal, xvi, 34, 42, 92–94, 309–10. *See also* Approval, papal.
  of approbation of Society, xv–xvi, xxi–xxii, xxxi–xxxii, 18–20, 415. See also *Exposcit; Regimini.*
Barnabite, 92, 94, 297, 514 n. 37, 530 n. 20
Cistercian, 320
Dominican, 78, 374, 455 n. 69, 528 n. 21, 530 n. 20
Dominican Third Order, 297
Franciscan, 18, 99, 171, 294, 513 n. 36
Franciscan Third Order, 93, 514 n. 37
Somaschi, 351, 513 n. 36, 530 n. 20
Theatine, 92, 94, 297, 321, 351, 514 n. 37, 530 n. 20
Trinitarian, 509 nn. 8 and 10
Bynum, Caroline Walker, 468 n. 16

Cáceres, Diego, 188, 253, 489 n. 12, 490 n. 15
Calveras, José, 26
Calvin, 183–84
Câmara, Luis Gonçalves da, 186, 217, 252, 430 n. 14
Camillians, 206, 507 n. 3, 514 n. 37
Campos, J., 523 n. 40
Canonicae sanctiones, normative teachings, 287, 319–21
Canons regular, 56, 75, 79, 322–23, 468 n. 16
Capdepós, Margarita, 136, 178
Capuchins, xxix, 137, 156, 206, 225, 293, 326, 468 n. 12, 507 n. 3, 513 n. 36
  Constitutions of, 137, 142, 156, 476 n. 73
Carafa, Cardinal Gianpietro
  cofounder of Theatines, 37, 141, 326, 433 n. 7
  and companions, 53, 195, 471 n. 39

and Ignatius, 37, 433 n. 7
Ignatius's letter to, 242,
    260–66, 503 n. 5
Memorial of, 141, 155–56,
    184, 202, 225, 487 n. 3,
    497 n. 37
as Paul IV, 437 n. 9
Carafa, Cardinal Vincenzo, 53,
    140, 147–48, 190, 471 n. 39
Carmelites, 296, 326, 350, 508
    n. 11, 519 n. 31
Carthusians, 56–57, 225, 321,
    324, 367–69
  companions meeting at, 44,
    86, 368
  Ignatius and, xvii, xxv, 66, 358,
    364, 367–68
  some terms in their *Consuetudines*, 244, 349, 503 n. 3
Cassian, John, 249, 281, 318, 493
    n. 7, 501 n. 6, 514 nn. 38
    and 42
Castello, Bishop Ottaviano de,
    134, 229
Castilla, Pedro de, 490 n. 16
Castro, Juan de, 160, 489 n. 9
Catarino, Ambrogio, 53, 193,
    201, 229
Catechism. *See* Christian doctrine, teaching.
Cathars, 57, 145, 147, 151, 373.
    See also Albigensians.
Cazador, Jaime, 143, 473 n. 47
Charles V, Emperor, 41, 52, 134,
    292–93, 434 n. 13
Chastity, 98, 167, 169, 231, 302–7,
    343–45. *See also* Angelic
    purity; Pilgrimaging, chastity
    as characteristic of.
  in the Constitutions, 499 n. 2,
    386–87
  in the Deliberation, 280, 313,
    379
  Favre's vow of, 72, 313

  in the Formula of the Institute,
    279, 314–15, 380,
    384–87, 530 n. 16
  Ignatius's vow of, 172, 313,
    359, 366, 524 n. 13
  as means of service, 314–15
  and mission, 279, 384–87, 530
    n. 16
  vow at Montmartre, 108–9,
    112, 377, 461–62 n. 24,
    481 n. 31
  vow in Venice, 280, 313, 453
    n. 59, 481 n. 31
Chenu, M.-D., 473 n. 50
Children, instruction of, 24,
    177–81, 198, 278, 385, 483
    n. 41, 484 n. 47, 486 n. 58
Christian doctrine, teaching,
    177–80, 205, 385
  Companions' practice of, 38,
    40, 178–80, 205, 227–28,
    240, 485 n. 51 and 54–55,
    486 nn. 56–58 and 60
  Ignatius's practice of, 136,
    164, 178–79, 484 n. 48
Christian life
  commitment to, 299, 302–4,
    317–18, 441 n. 33
  companions and, 230, 250–51,
    conversatio as, 213–16
  religio as, 243–44
  Vatican II on, 331–32, 510 n. 11
Christian religion, 244
Church, 66, 219–30. *See also*
    Approval, papal; Lay people,
    in the Church; Service of
    Christ and his vicar.
  as Body of Christ, 67, 74–75,
    117, 139, 298, 300, 366,
    414, 451 n. 49
  companions' commitment to,
    80, 298, 332, 402, 414,
    418–19

in need of renewal, 36, 170, 219–30, 314, 332
submitting *propositum* to, 368, 370, 372–74, 379–80
at time of Renaissance, 35–36, 140–42, 218, 225–26,
Cicero, 242–43, 277, 342, 354, 500 nn. 8 and 11
Cistercians, xvii, xxv, 321–22, 368, 370–71
  mission to Albigensians of, 145–46, 419
  some terms in early documents of, 56–57, 99, 244, 250, 258, 439 n. 20, 443 n. 42, 499 n. 4, 501 n. 11, 503 n. 3
Clement VII, Pope, 92, 141, 297, 321, 326, 340, 351, 489 n. 9, 507 n. 3
Clerical state and privileges, 65–68, 444 n. 10
Clergy. *See also* Priest and priesthood.
  companions as different from diocesan, 80, 328
  conflicts involving, 75, 157
  greed of higher, 67–69, 200, 225, 447 n. 17, 448 n. 21
  ignorance of, 68, 80, 177, 447 n. 17, 448 n. 19
  immoral conduct of, 68–69, 200–201, 220, 225, 448 n. 24
  poverty of lower, 68, 141, 199, 446 n. 15
  renewal of, 209, 449 n. 33
Clerks regular, 265, 519 n. 41
  companions as different from, 78–79, 297, 327
Clichtove, Josse, 221, 449 n. 33
Codacio, Pietro, 53, 174–75, 252, 502 n. 15
Codure, Jean, xxx–xxxii, 25, 41–42, 85–87, 160, 201, 265–66, 375, 405
  ministry of, 241, 246, 293
Colet, John, 200–201
Collège de Sainte-Barbe, 84–85, 119
Colonna, Vittoria, 39
Common life, 327, 332, 393
Communio, sharing, 304–6, 308, 316
Communion, frequent
  companions' advocating, 136, 149, 154–55, 157–58, 181
  companions' practice of, 44, 109, 157, 217, 368, 378, 476 n. 73
  Lateran IV on, 451 n. 48, 476 n. 69
Compañía, compañero, 256, 258–59, 504 nn. 14 and 16–17
Companionship in Christ, 235, 255–84, 332, 364–65. *See also* Friends in the Lord; Joining together.
  companions' experience and understanding of, 217–18, 256, 258–76, 378, 504 n. 17
  in the Deliberation, 13–14, 121–22, 267–70
  in the Formula, 328, 384–85, 387–88
  means to preserve, 276–84
Companionship in mission, xxiv–xxv, 14, 16, 90, 176, 395
  in the Formula, 384–86, 389–90
  obedience and, 281, 283–84
  today's challenges re, 416–17
Companions of Jesus
  La Storta experience, 105–6, 274, 410
  with Jesus, like Jesus, 206–7, 384–86, 390, 409, 421
Companions with same resolve, 374–80, 528 nn. 26–27
  parallels, 367–69, 371–74
  Paris experience, 365, 374–77

Company of Jesus, 88, 379, 383.
See also Society of Jesus.
  ecclesial dimension of, 397,
    402, 418–19
  spirit of, 414–16
Confession (sacrament), 141,
    155–58, 205, 475 n. 66, 476
    n. 73
  companions' ministry of hearing, 24, 39, 40, 164, 175,
    179, 181–82, 197, 227–28,
    377, 486 n. 60
  companions' practice of frequent, 44, 109, 157, 217,
    368, 378
  companions' urging frequent,
    136, 149, 154, 157–58, 181
  faculties to hear, xxxi, 38, 78,
    112, 142–43, 147, 156–57,
    181, 188, 434 n. 11, 468 n. 15
  Lateran IV on frequency of,
    451 n. 48, 476 n. 69
Confirmation of Society, xiii,
  xxxii, 20, 94. See also
  Exposcit.
Confirmation, step in discernment process, 357–58, 360
Congregatio, association, 272–74,
    282–303, 379
Consecration of virgins, 343–44
Consilium de emendanda ecclesia.
  See Reform.
Conspirasse, conspire, 94–95,
    419–20, 457 n. 6
Constitutions on Missions, xxxii,
    21, 123, 464–65 n. 40, 503 n. 7
Constitutions of Society of Jesus,
    138, 470 n. 32, 486 n. 56
  on chastity, 232, 386, 499 n. 2
  and *Cum ex plurium*, 27–28, 49,
    432 n. 42
  and the Formula, 298, 403–5
  writing of, xxxi, 41–42, 405

Contarini, Cardinal Gasparo,
    xxx–xxxi, 51–52, 79, 221,
    340, 437 nn. 1–2, 491 n. 19
  letter to Ignatius of, 19
  memo at end of *Cum ex
    plurium* and *CEP* ms,
    18, 26
  as portrayed in *Cum ex
    plurium*, 18, 27, 235, 247
  role ascribed to, 21–27
  role in presenting and
    expediting the Formula,
    19–20, 415
Contarini, Pietro, 52, 160, 164,
    437 n. 2, 491 n. 19
Conti, Cardinal Hugolino, 325,
    513 n. 35
Conti, Cardinal Raynaldo, 513
    n. 35
Conversatio, way of living, xxv,
    213–16, 347, 493 nn. 4 and
    8, 494 n. 13, 507 n. 6. See
    also Christian life.
  and *exemplum*, 227–28
  as used by or about the
    companions, 194, 196,
    216–18, 528 n. 22
Conversini, Bishop Benedetto,
  Governor of Rome, 22, 38,
    43, 135, 190, 196–97, 229,
    466 n. 7
Conversion, 215
  Ignatius's experience of, 101,
    103–5, 356, 371–72
Cortese, Gregorio, 221
Cosci, Francesco, 134
Councils, decrees of, 319–21. See
  also Lateran Council IV;
  Lateran Council V; Lyons II,
  Council of; Trent, Council of.
  on benefices, 448 n. 20, 449
    n. 26

Index   567

on clerical abuses, 448
    nn. 19–21 and 24
on establishing new orders,
    322–26, 329, 516 n. 7, 519
    n. 31
on evangelical counsels, 510
    n. 11, 515 n. 49
on frequent confession and
    communion, 451 n. 48,
    476 n. 69
on preaching and teaching
    Christian doctrine, 141,
    146, 178, 220, 468–69 n. 16
on priesthood, 454 nn. 60–61
Countercultural stance, 44, 57,
    127, 213–14, 390–93
Crusades, 169–70, 323
Cum ex plurium
  authorship of, xvi, 21–26, 90,
    202
  content of, xvi, xxii, 17–18, 26–29
  and Deliberation, 22–23,
    256–57
  interlinear text of, 33–34, 50,
    130–31, 210, 236, 288–89,
    336–37, 398–99, 400
  manuscript of, 17, 26, 55, 256,
    271, 437–38 n. 11.
  name of, xvi, xxii
  origins and context of, xxxi,
    18–21, 212, 292–93
  overview of, 47, 233, 333
  relationship to *Regimini* and
    Exposcit, xxii, 20, 294, 415,
    505 n. 20, 515 n. 47
  story of oral approval and
    sequel, 19–20, 93–94, 415
  structure of, 26–29, 50, 82, 89,
    131, 210, 237, 240, 289,
    336–37, 399, 400
Cupis, Cardinal Domenico de,
    293
Cura animarum, care of souls, 67,
    74–75, 143, 446 n. 15, 447
    n. 16, 452 n. 50

Cyprian, Saint, 343

Dallen, James, 475 n. 66
Dalmases, Candido de, 466 n. 10
de Bhaldraithe, Eoin, 227
De Nicolas, Antonio, 354
Decisions about the Company, 17,
    59, 253, 313
Dedication. *See* Service of God;
    Service of Christ and his
    vicar.
Deliberation
  in establishing new order, 368,
    370, 373–74
Deliberation of First Fathers
  and *Cum ex plurium*, 11–12,
    22–23, 413–15
  as an experience, 12–16,
    91–92, 95, 357, 408, 414
  and the Formula, 297–98,
    413–15
  matters touched upon, 180,
    272–73, 313, 379, 384, 504
    n. 16
  on obedience, 15–16, 122–23,
    280–84, 322, 327, 389–90
  some terminology in, 456 n. 8,
    457 n. 2
  time frame of, xxxi, 12, 369,
    428 n. 6
  on union, 14, 87, 121–22, 256–
    57, 267–70, 384, 503 n. 7
Deo militare, serve God, 315,
    384–85. *See also* Service of
    God.
Desert, 99, 232, 361–62, 368
Desert Fathers, 249, 281
Desire. *See also* Companions with
    same resolve.
  experienced in the Delibera-
    tion, 13, 16, 91–92, 123,
    256–57
  as expressed in *CEP*, 28, 248,
    255–57

of Ignatius. See *Propositum,* Ignatius's
shared amongst themselves, 112, 217, 355, 375, 377
to be like Jesus, 54, 60–62
to be martyred in service of Christ, 106, 110–11, 116, 413, 462 n. 26
to be pilgrims, 116, 124, 172, 245, 375, 413
to preserve their way of life, 20, 233, 255–57
to serve Christ and the Church, 50, 88, 90, 95, 180, 414. *See also* Service of Christ and his vicar.
to serve in companionship, 384. *See also* Companionship in mission.
De Vogüé, Adalbert, 303
Devotio moderna, 158–59
Diego, Luis de, 442 n. 40, 447 n. 17, 449 nn. 26, 30 and 32, 454 n. 66
Diego of Osma, Bishop, 145–46, 373
Díez, Ferdinando, 196
Discernment, xvi–xvii, xix, xxii–xxiii. *See also* Prayer, and discernment.
engaged in by Ignatius, 262, 356–58, 363
as experienced in the Deliberation, 11–16, 88, 91–92, 95, 457 n. 1
and listening, 29, 384, 408–10, 416–21
practiced by companions, 82, 111, 206, 462 n. 26
process of, xix, 11–16, 28–29, 54, 71, 285, 291, 413
in the Spiritual Exercises, 159, 310, 312, 354
today's need for, 416, 419

Discurrir, roam, 123–24, 464 n. 39
Dispersion of companions, 124, 257, 261, 265–66, 503 n. 7
Dittrich, Franz, 26
Doménech, Juan Jerónimo, 502 n. 23
Dominic de Guzman, Saint, 145–46, 216, 222, 382–83, 450 n. 40, 452 n. 50. *See also* Ignatius de Loyola, and Dominic.
Dominicans, early
beginnings of, 326, 373–74, 382–83, 530 n. 20
missionary activity of, 149, 261, 469 n. 20, 472 n. 44, 518 n. 25
parallels with Ignatius and companions, xvii, xxv, 230, 321, 373–74
preaching in poverty of, 57–58, 78, 144–48, 171, 175, 440 n. 28, 455 n. 69, 469 nn. 17 and 22
some terms in their early documents, 244, 257, 262, 507 n. 36, 521 n. 8, 528 n. 21
Dotti, Gasparo de', 160, 188, 192–93, 229, 489 n. 13
Dozzi, Dino, 302
Durand de Huesca, 57, 152
Durandus, William, the Elder, 498 n. 49
Durandus, William, the Younger, 494 n. 7

Eguía, Diego de, 160, 253
Eguía, Estevan de, 160, 253
End of the Society, 276–78, 379, 389, 404
Entregar, surrender, 103
Erasmus, Desiderius, 140

Esser, Cajetan, 144, 171, 480 n. 28, 494 n. 13, 508 n. 2, 509 n. 8
Este, Duke Ercole II d', 39, 121, 134, 140, 202
Estrada, Francisco, 160, 252
Evagrius of Antioch, 249, 347–48, 493 n. 4
Evangelical counsels, 299–318, 509 n. 8, 510 n. 11, 514 n. 39, 515 n. 49
  the companions and the, 287, 310–17, 321, 340
Examples of Christian living, 145, 214, 219–23, 261–62, 307, 496 n. 27. *See also* Preaching, by word and example.
  the Church's need for, 140–42, 202, 220–23,
  the companions as, 134, 140, 202, 209–10, 212, 219, 223, 227–32
Exhorting, 150–55
  companions' ministry of, 136, 140, 152–55, 182, 202, 205, 227–28, 391, 486 n. 60
Exile, 168–74, 366, 479 nn. 15–16, 481 n. 33
Exposcit debitum, xv, xxxii, 20, 94, 294–95, 459 n. 15, 515 n. 47, 530 n. 16

Farnese, Alessandro, future pope Paul III. *See* Paul III, Pope.
Farnese, Alessandro, grandson of Pope Paul III, 36, 433 n. 5
Farnese, Ottavio, grandson of Pope Paul III, 41, 293
Fasting, 136, 346, 361, 393
  companions' practice of, 91, 113, 196, 241, 312–13, 317
Fathers of the Church, 320–21

Favre, Blessed Pierre, xxix–xxxii, 19, 39, 259, 313, 434 n. 13, 504 n. 15
  on Montmartre vows, 108–9, 377
  on oblation to pope, 118–21, 267, 271
  ordination to priesthood of, 72, 135, 453 n. 56, 455 n. 68
  Paris experience of, 84–87, 106–9, 160, 217–18, 374–75, 377, 457 n. 1
  on preaching faculties, 148–49
  some terms used in his *Memoriale*, 217–18, 250, 269, 376
Ferrão, Bartolomeo, 26, 252
Ferrara, xxxi, 39, 42, 134, 140, 165, 179, 196, 266
Figueroa, Juan Rodríguez de, 186, 192–94, 245, 488 n. 6
Filonardi, Cardinal Enrico, 293
Firmicius Maternus, 507 n. 6
Following Jesus, 57–58, 78, 98–99, 301–4, 309, 317–18, 360, 365–66, 368. *See also* Gospel living.
  being and living like Jesus, 60–62, 86, 110, 116, 172–73, 175, 407
  carrying his cross, 121, 390, 410, 421
  Gospel call, xxvi, 98, 108, 113, 168–69, 407
  to Jerusalem, 88, 106, 388
  propositum of companions, xviii, 314, 346, 380, 384–85
  in Vatican II, xv, 331, 510 n. 11
  wherever the Spirit leads, 407–10, 420–21
Formula of the Institute, 314–17, 381–93. See also *Vivendi formula.*

570 Index

approval of, xv, xxi–xxii,
  18–20, 29, 380, 401–4, 415
on chastity and mission, xxii,
  278–79, 314–15, 384–87,
  530 n. 16
decrees [*capitula*] of, 278,
  320, 429 n. 8
Holy Spirit in, xxii–xxiii, 92,
  206, 409
on obedience to the pope,
  xxiii, 279, 315–16, 387–89
on obedience within the
  Society, 279, 316, 389–90
on poverty, 279, 316–17,
  390–91
relation to the Constitutions,
  403–5
relation to *Cum ex plurium*,
  xx–xxiv, 27–28, 248
relation to the Deliberation,
  408, 413–15
on religious observances, 279,
  317, 392–93
spirit of, xx–xxi, 278–80, 314,
  402, 460 n. 17
summary of the rule, 381–84,
  529 nn. 13–15
time frame of drafting, xxxi,
  341
way of life of companions, xv,
  251, 294–96, 298, 380
Founding experience, xxiv–xxv,
  11, 413–16
Fourth vow, 100. *See also* Service
  of Christ and his vicar.
Francis of Assisi, Saint, 67, 73, 99,
  222, 356, 445 n. 13, 450 n. 40,
  469 nn. 16 and 20–21. *See also*
  Ignatius de Loyola, and Francis of Assisi; Rule of Francis.
  and poverty, 57–59, 144–47,
    360, 440 n. 27, 445–46 n.
    14, 469 nn. 17 and 22

Franciscans, early
  beginnings of, 326, 371–72,
    382, 441 n. 31, 518 n. 25,
    530 n. 20
  form of life of, 215–16, 296,
    300–302, 508 n. 10
  itinerant preaching of, 57, 99,
    145, 148, 171, 261, 469 n.
    16, 472 n. 43, 480–81 nn.
    28–29
  parallels with Ignatius and
    companions, xvii, xxv, 56,
    81, 230, 262, 321, 371–72
  and poverty movement, 57
  some terms in Franciscan
    sources, 81, 215–16, 244,
    262, 371–72, 508 n. 10
Francis I, King of France, 134,
  259, 292
Frascati, xxxi, 191, 211–12, 355
Freedom, 54–55, 97–102
  companions' desire to work
    in, 140, 288, 329
  experienced in commitment,
    88, 282–83, 317–18, 387,
    395, 418
  sponte, freely choosing, 54–55,
    75, 79–80, 90, 94–95
Fregoso, Bishop Federigo, 221
Friars Minor, 294, 300. *See also*
  Franciscans, early.
"Friends in the Lord," 86–87,
  235, 256, 259, 269, 376, 414
Fulk of Toulouse, Bishop, 373,
  440 n. 28, 470 n. 31
Futrell, John, 456 n. 8, 457 n. 2

Gaetano da Thiene, Saint,
  449–50 n. 33
García, Lorenzo, 188, 252–53,
  489 n. 12, 490 nn. 15–16
García Madariaga, José, 464 n. 37
Gaudemet, Jean, 492 n. 1
Gelasius I, Pope, 451 n. 45

General Examen, 441–42 n. 34, 486 n. 58
Genestal, R., 444–45 n. 11
Ghinucci, Cardinal Girolamo, 19, 415, 429 n. 12, 468 n. 15, 531 n. 7
Giberti, Bishop Gian Matteo, 141, 221, 225, 260, 292, 449 n. 32
Giles of Viterbo, 226
Gioia, Mario, 529 n. 13
Giussano, Gian Pietro, 177
Gleason, Elisabeth, 437 n. 1, 468 n. 12, 494 n. 8, 495 nn. 14 and 17
Glory of God
   companions' purpose, 13, 111, 121, 124, 128, 199, 206, 328, 378, 404–5
   Irenaeus on the, 102, 405, 459 n. 12
Golden Legend, 261, 525 n. 15
Gonzalez, Luis, 457 n. 1
Gospel
   Beatitudes, 387, 419, 510 n. 11
   missionary discourse in, 62, 124, 143–47, 170–71, 182, 280, 442 n. 38, 469 n. 20, 472 n. 44
   norm for the companions, xvii, 61–62, 75, 182, 206, 331–32
   norm for Francis of Assisi, 144, 146, 262, 301–2, 372, 382, 508 n. 2, 515 n. 49
Gospel living, xv, 213–16, 218, 224, 241, 254, 297, 346, 365–66, 510 n. 11
   the companions and, 75, 212, 230, 246, 298, 312–17
   evangelical counsels and, 299–308, 310, 317–18,
   and preaching in poverty, 57–58, 61, 67, 144–47, 151–52, 170–71, 419

   today's challenges for, 419–20
Gouveia, Dr. Diogo de, 119, 267
Granvelle, Antoine de, 434 n. 13
Granvelle, Nicolas de, 434 n. 13
Gratian, 346
Gregory the Great, Saint, 458 n. 6
Gregory VII, Pope, 152
Gregory IX, Pope, 307, 445 n. 11, 513 n. 35
Gregory X, Pope, 516 n. 7
Gregory of Nyssa, Saint, 408, 482 n. 34
Guidiccioni, Cardinal Bartolomeo, 36, 292, 415, 531 n. 7
Guigo I, 56
Guillaumont, Antoine, 478 n. 8
Gyrovagi, gyrovagues, 169, 175–76, 215

"Helping souls." *See also* Ministry.
   companions' intent, 75, 111–12, 375–76, 378
   in the Formula, 380, 388–89, 391, 393, 395, 404
   propositum of Ignatius, 69–70, 104, 174, 362–65, 449 n. 29, 525 n. 17
Henry VIII, King of England, 52, 184, 293
Heresy, 146, 183–85, 293
   companions free from, 136, 184–99, 227–28,
Hermits, 56, 61, 169, 171, 232, 368, 482 n. 37
Hermits of St. Augustine, 326
Hertling, Ludwig, 511 n. 20
Hesychia, quiet, 232, 366
Holocaust, 113–14, 116, 120, 122
Holy Spirit, 89–95, 405–10, 413–21
   characteristics of, 97, 100, 240, 328, 331, 415
   in *Cum ex plurium*, xxii–xxiii, 92, 125, 128, 206, 316, 407

discerning presence of, 233, 291, 366, 416–17
impelling action of, 89–95, 199, 240, 248, 367–68
impelling the Company, xvii, xix, xxiii–xxiv, 49, 125, 139, 328, 333, 406–10, 414–16
responding to, 29, 240, 408–10, 416–21
today's challenge to listen to, 416–21
"The Spirit of God is here," 19, 94
Honorius III, Pope, 18, 78, 99, 171, 374, 383, 455 n. 69, 521 n. 8, 528 n. 21
Hospitality, 99, 161, 164, 170
Hospitals, serving in, 40, 63, 136, 164–65, 205, 261, 264
Hozes, Diego de, 41, 160, 164, 241, 265, 434 n. 11, 468 n. 15
Hugh of St. Victor, 512 n. 20
Humiliati, 57, 133, 151–52, 296, 350, 469 n. 16, 474 n. 54
Humphrey, Saint, 362, 376, 524 n. 9, 525 n. 15

Ignatius de Loyola, 353–66
 activities at or in
  Alcalá, xxix, 70, 84, 178, 185–86, 245, 263, 364–65
  Aránzazu, 166, 313, 359
  Azpeitia, xxx, 153, 173, 179
  Barcelona, xxix, 69, 84, 178, 245, 263, 364
  Jerusalem, xxix, 69, 178, 245, 363–64
  La Storta, xxxi, 60, 105–6, 115, 120, 274, 410
  Loyola, xxix, 66, 103–4, 172, 219, 356–59
  Manresa, xxix, 60, 69, 104, 133, 136, 159, 164, 178, 361–63, 466 nn. 8 and 10, 484 n. 48, 491 n. 31
  Montserrat, xxix, 59–60, 67, 105, 166, 360–61, 441–42 n. 34
  Paris, xxix–xxx, 43–44, 71–73, 84–87, 107, 111, 119, 159–60, 178, 186–87, 263–64, 365, 374–78, 433 n. 6, 460 n. 18
  Rome, xxx–xxxii, 38, 53, 149–50, 188–99, 405
  Salamanca, xxix, 70, 84, 152–53, 175, 178, 185–86, 365
  Venice, xxx, 52, 76, 87, 160, 164, 179, 187–88, 264, 433 n. 7
  Vicenza, xxxi, 88, 147, 193, 265, 379
 background and family, xxix, 24–25, 65, 68–69, 94, 443 n. 3, 448 n. 25, 523 n. 3
 caring for marginal, 69–70, 136, 164, 173, 178, 362–65
 catechist, 136, 164, 178–79
 within Christian tradition, 67, 102, 152, 158–59, 172, 365–66, 524 n. 13, 525 n. 14
 and Dominic, 78, 143, 146–47, 222, 261–62, 265, 373–74, 442 n. 38
 embracing poverty, 58–60, 67, 143–44, 172, 360, 363–64, 395
 and Francis of Assisi, 58–60, 67, 144, 146–47, 150, 153, 222, 261–62, 265, 314–15, 371–72, 374, 442 n. 38, 445 n. 13

giving the Spiritual Exercises, 52–53, 159–60, 164, 179, 186, 188, 195, 433 n. 6
imitating the Saints, 356–57, 361–62, 364–65, 376, 391, 395
mystic, xix, 355
opting for priesthood, 69–71, 449 n. 30
pilgrim, xxix, 69, 166, 172–74, 263, 356–64, 376, 395, 481 nn. 32–33, 492 n. 31
preacher, 147, 149–50, 152–54, 178, 471 n. 36
Illuminism, 152–53, 184, 186, 408
Imitation of Christ, 158
Innocent I, Pope, 345
Innocent III, Pope
and Cistercian mission to Albigensians, 145, 419
and Dominican beginnings, 373, 382–83
and Franciscan beginnings, 301, 371, 382, 446 n. 14
involvement in Lateran Council IV of, 322, 325–26
letter to Subiaco abbot, 306–8, 325
and new groups, 133, 151–52, 294, 296, 300–301, 509 n. 8
and preaching, 133, 149, 151–52, 446 n. 14, 468 n. 16
Innocent IV, Pope, 308–9, 325, 513 n. 35
Innocent VII, Pope, 297
Innocent VIII, Pope, 498 n. 49
Inquisition, 184, 186–87, 408, 488 n. 7
Institutio, institution, 322, 324–25, 382–83, 518 n. 24
propositum and, 349

Institutum, institute, 247–54, 347, 502 n. 12, 507 n. 6
grace of a particular, 355–56
from *propositum* to, 349–51, 369–70, 376–80, 528 n. 27
vite institutum, manner of life, 247–54. *See also* Formula of the Institute, way of life of companions.
Irenaeus, Saint, 102, 405, 459 n. 12
Iserloh, Erwin, 140
Iturrioz, Jesús, 21–22, 24–25, 505 n. 22

Jacques de Vitry, 56, 145, 167, 300–301, 469 n. 16, 472 n. 43
Jancolini, Faustina de, 73, 451 n. 44
Jay, Claude, xxx, xxxii, 39, 85–87, 135, 160, 375, 453 n. 56
on being poor with Christ, 61
ministry of, 41–42, 134, 140, 165, 229
Jerome, Saint, 57, 347, 473 n. 46, 480 n. 23, 493 n. 7
Jerusalem and Holy Land. *See also* Ignatius de Loyola, activities at or in, Jerusalem; Ignatius de Loyola, pilgrim; Pilgrimaging.
Italy as good Jerusalem, 388, 413, 504 n. 18
object of pilgrimage, 42, 166–67, 346, 480 n. 23, 481 n. 28
permission to go to, xxx, 37–38, 67, 355, 434 n. 11
vow to go to, 108–12, 115, 166, 173, 192, 375–76, 413, 462 n. 26
Jesus. *See also* Companions of Jesus; Company of Jesus;

Following Jesus; Service of
Christ and his vicar.
  centrality of, 310–12, 314–17,
    404–5
  as example, 59–61, 103, 219,
    295–96, 311–12, 316–17
  head of the Company, 88,
    271–72, 298, 314, 379,
    404, 409, 414, 506 n. 28
  name of the Society, 88,
    270–71, 384
John the Baptist, Saint, 76, 171,
  223, 362, 369
John of the Cross, Saint, xx, 280,
  441 n. 32
John III, King of Portugal, 119,
  185–87, 198–99
John XXII, Pope, 329
John XXIII, Pope, 224
Joining together, 14, 49, 54–55,
  81–88, 90, 267–70, 371–72,
  456 n. 3, 527 n. 14
Juan de Avila, Saint, 449 n. 33
Judicial inquiries, xxix–xxxi,
    185–99
  in Alcalá and Salamanca, 70,
    152, 185–86, 364–65, 488
    nn. 6 and 7
  in Paris, 186–87, 488 n. 9
  in Rome, 22, 38, 52, 129, 138,
    184, 188–98, 229–30, 490
    n. 15–17
  in Venice, 187–88, 192–93
Julius II, Pope, 220, 516 n. 7
Julius III, Pope, xv, xxxii, 94

King, Nicholas, 457 n. 6
Knights Templar, 350
Koinōnia, companionship,
  275–76
Kolvenbach, Peter-Hans, 462–63
  n. 29, 464 n. 39, 481 n. 32
Kunkel, Paul, 438 n. 14

Lactantius, 243, 245, 500 n. 11
Landívar, Miguel, 252, 260, 434
  n. 11, 453 n. 56, 490
  nn. 15–16
La Storta, xxxi, 60, 105–6, 274,
    459 n. 16
  the Formula reflects, 383–84,
    388
  significant for companions,
    115, 120, 409–10, 413, 421
Lateran Council IV, 296, 322,
    516 n. 7
  canon 13 on new religious
    orders, 244, 309, 322–26,
    329, 349, 373, 381–82,
    403, 517 n. 22, 518
    nn. 24–25
  other canons of, 448 nn. 21
    and 24, 449 n. 26, 451
    n. 48, 468–69 n. 16, 476
    n. 69, 496 n. 32
Lateran Council V, xxix, 133
  and Church reform, 36, 220,
    224–26
  decrees of, 141, 178, 220, 448
    nn. 20 and 24
Laurency, Thomas, 187–88
Lay brothers, 456 n. 74
Lay people
  in the Church, 66, 70–71, 146,
    151–52, 300, 474 n. 57
  the companions as different
    from, 79
  Ignatius as layman, 67, 137,
    152–54, 366, 526 n. 22
  13th c. movement of, 57, 67,
    146–47, 151–52, 296, 308,
    350, 382
Laynez, Diego, xxx–xxxii, 19, 39,
    44, 84–87, 107, 375
  on companions' way of life,
    62, 109–10, 143, 149, 253,
    377–78

on Ignatius, 105–6, 172, 274, 359, 524 n. 11, 525 n. 17
on origins of the Society, 19, 37, 272–75, 298, 415, 504 nn. 16–17
testimony about, 193, 229
Least Society, 56, 418–19
Leclercq, Jean, 170, 478 n. 5, 481 n. 33, 482 n. 37
Lecturing, ministry of, 23–24, 39–40, 78, 179, 181, 190, 195, 197, 455 n. 67, 486 n. 60
Le Goff, Jacques, 219
Leo the Great, Saint, 344
Leo X, Pope, 93, 133, 177, 294
Leturia, Pedro, 471 n. 36, 502 n. 13, 523 n. 3
Licentia predicandi. *See* Preaching, itinerant.
Liévin, Valentín, 186–87
Life of Antony, 98, 249, 303, 493 n. 4
Life of Bruno, 249, 458 n. 6
Life of Christ, 356, 524 n. 9
Liturgy, 317, 392
Livery of Christ, 199, 441–42 n. 34
Lives of Saints, 219, 356, 524 n. 9
Llorca, Bernardino, 488 n. 7
Longhurst, John, 488 n. 6
Loreto, xxx, xxxii, 37, 117, 165–66, 173–74, 241, 293
Loyola. *See* Ignatius de Loyola, activities at or in, Loyola.
Luther, Martin, 43, 184, 195, 220, 226, 483 n. 46
Lutheranism, 42, 183–86, 189, 194–95, 292, 388, 487 n. 3
Lyons II, Council of, 322, 326, 329, 516 n. 7, 519 n. 31

Madalena de Araoz, 448 n. 25
Mainardi, Agostino, xxxi, 129, 189

Manare, Olivier, 462 n. 24
Mandonnet, Pierre, 513 n. 34, 518 n. 24, 520 n. 1
Manresa. *See* Ignatius de Loyola, activities at or in, Manresa.
Marcellus, Archbishop Christopher, 220, 494 n. 4
Marcial, Dr., 160
Margaret of Austria, Queen, 41, 293
Martín García de Oñaz, Ignatius's brother, 68, 354, 358, 448 n. 25, 523 n. 3, 524 n. 10
Maruca, Dominic, 456 n. 8, 457 n. 2
Mary, Blessed Virgin, 102, 108, 113–16, 311
Ignatius's devotion to, 357–59, 524 n. 13
Massurius Sabinus, 243, 500 n. 9
Master of Arts, 44
Master of the Sacred Palace, 18–19, 340, 520 n. 1
"Masters of Paris," 42–45, 54, 79, 194, 206, 436 n. 36
McNally, Robert, 226
Mendicants, 75, 77–78, 140, 157, 326–327
companions as different from, 78–79
Mercurian, Everard, 111, 430 n. 15
Middle Ages, 56–57, 155, 168–70, 219, 249, 447 n. 16, 498 n. 44
Military orders, 323
Minims, 326
Ministry, 101, 452 nn. 50 and 54. See also *Cura animarum;* Priest and priesthood, and ministry.
companions' understanding and practice of, 73–75, 176, 314–17, 321, 393

in Ignatius's letter to Carafa, 264–65
to marginalized, xvii, 80, 129, 135–36, 163–65, 175, 177–81, 205–6, 362, 391, 418, 484 n. 47, 485 n. 52, 486 n. 60
of the Word, 80, 129, 134–35, 139–61, 179, 206, 227–28, 278, 385
Mission, 148–49, 152, 472 n. 44. *See also* Companionship in mission.
chastity and, 279, 314–15, 386–87, 530 n. 16
and evangelization, 180
obedience and, 281–83, 390
today's challenge, 417–19
Missionary journeys, 63, 165–76, 205, 232, 261, 481 n. 29
Monastic life and tradition, 56–57, 66, 98–99, 169, 214–15, 231–32, 303–4, 417–18, 441 nn. 31 and 33, 510 n. 15. *See also*, Carthusians; Cistercians.
commitment to, 102, 215, 281, 303–4, 317–18, 347–49, 381, 506–7 n. 36, 518 n. 25
companions' life different from, 79, 99, 176, 231–32, 281, 328, 417–18, 482 n. 37
Ignatius and, 66, 361–62, 366
Innocent III and, 306–8
key words in, 57, 102, 169, 214–15, 231, 243–44, 249–50, 347–49, 366
and pilgrimaging, 169–71, 176, 480 n. 23, 481 n. 33, 482 n. 37
and priestly ministry, 75, 79, 149, 221, 445 n. 12, 447 n. 16, 473 n. 46

Montmartre vows, xxx, 62, 87, 107–17, 313, 375, 460 n. 19, 461 nn. 21 and 24, 462 nn. 25–26 and 29
and the Formula, 107, 383, 388–89, 391
renewal of, 87, 378, 462 n. 27
Montserrat. *See* Ignatius de Loyola, activities at or in, Montserrat.
Moral conduct of companions, 193, 195–96, 200–203, 227–28,
Morone, Bishop John, 434 n. 13
Moscoso, Dr. Alvaro, 160, 434 n. 13
Mudarra, Francisco de, 490 n. 16
Myers, Ched, 170

Nadal, Jerónimo, xxxii, 21
on the companions, 161, 181, 453 n. 59, 482 n. 37, 492 n. 1, 505 n. 21
on Ignatius, 137, 147, 279–80, 355, 524 n. 7
"Spirit of God is here", 19, 93–94
Najera, Duke of, xxix, 25
Nascio, Doimi, 195, 202, 229, 491 n. 25
Negusanti, Bishop Vincenzo, 76, 453 n. 58
Nepotism, 36, 433 n. 5, 446 n. 15, 494 n. 8
Niermeyer, J. F., 295
Norbert of Xanten, Saint, 148
Nota, sign, 22, 184, 197

O'Malley, John, 220, 226, 465 n. 40, 467 n. 2, 471 n. 36, 482 n. 37, 496 nn. 32 and 35
Obedience, 281, 299–300, 302–7, 363, 506–7 n. 36

bond of, 280–84, 380
  as discussed during Deliberation, 15–16, 91–92, 122–23, 256–57, 280–84, 313, 379, 389–90, 505 n. 18
  document *On Making a Vow of Obedience*, xxxi, 16–17, 284, 428 nn. 5–6
  to the pope, 123–24, 279, 315–16, 379, 387–89. *See also* Service of Christ and his vicar.
  within the Society, 279, 313, 316, 379, 389–30
Oblation to the pope, xxxi, 118–25, 271, 281, 463 n. 33, 464 n. 36
  fulfillment of Montmartre experience, 108–13, 192, 375, 464 n. 37
Odo, Abbot of St. Genevieve, 304–6, 308, 511 n. 20
Oliger, Livarius, 513 n. 34
Olin, John, 481 n. 30
Opprobrium, 60–61, 105, 108, 198–99
Order of Preachers. *See* Dominicans.
Ordo, order, 168, 323–25
Orthodoxy of companions, 43, 131, 134–35, 140, 184–99, 209, 239
Ortiz, Dr. Pedro, xxxi, 52, 193–95, 252, 434 n. 13
  adversary [for a time], 37, 186, 433 n. 6, 477 n. 81, 488 n. 9
  friend, 37, 43, 135, 252
Ory, Dr. Matthieu, 186, 192–93, 196, 489 n. 9
Osuna, Javier, 429 n. 7

Pachomius, Saint, 133, 214
Padua, 41, 179, 265–66

Palmio, Francesco, 110
Pamplona, xxix, 72, 356
Paradigm shift, xix, 413
Paris, xxix–xxx, 37, 71–72, 83–87, 374–79, 456 n. 6. *See also* Ignatius de Loyola, activities at or in, Paris; Montmartre vows.
Paris, Council of, 141, 449 n. 32
Paris, University of, 43–44, 71, 436 n. 34
Parma, xxxi, 19, 35–36, 39, 293, 502 n. 23
Paschini, Pio, 265
Pascual, Matthaeo, 490 n. 16
Paul III, Pope, 35–42, 221–22, 494 n. 8
  appreciating the companions, 22, 211–12, 218, 233, 235, 239–40
  and approval of Society, xv, 93–94, 339–41, 380, 405–7, 415
  and Church reform, 209–10, 218, 221–27, 292, 495 n. 14
  coming to know the companions, xxx–xxxi, 37–42, 51, 134–35, 142, 293, 355
  conversation with Ignatius at Frascati, xxxi, 191, 211–12, 355
  discerning the companions' discernment, xvi–xvii, xxii, 80, 209, 219, 223
  1539 schedule of, 292–93
  missioning the companions, 12, 16, 38–42, 179–80
  oblation of companions to, 12, 118–25
  as portrayed in *Cum ex plurium*, 17–18, 20, 47, 235, 239–40, 285, 333

Paul IV, Pope. *See* Carafa, Cardinal Gianpietro.
Pauperes Christi, Poor of Christ, 56–57, 67, 128, 151, 418, 440 n. 27
Pauperes Christi sacerdotes, poor priests of Christ, 55–63, 65, 73, 77–79
Pavia, 241, 246
Peña, Juan de la, 85, 269
Penance, 91, 167, 368, 393
  propositum of Ignatius, 66, 104, 172, 357–64, 395
Peralta, Master Pedro de, 159–60, 488 n. 9
Perfectae caritatis, 331
Pero Lopez de Oñaz, Ignatius's brother, 65, 68–69
Persecution. *See* Judicial inquiries.
Peter Comestor, 512 n. 20
Peter of Vaux-de-Cernai, 145
Picalques, Francis, 466 n. 8
Pietas, faithful love, 240–42, 499 nn. 1 and 3–4
  pietas et religio, 235, 239–40, 246
Pilgrimaging, 165–76, 213, 346, 369, 478 n. 5, 479 nn. 15–16, 480 nn. 23 and 28, 481 nn. 29 and 33. *See also* Ignatius de Loyola, pilgrim; Jerusalem and Holy Land; Missionary journeys.
  chastity as characteristic of, 167, 172, 359–60, 363–64, 395, 481 n. 31
  the companions and, 37, 42, 62–63, 76, 117, 166–67, 172–76, 182, 205, 380, 443 n. 41, 481 n. 31
  companions' vow of, 108–12, 115, 173, 192, 245, 313, 375–77, 387–89, 461 n. 24, 505 n. 18. *See also* Service of Christ and his vicar.
  Nadal on, 482 n. 37
  poverty as characteristic of, 62–63, 115, 167, 169, 172–73, 377, 390, 443 n. 41, 481 n. 31, 483 n. 38
"Pilgrimaging in religion," 115–16, 175, 232, 389
Pilgrim priests. *See* Priest and Priesthood, Pilgrim priests.
Pius V, Pope, 326, 351
Polanco, Juan de, xxxii, 19
  on companions before Society's approbation, 173, 179, 271–72, 486 n. 60, 528 n. 26
  on formation and approbation of Society, 20, 83–84, 94, 298, 415, 508 n. 13, 528 n. 27
Pole, Cardinal Reginald, 53, 221, 340
Politeia, ascetical life, 249, 493 n. 4
Politi, Lancelloto de'. *See* Catarino, Ambrogio.
Poor Catholics, 57, 300, 350
Poor Clares, 57, 308–9, 325, 513 n. 35
Poor Lombards, 300, 350
Poverty, 56–57, 67, 231, 299–310. *See also* Begging; Benefices; Francis of Assisi, and poverty; Ignatius de Loyola, embracing poverty; *Pauperes Christi;* Pilgrimaging, poverty as characteristic of; Preaching, in poverty; Stipends.
  companions' choice of, 49, 54–55, 58–63, 72, 355
  companions' practice of, 62–63, 74, 142–43,

146–47, 156, 200, 206, 313, 390–91, 461 n. 20
  in the Formula, 279, 316–17, 380, 390–91
  in Ignatius's letter to Carafa, 260, 262, 264–65
  personal and communal, 146–47, 441 n. 31, 530 n. 20
  "poor with Christ poor," 54, 58, 60–63, 79–80, 99, 146, 390, 443 n. 42
  serving Christ in, 62, 109–10, 120, 253, 378
  sine proprio, with nothing of one's own, 302, 308, 313, 316, 323, 441 n. 31, 509 nn. 8 and 10
  today's call to gospel, 418–19
  vow at Montmartre, 62, 72, 108–10, 112, 115, 313, 377–78, 455 n. 68, 461 n. 24, 462 n. 25, 481 n. 31
  vow at Venice ordination, 76–79, 280, 313
Poverty movements, 57, 67, 146–47, 151–52, 323, 439–40 n. 24, 474 n. 52
Praise, companions' way of life worthy of, 22, 140, 184, 202–3, 209, 211–12, 239, 403, 406, 415
Prayer
  in companions' daily life, 99, 117, 161, 176, 201, 232, 241, 313, 317, 332, 384
  during the Deliberation, 12–17, 91–92, 256, 282
  and discernment, 63, 88, 97, 111, 271, 273, 384, 416
  while in Paris, 86, 109, 112, 378
Preaching, 66, 140–50, 373, 445 n. 12, 446 n. 14, 473 n. 46

companions' ministry of, 23–24, 39–42, 80, 112, 142–43, 146–50, 190, 197–98, 202, 205, 265, 377, 471 n. 36, 472 n. 45
faculties, xxxi, 78, 112, 142–43, 147–49, 181, 188, 471 n. 38
itinerant, 148–49, 166–67, 170–71, 175–76, 182, 472 nn. 42 and 44, 480 n. 28
in poverty, 63, 143–47, 150, 373–74, 391
testimony re companions', 140, 179, 181, 185, 195, 486 n. 60
by word and example [*verbo et exemplo*], 140, 144–46, 152, 222, 227–28, 468–69 n. 16
Precepts and counsels, 300–301, 305, 514 n. 39
Premonstratensians, 383
Priest and priesthood, 65–80, 221–22, 225, 385, 445 n. 12, 449 n. 33. *See also* Ignatius de Loyola, opting for priesthood.
  companions as secular priests, 55, 76–77, 79–80, 143, 157, 297, 328, 519 n. 41
  companions' free choice, 49, 54–55, 71–73, 355
  companions' understanding of, 44, 58–63, 78, 392, 452 n. 50
  and ministry, 68, 71, 73–75, 80, 139, 149, 163, 205–6, 451 n. 44, 452 n. 50
  ordination to, xxx, 37, 40, 58, 75–79, 142, 228–29, 369, 434 n. 11, 453 nn. 56–59, 454 nn. 60–66, 455 nn. 67–70, 498 n. 49

580 *Index*

"Pilgrim priests [*preti peregrini*]," 55, 174–75, 210
"Poor priests of Christ [*pauperes Christi sacerdotes*]," 55–63, 65, 73–74, 77–79
"Reformed priests [*preti reformati*]," 55, 158, 210, 227, 438 n. 14, 451 n. 44
Promise, 309, 318, 344, 507 n. 36
Prophetic commitment, 76, 80, 235, 239–46, 332
Propositum, 341–95, 416, 419
   in Christian tradition, 323, 335, 339, 341–52, 367–74, 507 n. 6
   of companions is "good and holy," 341, 381, 395, 415, 521 n. 8
   companions with the same, 365, 374–80, 528 nn. 26–27
   Ignatius's, 353–66
   and *institutum*, 349–51, 367, 369–71, 373–74, 376–80, 523 n. 40, 525 n. 16
   as summarized in the Formula, 381–95
   synonyms of term, 344–45, 355, 359, 361, 363, 367, 375, 379, 384, 523 n. 40, 524 n. 11, 525 n. 16, 528 n. 26
   tranformation of initial, 386, 389, 393, 395
Pucci, Cardinal Antonio, 76, 453 n. 56
Puig, Francis, 133

Rambla, José, 482–83 n. 38
Ravier, André, 456 n. 6, 484 n. 48, 486 n. 57
Reform [of the Church], 36, 183, 209–10, 218, 220–26, 292, 449 n. 32, 494 n. 4

Consilium de emendanda ecclesia, xxx, 142, 202, 222, 495 n. 17
   papal commission on, 52, 221–22, 292, 340
"reform in head and members," 221, 314, 494 n. 7
Regimini militantis Ecclesiae, xv, xxxi, 516 n. 7
   as different from *Cum ex plurium*, xxii, 20, 94, 294–95, 415, 505 n. 20, 515 n. 47
Regula, rule, 296, 322–27, 381–83, 529 nn. 13–14
regula et institutio, 323–25, 349, 403, 518 nn. 22 and 24
regula et vita, rule and life, 296, 301–2, 382, 529 n. 3
Regulares, those who follow a rule, 323
Rejadell, Teresa, 354
Religio, 242–46, 323–24, 351, 500 nn. 8–9, 11–12 and 15, 507 n. 6. *See also* Religious commitment; Religious Order(s).
   companions do not call themselves a [religious order], xxv, 327, 383
pietas et, 235, 239–40, 246
Religious commitment, 244–46, 309–10, 314, 317–18, 341–50, 375–77
Religious institute, genesis of, 367–74. *See also Institutum*.
Religious life, 216, 243–46, 296, 299–318, 324–26, 500 n. 14.
   companions' approach to, 279, 297, 314–17, 392–93
   "essentials" of, 307–10, 507 n. 36, 514 n. 37, 515 n. 45
   Vatican II on, xv, 331–32, 510 n. 11

Religious Order(s), 244–46, 249, 251, 254, 322–23, 326, 382–83, 519 n. 31. *See also* Approval, papal.
  Bobadilla on founding a, 17, 505 n. 18
  companions as different from other, 327–28, 391
  Ignatius thinking of entering a, 69, 245, 358, 364, 368
  Lateran IV and Lyons II on new, 322–26, 517 n. 22
  no intent of companions to found a, xxv, 88, 109–10, 230, 245, 253, 273, 327, 379
  similarities and parallels, 367–74
  in 16th century, 202, 206, 222, 225, 293, 297, 309–10, 415
  "substantials" of any, 308–9
Renaissance, 35–36, 199–200, 219. *See also* Church, at time of Renaissance.
Renewal, xv, 209–10, 212, 221, 223–26, 230–32, 331–32, 409, 416–21. *See also* Reform [of the Church].
Renunciation, 97–99, 169, 231, 303, 366
  companions', 172, 364, 380
  of property, 307–8
Reputation
  companions' need for good, 186–92, 198, 202, 282, 355
  testimony re companions', 193, 195, 209, 229
Requests of companions, 287, 291, 294, 339–40
Return to sources, xv, 226, 331–32
Ribadeneira, Pedro, 94, 375, 462 n. 24
Robert d'Arbrissel, 148

Robert of Molesme, 370
Rodrigues, Simão, xxix–xxxii, 41, 84–86
  anecdotes, 37, 41, 154, 201, 265–66
  on companions' commitment, 86, 107, 112, 241, 245–46, 265, 377, 464 n. 37
  on ministries, 149, 154, 157, 164–65
  on Montmartre vows, 62, 111–14, 245, 377, 462 n. 25, 471 n. 38
  on origins of the Society, 379, 430 n. 15
  on pilgrimaging, 62–63, 173–75, 443 n. 41, 461 n. 20
  terms used by, 241, 245–46, 250, 258, 298, 375–77, 466–67 n. 13, 504 n. 17
Rome, xxx–xxxii, 25–26, 37–42, 51–53, 129, 135, 140, 174–75, 379–80. *See also* Ignatius de Loyola, activities at or in, Rome; Judicial inquiries, in Rome.
  companions' ministry in, 147, 149–50, 160–61, 165, 179–80, 483 n. 46, 486 n. 60
Roser, Isabel, letter of Ignatius to, 23–24, 211–12, 251–52, 266, 355, 431 n. 26
  on trials in Rome, 189–93, 197–98, 245, 253, 273
Rossi de Gasperis, Francesco, 525 n. 14
Rufinus of Aquileia, 348
Ruiz Jurado, Manuel, 461 nn. 21 and 24
Rule, summary of, 381–84, 529 nn. 13–14. See also *Regula, rule.*

Rule of Augustine, 56, 79, 296,
304–6, 323–26, 382
   basis for later rules, 374, 383,
512 n. 20, 530 n. 20
Rule of Basil, 296, 323–24, 348,
381
Rule of Benedict, 296, 323–26,
381
   aspects of, 102, 215, 250,
303–4, 318, 493 n. 8, 499
n. 4, 501 n. 6, 506–7 n. 36
   the Cistercians and, 250, 322,
370
   Innocent III on, 306–7
   the Poor Clares and, 308–9,
325, 513 n. 35
Rule of Francis, 18, 301–2, 314,
326, 382, 513 n. 36, 515
n. 49. *See also* Gospel, norm
for Francis of Assisi.
Rule of the Master, 348, 458 n. 6,
506 n. 36
Rule of the Theatines, 155–56,
321

Sacraments, 75, 78, 112, 154–56,
175, 265, 377–78. *See also*
Communion, frequent; Confession (sacrament).
Sadoleto, Cardinal Jacopo, 221,
340
Salamanca. *See* Ignatius de
Loyola, activities at or in,
Salamanca.
Salmerón, Alfonso, xxx–xxxii,
25, 40–41, 84–86, 94, 107,
453 n. 56
   ministry of, 40, 134–35, 165,
193, 229
Sanctius, Bishop Berardo, 434
n. 13
Sapienza, xxxi, 39–40, 135, 197,
455 n. 67, 486 n. 60

Schillebeeckx, Edward, 450
n. 40, 451 n. 49, 474 n. 57
Scholz, Dieter, 485 n. 52
Schurhammer, Georg, 21–22,
165, 202
Scosi, Raphael, 491 n. 31
Scripture, 194, 381, 461 n. 22.
   See also Gospel, norm for the
companions; Word of God.
Search for God, 409, 417
Service of God, 56–57, 101–3,
231, 369–70. *See also* Christian
life; Evangelical counsels;
Propositum, in Christian
tradition; *Religio.*
   companions' dedication to
the, 106–7, 246, 376–78
   as experienced by Ignatius,
103–6, 358–64, 395
Service of Christ and his vicar,
108–25. *See also* Companionship in mission; Following
Jesus; Montmartre vows;
Oblation to pope.
   end of the Society, 276–78
   as experienced by Ignatius
and companions, 50, 108–
25, 128, 246, 271, 332,
408, 417, 459 n. 15, 462
n. 26, 463 n. 35, 464 n. 37
   in the Deliberation, 121–23,
256, 280–81
   in the Formula, 279, 314–16,
380, 384–93
Sforza, Guido, 36, 433 n. 5
Shakespeare, William, xxv, 213,
216
Sick, caring for the, 117, 136,
163–65, 175, 181–82
Siena, xxxi, 12, 25, 195–96, 200,
268, 293
   companions' ministry in,
40–41, 53, 134, 165,
179

Sine proprio. See Poverty, *sine proprio.*
Societas, socius, xxvi, 256, 258–59, 503 n. 3, 504 nn. 17–18, 505 n. 21. *See also* Companionship in Christ.
Society of Jesus, 270–71, 380, 415–16, 441 n. 31, 504 n. 17. *See also* Company of Jesus.
Solitude, 169, 171, 176, 232, 265, 366, 369, 482 n. 37, 525 n. 14
Somaschi, xxix, 206, 326, 351, 530 n. 20
Spirit and aims, xv–xvii, xxv, 331–33, 356, 414–16, 419
Spiritual conversation, 136–37, 178–79, 181, 486 n. 60
Spiritual Exercises, 158–61
  directed by companions, 24, 160–61, 181–82, 197, 205, 391, 486 n. 60
  directed by Ignatius, 51–53, 159–60, 164, 179, 187–88, 195
  and the Formula, xvi, xxi, 278–80, 385
  investigation of, 186–88, 194, 229
  made by companions, 72, 86, 91, 275, 376
  parts of
    "Annotations," 71–72, 217, 312, 514 n. 41
    "Call of King," 54, 60–61, 103–5, 310–11, 407, 514 n. 38
    "Contemplation to Attain Love," 103, 122, 242
    "First Week," 60, 102, 216–17, 242
    "Principle and Foundation," 54, 71, 102, 277, 404
    "Rules for Election," 69, 70–71, 449 n. 27

  "Two Standards," 60–61, 103, 105, 108, 274, 390
    other parts of, 60–61, 198, 261, 311, 354
    prominent persons who made them, 51–53, 164, 188, 195
    some terminology in, 54, 60–61, 205, 216–17, 245, 310–12, 353–54, 409
Stability, 169–70, 174, 176, 215, 318, 417–18, 507 n. 36, 518 n. 25
Steidle, Basilius, 463 n. 35
Stephen Salagnac, 216
Stipends, 199–200, 446 n. 15
  companions not accepting, 62, 77, 112, 146, 150, 156, 181, 200, 241, 377, 470 n. 32
Strada, Antonio de, 26
Substantialia, essentials, 308–10, 513 n. 34, 514 n. 37
Suckis, Cornelius de, 140

Tacchi Venturi, Pietro, 26, 279, 341
Teachings of the Church, 320–21, 340
Testimonies, xxxi, 51–53, 129–30, 134–35, 140, 185, 187–88, 193–97, 200–202, 229–30
Theatines, xxix, 141, 206, 225, 321, 326, 433 n. 7, 438 n. 14, 449 n. 33, 530 n. 20. *See also* Bulls and briefs, Theatine.
  companions and, 78–79, 297, 327
  Ignatius's letter to Carafa about, 260–66
Thomas à Kempis, 158, 222
Thomas Aquinas, Saint, 74–75, 223, 452 nn. 50 and 54, 500 n. 11

on religious life, 308, 510 n. 11, 514 nn. 37 and 39, 515 n. 46
Thomas of Celano, 81, 301, 371–72
Thomas of Spalato, 144
Tillard, J.-M.-R., 513 n. 34
Timothy, first letter to, 227–28, 232
Title, 43–44
  title of ordination, 77–79, 454 nn. 60–66, 455 nn. 67–68
Tivoli, 19, 21, 253, 292–93, 341
Tolomei, Lattanzio, 52–53, 195, 200, 203
Toner, Jules, 456 n. 8, 457 n. 2
Tonsure, 443 n. 2, 445 n. 11, 446 n. 14
  Ignatius and, 65–67, 443 n. 3, 526 n. 22
Torres, Jesús, 529 n. 14
Tradition, Christian, xxv–xxvi. See also Ignatius de Loyola, within Christian tradition.
  companions and, xxv, 195, 321, 342, 393,
  as norm, xvii, 320–21, 332, 381
Trent, Council of, 296, 320, 322
  companions appointed to, 39–40, 520 n. 41
  decrees of, 448 nn. 19–20, 454 n. 61, 510 n. 11
Trichet, Louis, 443 n. 2
Trinitarians, 509 nn. 8 and 10
Truchsess, Cardinal Otto, 39
Trust in God, 172, 263, 364, 376, 416
Tuchman, Barbara, 444 n. 10, 447 n. 17
Tugwell, Simon, 469 nn. 17 and 22
Turks, 14, 37, 113, 122, 292–93, 388

Ugoleto, Elpidio, 502 n. 23
Uninitiated, instruction of, 177–80, 278
Union in Christ, 95, 256–57, 267–76, 333, 391, 505 nn. 18 and 20. See also Deliberation of First Fathers, on union.
  means to preserve, 276–84, 291, 384, 387
Unity in diversity, 13–14, 83–84, 87–88, 95, 416–17, 456 n. 2. See also Joining together.
Urban II, Pope, 350

Valle, Dr., 160
Vatican Council II, xv, xxiv, 331–32, 452 n. 54, 496 n. 35, 510 n. 11
Velázquez de Cuéllar, Juan, xxix, 24–25
Velletri, 25, 293
Venice, xxx–xxxi, 37–38, 51–52, 76, 78, 83, 187–89, 192–93, 196, 375–76
  companions' ministry in, 40, 63, 142–43, 164–65, 261, 264
Veralli, Bishop Girolamo, 76, 142–43, 160, 188, 454 n. 59
Verdolay, Juan de, 259, 355, 453 n. 56
Viaticum, 313, 442 n. 39
Vicaire, M.-H., 472 n. 44
Vicar of Christ, 20, 100–101, 104, 176. See also Service of Christ and his vicar.
Vicenza, xxxi, 88, 181, 193, 196, 265, 273, 379, 491 n. 23
Vineyard of the Lord, 137–39, 150, 163, 183, 205, 282, 406, 409–10, 466–67 n. 13
Viola, Giovanni Battista, 502 n. 23
Virginity, commitment to, 343–46

Vita, life, 296–97, 350
  regula (rule) and, 296, 301–2, 382, 529 n. 3
Vita apostolica, apostolic life, 57, 151–52, 175, 301, 439–40 n. 24
Vivendi formula, "form of living," 291, 294–98, 507 n. 7, 508 nn. 10–11
  in the Deliberation, 13, 83, 257, 297–98, 313
  examining and approving the, 287, 294, 310, 314, 321, 329, 335, 340–41, 401–5
  and *regula*, 327, 383–84, 403, 529 nn. 13–14
  synonyms of term, 288–96, 350–51, 369, 371, 507 n. 7
  way of living of the Society, 294–98, 314, 327–28, 508 n. 13, 528 n. 27. *See also* Formula of the Institute.
Vocation (call), 261, 303, 369, 371, 523 n. 40.
  of the companions, 106, 120, 298, 317, 392, 504 n. 16
  in *Cum ex plurium*, xxiii, 18, 92, 317, 392, 407–8,
  in the Deliberation, 13, 83–84, 95, 257, 298, 313, 504 n. 16
  and *propositum*, 346, 349, 369, 377, 523 n. 40
Vows of religion, 273, 299–300, 309–10, 323, 344, 386, 505 n. 26, 515 n. 45
  of companions, xxxii, 310–17, 332, 386, 486 n. 56. *See also* Montmartre vows.
  the Gospel and, 312–15, 317–18

Waldensians, 57, 147, 152–53, 445 n. 13, 474 n. 57

Waldo of Lyons, 67, 153, 445 n. 13
Wauchope, Bishop Robert, 53, 434 n. 13
Way of life. See *Institutum*, from *propositum* to.
Wedericus, monk, 148, 472 n. 42
William of Monferrato, 216
Word and example, 189–97, 209, 227–28. *See also* Preaching, by word and example.
Word of God, 99, 150, 171, 261, 301, 303, 333. *See also* Ministry, of the Word.
Works of charity, 181, 227–28, 278, 385, 392. *See also* Ministry, to marginalized.
World, 98, 138, 213–14, 231, 303, 458 n. 3
  abandoning snares of the, 49–50, 97–100, 107–8, 145, 173, 368, 418–19, 458–59 nn. 5–9
World-wide apostolate, 148–49, 171, 371–74, 518 n. 25
Worship, 121, 241, 243
  service and, 101–3, 112, 116, 124–25

Xavier, Francisco, Saint, xxix, xxxi–xxxii, 22, 25–26, 40, 44, 72, 84–86, 107, 174–75, 263
  ministry of, 40, 185, 201, 485 n. 51
  roommate of Favre and Ignatius, 85, 217, 269, 374–75
Xeniteia, voluntary exile, 169, 232, 366

Zannetti, Agostino, 185

www.ingramcontent.com/pod-product-compliance
Lightning Source LLC
Chambersburg PA
CBHW021756220426
43662CB00006B/71